AI Applications and Pedagogical Innovation

Viktor Wang
California State University, San Bernardino, USA

IGI Global
Scientific Publishing
Publishing Tomorrow's Research Today

Vice President of Editorial	Melissa Wagner
Director of Acquisitions	Mikaela Felty
Director of Book Development	Jocelynn Hessler
Production Manager	Mike Brehm
Cover Design	Jose Rosado

Published in the United States of America by
IGI Global Scientific Publishing
701 East Chocolate Avenue
Hershey, PA, 17033, USA
Tel: 717-533-8845
Fax: 717-533-7115
Website: https://www.igi-global.com E-mail: cust@igi-global.com

Library of Congress Cataloging-in-Publication Data

Names: Wang, Viktor editor
Title: AI applications and pedagogical innovation / [edited by] Viktor Wang.
Other titles: Artificial intelligence applications and pedagogical innovation
Description: Hershey, PA : IGI Global Scientific Publishing, [2026] | Includes bibliographical references and index. | Summary: AI is rapidly transforming education, offering more opportunities for pedagogical innovation. By integrating AI tools and systems into teaching and learning environments, educators can now personalize instructions and enhance student engagement. As educational institutions continue to explore the potential of AI, it becomes increasingly important to understand how these innovations can be harnessed to improve learning outcomes and reshape traditional pedagogical models. -- Publisher
Identifiers: LCCN 2025026182 (print) | ISBN 9798337350936 | ISBN 9798337350929 | ISBN 9788337350920 | ISBN 833735092X | ISBN 9798337350943 electronic bk
Subjects: LCSH: Artificial intelligence--Educational applications | Computer-assisted instruction | Educational psychology | Artificial intelligence
Classification: LCC LB1028.43 .A78 2026 (print) | LCC LB1028.43 (ebook)
LC record available at https://lccn.loc.gov/2025026182
LC ebook record available at https://lccn.loc.gov/2025026183

British Cataloguing in Publication Data
A Cataloguing in Publication record for this book is available from the British Library.

Table of Contents

Foreword

As institutions of higher education continue to navigate the rapid convergence of digital innovation and global complexity, it becomes increasingly clear that artificial intelligence will not simply augment our work—it will redefine it. This latest book by Dr. Viktor Wang is both timely and essential. It offers not only a vision of the future, but also a practical framework for leading educational systems through profound transformation.

From my vantage point as a university administrator and advocate for academic excellence, I have seen firsthand the pressure facing our faculty, staff, and students. Institutions are tasked with ensuring access, equity, innovation, and relevance in an age when the pace of change outstrips conventional models of reform. Dr. Wang's work is a call to action for educational leaders to embrace AI thoughtfully—not as a threat, but as a strategic lever to rethink teaching, reimagine learning, and expand opportunity across borders.

What sets this book apart is its global lens. With contributions and insights shaped by cross-cultural experience and grounded in decades of educational leadership, Dr. Wang makes the case that AI is not just a Western technological development, but a global movement with implications for learners everywhere. Whether in traditional classrooms, adult education programs, or workforce development initiatives, the tools explored here have the potential to democratize knowledge, personalize learning, and close longstanding gaps in educational access.

This book will prove invaluable for university presidents, deans, provosts, and policymakers who are tasked with not only managing change but leading it. The chapters within challenge us to move beyond reactionary policies or short-term fixes. Instead, the book compels us to consider long-term strategies that align technological capacity with human values, educational equity, and institutional mission. In doing so, it provides a roadmap that is both bold and actionable.

At a time when higher education must demonstrate its relevance on a global stage, this volume offers a rare blend of academic rigor, visionary leadership, and strategic insight. It is a resource that should be studied, shared, and implemented by educational leaders who understand that the future of learning begins now—and that AI, used wisely, can be a bridge to a more inclusive, innovative, and informed world.

I commend this volume to readers across the academy and beyond in the hope that it may serve as a guidepost for a new era of leadership—one that is globally aware, ethically grounded, AI-literate, and ready to shape the next generation of learning.

Paul A. Bott
Independent Researcher, USA

Preface

INTRODUCTION

The idea for this book, *AI Applications and Pedagogical Innovation*, emerged from the convergence of two lifelong passions: my dedication to advancing adult, career, and higher education, and my deep curiosity about the potential of artificial intelligence to reshape the ways we teach, learn, and lead. As an educator, researcher, and mentor with more than two decades of global academic engagement, I have had the privilege of witnessing—and contributing to—many waves of educational reform. Yet none has been as rapid, as disruptive, or as full of possibility as the current era of AI innovation.

My academic foundation is rooted in one of the most influential departments in the history of adult education—the Department of Vocational and Adult Education at the University of Arkansas, where I earned both my doctoral degree in education and a master's degree in educational technology. This is the same department where the late Dr. Malcolm Knowles, the father of andragogy, taught until his passing in 1997. It is a profound honor to have graduated from a department so deeply connected to the origins of adult learning theory. I have proudly carried Dr. Knowles' torch of andragogical leadership forward, guiding research across disciplines and continents, and advancing his legacy through my own teaching, writing, and mentorship.

To date, I have published over 240 refereed works, including approximately 80 volumes of scholarly books. My publications are held in the libraries of leading universities such as Stanford, New York University, and Princeton, a testament to their relevance and scholarly impact. I have had the privilege of publishing articles and book chapters authored by some of the most respected figures in the field of education, including Dr. Stephen Brookfield. Furthermore, my *Encyclopedia of Strategic Leadership and Management* drew contributions from over 300 scholars worldwide, reflecting a truly global conversation around leadership and learning in a changing world.

I also take great pride in my long-standing relationship with Dr. John A. Henschke, one of Malcolm Knowles' own doctoral students and a towering figure in his own right. Dr. Henschke has been both a mentor and a friend, and it is with deep gratitude that I acknowledge his contribution of a foreword to this volume. His lifelong dedication to andragogical principles and international education has deeply shaped my thinking and my work.

The inspiration for this work also draws from a career in teaching that spans continents. I have had the distinct honor of teaching in both China and across many states in the United States, including California, Florida, Arizona, and Montana. My classrooms have included doctoral candidates, educational leaders, adult learners, and pre-service teachers—all eager to make sense of the complexities of learning in the 21st century. Across all these settings, a common thread emerged: the desire to understand how technology, when guided by values and vision, can support deeper, more inclusive learning experiences.

This book is the result of ongoing conversations with colleagues, students, institutional leaders, and policymakers from around the world. It is built upon decades of work in instructional leadership, curriculum development, and the integration of andragogical principles in both physical and virtual learning environments. Over time, I began to realize that while AI was gaining traction in the fields of industry, healthcare, and business, its application in education was often misunderstood, oversimplified, or siloed. There was—and still is—a need for thoughtful, ethical, and strategically guided exploration of what AI can actually do to support and uplift teaching and learning.

My intent with this book is not to celebrate technology for its own sake. Rather, it is to invite educators, leaders, and learners into a dialogue about how AI can be used to advance the values we hold most dear: access, inclusion, equity, adaptability, and lifelong learning. I firmly believe that AI tools, when integrated intentionally and reflectively, can serve as catalysts for educational transformation—not only enhancing instructional efficiency, but also deepening human connection and creativity in ways that support the full spectrum of learning.

ORGANIZATION OF THE BOOK

The book is organized into several volumes, each focused on a specific aspect of AI in education—from practical tools and case studies to theoretical frameworks and future-facing models of leadership. The contributors to this work represent a wide range of disciplines and global perspectives. Together, we aim to highlight both the promise and the limitations of AI, always with the understanding that technology must serve human development—not replace it.

Chapter 1: AI in Higher Education in the Context of Open and Distance Learning: Opportunities and Challenges

In this foundational chapter, the authors provide a timely and in-depth analysis of how Artificial Intelligence (AI) is reshaping higher education, with particular attention to Open and Distance Learning (ODL) environments. ODL institutions, operating within unique structural and pedagogical frameworks, face persistent challenges such as learner isolation, delayed feedback, and elevated dropout rates. This chapter argues that AI holds significant promise in addressing these challenges while acknowledging the practical and ethical complexities of implementing AI across diverse and often transnational educational contexts. Drawing on global case studies and institutional insights, the authors present evaluative frameworks and governance models that serve as a roadmap for sustainable and responsible AI integration. Their contributions offer critical guidance for policymakers, institutional leaders, technologists, and educators working to enhance equity, efficiency, and learner support in the digital education landscape.

Chapter 2: Artificial Intelligence and the Transformation of Career Technical Education

Chapter 2 explores how AI is catalyzing a new era in Career and Technical Education (CTE), redefining instructional delivery, learner support, and administrative efficiency. By automating routine tasks and enabling data-informed personalization, AI technologies empower educators to focus more deeply on learner interaction and hands-on skill development. However, the authors are careful to underscore the importance of ethical AI integration. They raise essential questions about data privacy, bias, and the need to preserve the irreplaceable human element that underpins effective teaching and learning. This chapter sets a critical tone for understanding how AI can enhance—not replace—human-centered educational practices in vocational and technical domains.

Chapter 3: Generative Artificial Intelligence Practices for Doctoral Student Engagement

Focusing on the often-overlooked realm of doctoral education, Chapter 3 offers a compelling examination of how generative AI is transforming doctoral learning ecosystems. Guided by the Community of Inquiry framework, the chapter outlines how AI tools foster deeper cognitive, social, and teaching presence within doctoral programs. From academic writing aids to intelligent feedback systems, AI emerges as a supportive co-participant in both student and faculty workflows. The authors argue convincingly for a balance between innovation and academic integrity, presenting ethical implementation as essential to equitable and meaningful engagement. This chapter is a significant contribution for institutions aiming to modernize advanced education without compromising rigor or scholarly values.

Chapter 4: Generative AI in Academic Research: A Practical Guide for Scholars

In Chapter 4, the authors provide an indispensable guide for integrating generative AI into the academic research process. Through tool trials, case scenarios, and ethical reflection, they demonstrate how large language models and AI-powered applications such as Scite and Elicit can assist scholars in every stage of research—from conceptualization to dissemination. A particularly valuable feature of this chapter is its inclusion of prompt design strategies and practical workflows that researchers can adopt immediately. Just as importantly, the authors address epistemological concerns, emphasizing the need for critical human oversight to maintain scholarly rigor and ethical standards. This chapter fills a pressing knowledge gap by offering actionable, critically engaged approaches to using AI in academic inquiry.

Chapter 5: AI-Driven Content Creation: Revolutionizing Open Educational Resources

Chapter 5 delves into the intersection of AI and Open Educational Resources (OER), exploring how content generation tools are revolutionizing the creation, adaptation, and dissemination of instructional materials. The authors present a balanced view of the efficiencies AI can bring to lesson planning, multimedia development, and curriculum design, while also drawing attention to the inherent risks of misinformation, bias, and quality dilution. Emphasizing the importance of human oversight, they propose models for maintaining intellectual integrity and promoting inclusivity in AI-generated content. This chapter offers educators and instructional designers a thoughtful pathway to integrate AI into OER initiatives without sacrificing creativity, pedagogical soundness, or ethical responsibility.

Chapter 6: AI and Gamification: Engaging Students in New Ways

The synergy between gamification and AI is the focus of Chapter 6, where the authors examine how these technologies can co-create immersive, adaptive learning experiences that motivate students and elevate performance. Through real-world case studies across K–12 and higher education, the chapter illustrates how AI enhances gamified learning by enabling real-time feedback, dynamic difficulty adjustment, and personalized learning trajectories. While the authors highlight numerous pedagogical benefits, they also caution against over-entertainment, equity gaps in access, and the potential loss of educational depth. The chapter ultimately positions AI-infused gamification as a promising, though complex, innovation that demands thoughtful implementation to maximize its educational value.

Chapter 7: AI in Assessment: From Standardized Testing to Dynamic Feedback

Chapter 7 reimagines the assessment landscape, tracing a shift from traditional standardized tests toward AI-enabled, responsive feedback systems. The authors argue that AI's capacity to process large-scale data sets in real time enables a transition from static evaluations to ongoing assessments that better support student growth. This chapter offers a nuanced discussion of the pedagogical, technological, and ethical considerations involved, including fairness, transparency, and accountability. The result is a forward-looking vision of assessment that leverages AI not just to evaluate learning, but to enhance it—reinforcing the role of assessment as a continuous, formative, and learner-centered process.

Chapter 8: AI Tools for Enhancing Student Engagement

In the final chapter, the authors present a sweeping overview of AI tools designed to enhance student engagement across educational contexts. From intelligent tutoring systems and predictive analytics to game-based learning and affective computing, the chapter surveys an expansive toolkit available to today's educators. Drawing from examples like DreamBox and Civitas Learning, the authors demonstrate how AI can personalize instruction, track student progress, and foster inclusive learning environments. Yet, they also issue a clarion call for ethical use, urging educators and developers alike to safeguard student agency, ensure data privacy, and remain vigilant against algorithmic bias. By envisioning AI not as a replacement but as a collaborative partner in education, this chapter provides a fitting conclusion to a volume dedicated to meaningful and responsible AI integration in teaching and learning.

Chapter 9: Exploring the Authenticity of AI-Generated Texts as Resources for Language Teaching and Learning: Challenges and Opportunities

This chapter engages with a central tension in modern language pedagogy: the use of AI-generated texts as learning resources and the degree to which they can be considered "authentic." Framed through the dual lenses of authenticity and resourcefulness, the authors delve into the pedagogical, policy, and market implications of employing AI texts in second language instruction. By juxtaposing the challenges—ranging from reliability to pedagogical alignment—with the opportunities for increased accessibility and linguistic diversity, the chapter provides a three-pronged exploration of how AI is reshaping classroom materials, teacher roles, and institutional strategies. This thoughtful analysis offers both a caution and a call to innovate, providing grounded insights for educators navigating the complex linguistic terrain of AI-mediated learning.

Chapter 10: Navigating AI in Teacher Education: Exploring the Interplay Between Artificial Intelligence Anxiety and Creative Cognition

Chapter 10 investigates a timely and underexplored facet of teacher education: the psychological and cognitive dynamics between AI-related anxiety and creative thinking among pre-service teachers. Through a robust empirical study involving education students in Punjab, the authors identify a paradoxical but revealing relationship—where heightened anxiety about AI is positively correlated with enhanced creative cognition. Their findings suggest that when channeled constructively, apprehension toward emerging technologies may actually stimulate imaginative pedagogical approaches. With practical implications for teacher training programs, this chapter encourages institutions to rethink how emotional responses to AI can be harnessed to build more resilient, adaptive, and forward-thinking educators.

Chapter 11: Leveraging Sports, AI, and Gamification for Transformative Learning: A Framework for Active, Inclusive, and Future-Ready Education

This chapter proposes an ambitious, interdisciplinary framework that unites sports, artificial intelligence, and gamification to reimagine education as an active, inclusive, and future-ready endeavor. Drawing on principles from experiential and transformative learning, the authors outline how physical engagement, real-time data analytics, and game mechanics can collectively empower students and promote deeper skill acquisition. Real-world applications in digital apps, classrooms, and athletic contexts demonstrate how this triad fosters not only cognitive and physical development, but also motivation, resilience, and collaboration. By situating this integrative model within broader conversations on inclusion and equity, the chapter provides a visionary path forward for designing dynamic, student-centered learning environments.

Chapter 12: The Role of Derivatives in Machine Learning: Optimization, Applications and Ethical Considerations for the Education Field

In Chapter 12, the authors turn to the mathematical heart of machine learning—derivatives—and explore their foundational role in optimizing neural networks and cost functions within educational applications. With a particular focus on platforms such as Khan Academy, the chapter addresses how derivatives drive precision and scalability in AI-driven learning systems, while also surfacing significant ethical concerns. The authors highlight how data-driven optimization can unintentionally reinforce biases, affect fairness, and raise sustainability questions. By integrating technical explanation with applied educational ethics, this chapter bridges the gap between computational methods and the human-centered values essential to equitable and effective educational technology.

Chapter 13: Transforming English Language Learning in South Asia: Role of AI Tools in India

Chapter 13 examines the evolving landscape of English language instruction in South Asia, with a focus on the adoption and perception of AI tools in India. Through a rigorous quantitative study involving students and teachers, the authors reveal high levels of awareness and usage of AI applications for tasks such as translation, pronunciation, writing, and interactive grammar practice. Despite this promising engagement, the chapter does not shy away from highlighting persistent challenges—including issues of trust, infrastructure, and digital literacy. The authors advocate for targeted teacher training and student support mechanisms to ensure that AI-facilitated language learning remains effective, inclusive, and accessible across diverse educational settings.

Chapter 14: AI and Emerging Digital Worlds as a Tool, Not a Replacement

Firmly grounded in the ethos of digital ethics and critical posthumanism, this chapter challenges the misconception of AI as a substitute for educators. Instead, it positions AI as a powerful tool that complements human insight, empathy, and pedagogical nuance. By exploring innovations such as explainable AI (XAI), digital twins, and immersive learning environments, the authors demonstrate how AI can support differentiated instruction, career readiness, and inclusion in both K-12 and vocational contexts. Importantly, the chapter emphasizes the continued importance of teacher agency, ethical policy frameworks, and transparency in data use. In doing so, it articulates a human-centered vision of education in which AI enriches—rather than replaces—the vital relational and ethical dimensions of teaching and learning.

Chapter 15: AI-Powered Knowledge Management in Curriculum Design and Content Delivery

In Chapter 15, the authors introduce an open-source, AI-driven Knowledge Management (KM) platform designed to modernize vocational curriculum development and content delivery in India. This solution integrates global AI trends with localized labor market needs, offering a responsive model for interdisciplinary education that transcends traditional computer science domains. By addressing environmental, technological, and non-technical barriers, the chapter situates AI not just as a pedagogical tool, but as an engine for workforce transformation. Its focus on curriculum customization, scalability, and cross-sector collaboration provides practical insights for educational leaders seeking to align AI education with global imperatives in sustainability, healthcare, and innovation.

Chapter 16: Personalized Learning Through AI on the Power of Tailored Education

Concluding this section of the volume, Chapter 16 underscores the transformative promise of AI-powered personalized learning. Moving beyond one-size-fits-all instruction, the authors explore how adaptive algorithms can respond to student needs in real time—adjusting pacing, scaffolding content, and targeting support to close learning gaps. These technologies, the chapter argues, promote engagement, enhance retention, and nurture deeper understanding by empowering students to take ownership of their learning journeys. With a strong focus on practical implementation and pedagogical benefits, the chapter presents AI as a catalyst for more equitable and effective learning environments—while reminding readers of the ethical and design choices that must guide such innovations.

CONCLUSION

It is no coincidence that this work includes contributions from educators and thought leaders across continents. We are in a moment of global transformation, and our responses must be equally global. AI is not a trend—it is an inflection point. And the choices we make now, as educators and institutions, will determine whether we amplify opportunity or exacerbate inequality. This book is a humble offering in service of the former.

I would like to express my deepest gratitude to my co-authors, contributors, reviewers, and institutional partners who have supported this project. Your insights and commitment have shaped every chapter. I also want to thank the students and doctoral candidates I've mentored over the years—you continue to inspire me with your questions, your resilience, and your determination to make education more inclusive and more effective for future generations.

I also wish to extend my heartfelt appreciation to IGI Global, the publisher of this volume, for their enduring commitment to scholarly excellence and their support in bringing this multi-volume work to fruition. Their dedication to disseminating transformative research in education and leadership has been instrumental throughout this process.

Special thanks are also due to the many reviewers whose critical feedback helped refine the clarity, depth, and coherence of the chapters included. Your thoughtful engagement enriched the work in ways too numerous to count.

To the global network of contributors who lent their voices, perspectives, and expertise—thank you. Your diverse insights and dedication to educational advancement have shaped this book into a truly international and collaborative effort.

Finally, I wish to express deep gratitude to the university libraries around the world—including Stanford University, New York University, and Princeton University—that continue to catalog and share my work. Your support ensures that knowledge remains accessible, visible, and impactful for future generations of learners and researchers.

To the readers: whether you are a faculty member rethinking your curriculum, a dean or provost leading systemic change, a policymaker designing new frameworks, or a student exploring the frontiers of digital learning—I hope you find in these pages not only knowledge, but encouragement. This is your invitation to engage, to question, and to lead. The future of education is not just about digital tools or predictive algorithms—it's about the people who wield them with wisdom and care.

In closing, I offer this book as both a scholarly resource and a starting point for transformation. May it spark ideas, challenge assumptions, and serve as a guide for all who believe in the power of education to shape a better, more equitable world—one learner, one classroom, one innovation at a time.

This book, *Foundations and Frameworks for AI in Education*, is the first in the *Transformative AI Tools for Use in Education and Learning* series. It focuses on foundational theories, ethical frameworks, and structural approaches to integrating AI into education. It sets the stage for the books that follow by offering conceptual clarity and thematic grounding, ideal for educators, researchers, and policy leaders seeking a broad understanding of AI's role in shaping the future of learning.

Viktor Wang
California State University, San Bernardino, USA

Chapter 1
AI in Higher Education in the Context of Open and Distance Learning: Opportunities and Challenges

Freeson Kaniwa
Botswana Open University, Botswana

Gbolagade Adekanmbi
https://orcid.org/0000-0002-3858-5994
Botswana Open University, Botswana

ABSTRACT

This chapter analyzes how Artificial Intelligence (AI) is transforming higher education, focusing on Open and Distance Learning (ODL) environments. ODL institutions encounter unique challenges and opportunities in AI implementation that differ from conventional universities. The authors examine AI's potential to address persistent ODL challenges—student isolation, feedback delays, varying preparation levels, and high dropout rates—while navigating implementation barriers in cross-border education. Through case studies from leading global ODL institutions, practical frameworks are presented for evaluating AI opportunities, developing governance structures, and creating sustainable implementation models. The chapter also emphasizes ethical considerations and provides actionable guidance for policymakers, institutional leaders, faculty, and technologists.

BACKGROUND

Artificial intelligence (AI) represents the most significant technological shift in higher education since the internet revolutionized teaching and learning methodologies. For Open and Distance Learning (ODL) institutions, the stakes in this transformation are very high (Bozkurt et al., 2021). While traditional brick-and-mortar universities have often struggled

DOI: 10.4018/979-8-3373-5092-9.ch001

to adapt to digital transformation, many distance education providers, particularly those in developed countries, have been digital pioneers, positioning them as natural early adopters of AI technologies (Zawacki-Richter et al., 2019). The landscape of AI in education was dramatically accelerated by the COVID-19 pandemic, which forced the entire educational world to embrace remote learning overnight (Pelletier et al., 2021). This global shift highlighted both the potential and limitations of existing distance education models, creating an urgent need for innovation in how we teach and learn across geographic boundaries.

The applications of AI in ODL range from basic chatbots answering student queries to sophisticated systems that personalize learning pathways for thousands of students simultaneously. What makes these applications particularly powerful is their capacity to directly address the persistent challenges that have historically limited ODL effectiveness (Lee, 2021). For example, students may feel isolated from instructors and peers, waiting for days for essential feedback, often entering programmes with dramatically different levels of preparation, and dropping out at frustratingly high rates (Lee, 2021). Thus, the evolution of AI in distance education represents more than merely doing things more efficiently; it potentially rewrites the rules of what is possible in teaching and learning when geographic constraints disappear. As Tlili et al. (2022) observe, AI technologies are increasingly enabling ODL providers to overcome traditional limitations. They also amplify their unique strengths, creating educational models that may ultimately prove superior to conventional approaches in specific contexts (Tlili et al. 2022).

However, this technological transformation through AI comes with significant challenges. ODL institutional environments are characterized by geographically distributed stakeholders, cross-border operations, diverse student populations, varying technological infrastructure, and complex regulatory landscapes. Generic approaches to AI implementation that might work well in traditional campus settings often fail to address these realities, creating the potential for both missed opportunities and unintended consequences (Rienties et al., 2020).

This chapter therefore aims to fill a critical gap in understanding how AI is transforming ODL specifically, rather than treating distance education as an afterthought in the broader conversation about technology in higher education. We provide insights directly relevant to institutions serving students across geographic boundaries through technology-mediated learning, focusing on four key arguments:

1. AI can solve some of distance education's toughest problems, transforming traditional ODL limitations into potential advantages.
2. Distance educators face AI implementation challenges that differ substantially from those encountered by traditional universities.
3. ODL requires ethical AI frameworks as diverse as its global student populations.
4. Successful AI implementation in ODL demands strategies specifically designed for distributed education contexts rather than adaptations of campus-based approaches.

This chapter, through literature review, empirical research, case studies, and practical frameworks, examines the role of AI in higher education, its expanding role in ODL, and the opportunities for innovation in ODL environments. It also examines the nature of ethical and operational challenges in ODL contexts. The chapter finally offers some strategic recommendations for ODL institutions. This comes in form of actionable guidance for institutional leaders, faculty, technologists, and policymakers navigating this complex terrain. Overall, the goal of this chapter is to help ODL institutions harness AI's potential while addressing the unique ethical, operational, and pedagogical challenges of ODL. This is done in ways that enhance educational quality, expand access, and potentially redefine what is possible when geographic constraints are removed.

AI IN HIGHER EDUCATION

The integration of artificial intelligence into higher education represents a fundamental shift in how institutions approach teaching, learning, and administrative functions. From personalized learning pathways to sophisticated analytics that inform strategic decision-making, AI technologies are redefining the possibilities and potential of modern higher education environments.

The Evolving Landscape of AI in Educational Contexts

Artificial intelligence in educational settings has undergone a remarkable evolution, progressing from experimental applications to mainstream implementation in a few decades. The contemporary understanding of AI in education encompasses a broad spectrum of technologies and approaches, including machine learning algorithms, natural language processing, intelligent tutoring systems, predictive analytics, and adaptive learning platforms (Zawacki-Richter et al., 2019). These technologies are increasingly capable of personalizing instruction, automating administrative tasks, providing intelligent feedback, and generating insights that would be impossible through manual analysis alone.

The history of AI in education traces back to early intelligent tutoring systems in the 1970s and 1980s, which attempted to model student knowledge and provide customized instruction (Holmes et al., 2019). However, it is only in the past decade that advances in computational power, algorithmic sophistication, and data availability have enabled AI to fulfill some of its long-promised potential in educational contexts. Today's educational AI systems can analyze vast datasets of student interactions, identify patterns in learning behaviors, predict outcomes with remarkable accuracy, and deliver personalized interventions at scale (Luckin & Cukurova, 2019). Also, recent developments have been particularly dramatic. Since 2022, large language models (LLMs) and generative AI have introduced capabilities that would have seemed far-fetched a few years earlier. These systems can now generate human-quality content across multiple formats, engage in sophisticated dialogues with learners, and serve as both creative tools and cognitive scaffolds (Kasneci et al., 2023). The emergence of these technologies has forced radical reconsideration of assessment practices, pedagogical approaches, and consequently, fundamental questions about the nature and purpose of education have been raised.

Current Applications in Conventional Higher Education

Many conventional institutions have implemented AI across various functional areas, though adoption patterns remain uneven across the sector. Administrative applications, including enrollment management, student success prediction, and institutional analytics, have seen the most widespread implementation, partly because they often require less fundamental change to teaching and learning practices (Gašević et al., 2016).

In teaching and learning, AI applications in traditional higher education include:

1. Intelligent tutoring systems: Programmes that adapt to student responses and provide customized guidance, particularly in well-structured domains like mathematics, computer science, and certain natural sciences.
2. Writing support tools: Applications that offer automated feedback on writing structure, grammar, and style, though their use in formal assessment remains controversial.
3. Content personalization: Systems that adjust learning materials based on student performance, preferences, and learning styles, though the evidence base for some approaches remains contested.
4. Virtual teaching assistants: AI-powered chatbots and conversational agents that answer student questions, explain concepts, and provide round-the-clock support.
5. Assessment tools: Programmes that assist with grading, feedback provision, and detecting academic misconduct, particularly in courses with large enrollments.

For research and knowledge creation, AI tools are helping scholars navigate the overwhelming volume of academic literature, identify patterns across large datasets, and collaborate across institutional boundaries. Administrative applications include predictive analytics for enrollment management, financial optimization, and resource allocation.

However, as Baker et al. (2019) note, implementation in traditional higher education has often been piecemeal rather than strategic, with initiatives frequently driven by individual departments or faculty members rather than institutional vision. This fragmented approach has limited the transformative potential of AI in many campus-based settings.

These institutional implementation patterns, however, tell only part of the story. Student experiences with AI in higher education vary dramatically based on individual circumstances, institutional approach, and contextual factors. Students from technologically privileged backgrounds often navigate AI systems with confidence and strategic sophistication. They leverage these tools to enhance their learning while maintaining critical perspective on algorithmic limitations. In contrast, those with limited prior technological exposure or from contexts where AI systems are culturally unfamiliar often experience greater anxiety, skepticism, or difficulty in beneficial engagement.

Beyond these demographic variations, individual student experiences are shaped by the design of AI implementation. Implementations emphasizing transparency, student agency, and clear educational purpose typically generate more positive experiences than those perceived as surveillance-oriented or primarily serving institutional efficiency goals. As Lee (2021) highlights, students' engagement with AI systems is shaped by the way these systems are implemented, which can either empower or diminish their sense of agency, capability, and belonging. This student-centered approach reminds us that the effectiveness of educational technologies is not solely determined by their sophistication, but by how well they are integrated with the needs and perspectives of students.

Unique Potential in Higher Education Transformation

Beyond specific applications, AI has the potential to fundamentally transform higher education in several dimensions:

1. Personalization at scale: AI enables the seemingly contradictory goals of mass higher education and individualized learning experiences to be reconciled, allowing institutions to customize pathways for each student while maintaining economic viability (Popenici & Kerr, 2017).
2. Continuous assessment and feedback: Rather than relying primarily on high-stakes examinations, AI systems can enable continuous, low-stakes assessment that provides immediate feedback and adjusts instruction accordingly.
3. Expanded access: AI reduces certain labor-intensive aspects of education and enabling more efficient resource allocation. But in addition, it also has the potential to make quality higher education accessible to populations previously excluded due to geographic, economic, or personal constraints.
4. New forms of student support: AI systems can identify struggling students earlier and with greater accuracy than traditional methods, enabling proactive interventions before problems escalate.
5. Faculty augmentation: Rather than replacing educators, sophisticated AI tools can amplify faculty expertise, freeing human instructors from routine tasks to focus on complex coaching, mentoring, and the development of higher-order thinking skills (Aoun, 2017).
6. Reimagined credentials: AI-driven assessment systems may enable more granular, skills-based credentialing that better aligns with workforce needs than traditional degree structures.

These transformative possibilities align with many of the longstanding aspirations of higher education reformers, and enable universities to become more student-centered, outcomes-focused, and accessible while maintaining or enhancing quality. However, realizing this potential requires addressing significant challenges, including ethical concerns around data privacy and algorithmic bias. It also addresses faculty resistance to changing roles, institutional capacity for implementation, and ensuring that technological innovation serves educational values rather than diluting them.

Implementation Challenges and Limitations

Despite its potential, AI implementation in higher education faces substantial barriers. These challenges include:

1. Technical complexity: Developing, implementing, and maintaining sophisticated AI systems requires specialized expertise that many institutions lack internally, creating dependency on external vendors whose interests may not perfectly align with educational goals.
2. Data limitations: AI systems require large quantities of high-quality data, yet many institutions struggle with fragmented data systems, inconsistent data collection practices, and limited analytical capacity.
3. Ethical concerns: Questions about data privacy, consent, surveillance, algorithmic bias, and the appropriate boundaries of AI-driven interventions have rightfully slowed implementation in many contexts (Prinsloo, 2020).
4. Faculty skepticism: Educators often view AI initiatives with suspicion, concerned about job displacement, deskilling, loss of autonomy, and the imposition of corporate values on academic practice.
5. Organizational readiness: Successfully implementing AI requires not just technological capacity but organizational change management skills that many institutions have not developed (Rienties et al., 2020).
6. Cost and sustainability: Initial implementation and ongoing maintenance costs can be substantial, raising questions about long-term sustainability, particularly for resource-constrained institutions (ICDE, 2019).
7. Regulatory uncertainty: Evolving regulations around data protection, algorithmic transparency, and digital rights create compliance challenges, especially for institutions operating across different (Jarke & Breiter, 2019).

While these challenges affect all higher education institutions, they manifest differently across contexts. As we will explore in subsequent sections, ODL institutions face unique variants of these challenges while also encountering implementation barriers specific to ODL environments.

AI'S EXPANDING ROLE IN ODL INSTITUTIONS

Artificial intelligence is rapidly transforming the landscape of open and distance learning, creating unprecedented opportunities for institutional growth and student engagement. As educational paradigms shift toward more personalized and accessible models, AI technologies are becoming essential tools in the evolution of ODL frameworks.

ODL Emergence and its Technologies

ODL has evolved through distinct technological phases, each expanding educational access while presenting unique challenges and opportunities. Understanding this evolution provides crucial context for appreciating AI's transformative potential in contemporary ODL environments. The earliest formal distance education programmes relied on postal correspondence, with students receiving printed materials, completing assignments independently, and returning them for assessment (Keegan, 1996; Adekanmbi & Boitshwarelo, 2010). This model dramatically expanded access but created significant temporal delays in feedback and limited opportunities for interaction. The next phase of intervention incorporated broadcast media, radio, and television, enabling richer content delivery but maintaining essentially one-way communication (Moore & Kearsley, 2012) with obvious limited pedagogical gains for learners.

The emergence of the internet in the 1990s revolutionized ODL, enabling synchronous and asynchronous interaction, multimedia content delivery, and collaborative learning environments (Anderson & Dron, 2011). Learning management systems became central infrastructure, facilitating course organization, content delivery, assessment, and communication. Video conferencing enabled real-time interaction regardless of physical location, while digital repositories expanded access to learning resources (Bates, 2019).

Mobile learning represents a more recent evolution, extending educational access to previously underserved populations through smartphone-based learning applications. This shift has been particularly significant in developing regions where mobile penetration exceeds traditional internet access (Traxler, 2018). Meanwhile, learning analytics has enabled institutions to gather and analyze data about student behaviors, identifying patterns that predict success or failure and informing interventions (Long & Siemens, 2011).

Contemporary ODL technologies increasingly focus on creating engaging, interactive experiences that overcome traditional limitations of distance education. Virtual and augmented reality applications enable immersive learning experiences, particularly valuable for practical skills development that has historically been challenging in distance contexts (Tlili et al., 2022). Simulation technologies allow students to practice complex procedures in safe, controlled environments before applying them in real-world settings. Throughout this technological evolution, ODL institutions have continuously balanced innovation with accessibility, ensuring that technological advances do not exclude learners with limited resources or technical proficiency. This tension remains central to AI implementation in ODL contexts, as institutions seek to harness sophisticated technologies while maintaining their core mission of expanding educational access. Notably, progress in this area has not been the same in developed and developing countries, with institutions in Africa often playing catch up to their counterparts in the more affluent contexts. South Africa however has a few examples worth noting as the authors show later in this chapter.

Table 1 shows a timeline which illustrates how distance education has evolved from correspondence-based models through broadcast media, digital platforms, mobile learning, and now AI-enhanced environments, with each stage introducing new capabilities while presenting unique implementation challenges (Anderson & Dron, 2011; Moore & Kearsley,

2012; Bates, 2019). The transition from text-based correspondence courses to sophisticated AI-enhanced learning environments represents a fundamental shift in how distance education addresses traditional limitations of separation between teachers and learners (Keegan, 1996; Adekanmbi & Boitshwarelo, 2010).

Table 1 presents a synthesis of ODL technological evolution based on the work of multiple scholars in the field. This framework integrates perspectives from prominent distance education researchers including Keegan (1996), Anderson and Dron (2011), Moore and Kearsley (2012), Zawacki-Richter et al. (2019), and others to provide a comprehensive overview of how distance education technologies and approaches have evolved over time. While individual authors may emphasize different aspects or use varying terminology to describe these developments, this integrated timeline captures the major technological shifts that have shaped the field of open and distance learning across five distinct eras

Table 1. Evolution of ODL technologies in distance education

Era	Time Period	Key Technologies	Primary Characteristics	Learning Approach	References
Era 1	1800s-1950s	• Print materials • Postal services • Written correspondence	• Asynchronous communication • Long feedback cycles • Individual study	Correspondence Education Postal tuition	Keegan (1996); Anderson & Dron (2011) Adekanmbi (1992)
Era 2	1950s-1980s	• Radio broadcasting • Television • Audio cassettes	• One-way communication • Standardized content • Limited interaction	Broadcast Media Learning	Moore & Kearsley (2012); Bozkurt et al. (2019)
Era 3	1980s-2000s	• Learning Management Systems • Email • Web resources • Early video conferencing	• Digital content delivery • Enhanced communication • Early online collaboration	Digital Revolution	Bates (2019); Zawacki-Richter et al. (2019)
Era 4	2000s-2015	• Smartphones • Mobile apps • Social media • Learning analytics	• Anytime, anywhere access • Data-driven insights • Expanded connectivity	Mobile & Analytics Learning	Traxler (2018); Long & Siemens (2011)
Era 5	2015-Present	• Artificial intelligence • Adaptive learning • Automated feedback • Predictive analytics	• Personalized learning paths • Intelligent tutoring • Proactive interventions	AI Integration	Kasneci et al. (2023);Zawacki-Richter et al. (2019)

Evolution of AI in ODL Contexts

Artificial intelligence has entered ODL environments through several distinct pathways, each reflecting particular institutional priorities and technological capacities. The earliest AI applications in distance education focused primarily on automating administrative functions and providing basic student support, often through rule-based systems with limited adaptive capabilities (Zawacki-Richter et al., 2019).

Chatbots represent one of the most widely implemented AI technologies in ODL, providing all-round student support for common questions about courses, procedures, and technical issues. Early implementations relied on pre-programmed responses to anticipated queries, but contemporary systems use natural language processing to understand a wider range of questions and machine learning to improve responses over time (Abdelkefi & Kallel, 2021). For institutions serving students across time zones, these systems have proven particularly valuable in providing immediate assistance when human support staff are unavailable.

Predictive analytics emerged as another early focus, with institutions using historical data to identify factors associated with student success or failure. The UK Open University's OU Analyse system represents one of the most sophisticated and well-documented examples, using machine learning algorithms to predict student outcomes with remarkable accuracy and enable targeted interventions (Herodotou et al., 2020). Similarly, South Africa's UNISA has developed predictive models tailored to its student population, demonstrating how these approaches can be adapted to diverse educational contexts (Makhanya, 2020). Automated assessment and Feedback systems have gained traction as ODL enrollments have grown, helping institutions manage evaluation at scale while providing more timely feedback than traditional methods would allow. These range from relatively simple multiple-choice assessment tools to sophisticated systems that can evaluate written work, programming assignments, and other complex tasks (Alqassab et al., 2018).

More recently, adaptive learning systems have begun to personalize educational experiences based on individual student characteristics, performance, and behavior. These systems continuously adjust content, pacing, and assessment based on student interactions, potentially addressing the challenge of serving diverse student populations with varying levels of preparation and learning preferences (Holmes et al., 2019). Noably, the evolution of AI in ODL has not followed a uniform pattern across all institutions. Resource-rich universities in developed regions have generally implemented more sophisticated systems earlier, while those in resource-constrained environments have often focused on solutions requiring less technical infrastructure and expertise. This uneven adoption raises important questions about potential new forms of educational inequality, a theme we explore further in subsequent sections. Africa tends to be affected more in such inequalities.

Current Landscape of AI Adoption Across ODL Institutions

The current landscape of AI adoption in ODL institutions reveals significant variation in implementation maturity, strategic approach, and technological sophistication. Several factors influence this diversity, including institutional resources, technical capacity, regulatory environments, and organizational cultures. Leading ODL universities in developed regions have generally implemented the most comprehensive AI ecosystems. The UK Open University, for example, has developed sophisticated learning analytics infrastructure that tracks student engagement across digital platforms, predicts outcomes, and triggers interventions when concerning patterns emerge. Similarly, Western Governors University in the United States has integrated AI throughout its competency-based model, using machine learning to personalize learning pathways and optimize assessment approaches (Bodily & Verbert, 2017).

In contrast, many ODL institutions in developing regions have adopted more targeted approaches, focusing AI implementation on specific high-priority challenges rather than comprehensive transformation. The African Virtual University, for instance, has prioritized AI solutions that function effectively in low-bandwidth environments, enabling students to access key resources despite connectivity limitations (Nafukho & Muyia, 2018). Cross-institutional collaborations have also emerged, enabling resource-sharing and collective development of AI capabilities that individual institutions might struggle to create independently. The Commonwealth of Learning (McGreal, 2020) has facilitated several partnerships, bringing together ODL providers from multiple countries to develop shared technical infrastructure and implementation frameworks. Regulatory environments significantly influence adoption patterns, with institutions in regions having strict data protection laws often taking more cautious approaches to AI implementation. European ODL providers, operating under General Data Protection Regulation (GDPR) constraints, have generally developed more robust data governance frameworks than those in less regulated environments; the requirements can sometimes slow innovation (Jarke & Breiter, 2019).

For ODL institutions planning AI initiatives, understanding the interrelationships between these technical components is essential. Sophisticated applications typically require integration across multiple systems, creating complex dependencies that must be carefully managed. While the current landscape reveals significant implementation variation, the next section examines how these emerging technologies can be strategically deployed to address challenges that limit ODL effectiveness.

Opportunities for Innovation In ODL Environments

The integration of AI in ODL presents unique opportunities to address longstanding challenges that have historically limited effectiveness. This section explores four key areas where AI can transform distance education. Thy include creating personalized learning ecosystems for diverse learners, enhancing student support across geographic boundaries, enabling new approaches to research in distributed academic communities, and improving operational efficiency in complex distributed organizations.

Personalized Learning Ecosystems for Diverse Distance Learners

One of AI's most promising applications in ODL environments is creating truly personalized learning experiences that adapt to individual student needs, preferences, and circumstances. Unlike traditional approaches that typically offer identical content and pacing to all learners, AI-enabled personalization can dynamically adjust multiple dimensions of the educational experience based on continuous assessment of student performance and engagement (Holmes et al., 2019).The potential for personalization is particularly significant where student populations tend to be exceptionally diverse in terms of academic preparation, learning preferences, cultural backgrounds, and contextual circumstances. Kasneci et al. (2023) note that traditional "one-size-fits-all" approaches are especially problematic in distance education, where instructor observations that might enable informal personalization in face-to-face settings are often unavailable. Several dimensions of personalization in innovative ODL implementation have been discussed in the literature, as reflected below:

1. Content adaptation adjusts learning materials based on student performance and preferences. This can include providing alternative explanations of difficult concepts and offering additional practice for struggling students (Khosravi et al., 2020). It also includes suggesting enrichment activities for those who have mastered basic content and presenting information in formats that align with individual learning preferences (Khosravi et al., 2020).
2. Pathway personalization enables flexible navigation through curriculum requirements, allowing students to take different routes to demonstrating competency based on their prior knowledge, interests, and goals. Western Governors University has been a pioneer in this approach, using AI to create individualized learning paths that optimize time-to-completion while ensuring mastery of essential outcomes (Bodily & Verbert, 2017).
3. Pacing adaptation allows students to progress through material at different speeds, based on their understanding and circumstances (Holmes et al., 2019). It also includes addressing a persistent challenge in traditional cohort-based models where fixed schedules may force some students to move forward before achieving mastery while unnecessarily constraining others who could progress more rapidly (Holmes et al., 2019).
4. Assessment personalization tailors evaluation methods to individual students, potentially allowing them to demonstrate competency through different means based on their strengths and preferences. This might include adjusting question difficulty based on previous responses, varying assessment formats, or allowing students to choose from multiple options for demonstrating mastery (Alqassab et al., 2018).
5. Support customization provides interventions and assistance tailored to specific student needs, from technical help to academic guidance to motivational strategies. The University of South Africa has developed sophisticated systems that customize support based on multidimensional student profiles, addressing both academic and non-academic factors that influence success in distance learning environments (Makhanya, 2020).

While the above are notable, effective personalization requires overcoming significant challenges. These include ensuring sufficient data quality for accurate decision-making, addressing privacy concerns related to extensive data collection, maintaining student agency rather than creating dependency on algorithm-driven decisions, and developing interfaces that make personalization transparent and controllable rather than mysterious and imposed (Knox et al., 2020). Perhaps most fundamentally, personalization must be designed to expand students' horizons rather than constraining them to what algorithms predict they might prefer or perform well on. This is particularly required across time zones.

Enhanced Student Support Systems across Time Zones and Geographies

AI-enabled support systems offer great benefits for ODL institutions serving students across multiple time zones and geographic contexts. Traditional models of student support, typically based on synchronous interaction with support staff during business hours, create inherent inequities in global distance education ((Zawacki-Richter & Qayyum, 2019).This disadvantages students in time zones distant from institutional headquarters and those with work or family responsibilities that limit availability during conventional hours (Zawacki-Richter & Qayyum, 2019). AI technologies enable several innovations that address these limitations in the following ways:

1. All round Multilingual Support through conversational agents provides immediate assistance regardless of time zone or language preference. Georgia Tech's pioneering "Jill Watson" virtual teaching assistant demonstrates the potential of these approaches, answering student questions with such natural language capabilities that many students could not distinguish the AI from human teaching assistants (Goel & Polepeddi, 2016).
2. For global ODL providers, multilingual capability is particularly valuable, allowing students to receive support in their preferred language even when staff with those language skills are unavailable.
3. Proactive Intervention Systems identify potential problems before students themselves may recognize them, enabling timely support that prevents minor issues from escalating into serious barriers to success. The OU Analyse system at the UK Open University exemplifies this approach, using predictive analytics to identify struggling students as early as the third week of a course and triggering targeted interventions (Herodotou et al., 2020). This proactive approach is especially valuable in distance education contexts where traditional cues of student difficulty may be less visible to instructors.
4. Automated Formative Feedback provides immediate guidance on assignments and activities, addressing the critical need for timely feedback in distance learning environments. While not replacing substantive instructor evaluation, these systems can help students identify basic issues and iteratively improve their work before submission . For students in time zones that limit synchronous interaction with instructors, this immediate feedback can maintain momentum and engagement.
5. AI-Facilitated Peer Support connects students with appropriate peers for collaboration and assistance, potentially overcoming isolation that has historically characterized many distance learning experiences. These systems can match students based on complementary knowledge, learning preferences, or schedules, creating more effective learning communities across geographic boundaries (Cela et al., 2015).

Implementation of these systems in global ODL contexts requires careful attention to cross-cultural dimensions of support. As Prinsloo (2020) observes, most educational AI systems have been developed in Western contexts and may embed assumptions that do not transfer seamlessly to other cultural environments. Effective global implementation requires cultural adaptation of both technical systems and the interventions they trigger, ensuring relevance across diverse student populations.

Several ODL institutions have demonstrated the positive impact of AI-enhanced support systems on student outcomes. The University of South Africa found that students receiving AI-triggered interventions were more likely to complete their courses successfully compared to those receiving traditional support, with particularly strong results for first-generation students (Makhanya, 2020). However, thoughtful implementation must navigate several challenges, including ensuring systems can function in low-bandwidth environments, maintaining appropriate human oversight of automated support, addressing privacy concerns related to continuous monitoring, and ensuring that technological solutions complement rather than replace human connection. As Selwyn (2019) cautions, there is a risk that AI-driven efficiency in support systems might inadvertently diminish the relational aspects of education that many students value, particularly in distance contexts where human connection is already constrained.

Research and Knowledge Creation in Distributed Academic Communities

AI technologies are transforming research practices in ODL communities, enabling new forms of collaboration, data analysis, and knowledge discovery that are particularly valuable in such contexts where research teams may be geographically dispersed. These innovations address longstanding challenges in distance-based research, including limited access to specialized equipment, difficulties in collaborative data analysis, and barriers to serendipitous knowledge exchange.

Based on the available literature, several emerging applications demonstrate a lot of promise:

1. Collaborative Knowledge Management systems organise information and maintain collective awareness across geographically dispersed research teams (Bozkurt et al., 2021).
2. Intelligent Research Assistants supports literature review processes, particularly valuable for ODL scholars in regions with limited library resources.
3. Automated Data Analysis accelerates pattern identification in complex educational datasets(Gašević et al., 2016).
4. AI-Enhanced Virtual Research Environments create immersive spaces for distributed collaboration (Tlili et al., 2022).
5. Multilingual Research Tools reduce language barriers in international research collaboration (Bozkurt et al., 2021).

While these are noted, ethical and practical challenges must be addressed for these technologies to fulfill their potential. These include ensuring equitable access to AI research tools across resource contexts, maintaining appropriate human judgment in research processes, addressing potential biases in automated analysis systems, and developing governance frameworks for AI use in research that align with disciplinary standards and institutional values (Prinsloo, 2020). What could be a significant concern is the risk of creating new forms of research inequality. In such scenarios, well-resourced institutions leverage sophisticated AI systems to accelerate knowledge production while those in resource-constrained environments fall further behind. As Czerniewicz (2018) argues, without deliberate attention to accessibility and capacity building, AI in research could exacerbate rather than ameliorate existing global inequalities in knowledge production. This risk is particularly relevant for ODL institutions in developing regions, which already face significant barriers to research participation.

Operational Efficiency for Complex Distributed Operations

AI technologies offer substantial opportunities to enhance operational efficiency in ODL institutions, which typically manage complex distributed operations across multiple geographic contexts, time zones, and regulatory environments. These institutions face distinctive operational challenges, including coordinating geographically dispersed staff, managing multi-modal educational delivery systems, ensuring consistent quality across diverse learning centers, and navigating multiple regulatory frameworks (Pelletier et al., 2021).Several AI applications demonstrate particular value in addressing these operational complexities in the following ways:

1. Intelligent Resource Allocation systems optimize the distribution of institutional resources, including faculty time, support staff, technical infrastructure, and learning materials, based on predicted student needs and institutional priorities. These systems can potentially improve both efficiency and equity by ensuring resources are directed where they will have the greatest impact (Zawacki-Richter et al., 2019).
2. Automated Administrative Processes reduce manual workload for routine tasks such as enrollment management, scheduling, document processing, and basic student service requests. AI-driven document processing systems can significantly reduce turnaround times for credential verification, enabling faster enrollment decisions despite operating across multiple national education systems (Nafukho & Muyia, 2018).
3. Predictive Maintenance for technical infrastructure anticipates potential failures in critical systems before they occur, particularly valuable for ODL institutions whose operations depend heavily on continuous availability of digital platforms. By analyzing patterns in system performance data, these approaches enable proactive maintenance that minimizes disruption to learning activities (ICDE, 2019).
4. Supply Chain Optimization for physical materials improves the logistics of delivering learning resources to distributed locations, addressing a persistent challenge for ODL providers operating in regions with limited infrastructure. AI-enhanced logistics systems

can reduce delivery times for course materials while decreasing costs, significantly improving student experience in remote areas (Makhanya, 2020).

5. Compliance Management systems track regulatory requirements across multiple contexts, alert staff to potential compliance issues and generate necessary documentation for different regulatory frameworks (Coglianese & Nash, 2021). These capabilities are particularly valuable for ODL institutions operating across national boundaries, where keeping pace with evolving regulations in multiple jurisdictions creates significant administrative **burdens** (Jarke & Breiter, 2019).
6. Smart Scheduling Systems coordinate activities across time zones, optimizing availability of synchronous learning opportunities, support services, and assessment activities. These help to maximize accessibility for geographically dispersed participants. These systems can potentially reduce the inequities that arise when institutional schedules privilege certain time zones over others (Zawacki-Richter & Qayyum, 2019).

The potential efficiency gains from these applications are substantial. The UK Open University has reported on significant reduction in administrative staff time spent on routine enrollment processes after implementing AI-driven automation, thus allowing reallocation of resources to more complex student support needs. This notwithstanding, realizing these benefits requires navigating several challenges. First, Rienties et al. (2020) have noted that initial implementation often requires significant investment before efficiency gains materialize, creating financial barriers for resource-constrained institutions. Second, they further note that successful implementation typically requires substantial process redesign rather than simply layering technology onto existing procedures, necessitating change management capabilities many institutions have not developed (Rienties et al., 2020). Third, automation of administrative functions raises important questions about potential workforce displacement and changing skill requirements for staff roles that remain (Castañeda & Selwyn, 2018). Perhaps most fundamentally, institutions must balance efficiency considerations with human needs and educational values. The most successful implementation maintains a focus on how operational improvements ultimately contribute to enhanced educational experiences and outcomes rather than treating efficiency as an end in itself.

A Case Study: Botswana Open University's AI Chatbot for Research Ethics Support

A particularly innovative application of AI in ODL contexts comes from Botswana Open University (BOU), where this chapter's authors work. It involved the implementation of an AI-powered chatbot system specifically designed to support research ethics applications and procedures (Botswana Open University, 2022). This implementation demonstrates how AI can address specific challenges in distributed learning environments while accounting for local context and needs.

The BOU Research Ethics Management Information System (REMIS) was developed to address a persistent challenge faced by the university's geographically dispersed postgraduate student population. Prior to implementation, students conducting research requiring ethical approval often faced significant delays in receiving guidance on application procedures, with inconsistent advice sometimes provided across different regional centers. This was particularly problematic for students in remote regions of Botswana and international students in other African countries, who often had limited access to face-to-face consultation with research supervisors and the Ethics Committee members. Figure 1 shows a screenshot of the AI chatbot and the interface of the REMIS system.

Figure 1. REMIS AI chatbot for Botswana Open University

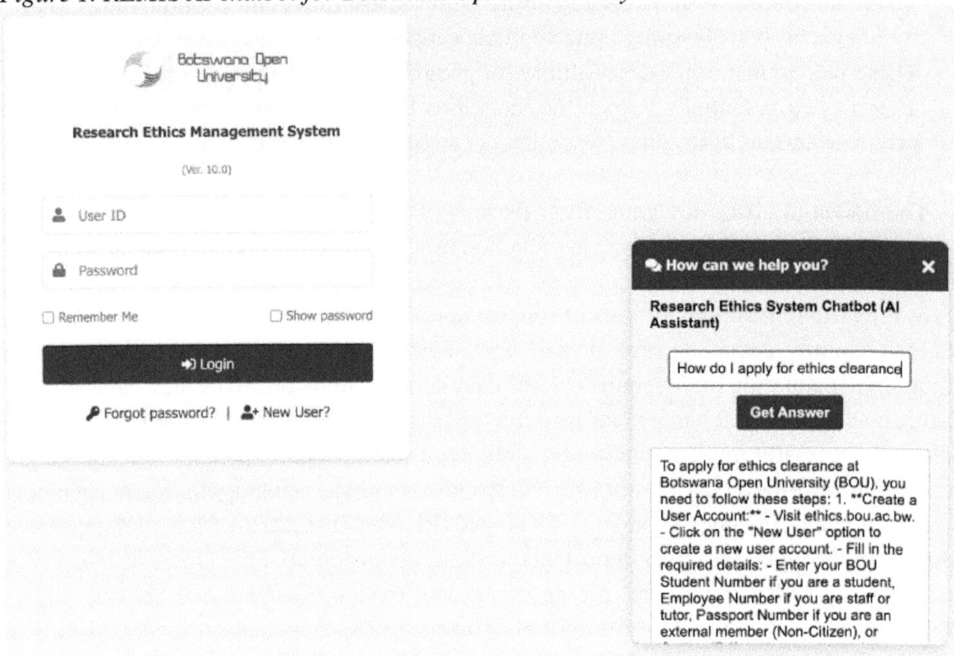

The REMIS chatbot system was developed using a combination of natural language processing and a knowledge base specifically constructed around the university's research ethics policies, common procedural questions, and typical challenges faced by distance students conducting research in diverse contexts. Key features of the system include:

1. All round guidance on research ethics application procedures, documentation requirements, and common issues that typically cause approval delays.
2. Context-aware support that recognizes different requirements for various research methods and subject areas.
3. Multilingual capability supporting English and Setswana, with planned expansion to other languages common among the student population.
4. Progressive complexity design that provides basic information for initial queries while offering increasingly detailed guidance for students with more advanced needs.

Evaluation data from the first 18 months of implementation showed promising results, with a 34% reduction in the average time required for students to prepare complete ethics applications and a 28% decrease in applications returned for revision. Students found the system helpful or very helpful, with particularly positive feedback from those in remote regions who previously had limited access to timely support. The BOU case demonstrates several important principles for successful AI implementation in ODL contexts:

1. Targeted application addressing a specific, well-defined challenge rather than attempting comprehensive AI transformation without clear purpose
2. Contextual adaptation ensuring the system reflects local needs, policies, and circumstances rather than imposing generic solutions
3. Accessibility focus maintaining service availability across varying technology environments, including designing for low-bandwidth access and mobile interfaces
4. Complementary design positioning AI as an enhancement to human support rather than a replacement, with clear integration between automated and human assistance
5. Continuous improvement through regular evaluation and refinement based on usage patterns and feedback

The BOU implementation exemplifies how ODL institutions in resource-constrained environments can achieve significant benefits through targeted, contextually appropriate AI applications. These help to address specific institutional priorities rather than attempt to replicate comprehensive implementations from more resourced contexts.

ETHICAL AND OPERATIONAL CHALLENGES IN ODL CONTEXTS

While AI offers significant opportunities for enhancing ODL, its implementation presents unique challenges in distance education environments. This section examines four critical areas of concern: data privacy and security in global learning contexts, algorithmic bias affecting diverse student populations, implementation barriers in resource-constrained institutions, and academic integrity considerations in unproctored environments. Understanding these challenges is essential for developing responsible, effective AI strategies in ODL settings.

Data Privacy and Security Concerns in Global Distance Learning

Data privacy and security issues take on distinctive dimensions in global ODL contexts, where institutions typically collect, process, and store student data across multiple jurisdictions with varying regulatory frameworks, technological infrastructures, and cultural expectations regarding privacy. These complexities create significant challenges for institutions attempting to implement AI systems that fundamentally depend on data access and processing (Prinsloo & Slade, 2018).

The regulatory landscape for data protection varies dramatically across regions, creating compliance challenges for ODL institutions serving global student populations. While the European Union's General Data Protection Regulation (GDPR) establishes comprehensive requirements including explicit consent, data minimization, and the right to explanation for algorithmic decisions, many other regions have less stringent frameworks or focus on different aspects of data governance (Jarke & Breiter, 2019). For global ODL providers, these variations create potential conflicts when data flows across regulatory boundaries or when institutional practices developed for one context are applied in another.

Beyond formal regulations, cultural expectations regarding privacy differ significantly across contexts. Research has found that students from different cultural backgrounds vary substantially in their comfort with educational data collection and their expectations regarding institutional uses of that data. For example, students from some East Asian contexts reported greater comfort with comprehensive monitoring if positioned as supporting educational goals. On the other hand, those from Western European backgrounds expressed stronger concerns about potential surveillance implications. These differences create challenges for global ODL institutions attempting to develop consistent data policies while respecting diverse cultural perspectives (Viberg et al., 2024).

Technical security requirements present additional complexity in global contexts. Students accessing learning systems from regions with limited cybersecurity infrastructure may face greater risks of data compromise, creating potential liability for institutions and undermining student trust. To address these complexities, several ODL institutions have developed innovative approaches. Among others:

1. Federated Learning Architectures enable AI models to be trained across distributed data without centralizing sensitive information, potentially addressing both regulatory requirements for local data storage and security concerns related to data transmission. These approaches enable collaborative development of predictive models while maintaining compliance with diverse local regulations (Commonwealth of Learning, 2020).
2. Tiered Privacy Frameworks apply different standards based on data sensitivity and student preferences, potentially enabling more complex approaches than blanket policies. The UK Open University has implemented such a framework, classifying data into distinct categories with corresponding limitations on collection, processing, and retention (Herodotou et al., 2020).
3. Transparent AI Design makes data collection and algorithmic decision-making visible and comprehensible to students, addressing concerns about "black box" systems that may undermine trust. This includes accessible explanations of how predictive systems function and clear disclosure of data uses (Prinsloo & Slade, 2017).
4. Privacy-preserving Analytics Techniques enable certain insights to be derived from educational data while limiting risks to individual privacy. These include differential privacy approaches that introduce calibrated noise into datasets and synthetic data

techniques that generate artificial data preserving statistical properties of original information without exposing actual student records.

Despite these innovations, fundamental tensions remain between data-intensive AI implementations and privacy protection in global ODL contexts. Prinsloo (2020) argues that these tensions cannot be resolved through technical or regulatory approaches alone but require ongoing ethical engagement with questions about power, consent, and educational purpose in specific institutional contexts. This perspective suggests that privacy in global ODL should be understood not as a fixed set of requirements but as an ongoing process of negotiating appropriate data practices across diverse stakeholder communities.

Algorithmic Bias and Equity Issues across Diverse Student Populations

Algorithmic bias presents particular concerns in ODL environments, where student populations typically span diverse demographic, cultural, and socioeconomic contexts. While AI systems promise to personalize education and identify students needing support, they may inadvertently reproduce or amplify existing inequalities if not designed with careful attention to potential biases affecting different student groups (Knox et al., 2020). Several mechanisms can introduce bias into educational AI systems in ODL contexts:

1. Training data limitations occur when historical data used to develop predictive models underrepresents certain student populations or reflects past patterns of inequitable educational practices. For example, a study by Lee (2021) found that predictive models trained primarily on data from students in urban contexts with reliable internet access performed significantly worse when applied to rural students with intermittent connectivity, potentially leading to inappropriate interventions or missed support opportunities.
2. Proxy variable effects emerge when seemingly neutral variables correlate with protected characteristics in ways that introduce indirect bias. Gašević et al. (2016) documented how time-of-day patterns in learning platform access, often used in engagement models, can systematically disadvantage students with caretaking responsibilities or non-traditional work schedules, groups that include disproportionate numbers of women and lower-income students in many contexts.
3. Cultural assumption embedding occurs when AI systems incorporate assumptions from the cultural contexts where they were developed, potentially disadvantaging students from other backgrounds. Research by Bozkurt et al. (2021) demonstrated how natural language processing systems used to analyze student discussions often misinterpreted communication patterns common in certain cultural contexts, incorrectly flagging them as indicating confusion or disengagement.
4. Feedback loop reinforcement happens when algorithmic decisions influence future data collection in ways that confirm initial biases. For example, if an early intervention system disproportionately flags certain student groups for remediation, those interventions may change student behavior in ways that generate data confirming the system's initial

assessment, creating what Prinsloo (2020) describes as "algorithmic self-fulfilling prophecies."

5. Infrastructure-based exclusion affects students with limited technological access or digital literacy, who may generate less detailed data for AI systems to analyze or interact with systems in ways that algorithms misinterpret. This form of bias disproportionately affects students in developing regions and those from lower socioeconomic backgrounds, potentially exacerbating existing educational divides (Czerniewicz, 2018).

The consequences of these biases can be particularly severe in ODL contexts, where algorithmic decisions often occur without the mitigating effect of direct human observation and where students may have limited channels for contesting inappropriate determinations. As Prinsloo and Slade (2018) observe, students experiencing algorithmic bias in distance education may lack the institutional connections and advocacy resources that might be available in campus-based settings.

Several approaches show promise for addressing these challenges:

1. Inclusive design methodologies involve diverse stakeholders in AI system development, potentially identifying and mitigating bias risks before implementation. The UK Open University has pioneered participatory design approaches for learning analytics that specifically include students from historically marginalized groups in development processes.
2. Algorithmic impact assessments systematically evaluate potential bias effects before systems are deployed, enabling proactive mitigation. These assessments address both technical and contextual dimensions of algorithmic equity (Commonwealth of Learning, 2020).
3. Continuous monitoring for differential impacts across student groups can identify emerging bias issues that may not have been apparent during system development. This involves disaggregating system performance data across multiple demographic dimensions, enabling ongoing refinement to address bias effects (Nguyen et al., 2021).
4. Multimodal approaches combine different data sources and analytical techniques, potentially reducing over-reliance on any single approach that might disadvantage particular student groups. These approaches recognize that no single data source or algorithm will be equally effective across diverse student populations.
5. Human-in-the-loop systems maintain meaningful human oversight of algorithmic decisions, particularly for high-stakes determinations affecting student progression or support allocation. These approaches recognize the limitations of purely automated decision-making in complex educational contexts with diverse student needs (Selwyn, 2019).

While these approaches can significantly reduce bias risks, Czerniewicz (2018) argues that addressing algorithmic bias in global ODL contexts ultimately requires confronting broader questions about power, representation, and resource allocation in educational technology development. When most educational AI systems are developed in resource-rich,

Western contexts and subsequently deployed globally, structural inequalities in development processes may limit the effectiveness of technical solutions to bias. This perspective suggests that genuinely equitable AI implementation in ODL may require not just refined algorithms but transformative approaches to technology development that center currently marginalized perspectives.

Implementation Barriers in Resource-Constrained ODL Institutions

Resource constraints present significant barriers to AI implementation for many ODL institutions, particularly those in developing regions or serving primarily disadvantaged student populations. While well-resourced universities can invest in sophisticated infrastructure, technical expertise, and comprehensive implementation processes, institutions with limited resources face difficult choices about where to focus their AI efforts and how to develop sustainable approaches despite constraints (ICDE, 2019). Based on available literature, several specific barriers affect resource-constrained ODL institutions and a few examples are highlighted:

1. Technical infrastructure limitations include insufficient computing resources, inadequate data storage capacity, unreliable internet connectivity, and outdated systems that cannot easily integrate with modern AI applications. A survey by the International Council for Open and Distance Education found that 62% of ODL institutions in low-income countries identified infrastructure limitations as their primary barrier to AI implementation, compared to 17% in high-income regions (ICDE, 2019).
2. Expertise gaps emerge when institutions lack specialized personnel with skills in data science, machine learning, and AI implementation. Smaller ODL providers often struggle to compete with private sector compensation for these roles, creating persistent capacity limitations. The African Virtual University reported that positions for data scientists remained unfilled for average periods of 14 months, significantly delaying planned analytics initiatives (Nafukho & Muyia, 2018).
3. Financial constraints affect both initial implementation and ongoing maintenance of AI systems. While certain AI applications ultimately generate operational efficiencies and cost savings, realizing these benefits typically requires substantial upfront investment that resource-constrained institutions struggle to secure. Traditional funding models for educational technology may not adequately account for the continuous development requirements of sophisticated AI systems.
4. Vendor dependence risks arise when resource limitations lead institutions to rely heavily on external providers for AI capabilities, potentially sacrificing strategic control and creating long-term financial obligations. Commercial solutions may not be designed for the specific needs and constraints of ODL contexts in developing regions, creating misalignment between institutional requirements and available options (Selwyn, 2019).
5. Scale limitations can prevent smaller institutions from generating sufficient data for effective machine learning implementations, particularly for applications requiring large training datasets. While large ODL universities like the UK Open University or India's

IGNOU can leverage massive student populations for AI development, smaller institutions face fundamental challenges in data-driven approaches Nguyen and Karunaratne (2024).

Several strategies have emerged for addressing these challenges, based on the literature:

1. Phased implementation approaches prioritize high-impact, lower-resource applications while building organizational capacity for more sophisticated implementations over time. Strategic roadmaps often begin with rule-based chatbots and basic learning analytics before progressing to more complex applications, ensuring sustainable development despite resource limitations (Commonwealth of Learning, 2020).
2. Collaborative development models enable resource-sharing across multiple institutions, distributing costs and leveraging collective expertise. The Commonwealth of Learning has facilitated several such collaborations, including shared predictive analytics frameworks now used by ODL providers across multiple African countries (Commonwealth of Learning, 2020).
3. Open source solutions reduce licensing costs and enable adaptation to specific institutional contexts, potentially addressing both financial constraints and alignment challenges. The Open Education Analytics initiative has developed freely available tools specifically designed for resource-constrained educational contexts, with implementations across several developing regions (Mavengere, Ruohonen, & Nleya, 2013).
4. Cloud-based architectures can reduce on-premises infrastructure requirements, enabling sophisticated applications despite local hardware limitations. However, these approaches require careful attention to data sovereignty concerns, connectivity constraints, and long-term cost implications (Jarke & Breiter, 2019).
5. Hybrid human-AI systems combine strategic automation with human expertise, potentially achieving meaningful benefits despite limited technical capacity. These approaches recognize that full automation may be neither feasible nor desirable in many resource-constrained contexts (Selwyn, 2019).

Capacity building remains a central challenge for sustainable AI implementation in resource-constrained ODL institutions. The African Virtual University's approach demonstrates promising directions, developing internal expertise through targeted professional development while strategically engaging external partners for specialized capabilities. This model has enabled meaningful AI implementation despite resource limitations, with documented improvements in student retention and satisfaction (Nafukho & Muyia, 2018). We provide practical approaches adapted from various sources in Table 2 in matrix form as ways of overcoming common implementation challenges faced by ODL institutions with limited resources.

Table 2. AI implementation barriers and strategic responses in resource-constrained ODL contexts

Implementation Barrier	Strategic Responses	Institutional Examples
Technical Infrastructure Limitations	• Cloud-based approaches requiring minimal local computing • Progressive enhancement design for varying connectivity • Offline capability for intermittent access • Mobile-first development for smartphone access	• African Virtual University's lightweight chatbots functioning in low-bandwidth contexts (Nafukho & Muyia, 2018) • BOU's offline-capable REMIS system (Botswana Open University, 2022)
Expertise Gaps	• Distributed expertise networks across institutions • Tiered capability development focusing on high-priority areas first • Strategic partnerships with technical providers that include knowledge transfer • Faculty fellowship programmes developing internal champions	• Commonwealth of Learning's shared analytics expertise network (Commonwealth of Learning, 2020) • UNISA's AI implementation mentorship programme (Makhanya, 2020)
Financial Constraints	• Open-source solutions adapted to institutional contexts • Phased implementation targeting high-ROI applications first • Collaborative development across multiple institutions • Subscription models rather than capital-intensive infrastructure	• Open Education Analytics Initiative • ICDE shared implementation frameworks (ICDE, 2019)
Vendor Dependence Risks	• Hybrid models combining commercial and open-source components • Multi-vendor strategies avoiding single-provider lock-in • Requirement for open data standards and portability • Progressive development of internal capability	• UK Open University's mixed vendor strategy • Commonwealth of Learning's vendor evaluation framework (Commonwealth of Learning, 2020)
Scale Limitations	• Data pooling across partner institutions (with appropriate privacy protections) • Transfer learning approaches requiring less training data • Rule-based systems complementing machine learning for smaller datasets • Progressive implementation expanding with data accumulation	• Small ODL providers in Pacific region data collaborative (Bozkurt et al., 2021) • ICDE analytics models for smaller institutions (ICDE, 2019)

As Prinsloo (2020) argues, resource constraints in AI implementation reflect broader geopolitical inequalities in educational technology development. When most research, development, and standard-setting occurs in resource-rich contexts, the resulting technologies may be fundamentally misaligned with the realities of resource-constrained institutions. Addressing these disparities may require not just capacity building within individual institutions but broader structural changes in how educational AI is developed, funded, and governed globally.

Academic Integrity Considerations in Unproctored Environments

The unproctored nature of most distance learning environments creates particular challenges for maintaining academic integrity. This is because AI technologies simultaneously enable new approaches to academic misconduct detection and create unprecedented tools for academic dishonesty. This tension has intensified dramatically since late 2022, when advances in large language models made sophisticated AI writing tools widely available, creating what Kasneci et al. (2023) describe as a "fundamental disruption in traditional approaches to assessment and academic integrity."

ODL institutions face several distinct challenges in this area:

1. Identity verification is a persistent concern in distance assessment, where traditional approaches to confirming student identity through physical presence are unavailable. While various technical solutions exist, including biometric verification, credential authentication, and pattern analysis, each presents limitations in global ODL contexts where students may access learning systems from diverse devices and connectivity environments (Selwyn et al., 2020).
2. Unauthorized collaboration detection becomes increasingly difficult in ODL environments where traditional monitoring approaches are infeasible. Research by Lee (2021) reported increased concerns about collusion during online assessments since the COVID-19 pandemic accelerated distance education adoption.
3. Contract cheating, where students engage third parties to complete academic work, presents growing challenges that traditional plagiarism detection tools cannot adequately address. The commercial market for ghostwritten assignments has expanded dramatically with the growth of online learning, creating what Ellis et al. (2020) describe as an "integrity crisis" particularly affecting distance education providers.
4. AI-generated content represents the newest and perhaps most challenging frontier, as large language models can now produce essays, code, and other assignments that increasingly resemble authentic student work. Unlike previous forms of academic misconduct that involved human production, AI-generated content may be undetectable through traditional means and can be produced at unprecedented scale and speed (Kasneci et al., 2023).
5. Cultural variation in understanding and applying academic integrity standards creates additional complexity in global ODL contexts. Research by Bozkurt et al. (2021) found significant differences in how students from different cultural backgrounds conceptualize plagiarism, collaboration, and appropriate attribution, creating challenges for developing consistent approaches across diverse student populations.

Several approaches show promise for addressing these challenges:

1. Assessment redesign represents perhaps the most fundamental response, creating evaluation approaches that emphasize process over product, incorporate personalized elements resistant to outsourcing, require application in authentic contexts, or leverage

students' unique perspectives and experiences. The UK Open University has pioneered assessment designs specifically developed for integrity in distance contexts, focusing on demonstrated reasoning rather than easily reproducible outputs.

2. Multimodal verification systems combine different approaches to student authentication, potentially providing more robust security than any single method. These might include knowledge-based verification (information only the student should know), possession-based approaches (access to enrolled devices or accounts), and biometric elements where appropriate and legally permissible (Selwyn et al., 2020).
3. Digital forensic techniques analyze patterns in student submissions to identify potential irregularities, including stylistic inconsistencies, unusual submission patterns, or document metadata suggesting third-party involvement. These approaches focus on behavioral indicators rather than content matching, potentially addressing forms of misconduct that traditional plagiarism detection misses (Ellis et al., 2020).
4. AI detection tools attempt to identify AI-generated content through statistical analysis, though the effectiveness of these approaches remains contested as generative models continue to evolve. Some institutions have implemented policies requiring students to disclose AI use in completing assignments, shifting emphasis from detection to appropriate attribution (Kasneci et al., 2023).
5. Honor codes and integrity education approaches focus on developing student understanding and commitment to academic integrity rather than relying primarily on detection and punishment. Research by Ellis et al. (2020) suggests that ODL institutions with well-developed integrity education programmes experience lower rates of misconduct, though these approaches require thoughtful adaptation across cultural contexts.

Beyond specific technical or pedagogical interventions, many ODL institutions are reconsidering fundamental assumptions about assessment in light of the changing technological landscape. As Kasneci et al. (2023) argue, the emergence of sophisticated AI writing tools challenges traditional distinctions between acceptable and unacceptable assistance, potentially requiring new conceptualizations of what constitutes original student work in an age of human-AI collaboration. This reconceptualization is particularly relevant for ODL institutions, which have historically been at the forefront of navigating tensions between technological innovation and academic tradition. Makhanya (2020) suggests promising directions, combining redesigned assessments that remain meaningful in an AI-enabled environment with clear guidelines for appropriate technology use and educational initiatives that help students understand the value of authentic academic work beyond credentialing requirements. While these approaches can significantly mitigate integrity risks, no single strategy or combination of strategies can eliminate all possibilities for academic misconduct in unproctored environments. As Selwyn (2019) observes, ODL institutions must ultimately balance integrity assurance with other important values, including accessibility, student privacy, and the development of authentic assessment approaches that prepare students for real-world contexts where collaboration and resource use are normal and expected.

The ethical and operational challenges examined in this section, data privacy across jurisdictions, algorithmic bias affecting diverse student populations, resource constraints limiting implementation, and academic integrity concerns in unproctored environments, create a complex terrain that ODL institutions must navigate carefully. While these challenges are significant, they are not insurmountable. The following section offers strategic recommendations and practical frameworks to help institutions develop context-appropriate approaches that leverage AI's potential while addressing these multifaceted concerns.

STRATEGIC RECOMMENDATIONS FOR ODL INSTITUTIONS

Based on research evidence and case studies of successful implementation, this section offers strategic recommendations for ODL institutions navigating the AI landscape. These recommendations address governance structures for cross-border education, institutional capacity building, curriculum redesign for AI-enhanced learning, ethical implementation frameworks, and sustainable funding models for resource-constrained providers. While specific implementation details will necessarily vary across institutional contexts, these general principles provide guidance for developing context-appropriate AI strategies in ODL environments.

Developing Comprehensive AI Governance Structures for Cross-Border Education

Effective governance represents perhaps the most fundamental requirement for responsible AI implementation in ODL contexts, particularly for institutions operating across multiple contexts with varying regulatory frameworks, cultural expectations, and student needs. While traditional governance approaches often assume relatively homogeneous stakeholder communities and consistent regulatory environments, cross-border ODL institutions must develop more complex structures that accommodate diverse contexts while maintaining coherent institutional direction (Prinsloo & Slade, 2018).

Several principles emerge from successful governance implementations:

1. Multi-level frameworks establish core institutional principles that apply across all contexts while enabling contextual adaptation to different regulatory environments and student populations. The University of South Africa's approach exemplifies this balance, with university-wide ethical guidelines for AI use complemented by region-specific implementation protocols that address varying data protection requirements and cultural considerations (Makhanya, 2020).
2. Stakeholder representation ensures that governance structures include diverse perspectives reflecting the institution's full range of contexts and constituencies. The UK Open University's AI Ethics Board includes not only technical and academic experts but also student representatives from different regions and demographic backgrounds, specifically ensuring inclusion of historically marginalized perspectives.

3. Transparent decision processes make visible how AI-related determinations are made, who is involved in making them, and what values and priorities inform them. Transparency is particularly important in cross-border contexts where differences in power and privilege might otherwise lead to some stakeholder perspectives being privileged over others (Knox et al., 2020).
4. Continuous assessment mechanisms regularly evaluate AI systems' impacts across different student populations and contexts, enabling ongoing refinement in response to emerging issues or unexpected consequences. These mechanisms recognize that governance cannot be established once and left static but must evolve as technologies develop and implementation contexts change.
5. Clear accountability structures establish responsibility for AI-related decisions and provide mechanisms for addressing concerns when systems function inappropriately. In cross-border contexts, these structures must be accessible to stakeholders across all operational regions, with appropriate accommodation for language differences and varying levels of institutional familiarity (Prinsloo, 2020).

A number of governance models are seen to demonstrate particular promise for cross-border ODL contexts:

1. Ethical review boards specifically focused on AI implementation can provide oversight similar to institutional review boards for research, evaluating proposed applications against ethical principles and institutional values. These bodies typically include diverse expertise spanning technical, legal, educational, and ethical domains (Selwyn, 2019).
2. Algorithmic impact assessment processes systematically evaluate potential effects of AI systems before implementation, with particular attention to how impacts might vary across different student populations and contexts. These processes can identify potential issues early enough to implement mitigating strategies before problems emerge at scale (Prinsloo & Slade, 2018).
3. Federated governance structures distribute certain decision-making authority to regional or contextual units while maintaining centralized oversight for institution-wide concerns. This approach recognizes that many AI governance questions cannot be appropriately addressed through one-size-fits-all determinations applied across diverse contexts (Jarke & Breiter, 2019).
4. Student participation mechanisms formally incorporate student perspectives in governance processes, recognizing that those most affected by AI systems should have meaningful voice in how those systems are designed and implemented. These mechanisms require careful design to ensure diverse student representatives can participate effectively despite potential barriers related to technical knowledge, institutional power dynamics, or practical constraints (Knox et al., 2020).
5. Cross-institutional collaborations enable ODL providers to share governance frameworks, ethical guidelines, and implementation protocols, potentially addressing capacity limitations while promoting standardization where appropriate. The Commonwealth of Learning has facilitated several such collaborations, developing shared governance

resources adaptable to different institutional contexts (Commonwealth of Learning, 2020).

As Prinsloo (2020) argues, effective AI governance in cross-border ODL contexts ultimately requires engaging with fundamental questions about institutional purpose, educational values, and power relationships across diverse stakeholder communities. Technical and procedural mechanisms can support this engagement but cannot substitute for the essential work of clarifying institutional values and establishing processes that apply those values consistently across varying contexts while respecting legitimate differences in stakeholder priorities and needs.

Building Institutional Capacity For Distributed Implementation

Successful AI implementation in ODL environments requires developing various forms of institutional capacity beyond technical infrastructure and expertise. For distributed organizations operating across multiple contexts, this capacity-building challenge takes on distinctive dimensions related to coordination across distance, adaptation to diverse environments, and alignment of efforts despite varying local conditions (Rienties et al., 2020).

Some forms of forms of capacity are particularly important for distributed implementation:

1. Technical capabilities include not only centralized expertise but distributed technical capacity appropriate to local implementation contexts. While certain specialized functions may be maintained centrally, successful distributed implementation requires local technical staff who understand both the AI systems being implemented and the specific contextual factors that influence their operation in particular environments.
2. Data literacy across academic and administrative staff enables informed engagement with AI systems, including appropriate interpretation of insights and recognition of limitations.
3. Change management expertise supports the organizational transitions necessary for effective AI implementation, which typically require not just adopting new technologies but fundamentally rethinking processes and practices. In distributed contexts, this expertise must address the particular challenges of coordinating change across geographic, cultural, and operational boundaries (Rienties et al., 2020).
4. Ethical reasoning capabilities enable thoughtful navigation of the complex questions that inevitably arise in AI implementation, especially in diverse global contexts where different stakeholder communities may hold varying perspectives on appropriate data use, algorithmic decision-making, and related concerns (Prinsloo, 2020).
5. Cross-cultural competence supports effective adaptation of AI implementations across different cultural contexts, recognizing that technologies developed in one environment may require significant modification to function appropriately in others. This competence includes understanding how cultural factors influence technology perception, use patterns, and appropriateness of various interventions (Bozkurt et al., 2021).

In the same manner, various capacity-building approaches that show particular promise for distributed ODL contexts are now outlined:

1. Communities of practice connect practitioners across distributed locations, enabling knowledge-sharing, collaborative problem-solving, and development of context-appropriate implementation approaches. The UK Open University has developed sophisticated communities of practice around learning analytics implementation, connecting staff across regional centers through both technological platforms and periodic in-person exchanges.
2. Phased implementation models build capacity progressively through carefully sequenced initiatives that develop institutional capabilities while delivering concrete benefits at each stage. This approach begins with focused applications requiring limited technical sophistication while systematically developing the expertise and infrastructure needed for more ambitious implementations (Koole et al., 2021).
3. Strategic partnership approaches complement internal capacity with external expertise where appropriate, particularly for specialized technical functions that may be difficult to maintain internally. Successful partnerships typically focus not only on immediate implementation support but also on knowledge transfer that builds institutional capacity over time.
4. Distributed training models develop capabilities across institutional locations rather than concentrating expertise centrally. "Train-the-trainer" approaches for learning analytics implementation enable local capacity development while maintaining consistency through carefully designed training materials and ongoing support networks (Nafukho & Muyia, 2018).
5. Simulation and scenario planning builds capability for addressing potential implementation challenges before they emerge in practice. These approaches are particularly valuable for preparing distributed teams to handle variations in how AI systems might function across different contexts and student populations.

The University of South Africa's capacity-building approach demonstrates effective practices for large-scale distributed implementation. Rather than attempting to develop comprehensive AI capabilities simultaneously across all regional centers, the university identified pilot locations for initial implementation, using these experiences to develop context-appropriate training materials and implementation protocols. Regional implementation teams combine central technical experts with local staff familiar with specific operational contexts, creating what Makhanya (2020) describes as "contextually-aware technical capacity." Regular cross-regional exchanges enable sharing of emerging practices and collaborative problem-solving for common challenges. This approach has enabled successful implementation across dramatically different operational contexts while developing sustainable internal capacity rather than creating ongoing dependency on external vendors. As Rienties et al. (2020) observe, capacity building for AI in distributed ODL environments is not simply about developing technical capabilities but about creating "socio-technical readiness" that encompasses human, organizational, and technical dimensions. This perspective recognizes that successful implementation depends not only on technological sophistication but on developing the human and organizational capabilities to use these technologies effectively in service of educational goals across diverse implementation contexts.

Redesigning Curricula and Pedagogies for AI-Enhanced Distance Learning

Realizing AI's potential in ODL requires more than adding technological capabilities to existing educational approaches. It necessitates thoughtful redesign of curricula and pedagogies to leverage AI's strengths while preserving essential human elements of effective distance education.

Developing AI Literacy Among Faculty and Students

Effective AI implementation in ODL environments requires not only institutional capacity but also AI literacy among the primary users of these systems, faculty and students. AI literacy encompasses understanding AI capabilities and limitations, developing skills for effective human-AI collaboration, and cultivating critical perspectives on algorithmic systems (Ng & Kolko, 2023). This literacy is particularly important in cross-border ODL contexts, where varying levels of technological familiarity, cultural perspectives on technology, and access to digital resources create significant disparities in readiness for AI-enhanced education.

For faculty in ODL environments, AI literacy development faces unique challenges compared to traditional settings. Faculty are often geographically dispersed, may work part-time across multiple institutions, and typically have varied levels of technical background and support. Effective AI literacy programmes for ODL faculty should include:

1. Contextually relevant training that addresses how AI functions within specific ODL educational models rather than generic AI awareness
2. Discipline-specific application examples showing how AI can enhance teaching in particular subject areas
3. Staged competency development that begins with basic AI interaction skills and progressively builds toward advanced implementation capabilities
4. Peer learning communities that connect faculty across locations for collaborative skill development and practice sharing
5. Just-in-time support resources accessible at the moment of need rather than solely through scheduled formal training

Several ODL institutions have developed promising approaches to faculty AI literacy. The UK Open University's "AI for Educators" programme combines self-paced online modules with facilitated community discussions and practical implementation projects. Similarly, the African Virtual University has created a distributed mentorship model pairing faculty experienced in AI implementation with colleagues new to these technologies, supported by localized resource materials addressing specific regional contexts and constraints.

For students, AI literacy development must be embedded within the ODL experience rather than treated as a separate prerequisite. Effective approaches include:

1. Orientation modules introducing available AI tools with scaffolded practice opportunities
2. Progressive skill development integrated into course activities, building capabilities throughout the programme
3. Clear ethical guidelines for appropriate AI use that emphasize augmentation rather than replacement of learning
4. Explicit instruction in distinguishing between AI-generated content and developing original thinking
5. Metacognitive activities that help students understand how AI can support their unique learning processes

The University of South Africa has implemented a particularly effective approach by developing an "AI Assistant Orientation" that introduces students to institutional AI tools through practical problem-solving scenarios relevant to their specific programmes. This approach develops not only technical skills but also nuanced understanding of when and how to use AI appropriately in different learning contexts.

As Khare, Stewart, and Khare (2018) observe, the integration of AI into ODL must be approached with careful consideration of equity, ensuring that students and faculty with limited technological access or digital experience are not further disadvantaged. This includes providing alternative approaches for low-bandwidth environments, offline components for those with intermittent connectivity, and additional support resources for individuals with limited digital backgrounds. Without such equity-focused strategies, AI implementation risks creating new forms of educational exclusion, undermining ODL's mission to expand educational access.

This redesign process presents both opportunities and challenges, requiring careful attention to how AI capabilities can enhance rather than undermine educational quality and human connection in distance learning environments (Holmes et al., 2019).A few principles emerge from successful curriculum and pedagogy redesign initiatives, based on available literature are worth highlighting:

1. Complementarity approaches identify which educational functions are best performed by human educators and which can be effectively supported or enhanced by AI, developing models that leverage the distinctive strengths of each. Research by Holmes et al. (2019) suggests that AI systems typically excel at content delivery, immediate feedback on structured tasks, and identifying patterns across large datasets, while human educators bring irreplaceable value in motivating students, contextualizing knowledge, modeling expert thinking, and supporting socio-emotional development.
2. Design for diverse contexts ensures that AI-enhanced curricula function effectively across the varying technological, cultural, and social environments characteristic of global ODL student populations. This principle recognizes that approaches developed

for resource-rich, high-connectivity contexts may require significant adaptation to serve students in different circumstances (Bozkurt et al., 2021).

3. Student agency preservation maintains learner control and decision-making rather than creating passive relationships with algorithmic systems. While AI can provide recommendations and personalized pathways, effective designs ensure students understand options, participate in key decisions, and develop the self-regulation capabilities essential for lifelong learning (Knox et al., 2020).
4. Assessment transformation moves beyond traditional testing approaches vulnerable to academic integrity concerns toward authentic evaluation methods that leverage AI's capabilities while remaining meaningful in an age of AI-generated content. This transformation involves not only technical changes in assessment tools but fundamental reconsideration of what should be assessed and how (Kasneci et al., 2023).
5. Collaborative intelligence integration develops students' capabilities to work effectively with AI tools as partners in learning and problem-solving rather than treating AI merely as a delivery system for educational content. This approach recognizes that graduates will increasingly work alongside AI systems in professional contexts, making human-AI collaboration an essential competency (Luckin & Cukurova, 2019).

Among specific redesign strategies that demonstrate particular promise, the following are notable:

1. Flipped learning models leverage AI for content delivery and basic concept mastery, freeing synchronous interaction time (whether in-person or virtual) for higher-order discussion, problem-solving, and application.
2. Competency-based frameworks combined with AI-driven personalization enable students to progress based on demonstrated mastery rather than time-based cohort models. These approaches can be particularly effective in ODL contexts with diverse student populations entering with varying levels of preparation and progressing at different rates (Bodily & Verbert, 2017).
3. Project-based learning designs engage students in authentic tasks requiring integration and application of knowledge, with AI systems providing scaffolding, resources, and feedback throughout the process. These approaches can address both engagement challenges common in distance education and assessment integrity concerns by creating personalized learning products difficult to outsource (Ellis et al., 2020).
4. Collaborative learning structures supported by AI facilitation tools enable meaningful peer interaction despite geographic separation, addressing the isolation that has historically characterized many distance learning experiences. These structures can be particularly valuable in cross-cultural ODL contexts where peer learning also develops intercultural competencies (Cela et al., 2015).
5. Multimodal learning pathways offer content and assessment through different modalities, with AI systems helping students identify which approaches best suit their learning preferences, circumstances, and goals. This flexibility is especially important in global

ODL contexts where students access learning through varying devices and connectivity environments (Tlili et al., 2022).

Research on adaptive learning redesign in psychology curricula demonstrates effective integration of these principles. Rather than simply adding AI tools to existing course structures, some universities have fundamentally reimagined curricula around competency-based models where AI systems help students identify appropriate learning pathways based on their current knowledge, learning preferences, and professional goals. Adaptive learning modules provide personalized content and practice for foundational concepts, freeing instructor time for synchronous sessions focused on complex problem-solving and professional application. Assessment combines AI-supported formative feedback with authentic projects requiring students to apply psychological concepts to real-world scenarios in their local contexts. This integrated redesign has significantly improved completion rates while maintaining academic standards and enhancing student satisfaction (ICDE, 2019).

As Holmes et al. (2019) observe, effective curriculum and pedagogy redesign for AI-enhanced ODL requires moving beyond questions of technical implementation to engage fundamental questions about educational purpose, the nature of expertise, and the kinds of human capabilities that remain essential in an increasingly AI-mediated world. This perspective suggests that the most successful redesign approaches will be those grounded in clear educational philosophy rather than driven primarily by technological possibility.

Ensuring Ethical and Equitable Implementation across Diverse Contexts

Ethical and equitable AI implementation takes on distinctive dimensions in ODL environments serving diverse student populations across multiple geographic, cultural, and socioeconomic contexts. While all educational institutions face ethical challenges in AI adoption, global ODL providers must navigate particular complexities related to cross-border data flows, varying cultural norms, disparate regulatory frameworks, and dramatic differences in technological access and digital literacy (Prinsloo, 2020).

The following principles have been seen to guide effective ethical implementation in these complex environments:

1. Contextual adaptation recognizes that ethical frameworks developed in one context may not transfer seamlessly to others, requiring thoughtful consideration of how principles should be applied across diverse environments. This approach rejects both rigid universalism that ignores legitimate contextual differences and relativism that abandons core ethical commitments in the name of cultural sensitivity (Prinsloo & Slade, 2018).
2. Participatory justice ensures that stakeholders from all institutional contexts, particularly those from historically marginalized communities, have meaningful voice in decisions about AI system design, implementation, and governance. This principle recognizes that technical decisions embed values and priorities that should reflect diverse perspectives rather than defaulting to assumptions from dominant groups (Knox et al., 2020).

3. Transparency requirements make visible how AI systems function, what data they collect, and how algorithmic determinations are made, enabling informed consent and meaningful accountability across diverse stakeholder communities. These requirements take on particular importance in cross-cultural ODL contexts where different assumptions about institutional authority and technological acceptance may influence how systems are perceived (Selwyn, 2019).
4. Equity by design builds fairness considerations into system development from the beginning rather than treating bias as an afterthought to be addressed once problems emerge. This approach requires proactive consideration of how systems might function differently across varied student populations and implementation contexts.
5. Progressive realization acknowledges that perfect ethical implementation may not be immediately achievable, establishing processes for continuous improvement while ensuring that interim approaches do not create unacceptable harms. This principle is particularly important for resource-constrained institutions navigating complex ethical terrain with limited specialized expertise (Prinsloo, 2020).

The following strategies demonstrate effectiveness in operationalizing the highlighted principles:

1. Ethics review processes adapted for educational technology evaluate proposed AI implementations against institutional values and ethical principles before deployment. The UK Open University provides a model for such processes, with representation from diverse stakeholder groups and explicit consideration of cross-cultural dimensions.
2. Tiered implementation models deploy different approaches in different contexts based on local regulatory requirements, technological infrastructure, and cultural expectations. These models maintain consistent ethical principles while recognizing that specific practices may legitimately vary across diverse implementation environments (Jarke & Breiter, 2019).
3. Algorithmic impact assessments systematically evaluate potential effects of AI systems before implementation, with particular attention to how impacts might vary across different student populations and contexts. These assessments typically consider both intended functions and potential unintended consequences (Prinsloo & Slade, 2018).
4. Ethical capacity building develops capability for addressing complex questions throughout the institution rather than concentrating expertise in specialized units. This distributed approach enables context-appropriate ethical implementation across diverse environments while maintaining consistent institutional values (Rienties et al., 2020).

The University of South Africa's approach to ethical implementation demonstrates these principles in practice across a complex multi-country operation. The university developed a tiered ethical framework establishing non-negotiable principles that apply across all contexts while enabling contextual adaptation for specific implementation environments. Algorithmic impact assessments conducted before system deployment specifically consider effects across different student populations, with particular attention to potentially vulnerable groups. Ethics training for all staff involved in AI implementation, not only technical specialists, builds distributed capacity for addressing ethical questions as they emerge in different contexts. A formal review process evaluates system performance against ethical criteria after implementation, identifying needed adjustments and ensuring continuous improvement. This comprehensive approach has enabled the university to implement AI innovations while maintaining stakeholder trust across dramatically different operational contexts (Makhanya, 2020).

As Prinsloo (2020) argues, ethical implementation in global ODL contexts ultimately requires moving beyond compliance-oriented approaches focused primarily on risk mitigation toward positive ethical vision that articulates how AI technologies can affirmatively serve values of educational access, quality, and empowerment across diverse global communities. This perspective suggests that ethics should not be treated as a constraint on implementation but as a central aspect of institutional purpose that shapes how AI technologies are designed, deployed, and governed.

Creating Sustainable Funding Models for Resource-Constrained Providers

Developing sustainable funding approaches for AI implementation represents a critical challenge for many ODL institutions, particularly those operating in resource-constrained environments or serving primarily disadvantaged student populations. While well-resourced universities can make substantial upfront investments with confidence in long-term returns, institutions facing tighter financial constraints require more creative approaches that deliver meaningful benefits while managing costs and risks (ICDE, 2019).

Some principles are seen to guide effective funding strategy in these contexts:

1. Value-based prioritization focuses limited resources on applications with clear connections to institutional priorities and demonstrated potential for meaningful educational or operational benefits. This approach rejects both uncritical adoption of fashionable technologies and excessive risk aversion that prevents strategic innovation (Rienties et al., 2020).
2. Phased implementation sequences AI initiatives to generate early returns that can support subsequent development, creating sustainable growth trajectories rather than requiring massive upfront investment. This approach recognizes that successful AI implementation typically involves organizational learning that is difficult to compress into condensed timeframes regardless of available resources.
3. Total cost accounting considers the full financial implications of AI initiatives, including not only initial development or procurement but also ongoing maintenance, training, integration, and adaptation requirements. This comprehensive perspective prevents unpleasant surprises that can undermine sustainability and institutional confidence.
4. Strategic outsourcing balances internal capability development with external partnerships where appropriate, recognizing that certain specialized functions may be more economically provided by partners while maintaining internal control of core strategic

capabilities. This balanced approach prevents both wasteful duplication of readily available external capabilities and dangerous dependency on vendors for mission-critical functions (Selwyn, 2019).

Based on the literature, specific strategies demonstrate effectiveness in operationalizing the principles just highlighted:

1. Incremental deployment models begin with targeted implementations addressing high-priority needs, using demonstrated success to build institutional confidence and financial support for subsequent phases. These approaches begin with focused AI implementation for specific high-value applications before expanding to broader AI applications based on documented benefits from the initial project (Commonwealth of Learning, 2020).
2. Open source utilization leverages freely available tools and platforms where appropriate, reducing licensing costs while enabling customization to specific institutional contexts. The Open Education Analytics initiative provides particularly valuable resources for resource-constrained institutions, offering pre-built components that can be adapted to different educational environments.
3. Strategic vendor relationships structure external partnerships to include knowledge transfer and capacity building alongside service provision, gradually reducing dependency over time as internal capabilities develop. This approach recognizes that while complete self-sufficiency may be unrealistic for many institutions, continued absolute dependency creates both financial and strategic vulnerabilities.
4. Return-on-Investment-driven (ROI-driven) expansion bases decisions about scaling successful pilot implementations on documented return on investment, whether measured through improved educational outcomes, operational efficiencies, enhanced competitiveness, or other institutional priorities. This evidence-based approach builds sustainable financial support by demonstrating concrete value to institutional stakeholders (Rienties et al., 2020).

The African Virtual University's funding approach for learning analytics implementation demonstrates these principles in practice. Rather than attempting comprehensive development using internal resources alone, the university established strategic partnerships with both commercial providers and other educational institutions, creating a hybrid model that combined external expertise with internal direction. Initial implementation focused on applications with clear connections to student retention, a critical priority with direct financial implications, generating measurable returns that supported subsequent phases. Open source components reduced licensing costs, while shared development arrangements with partner institutions distributed expenses for custom elements. Staff training emphasized developing internal capacity over time, gradually reducing dependency on external consultants. This multifaceted approach enabled sophisticated AI implementation despite significant resource constraints, creating sustainable funding through demonstrated value rather than requiring speculative upfront investment (Nafukho & Muyia, 2018).

As ICDE (2019) observes, sustainable funding for AI in resource-constrained ODL institutions ultimately requires moving beyond traditional project-based approaches toward integrated planning that connects technology investments to core institutional strategy and budget processes. This perspective suggests that rather than treating AI as a separate initiative requiring special funding, successful institutions increasingly incorporate these capabilities into fundamental operational and educational planning, allocating resources based on strategic priorities rather than technological categories.

Conceptual Framework for AI Implementation in Cross-Border Education

The Conceptual Framework for AI Implementation in Cross-Border Education, being proposed, provides ODL institutions with a comprehensive structure for developing and evaluating AI initiatives through a systematic approach addressing the complexity of implementing AI in globally distributed educational contexts. The practical application process begins with context assessment, mapping student and faculty distribution, cultural diversity, regulatory environments, technological capabilities, and student needs. This is followed by dimensional analysis across six key areas: technological infrastructure, ethical framework, governance structure, educational strategy, stakeholder engagement, and resource allocation. The framework integrates cross-cutting principles of contextual adaptation, inclusive design, transparency, and sustainability while accommodating external factors like diverse regulations, economic constraints, cultural expectations, and access inequalities. Implementation follows a staged approach of foundation building, pilot testing, phased expansion, continuous refinement, and knowledge sharing, all supported by ongoing evaluation. Figure 2 shows the framework. This framework illustrates the six interconnected dimensions essential for effective AI implementation in cross-border ODL contexts.

Figure 2. Conceptual framework for AI implementation in cross-border education

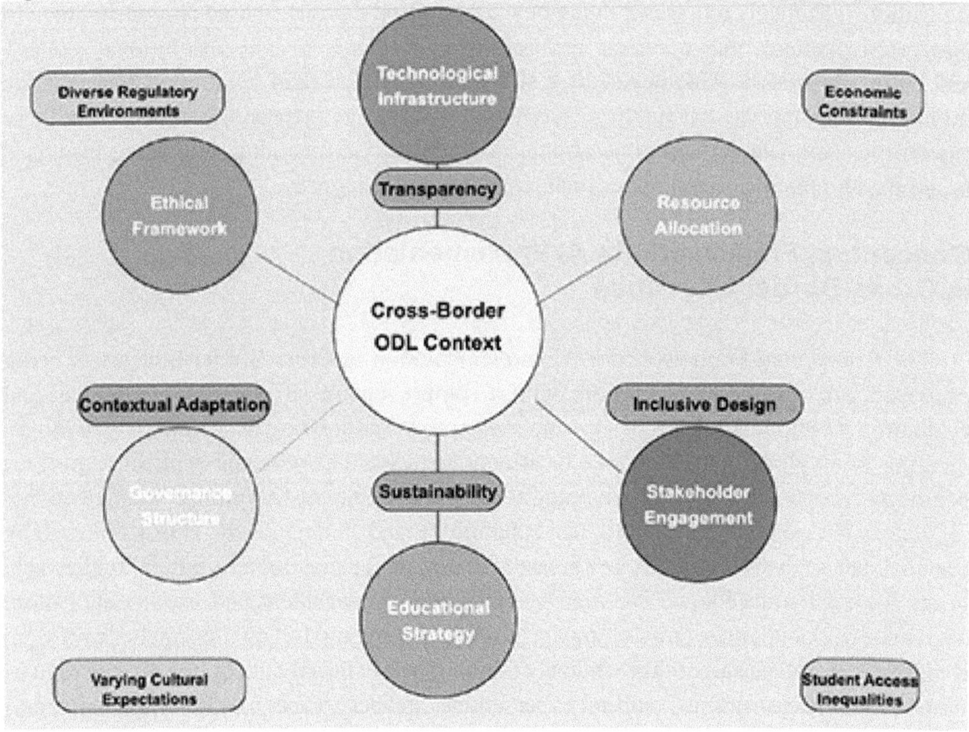

Botswana Open University's AI chatbot for research ethics support illustrates effective application of this framework. BOU assessed their distributed student population across multiple regions and in some cases, multiple countries, designed lightweight technology with offline capabilities, established ethical boundaries, created tiered governance, focused on specific educational pain points, engaged stakeholders through consultation, and allocated resources strategically within constraints. They integrated cross-cutting principles by adapting for varying connectivity, designing inclusive interfaces, creating transparent documentation, and developing sustainable approaches with minimal ongoing resource requirements. By addressing external factors including diverse regulations, resource limitations, cultural variations, and connectivity disparities, BOU successfully implemented an AI solution that addressed a specific institutional challenge while accounting for their unique cross-border context, demonstrating how the framework guides practical implementation in resource-constrained environments. We also share in Appendix A, a Sample AI Readiness Assessment Framework for ODL Institutions. This assessment framework is designed to help ODL institutions evaluate their readiness for AI implementation across key dimensions.

CONCLUSION

This chapter has explored how artificial intelligence is transforming Open and Distance Learning. We examined both the unprecedented opportunities these technologies present and the distinctive challenges they create for institutions serving students across geographic boundaries. Our analysis has highlighted how AI is enabling ODL providers to address persistent challenges including student isolation, delayed feedback, variable preparation levels, and high attrition rates, while also creating new considerations related to data privacy, algorithmic bias, implementation barriers, and academic integrity. Several key themes emerge from this examination:

First, AI in ODL represents not merely an incremental enhancement to existing approaches but a potential paradigm shift in how distance education functions. The capabilities now emerging, personalized learning at massive scale, real-time support across time zones and languages, predictive interventions before problems become critical, are notable. So also, is adaptive assessment, with a focus on demonstrated competency rather than standardized processes. These therefore address fundamental limitations that have historically constrained ODL effectiveness. While these capabilities remain unevenly implemented across the sector, leading institutions are demonstrating that thoughtful AI integration can transform educational experiences and outcomes—potentially making certain forms of open and distance learning (ODL) superior to traditional approaches in specific contexts

Second, successful AI implementation in ODL requires approaches specifically designed for distributed educational environments rather than adaptations of campus-based models. The unique characteristics of ODL, geographically dispersed stakeholders, cross-border operations, dramatically diverse student populations, varying technological infrastructure, and complex regulatory landscapes, create implementation requirements that generic approaches often fail to address. Institutions that have achieved the most significant benefits have developed strategies explicitly tailored to these realities, with particular attention to cross-cultural dimensions, varying resource constraints, and the need for flexible adaptation across different operational contexts.

Third, ethical implementation takes on distinctive dimensions in global ODL environments, requiring frameworks as diverse as the student populations these institutions serve. When data flows across jurisdictional boundaries, algorithms affect students from dramatically different cultural and socioeconomic contexts. Also, implementation occurs in environments with varying resources and constraints while ethical approaches cannot rely on one-size-fits-all determinations developed in single cultural contexts. Successful institutions have developed tiered frameworks that maintain consistent principles while enabling contextual adaptation, with particular attention to participatory approaches that include diverse stakeholder perspectives in system design, implementation, and governance.

Fourth, the uneven distribution of AI capabilities across global ODL institutions raises significant concerns about new forms of educational inequality. Current patterns suggest a troubling divergence between well-resourced providers implementing sophisticated systems that enhance educational quality and access, and resource-constrained institutions struggling with basic implementation barriers related to infrastructure, expertise, and funding. Without deliberate attention to capacity building, resource sharing, and affordable implementation models, AI could potentially widen rather than narrow educational divides, undermining ODL's historical mission of democratizing access to quality higher education.

Looking ahead, several developments will shape AI's continued evolution in ODL contexts:

a) Multimodal AI systems capable of functioning effectively across varying bandwidth constraints and device limitations will be essential for ensuring students are not disadvantaged by their technical circumstances. As these systems develop, they may help address some current implementation barriers for resource-constrained institutions and student populations, though concerns about equitable access will likely persist.
b) Cross-institutional AI collaborations will become increasingly important as development costs continue rising, enabling resource-sharing that makes sophisticated capabilities accessible to institutions that could not independently develop them. These collaborations will require careful attention to governance, intellectual property, and value alignment across diverse institutional contexts.
c) AI-enhanced virtual reality and simulation environments will increasingly address ODL's persistent limitations in providing authentic hands-on learning experiences, particularly for fields like healthcare, engineering, and other disciplines requiring practical skills development. These developments may significantly expand the range of programmes that can be effectively delivered through distance modes. Also, hybrid human-AI instruction models will continue evolving, creating new faculty roles focused on areas where human expertise remains irreplaceable while leveraging AI for functions where automation brings clear benefits. These models will require significant professional development for educators and thoughtful change management by institutional leaders.
d) Transnational governance frameworks for educational AI will emerge in response to the challenges of operating across jurisdictional boundaries, attempting to harmonize varying regulatory requirements while protecting student interests regardless of location. These frameworks will require careful balancing of universal principles with legitimate contextual variation.

For institutional leaders navigating this complex landscape, this chapter offers several core recommendations:

1. Develop comprehensive AI strategies aligned with institutional mission and values rather than implementing disconnected technologies without clear purpose. These strategies should articulate how AI specifically addresses institutional priorities and challenges, with particular attention to the distinctive characteristics of distance education in your operational contexts.
2. Invest in human capacity alongside technological capability, recognizing that successful implementation depends as much on organizational readiness and staff skills as on technical sophistication. This capacity development should span technical, educational, ethical, and operational domains, with particular attention to distributed capability across different institutional locations and functions.

3. Create robust governance structures appropriate to your institutional context, ensuring clear direction, appropriate oversight, and meaningful stakeholder participation in decisions about AI design and implementation. These structures should explicitly address cross-cultural dimensions if you operate across multiple contexts, with particular attention to including perspectives from historically marginalized communities.
4. Prioritize ethical considerations throughout the implementation process rather than treating them as compliance requirements to be addressed after technical decisions are made. This approach requires ongoing engagement with questions about data privacy, algorithmic transparency, equity across diverse student populations, and appropriate boundaries of AI-driven interventions.
5. Design for inclusion across your full range of student populations and contexts, ensuring AI implementations do not inadvertently disadvantage certain groups through unexamined assumptions or requirements that some students cannot meet. This inclusive design should consider not only technical access but cultural appropriateness, linguistic accessibility, and alignment with diverse learning preferences.
6. Balance innovation with sustainability, developing implementation approaches appropriate to your resource context and institutional capabilities. While ambition drives progress, approaches that outstrip available resources or organizational readiness typically fail regardless of their theoretical potential.
7. Share experiences and resources with other institutions navigating similar challenges, contributing to collective knowledge development while benefiting from others' insights. The complexity of AI implementation in ODL contexts means no single institution can develop comprehensive solutions independently, making collaboration essential for sector-wide progress.

AI in ODL represents both extraordinary opportunity and significant responsibility. These technologies have the potential to help higher education institutions serve more students more effectively than ever before, potentially transforming access to quality learning experiences regardless of geographic location or personal circumstances. Realizing this potential while navigating the ethical complexities and implementation challenges requires thoughtful leadership, clear institutional values, and commitment to educational mission over technological novelty. The institutions that successfully navigate this terrain will not merely enhance existing educational approaches but potentially redefine what's possible when geographic constraints no longer limit educational opportunity.

ACKNOWLEDGEMENTS

The authors wish to express their gratitude to the leadership of Botswana Open University for their support of this research. We are particularly grateful to our students and colleagues whose feedback and participation have shaped our understanding of AI's potential in distance education contexts.

REFERENCES

Adekanmbi, G. (1992). The transformation of correspondence education to distance education in Nigeria, 1927-1987. Unpublished PhD dissertation of the University of Ibadan.

Adekanmbi, G., & Boitshwarelo, B. (2010). International collaboration in distance education in Sub-Saharan Africa: Trends, trials and tomorrow's thrusts. Mukerji, S. & Tripathi, P. (Eds.). *Cases on interactive technology environments and transnational collaboration: Concerns and perspectives*. (pp. 39-55). IGI Global.

Anderson, T., & Dron, J. (2011). Three generations of distance education pedagogy. *International Review of Research in Open and Distance Learning*, *12*(3), 80–97. DOI: 10.19173/irrodl.v12i3.890

Aoun, J. E. (2017). *Robot-proof: Higher education in the age of artificial intelligence*. MIT Press. DOI: 10.7551/mitpress/11456.001.0001

Baker, T., Smith, L., & Anissa, N. (2019). Educ-AI-tion rebooted? Exploring the future of artificial intelligence in schools and colleges. Nesta. https://media.nesta.org.uk/documents/Future_of_AI_and_education_v5_WEB.pdf

Bodily, R., & Verbert, K. (2017). Review of research on student-facing learning analytics dashboards and educational recommender systems. *IEEE Transactions on Learning Technologies*, *10*(4), 405–418. DOI: 10.1109/TLT.2017.2740172

Bozkurt, A., Jung, I., Xiao, J., Vladimirschi, V., Schuwer, R., & Egorov, G. (2021). A global outlook to the interruption of education due to the COVID-19 pandemic: Navigating in a time of uncertainty and crisis. *Asian Journal of Distance Education*, *15*(1), 1–126.

Castañeda, L., & Selwyn, N. (2018). More than tools? Making sense of the ongoing digitizations of higher education. *International Journal of Educational Technology in Higher Education*, *15*(1), 22. DOI: 10.1186/s41239-018-0109-y

Coglianese, C., & Nash, J. (2021). Compliance management systems: Do they make a difference? In van Rooij, B., & Sokol, D. (Eds.), *The Cambridge handbook of compliance* (pp. 280–292). Cambridge University Press. DOI: 10.1017/9781108759458.039

Gašević, D., Dawson, S., & Siemens, G. (2016). Let's not forget: Learning analytics are about learning. *TechTrends*, *60*(1), 64–71. DOI: 10.1007/s11528-014-0822-x

Goel, A. K., & Polepeddi, L. (2016). Jill Watson: A virtual teaching assistant for online education. Georgia Institute of Technology. Retrieved from https://smartech.gatech.edu/handle/1853/59104

Herodotou, C., Rienties, B., Boroowa, A., Zdrahal, Z., & Hlosta, M. (2020). A large-scale implementation of predictive learning analytics in higher education: The teachers' role and perspective. *Educational Technology Research and Development*, *68*(1), 2193–2213.

Holmes, W., Bialik, M., & Fadel, C. (2019). *Artificial intelligence in education: Promises and implications for teaching and learning*. Center for Curriculum Redesign.

Kasneci, E., Sessler, K., & Bannert, M. (2023). ChatGPT for good? On opportunities and challenges of large language models for education. *Learning and Individual Differences*, *103*, 102274. DOI: 10.1016/j.lindif.2023.102274

Keegan, D. (1996). *Foundations of distance education* (3rd ed.). Routledge.

Khare, K., Stewart, B., & Khare, A. (2018). Artificial intelligence and the student experience: An institutional perspective. *IAFOR Journal of Education*, *6*(3), 63–78. DOI: 10.22492/ije.6.3.04

Lee, J. C. (2021). Artificial intelligence and the student experience: An institutional perspective. IAFOR Journal of Education, 6(3).

Luckin, R., & Cukurova, M. (2019). Designing educational technologies in the age of AI: A learning sciences-driven approach. *British Journal of Educational Technology*, *50*(6), 2824–2838. DOI: 10.1111/bjet.12861

Mavengere, N., Ruohonen, M., & Nleya, P. (2013). E-learning using open source software in African universities. In Ley, T., Ruohonen, M., Laanpere, M., & Tatnall, A. (Eds.), *Open and social technologies for networked learning* (pp. 197–202). DOI: 10.1007/978-3-642-37285-8_23

McGreal, R. (2020). Evaluation report on three regional centres established by the Commonwealth of Learning. Commonwealth of Learning.

Nguyen, N. B. C., & Karunaratne, T. (2024). Learning analytics with small datasets—State of the art and beyond. *Education Sciences*, *14*(6), 608. DOI: 10.3390/educsci14060608

Pelletier, K., McCormack, M., Reeves, J., Robert, J., & Arbino, N. (2021). *2021 EDUCAUSE Horizon Report, Teaching and Learning Edition*. EDUCAUSE.

Popenici, S. A. D., & Kerr, S. (2017). Exploring the impact of artificial intelligence on teaching and learning in higher education. *Research and Practice in Technology Enhanced Learning*, *12*(1), 22. DOI: 10.1186/s41039-017-0062-8 PMID: 30595727

Prinsloo, P. (2020). The ethics of learning analytics: A South African perspective. *British Journal of Educational Technology*, *51*(6), 2142–2156.

Rienties, B., Herodotou, C., Olney, T., Schencks, M., & Boroowa, A. (2020). Making sense of learning analytics dashboards: What do teachers want? *European Journal of Open. Distance and E-Learning*, *23*(1), 1–19.

Selwyn, N., Pangrazio, L., Nemorin, S., & Perrotta, C. (2020). What might the school of 2030 be like? An exercise in social science fiction. *Learning, Media and Technology*, *45*(1), 90–106. DOI: 10.1080/17439884.2020.1694944

Tlili, A., Huang, R., Shehata, B., Liu, D., Zhao, J., & Agyemang, B. (2022). What if the devil is my guardian angel: ChatGPT as a case study of using chatbots in education. *Smart Learning Environments*, *9*(1), 1–14. PMID: 40477962

Viberg, O., Kizilcec, R. F., Jivet, I., Martínez Monés, A., Oh, A., Mutimukwe, C., Hrastinski, S., & Scheffel, M. (2024). Cultural differences in students' privacy concerns in learning analytics across Germany, South Korea, Spain, Sweden, and the United States. *Computers in Human Behavior Reports*, *14*, 100416. DOI: 10.1016/j.chbr.2024.100416

Zawacki-Richter, O., Marín, V. I., Bond, M., & Gouverneur, F. (2019). Systematic review of research on artificial intelligence applications in higher education–where are the educators? *International Journal of Educational Technology in Higher Education*, *16*(1), 39. DOI: 10.1186/s41239-019-0171-0

KEY TERMS AND DEFINITIONS

Adaptive Learning Systems: Educational technologies that adjust content, pacing, and assessment based on individual learner performance and characteristics.

Algorithmic Bias: Systematic errors in AI systems that create unfair outcomes for certain groups of users, often reflecting historical inequities in training data.

Artificial Intelligence (AI): Computer systems capable of performing tasks that normally require human intelligence, including learning, reasoning, and self-correction.

Data Literacy: The ability to read, understand, create, and communicate data as information, essential for educators working with AI systems.

Differential Privacy: Mathematical frameworks that enable data analysis while providing formal guarantees against privacy violations.

Federated Learning: Machine learning approach that trains algorithms across multiple decentralized devices or servers holding local data samples without exchanging the data itself.

Large Language Models (LLMs): AI systems trained on vast corpora of text data that can generate human-like text, understand natural language, and perform various linguistic tasks.

Learning Analytics: The measurement, collection, analysis, and reporting of data about learners and their contexts for purposes of understanding and optimizing learning environments.

Machine Learning: Subset of AI focused on developing systems that learn from data without being explicitly programmed for specific tasks.

Natural Language Processing (NLP): Branch of AI concerned with the interaction between computers and human language, particularly programming computers to process and analyze large amounts of natural language data.

Open and Distance Learning (ODL): Educational approaches characterized by the separation of teacher and learner in time or place, or both, with learning materials and interaction provided through technology.

Personalized Learning: Educational approaches that tailor learning experiences to individual students' needs, interests, and abilities.

Predictive Analytics: Use of statistics, modeling, machine learning, and data mining to analyze current and historical data to make predictions about future events or behaviors.

ENDNOTES

1. The term "bias" is used in this chapter to refer to systematic disparities in how AI systems function across different student populations or contexts, particularly those that create or reinforce educational inequalities. This usage differs from the technical meaning of bias in statistics and machine learning.

2. The concept of "resource-constrained" encompasses not only financial limitations but also constraints related to technical infrastructure, human expertise, and organizational capacity. These constraints often co-occur but may manifest differently across institutional contexts.

APPENDIX I

Sample AI Readiness Assessment Framework for ODL Institutions

This assessment framework is designed to help ODL institutions evaluate their readiness for AI implementation across key dimensions. The framework enables institutions to identify strengths, gaps, and priorities for development before embarking on AI initiatives.

Instructions for Use:

1. Rate your institution on each indicator using the 1-5 scale described below
2. Calculate dimension averages to identify overall areas of strength and weakness
3. Use results to prioritize capacity-building initiatives and develop phased implementation plans
4. Reassess periodically (recommended annually) to track progress

Rating Scale:

1. **Initial/Ad Hoc**: No formalized approach; activities are reactive and inconsistent
2. **Developing**: Basic systems in place but significant gaps remain; limited coordination
3. **Defined**: Clear processes established with moderate consistency; some cross-functional coordination
4. **Managed**: Comprehensive approaches with good consistency; strong cross-functional integration
5. **Optimized**: Sophisticated systems with continuous improvement; exemplary integration and proactive adaptation

Assessment Dimensions:

Table 3. Strategic alignment

Indicator	Rating (1-5)	Evidence/Notes
Clear institutional vision for AI use		
AI initiatives linked to strategic priorities		
Executive leadership commitment		
Cross-functional governance structures		
Defined success metrics for AI initiatives		

Table 4. Technical infrastructure

Indicator	Rating (1-5)	Evidence/Notes
Computing resources adequacy		
Data storage capacity		
Network reliability across service regions		
System integration capabilities		
Technical support capacity		

Table 5. Data management

Indicator	Rating (1-5)	Evidence/Notes
Data quality standards and processes		
Data governance frameworks		
Cross-border data management protocols		
Data security systems		
Learning analytics capabilities		

Table 6. Human capacity

Indicator	Rating (1-5)	Evidence/Notes
AI/data science expertise		
Faculty data literacy		
Professional development programs		
Change management capabilities		
Cross-cultural implementation expertise		

Table 7. Ethical & regulatory readiness

Indicator	Rating (1-5)	Evidence/Notes
AI ethics framework		
Privacy protection protocols		
Regulatory compliance systems		
Algorithmic bias mitigation approaches		
Transparency practices		

Table 8. Educational integration

Indicator	Rating (1-5)	Evidence/Notes
Pedagogical frameworks for AI integration		
Faculty acceptance and engagement		
Assessment adaptation capabilities		
Student digital literacy development		
Learning design flexibility		

Table 9. Resource sustainability

Indicator	Rating (1-5)	Evidence/Notes
Sustainable funding models		
Resource allocation processes		
Partnership/collaboration frameworks		
Long-term maintenance planning		
ROI measurement systems		

Interpretation Guide:
Dimension Averages:

- **4.0-5.0**: Area of strength; ready for advanced implementation
- **3.0-3.9**: Moderate readiness; appropriate for targeted implementation with ongoing development
- **2.0-2.9**: Development needed; focus on capacity building before major implementations
- **1.0-1.9**: Significant gaps; requires fundamental development before implementation

Implementation Recommendations:

- Focus initial efforts on dimensions scoring 3.0 or higher
- Develop capacity-building plans for dimensions below 3.0
- Prioritize "quick wins" where moderate effort can significantly increase readiness
- Consider phased implementation approaches aligned with progressive capacity development

Chapter 2
Artificial Intelligence and the Transformation of Career Technical Education

Angela R Crevar
https://orcid.org/0000-0002-0596-9174
Mercer University, Atlanta, USA

Praveen K. Dubey
Montana State University - Northern, Havre, USA

Mattius Rischard
Montana State University - Northern, Havre, USA

ABSTRACT

Artificial Intelligence is revolutionizing Career and Technical Education (CTE) by enhancing instructional practices, increasing efficiency, and personalizing learning experiences. As CTE programs integrate AI technologies, educators are empowered to focus more on impactful teaching while AI reduces administrative tasks and provides real-time data for targeted interventions. However, successful AI implementation requires careful consideration of ethical concerns, algorithmic bias, data privacy, and maintaining the human element in education.

INTRODUCTION

Artificial intelligence (AI) is considered to be the fourth Industrial Revolution, making training with AI essential to prepare students for evolving workforce needs (Ally & Perris, 2022; Gates et al., 2024). AI is the development of computers which can perform complex tasks that imitate human-like intelligence such as learning, reasoning, or problem solving. Machine learning, natural language processing, robotics, and virtual simulations are forms

DOI: 10.4018/979-8-3373-5092-9.ch002

of AI found in industry and education (Rosyadi et al., 2023). Tyson and Zysman (2022) predict three outcomes regarding the workforce with the onset of the AI revolution: displacement, productivity, and reinstatement. Displacement is the decrease in labor demand for tasks that can be automated with AI. Productivity refers to the increase in demand for workers for non-automated tasks, and reinstatement calls for labor skilled in the new tasks created by the AI technologies. Each of these three outcomes presents implications for career technical education (CTE) programs and their ability to adapt and equip students with the skills required for an evolving job market.

CTE programs focus on developing industry relevant competencies, including both technical and soft skills such as communication, problem solving, and collaboration (Haviland and Robbins, 2021). Since the implementation of the Strengthening Career and Technical Education for the 21st Century Act, CTE programs must align with local industry standards and needs, offering students opportunities to earn credentials of value that enhance their competitiveness in the marketplace (Perkins V, 2018). CTE includes secondary, postsecondary and adult education programs while reaching a wide range of learners (ACTE, 2025).

This chapter explores the importance of integrating AI in CTE. Just as AI transforms the field of education through increased efficiency of administrative tasks, data analysis, and personalized feedback (Chen et al., 2020), AI also transforms industry. Because CTE bridges the gap between education and industry expectation, it is essential for CTE programs to evolve to include AI education and to develop skills that complement AI technologies. CTE programs will need to offer training in developing, maintaining, and operating AI systems. Beyond generative AI as a specific field of study, CTE must address the integration of AI into the workplace across multiple industries and applications. Integration of AI into CTE prepares students for the emerging opportunities and challenges across differing industries. While students will continue to need strong technical skills, CTE programs must also acquire practice generating, auditing, and assessing AI output across disciplines (Sublett et al., 2025). Jensen Huang (2024) emphasizes that individuals are more likely to be replaced with workers who use AI rather than be replaced by the entity of AI.

The incorporation of AI into CTE enables students to gain hands-on experience with cutting edge tools, improving their technical proficiency and adaptability. Such skills ensure students are well prepared for new technologies in high-demand careers. AI is poised to enhance the relevance, effectiveness, and innovation within CTE programs, ultimately fostering a workforce capable of driving economic growth and technological advancement (Cazaniga et al., 2024). CTE programs are uniquely situated to fill the growing demand for workers who possess strong technical skills in AI. CTE coursework places an emphasis on hands-on-learning that draws on industry knowledge and skill sets. CTE instruction must grow with the continually evolving technologies that are placing new demands on the workforce to update or acquire new technological skills (Cade et al., 2023).

Rapid data analysis with AI enables in-time adjustment of curricula that is better aligned with industry developments for more authentic work-based learning (Rosyadi et al., 2023). Incorporating AI into existing CTE coursework aligns instruction to AI usage and developments within those specific industries. Educationally, embedding AI technologies in CTE instruction increases personalized learning, enhances curricular development with data driven insight, and fosters innovative instructional pedagogy. AI can be a catalyst for advancing CTE, improving educational outcomes, and improving workforce development (Ng, 2024). Educators, policymakers, and industry leaders stand to benefit from recognizing the long-term value of AI in shaping a more dynamic, responsive, and forward thinking CTE approach.

INTEGRATION OF AI INTO CTE

As the economy enters the fourth industrial revolution, driven by the rise of artificial intelligence, the demand for a workforce skilled in AI technologies continues to increase (Ally & Perris, 2022). The revolution is not confined to technical advancements in industry alone but also transforms the way we educate and prepare the next generation for the workforce. Career technical education (CTE) serves as a critical bridge between education and industry, but CTE must evolve with the changing landscape of workforce demands (Crevar, 2023). Just as AI is transforming industries by enhancing efficiency, productivity, and innovation, AI holds the promise to transform CTE education through these same advancements (Vervinck, 2024). AI plays a crucial role in reshaping CTE, offering students the opportunity to gain hands-on experience with integrated technology while ensuring they are equipped to enter the workforce, regardless of the industry type (Malyn-Smith et al., 2021). By embedding AI into CTE curricula, educational institutions stand to cultivate a generation of highly adaptable and skilled workers ready to drive economic growth and technological advancement.

CTE coursework differs from traditional grade level coursework, as CTE coursework is application based and relates directly to specific career programs of study (Sun & Pratt, 2024). CTE stands to benefit from the augmentation of AI technologies through several critical areas: increased preparedness for technological advances in industry, improved educational efficiency and effectiveness, innovation in pedagogy in instructional practices, personalization of learning and adaptive instruction, and increased student engagement and motivation (Ayers, 2024).

A workforce skilled in AI technologies stands to enter high-demand, high-wage occupations (Carnevale et al., 2023). These high-skill occupations benefit from increasing wages as compared to those occupations that remain stagnant or are displaced with AI integration (Hoffman et al., 2020). Integrating AI into CTE ensures that students are prepared to meet the demands of the workplace by equipping students with practical, hands-on experience that aligns with real-world job requirements in a wide berth of industries which are integrating AI such as automation, data analysis, healthcare, and the service industries (Lindsay et al., 2024). AI in CTE stands to not only better equip students for the workforce, but to also better equip CTE educators for instruction.

INCREASED PREPAREDNESS FOR TECHNOLOGICAL ADVANCES IN INDUSTRY

Students gain experience working with the same technologies prevalent in multiple industries when AI is incorporated into CTE programs. Proficiency in AI tools and applications equips students with transferable skills that are directly applicable to future careers (Oschinski et al., 2024). As automation with AI increases in the skilled trades, workers must be able to work within these networked thinking systems (Windelband, 2023). The requirement of interfacing with AI is increasing and becoming more of a collaborative between AI and the workforce (Traumer et al., 2017). Workers are required to have an understanding of production, interface ability, and how to adapt with increasing amounts of information to process (Windelband, 2023). For instance, in the manufacturing sector, AI technologies are employed to improve efficiency, reduce costs, conduct risk analysis, and improve customer experiences (Holland, 2024). AI technologies are instrumental in detecting equipment failures, subtle leaks or emissions, and safety violations (Fisher et al., 2023).

The same need exists across different industries. In cosmetology, AI driven virtual visualizations of cosmetic products and procedures, such as hair styles and color simulations, assist customers in making informed product selections (Gates et al., 2024). Similarly, the real estate industry uses AI to refine real estate searches, analyze market trend data, or evaluate property values (Fitzpatrick et al., 2023). Retail and service industries integrate AI in platforms for selling goods, providing services, and asset rentals such as clothing or short-term rentals (Bearson et al., 2021). In the medical and education fields, AI is increasingly used for data analysis, diagnostics, and forecasting (Tyson & Zysman, 2022). By incorporating AI training and usage into CTE programs, educational institutions can bridge the skills gap, ensuring that students are equipped with the critical competencies required by the evolving job market.

IMPROVED EDUCATIONAL EFFICIENCY

Research by Bryant and colleagues (2020) indicates that teachers spend 20 to 40 percent of their time on administrative tasks which could be automated by AI. AI technologies streamline administrative tasks such as attendance, grading, scheduling, career guidance, and resource management, which allows educators to focus on instruction and individualized student support rather than administrative duties (Chen et al., 2020). This increased efficiency helps make CTE programs more effective by enabling educators to devote more time to hands-on-training and skill development (Wang et al., 2024). AI's use of predictive analytics facilitates the alignment of content creation to emerging workforce trends (Ng, 2024). Predictive analysis enables career education programs to analyze marketplace growth, student outcomes, and hiring trends and then adjust curricula in real-time to those forecasted skill gaps (Sandhu, 2025). Large scale data analytics rapidly identify emerging gaps ahead of trends, giving career technical education providers the opportunity to collaborate with industry and community stakeholders to adjust curricular priorities to match emerging needs.

Immediate data analysis offers early identification of learning gaps with optimized resource allocation and guidance structures for instructional use.

Attendance

With automated processes in place for these routine tasks, educators are freed to focus on improving instruction and responding to the individual needs of students (Selwyn, 2022). Developments in administrative tasks include the ability for students to check-in online without need for the instructor to take attendance, which saves time. More advanced learning management systems use facial recognition to take attendance (Chen, 2025). Others use login information, track the amount of time a student is engaged, and how long the student is present. Numbers of absences and attendance patterns are analyzed with AI generated feedback which the educator may use to guide the student or for outreach increasing the educator's responsiveness to student attendance (Smitha et al., 2020). Analysis of attendance patterns with correlation to academic performance aids in identification of students who are at-risk due to frequent absences (Bryant et al., 2020). Attendance patterns may also be analyzed over time to identify attendance patterns, such as absence spikes or classes with high absenteeism rates. Such analysis aids in oversight and intervention.

Automated Assessment and Feedback

The use of AI is transforming career technical education from traditional pedagogies toward data-driven individualized approaches (Liu et al., 2025). With AI, large amounts of student data are available on-demand (Kurtz et al., 2024). AI enables learning management systems to provide immediate grading with feedback to students on submitted work, reducing the grading load while providing instantaneous data analysis of student performance individually, within a class, between classes, and over time. Both educators and administrators can access student strengths and weaknesses immediately (Kew & Tasir, 2022). Information regarding gaps in achievement is rapidly available, opening avenues to intervention in real-time rather than at the end of instruction following summative assessment.

Across engineering disciplines, automated assessment can fall into multiple categories, one being student assessment as mentioned above and the other is programming or code quality assessment (Liu, et al., 2025). Automated programming assessment systems not only evaluate the quality of code for the assessment for a group assignment but are also able to isolate the quality of individual contributions (Chen et al., 2022). Applications range in complexity with applications accessing functionality and quality, to identifying the source of coding, and detecting AI generated code for authenticity (Insa et al., 2021; Nazar et al., 2023; Nguyen et al., 2024). Automated tools such based on CAD applications support student learning in digital environments while providing learning scenarios for practical engineering skills and proficiency (Bourrie et al., 2015).

Scheduling

AI integration optimizes the nuanced scheduling needs that occur between course timing needs, resource allocation, simultaneous teacher and student availability, and space availability, especially in online or hybrid school formats where scheduling demands become cumbersome (Ounejjar et al., 2024). AI blends large language models with generative AI to assist with the complex task of course and student scheduling (He & Liu, 2023). Increased administrative efficiency results when scheduling platforms use query loops to refine decision making and determine priorities in the scheduling process (Ballard, 2025). Scheduling algorithms even facilitate the incorporation of pedagogical instructional decisions such as course timing for attendance purposes or increased cognitive engagement (Mon et al., 2023).

Using AI to transform scheduling facilitates alignment of strategic goals to scheduling, aids in identifying and meeting the needs of special education students, and builds flexibility into the schedule (Lu et al., 2025). Generative AI permits stakeholder input. Students may self-select parameters such as preferred course times, course modalities, or individual constraints which have been associated with increased academic achievement (Cordis & Pierce, 2017). Scheduling with AI also allows for adjustments in real-time as needs arise which reduces scheduling conflicts and offers additional flexibility without taxing administrative time and attention (He & Liu, 2023). Use of these programs also aids in identification of historical scheduling patterns, potential schedule conflicts, and optimizes available resources of both faculty time and facility availability lending a data-driven approach to scheduling.

These benefits come with conditions. Maximizing the benefits of AI based scheduling requires a robust data infrastructure as well as a thorough working understanding of the scheduling platform as demonstrated with Ounejjar et al.'s work (2024). Educational leadership benefits from experience with sophisticated digital tools or will require extensive support and training when using such a platform. Refining systems as scheduling platforms learn from data inputs becomes necessary (Ounejjar et al., 2024). As scheduling improves efficiency, systematic evaluations need to occur to ensure the algorithms remain unbiased by examining scheduling outputs for fairness and balance (Lu et al., 2025). CTE programs serve a diverse body of students, including secondary school students, college students, working adults, and career changers; therefore, a more flexible and intuitive scheduling system can accommodate the nuances of varied needs, including those that extend to apprenticeship and workbased learning experiences (He & Liu, 2023; Ng, 2024).

Career Guidance

Just as AI improves efficiency in education, AI stands to increase the opportunities available in career guidance to reduce attrition and increase completion rates for industry credential attainment (Westman et al., 2021). Guidance counseling provides current information on available careers, career aptitude assessment, and educational recommendations. A key component of career guidance is recognizing an individual's strengths and matching those with the opportunities that are available in the marketplace, especially for students who may be overlooked (Barnes et al., 2020; Morrell, 2025). Traditionally, this matching has been completed through individual placement tests and the knowledge of individual guidance counselors. Instead, AI embedded career guidance stands to increase the efficiency and accuracy of career guidance counselors (Wilson et al., 2024). AI is able to analyze vast amounts of labor market data and match that information to individual skills and strengths to provide personalized career recommendations (Bimrose, 2020). However, the success of AI implementation relies on the ability of guidance staff to effectively integrate AI technologies with guidance personnel expertise (Hooley et al., 2015).

AI enabled career assessment proffers rapid identification of student strengths with newly emerging careers in the desired marketplace. With this AI powered groundwork, individual guidance counselors can focus on meaningful work with the students such as setting educational goals with the match data produced by AI, vastly reducing the manpower required (Toni & Vuorinen, 2020). The same process is available for use to match students to CTE apprenticeship programs (Ng, 2024). AI technologies do not replace human services but rather enhance the scope and availability of services career guidance counselors provide (Hooley et al, 2015). AI in career guidance provides increased accessibility and availability to such services at lower costs to CTE programs.

INNOVATION IN PEDAGOGY AND IMPROVED INSTRUCTIONAL PRACTICES

AI technologies spawn new and innovative instructional applications, such as intelligent tutoring systems (ITS), AI driven simulations, virtual reality, and gamification that further instruction in CTE . Such tools provide interactive learning experiences which mimic real-world scenarios, providing the opportunity to improve technical skills and practice problem solving (Johri et al., 2023). For example, Fusion 360 offers design students the opportunity to design components that are then able to be sent to machining students to program to the tool pathway, or AI can be used to analyze the quality of welding beads during real time (Micic, 2024). Additionally, CTE educators are typically less likely to have attended a traditional teacher preparation program but enter education as experts in their industry field (Ayers, 2024; Windelband, 2023). These applications often rely on machine learning and large language models of AI. Intelligent tutoring systems are computerized learning platforms that offer automatic assessment with feedback; however, in an AI enhanced ITS, combines advanced algorithms, statistics, and language learning models to provide personalized and adaptive instruction that mimics the approach of an individual tutor (Cardona et al., 2023). The tutoring component may remain working behind the scenes selecting instructional pathways and steps, or the tutor may function as an avatar and directly dialog with the student (Niño-Rojas et al., 2023). Hints and next steps are offered in real-time as students experience difficulty. An ITS offers multiple types of supports such as tutorials, instructional videos, reviews, hints, and dialog which offer student agency in learning (Feng et al., 2021). AI uses data analytics analyze mistakes that are made and provide instruction to scaffold instruction tailored to the student's need while educators are easily able to monitor progress and provide instructional support for more targeted intervention (Kulik & Fletcher, 2016).

Such AI applications function to bridge the gap between learning and application in CTE. For instance, Java programming instruction through ITS responds dynamically to adjust instruction based on student coding errors, thereby addressing those errors immediately without loss of time or continuing to build on misunderstandings (Gavrilović et al., 2018). The Per Scholas ITS embeds real-life scenarios for the CompTIA A+ certification course with two tutoring agents, one a fellow learner and the other the tutor. The student has the option to work with a fellow learner, engage with feedback, and then have multiple opportunities to answer questions which simulate the certification exam (Cade et al., 2023). Research indicates that lifelike chat boxes and tutors are shown to reduce learner loneliness by approximately 30 percent and have positive associations with emotional well-being (Dhimola et al., 2022; Wu et al., 2020).

Professional Development

With a majority of CTE educators taking non-traditional pathways into CTE, educator pedagogy is an area to be addressed with professional development (Sun & Pratt, 2024). Green and Moore's (2016) work finds that CTE teachers desire professional development in the following areas: creating simulated learning environments with learning technologies; aligning curriculum, instruction and assessment; engaging students; and eliciting critical thinking. Qualitative research indicates the need for additional professional development in onboarding and translating work experience to instruction in CTE (Clark et al., 2014; Deever et al., 2020) AI stands to enhance each of these professional development needs in CTE through new technologies which are designed to improve instructional practices and enhance pedagogy giving attention to the gaps between competencies teachers have and those competencies that are needed (Tan et al., 2025).

Research indicates that students with lower standardized test scores and less advanced math coursework tend to be overrepresented in CTE coursework (Anglum et al., 2023). A deeper understanding of CTE pedagogy is essential for teachers who work with students who may face greater challenges during and after high school (Theobald et al., 2022). As these students experience barriers to success, enhancing CTE teachers' professional development equips CTE teachers to meet student needs (al-Zyoud, 2020). AI enhanced professional development programs offer adaptability and personalization for teachers to provide the skills and opportunities for practice needed to succeed in CTE classrooms. The flexibility of on-demand AI enhanced professional development strengthens CTE educators' ability to balance scheduling with their responsibilities. Providing professional development on how to address student need promotes equitable educational outcomes for the most vulnerable students (Ecton & Dougherty, 2023).

Teacher attrition is also a concern among education leaders and stakeholders at large with both economic and educational implications (Hasselquist & Graves, N. 2020). These concerns extend to CTE, especially with the specialized industry knowledge CTE teachers must have (Clark et al., 2014). Heavy workloads and time demands of administrative tasks contribute to CTE teachers' decisions to leave education (Lemons et al., 2015). Providing professional development through AI on AI embedded learning applications addresses these needs and provides support in areas that directly address issues in CTE teacher retention. AI enhanced professional development offers flexibility in access with individual pacing which allows CTE educators to balance their time commitments (Rosyadi et al., 2023). AI embedded professional development provides virtual simulations, collaboration tools, and additional resources which are also built into AI student learning systems (Santosa et al., 2023). Training CTE educators with professional development using these components directly equips and familiarizes CTE educators with the same features they will use with students.

Content Creation

Content creation with AI encompasses a number of facets. Generative AI applications create content for instructional purposes at the behest of education leaders, teachers, and students. Education leaders use AI to assess and address curricular trends and gaps. Teachers use AI to create instructional content to fulfill curricular gaps within their class. AI serves as a powerful curricular enhancement tool by supporting the creation of course structures, rubrics, and suggested pacing (Tomsio, 2024). Generation of unique images, code, and practice datasets offers educators content on-demand (Kohnke et al., 2025). Additionally, educators are able to tweak the content with additional prompts or requests.

Generative AI creates content on demand through the entering of prompts by users. Prompts are directions that users provide to the AI application to elicit desired content. The functionality of AI is improved by targeted prompts with is often referred to as prompt engineering (Waterfield et al., 2024). Through effective prompts, teachers use generative AI to create new lessons, create case studies, scenarios, how-to guides, and support resources to augment instruction (Bai et al., 2024). Work by Jia and colleagues (2024) show that how-to math guides and supports generated by AI were often indistinguishable from human generated products. Lee and Zhai (2024) found that generative AI produced appropriate support information as well as created informative role-play activities. For example, generative AI was shown to increase teacher productivity by generating engaging example sentences from curricular vocabulary lists (Alali, & Al-Barakat, 2023). While effective in some areas, studies on course and lesson generation show limitations in generative AI's ability to integrate prior and current learning. Instead, generative AI applications tend to create standalone lessons which do not scaffold well to one another (Davis & Lee, 2023).

Special Education

Additionally, multiple studies find generative AI an effective resource for content creation for teachers with students who have unique learning needs (Hopcan et al., 2023). Special education teachers maximize AI applications to curate content that is specific to the individual learning needs of students. Infographics, educational games, study guides, and learning mnemonics are quickly produced as needs are identified (Waterfield et al., 2024). AI offers the ability to instantly create instructional modifications in real-time to differentiate assignments. Modifications include scaffolded text, multiple reading levels, and adapted comprehension questions or activities (Marino et al., 2023). For example, a CTE instructor could have students on multiple reading levels and needs to differentiate the reading assignment. The teacher can prompt the AI application to create passages on multiple reading levels for students with reading difficulties. The teacher can also prompt AI to create a more advanced passage for enrichment for advanced students. The teacher may also request for the application to create accompanying comprehension questions for each passage. Both types of passages and questions are generated within minutes, and the teacher can input additional prompts for any desired changes.

Generative AI can augment the writing of individual education plans in CTE (Waterfield et al., 2024). AI applications suggest goals and expectations for students with appropriate inputs regarding student difficulties and achievement. While accommodation recommendations can be created, the expertise of the teacher is essential in determining what is best for each student. AI is resource which can reduce the time to write the plan by organizing and incorporating notes from multiple sources, creating monitoring forms, and drafting section comments. AI can be used to create communication templates and notification forms for students and families to reduce the administrative load on the teacher. Some LLM generative AI tools are designed specifically for special education. Applications such as Educaide AI work with school learning management systems to design individual education plan goals based on student performance analytics and career goals. Such systems work to scaffold instructional steps with universal design for learning (Rose, 1999). The application also provides research articles with evidenced based interventions appropriate to the students' needs (Waterfield et al., 2024). Finally, AI video applications also offer avatars to read aloud instructions or text for students freeing the teacher to focus on in depth instructional support. This provides an auditory input to support learning. Such avatars also present material in multiple languages to address the needs of English language learners in CTE. Additional care regarding student privacy policies is a prevailing concern. School districts may not allow private student information to be entered into unsecured or non-approved databases, or AI policies may lag behind AI technology advances.

English Language Learners

English language learners also benefit from the rich availability of generative AI content (Ji et al., 2024). Generative AI can translate text, provide alternate text, suggest grammar and vocabulary improvements, and simulate conversations for low-pressure language practice geared to CTE topics (Mogavi et al., 2024). Generative AI applications function as translators for teachers. Not only do these applications translate, but they also create additional support materials, create alternate activities, and work interactively with students. The creation of vast amounts of text in natural language as needed, on requested topics, offers unlimited opportunities to practice language acquisition through reading and writing in CTE (Lee et al., 2023). Students practice vocabulary and refine pronunciation with feedback on pronunciation and phrasing from AI large language models. Use of these interactive components increases student engagement which has been shown to correlate to achievement (Wang & Xue, 2024).

Students use AI to create personalized instructional pathways through a course. Due to rapid data analysis, personalized prescriptive paths of adaptive learning are created based on student inputs during work with the learning platform (Walter, 2024). These pathways include customized pacing and content to support students to mastery known as adaptive learning applications, which are addressed further in the Personalization and Adaptive Learning section of the chapter.

INCREASED STUDENT ENGAGEMENT AND MOTIVATION

Virtual reality simulations, augmented reality, and gamified learning platforms increase student interaction and engagement (Mann, 2022). Through the provision of dynamic, hands-on experiences, AI improves motivation and interest which is consistently associated with retention of knowledge and improved skill development (Tobarra et al., 2021). Prior research indicates that students are more motivated when interested and find purpose to the instruction (Makransky et al., 2021). Virtual reality provides simulated training and work-based experiences which are purposeful to students with a low safety risk (Antrium, 2025). Beyond increasing engagement, virtual reality simulations are able to provide real-world experiences and career exploration, particularly when those actual experiences are unavailable to students or are unsafe (Amin et al., 2022). Virtual reality lends itself well to the applied nature of CTE instruction (Plasman et al., 2021; Sun & Turner, 2022).

Virtual Reality

Virtual reality is represented by both immersive and desktop applications (Hamilton et al., 2021). Immersive virtual reality provides 360-degree visual representation with headphones for wrap-around sound and lifelike control, while desktop virtual reality issues from a screen without 360-degree visuals, the need for headphones, and interaction is through the computer controls (Murcia-Lopez & Steed, 2016). Immersive virtual reality was found to be effective in both architectural and engineering CTE pathways, particularly with structural concepts and retention of mechanical concepts (Fogerty, 2018; Webster, 2016). In education fields, simulations are used to prepare students for classroom simulations with students who are English language learners (Neeley, 2017). In the health services pathways, patient simulations allow those training in the health fields to practice minimally invasive techniques in a simulated environment without the threat of potential harm to a patient (Atrium, 2025). In Pirker and colleagues (2021) work found virtual reality instruction improved conceptual understanding and perception in computer science courses making abstract concepts appear more concrete to students with positive affective responses. In overall education and training contexts, Conrad et al., (2024) report that immersive virtual reality is more advantageous for both content mastery and procedural knowledge than other types of media.

Desktop virtual realities provide interactive learning experiences which mimic real-world scenarios, providing the opportunity to improve technical skills and practice problem solving in a more accessible form (Johri et al., 2023). For example, Fusion 360 offers design students the opportunity to design components and then integrates that design with machining courses. Machining students then use the student designed components to program to the tool pathway. AI applications can be used to analyze the quality of welding beads during real time to augment the instructor's feedback (Micic, 2024). As noted previously, CTE educators are typically less likely to have attended a traditional teacher preparation program but enter education as experts in their industry field, and the AI imbedded applications bridge education to meaningful field experience (Ayers, 2024).

Gamification

Gamification is defined as the use of game design elements in educational contexts to improve learning (Jayalath & Esichaikul, 2022). During gaming scenarios increased dopamine, epinephrine, and norepinephrine levels are released in players which correlates with improved motivation and engagement (Bateman & Nacke, 2010). Webster's (2016) research with Army training found that gamification combined with immersive virtual reality produced the highest levels of gain in conceptual understanding and knowledge acquisition in both corrosiveness and warfare. However, since the year 2020, the majority of gamification research in CTE has centered on healthcare and engineering fields (Dahalan et al., 2024). Studies occurring since 2019 indicate positive returns for improving knowledge and skill acquisition as well as improving the quality of instruction (Dahalan et al., 2024; Samah et al., 2022).

AI also promotes engagement through collaboration as teams can work together to accomplish tasks and reach goals within workplace simulations, virtual realities, desktop realities, and gamification applications (Ng, 2024). AI further promotes engagement and collaboration by matching students with similar instructional goals to create teams in these applications. Furthermore, AI uses course data to connect students with mentors who are able to guide teamwork through such online environments (Sandhu, 2025).

PERSONALIZATION OF LEARNING AND ADAPTIVE INSTRUCTION

Personalized learning requires departure from traditional pedagogies in which the teacher introduces the material, lectures, instructionally models concepts, and offers a gradual release of responsibility for the learning to students (Foster, 2024). Instead, personalized learning shifts the responsibility of the teacher to the role of facilitator and supporter (Alamri et al., 2021). Students have some autonomy and choice in how they receive instruction. Personalized learning adapts instruction by accounting for the student's prior knowledge, interests, skills, culture, and motivation (Bernaki et al., 2021). Simply defined, personalized learning is "instruction that is paced to learning needs, tailored to learning preferences, and tailored to specific interests of different learners" (U.S. DoE, 2010)

By taking individual preferences into account, personalized learning offers multiple pathways of learning experiences to ensure unique learning needs and multiple learning styles are available. Personalized learning relies heavily on predictive learning models with heavy data analytics and is often executed through an ITS platform whether the learning occurs in face to face or digital contexts (Liu et al., 2025). AI offers differentiation of instruction on a scale that would be unattainable for a single teacher (Lin et al., 2023).

Blended learning is a form of personalized learning which combines the traditional role of the teacher with adaptive learning pedagogy. Blended learning combines direct instruction from the teacher and peer interaction of typical in-person instruction with ITS platforms. Through daily formative assessment in blended learning, students and teachers are able to immediately select tailored support and instruction through AI supported technologies. Allowing students to act autonomously to improve their instruction increases their ownership in the learning process and increases their cognitive engagement.

Personalized and adaptive learning platforms continually analyze student performance data to adjust instruction in real-time. Advantages of AI powered learning platforms include personalized feedback, identification of areas for improvement, adaptability of the instructional pace to the individual student, and prediction of student performance and completion in the course (Liu et al., 2025). Students progress at individual paces and receive targeted support in real time through rapid analysis of student performance data (Cardona et al., 2023). This data enables the instantaneous identification of trends, assessment of the effectiveness of instructional methods, and for the adjustment of instructional strategies in real-time (Batsaikhan & Correia, 2024). Students progress at individual paces while receiving targeted, personalized support through rapid analysis of student performance data (Cardona et al., 2023). This data enables the evaluation of the effectiveness of instructional pedagogies for the course (Feng et al., 2021). Personalized learning is often combined with traditional coursework; however, student learning is most often personalized through the implementation of ITS within a learning management system.

PRACTICAL IMPLICATIONS

The practical implications of AI in CTE stand to be transformative; however, several considerations must be addressed to ensure sustainability and effectiveness. First, CTE educators must be provided with comprehensive training to implement AI technologies meaningfully into their coursework (Zhang & Aslan, 2021). Virtual reality and AI augmented systems offer instructional supports for CTE teachers while reducing the administrative burden of teaching; however, how teachers elect to implement such supports will garner different results. Human discernment is needed to determine the best supports for CTE content areas and CTE students. AI generated instructional pathways, monitoring, problem- and practice-based exercises reduce the instructional workload of CTE teachers but do not replace teachers (Sun & Pratt, 2024). The data analytics of AI provide wrap-around supports for students under the guidance of teachers. The quality instructional pedagogies built into AI systems further support CTE teachers who enter education from industry backgrounds.

Next, professional development should focus on how to use AI technologies to augment instruction, while addressing any concerns regarding ethical use and potential bias (Farrelly & Baker, 2023). AI tools should be carefully evaluated for effectiveness and alignment with current industry standards to ensure such tools are relevant to the specific needs of the workforce. Educators should regularly assess AI tools to ensure they enhance rather than replace critical human interactions and social learning. Thorough planning, ongoing professional development, and regular evaluation are essential to ensure that the integration of AI in CTE equips students for the future workforce. Successful implementation of AI in CTE will includes effective professional development to equip CTE educators to maximize the instructional benefits of AI (Rosyadi et al., 2023).

CONCERNS AND CHALLENGES

While AI holds the promise of transforming CTE, a number of challenges exist. The process of selecting the optimal AI tools for the spectrum of CTE courses is time consuming (Waterfield et al., 2024). Each application touts multiple benefits that may not translate across different CTE content courses and must be evaluated. Beyond the time commitment of AI application selection is the consideration of cost. Applications which interface with school learning management systems are often cost prohibitive. Additionally, AI applications often have specific industry designs that are not broadly applicable to CTE programs.

Concerns regarding data privacy and security policies are of paramount importance, especially when using systems that collect and analyze student data (Mühlhoff, 2023). While AI introduces numerous advantages for CTE, this technology comes with a caution. The large-scale data collection in AI platforms raises concerns about data storage and the ethical use of such large-scale data (Oschinski et al., 2024). CTE programs using such data will need to implement robust policies on access and storage which are in line with policies on student privacy and protection, including such options as dual authentication and data encryption (Suparyati et al., 2023). Regulations and policies governing AI arise from both industry sectors and education institution governance systems. CTE instruction intersects both systems of governance, increasing the complexity of policy navigation.

Algorithmic biases exist in AI technologies and may amplify societal biases, particularly when these biases are embedded in training data (Kizilcec & Lee, 2022). Over the past decade, scholars have warned about the limited generalizability of algorithms in education, especially for historically marginalized student populations such as socio-disadvantaged learners, students of color, and those with disabilities (Baker & Hawn, 2021; Ocumpaugh et al. 2014). This concern is particularly relevant in the context of CTE, given the goals outlined in the Perkins V legislation. The latest iteration of Perkins seeks to expand access and opportunity for students who have been traditionally underserved by the education system. If AI systems in CTE perpetuate or amplify biases, they could undermine these goals and further disadvantage the very groups they aim to support (Sandhu, 2025). Therefore, ensuring transparency in the training of AI models is crucial for maintaining accountability. Furthermore, the integration of bias detection mechanisms in deployment plans is essential to mitigate the risks of discriminatory outcomes (Farrelly & Baker, 2023). As AI becomes increasingly prevalent in CTE, educators face the challenge of balancing industry-driven advancements with educational ethics. Navigating the tension between technological innovation and the imperative to protect student privacy is best navigated by CTE educators with experience from both perspectives.

Concerns regarding the role of teachers in instruction are central to the discussion of AI in CTE. Over reliance on AI in CTE may diminish the educator-student interactions, which are vital to teaching and learning process. AI in CTE should not replace, but augment, the interactions between educators and students. While AI may bring increased efficiency, it also raises concerns about the potential displacement of human educators by technology (Tyson and Zysman, 2022). However, CTE teachers, with their professional expertise, are well positioned to integrate AI effectively into their teaching practices. Effective AI implementation in CTE requires educators to undergo substantial professional development, ensuring they possess the necessary technical and pedagogical skills to use AI responsibly (Sun & Pratt, 2024).

Moreover, the implementation of AI in CTE must also address the challenges posed by the digital divide. AI driven technologies often come with substantial costs for both equipment and platforms, making these technologies less accessible to underfunded institutions. Furthermore, successful integration of AI requires extensive knowledge not only in information technology but also in educational methodologies, encompassing everything from initial implementation to ongoing maintenance. This broad range of expertise is crucial for ensuring the sustained effectiveness of AI systems in CTE environments.

FUTURE DIRECTIONS

AI technologies continue to advance rapidly in education, offering the potential to expand personalized learning opportunities and enhance workforce skills training (Advance CTE, 2020). To fully leverage AI in CTE, it is crucial that both hard and soft skills training be integrated, particularly those skills that align directly with industry demands (Cardona et al., 2023). Successful workforce transitions depend on preparing students with the AI technologies that are used in their respective industries. The integration of AI in CTE education requires interdisciplinary training that bridges education with industry needs, ensuring that students are equipped for the future workforce.

While the integration of AI in CTE offers numerous benefits, there is still a significant gap in understanding the most effective strategies for recruiting, preparing, and retaining educators who can successfully adapt to these technologies (Anglum et al., 2023). The evolving nature of AI tools in CTE requires a workforce of educators who not only have strong pedagogical skills but also the technical expertise to incorporate these tools into instruction. Research is essential to identify the most effective recruitment methods, including outreach to underrepresented groups, and the best strategies for ongoing professional development that keeps pace with technological and AI advancements. Policy makers are crucial in addressing this gap, as they shape the infrastructure and requirements for teacher education, which has implications regarding professional development and certification for CTE. In particular, ensuring that funding is available for upskilling CTE teachers and ensuring that there are pathways for career advancement within CTE programs will sustain retention of qualified CTE educators.

Policymakers

Policymakers should begin by addressing thorough local needs assessments, as mandated by Perkins V, to identify gaps between the skills students are developing in CTE programs and the demands of the local workforce. These assessments can help reveal the misalignment between AI applications prevalent in local industry and the current curricula of local CTE programs. To ameliorate these gaps, CTE programs must gain access to the same AI technologies that are adopted by local industry. Alleviation of these gaps ensures that students are equipped with the skills necessary to succeed in the AI-driven job market. Strong industry and education partnerships are vital in facilitating this access, as they bridge the divide between educational institutions and leading industries (Sun & Pratt, 2024). Apprenticeships, access to advanced technologies, and work-based learning partnerships thrive with collaborative effort between educational institutions and industry (Sublett et al., 2025). Policymakers can support these partnerships by directing resources to strengthen industry-education collaborations.

Furthermore, CTE programs require increased investment in resources and funding to keep pace with industry developments with AI, particularly those occupations at greatest risk from disruption (Cazzaniga et al., 2024). As AI continues to disrupt various industries, CTE programs must focus on preparing students for the careers most vulnerable to automation, ensuring that workers are equipped with both technical and transferable skills to remain competitive in the evolving workforce (Morrell, 2025). Lastly, institutional and governmental policies must develop alongside AI technologies to address the emerging concerns related to data privacy and algorithmic bias. As AI applications become more integrated into education and workforce preparation, it is essential for policymakers to create regulatory frameworks that protect student data and ensure fairness in AI-driven decision making.

CONCLUSION

CTE sits at the nexus of both education and the workforce, positioned to uniquely leverage the transformative potential of AI technologies. As AI continues to drive the fourth industrial revolution, the integration into CTE programs promises to reshape not only how students learn, but also how CTE teachers teach (Ally & Perris, 2022). In this evolving landscape, CTE educators must also prepare to embrace the promises while also preparing to navigate the challenges that accompany AI integration. The promises of AI integration range from enhanced educational practices by improved efficiency, innovation of pedagogy, and increased student motivation to the personalization of learning (Liu et al., 2025). Improved efficiency in administrative tasks decreases time educators spend taking attendance, grading, or scheduling to increase the time to focus on impactful educational practices (Feng et al., 2021). In addition to administrative efficiencies, more complex tasks such as content creation or ITS systems bolster sound pedagogical practices that inform CTE teachers as they guide learning and develop targeted interventions based on real-time data analysis of student performance (Cardona et al., 2023).

Ultimately, AI serves as an enhancement, not a replacement to CTE instruction. While AI tools augment the learning process, such tools are not able to replicate the nuanced, social process through which knowledge is made meaningful (Bourrie et al., 2015). The process of making knowledge meaningful is inherently a social process, requiring human interaction and guidance which are factors AI is unable to fully replicate (Ayers, 2024; Vygotsky, 1978). It is the responsibility of the CTE educator to evaluate and select AI tools which align with instructional goals (Ng, 2024). Furthermore, it is the educator who inspires and motivates students, fostering an environment where students acquire the skills and knowledge necessary for career success. Beyond the role of technology, CTE educators inspire and motivate students, cultivating an environment in which students develop both the technical skills and the critical thinking skills necessary to succeed in the workforce.

AI implementation is not without challenges and potential pitfalls. One of the foremost concerns is the balance of human and computer decision making. While AI serves as an enhancement to instruction, use should not overshadow the educator's judgement and ability to foster supportive learning environments (Ayers, 2024). Additionally, algorithmic bias presents a persistent challenge, with the potential to perpetuate skewed outcomes for certain groups of students if left unchecked (Baker & Hawn, 2022). AI systems require technical and institutional oversight through data monitoring to ensure accurate outcomes for students. Data privacy also presents a critical challenge, as the collection and analysis of student data by AI systems raise significant questions about database security and student safety (Mühlhoff, 2023). As AI systems become increasingly integrated into CTE programs, policies and frameworks must be developed to protect personal student information and ensure that data collection process adhere to ethical standards.

In addition to these concerns, the financial and time costs of implementing AI in CTE programs must be carefully weighed. While AI technologies offer much promise, the infrastructure required for support is expensive and resource intensive (Kaplan-Rakowski et al, 2023). These costs, if unaddressed, may undermine the benefits of AI integration. However, with appropriate oversight, planning, and funding, the integration of AI stands to enhance CTE programs by making CTE curricula more relevant and responsive to the rapidly evolving needs of the marketplace. Ultimately, with AI implementation properly addressed, an AI transformed CTE supports student outcomes and prepares a future workforce with the knowledge and skills necessary to thrive in an increasingly AI-driven economy.

REFERENCES

Advance, C. T. E. (2020). *CTE prepares learners for the future of work.* Advance CTE. https://careertech.org/wp-content/uploads/2023/01/CTE_Prepares_Learners_Future_Work_2020.pdf

al-Zyoud, M. (2020). The role of artificial intelligence in teacher professional development. *Universal Journal of Educational Research, 8*(11B), 6263–6272. DOI: 10.13189/ujer.2020.082265

Alali, R., & Al-Barakat, A. (2023). Leveraging the revolutionary potential of chatgpt to enhance kindergarten teachers' educational performance: A proposed perception. *Eurasian Journal of Educational Research, 106*, 50–69. DOI: 10.14689/ejer.2023.106.004

Alamri, H. A., Watson, S., & Watson, W. (2021). Learning technology models that support personalization within blended learning environments in higher education. *TechTrends, 65*(1), 62–78. DOI: 10.1007/s11528-020-00530-3

Ally, M., & Perris, K. (2022). Artificial intelligence in the fourth industrial revolution to educate for sustainable development. *Canadian Journal of Learning and Technology, 48*(4). Advance online publication. DOI: 10.21432/cjlt28287

Amin, W., I., Yulia, C., & Abdullah, A. G. (2022). *The application of virtual reality (VR) in vocational education: A systematic review.* 4th International Conference on Innovation in Engineering and Vocational Education (ICIEVE 2021), Bandung, Indonesia. https://doi.org/DOI: 10.2991/assehr.k.220305.024

Anglum, J. C., Diemer, A. R., Ecton, W. G., & Nguyen, T. D. (2023). We need to know more about CTE teachers. *Phi Delta Kappan, 104*(6), 18–23. DOI: 10.1177/00317217231161535

Atrium. (2025). *Simulation laboratory open.* Navicent Health. https://navicenthealth.org/service-center/mercer-university-school-of-medicine/simulation-laboratory-open

Ayers, J. (2024, September 15). *How can AI transform CTE curricula?* ACTE Online. https://www.acteonline.org/blog/2024/09/15/ai-can-transform-cte/

Bai, S., Gonda, D. E., & Hew, K. F. (2024). Write-curate-verify: A case study of leveraging generative AI for scenario writing in scenario-based learning. *IEEE Transactions on Learning Technologies, 17*, 1301–1312. DOI: 10.1109/TLT.2024.3378306

Ballard, S. (2025, February 28). *AI tool helps make trustworthy, explainable scheduling decisions.* https://engineering.washu.edu/news/2025/AI-tool-helps-make-trustworthy-explainable-scheduling-decisions.html

Barnes, S. A., Bimrose, J., Brown, A., Kettunen, J., & Vuorinen, R. (2020). *Lifelong guidance policy and practice in the EU: Trends, challenges and opportunities.* University of Warwick's Institute for Employment Research. [European Commission Directorate-General for Employment Social Affairs and Inclusion], https://data.europa.eu/doi/10.2767/91185

Bateman, C., & Nacke, L. E. (2010). The neurobiology of play. *Proceedings of the International Academic Conference on the Future of Game Design and Technology*, 1–8. https://doi.org/DOI: 10.1145/1920778.1920780

Batsaikhan, B., & Correia, A.-P. (2024). The effects of generative artificial intelligence on intelligent tutoring systems in higher education: A systematic review. *Studies in Technology Enhanced Learning*, *4*(1). Advance online publication. DOI: 10.21428/8c225f6e.33570bb1

Bearson, D., Kenney, M., & Zysman, J. (2021). Measuring the impacts of labor in the platform economy: New work created, old work reorganized, and value creation reconfigured. *Industrial and Corporate Change*, *30*(3), 536–563. DOI: 10.1093/icc/dtaa046

Bimrose, J. (2020). Labour market information for career development: Pivotal or peripheral? In Robertson, P. J., Hooley, T., & McCash, P. (Eds.), *The Oxford Handbook of Career Development* (1st ed., pp. 283–296). Oxford University Press., DOI: 10.1093/oxfordhb/9780190069704.013.21

Bourrie, D., Sanker, C., & Jones-Farmer, L. (2015). Conceptualizing interactions between innovation characteristics and organizational members' readiness to adopt educational innovations. *International Journal of Engineering Education*, *31*(4), 967–985. https://www.researchgate.net/publication/281099208_Conceptualizing_Interactions_between_Innovation_Characteristics_and_Organizational_Members'_Readiness_to_Adopt_Educational_Innovations

Bryant, J., Heitz, C., Sanghvi, S., & Wagle, D. (2020). *How artificial intelligence will impact K–12 teachers*. McKinsey and Company. https://www.mckinsey.com/industries/education/our-insights/how-artificial-intelligence-will-impact-k-12-teachers#/

Cade, W., Amin, S., Bishop, A., & Zhang, C. X. (2023). *Piloting intelligent tutoring systems to enhance sectoral training programs*. American Institutes for Research. https://www.air.org/sites/default/files/2023-06/Piloting-Intelligent-Tutoring-Systems-to-Enhance-Sectoral-Training-Programs-Early-Findings-Lessons-Learned-June-2023.pdf

Cardona, M. A., Rodríguez, R. J., & Ishmael, K. (2023). *Artificial intelligence and the future of teaching and learning*. US Department of Education. https://www.ed.gov/sites/ed/files/documents/ai-report/ai-report.pdf

Carnevale, A. P., Mabel, Z., Campbell, K. P., & Booth, H. (2023). *Ten education, training, and work-based pathway changes that lead to good jobs*. Georgetown University Center on Education and the Workforce., https://cew.georgetown.edu/wp-content/uploads/cew-ten_pathway_changes-fr.pdf

Cazzaniga, M., Jaumotte, F., Li, L., Melina, G., Panton, A., Pizzinelli, C., Rockall, E., & Mendes Tavares, M. (2024). *Gen-AI: Artificial intelligence and the future of work*. International Monetary Fund., https://www.imf.org/en/Publications/Staff-Discussion-Notes/Issues/2024/01/14/Gen-AI-Artificial-Intelligence-and-the-Future-of-Work-542379 DOI: 10.5089/9798400262548.006

Chen, H. M., Nguyen, B. A., & Dow, C. R. (2022). Code-quality evaluation scheme for assessment of student contributions to programming projects. *Journal of Systems and Software, 188*, 111273. DOI: 10.1016/j.jss.2022.111273

Chen, L. (2025). Analysis of facial recognition attendance technology based on artificial intelligence algorithms in political course e-learning teaching. *Entertainment Computing, 52*, 100821. DOI: 10.1016/j.entcom.2024.100821

Chen, L., Chen, P., & Lin, Z. (2020). Artificial intelligence in education: A review. *IEEE Access : Practical Innovations, Open Solutions, 8*, 75264–75278. DOI: 10.1109/ACCESS.2020.2988510

Clark, M. S., Kelsey, K. D., & Brown, N. R. (2014). The thornless rose: A phenomenological look at decisions career teachers make to remain in the profession. *Journal of Agricultural Education, 55*(3), 43–56. DOI: 10.5032/jae.2014.03043

Conrad, M., Kablitz, D., & Schumann, S. (2024). Learning effectiveness of immersive virtual reality in education and training: A systematic review of findings. *Computers & Education: X Reality, 4*, 100053. https://doi.org/DOI: 10.1016/j.cexr.2024.100053

Cordis, A. S., & Pierce, B. G. (2017). The impact of class scheduling on academic performance in quantitative and qualitative business disciplines. *Global Perspectives on Accounting Education, 14*, 44–66. https://www.semanticscholar.org/paper/The-Impact-of-Class-Scheduling-on-Academic-in-and-Cordis-Pierce/9d406c6522cd1898b879130d9b655f6e8927a375

Crevar, A. (2023). *Building bridges from high school career technical education to post-secondary and career success with CTE math, endorsements, and dual enrollment* [Texas Tech University]. https://hdl.handle.net/2346/96315

Dahalan, F., Alias, N., & Shaharom, M. S. N. (2024). Gamification and game based learning for vocational education and training: A systematic literature review. *Education and Information Technologies, 29*(2), 1279–1317. DOI: 10.1007/s10639-022-11548-w PMID: 36688221

Davis, R. O., & Lee, Y. J. (2023). Prompt: ChatGPT, Create My Course, Please! *Education Sciences, 14*(1), 24. DOI: 10.3390/educsci14010024

Deever, D., Grubaugh, S., Levitt, G., & Gonzales, G. (2020). Why new career & technical education teachers leave, why new ones stay and how principals affect attrition and retention rates. *Journal of Education and Human Development, 9*(2). Advance online publication. DOI: 10.15640/jehd.v9n2a1

Ecton, W. G., & Dougherty, S. M. (2023). Heterogeneity in high school career and technical education outcomes. *Educational Evaluation and Policy Analysis, 45*(1), 157–181. DOI: 10.3102/01623737221103842

Farrelly, T., & Baker, N. (2023). Generative artificial intelligence: Implications and considerations for higher education practice. *Education Sciences, 13*(11), 1109. DOI: 10.3390/educsci13111109

Feng, S., Magana, A. J., & Kao, D. (2021). A systematic review of literature on the effectiveness of intelligent tutoring systems in STEM. *2021 IEEE Frontiers in Education Conference (FIE)*, 1–9. https://doi.org/DOI: 10.1109/FIE49875.2021.9637240

Fisher, E., Flynn, M. A., Pratap, P., & Vietas, J. A. (2023). Occupational safety and health equity impacts of artificial intelligence: A scoping review. *International Journal of Environmental Research and Public Health, 20*(13), 6221. DOI: 10.3390/ijerph20136221 PMID: 37444068

Fitzpatrick, M., Gujral, V., Kapoor, A., & Wolkomir, A. (2023, November). *The power of generative AI in real estate*. McKinsey. https://www.mckinsey.com/industries/real-estate/our-insights/generative-ai-can-change-real-estate-but-the-industry-must-change-to-reap-the-benefits

Foster, J. (2024, February). *Educator's journey through personalized learning to AI integration*. University of North Carolina, Charlotte. https://www.ednc.org/educators-journey-personalized-learning-artificial-intelligence-ai-integration/

Gates, A., Jones, A., & Wikkeling-Miller, C. (2024, November). *The nexus of career and technical education and artificial intelligence*. https://www.asccc.org/content/nexus-career-and-technical-education-and-artificial-intelligence

Gavrilović, N., Arsić, A., Domazet, D., & Mishra, A. (2018). Algorithm for adaptive learning process and improving learners' skills in Java programming language. *Computer Applications in Engineering Education, 26*(5), 1362–1382. DOI: 10.1002/cae.22043

Green, C., & Moore, C. (2016). Professional learning: What CTE teachers want. *Techniques*, 1–3. https://www.acteonline.org/wp-content/uploads/2018/05/Techniques-May2016-ProfessionalLearningCTETeachers.pdf

Hamilton, D., McKechnie, J., Edgerton, E., & Wilson, C. (2021). Immersive virtual reality as a pedagogical tool in education: A systematic literature review of quantitative learning outcomes and experimental design. *Journal of Computers in Education, 8*(1), 1–32. DOI: 10.1007/s40692-020-00169-2

Hasselquist, L., & Graves, N. A. (2020). CTE teacher retention: Lessons learned from mid-career teachers. *Career and Technical Education Research, 45*(1), 3–16. DOI: 10.5328/cter45.1.3

Haviland, S., & Robbins, S. (2021). Career and technical education as a conduit for skilled technical careers: A targeted research review and framework for future research. *ETS Research Report Series, 2021*(1), 1–42. DOI: 10.1002/ets2.12318

He, J., & Liu, X. (2023). Hybrid teaching–learning-based optimization for workflow scheduling in cloud environment. *IEEE Access : Practical Innovations, Open Solutions, 11*, 100755–100768. DOI: 10.1109/ACCESS.2023.3314735

Holland, M. F. (2024). *Working smarter: How manufacturers are using artificial intelligence*. National Association of Manufacturers., https://nam.org/wp-content/uploads/2024/05/NAM-AI-Whitepaper-2024-1.pdf

Hooley, T., Shepherd, C., & Dodd, V. (2015). *Get yourself connected: Conceptualising the role of digital technologies in Norwegian career guidance*. International Centre for Guidance Studies, University of Derby. https://doi.org/DOI: 10.48773/93Y86

Hopcan, S., Polat, E., Ozturk, M. E., & Ozturk, L. (2023). Artificial intelligence in special education: A systematic review. *Interactive Learning Environments*, *31*(10), 7335–7353. DOI: 10.1080/10494820.2022.2067186

Huang, J. (2024, May 21). A conversation with NVIDIA's Jensen Huang [Interview]. https://www.youtube.com/watch?v=8Pfa8kPjUio&t=2983s

Insa, D., Pérez, S., Silva, J., & Tamarit, S. (2021). Semiautomatic generation and assessment of Java exercises in engineering education. *Computer Applications in Engineering Education*, *29*(5), 1034–1050. DOI: 10.1002/cae.22356

Jayalath, J., & Esichaikul, V. (2022). Gamification to enhance motivation and engagement in blended eLearning for technical and vocational education and training. *Technology. Knowledge and Learning*, *27*(1), 91–118. DOI: 10.1007/s10758-020-09466-2

Ji, H., Han, I., & Park, S. (2024). Teaching foreign language with conversational AI: Teacher-student-AI interaction. *Language Learning & Technology*, *28*(2), 91–108. https://hdl.handle.net/10125/73573

Jia, J., Wang, T., Zhang, Y., & Wang, G. (2024). The comparison of general tips for mathematical problem solving generated by generative AI with those generated by human teachers. *Asia Pacific Journal of Education*, *44*(1), 8–28. DOI: 10.1080/02188791.2023.2286920

Johri, A., Katz, A. S., Qadir, J., & Hingle, A. (2023). Generative artificial intelligence and engineering education. *Journal of Engineering Education*, *112*(3), 572–577. DOI: 10.1002/jee.20537

Kaplan-Rakowski, R., Grotewold, K., Hartwick, P., & Papin, K. (2023). Generative AI and teachers' perspectives on its implementation in education. *Journal of Interactive Learning Research*, *34*(2), 313–338. https://www.learntechlib.org/primary/p/222363/. DOI: 10.70725/815246mfssgp

Kew, S. N., & Tasir, Z. (2022). Learning analytics in online learning environment: A systematic review on the focuses and the types of student-related analytics data. *Technology. Knowledge and Learning*, *27*(2), 405–427. DOI: 10.1007/s10758-021-09541-2

Kizilcec, R. F., & Lee, H. (2022). Algorithmic fairness in education. In W. Holmes & K. Porayska-Pomsta, *The Ethics of Artificial Intelligence in Education* (1st ed., pp. 174–202). Routledge. https://doi.org/DOI: 10.4324/9780429329067-10

Kohnke, L., Zou, D., & Su, F. (2025). Exploring the potential of GenAI for personalised English teaching: Learners' experiences and perceptions. *Computers and Education: Artificial Intelligence*, *8*, 100371. DOI: 10.1016/j.caeai.2025.100371

Kulik, J. A., & Fletcher, J. D. (2016). Effectiveness of intelligent tutoring systems: A meta-analytic review. *Review of Educational Research*, *86*(1), 42–78. DOI: 10.3102/0034654315581420

Kurtz, G., Amzalag, M., Shaked, N., Zaguri, Y., Kohen-Vacs, D., Gal, E., Zailer, G., & Barak-Medina, E. (2024). Strategies for integrating generative AI into higher education: Navigating challenges and leveraging opportunities. *Education Sciences*, *14*(5), 503. DOI: 10.3390/educsci14050503

Lee, G., & Zhai, X. (2024). Using ChatGPT for Science Learning: A Study on Pre-service Teachers' Lesson Planning. *IEEE Transactions on Learning Technologies*, *17*, 1643–1660. DOI: 10.1109/TLT.2024.3401457

Lee, U., Jung, H., Jeon, Y., Sohn, Y., Hwang, W., Moon, J., & Kim, H. (2023). Few-shot is enough: Exploring ChatGPT prompt engineering method for automatic question generation in English education. *Education and Information Technologies*, *29*(9), 11483–11515. DOI: 10.1007/s10639-023-12249-8

Lemons, L. L., Brashears, M. T., Burris, S., Meyers, C., & Price, M. A. (2015). Factors contributing to attrition as reported by leavers of secondary agriculture programs. *Journal of Agricultural Education*, *56*(4), 17–30. DOI: 10.5032/jae.2015.04017

Lin, C. C., Huang, A. Y., & Lu, O. H. (2023). Artificial intelligence in intelligent tutoring systems toward sustainable education: A systematic review. *Smart Learning Environments*, *10*(1), 41. DOI: 10.1186/s40561-023-00260-y

Lindsay, J., Hughes, K., Dougherty, S., Reese, K., & Joshi, M. (2024). *What we know about the impact of career and technical education: A systematic review of the research*. American Institutes for Research, Career and Technical Education Research Network., https://cteresearchnetwork.org/resources/2024-systematic-review

Liu, C., Wang, G.-C., & Wang, H.-F. (2025). The application of artificial intelligence in engineering education: A systematic review. *IEEE Access : Practical Innovations, Open Solutions*, *13*, 17895–17910. DOI: 10.1109/ACCESS.2025.3532595

Lu, A., Rouhanifard, P., Cleveland, C., Gilbert, E., & Loeb, S. (2025, March). *The key resource of time: Master schedules and effective allocation of students and educators | SCALE initiative*. Stanford Publications. https://scale.stanford.edu/publications/master-scheduling

Makransky, G., Andreasen, N. K., Baceviciute, S., & Mayer, R. E. (2021). Immersive virtual reality increases liking but not learning with a science simulation and generative learning strategies promote learning in immersive virtual reality. *Journal of Educational Psychology*, *113*(4), 719–735. DOI: 10.1037/edu0000473

Malyn-Smith, J., Juliuson, J., & MacGillivray, S. (2021, May 4). *Innovation at the forefront: CTE & the future of work*. ACTE Online. https://www.acteonline.org/tech-may-future-innovation/

Mann, R. (2022, January 10). *Leveraging VR, AR & AI for CTE student success*. ACTE Online. https://www.acteonline.org/tech-changes-how-we-learn/

Marino, M. T., Vasquez, E., Dieker, L., Basham, J., & Blackorby, J. (2023). The future of artificial intelligence in special education technology. *Journal of Special Education Technology*, *38*(3), 404–416. DOI: 10.1177/01626434231165977

Micic, M. (2024, November). *Artificial intelligence in career technical education*. Academic Senate for California Community Colleges. https://www.asccc.org/content/artificial-intelligence-career-technical-education

Mogavi, R., Deng, C., Juho Kim, J., Zhou, P., & Kwon, D., Y., Hosny Saleh Metwally, A., Tlili, A., Bassanelli, S., Bucchiarone, A., Gujar, S., Nacke, L. E., & Hui, P. (. (2024). ChatGPT in education: A blessing or a curse? A qualitative study exploring early adopters' utilization and perceptions. *Computers in Human Behavior: Artificial Humans*, *2*(1), 100027. DOI: 10.1016/j.chbah.2023.100027

Mon, B. F., Wasfi, A., Hayajneh, M., & Slim, A. (2023). A study on role of artificial intelligence in education. *2023 International Conference on Computing, Electronics & Communications Engineering (iCCECE)*, 133–138. https://doi.org/DOI: 10.1109/iCCECE59400.2023.10238613

Morrell, C. (2025.). *The influence of artificial intelligence on career and technical education and its diverse students*. STEM Equity Initiative. Retrieved March 22, 2025, from https://stemeducatorinitiative.org/blog/the-influence-of-artificial-intelligence-on-career-and-technical-education-and-its-diverse-students

Mühlhoff, R. (2023). Predictive privacy: Collective data protection in the context of artificial intelligence and big data. *Big Data & Society*, *10*(1), 20539517231166886. DOI: 10.1177/20539517231166886

Murcia-López, M., & Steed, A. (2016). The effect of environmental features, self-avatar, and immersion on object location memory in virtual environments. *Frontiers in ICT (Lausanne, Switzerland)*, *3*. Advance online publication. DOI: 10.3389/fict.2016.00024

Nazar, N., Chen, N., & Chong, C. Y. (2023). CodeLabeller: A web-based code annotation tool for java design patterns and summaries. *International Journal of Software Engineering and Knowledge Engineering*, *33*(07), 993–1009. DOI: 10.1142/S0218194023500213

Neeley, T. (2017). *Engaging students emotionally through online simulations*. Harvard Business School. https://www.hbs.edu/faculty/Pages/item.aspx?num=52283

Ng, A. (2024, December 5). *Could AI transform career-technical education?* EdWeek Market Brief. https://marketbrief.edweek.org/education-market/could-ai-transform-career-technical-education/2024/12

Nguyen, P. T., Di Rocco, J., Di Sipio, C., Rubei, R., Di Ruscio, D., & Di Penta, M. (2024). GPTSniffer: A CodeBERT-based classifier to detect source code written by ChatGPT. *Journal of Systems and Software, 214*, 112059. DOI: 10.1016/j.jss.2024.112059

Niño-Rojas, F., Lancheros-Cuesta, D., Jiménez-Valderrama, M. T. P., Mestre, G., & Gómez, S. (2023). Systematic Review: Trends in Intelligent Tutoring Systems in Mathematics Teaching and Learning. *International Journal of Education in Mathematics. Science and Technology, 12*(1), 203–229. DOI: 10.46328/ijemst.3189

Ocumpaugh, J., Baker, R., Gowda, S., Heffernan, N., & Heffernan, C. (2014). Population validity for educational data mining models: A case study in affect detection. *British Journal of Educational Technology, 45*(3), 487–501. DOI: 10.1111/bjet.12156

Oschinski, M., Crawford, A., & Wu, M. (2024). *AI and the future of workforce training*. Center for Security and Emergent Technologies. https://cset.georgetown.edu/publication/ai-and-the-future-of-workforce-training/

Ounejjar, L. A., Lachgar, M., Ouhayou, O., Laanaoui, M. D., Refki, E., Makaoui, R., & Saoud, A. (2024). SmartBlendEd: Enhancing blended learning through AI-optimized scheduling and user-centric design. *SoftwareX, 27*, 101891. DOI: 10.1016/j.softx.2024.101891

Pirker, J., Kopf, J., Kainz, A., Dengel, A., & Buchbauer, B. (2021). The Potential of Virtual Reality for Computer Science Education -Engaging Students through Immersive Visualizations. *2021 IEEE Conference on Virtual Reality and 3D User Interfaces Abstracts and Workshops (VRW)*, 297–302. https://doi.org/DOI: 10.1109/VRW52623.2021.00060

Plasman, J. S., Gottfried, M. A., & Klasik, D. J. (2021). Do Career-Engaging Courses Engage Low-Income Students? *AERA Open, 7*, 23328584211053324. DOI: 10.1177/23328584211053324

Rose, D. (1999). Universal design for learning. *Journal of Special Education Technology, 15*(1), 67–70. DOI: 10.1177/016264340001500108

Rosyadi, M. I., Kustiawan, I., Tetehfio, E. O., & Joshua, Q. (2023). The role of AI in vocational education: A systematic literature review. *Journal of Vocational Education Studies, 6*(2), 244–263. DOI: 10.12928/joves.v6i2.9032

Samah, L. A., Ismail, A., & Hasan, M. K. (2022). The effectiveness of gamification for students' engagement in technical and vocational education and training. *International Journal of Advanced Computer Science and Applications, 13*(9). Advance online publication. DOI: 10.14569/IJACSA.2022.0130920

Sandhu, S. (2025, February 25). *How Artificial Intelligence is Transforming the Vocational Education a.* CAQA Compliance. https://caqa.com.au/blogs/news/how-artificial-intelligence-is-transforming-the-vocational-education-and-training-vet-sector

Santosa, S., Suharto, S., Purbo Santosa, Y., Alzami, F. A., & Moses Setiadi, D. R. I. (2023). Design and evaluation of virtual compression testing machine based on multilayer perceptron for vocational-education virtual laboratory. *TEM Journal*, 710–720. https://doi.org/DOI: 10.18421/TEM122-14

Selwyn, N. (2022). The future of AI and education: Some cautionary notes. *European Journal of Education*, *57*(4), 620–631. DOI: 10.1111/ejed.12532

Smitha, H., & Afshin, Pavithra S Hegde. (2020). Face recognition based attendance management system. *International Journal of Engineering Research & Technology (Ahmedabad)*, *9*(5). Advance online publication. DOI: 10.17577/IJERTV9IS050861

Strengthening Career and Technical Education for the 21st Century Act (Perkins V). Pub. L. No. 115-224). https://www.govinfo.gov/app/details/PLAW-115publ224/related

Sublett, C., Mason, L., Rimbach-Jones, D., Beltran, K., & Fresard. (2025). *Fostering AI ready building and moving CTE pipelines* (pp. 1–13). The Education Research & Opportunity Center, The University of Tennessee Knoxville. https://cehhs.utk.edu/ero/wp-content/uploads/sites/2/2025/02/Fostering-AI-Ready-Building-and-Moving-CTE-Pipelines-compressed.pdf

Sun, J. C., & Pratt, T. L. (2024). Navigating AI integration in career and technical education: Diffusion challenges, opportunities, and decisions. *Education Sciences*, *14*(12), 1285. DOI: 10.3390/educsci14121285

Sun, J. C., & Turner, H. A. (2022). Induction by quarantine: Stages and effects of new career and technical education teachers' development. *Career and Technical Education Research*, *47*(2), 60–82. DOI: 10.5328/cter47.2.60

Suparyati, A., Widiastuti, I., Saputro, I. N., & Pambudi, N. A. (2023). The role of artificial intelligence (AI) in vocational education. *Jurnal Ilmiah Pendidikan Teknik Dan Kejuruan*, *17*(1). Advance online publication. DOI: 10.20961/jiptek.v17i1.75995

Tan, X., Cheng, G., & Ling, M. H. (2025). Artificial intelligence in teaching and teacher professional development: A systematic review. *Computers and Education: Artificial Intelligence*, *8*, 100355. DOI: 10.1016/j.caeai.2024.100355

Theobald, R., Plasman, J., Gottfried, M., Gratz, T., Holden, K., & Goldhaber, D. (2022). Sometimes less, sometimes more: Trends in career and technical education participation for students with disabilities. *Educational Researcher*, *51*(1), 40–50. DOI: 10.3102/0013189X211006361

Tobarra, L., Utrilla, A., Robles-Gómez, A., Pastor-Vargas, R., & Hernández, R. (2021). A cloud game-based educative platform architecture: The CyberScratch project. *Applied Sciences (Basel, Switzerland)*, *11*(2), 807. DOI: 10.3390/app11020807

Tomsio, L. (2024, December 31). *AI in career education: Future of workforce readiness*. TxDLA. https://www.txdla.org/ai-intelligence-in-career-educaiton/

Toni, A., & Vuorinen, R. (2020). Lifelong guidance in finland: Key policies and practices. In Haug, E. H., Hooley, T., Kettunen, J., & Thomsen, R. (Eds.), *Career and Career Guidance in the Nordic Countries* (pp. 127–143). BRILL., DOI: 10.1163/9789004428096_009

Traumer, F., Oeste-Reii, S., & Leimeister, J. M. (2017). Towards a future reallocation of work between humans and machines taxonomy of tasks and interaction types in the context of machine learning. SSRN *Electronic Journal*. https://doi.org/DOI: 10.2139/ssrn.3159131

Tyson, L. D., & Zysman, J. (2022). Automation, AI & work. *Daedalus*, *151*(2), 256–271. DOI: 10.1162/daed_a_01914

U.S. DoE. (2010). *ED512681.pdf* (Supporting American Education Learning: Powered by Technology, pp. 1–124). U.S. Department of Education. https://files.eric.ed.gov/fulltext/ED512681.pdf

Vervinck, M. (2024, June). *Embracing AI tools as an educator: Adapting for the future*. Alliant International University. https://cte.alliant.edu/wp-content/uploads/2024/06/2024-June-Newsletter.pdf

Vygotsky, L. S. (1978). *Mind in society: Development of higher psychological processes* (Cole, M., John-Steiner, V., Scribner, S., & Souberman, E., Eds.). Harvard University Press.

Walter, Y. (2024). Embracing the future of Artificial Intelligence in the classroom: The relevance of AI literacy, prompt engineering, and critical thinking in modern education. *International Journal of Educational Technology in Higher Education*, *21*(1), 15. DOI: 10.1186/s41239-024-00448-3

Wang, S., Wang, F., Zhu, Z., Wang, J., Tran, T., & Du, Z. (2024). Artificial intelligence in education: A systematic literature review. *Expert Systems with Applications*, *252*, 124167. DOI: 10.1016/j.eswa.2024.124167

Wang, Y., & Xue, L. (2024). Using AI-driven chatbots to foster Chinese EFL students' academic engagement: An intervention study. *Computers in Human Behavior*, *159*, 108353. DOI: 10.1016/j.chb.2024.108353

Waterfield, D. A., Watson, L., & Day, J. (2024). Applying artificial intelligence in special education: Exploring availability and functionality of AI platforms for special educators. *Journal of Special Education Technology*, *39*(3), 448–454. DOI: 10.1177/01626434241257237

Webster, R. (2016). Declarative knowledge acquisition in immersive virtual learning environments. *Interactive Learning Environments*, *24*(6), 1319–1333. DOI: 10.1080/10494820.2014.994533

Westman, S., Kauttonen, J., Klemetti, A., Korhonen, N., Manninen, M., Mononen, A., Niittymäki, S., & Paananen, H. (2021). Artificial intelligence for career guidance – current requirements and prospects for the future. *IAFOR Journal of Education*, *9*(4), 43–62. DOI: 10.22492/ije.9.4.03

Wilson, M., Robertson, P., Cruickshank, P., & Gkatzia, D. (2024). Opportunities and risks in the use of AI in career development practice. *Journal of the National Institute for Career Education and Counselling*, *48*(1), 48–57. DOI: 10.20856/jnicec.4807

Windelband, L. (2023). Artificial intelligence and assistance systems for technical vocational education and training – Opportunities and risks. In Shajek, A., & Hartmann, E. A. (Eds.), *New Digital Work* (pp. 195–213). Springer International Publishing., DOI: 10.1007/978-3-031-26490-0_12

Wu, E. H. K., Lin, C. H., Ou, Y. Y., Liu, C. Z., Wang, W. K., & Chao, C. Y. (2020). Advantages and constraints of a hybrid model K-12 E-learning assistant chatbot. *IEEE Access : Practical Innovations, Open Solutions*, *8*, 77788–77801. DOI: 10.1109/ACCESS.2020.2988252

Zhang, K., & Aslan, A. B. (2021). AI technologies for education: Recent research & future directions. *Computers and Education: Artificial Intelligence*, *2*, 100025. DOI: 10.1016/j.caeai.2021.100025

Chapter 3
Generative Artificial Intelligence Practices for Doctoral Student Engagement

Lynne Orr
https://orcid.org/0000-0002-6238-0761
Walden University, Minneapolis, USA

Kimberly Burton
https://orcid.org/0009-0004-9273-4737
Walden University, Minneapolis, USA

Judith Blakely
Walden University, Minneapolis, USA

Sherry Harrison
https://orcid.org/0000-0002-8121-0717
Walden University, Minneapolis, USA

ABSTRACT

Artificial intelligence (AI) is rapidly transforming the landscape of higher education, offering scalable, adaptive, and personalized tools that enrich the doctoral learning experience. This chapter examines how AI is reshaping doctoral education through enhanced student engagement, increased faculty effectiveness, and dynamic content interaction. Anchored in the Community of Inquiry framework, the chapter explores AI tools that support doctoral candidates with writing, research, and academic planning, while enabling faculty to deliver timely feedback and proactive support. Additionally, it highlights how adaptive and generative technologies personalize content engagement to elevate knowledge construction and scholarly inquiry. As AI becomes a strategic partner in doctoral education, ethical implementation and purposeful design are essential to ensuring its alignment with academic

DOI: 10.4018/979-8-3373-5092-9.ch003

integrity, equity, and learner success.

INTRODUCTION

Although, Mujtaba (2024) attested that AI has been discussed for over half a century, during the last two years various facets of AI functions for education have proliferated across global higher education campuses. The AI functions seem to be expanding moment by moment during the last year 2024-2025. Tayan et al. (2024) described the field of education being a predominant field influenced by the advancements in AI. Universities need to ensure the proper usage by students, developing policies, while also educating faculty, staff and students (Tayan et al., 2024). The number of uses and functions for doctoral students of AI to promote student engagement also has amplified throughout educational systems. Higher education has begun to fully embrace the various AI text-based tools to ensure the proper use of AI tools. This chapter specifically focused on the AI text-based tools used for doctoral student engagement. The purpose of this chapter is to review the recommendations and practices for effectively using AI to promote doctoral student engagement. The chapter applies the conceptual framework from Garrison's community of inquiry as the engagement definition to promote both student and faculty presence (Garrison et al., 2000).

The background portion of the chapter begins with the generative AI use in higher education and doctoral education. Next, the AI tools used for doctoral student engagement were reviewed in the background information. This information is followed by the AI tools used to enhance faculty engagement and content engagement. While the background information concludes with the summary of the impact of AI tools on learning analytics and student engagement.

The issues portion of the chapter begins with a short review of the importance of doctoral students using their original writing throughout their dissertation journey. Ethical considerations for doctoral students were the next portion of the issues section of the chapter. While the issue of data mining and the training of a generative artificial intelligence model was the issue reviewed. And the issue portion of the chapter concludes with the impact of artificial intelligence on student academic performance in higher education.

The chapter concludes with the recommendations portion of the chapter. The recommendations portion of the chapter begins with the suggestions for using AI tools for promoting doctoral student engagement. This ration of the promptings continues by reviewing the use of AI tools in different stages of students' research, specifically finding a research problem, writing the literature review, and outlining and editing research papers. Next are the commendations for facilitating active learning using AI tools. While this is followed by the suggestions for supporting doctoral student engagement as well as AI tool usage too promote doctoral mentoring relationship. While the background section includes the various functions of AI tools used in higher education.

BACKGROUND

Higher education has embraced the use of AI tools for text based generative artificial intelligence with the use of ChatGBT (Tayan et al., 2024). Tayan et al. mentioned how higher education has primarily focused on the use of AI to improve teaching and learning experiences, as well as increase student engagement. Doctoral education has also applied AI tools for student engagement (Tayan et al.). The background for this chapter includes the Community of Inquiry (CoI) as the conceptual framework (Garrison et al., 2000, 2001). There are three components discussed on engagement. One part includes the perspective on student engagement and how it is defined. The second portion includes the faculty engagement and the description of faculty engagement. While the third aspect of learner engagement focuses on content engagement and a explanation of content engagement. The background information concludes with the AI tool use to enhance student engagement in higher education and student learning.

AI Use in Higher Education

The rapid integration of artificial intelligence (AI) into higher education has initiated a paradigm shift in how teaching, learning, and engagement are conceptualized—particularly within the rigorous and self-directed landscape of doctoral education. AI offers innovative opportunities to personalize instruction, streamline academic support services, and foster meaningful connections between learners, faculty, and content. This section explores the critical role AI plays in enhancing doctoral engagement across three primary areas: student engagement, faculty engagement, and content engagement. These domains reflect the foundational elements of the Community of Inquiry (CoI) framework, which emphasizes the interplay between social, cognitive, and teaching presence in promoting a successful and engaging learning environment (Garrison et al., 2000, 2001).

AI in higher education serves both as an academic assistant and as a strategic educational partner. Doctoral students—often working professionals balancing research, teaching, and personal obligations—benefit from AI's capacity to deliver efficient, individualized support. Generative tools such as ChatGPT and Microsoft Copilot can help students brainstorm research questions, outline literature reviews, refine arguments, and check formatting for scholarly writing. These tools reduce cognitive load and support students in progressing more confidently through the dissertation process (Mollick & Mollick, 2023).

Institutions leverage AI-driven analytics platforms such as Civitas Learning or Brightspace Insights to monitor student engagement, predict risk, and facilitate timely intervention (Ifenthaler & Yau, 2020). For doctoral students, this means that support services can be proactively tailored to individual learning behaviors and academic trajectories, which is especially important in online, asynchronous environments. Additionally, AI enhances equity in higher education by providing accessible support tools for students with disabilities or non-native English speakers through real-time translation, voice-to-text capabilities, and adaptive content suggestions (Popenici & Kerr, 2017).

These tools, while powerful, must be framed within a commitment to ethical AI use. Doctoral programs must promote transparency and academic integrity by clearly defining acceptable use and ensuring students receive guidance on how to responsibly integrate AI into their scholarly work (Flanagan & Shoffner, 2023). AI tools are also available to measure student engagement.

AI Tools for Student Engagement

Engagement is a multifaceted construct in doctoral education, comprising emotional investment, behavioral participation, and cognitive immersion. AI enhances each of these elements by offering timely feedback, responsive tutoring, and adaptive resources that respond to the student's evolving needs. Intelligent tutoring systems, such as Carnegie Learning or Querium, simulate one-on-one instruction, helping students grasp complex methodological concepts or statistical techniques (VanLehn, 2011).

Chatbots and virtual research assistants provide around-the-clock access to academic support. For example, AI-powered platforms like Elicit or Scite allow students to efficiently synthesize relevant literature and assess the credibility of sources—an essential skill in evidence-based doctoral work. Moreover, AI fosters learner autonomy by enabling doctoral students to set and monitor academic goals using intelligent planning tools integrated into learning management systems.

These innovations promote social presence by supporting dialogue and peer feedback through AI-curated discussion prompts or real-time language enhancements. Furthermore, they encourage cognitive presence by facilitating iterative exploration, integration, and resolution of academic challenges (Garrison et al., 2000, 2001).

AI Tools for Faculty Engagement

Faculty are central to sustaining quality in doctoral education. Their teaching presence, mentorship, and scholarly expertise shape students' academic identity and intellectual development. AI supports faculty by automating routine administrative and instructional tasks, freeing time for deeper mentorship and pedagogical innovation. For example, AI-enabled grading tools can assess grammar, APA formatting, and structure in formative writing assignments, allowing instructors to concentrate on content-specific feedback (Holstein et al., 2019).

AI tools also aid in identifying patterns in student performance, alerting faculty when doctoral candidates disengage or demonstrate inconsistent progress. These insights allow for timely intervention, which is critical in reducing attrition—a persistent challenge in doctoral education. Faculty dashboards powered by AI provide actionable analytics that inform personalized outreach and differentiated instruction. Furthermore, AI tools facilitate professional development by recommending research articles, pedagogical strategies, and scholarly networks relevant to faculty interests. As faculty engage with AI as collaborators rather than competitors, their role in curating, mentoring, and modeling ethical research practices becomes even more essential (Luckin, 2018). Next, AI tools are available to assist with increasing learner's content engagement.

AI Tools Content Engagement

Content engagement involves the learner's interaction with course material, and AI is reshaping this process through personalization and interactivity. AI can dynamically adjust content based on a learner's prior knowledge, interests, and progress, which enhances relevance and retention. Adaptive learning platforms such as Smart Sparrow and Knewton tailor content delivery to student performance, enabling doctoral learners to move through challenging concepts at a personalized pace.

Generative AI supports content engagement by helping students deconstruct complex theories or visualize data through interactive simulations and data dashboards. For example, doctoral candidates working on qualitative dissertations can use tools like QuillBot or Trint to transcribe interviews and identify thematic patterns. Meanwhile, data science students can use AI platforms such as Tableau with embedded machine learning algorithms to explore and present findings in real time.

This level of engagement strengthens cognitive presence, as students are not only consuming content but actively constructing knowledge, applying theory, and generating new insights. Furthermore, AI supports cross-disciplinary exploration by linking content across fields, which is particularly valuable in interdisciplinary doctoral research. While AI and learning analytics can impact student engagement, is addressed in the next portion of the writing.

Impact of AI and Learning Analytics on Student Engagement

Artificial Intelligence (AI) tools can enhance student engagement when providing personalized learning opportunities. Altememy et al. (2023) found that AI applications such as ChatGPT and intelligent tutoring systems delivered personal supports to students such as immediate feedback and clarification, encouraging students in Iraq to actively participate in learning. Nuangchalerm and Prachagool (2023) shared that the use of possible AI enabled gamification, and other strategies can be used to keep learners motivated and engaged throughout the entire learning process in STEM classroom. Nuangchalerm and Prachagool shared that AI tools can provide powerful data analytics for tracking STEM student performance, and providing customized assistance to students, helping to ensure students remain engaged.

Chen et al., (2025) established that AI tools positively impacted student engagement in many ways, such as serving as a tutor, providing personalized instruction, providing adaptive feedback, and giving real-time assistance, fostering cognitive and emotional engagement. Chen et al. also found that AI chatbots can promote higher order thinking skills in learners, improving learner engagement. Ezeoguine and Eteng-Uket (2024) established that AI tools can provide interactive and immersive learning environments that can help maintain student motivation and interest. Ezeoguine and Eteng-Uket also stated that the personalized learning experiences provided through AI tools such as chatbots, writing assistant tools, and plagiarism detection software can help support the diverse learning needs of students, promoting student engagement. Ezeoguine and Eteng-Uket stressed the importance of inclusivity of the use of AI Tools for all types of learners, regardless of gender of age. In addition, Exeoguine and Eteng-Uket shared that AI tools can provide learners with support ensuring efficient use of time management helping prevent frustration and boredom and increasing student motivation.

AI tools promote student engagement for student diverse needs and lifestyles. Ngyen et al. (2024) found that Generative AI (GenAI) provides personalized learning, convenience, real-time interaction, and allows for learning to occur anywhere at any time. Ngyen et al. also shared that learning engagement can be increased for learners who prefer studying outside the conventional classroom using AI Tools providing that flexibility. By using GenAI to create personalized content, personalized assessments, and personalized feedback, the diverse needs and lifestyles of students can be taken into consideration and learner engagement of those students can be increased (Ngyen et al.). Next, are the issues and concerns which arise with the use of AI tools.

ISSUES

There were four issues included in this chapter. The first challenge involves the importance of doctoral students using their original writing for their doctoral manuscript, course discussion boards, and assignments (Johnson et al., 2024). Reviewing ethical considerations related to plagiarism was the second concern included in this chapter (Ahmad and Fauzi, 2024; Cotton et al., 2023; Liang et al., 2023; Prashar et al., 2023). While the third problem included data mining and ChatGPT initial training model as the concern contained in this chapter (López-Meneses et al., 2025). And to conclude this portion of the chapter writing were the AI tools for improving academic performance (Fazil et al., 2024; Adewale et al., 2024; Ajani et al., 2025; Fazil et al., 2024).

Original Writing

Students seeking doctoral degrees need to have proficient research and writing skills. The importance of original writing is critical to demonstrate the contextual understanding of a concept, identify gaps in the literature, conduct empirical research, and apply findings to solve issues and problems in society or practice (Nguyen et al., 2024). Original writing establishes credibility for the author and helps maintain academic rigor (Johnson et al., 2024). AI tools can contribute to these skills by improving efficiency, organization, and editing, as well as increasing motivation and engagement in students.

The Use of AI and Ethical Considerations in Higher Education

Plagiarism has been a concern in higher education for a long time. Modern technology such as word processors, and communication advances has made academic dishonesty perhaps easier or more appealing to some learners for various reasons in more recent times. Artificial Intelligence (AI) tools continue to impact ethics and plagiarism in higher education.

Ensuring assessments are measuring the performance of the actual learner being assessed is extremely important in maintaining academic integrity. Ensuring writing is the original writing of the learner is also important in maintaining high academic standards and ensuring academic integrity. Cotton et al. (2023) examined research that discussed both opportunities such as increased student engagement and collaboration for the use of versions of Chat Generative Pre-Trained Transformer (ChatGPT) in higher education as well as the challenges created with the opportunities for the use of ChatGPT in higher education. AI tools have impacted academic dishonesty over time. While there are many opportunities to enhance learning experiences for students by the use ChatGPT, Cotton et al. pointed out the research supports that Artificial Intelligence (AI) tools can make plagiarism more accessible to students who may not have even considered being academically dishonest previously.

Ahmad and Fauzi (2024) shared multiple contributing factors such as students feeling increased pressure for higher academic performance, students not having clear academic integrity awareness, and students not having a clear understanding of academic policies or codes. There are contributing factors for possible academic dishonesty to be proactively addressed. Ahmad and Fauzi recommended that students could be provided with resources such as tutoring to assist them with their academic writing. In addition to providing tutorials for improving academic writing, Ahmad and Fauzi also shared those tutorials focusing on the ethical and morally responsible use of AI Tools, and on effectively understanding and using AI and plagiarism detection tools. With the continual integration of AI tools in higher education, it is imperative that strategies and procedures are created, reviewed, implemented, and continually updated to maintain academic integrity and degree standards for learners.

There are institutional interventions which help facilitate responsible use of AI tools. Ethical decisions and judgements need to be determined by educators for possible plagiarism reports. Many plagiarism and AI detection tools are already available and are in use in higher education institutions. While GPT detectors can be helpful in determining possible academic dishonesty cases where written work was generated through GPT rather than by the student, Liang et al. (2023) found that GPT detectors exhibit bias against authors who do not speak English as their first language. Liang et al. found that GPT detectors may penalize non-native English speakers by identifying the limited linguistic phrases that non-native English speakers may use as possible GPT generated text. Liang et al. shared the importance of instructors being aware of possible false positives with GPT detectors, and the possible need for reviewing additional factors when determining if text was generated by GPT to avoid possible unfair consequences and bias academic integrity decisions for non-native English-speaking learners.

Prashar et al. (2023) examined unintentional plagiarism using a longitudinal quasi-experimental study with 294 postgraduate students in India. Prashar et al. established that there were personal factors that institutional efforts to increase plagiarism awareness for students positively strengthened students' ethical awareness of fairness, contextual ethics, and academic agreements. In addition, Prashar et al. initiated that students' personal religious background, gender, and professional experience impacted how the institutional efforts to increase plagiarism awareness affected each student's ethical perspectives on fairness. Prashar et al. stressed that it is important when higher education institutions are putting proactive procedures in place to prevent academic dishonesty that the use of targeted educational interventions are implemented to promote student understanding of plagiarism as a matter of ethics, rather than just plagiarism as an academic integrity violation.

The work of Prashar et. Al (2023), Ahmad and Fauzi (2024), Cotton et al. (2023), and Liang et al (2023) all support the importance of proactive approaches to prevent academic dishonesty and to ensure possible academic dishonesty cases are reviewed through a fair and non-bias approach. Supporting learners in their education and understanding of ethical standards, helping learners fully understand what academic honor codes mean, and providing an environment where students know and understand expectations of responsible academic behaviors, higher education institutions can help prevent academic dishonesty in a world of rapidly advancing technology tools. There are continued ethical concerns with data mining and training which collide with privacy issues.

Data Mining and Training/ChatGBT

Through personalized learning and Educational Data Mining (EDM) Artificial Intelligence (AI) is transforming higher education. López-Meneses et al. (2025) found that EDM allows for the analysis of student data to predict student performance and needed interventions; however, López-Meneses et al. also highlighted the importance of a human being in the loop to ensure that the information is correct, and that the correct needed interventions are implemented. DataCamp (2024) indicates that fine-tuning Generative AI models is an important task to ensure information received is accurate and the information desired. DataCamp stresses the need for human supervision through evaluating the model to track the progress during training to determine the effectiveness and if modifications need to be made. Both López-Meneses et al. and DataCamp support the need for human guidance on the use of data mining and training of AI Tools. Building on the use of AI Tools Data Mining and Training combined with human oversight to address learning needs, Chen et al. (2025) explored AI-supported student engagement through a comprehensive text mining and systematic analysis. Chen et al. found that AI is mostly used as tutoring systems for personalized instruction.

Dornis (2025) shared that traditional text and data mining versus generative AI training has important copyright implications. There are some other challenges in addition to copyright implications with data mining and AI training that need to be taken into consideration. The challenges of AI bias, not just the AI-generated content, but also how the tools to detect AI content should be taken into consideration. Liang et al. (2023) revealed significant bias issues in AI detection systems used in educational settings, finding that GPT detectors demonstrate consistent bias toward non-Native English writers identifying over 60% of TOEFL essays written by Non-Native English Writers as AI generated.

López-Meneses et al. (2025), DataCamp (2024), Chen et al. (2025), Dornis (2025), and Liang et al. (2023) all emphasized the need for human oversight, consideration of intellectual property/copyright, and monitoring for bias in AI systems or detection tools. Liang et al. (2023) discovered that simple language modifications dramatically reduced detection rates in AI generated detection tools. These considerations are essential for data mining and training AI systems that enhance learning in higher education while ensuring academic integrity, protecting intellectual property, and ensuring AI systems are not producing bias information. There still remains an issue with accessibility of resources and availability of AI tools.

Impact of Artificial Intelligence on Student Academic Performance in Higher Education

From providing personalized learning experiences to improving administrative processes for educators, AI tools are continually evolving and providing more and more resources to use for improving student academic achievement. AI tools are impacting academic achievement. And there are challenges with implementing available technology tools in higher education.

Fazil et al. (2024) found students at Kabul University demonstrated a high level of AI knowledge in their daily lives, however, there were still opportunities for better integration of AI tools into the academic curriculum. Fazil et al. found that the length of engagement with AI tools only influenced students' perceptions minimally regarding the potential for positive impact of AI tools on academic achievement, suggesting that deeper interactions with the use of AI tools in student education may be important in positively impacting student academic achievement.

Adewale et al. (2024) conducted a systematic review of studies of the impact of machine learning methods in predicting and enhancing academic performance in Open and Distance Learning (ODL) environments. Adewale et al. found machine learning methods were used in 29.69% of the studies reviewed, demonstrating substantial effectiveness in predicting student performance and providing timely interventions. Adewale et al. also found in the systematic review that the integration of AI tools in ODL, using personalized learning experiences with AI-tutoring systems providing personalized instruction, learning outcomes could be significantly improved.

There are other AI tools and opportunities can aid in improvement of academic performance in higher education beyond personalized learning and tutoring opportunities for students. AI tools can help streamline administrative tasks, providing educators more time to focus their teaching on their learners' needs. Ajani et al. (2025) noted from studies systematically reviewed that AI tools could provide grading assistance, and routine tasks which allow more time to focus on student learning needs, also providing for more efficient decision-making and resource allocation. While AI tools can provide grading assistance, and assistance with routine tasks, there are also challenges with AI performing grading and other administrative tasks. For example, Ajani et al. (2025) shared that research reviewed shows that AI systems require access to extensive amounts of student data to complete tasks, and that the data must be handled in ways that maintain compliance with privacy and security legal requirements. Another challenge Ajani et al. pointed out from review of research that it is possible there are inequalities with available AI tools, such as gender and regional disparities. Ajani et al. stressed that those disparities should be considered, and any access gaps addressed when determining factors affecting the impact of AI on ODL.

AI offers the potential to positively impact academic performance through many ways, such as providing personalized learning opportunities, focused interventions, grading assistance, and administrative routine task assistance. The work of Fazil et al. (2024), Adewale et al. (2024), and Ajani et al. (2025) supported that when implemented purposefully, ethically, and responsibly, AI tools can significantly improve student academic performance. Ensuring challenges such as privacy, security, and equitable access are mitigated, and ethical considerations are taken in account, AI tools can help higher education institutions provide more effective, inclusive, and personalized learning opportunities for students, thus positively impacting student academic performance. These issues need continued evaluation along with updated recommendations for AI use for doctoral student engagement.

RECOMMENDATIONS

Recommended AI Practices for Doctoral Student Engagement

AI tools have been shown to promote active participation, making the research process more interesting and enjoyable. In doing so, it improves students' engagement and motivation (Ringo, 2025). The interactive formats also increase autonomous motivation (Li et al., 2025), while personalized, immediate feedback positively influences students' self-efficacy. The increased efficiency can help students complete projects promptly and contribute to their overall academic achievement (Li et al., 2025; Ringo, 2025).

Artificial Intelligence, in its many forms and applications, has become not just tools students in higher education use, they now rely on these tools. From proofreading to generating an outline to synthesizing current literature, it is a resource that needs to be integrated into higher education curriculums. Students are using it, and they will use it after they graduate. Higher education needs to embrace these tools and integrate them into the curriculum (Keykha et al., 2024; Salhab, 2024). The more familiarity with AI tools students have, the more efficiently they can use and benefit from them (Andersen et al., 2025; Nguyen et al., 2024).

Using AI to Find a Research Problem

Three areas that have demonstrated success when employing AI tools include finding a research problem, researching and synthesizing resources for the literature review, and helping with outlines and editing. A common problem facing many doctoral students is finding a researchable problem. One issue is when students choose a topic before searching the literature. They see a problem in their jobs or lives, and they want to fix that problem

(Zafar et al., 2024). They are then unsuccessful in finding research that addresses the problem or phenomenon and assume it is a gap. Unfortunately, the absence of literature does not necessarily mean it is a viable dissertation topic. There needs to be research to support the need for a study. This paradox often leads to frustrating attempts by students searching for articles to support a topic that is too broad or does not align with the rest of their study (Zafar et al., 2024).

Artificial intelligence can help students find viable research problems. Uploading articles into an AI search engine can quickly find trends in the literature (Keykha et al., 2024). The summarization and synthesis features of AI tools extract key points from research, often voluminous works, to generate thematic summaries and sources that align with the researchers' study (Keykha et al., 2024). For visual learners, there are AI tools that can create conceptual maps to show the connections between existing research (Kumar & Gunn, 2024). Leveraging these tools can help students be flexible in their topics. They can still work with something they are passionate about, but also find a topic supported by the literature. These tools can, therefore, help isolate contradictions and possible research gaps.

Natural Language Processing (NLP) is a feature that students gravitate to. Being able to type a question into a search engine, rather than breaking it out into concepts and Boolean operators, is appealing and quick. When NLP is not available, AI can help researchers generate keywords to use in Boolean searching (Keykha et al., 2024). This can make research in library databases more user-friendly. These keywords, used in library databases, can find relevant, peer reviewed, and empirical research in a structure that is comfortable to students. The relevant articles can show the current landscape of a problem and provide potential gaps to be explored.

Students must always be aware of the evolving technology and the creation of AI features and tools. An iterative process of searching can help them stay on top of this new technology. AI concept maps are a helpful way to see the larger picture of a topic and possible avenues for future research. As always, students must diligently review all AI-generated information for credibility and validity. Taking the extra steps to research the generated ideas is necessary when using AI tools.

Enhancing the Literature Review with AI

The literature review for a doctoral dissertation, provides a comprehensive overview of a topic, analyzing the existing research and showing how the researcher's topic contributes to the current conversation. AI can play an integral role in the literature review process if used appropriately. AI's large language model (LLM) can rapidly identify relevant papers, summarize those articles, and even point out themes and patterns between those sources (Kumar & Gunn, 2024; Storey, 2023). Since the literature review is an iterative process, it can be quickly updated to stay current.

Numerous AI tools are available today, many of which are widely available for free online. These platforms can help organize papers by pointing out the recurring ideas between them. They can help researchers locate relevant research. There are also many AI-based literature mapping tools. Conceptual maps provide a visual tool to identify insights and connections between research studies. Drawing relationships across various authors' works can give a better understanding and context to the researcher (Wong & Li, 2023). This added efficiency helps produce a simplified workflow structure, saving time and reducing stress while increasing engagement. (Kumar & Gunn, 2024; Wong & Li, 2023) It

Citation management software is not new to the research field; however, AI has improved this already useful tool. The introduction of "AI assistants" to these platforms allows researchers to ask questions to find related research, locate DOIs, proofread, and make grammatical corrections based on the citation style being used (Subramanian et al., 2025). The citations generated by these software programs are only as good as the information put into the software. Many platforms add an extra layer of protection by finding and alerting the researcher to possible errors. The final product will always depend on the due diligence of the researcher. Citations should always be double (or triple) checked to ensure they are formatted correctly.

While AI helps to make the literature review process less intimidating (Kumar & Gunn, 2024). Students need to review any information generated by AI manually. Literature summaries are convenient, but it is essential that the researchers review the literature manually to make sure they provide the correct information in the context it was delivered. Performing a rigorous review of citations is also important. This is an area where mistakes can easily be overlooked. Having an extra set of eyes from AI is helpful, but the end product is entirely on the student (Ringo, 2025). AI tools are helpful for outlining and editing, while ensuring ethical practices are followed.

AI Tools for Outlining and Editing

One of the most daunting tasks in writing research is where to begin. Staring at a blank screen can be overwhelming. AI has many tools to help in this area. AI is an ideal tool to use for organizing your writing. Templates can be generated to help create an outline. The templates have areas for main points, subtopics, and supporting details to help conceptualize the organization and flow of the paper.

The image below is an example of an outline for a research paper generated in a popular online chatbot (see Figure 1). This is the prompt:

Create an outline for a research paper on the pros and cons of using AI in research. The paper is for an undergraduate English class.

Figure 1. Sample outline for a research paper

Outline

- **Abstract**
  - Brief summary of research (150-250 words)
  - Research question, methods, main findings, and conclusions
- **Introduction**
  - Background information on research topic
  - Purpose of the study
  - Research question
  - Significance of the study
- **Literature Review**
  - Summary of relevant previous research
  - Key studies, theories, and findings
  - Context for the current research
- **Methodology**
  - Description of research methods
  - Participants, materials, and procedures
  - Data analysis techniques
- **Results**
  - Presentation of research findings
  - Use of tables, charts, or figures if necessary
  - Objective and clear descriptions
- **Discussion**
  - Interpretation of results
  - Relationship to hypothesis and previous research
  - Implications, limitations, and future research directions
- **Conclusion**
  - Summary of key findings and their significance
  - Restatement of research importance
  - Suggested next steps
- **References**
  - List of all sources cited
  - Proper citation style (APA, MLA, Chicago, etc.)

AI can also be used for creating more detailed outlines. Instead of putting in a generic prompt of "I need an outline for a research paper," you can put in the topic and specific points you would like to address. This is an example of a possible prompt to create an outline with AI:

Create an outline for a research paper on the pros and cons of using AI in literary research. The paper is for an undergraduate English class and will be part of an oral presentation.

AI immediately generated an outline, including a title, an introduction with subparts, a section for advantages and disadvantages, listing the pros and cons that can be explored, case studies and examples, and a conclusion. It provided the time allotted to each section for the oral presentation. The extremely detailed outline below provides a blueprint for the entire project (see Figure 2).

Figure 2. Sample outline for a research paper on the pros and cons of using AI in literary research

Title: The Pros and Cons of AI in Literary Research

1. **Introduction (1–2 minutes)**
    a. **Hook** – Start with an engaging quote or question (e.g., "Can AI truly understand Shakespeare?")
    b. **Background** – Brief overview of AI's increasing role in analyzing literature
    c. **Thesis Statement** – While AI enhances literary analysis through pattern recognition and efficiency, it also raises concerns about creativity, interpretation, and academic integrity
2. **Advantages of AI in Literary Research (3–4 minutes)**
    a. **Speed and Efficiency**
        i. AI quickly processes vast amounts of literary texts
        ii. Saves researchers time on data gathering and textual analysis
    b. **Pattern Recognition and Thematic Analysis**
        i. AI detects literary trends, recurring themes, and stylistic patterns
        ii. Helps analyze large corpora of literature (e.g., sentiment analysis, authorship attribution)
    c. **Access to Vast Digital Archives**
        i. AI can compare historical texts, translations, and adaptations
        ii. Enhances intertextual studies by cross-referencing works
    d. **Assistance in Linguistic and Stylistic Studies**
        i. AI can analyze an author's unique style or detect forgeries
        ii. Useful in comparative literature and translation studies
3. **Disadvantages of AI in Literary Research (3–4 minutes)**
    a. **Lack of Deep Understanding and Interpretation**
        i. AI lacks human intuition and emotional intelligence
        ii. Cannot fully grasp metaphor, irony, and cultural nuances
    b. **Risk of Oversimplification and Bias**
        i. AI models may misinterpret literary meanings due to biased training data
        ii. Overreliance on quantifiable aspects can reduce the richness of analysis
    c. **Ethical Concerns and Academic Integrity**
        i. AI-generated analysis may lead to plagiarism or lack of original thought
        ii. Students may misuse AI tools instead of engaging critically with texts
    d. **Challenges in Creativity and Subjectivity**
        i. Literary research often requires subjective interpretation, which AI struggles with
        ii. Over-dependence on AI may discourage independent critical thinking
4. **Case Studies and Examples (2–3 minutes)**
    a. **Example of AI Success** – AI-driven authorship analysis (e.g., identifying anonymous writers)
    b. **Example of AI Limitation** – AI misinterpreting literary themes or failing to recognize satire
5. **Conclusion (1–2 minutes)**
    a. **Restate Key Points** – AI is a powerful tool, but it cannot replace human literary analysis
    b. **Encourage a Balanced Approach** – Use AI as an aid, not a substitute for critical reading
    c. **Closing Thought** – Pose a thought-provoking question (e.g., "Can AI ever truly appreciate poetry?")

AI content development and refinement tools can help with grammar, tone, summarization, engagement, and flow. These tools are extremely helpful for students when proofreading and reviewing work. They can quickly assess the paper and suggest personalized recommendations for improvement in these areas (Storey, 2023). This added efficiency allows more time for researching, analyzing, and writing rather than proofreading and reviewing.

Editing for cohesiveness and style is another area where AI tools shine. AI's ability to pull context from a submitted paper can immediately assist in readability and consistency. AI can identify errors or areas of weakness repeated in a document and suggest possible solutions. It can also review a resource in a specific discipline and adopt the terminology and formatting regularly employed in that field.

Outlining and editing tools for AI can be minutely specified according to discipline, formatting style, tone, audience, and purpose. The dynamic and modifiable outlines created at the start of the process can help with organization and ease anxiety if the writer is unsure where to begin. However, AI-generated content must be integrated with personal voice and critical analysis. It is important to know the line between how far you can apply AI and when to use your analysis. AI is ideal for larger reviews to help identify repeating areas for improvement and iterative editing. As always, the final product depends on the writer's oversight.

Recommendations for Promoting Active Learning Through AI Tools

The authors of this chapter recommend AI tools to promote active learning with doctoral students. Martinez et al. (2025) described how educators are using active learning strategies together with AI tools to personalize learning. Martinez et al. suggested that AI tools can move beyond personalization and support collaborative and experiential learning. Pahi et al. (2024) also suggested the practice of combining AI tools with teaching assistance to help increase active learning. The combination of both provides a more supportive and interactive environment. Were as, Jimenez et al (2024) integrated AI tools with active learning strategies and found that there was a significant impact on critical thinking and innovative instructional practices. While Jimenez et al (2024) integrated AI tools with active learning strategies and found that there was a significant impact on critical thinking and innovative instructional practices. Lastly, Oliinyk et al. (2024) found that the research competence of doctoral students increased when using AI to build and develop research competencies of PhD students.

Recommendations for Stakeholder Engagement with AI Tools

Like AI tools promoting active learning, AI tools can also increase student engagement. Mirdad et al. (2024) found the positive benefits to implementing AI technology tools for improving student engagement. Perera and Lankathilake (2023) also discussed how one of the pros to using Open AI was the increase in student engagement. Also, Alordiah, C. O. (2023) discussed how Georgia State University of Technology used an AI automated response to student questions, termed Jane Watson. Through this experience, it was determined that there was an increase in student assistance and engagement (Alordiah, 2023). Overall, Ezeoguine and Eteng-Uket (2024) also discovered that the use of AI tools increased student engagement.

Recommendations for Enhancing the Doctoral Mentoring Relationship

The doctoral supervision relationship includes both the iterative writing process and the relationship development process. Developing a relationship of trust with a supportive positive environment helps strengthen the guidance throughout the iterative writing process. Oliveira et al. (2024) discussed the integration of AI tools can expediate data collection, analysis as well as advance communication and collaboration. Parker et al. (2024) studied the integration of AI tools with doctoral student writing. Parker et al. introduced various functions of writing which included the hybrid-human AI writing process. Dynamic brainstorming and ideation, continuous negotiation of meaning, comparative evaluation, cognitive and metacognitive engagement, confidence, and learner agency, and AI for formative feedback were all reviewed as tools included into the co-supervision writing process. Parker et al. (2024) introduced the concept of hybrid-human AI writing concerning the doctoral student's dissertation process which was developed by Eaton (2023). Eaton referred to the challenging writing process of doctoral students incorporating the concern for *post-plagiarism* while integrating AI tools raising concerns for ethics and integrity. While Oliveira et al. (2024) mentioned the importance of using AI for research fluency and maintaining the importance of maintaining the student voice. Thong et al. (2025) investigated the use of generative AI with doctoral co-supervision and found the AI tools were advantageous for enhancing collaboration within the student and doctoral supervisor.

CONCLUSIONS

AI tools in the higher education arena are quickly changing the landscape. If the university continues to develop policies and standards of use (Perera & Lankathilake (2023) and continually educate doctoral students along the lines of privacy, ethical concerns, information literacy, and positive uses for the research process, AI will continue to prosper in higher education. If we remember what Sutomo et al. (2024, May) presented as the challenges of the use for AI in higher education as: "ethical consideration of AI, data privacy, and the digital divide" (para. 1). Also, Alordiah (2023) indicated additional risks to AI use in colleges as, "risks to human interaction, critical thinking, and creativity" (p. 62).

As AI continues to evolve, it will be important for educators to continue to research possible ways to maximize the potential of AI tools for engaging students in the learning process. Lesh and Lancaster (2024) conducted a study with EdD students and the use of generative AI tools to support their research skills and the doctoral process. Lesh and Lancaster suggested a balanced approach which incorporates the ethical considerations, accuracy, compliance rules, and continuous training. Tayan et al. (2024) also advocated that university administrators continual update the course policies and guidelines regarding the use of AI texted based tools.

Administrators, faculty, and students require the knowledge of the potential benefits and limitations of using AI for learning (Tayan et al., 2024). It should not replace the instructor for learning and students still need to enhance their knowledge on key course concepts. Overall, Perera and Lankathilake (2023) made excellent proposals on AI usage guidelines. These commendations were the advised practices for higher education institutions to follow; a. raise awareness of the potential uses and limitations, b. use ChatGPT as a complementary tool, c. incorporate proctored, in-person assessments, d. develop ethical principles and guidelines, e. prevent plagiarism, f. provide personalized feedback, and g. use formative assessments (Perera & Lankathilake, 2023). Following these guidelines will help guide the proper use of AI tools for graduate education. In conclusion, as Alawida et al. (2023) mentioned, an AI large language model has the potential to revolutionize research, yet there remains a need for scrutiny to assess the information and preserve the integrity of research.

REFERENCES

Adewale, M. D., Azeta, A., Abayomi-Alli, A., & Sambo-Magaji, A. (2024). Impact of artificial intelligence adoption on students' academic performance in open and distance learning: A systematic literature review. *Heliyon*, *10*(22), e40025. DOI: 10.1016/j.heliyon.2024.e40025 PMID: 39605813

Ahmad, H., & Fauzi, M. A. (2024). Plagiarism in academic writing in higher education institutions: A bibliometric analysis. [IJonSES]. *International Journal on Social and Education Sciences*, *6*(1), 64–84. DOI: 10.46328/ijonses.623

Ajani, O. A., Gamede, B., & Matiyenga, T. C. (2025). Leveraging artificial intelligence to enhance teaching and learning in higher education: Promoting quality education and critical engagement. *Journal of Pedagogical Sociology and Psychology*, *7*(1), 54–69. DOI: 10.33902/JPSP.202528400

Alawida, M., Mejri, S., Mehmood, A., Chikhaoui, B., & Isaac Abiodun, O. (2023). A Comprehensive Study of ChatGPT: Advancements, Limitations, and Ethical Considerations in Natural Language Processing and Cybersecurity. *Information (Basel)*, *14*(8), 462. DOI: 10.3390/info14080462

Alordiah, C. O. (2023). Proliferation of artificial intelligence tools: Adaptation strategies in the higher education sector. *Propellers Journal of Education*, *2*(1), 53–65.

Altememy, H. A., Neamah, N. R., Mazhair, R., Naser, N. S., & Fahad, A. A., Abdulghffar al-sammarraie, N., ... & Al-Muttar, M. Y. O. (2023). AI Tools' Impact on Student Performance: Focusing on Student Motivation & Engagement in Iraq. [Social Space]. *Przestrzeń Społeczna*, *23*(2), 143–165.

Andersen, J. P., Degn, L., Fishberg, R., Graversen, E. K., Horbach, S. P. J. M., Schmidt, E. K., Schneider, J. W., & Sørensen, M. P. (2025). Generative Artificial Intelligence (GenAI) in the research process – A survey of researchers' practices and perceptions. *Technology in Society*, *81*, 102813. DOI: 10.1016/j.techsoc.2025.102813

ChatGPT. (2025, April 1). *The pros and cons of AI in literary research* [Outline]. Personal communication.

Chen, X., Xie, H., Qin, S. J., Wang, F. L., & Hou, Y. (2025). Artificial Intelligence-Supported Student Engagement Research: Text Mining and Systematic Analysis. *European Journal of Education*, *60*(1), e70008. DOI: 10.1111/ejed.70008

Cotton, D., Cotton, P., & Shipway, R. (2023). Chatting and cheating: Ensuring academic integrity in the era of ChatGPT. *Innovations in Education and Teaching International*. Advance online publication. DOI: 10.1080/14703297.2023.2190148

DataCamp. (2024, March 14). Fine-tuning OpenAI's GPT-4: A step-by-step guide. https://www.datacamp.com/tutorial/fine-tuning-openais-gpt-4-step-by-step-guide

Dornis, T. W. (2025). The training of generative AI is not text and data mining. *Applied Sciences (Basel, Switzerland)*, *15*(3), 1–28.

Eaton, S. E. (2023). Postplagiarism: Transdisciplinary ethics and integrity in the age of artifcial intelligence and neurotechnology. *International Journal for Educational Integrity*, *19*(23), 23. Advance online publication. DOI: 10.1007/s40979-023-00144-1

Ezeoguine, E. P., & Eteng-Uket, S. (2024). Artificial intelligence tools and higher education student's engagement. *Edukasiana: Jurnal Inovasi Pendidikan*, *3*(3), 300–312. DOI: 10.56916/ejip.v3i3.733

Fazil, A. W., Hakimi, M., Shahidzay, A. K., & Hasas, A. (2024). Exploring the broad impact of AI technologies on student engagement and academic performance in university settings in Afghanistan. *RIGGS: Journal of Artificial Intelligence and Digital Business*, *2*(2), 56–63. DOI: 10.31004/riggs.v2i2.268

Flanagan, S. M., & Shoffner, M. (2023). Academic integrity in the age of artificial intelligence: Policy, pedagogy, and practice. *Journal of Ethics in Education*, *27*(3), 105–120.

Garrison, D. R., Anderson, T., & Archer, W. (2000). Critical inquiry in a text-based environment: Computer conferencing in higher education. *The Internet and Higher Education*, *2*(2–3), 87–105.

Garrison, D. R., Anderson, T., & Archer, W. (2001). The first decade of the Community of Inquiry framework: A retrospective. *The Internet and Higher Education*, *13*(1–2), 5–9.

Holstein, K., McLaren, B. M., & Aleven, V. (2019). Designing for complementarity: Teacher and student needs for orchestration support in AI-enhanced classrooms. *Artificial Intelligence in Education*, *11625*, 157–171.

Ifenthaler, D., & Yau, J. Y.-K. (2020). Utilising learning analytics to support study success in higher education: A systematic review. *Educational Technology Research and Development*, *68*(4), 1961–1990. DOI: 10.1007/s11423-020-09788-z

Jiménez, O. R., Gastélum, V. S., Ramírez, C. Z., & Almaguer, C. G. (2024). Application of active learning techniques supported by generative AI in education. In *ICERI2024 Proceedings* (pp. 10408-10417). IATED. DOI: 10.21125/iceri.2024.2662

Johnson, J. E., Goodman, P., & Robert, R. (2024). Indicators of rigor in dissertation research. *Journal of Professional Nursing*, *55*, 57–64. https://doi.org/DOI: 10.1016/j.profnurs.2024.07.011

Keykha, A., Behravesh, S., & Ghaemi, F. (2024). ChatGPT and medical research: A metasynthesis of opportunities and challenges. *Journal of Advances in Medicine Education & Professionalism*, *12*(3), 135–147. DOI: 10.30476/JAMP.2024.101068.1910 PMID: 39175584

Kumar, S., & Gunn, A. (2024). Doctoral students' reflections on generative artificial intelligence (GenAI) use in the literature review process. *Innovations in Education and Teaching International*, •••, 1–14. DOI: 10.1080/14703297.2024.2427049

Lesh, J. J., & Lancaster, J. J. (2024). AI-Assisted Academia: Unveiling Doctoral Students' Perspectives on Dissertation in Practice Innovation. *Bulletin of Educational Studies, 3*(2). DOI: 10.61326/bes.v3i2.288

Li, Y., Sadiq, G., Qambar, G., & Zheng, P. (2025). The impact of students' use of ChatGPT on their research skills: The mediating effects of autonomous motivation, engagement, and self-directed learning. *Education and Information Technologies, 30*(4), 4185–4216. DOI: 10.1007/s10639-024-12981-9

Liang, W., Yuksekgonul, M., Mao, Y., Wu, E., & Zou, J. (2023). GPT detectors are biased against non-native English writers. *Patterns (New York, N.Y.), 4*(8), 100779. Advance online publication. DOI: 10.1016/j.patter.2023.100779 PMID: 37521038

López-Meneses, E., López-Catalán, L., Pelícano-Piris, N., & Mellado-Moreno, P. C. (2025). Artificial intelligence in educational data mining and human-in-the-loop machine learning and machine teaching: Analysis of scientific knowledge. *Applied Sciences (Basel, Switzerland), 15*(2), 772. DOI: 10.3390/app15020772

Martinez, M. E., & Gomez, V. (2025). Active Learning Strategies: A Mini Review of Evidence-Based Approaches. *Acta Pedagogia Asiana, 4*(1), 43–54. DOI: 10.53623/apga.v4i1.555

Mirdad, K., Daeli, O. P. M., Septiani, N., Ekawati, A., & Rusilowati, U. (2024). Optimizing student engagement and performance usingai-enabled educational tools. *Journal of Computer Science and Technology Application, 1*(1), 53–60. 10.34306

Mollick, E., & Mollick, L. (2023). Using AI to increase student engagement, writing quality, and critical thinking. *Innovations in Education and Teaching International*. Advance online publication. DOI: 10.1080/14703297.2023.2250023

Mujtaba, B. (2024). Clarifying Ethical Dilemmas in Sharpening Students' Artificial Intelligence Proficiency: Dispelling Myths About Using AI Tools in Higher Education. [BEL]. *Business Ethics & Leadership, 8*(2), 107–127. DOI: 10.61093/bel.8(2).107-127.2024

Nguyen, A., Hong, Y., Dang, B., & Huang, X. (2024). Human-AI collaboration patterns in AI-assisted academic writing. *Studies in Higher Education, 49*(5), 847–864. DOI: 10.1080/03075079.2024.2323593

Nguyen, A., Kremantzis, M., Essien, A., Petrounias, I., & Hosseini, S. (2024). Enhancing student engagement through artificial intelligence (AI): Understanding the basics, opportunities, and challenges. *Journal of University Teaching & Learning Practice, 21*(6), 1–13. https://orcid.org/0000-0002-0759-9656. DOI: 10.53761/caraaq92

Nuangchalerm, P., & Prachagool, V. (2023). AI-driven learning analytics in STEM education. *Online Submission, 5*(2), 77–84.

Oliveira, J., Murphy, T., Vaughn, G., Elfahim, S., & Carpenter, R. E. (2024). Exploring the adoption phenomenon of artificial intelligence by doctoral students within doctoral education. *New Horizons in Adult Education and Human Resource Development, 36*(4), 248–262. DOI: 10.1177/19394225241287032

Pahi, K., Hawlader, S., Hicks, E., Zaman, A., & Phan, V. (2024). Enhancing active learning through collaboration between human teachers and generative AI. *Computers and Education Open, 6*, 100183. DOI: 10.1016/j.caeo.2024.100183

Parker, J. L., Richard, V. M., Acabá, A., Escoffier, S., Flaherty, S., Jablonka, S., & Becker, K. P. (2024). Negotiating Meaning with Machines: AI's Role in Doctoral Writing Pedagogy. *International Journal of Artificial Intelligence in Education*, •••, 1–21. DOI: 10.1007/s40593-024-00425-x

Perera, P., & Lankathilake, M. (2023). AI in higher education: A literature review of chatgpt and guidelines for responsible implementation. **https://dx.doi.org/**DOI: 10.47772/IJRISS.2023.7623

Popenici, S. A. D., & Kerr, S. (2017). Exploring the impact of artificial intelligence on teaching and learning in higher education. *Research and Practice in Technology Enhanced Learning, 12*(1), 1–13. DOI: 10.1186/s41039-017-0062-8 PMID: 30595727

Prashar, A., Gupta, P., & Dwivedi, Y. K. (2023). Plagiarism awareness efforts, students' ethical judgment and behaviors: A longitudinal experiment study on ethical nuances of plagiarism in higher education. *Studies in Higher Education, 49*(6), 929–955. DOI: 10.1080/03075079.2023.2253835

Ringo, D. S. (2025). The effect of generative AI use on doctoral students' academic research progress: The moderating role of hedonic gratification. *Cogent Education, 49*(5), 847–864. DOI: 10.1080/2331186X.2025.2475268

Salhab, R. (2024). AI Literacy Across Curriculum Design: Investigating College Instructors' Perspectives. *Online Learning : the Official Journal of the Online Learning Consortium, 28*(2), 29–49. DOI: 10.24059/olj.v28i2.4426

Storey, V. A. (2023). AI technology and academic writing: Knowing and mastering the "craft skills.". *International Journal of Adult Education and Technology, 14*(1), 1–15. DOI: 10.4018/IJAET.325795

Subramanian, P., Soundararajan, R., & Makol, J. (2025). Building Credibility with Comprehensive Citation Practices. *The Indian Journal of Radiology & Imaging, 35*(3), S95–S101. DOI: 10.1055/s-0044-1796641 PMID: 39802710

Sutomo, A. D., Nurhasanah, F., Marmoah, S., Saddhono, K., & Rahardjo, S. S. (2024, May). Adaptation of Change in the Learning System with the use of Artificial Intelligence to Ensure Better Strategy. In *2024 4th International Conference on Advance Computing and Innovative Technologies in Engineering (ICACITE)* (pp. 912-917). IEEE. DOI: 10.1109/ICACITE60783.2024.10616824

Tayan, O., Hassan, A., Khankan, K., & Askool, S. (2024). Considerations for adapting higher education technology courses for AI large language models: A critical review of the impact of ChatGPT. *Machine Learning with Applications*, *15*, 100513. DOI: 10.1016/j.mlwa.2023.100513

Thong, C. L., Atallah, Z., Islam, S., Lim, W., & Cherukuri, A. K. (2025). AI-powered Tools for Doctoral Supervision in Higher Education: A Systematic Review. *Journal of Information & Knowledge Management*, *2530001*(2), 2530001. Advance online publication. DOI: 10.1142/S0219649225300013

VanLehn, K. (2011). The relative effectiveness of human tutoring, intelligent tutoring systems, and other tutoring systems. *Educational Psychologist*, *46*(4), 197–221. DOI: 10.1080/00461520.2011.611369

Wong, G. K. W., & Li, S. Y. K. (2023). An Exploratory Study of Helping Undergraduate Students Solve Literature Review Problems Using Litstudy and NLP. *Education Sciences*, *13*(10), 987. DOI: 10.3390/educsci13100987

Zafar, S., Maqbool, D. R., Kamran, Z., & Zafar, F. (2024). Exploring Doctoral Students' Lived Experiences While Selecting Research Topic: A Phenomenological Study. *Journal of Information Management and Practices*, *4*(1), 1. Advance online publication. DOI: 10.52461/jimp.v4i1.2523

Chapter 4
Generative AI in Academic Research:
A Practical Guide for Scholars

Angela Elkordy
https://orcid.org/0000-0001-5154-9368
National Louis University, Wheeling, USA

Doug van Dyke
National Louis University, Wheeling, USA

Katie Giradot
National Louis University, Wheeling, USA

Lauren Anderson
https://orcid.org/0009-0007-9978-6750
National Louis University, Wheeling, USA

ABSTRACT

This chapter explores the integration of generative AI (genAI) tools into academic research workflows to enhance scholarly productivity, synthesis, and inquiry. Drawing on reflective practice, tool trials, and theoretical frameworks, it addresses AI as a research partner across all stages of the research process. The chapter examines large language models (LLMs) like ChatGPT and Claude, along with specialized tools like Scite and Elicit, which streamline research from conceptualization to data analysis. Practical strategies for prompt engineering and ethical use are included, along with sample prompts to guide researchers through each phase. The chapter also critically addresses the epistemic challenges of using AI in scholarly work, including issues of accuracy, reliability, bias, and academic integrity. It advocates for human oversight and critical engagement to preserve researcher agency, rigor, and scholarly standards, filling a critical literature gap with structured, actionable guidance.

DOI: 10.4018/979-8-3373-5092-9.ch004

INTRODUCTION: THE AI-RESEARCH PARTNERSHIP PARADIGM

In the brief two-year span since the public release of OpenAI's ChatGPT in November 2022, followed rapidly by other large language models (LLMs) such as Anthropic's Claude and Google's Bard (now Gemini), the discourse around using generative artificial intelligence (genAI) in academic research has evolved significantly. While initial reactions from educators and academics were cautious, the conversation has shifted toward nuanced discussions of how to responsibly integrate and acknowledge AI assistance rather than impose outright bans on its use. Yet significant concerns persist that require careful consideration. These include risks of plagiarism and threats to scholarly originality, challenges with intellectual property rights, the phenomenon of AI *hallucinations* (where models present false, inaccurate, or contrived information with confidence), and the potential propagation of existing errors. Despite these challenges, when genAI is implemented with integrity, human oversight, and ethical practices, its integration into academic research offers opportunities for transformative shifts in how scholarly knowledge is created or co-constructed, analyzed, and disseminated.

The large-scale growth of AI in academia has prompted debates about foundational scholarly practices and ways of thinking. One prominent question has been whether AI tools can or should be recognized as *authors* of academic works. Leading scientific publishers and ethics organizations have taken a clear stance that they cannot. For instance, *Nature* stipulates that no LLM tool will be accepted as a credited author on a research paper because *"any attribution of authorship carries accountability for the work, and AI tools cannot take such responsibility"* (Riedlinger & Mitchell, 2023). Likewise, the Committee on Publication Ethics (COPE) affirms that AI tools fail to meet authorship criteria since they cannot consent to responsibility, declare conflicts of interest, or manage copyright agreements (2023). These early policy responses highlight the consensus that AI can be a powerful tool for researchers and academics—but should not be a substitute for human authorship and accountability in scholarly research.

Beyond questions of authorship and attribution, scholars are increasingly examining genAI's broader implications for research epistemology, such as how research questions are framed, methods selected, and results interpreted. Some view AI as a catalyst for methodological innovation, fostering new, digitally-enabled and AI-enhanced methods such as natural language processing, adaptive research designs, computational ethnography, and data mining of crowdsourced or public internet data (Amoako, n.d.). Others caution that reliance on AI could undermine core aspects of academic rigor. The reality likely involves finding an appropriate balance: leveraging AI's capacity to augment research processes while implementing critical oversight to preserve scholarly integrity.

Our goal in this chapter is to examine how generative AI can be practically and ethically integrated into academic research workflows as a *partner* in inquiry. We take a human-centric approach: AI is viewed not as an independent agent but as a powerful assistant or collaborator that operates under human direction and iterative guidance. We explore concrete strategies for using genAI tools across various stages of research—from planning and conceptualizing of topics and research questions, to literature reviews, data collection and analysis, to writing—while highlighting safeguards to maintain the quality and trustworthiness of scholarly work.

By drawing on recent research findings, tool trials, and our reflective practice, we present a balanced approach in which AI's affordances are leveraged to enhance (not replace) human scholarship. Anchored in a conceptual framework of human–AI collaboration, this chapter offers structured guidance on using genAI tools to streamline and enrich the research process, discusses their limitations (such as accuracy, bias, and transparency issues), and provides recommendations for ethical use. In doing so, we aim to fill a gap in the literature by moving beyond abstract debate to practical insights for researchers navigating the new paradigm of AI-assisted scholarship. *The following discussion areas will address specific research tools, including their uses and limitations. Additionally, we examine models of AI-human collaboration and the use of these tools for the augmentation of researchers' capacities.*

As this chapter will demonstrate, effectively integrating AI into academic workflows requires a structured approach, shaped and refined by human judgment. This partnership between human researchers and AI systems forms the foundation for the practical guidance presented in the following sections.

GENERATIVE AI TOOLS FOR RESEARCH

Contemporary genAI tools and systems, including ChatGPT and other large language models (LLMs), have powerful and unique capabilities that have the potential to make distinct contributions to academic research. Understanding their characteristics, affordances, and limitations is critical for effective use. Below, we summarize key strengths and weaknesses of genAI in the context of academic research (Figure 1 and the following text):

Figure 1. Affordances of GenAI tools (LLMs) for research

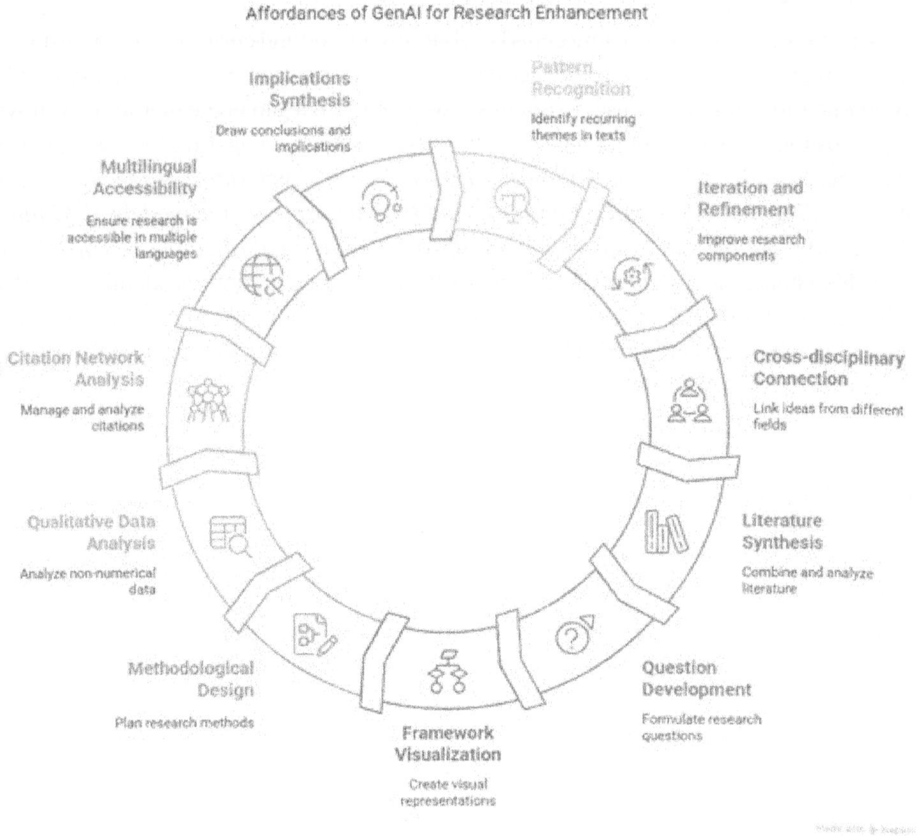

Characteristics and Affordances of AI in Research

- **Pattern recognition across academic texts:** AI can rapidly detect connections, themes, and patterns in large bodies of literature or data that would be onerous for a human to identify manually. This capability can help researchers synthesize findings across many sources (Butson & Spronken-Smith, 2024).
- **Rapid iteration and refinement of research components:** Generative models facilitate quick drafting and revision of research elements (problem statements, hypotheses, methodological descriptions), accelerating the ideation and refinement process while maintaining scholarly rigor.
- **Cross-disciplinary connection identification:** AI systems reveal unexpected links between academic disciplines, fostering interdisciplinary insights. For instance, AI

might connect educational psychology theories with neuroscience findings, generating novel research directions.

- **Advanced literature synthesis and thematic analysis:** LLMs provide sophisticated summarization of articles and paper collections, extract nuanced themes, and generate comparative analyses. This supports comprehensive literature reviews by producing cogent summaries and revealing gaps, contradictions, or convergent findings across studies (Liu & Xu, 2024; Slavin, 1986).
- **Research question development and hypothesis generation:** By engaging in a dialogue about a topic, genAI can help researchers brainstorm research questions or refine hypotheses. It can propose alternative framings, identify implicit assumptions, and suggest hypotheses based on various theoretical perspectives.
- **Theoretical framework visualization:** AI assists in mapping theoretical relationships, identifying conceptual gaps, and generating visual representations of complex theoretical frameworks, supporting theory development, refinement, and application.
- **Methodological design assistance:** AI provides guidance on research design selection, identifies potential methodological limitations, suggests appropriate sampling strategies, and recommends data collection methods aligned with research questions. It can also draft data collection tools and interview protocols.
- **Enhanced qualitative data analysis:** Aided by natural language processing capabilities, LLMs support coding processes by identifying patterns in textual data, generating preliminary coding frameworks, and assisting in theme development while preserving researcher interpretation and agency. "They [LLMs] can discern not just which words co-occur, but how phrases, sentences, and paragraphs interrelate, and how these relationships shift across contexts" (Hayes, 2025, p.3).
- **Citation network analysis and intelligent reference management:** Advanced AI tools (e.g., Scite, Semantic Scholar) map and analyze citation relationships or networks, identify seminal or seed works, track claim support/contradiction patterns, and automate reference organization while ensuring proper formatting across citation styles.
- **Multilingual research accessibility:** AI facilitates cross-language literature review, enables research translation, and supports creation of accessible summaries for diverse audiences, breaking down language barriers in global scholarship.
- **Implications synthesis and conclusion generation:** LLMs can analyze research findings to draft comprehensive implications across multiple domains (theoretical, practical, policy), identify potential future research directions, and generate well-structured conclusions that connect findings back to original research questions. This helps researchers articulate the broader significance of their work while ensuring no key implications are overlooked.

While genAI tools offer powerful capabilities for accelerating research, their use must be accompanied by a critical awareness of their limitations and appropriate oversight. To integrate these technologies responsibly into academic practice, researchers must carefully balance their potential benefits against the inherent risks. The following section explores some of the limitations and critical considerations.

Limitations and Potential Issues

While powerful assistants, GenAI tools have limitations inherent to LLMs and natural language processing, such as bias, lack of context for framing responses, and inaccurate information due to errors in training or the data used for training. Understanding potential issues and concerns with the use of genAI tools can help researchers to critically evaluate output with these limitations in mind. The following section discusses some of the more prominent and persistent issue or concerns with genAI tool (Figure 2).

Figure 2. Limitations of GenAI tools (LLMs) for research

- **Hallucination of citations and facts:** GenAI can produce plausible-sounding but entirely fabricated information. It may invent bibliographic references, or make claims that do not have real-world data or evidence, or misquote sources, which is a serious concern in academic use. AI hallucinations are also known as artificial hallucinations or confabulations (Jamaluddin et al., 2023). All AI-generated content must be verified against primary sources.

- **Bias in training data:** AI models inherit biases in their training data, which can lead to skewed outputs. For instance, as Buolamwini (2023) discusses, an LLM might under-represent perspectives from the Global South or marginalized groups if those were underrepresented in its data/ text corpus. Users must be mindful of potential biases in AI outputs, especially on sensitive topics, and counteract them with diverse source material.
- **Knowledge cutoff and versioning constraints:** AI tools have *knowledge cutoffs* after which they lack information (ChatGPT, for example, was initially trained on data up to 2021). They may not be aware of the latest research developments or data unless specifically updated or fine-tuned with new information.
- **Privacy and data security concerns:** Using genAI tools for research data or draft text raises issues of confidentiality when personal data or identifiable data are used. Inputting unpublished data or sensitive information into cloud-based AI services could violate privacy or data protection standards, confidentiality agreements, or breach institutional review board guidelines.
- **Over-reliance risks and authenticity challenges:** There is a risk of researchers relying too heavily on AI-generated text or analysis. Moreover, journals and peers may raise concerns about the authenticity of work heavily assisted by AI. Authors should disclose and document how AI was used in academic research.
- **Authentication and transparency challenges:** It can be difficult to distinguish AI-generated content from human-written text. This complicates the process and purpose of peer review and academic evaluation if not disclosed. Additionally, the *black-box nature* of many AI models means their reasoning for a given output is often opaque, making it hard to fully trust their conclusions without a way to trace or verify sources.

Understanding these affordances and limitations is the first step to effectively incorporating AI into research. In the next section, we turn to practical applications of AI tools in the research workflow, beginning with the foundational task of discovering and reviewing literature.

HUMAN-AI COLLABORATION IN RESEARCH

While generative AI can automate and augment human cognition for many research tasks, it does not obviate the need for human expertise. In fact, the partnership between human researchers and AI systems is emerging as the defining paradigm for scholarly innovation. In this section, we discuss how to balance automation with human oversight and examine frameworks for effective human–AI collaboration. We introduce three modes of human–AI working: co-intelligence, collaborative intelligence, and collective intelligence – and argue that treating AI as an augmentative partner (rather than a replacement) is key to preserving scholarly rigor and integrity.

Balancing Automation and Human Oversight

No matter how helpful an AI assistant may seem, maintaining human oversight over AI outputs is indispensable. At the current stage of AI development, *there is no such thing as not checking the AI's work.* Every piece of information or analysis that an AI contributes should be reviewed by a human. Successful human–AI collaborations thus require continuous human agency: researchers must verify AI-generated content, cross-check sources, and correct errors.

This need for oversight stems from the well-documented trust problem with AI. LLMs often produce fluent and confident answers that can mask subtle errors or outright falsehoods. Some users, especially those unfamiliar with AI's limitations, might be tempted to accept AI outputs at face value. This is analogous to how one might initially trust a new colleague: if you don't know their reliability, taking their work without question is risky. Such uncritical acceptance is happening even as the research community grapples with an erosion of trust in information sources generally. Trust is an essential element of the human-information relationship, and it must be earned in the human–AI relationship as well.

Establishing trust with AI tools requires transparency and accountability that are currently not fully achievable. AI systems are often *black boxes* – their decision processes are opaque, and they might not explain why they produced a given output. Moreover, many genAI providers do not disclose their training data or model architectures, making it hard to know *what* information the AI is drawing on or *how* it is reasoning. With so many unknowns, how can we trust these tools in critical research tasks? The answer is that trust must be built gradually, through consistent verification and bounded use. Researchers should treat AI suggestions as provisional, to be accepted only once confirmed. In educational and research contexts, some researchers have recommended implementing formal *"human-in-the-loop"* structures – for example, requiring that any AI-generated text in a manuscript is highlighted and then checked by a second person, or using AI outputs only as drafts that go through the normal peer review process with humans (Karaoke, et al., 2023; Yang, et al. 2024).

Frameworks and best practices are beginning to emerge for maintaining human oversight of AI in research. For instance, Yang et al. (2024) propose an *interactive auditing* approach for human–AI writing teams, where each suggestion from the AI is explicitly evaluated by the human for accuracy and relevance. Ensuring cognitive agency remains with the human is also vital; Liu et al. (2024) discuss techniques for preserving the researcher's active role in driving the inquiry, such as by using AI to handle low-level tasks while the human focuses on high-level interpretation. In sum, the guiding principle is *trust, but verify*: AI can accelerate research tasks, but researchers must continuously supervise and correct the AI's contributions.

Despite the optimistic language of *"AI collaborators"* or *"AI teammates"*, we must remember that current AI tools do **not** possess understanding, accountability, or true autonomy. Biases, hallucinations, privacy issues, and opacity remain unresolved problems. Therefore, maintaining a healthy skepticism and a robust oversight mechanism is not optional – it is the cost of doing research in the age of AI. The next sections will consider how, with such safeguards in place, researchers can conceptualize productive partnerships with AI under paradigms of co-intelligence, collaborative intelligence, and collective intelligence.

Modes of Human–AI Collaboration: Co-Intelligence, Collaborative Intelligence & Collective Intelligence

When researchers and AI systems work together, how should we characterize their joint intelligence? Recent literature introduces several terms to describe human–AI partnership modes:

- **Co-intelligence** refers to a synergistic relationship where humans and AI contribute complementary strengths to achieve a goal. The emphasis is on AI acting as a *partner* that extends human cognition without replacing human agency. In co-intelligent workflows, **agency is shared**: the human guides the process, makes judgments, and provides context, while the AI offers suggestions, identifies patterns, or generates materials that the human then evaluates. The concept of co-intelligence is rooted in systems thinking and ethics, highlighting that meaning-making is a joint effort between human insight and machine computation. For example, a human–AI pair might jointly write a literature review: the AI summarizes sources and the human critiques and integrates those summaries into a coherent narrative. The human's creative insight and the AI's speed and breadth of information processing together yield a result neither could easily produce alone.
- **Collaborative intelligence** in research contexts often means a team-like interaction: the AI functions as a *collaborator* or team member with a defined role, working alongside humans on a project (Cui & Yasseri, 2024). This idea stems from studies of human–AI interaction in workplaces. The AI might take on specific tasks delegated to it by human team members. For instance, an AI could be in charge of running many regressions to test the robustness of results, while the human researchers focus on interpreting those results and designing the next experiment. The key notion here is a division of labor that leverages what each does best. Humans bring critical thinking, domain expertise, ethical judgment, and creativity; AI brings tireless computation, pattern detection, and speed. When collaboration is effective, the weaknesses of one are covered by the strengths of the other (Cui & Yasseri, 2024). However, collaborating with AI also means humans must accept and manage the AI's "imperfections" (like errors, biased suggestions, irreproducibility, transparency, etc.) (Jain & Jain, 2023), which is not dissimilar to how one manages the imperfections of a human colleague. Establishing clear protocols for interaction (much like a team charter) can help, such as deciding in advance which tasks the AI will handle and how its outputs will be reviewed by humans.
- **Collective intelligence** traditionally refers to the enhanced capacity that emerges from the collaboration or competition of many individuals (e.g. the "wisdom of the crowd"). In a human–AI hybrid setting, **collective intelligence** involves groups of humans and AI agents working together, each contributing their knowledge or computations, to solve problems beyond the reach of a single human or AI. This can be thought of as the macro-scale of collaboration, potentially involving multiple researchers and multiple AI systems in networks. For instance, one could imagine an

online research community where scholars use various AI tools to analyze data, and the aggregated results (human-curated AI outputs) lead to new discoveries that no individual or machine could have achieved alone. Collective intelligence in hybrid teams can amplify creativity by drawing from a diverse set of contributors. A recent study by Cui and Yasseri (2024) suggests that human collectives augmented by AI can work interdependently, adaptively, and dynamically, achieving a level of integrated problem-solving that exceeds traditional crowdsourcing (Cui & Yasseri, 2024). However, true hybrid collective intelligence also faces challenges in coordination and trust—ensuring that the *human* members ultimately guide the collective effort in a meaningful direction, and that the AI members are used to enhance rather than distort the group's work.

It is worth noting that these terms overlap and are sometimes used inconsistently in the literature. In practice, they all gesture toward the central idea that humans + AI together can form a new kind of "augmented intelligence." The degree of AI's autonomy and role can vary. As one overview put it, *"AI's role in hybrid groups varies… AI may serve as a technical tool for human assistance or as an active agent that interacts with and influences humans. Functionally, AI's role can range from an assistant to a teammate, coach, or manager."* (Cui & Yasseri, 2024, p. 11). In some scenarios, AI is just a smart tool (e.g., a sophisticated calculator or text editor); in others, it behaves more like a junior researcher (e.g., providing an initial draft of an introduction which the human then rewrites).

To harness co-intelligence or collaborative intelligence effectively, researchers should be deliberate in assigning roles to AI. For example, one might decide: *"For this project, I will use an AI assistant to act as a brainstorming partner and proofreader, but I (the human) will do the interpretation and final writing."* Or in a group project: *"Let's have the AI take minutes of our meeting and suggest action items, then we will confirm and implement them."* Clarity in how AI is integrated prevents misunderstandings and ensures that the human team maintains control over the research narrative and decisions.

Finally, integrating AI into collective human efforts can democratize certain aspects of research. Researchers with limited access to mentoring or large laboratories might use AI tools to obtain guidance or analyze data, partially bridging resource gaps. On the other hand, if not handled inclusively, AI could exacerbate disparities (for instance, if only well-funded researchers can train custom AI models). Thus, as we explore human–AI collective workflows, considerations of access and ethical use remain paramount.

With a clear understanding of the risks and rewards of AI collaboration, researchers can more confidently select and implement the right tools for their work. The next section provides a practical guide to genAI tools for research and their capabilities, assisting scholars to choose the best technologies for their specific needs

AI TOOLS FOR RESEARCH: CAPABILITIES AND SELECTION

GenAI-powered tools are now available to support virtually every phase of research, from literature discovery to data analysis and writing. Table 1 provides an overview of several representative AI-enabled research tools and their primary uses. We focus especially on tools for literature review and citation management, as this is often the stage where many researchers first encounter AI assistance.

Table 1. Comparison of selected AI-powered research tools

Tool	Description and Capabilities
Consensus	An AI-powered academic search engine that provides direct answers to research questions by extracting and summarizing findings from scholarly papers. It delivers evidence-based responses with citations from the literature (useful for quickly gauging what the literature says on a question).
Semantic Scholar	An academic search engine (by AI2) that uses AI to filter results, highlight important citations, and map connections between papers. It offers features like citation graphs and influence scores, helping researchers identify key works and follow citation trails.
Google Scholar	A broadly used search engine for scholarly literature. While not a genAI tool per se, it's a baseline for literature search. It ranks papers by relevance and citations and is often a starting point for finding sources (though it lacks advanced AI summarization features).
Elicit	A research assistant that uses language models to automate parts of the literature review. It can answer questions by finding relevant papers, summarizing the findings, and extracting specific information (such as sample sizes or conclusions) from PDFsfile-wtnaldqymqzdntynmbcycgfile-wtnaldqymqzdntynmbcycg. Elicit helps in triaging large search results and getting quick insights from papers.
Scite	An AI-powered citation analysis tool that checks how a paper or claim has been cited by others. Scite classifies citations as supporting, contradicting, or just mentioning, thus helping researchers assess the consensus around a claim. This can alert scholars to disputed findings or potential controversies in the literature.
Notebook LM	A "literature management" notebook that integrates LLM capabilities for note-taking and synthesis. It can help researchers organize their reading notes, auto-summarize PDFs, and even draft syntheses across multiple sources. LM Notebook and similar tools aim to reduce the manual effort of organizing literature and spotting connections across readings.

Table 1 Continued

Feature	Consensus	Semantic Scholar	Google Scholar	Elicit	Scite	Notebook LM
Link to Tool	https://consensus.app/search/	https://www.semanticscholar.org/	https://scholar.google.com	https://elicit.com/	https://scite.ai/	https://notebooklm.google.com/
Primary Use	AI-powered academic search with summarized answers from research papers	AI-powered academic search engine with citation mapping	Comprehensive scholarly search engine	AI-assisted literature review & research organization	Citation analysis and smart referencing	AI-powered notebook for research documentation and collaboration
AI Integration	Summarizes findings from peer-reviewed sources	Uses NLP to extract key insights	Ranks results based on citations but lacks AI summaries	Uses AI to extract key points and generate structured summaries	Tracks citation contexts to assess credibility	Integrates LLMs for summarization, code generation, and text analysis

continued on following page

Table 1 Continued

Feature	Consensus	Semantic Scholar	Google Scholar	Elicit	Scite	Notebook LM
Source Type	Peer-reviewed journal articles	Open-access research papers & preprints	All scholarly articles (some behind paywalls)	Research papers and datasets	Peer-reviewed papers with citation context	User-provided research data, code, and notes
Search Experience	Provides AI-generated summaries of research findings	Allows filtering by field and influential papers	It is a powerful search, but no AI summaries	AI suggests papers based on questions and develops a combined report involving all of the chosen research	Highlights supporting and contradicting evidence	Combines search, note-taking, and coding in one environment
Prompting Notes	Prompt engineering and specifics can be added to create a more targeted database search.	Keyword only (limited)	Keyword only (limited)	Prompt engineering and specifics can be added to create a more targeted database search. Also provides feedback on the quality of the question entered.	Prompt engineering and specifics can be added to create a more targeted database search.	There is no specific prompt, but rather the app reviews uploaded articles chosen by the researcher
Accessibility	Free	Free	Free, but some sources require subscriptions	Free	No features are available until the user activates the trial by giving credit card information	Free for individuals, paid for teams
Best For	Quickly understanding the academic consensus on specific questions	Finding influential papers and citation networks	Finding a broad range of academic papers	Literature reviews and hypothesis exploration	Understanding how a paper has been used in citations	Collaborative research documentation and iterative analysis
Other notes	The prompt into Consensus allows for a ChatGPT-type interaction to go deeper into the searched topic	Like Google Scholar, it gives just a brief synopsis and information around each article selected via keyword	The keyword search limits results. The layout is almost the same as the Semantic Seminar	Pulls the top 50 articles (paid versions allow for more). Creates a summary of ALL compiled articles.	A trial activation and credit card number are required. Was unable to access and compare	This app can sound repetitive, particularly in the way the podcast is created and performed. The initial experience of the technology is impactful, but repetitive use is not recommended

Many other tools exist (with new ones emerging continuously), but those listed above illustrate the range of genAI applications for literature discovery and knowledge extraction. Some, like Consensus, aim to give direct answers from papers; others, like Elicit, assist in finding and distilling relevant studies; and others, like Scite, focus on the *quality* of evidence by analyzing citations. It should be noted that no single tool is comprehensive, and each comes with its own learning curve and quirks. Researchers often need to experiment with multiple tools to see which fits their needs, or even use them in combination (for example, using Semantic Scholar to find papers, then Scite to evaluate citation context).

One area where AI tools have made a significant impact is the literature review process. Conducting a thorough literature review is foundational to any research project, yet the explosion of publications has made this task increasingly daunting. Researchers must "present a comprehensive, critical, and accurate understanding of the current state of knowledge; compare different studies and theories to reveal gaps; and indicate what needs to be done to advance the field" (Efron & Ravid, 2019, p. 2). Achieving this is harder than ever when hundreds or thousands of papers might relate to a given topic. GenAI tools like those in Table 1 are designed to alleviate some of the burden of volume and synthesis by quickly summarizing large collections of texts and identifying key themes.

Sidebar: A Researcher's Reflection on Literature Review Challenges

"That phrase, 'current state of knowledge,' felt almost inconceivable to me. As a doctoral researcher, I found it incredibly intimidating. I want to contribute to the body of research, but finding where my contribution fits sometimes seems like looking for a needle in a haystack. The sheer volume of new studies is overwhelming. Compiling, reviewing, and connecting all the relevant literature often feels like an impossible task."

This reflection highlights a common sentiment among scholars facing an information deluge. AI tools, used judiciously, can mitigate some of these challenges. For instance, an LLM-based assistant can summarize dozens of articles in minutes, or tools like Connected Papers and Litmaps can visually map out networks of related work, helping researchers discover relevant papers they might have missed. Table 1 gives examples of systems that can accelerate searching and synthesizing literature. Indeed, recent AI applications have shown an incredible capacity for analyzing and reviewing a vast volume of research, pulling out evidence to support arguments or identify where knowledge is lacking. These capabilities allow researchers to devote more time to interpreting findings and developing insights rather than simply gathering and managing sources.

At the same time, it is crucial to approach these AI-generated summaries and suggestions with a critical eye. No matter how advanced the tool, the researcher must remain in the loop, verifying the accuracy of summaries against the original papers and ensuring that nuanced or conflicting views are not lost. As we use AI to lighten the load of literature reviews, we must also heed the principle of *trust but verify* for any content the AI provides. In practice, this means double-checking that any quote or citation an AI tool gives actually exists in the source, and reading important papers in full rather than relying solely on an AI synopsis. By doing so, researchers can benefit from genAI's efficiency gains without compromising the thoroughness and critical evaluation that a good literature review requires.

Augmentation, Not Replacement

A recurring theme in our discussion is that AI should augment human intellect and labor, not replace the human researcher. Generative AI is best understood as an extension of our human capabilities—a set of tools that can relieve us of tedious tasks and amplify our productivity, but not a substitute for human expertise and judgment. In an era of rapid automation, it is tempting for institutions to imagine AI completely taking over certain scholarly tasks (like automated essay grading or fully AI-written literature reviews). However, such an approach risks undermining the quality and integrity of research. Meaningful scholarly work relies on human qualities like curiosity, critical thinking, ethical reasoning, and contextual understanding—qualities that AI, as of yet, does not possess (Jain & Jain, 2023).

Economists and technologists have often framed AI's impact on work in terms of substitution vs augmentation. In academia, we argue for an augmentation paradigm. Even if an AI could perform a task capably, there may be educational or epistemic reasons to keep a human in the loop. For example, assembling a bibliography is time-consuming and arguably tedious; AI can do it faster. Yet if a student or researcher never learns how to evaluate sources for inclusion (because an AI is auto-selecting and formatting citations), they may miss out on understanding the foundations of their field. A balanced approach might be: use AI to format the bibliography (saving time and avoiding typos), but the human still decides which references to include and double-checks that all are correct.

Effective use of artificial intelligence hinges on a deep human understanding of the variables underlying the problems we aim to solve. AI cannot substitute for humans' nuanced insights—insights shaped by lived experience, contextual awareness, and critical reasoning. Rather than viewing AI as a replacement, we should see it as a collaborator in a reciprocal learning process. When a complex, subjective, and richly contextual human perspective is paired with AI's ability to analyze and synthesize information rapidly, the results can exceed the capabilities of either working alone. This synergy depends on thoughtful prompting. Successful prompts are not merely commands; they embed context, clarify intent, and frame parameters—or, at times, deliberately leave space for exploration and discovery.

While AI excels at scaling output, its true potential lies in deepening the quality and interconnectedness of our thinking. It is through intentional, reflective engagement that human-AI collaboration becomes not just efficient, but transformative.

Business scholars Paavo Ritala and colleagues (2024) suggest thinking in terms of an "algorithmic assistance matrix" that delineates areas of work where AI excels vs areas where humans excel. Their analysis of ChatGPT's impact on knowledge work illustrates that tasks in which AI is strong (e.g., information retrieval, basic text generation) tend to be those that are routine or formulaic parts of knowledge work, whereas tasks requiring originality, complex judgment, or ethical considerations remain human strongholds. The danger is if we attempt to offload *too much* to AI—especially tasks that *seem* routine but actually benefit from human nuance. For instance, summarizing an article might appear straightforward for AI, but an AI might omit subtle implications that a trained researcher would notice; if researchers stop practicing summarizing papers themselves, their grasp of nuance could atrophy.

To guard against this, researchers and educators can explicitly identify which aspects of a task must remain human. Perhaps hypothesis generation is kept human (to encourage creativity), while AI is used to suggest experiment designs or analyze data under human guidance. Perhaps AI drafts a portion of a paper, but the human thoroughly edits it to infuse a scholarly voice and ensure coherence. By consciously keeping humans in charge of the *core intellectual narrative*, we uphold a standard wherein AI contributes without usurping.

In practical terms, treating AI as an augmentation means using it to *reduce drudgery*. Many researchers find tasks like transcription, formatting, or data cleaning to be laborious; these are ideal candidates for AI automation. Freed from these chores, researchers can spend more time on interpretation, theory development, and creative design of studies. One researcher in our team reflected on this trade-off:

Sidebar: A Digital Immigrant's GenAI Journey

Born in 1981, I'm not a digital native. My early experiences with technology – an Atari console, my father's word processor – often slowed me down. These machines were clunky and made simple tasks take longer. In contrast, genAI tools for research have dramatically increased my efficiency and work quality.

Growing up, I was taught the value of hard work and persistence – spending long hours on tasks was seen as virtuous. And indeed, working through difficulties was part of learning. But in research, I've realized that not every tedious task deserves my struggle.

Citation management is a perfect example. Manually formatting references or checking APA vs MLA style isn't intellectual work; it's clerical. My time is better spent analyzing implications and developing arguments.

GenAI-powered citation tools have saved me countless hours. With a single click, I can organize sources and generate properly formatted references. Of course, I still verify outputs – 'trust but verify' is my motto. But 90% of the mechanical effort is gone.

The net effect is overwhelmingly positive. With hours saved, I can focus on tasks that truly require human insight: interpreting data, writing insightful discussions, and developing new arguments. My younger self would be jealous of these tools, but they bring responsibility. I can't use 'I ran out of time' as an excuse anymore. Instead, I must use this bandwidth to deepen my work.

This, I believe, is genAI's real promise: not to do our thinking for us, but to give us more space to think deeply.

This personal account underscores how, when used appropriately, AI tools can liberate researchers from menial tasks and even *improve* the overall quality of work by allowing more focus on high-level thinking. Yet it also wisely notes the need to reinvest the saved time into the research process, and to remain alert to the limitations of the tools (e.g., verifying their output). In essence, the mindset should be: *AI gives me power to handle some of the more tedious work, but I must use those powers responsibly to enhance – not shortcut – the scholarly process.*

Looking forward, the vision of *"AI-augmented scholarship"* is one where emerging technologies and human expertise are thoroughly intertwined. Researchers will increasingly function as orchestrators, directing ensembles of AI tools to do various tasks, then synthesizing and evaluating the results. In such a future, skills like prompt engineering (crafting effective queries for AI), AI result interpretation, and cross-validation of AI outputs will become as important as traditional research skills. Educational institutions are beginning to recognize this; many top universities are now issuing guidelines on how students and faculty can use AI in research and writing ethically (Merod, 2023). The consensus is that we must adapt our practices and policies so that we embrace AI's potential while safeguarding academic integrity and the values of scholarship. In the final section, we distill some implementation guidelines and best practices that scholars and institutions can follow to achieve this balance.

IMPLEMENTATION STRATEGIES: SAMPLE AI PROMPTS FOR RESEARCHERS

Having outlined the capabilities and limitations of available tools, and paradigms for AI-human collaborations, the next step is to consider how researchers can effectively integrate these technologies into their workflows. The following section provides practical examples of AI prompts to support various stages of the research process. These prompts may be used with LLMs such as ChatGPT, Claude, and similar tools.

Research Development:

- *Prompt:* "Analyze this research area and identify the following:

  1. Current state of knowledge
  2. Theoretical frameworks
  3. Methodological trends
  4. Research gaps
  5. Potential research questions"

Literature Review Enhancement:

- *Prompt:* "Summarize key themes from these academic sources and identify:

  1. Major findings
  2. Methodological approaches
  3. Theoretical connections
  4. Research gaps and limitations"

Organizing the Literature Review:

- *Pre-prompt step*: Organize your information in a table to upload:

Table 2.

Citation (Author, Year)	Title	Source (Journal, Publisher)	DOI/URL	Key Points Summary	Important Quotes (with page #)	Your Analysis & Thoughts	Connections to Other Sources	Potential Use in Lit. Review

- *Prompt*: "Using the attached document and carefully retaining citations, create an outline for a literature review in a project that seeks to explore this research question [include a summary of your project information]"

Synthesizing a Cohesive Proposal:

- *Prompt:* "Using the attached documents [include notes] create an outline for a qualitative research proposal that includes the following:

  1. Study purpose and research questions
  2. Brief literature review
  3. Methodology"

Evaluating a Research Plan or Proposal

- *Prompt*: [Attach research plan] "Evaluate this draft according to the criteria of this call for proposals"[Attach call for proposals]:
- *Prompt*: [Attach research plan] "Evaluate this qualitative research project, commenting on:

  1. Explicit and thoroughly described methodology?
  2. Congruence among questions, methods, findings?
  3. Researcher's craft?
  4. Innovation/Creativity?
  5. Artfulness?
  6. Vividness?
  7. Transferability?"

  (Criteria described in Leavy, 2017, p. 154)

- *Prompt: [Attach research plan]* "Evaluate this research proposal for potential issues in methodology, including an evaluation of the potential impact on participants."

Academic Writing Enhancement:

- *Prompt:* "Evaluate this draft for:

1. Argument structure
2. Evidence integration
3. Citation accuracy and consistency

Writing clarity and coherence"

Interview Protocol Development

- *Prompt:* "Analyze this interview transcript to identify if speaker 2 shows any bias as an interviewer that would influence the answers of speaker 1"
- *Prompt:* "Suggest changes to these interview questions in order to elicit more developed answers"

Analyzing Qualitative Data

- *Prompt 1:* "Identify and fix the mistakes in this transcript of an interview"
- *Prompt 2:* "Extract significant statements related to [topic key term] and [topic key term] from the uploaded interview data"
- *Prompt 3*: "Make no more than 6 bullet points that describe meaning units in the following text based on [topic key term] and [topic key term]"
- *Prompt 4*: "Synthesize the following points into a structural description of the phenomenon of feeling valued for speaking more than one language [enter summary of data analysis]"

Analyzing Quantitative Data

- *Prompt 1:* "Analyze this file and tell me if there is a statistically significant correlation between attendance (attending regularly or not attending regularly) and the number of courses in which a student earned a grade of C or better."
- *Prompt 2:* "Analyze this file to determine if there is a statistically significant correlation between Lab Grade and the number of courses in which a student earned a grade of C or better?"
- *Prompt 3:* "If I were to perform an analysis to determine whether lab grade was the most significant factor in a student's ability to earn a grade of C or higher in their other courses, what data points might I need, and what kind of analysis would I perform?"

Sidebar: Who's Prompting Whom?
In the midst of a project, I tend to become deeply immersed in the topic. Devoting time and attention to the details can make it feel disorienting when it is time to pull back and put a web of thoughts into order. Tools like ChatGPT are excellent at helping analyze and rearrange the words I give it. Seeing a mountain of my own ideas neatly sorted into

a manageable pile can offer a roadmap at the start of the writing journey, when I tend to feel the most lost.

When using AI tools to generate outlines and suggest possible organization, it is important to not feel too dazzled by the initial output. Presented with all of my own thoughts and ideas now drafted into an outline, it is tempting to say "aha! This is exactly what I meant." Remembering that AI tends to be agreeable reminds me to put my feelings of genius aside and keep my scholarship at the center. Taking the suggested order as a starting place, the work is to breathe life and voice into the writing, using my knowledge and experiences to animate the words.

When planning to use AI for these purposes, the first step is to use a note-taking format that is going to clearly organize and label the information. AI can provide suggestions for this, too – another way I can prompt AI to prompt me with ways to untangle my knot of thoughts. Providing an input format that includes key terms, concepts, and quotes, along with notes about connections, will give the AI tool what it needs to build output suggestions that represent my thinking.

CONCLUSION AND RECOMMENDATIONS FOR PRACTICE

This chapter has outlined a comprehensive framework for integrating generative AI into academic research workflows while maintaining scholarly rigor and ethical standards. By adopting a human-centered approach that treats AI as an augmentative partner rather than a replacement for human expertise, researchers can leverage these powerful tools while preserving the critical thinking, ethical judgment, and contextual understanding that define quality scholarship. As AI technologies continue to evolve, the academic community must remain actively engaged in developing best practices, institutional policies, and ethical guidelines that ensure these tools enhance rather than diminish the pursuit of knowledge. The future of research will likely be characterized by sophisticated human-AI collaboration, where technology amplifies human capabilities while researchers maintain ultimate responsibility for the integrity and direction of scholarly inquiry. By way of conclusion, we offer a summary of best practices and guiding principles for using AI in research in an ethical, effective manner:

- **Emphasize augmentation over automation:** Use AI to **augment** human skills, not replace them. Let AI handle repetitive, time-consuming tasks (data parsing, formatting, basic summarizing) so that you can focus on critical analysis and creative thinking. Even when AI generates content or suggestions, treat those as drafts or inputs to be refined by your expertise, rather than final products. This ensures that the researcher's intellectual contribution remains central and identifiable.
- **Keep humans in the loop at all critical junctures:** Maintain human oversight for anything that impacts the integrity of research conclusions. Always verify AI-generated text, calculations, or citations against original sources (Nakazawa et al., 2022). If an AI tool translates or transcribes data, have a human spot-check portions

for accuracy. Retain control over analytical decisions (like choosing which variables to analyze or which theory to apply) – an AI might inform those decisions, but should not make them autonomously. In peer review or collaboration, be transparent about any AI assistance used, so others know that additional scrutiny may be needed in those areas (Riedlinger & Mitchell, 2023)

- **Cultivate a critical mindset toward AI output:** Approach any AI-derived result with a scientist's skepticism. Ask: *Where might errors have crept in? What biases could have influenced this output? Is the reasoning sound?* Compare AI outputs with known findings to gauge reliability. For example, if an AI-written summary of literature doesn't mention a seminal paper you know, that's a red flag. Use multiple AI tools or iterations to see if they converge on the same answer; if not, further investigation is needed. In sum, never assume the AI is correct – corroborate important information via independent means (other literature, experts, or your own analysis).
- **Address ethical and bias considerations proactively:** Be aware of how using AI might introduce ethical issues. For instance, if an AI language model is used to suggest related work, it might systematically overlook research by underrepresented groups (due to biases in training data). As a researcher, you can counteract this by supplementing AI searches with your own searches focused on diverse voices or by using multiple databases. When writing, ensure that AI usage does not lead to inadvertent plagiarism—always trace ideas back to their source and cite appropriately, even if an AI helped you locate them. Protect confidential data: do not feed sensitive or proprietary information into external AI services without clarity on how that data will be used or stored. Institutional review boards and ethics committees are beginning to issue guidance on these matters; when in doubt, consult such guidelines or err on the side of caution.
- **Follow institutional and publisher guidelines for AI usage:** Academic institutions and journals are rapidly developing policies on AI. Many universities now require disclosure if AI was used in coursework or publications, and top journals have policies on forbidding AI from being listed as an author and requiring authors to attest that they take responsibility for content (even content drafted by AI). Keep updated on these evolving norms. If you're a supervisor or mentor, discuss AI use openly with students and junior researchers—set expectations for what is acceptable assistance and what crosses into academic misconduct. A good rule of thumb is transparency: if you are comfortable disclosing your AI use and can defend how it didn't compromise your scholarly rigor, you are likely on solid ethical ground.
- **Invest in learning and improving AI tools:** As a scholar, treating AI as a static, off-the-shelf product would be a mistake. These tools can often be customized or improved with your feedback. Fine-tuning an AI model on your specific subfield literature, for example, might yield more relevant insights (though this requires technical know-how and caution). Even simpler: when an AI tool allows user feedback (like flagging an incorrect answer or refining a prompt), take the time to provide it. This not only potentially improves the tool for your next use but also contributes to better

AI systems for the community at large. In a way, we are all co-creators in shaping how AI will serve academia.

In conclusion, generative AI has the potential to significantly enhance scholarly productivity, creativity, and collaboration. By automating laborious tasks and offering new ways to process information, AI can free researchers to focus on higher-order intellectual efforts. Yet, this potential will only be realized if we integrate AI thoughtfully and ethically into our workflows. The core values of research—rigor, integrity, originality, and critical inquiry—must remain paramount. AI should be harnessed in the service of these values, not as a shortcut that bypasses them. Researchers who adopt a reflective, hands-on approach with AI—treating it as a junior colleague who requires supervision and mentorship—are likely to reap substantial benefits. Those who over-rely or under-scrutinize will, conversely, encounter problems ranging from embarrassing errors to breaches of trust.

The academic community is still in the early days of understanding the long-term implications of AI in research. Ongoing dialogue and knowledge-sharing will be crucial. By openly sharing successes and failures in our experiments with AI, scholars can collectively develop best practices. Institutions have a role to play in training researchers to use AI effectively and in updating curricula to include AI literacy. Publishers and conferences likewise are adapting peer review and submission guidelines to account for AI-assisted works.

Ultimately, the partnership between human scholars and AI holds great promise: together, they can achieve what neither could alone. Leveraging AI responsibly can help accelerate discoveries and perhaps democratize certain aspects of research by lowering barriers to entry. But realizing this promise requires a commitment to *responsible AI use*, where the researcher remains the ultimate arbiter of quality and truth. With vigilance and virtue, scholars can navigate the AI revolution while upholding the standards of their craft. The message is clear – embrace the transformative tools at our disposal, but do so with eyes wide open and with our principles intact. The future of academic research will likely be characterized by this symbiosis of human and artificial intelligence to push the frontiers of knowledge.

AI Use Acknowledgment Statement

This chapter was developed with the support of generative AI tools, including ChatGPT, for ideation, text generation, editing, and formatting. These tools were used to refine language, structure content, and enhance clarity, while maintaining the authors' original voice and scholarly intent. All AI-generated outputs were carefully reviewed and edited by the authors to ensure accuracy, academic rigor, and alignment with research ethics. The authors remain fully responsible for the final content, including any errors or omissions, and affirm that the primary intellectual contributions reflect their original work.

REFERENCES

Amoako, R. (n.d.). Emerging research methodologies in the age of artificial intelligence and big data. https://cehhs.utk.edu/elps/emerging-research-methodologies-in-the-age-of-artificial-intelligence-and-big-data/

Buolamwini, J. (2023). *Unmasking AI: My mission to protect what is human in a world of machines*. Random House.

Butson, R., & Spronken-Smith, R. (2024). AI and its implications for research in higher education: A critical dialogue. *Higher Education Research & Development*, *43*(3), 563–577. DOI: 10.1080/07294360.2023.2280200

Committee on Publication Ethics. (2023). *Authorship and AI tools*. https://publicationethics.org/guidance/cope-position/authorship-and-ai-tools

Cui, H., & Yasseri, T. (2024). *AI-enhanced Collective Intelligence: The State of the Art and Prospects* [Conference presentation]. ACM Collective Intelligence Conference, Boston, MA, United States.

Efron, S. E., & Ravid, R. (2019). *Writing the literature review: A practical guide*. The Guilford Press.

Hayes, A. S. (2025). "Conversing" With Qualitative Data: Enhancing Qualitative Research Through Large Language Models (LLMs). *International Journal of Qualitative Methods*, *24*, 16094069251322346. DOI: 10.1177/16094069251322346

Jain, R., & Jain, A. (2023). *Generative AI in writing research papers: A new type of algorithmic bias and uncertainty in scholarly work*. arXiv. https://doi.org//arXiv.2312.10057DOI: 10.48550

Jamaluddin J, Gaffar N.A., Din, N.S.S. (2023). Hallucination: A key challenge to Artificial Intelligence-Generated writing. *Malaysia Family Physician*. Nov 28;18:68. .DOI: 10.51866/lte.527

Leavy, P. (2017). Research design: Quantitative, qualitative, mixed methods, arts-based, and community-based participatory approaches. Guilford.

Liu, Y., & Xu, L. (2024). Multi-dimensional path exploration of artificial intelligence empowering postgraduate research ability improvement. *Journal of Educational Research and Policies*, *6*(11), 72–75. DOI: 10.53469/jerp.2024.06(11).16

Merod, A. (2023, May 26). Office of Ed Tech: 'Keep humans in the loop' when using AI in schools. *K-12 Dive*. https://www.k12dive.com/news/Education-department-AI-schools-guidance/651409/

Nakazawa, E., Udagawa, M., & Akabayashi, A. (2022). Does the Use of AI to Create Academic Research Papers Undermine Researcher Originality? *AI*, *3*(3), 3. Advance online publication. DOI: 10.3390/ai3030040

Riedlinger, M., & Mitchell, P. (2023). *What is an author? How communication research journals and academic publishers are responding to the AI authorship dilemma* [Conference presentation]. ANZCA 2023 Conference.

Slavin, R. E. (1986). Best-Evidence Synthesis: An Alternative to Meta-Analytic and Traditional Reviews. *Educational Researcher*, *15*(9), 5–11. DOI: 10.3102/0013189X015009005

Wee, B. V., & Banister, D. (2016). How to write a literature review paper? *Transport Reviews*, *36*(2), 278–288. DOI: 10.1080/01441647.2015.1065456

KEY TERMS AND DEFINITIONS

Co-Intelligence: A collaborative relationship between human and artificial intelligence where both contribute to achieving objectives.

Generative AI (GenAI): Artificial intelligence systems capable of creating original content, including text, images, and code (programming) based on training data and user prompts.

Human-in-the-Loop: An approach where human oversight and verification remain integral and essential to AI-assisted processes and outcomes.

Large Language Models (LLMs): AI systems trained on vast text datasets to interpret and generate human-like text responses using natural language processing.

Prompt Engineering: The practice of crafting effective instructions or queries to extract more accurate responses from AI systems.

Chapter 5
AI-Driven Content Creation:
Revolutionizing Open Educational Resources

Sukanda Jongsermtrakoon
https://orcid.org/0009-0004-0896-1671
Kasetsart University, Thailand

ABSTRACT

This chapter discusses how AI-driven content creation is transforming the development of learning resources, enabling educators to create, adapt, and share Open Educational Resources (OERs) more efficiently and inclusively. It highlights the use of AI technologies in lesson planning, instructional material development, and multimedia content generation. The chapter also explores key considerations such as intellectual property rights, ensuring pedagogical quality and content accuracy, and addressing bias, misinformation, and credibility issues in AI-generated OERs. Furthermore, it proposes approaches for fostering inclusivity and diversity through AI-supported educational resources while emphasizing the importance of balancing AI automation with human expertise. By addressing these opportunities and challenges, the chapter encourages educators to thoughtfully integrate AI tools into OER initiatives to enhance educational access, equity, and innovation while maintaining educational integrity.

INTRODUCTION

Using external resources in teaching and learning is not a novel concept. Over the years, numerous definitions of Open Educational Resources (OERs) have been proposed. However, many people view OERs simply as any resource that is freely available, particularly through the Internet, without fully considering the broader principles of openness, licensing, and adaptability that truly characterize OERs (Mishra, 2017).OERs are freely accessible, openly

DOI: 10.4018/979-8-3373-5092-9.ch005

licensed educational materials designed to promote equitable access to high-quality learning resources, allowing educators and learners to use, adapt, and share content without financial barriers (Hilton et al., 2019; Smith, 2006). Beyond accessibility, OERs facilitate reusability and collaborative sharing, amplifying their impact on global education (Tella, 2020). One of the key factors influencing the effectiveness of OERs is their level of openness, which pertains to the rights granted for their use, specifically, the ability to Reuse, Revise, Remix, and Redistribute them (Hilton et al., 2010). This openness plays a crucial role in democratizing education by allowing institutions and educators to offer high-quality resources to a wider audience, ultimately promoting greater educational equity (Clinton-Lisell et al., 2023).

The essential skills in teaching strategies include adapting curriculum content to meet students' needs, selecting the most effective teaching approaches, designing inclusive classroom activities, and utilizing various instructional strategies effectively. Beyond teaching strategies, adapting lesson materials is also crucial, as learning materials serve as a medium for knowledge transfer (Rabi & Zulkefli, 2018). However, due to constraints in time, resources, or expertise, many educators still rely on outdated and generalized materials that fail to meet the diverse needs of learners. Adapting or repurposing existing materials offers an alternative approach for teachers to enhance the variety of learning resources used in their instruction. One accessible source of free educational content is Open Educational Resources (OERs).

Traditional OER creation and adaptation require significant effort, often posing challenges for educators seeking to customize materials for specific learning needs. AI-driven content creation presents a transformative solution by automating and streamlining the production, modification, and dissemination of OERs (Bozkurt, 2023), enabling more personalized, inclusive, and engaging learning experiences. By reducing the time, expertise, and resources needed for content development, generative AI expands the openness of OERs, allowing educators to create, modify, and share dynamic, customizable resources across various media formats with minimal effort. AI-powered tools democratize content creation, making it more accessible to educators without advanced technical skills. Generative AI plays a pivotal role in supporting educators by streamlining the development of lesson plans that promote active learning or comprehensive lesson frameworks incorporating personalized learning pathways. It also enables the creation of adaptive quizzes tailored to different learning levels and the production of engaging instructional media (Chaivisit et al., 2024).

Utilizing natural language processing and large language models streamlines the planning process, enabling educators to create structured, engaging, and personalized lesson plans more efficiently. For example, Empirical findings stemming from ChatGPT's testing in creating lesson plans for various subjects reveal that through the input of information on curriculum, learning objectives, learning theories, instructional models, and student requirements, ChatGPT can swiftly generate lesson plans and educational materials of high quality that are customized to address the particularities of each class and student (Hashem et al., 2023; Kehoe, 2023). This capability not only simplifies the planning process but also ensures that instructional content is relevant and aligned with desired learning outcomes. Additionally, it helps educators expand their pedagogical vocabulary and refine their teaching strategies to better accommodate diverse learning contexts (Karina & Kastuhandani, 2024).

In addition to supporting the design of personalized lesson plans and learning activities, Generative AI also plays a key role in developing assessment tools. One of its major advantages is the ability to create adaptive assessments, which dynamically adjust question difficulty based on a student's responses (Chaivisit et al., 2024). Unlike traditional standardized tests, AI-powered adaptive assessments offer a more accurate measure of student proficiency while minimizing test anxiety. This personalized approach enhances the assessment experience, making it more responsive to individual learning needs (Kadaruddin, 2023). Beyond using Generative AI to develop assessment tools, educators should also establish guidelines for leveraging AI in evaluating student learning outcomes and sharing these as part of OERs. Some researchers have emphasized the potential of reimagining assessment practices by integrating AI with human creativity. One promising approach is the hybridization of AI-assisted and human-led evaluation. While AI-powered grading systems can enhance efficiency by reducing time and pinpointing key assessment insights, teachers remain essential in interpreting these findings and providing meaningful feedback to support student development. The integration of AI in assessment highlights the need for educators to design innovative, targeted evaluation strategies that align with student learning objectives, fostering a more personalized and effective assessment experience (Creely & Blannin, 2023).

By integrating AI-driven tools into educational settings, teachers can efficiently design, customize, and refine learning materials, enhancing interactivity, personalization, and student engagement (Chaivisit et al., 2024). Generative AI has the potential to transform the creation of diverse learning materials by automating content generation and improving instructional design efficiency. It empowers educators to develop a wide range of multimedia contents (Chaivisit et al., 2024; Jovanovic & Campbell, 2022). For instance, visual content generation, such as images and infographics, can be approached as a multi-stage process, where well-structured pipelines combining large language models (LLMs) and image generation models (IGMs) effectively create data-driven visualizations (Dibia, 2023). AI-generated video tools are also playing an increasingly crucial role in digital content creation by lowering technical barriers to production, enabling automatic generation of high-quality videos that streamline content development and dissemination (Hu, 2024). Furthermore, Generative AI extends to music creation, allowing for the composition of lyrics, synthesis of melodies, and even generation of sound effects that align seamlessly with the intended auditory experience (Dong et al., 2022).

Beyond traditional media, AI can generate immersive content for virtual environments, including complex, interactive spaces in the Metaverse, further expanding the possibilities for digital learning experiences (Borocki et al., 2023). The ability of Generative AI to create diverse forms of media allows educators to develop OERs that cater to a wide range of learning needs. For example, educators can use Generative AI to generate storybooks by creating narratives and accompanying graphics. These materials can further be transformed into animated learning media, where AI-generated storylines are used to develop characters and produce animation, complete with AI-composed background music. This flexibility enables educators to design engaging, multimodal educational content that enhances accessibility and learning experiences.

Additionally, Generative AI serves as a valuable tool for teachers by enabling seamless translation of content into multiple languages (Powell & Courchesne, 2024). AI-driven transcription and translation tools enhance adaptability across diverse learning environments, breaking down language barriers and ensuring that OERs remain accessible to non-native speakers, learners with disabilities, and underserved communities. By facilitating multilingual content creation, AI expands educational inclusivity and equity on a global scale.

However, as AI continues to transform the creation and distribution of OERs, it is crucial to address ethical considerations, licensing compliance, and content validation. Generative AI tools challenge academic integrity, raise concerns about information accuracy, and necessitate strategies to ensure the credibility of AI-generated content (Simms, 2024). The adoption of AI-generated OERs must uphold intellectual property rights, licensing agreements, and educational integrity to maintain trust in open educational materials. To ensure responsible use, open licensing frameworks, such as Creative Commons licenses (Cuttler, 2018), should explicitly define the extent to which AI-assisted materials can be modified, redistributed, or remixed, clarifying ownership and attribution guidelines. Additionally, quality control mechanisms are essential to verify the accuracy, relevance, and pedagogical soundness of AI-generated educational materials before they are openly shared. Establishing review processes and human oversight can help mitigate misinformation and uphold the reliability of AI-driven OERs in educational contexts.

UNDERSTANDING OPEN EDUCATIONAL RESOURCES

Definition and Principles of OERs

Free educational resources have existed for several decades, long before the internet became widely known and utilized. In earlier periods, such resources were primarily disseminated through printed documents or books, intended to share knowledge across various academic and professional fields. However, due to significant budgetary constraints, the widespread printing and global distribution of these materials proved to be impractical. The advent of the internet has substantially addressed these limitations by enabling educational resources to be accessed, reused, and redistributed without restrictions on the number of users or the frequency of use. Consequently, educational resources can now be disseminated globally to any location with internet connectivity, thereby democratizing access to knowledge.

The concept of utilizing Open Educational Resources (OERs) is rooted in the promotion of lifelong learning, highlighting the importance of freely sharing high-quality educational resources to benefit global education. OERs are learning, teaching, and research materials available in any format or medium that reside in the public domain or are protected by copyright but have been released under an open license. Such licenses allow no-cost access, reuse, repurposing, adaptation, and redistribution by others while respecting the intellectual property rights of the original copyright holders. Open licenses grant the public explicit permissions to engage with educational materials in ways that promote wider dissemination and use. The Recommendation on OER, adopted by UNESCO's General Conference at its

40th session on 25 November 2019, serves as the first international normative instrument dedicated to the advancement of openly licensed educational materials and technologies in education (UNESCO, n.d.).

Open Educational Resources refer to teaching, learning, and research materials that are made available to the public under intellectual property licenses that permit others to use or adapt the resources according to their needs at no cost. OERs include full courses, course materials, learning modules, textbooks, streaming videos, tests, software, and other tools, as well as methodologies that facilitate access to knowledge (Jongsermtrakoon & Attaporn, 2012).

A widely cited definition by the William and Flora Hewlett Foundation (2017) states: "*Open Educational Resources are teaching, learning, and research resources that reside in the public domain or have been released under an intellectual property license that permits their free use and repurposing by others. OER include full courses, course materials, modules, textbooks, streaming videos, tests, software, and any other tools, materials, or techniques used to support access to knowledge.*"

Benefits of OERs in Education

Open Educational Resources, encompassing a broad spectrum of digital materials such as textbooks and complete online courses, play a pivotal role in cultivating collaborative learning environments and supporting educators in staying abreast of technological advancements. These openly licensed resources present a strategic opportunity to elevate educational quality, foster policy dialogue, and advance knowledge sharing and capacity building, particularly by enabling the free adaptation and reuse of existing knowledge assets. Educators have increasingly recognized the value of OERs for students, especially those who require alternative explanations of complex concepts or who face barriers to accessing conventional textbooks (Bucchiarone et al., 2024). Building on this foundational value, recent studies have highlighted the tangible benefits of OERs in terms of both cost efficiency and academic performance.

Open Educational Resources (OERs) have been demonstrated to significantly reduce educational expenses for college students without compromising academic achievement and, in some instances, to enhance student performance and retention rates (Tang, 2020). In addition to these economic benefits, OERs provide instructors with versatile instructional tools that can be adapted to diverse learning contexts. These resources equip instructors with a diverse array of enriched, easily accessible materials, such as open textbooks and online repositories, spanning multiple disciplines, including science, psychology, and mathematics. Educators can tailor these materials through processes of retention, reuse, revision, remixing, and redistribution to meet diverse learner needs and enhance instructional effectiveness (Hilton, 2016).

Such adaptability is not only pedagogically advantageous but also socially impactful, particularly in addressing issues of educational equity. Beyond their economic benefits, OERs contribute to promoting social justice in digital education, particularly in times of societal disruption. They offer high-quality, freely available content comparable to commercial textbooks, thereby expanding educational access for all learners, especially those from low socioeconomic backgrounds. In addition to serving as cost-effective, openly licensed alternatives to traditional textbooks in higher education, OERs also support cost reduction and differentiated instruction in K–12 educational settings (Hilton, 2016).

As the demand for timely and customized learning materials continues to grow, technological advancements further enhance the efficiency of OER development. The interactive process, guided by user-generated prompts, enables the rapid development of high-quality educational resources that can serve as foundational materials for instructional use or for further content adaptation. This streamlined mechanism substantially shortens the resource development cycle, thereby alleviating educators' workload and allowing them to devote more attention to instructional design and learner engagement (Tang & Zhao, 2024). This evolution in OER production not only supports instructional innovation but also reinforces the broader objectives of accessibility, personalization, and equity.

Levels of Openness in OERs

The concept of "open" in the context of Open Educational Resources is fundamentally tied to the principles of free and permissive use. At its core, "open" implies that a resource is freely available for others to access, use, and repurpose across different educational contexts. However, openness is not a binary state, but rather exists along a continuum. Hilton et al. (2010) conceptualized this continuum through the Four R's framework, which articulates the progressive levels of openness that an educational resource may possess. These levels include:

- Reuse — the foundational level of openness, which permits users to utilize all or part of the work without modification (e.g., downloading a copy of a digital textbook for later reference);
- Redistribute — which grants permission to share the original work with others (e.g., forwarding a digital article to a colleague);
- Revise — which enables users to modify, adapt, or translate the resource into a different format (e.g., converting an English-language textbook into a Spanish audiobook); and
- Remix — which allows the combination of multiple existing resources to produce a new, derivative work (e.g., integrating audio lectures with complementary visual content to construct a multimedia course module).

This framework underscores that while all open resources must allow reuse, greater degrees of openness extend further rights to redistribute, revise, and remix. The more permissions granted, the more flexible and adaptable the resource becomes for diverse teaching and learning contexts.

Crucially, the actual level of openness afforded by any given OER is not intrinsic to the material itself but is determined by the creator's intent. These intentions are formally conveyed through licensing mechanisms—most commonly, Creative Commons licenses—which clearly articulate the permissible scope of use. As defined by Creative Commons (n.d.) these licenses offer a standardized method for content creators to grant public permission for specific types of engagement with their work. The structure and implications of these licenses are further detailed in Table 1, providing clarity on how legal frameworks intersect with the practical implementation of openness in educational environments.

Table 1. The CC license options (Creative Commons, n.d.)

Logo/Symbol	License Type	Description
	CC0 (CC Zero)	CC0 is a public domain dedication tool that allows creators to waive their copyright and place their works into the global public domain. It permits users to distribute, remix, adapt, and build upon the material in any medium or format without any conditions or restrictions.
	CC BY	This license allows users to distribute, remix, adapt, and build upon the material in any medium or format, provided that proper attribution is given to the creator. It also permits commercial use of the material.
	CC BY-SA	This license allows users to distribute, remix, adapt, and build upon the material in any medium or format, provided that proper attribution is given to the creator. It also permits commercial use. If the material is remixed, adapted, or built upon, the resulting work must be licensed under the same terms as the original.
	CC BY-NC	This license allows users to distribute, remix, adapt, and build upon the material in any medium or format for noncommercial purposes only, provided that proper attribution is given to the creator.
	CC BY-NC-SA	This license allows users to distribute, remix, adapt, and build upon the material in any medium or format for noncommercial purposes only, provided that proper attribution is given to the creator. If the material is remixed, adapted, or built upon, the resulting work must be licensed under the same terms as the original.
	CC BY-ND	This license allows users to copy and distribute the material in any medium or format, but only in its original, unadapted form, provided that proper attribution is given to the creator. It also permits commercial use.
	CC BY-NC-ND	This license allows users to copy and distribute the material in any medium or format, but only in its original, unadapted form, and solely for noncommercial purposes, provided that proper attribution is given to the creator.

Remark

- *BY: credit must be given to the creator.*
- *NC: Only noncommercial uses of the work are permitted.*
- *SA: Adaptations must be shared under the same terms.*
- *ND: No derivatives or adaptations of the work are permitted.*

Creative Commons (CC) licenses serve as a foundational mechanism for communicating the intended level of openness in Open Educational Resources (OERs). As presented in Table 1, these licenses span a continuum of permissions, offering varying degrees of flexibility in how educational content may be used, adapted, and shared. At the most permissive end of the spectrum lies the CC0 (Public Domain Dedication) license, which relinquishes all copyright protections, allowing unrestricted reuse, adaptation, and distribution of materials without the need for attribution. In contrast, the most restrictive license—CC BY-NC-ND—permits only noncommercial redistribution in its original form and mandates attribution to the original creator.

At the core of most CC licenses is the "BY" condition, which requires appropriate credit be given to the original author. Beyond this, three additional conditions define the scope of reuse: NC (NonCommercial) restricts usage to noncommercial purposes; ND (NoDerivatives) prohibits modifications, thus preserving the integrity of the original work; and SA (ShareAlike) mandates that any derivative works be distributed under identical licensing terms, reinforcing a cycle of openness and collaborative development. For example, a CC BY-SA license permits adaptation and commercial use, provided that derivative works remain under the same license, while CC BY-ND allows commercial sharing only in unaltered form.

Educators and content developers must carefully select licenses that align with their intended level of openness, balancing the need for attribution, commercial use, and content modification. In the context of Open Educational Resources, understanding these licensing options is essential for promoting responsible reuse, facilitating global collaboration, and expanding equitable access to high-quality learning materials.

Applying a Creative Commons (CC) license to your work is straightforward. You simply need to select the CC license that best fits your needs and communicate this choice to others who encounter your work. As part of this communication, it is important to include a link to the license you have chosen. You must also own or control the copyright in the work, as only the copyright holder—or someone with explicit permission from the copyright holder—can apply a CC license or CC0 to a copyrighted work. If the work was created within the scope of your employment, you may not hold the copyright yourself. Communicating your chosen license can be as simple as including a copyright notice, such as "© 2019. This work is openly licensed via CC BY 4.0," along with a link to the license, or by displaying the CC license symbol directly on the work (Creative Commons, n.d.).

Barriers to OER Adoption and Creation

Although Open Educational Resources have been developed across diverse educational levels and subject domains, a significant limitation lies in the linguistic accessibility of the content. Most OERs are originally produced in a single source language—commonly English—thereby restricting their effectiveness in reaching and engaging learners in multilingual or non-English-speaking regions. This limitation diminishes the inclusivity and global utility of OERs. Tang (2020) emphasizes that simply translating content is insufficient; educators from underserved or underrepresented groups must consider whether the adapted material authentically reflects local contexts and voices, rather than relying on direct translations that may obscure cultural and pedagogical nuances.

Beyond linguistic challenges, the underrepresentation of marginalized communities in the creation of OERs further exacerbates issues of equity in open education. Underserved groups frequently struggle to have their perspectives included in global OER discourse. Therefore, meaningful engagement in OER development must involve more than content adaptation—it must also empower local educators to shape knowledge in ways that are contextually relevant and culturally affirming. A further challenge involves the timeliness and reliability of OERs. Users have expressed concerns regarding outdated content, particularly in rapidly evolving disciplines. For example, Bucchiarone et al. (2024) reported OER user feedback stated, *"OERs are not updated regularly, which is a problem in many fields... You have to review the content thoroughly to ensure it is still relevant."* This lack of consistent maintenance can undermine the credibility and pedagogical value of open resources, necessitating robust quality assurance and content review mechanisms.

In addition, several systemic barriers continue to hinder the adoption of OERs within formal education systems. Mishra (2017) outlines key challenges such as limited institutional incentives for educators, insufficient awareness of copyright and licensing issues, doubts about the quality and contextual relevance of available materials, and concerns about the long-term sustainability of OER initiatives. Collectively, these factors contribute to the slow and fragmented uptake of OERs, despite their well-documented potential to enhance access, reduce costs, and support pedagogical innovation.

THE ROLE OF GENERATIVE AI IN OER DEVELOPMENT

How AI-Driven Content Creation Transforms OER Development

The limitations and challenges associated with traditional Open Educational Resource development—ranging from linguistic barriers to sustainability issues—have prompted educators and researchers to explore innovative solutions for more efficient and inclusive content production. Among these, Generative Artificial Intelligence (Generative AI) has emerged as a transformative force. With capabilities such as natural language generation, multimodal content creation, and intelligent adaptation, generative AI offers significant potential to streamline the OER development process, reduce manual workload, and improve the responsiveness of educational resources to local and contextualized needs.

AI-driven content creation redefines how educational materials are designed, adapted, and disseminated. Through intelligent prompt-response interactions, large language models (LLMs) such as ChatGPT can generate customized lesson plans, assessment tools, summaries, and explanations that align with learning outcomes and instructional goals. This interactive process not only accelerates production but also enables the generation of multiple content versions tailored to learners with varying backgrounds, needs, and abilities. While the previous section highlighted barriers such as outdated content and underrepresentation in OER ecosystems, generative AI opens up new pathways to expand participation and diversity in OER authorship. It enables educators not only to consume but also to co-create content efficiently, thereby enhancing the sustainability and inclusiveness of open education initiatives. The following sections will explore in greater detail how generative AI tools contribute to lesson planning, assessment design, multimedia development, and language localization—core elements of high-quality, inclusive, and sustainable OER development.

By streamlining the content creation process, Generative AI serves as a powerful time-saving tool for educators. Its ability to generate educational content, integrate digital materials, and support basic programming tasks through natural language prompts allows instructors to develop high-quality learning resources with significantly reduced effort. Educators with strong pedagogical expertise but limited time can leverage generative AI to create lesson plans, presentations, assessments, and other instructional materials more efficiently. This time-saving function enables them to redirect their efforts toward learner engagement, instructional design, and classroom innovation—areas that have a greater impact on student development (Chaivisit et al., 2024; Veluru, 2024) . In this sense, generative AI acts not merely as a content generator but as an intelligent co-developer in the educational process.

Moreover, Generative AI enhances accessibility for non-technical users, particularly educators who may lack advanced ICT skills but possess creative ideas for designing learning experiences. The availability of user-friendly AI interfaces—such as text-to-image generators (e.g., DALL·E), video creators, slide deck assistants, and AI-supported website builders—makes it possible for teachers to produce multimedia-rich content without the need for specialized design or coding expertise. Multimodal generative AI systems, such as those that enable text-to-image generation from simple prompts, allow users to quickly create digital visuals and artworks regardless of their design or technical background (Rapp et al., 2025). These capabilities lower the barriers for many teachers to participate in OER creation or to enhance and republish existing content as high-quality open resources. These tools rely on intuitive, prompt-based interactions that lower the technical threshold for participation in OER development. As a result, more educators are empowered to contribute to the creation, adaptation, and dissemination of open resources, which in turn promotes a more inclusive and collaborative OER ecosystem (Mittal et al., 2024).

Furthermore, generative AI supports language translation and accessibility, which are critical for localizing educational resources in multilingual contexts. Educators can use AI-powered tools to create new OERs or to reuse and adapt existing ones originally written in languages other than their own (Sandhu et al., 2024). This capability enhances the global applicability and sustainability of OERs by removing language barriers, thereby fostering educational equity and supporting the broader mission of using open resources to uplift learning quality worldwide.

AI-Powered Automation in Lesson Planning and Instructional Materials

Building on the transformative potential of generative AI in OER development, its application in automating lesson planning and instructional material creation represents a particularly impactful area. AI-powered tools can assist educators in generating lesson structures, activity suggestions, learning objectives, and even complete instructional units aligned with curriculum standards. These tools not only reduce the preparation time but also allow for rapid customization to meet diverse learner needs and contexts.

At the core of this automation lies the technical strength of generative AI models, which operate based on extensive pre-trained datasets and advanced data processing capabilities. These models can efficiently extract relevant pedagogical content from large corpora of educational materials and synthesize it into coherent instructional components. As a result, AI systems can generate a wide variety of outputs—from textual explanations and reading passages to quizzes, charts, and even full curricula—that are well-aligned and tailored to the specific needs and learning levels of students (Yadav, 2024).

Beyond the generation of static content, generative AI provides substantial support in the lesson design process. For example, educators can use AI as a brainstorming partner, prompting it to suggest ten to twenty task ideas or inquiry-based activities for a given topic. These suggestions can serve as a creative catalyst, enabling teachers to select and adapt the most appropriate options based on their professional judgment and classroom needs (Chaivisit et al., 2024). In this sense, AI acts as a collaborative assistant that enhances, rather than replaces, the teacher's decision-making.

Nevertheless, while AI-generated lesson plans offer time-saving benefits, they may follow overly prescriptive structures that require further adaptation to align with specific instructional styles or learner profiles. This reinforces the importance of human oversight and contextual judgment in the lesson design process (Chaivisit et al., 2024).

In addition to lesson planning, generative AI significantly contributes to the creation of formative and summative assessments. Its ability to generate quizzes, exercises, and comprehension questions tailored to varying levels of difficulty enables teachers to assess student understanding more efficiently. Moreover, AI can assist in automating corrections or providing suggested feedback, relieving educators from time-consuming grading tasks (Mittal et al., 2024).

More broadly, generative AI serves as a tool for developing up-to-date and responsive instructional materials. By continuously incorporating new knowledge and aligning with evolving educational standards, AI systems can help educators maintain content relevance and richness, thereby supporting personalized learning pathways and improved student engagement (Yadav, 2024).

In addition to text-based generation, the fusion of multimodal AI systems has unlocked new frontiers in content creation by enabling AI to process and interpret diverse data modalities, including text, images, audio, and video (Veluru, 2024). GenAI text-to-image models, such as DALL·E and Adobe Firefly, employ deep neural networks trained on extensive multimodal datasets to generate high-quality synthetic visuals from natural language prompts. These tools present substantial opportunities for educators to create engaging visual content for lessons, learning modules, and instructional media (Rapp et al., 2025). The growing ecosystem of generative AI tools now supports diverse instructional tasks, ranging from text and image generation to video and voice synthesis. Educators can choose from tools like ChatGPT, Gemini, and Claude for drafting content; DALL·E and Midjourney for illustrations; Steve AI and Deepbrain IO for videos; and Soundraw or SUNO for audio elements. Moreover, tools like Synthesia and Steve AI facilitate the generation of educational videos from scripts, while platforms such as Gamma and Simplified assist in automated presentation design (Chaivisit et al., 2024; Mittal et al., 2024). This rich toolkit enables educators to craft multimodal OERs that appeal to various learning styles and enrich classroom experiences (Sandhu et al., 2024).

This expansion into multimodal content creation not only extends the utility of generative AI beyond text but also aligns seamlessly with the goals of OER development, enhancing inclusivity, accessibility, and learner engagement through diverse and adaptable formats.

AI-Assisted Content Adaptation for Different Learning Levels and Contexts

Expanding from the role of generative AI in automating lesson planning and instructional design, its capacity to tailor educational resources to different learning levels and contextual needs marks a pivotal advancement in the development of Open Educational Resources. This alignment between AI-driven adaptability and OER principles of openness and inclusivity positions generative AI as a catalyst for more personalized and engaging learning experiences.

- The integration of generative AI with OERs thus holds enormous potential not only for expanding access but also for reimagining how knowledge is represented and delivered. As Bozkurt (2023) provocatively suggests, future educators might design collections of structured prompts instead of writing traditional textbooks, transforming OERs into dynamic, dialogue-based explorations rather than static repositories of information.
- Generative AI enables educators to create content that is responsive to individual student needs, adjusting materials in real time based on learners' performance, interests, or background. For instance, adaptive worksheets can increase or decrease in difficulty depending on student progress, while interactive lessons can evolve to reinforce weaker areas or challenge advanced learners. This dynamic content generation supports differentiated instruction and helps ensure that educational materials are neither too easy nor too difficult, maximizing learner engagement and retention (Mittal et al., 2024; Veluru, 2024). In addition to real-time adaptability, generative AI facilitates personalized educational experiences that incorporate student interests and cultural contexts. AI can embed relevant topics such as music, art, or local histories into standard curricula, thereby making learning more relevant and meaningful.
- Another transformative application lies in immersive learning environments enabled by the fusion of generative AI with virtual, augmented, and extended reality (VR/AR/XR). These technologies allow educators to create engaging simulations that mimic real-world environments, ranging from virtual chemistry labs to aviation flight simulators, offering hands-on learning experiences without physical risks (Yadav, 2024). The integration of generative AI enhances these simulations with lifelike scenarios and responsive feedback loops, helping learners build both cognitive and procedural knowledge through experiential learning (Mittal et al., 2024; Sandhu et al., 2024). This immersive potential reaches new heights when combined with metaverse-based

educational settings, where generative AI powers interactive avatars, simulations of historical events, or dynamic visualizations of abstract scientific phenomena. Within these environments, learners can "walk alongside electrons" to understand atomic structures or simulate complex medical procedures in a risk-free digital space. These advancements not only increase accessibility to high-quality education but also prepare students for real-world challenges through authentic learning contexts (Mittal et al., 2024). Generative AI facilitates the creation of virtual laboratories and simulations, enabling students to engage in hands-on learning experiences, particularly in fields such as science and engineering. These tools serve to complement theoretical instruction by making learning more interactive and immersive. By offering realistic and practical environments, generative AI enhances traditional pedagogical approaches and fosters deeper comprehension of complex concepts.

ETHICAL CONSIDERATIONS AND CHALLENGES

Licensing and Ownership of AI-Generated Content

A common misunderstanding, particularly in academic settings, is the belief that any content accessible online is automatically free to use. This confusion often arises from a failure to distinguish between truly open resources, such as those released under public domain licenses like CC0 or open licenses like CC BY, and other materials that are merely available at no cost. Open Educational Resources (OERs) governed by Creative Commons licenses, or royalty-free resources, explicitly grant users permission to reuse, revise, remix, and redistribute content without financial cost, provided the licensing terms are followed.

In contrast, many freely accessible materials on the internet lack clear licensing or usage terms. Although they may not require payment to access, they remain under copyright protection, and using or adapting them without explicit permission may constitute a violation of intellectual property rights. It is essential to differentiate between content that is openly licensed and content that is merely cost-free to avoid legal and ethical misuse in educational contexts. As Mishra (2017) noted, the concept of OER often requires prefacing with foundational explanations of copyright, as a significant portion of the academic community lacks a clear understanding of these legal principles.

As the integration of generative AI into Open Educational Resource (OER) development continues to advance, one of the most pressing ethical and legal concerns centers on content ownership and licensing. While OERs are fundamentally based on principles of open access, free reuse, and collaborative adaptation, the emergence of AI-generated outputs complicates longstanding frameworks of authorship and intellectual property rights. In particular, the use of large datasets to train generative AI, often without explicit licensing for educational reuse, raises concerns about potential copyright infringement and the provenance of the outputs generated by such systems. To appreciate the legal complexity of AI-generated educational content, it is necessary to understand how copyright applies not only to final materials but also to the data used in AI training, as well as to the role of the human in shaping AI outputs.

Technically, every piece of content published online or in any other format is automatically protected by copyright unless the author has formally relinquished those rights or the copyright has expired. Although materials found on the web can typically be shared for personal use, their reuse, revision, remixing, or redistribution requires explicit permission from the copyright holder. Some exceptions exist under fair use or fair dealing provisions in copyright law; however, the boundaries of these exceptions are frequently ambiguous and open to interpretation. The foundational ethos of OER lies in enabling educators and learners to reuse and adapt educational materials without seeking further permission from the original authors—an essential relief for higher education systems that often depend on curated course packs.

However, this openness must be supported by a thorough understanding of copyright law, particularly in light of AI-generated content. Copyright protection exists to safeguard the rights of original creators and ensure they receive economic recognition, often through licensing or sales. Accordingly, the use of someone else's content, particularly for commercial purposes, as part of an OER raises legitimate concerns about the potential loss of economic benefits to the original author. These issues become more complex when content is produced by generative AI, which may draw from copyrighted materials in its training data or unintentionally reproduce existing works. In the context of AI-driven OER creation, navigating licensing and ownership is not merely a legal formality but a critical step in preserving the integrity and sustainability of open education.

The question of ownership over AI-generated works remains a topic of ongoing debate among educators and legal scholars. One perspective emphasizes that generative AI does not truly create novel content; rather, it synthesizes outputs based on patterns learned from pre-existing data during its training. A significant concern arises when portions of this training data have been incorporated without explicit authorization from the original content owners (Yadav, 2024). From this standpoint, the outputs generated by AI are seen not as original creations but as derivative works lacking a clear attribution of authorship. Consequently, the legal grounds for assigning copyright ownership, particularly to the individual who merely inputs prompts, remain uncertain and contested. This issue becomes especially critical in the context of Open Educational Resources (OERs), where questions of reuse, adaptation, and open licensing intersect with unresolved concerns around the provenance of AI-generated materials. As discussed in the following sections, clarifying the origin and legal standing of such content is essential for ensuring ethical and responsible integration of AI in educational content creation.

In addition to questions of ownership, the process of training generative AI systems introduces new layers of legal and ethical complexity related to data provenance and content reproduction. Training generative AI models with specific prompts to produce educational content, such as quizzes, summaries, and instructional materials, raises important concerns related to copyright compliance and potential plagiarism. The outputs generated by these models may inadvertently infringe on copyright laws, particularly if they reproduce elements from protected sources without proper attribution. Furthermore, there is an ongoing risk that user-provided input might be stored and reused as training data without explicit consent, thereby compromising user privacy and data ownership. These challenges underscore the urgent need for robust ethical guidelines and technical safeguards to protect intellectual property rights and user data in educational AI applications. Copyright concerns are especially pertinent in areas such as early childhood education, medical training, historical education, entrepreneurship, skills development, and general content creation, including image, video, and text generation, where AI-generated outputs (e.g., test papers, exercises, or instructional media) are commonly deployed. Similar issues also arise in teaching support scenarios, where AI-generated materials may be directly used in instructional settings (Mittal et al., 2024).

In response to these concerns, another perspective among scholars and educators views generative AI not as a content originator but as a sophisticated tool that enhances human creativity. From this standpoint, when humans actively engage in the creation process—by proposing ideas, crafting prompts, reviewing and refining AI-generated outputs, and synthesizing them into new educational resources—they serve as co-creators. In such cases, authorship and the right to distribute the work justifiably reside with the human collaborator. However, transparency remains critical: it is essential to disclose the sources of input and clarify the role of AI in the content creation process. Rather than positioning AI as the sole author, this approach frames it as a supportive instrument within the educator's toolkit. Through prompt engineering and iterative collaboration, generative AI can enable the creation of richer, more inclusive OERs. By recognizing the human-AI partnership as a co-creative process, this model offers a pragmatic solution to ownership concerns, aligning innovative content development with existing legal and ethical standards (Bozkurt, 2023).

Following this line of reasoning, it becomes evident that when Generative AI is employed in the development of OERs, creators must go beyond simply applying a Creative Commons license to the educational resources. They must also clearly declare their role as human co-creators and specify the extent and nature of AI involvement in the content creation process. Transparency regarding which parts of the work were generated, edited, or curated through AI tools is essential to maintain academic and ethical integrity. For example, educators might include statements such as "*This lesson plan was developed using generative AI to support content drafting, with final edits and adaptations made by the author*". Striking an appropriate balance between human input and AI contribution is therefore a critical consideration in OER development—a theme that will be further explored in the following section of this chapter.

Ensuring Pedagogical Quality, Accuracy, and Credibility

The integration of generative AI into educational contexts raises critical concerns regarding academic integrity, particularly concerning plagiarism and the reliability of AI-generated content. To ensure meaningful implementation, educators must navigate technical complexities while also verifying that such tools align with sound pedagogical principles and effectively support learning outcomes (Barus et al., 2025).

In addition to concerns about content accuracy, the timeliness of AI-generated outputs poses further limitations. A central technical challenge in the educational application of generative AI lies in the quality and impartiality of the content it produces. Because generative AI models are trained on large datasets drawn from existing sources, they are susceptible to reproducing and even reinforcing biases embedded within that data. This can result in the creation of educational materials that are not only inaccurate but also potentially biased or discriminatory. Furthermore, the advanced capabilities of generative AI to produce highly realistic content raise concerns about the dissemination of misinformation, including the generation of deepfakes that may undermine trust in educational resources (Yadav, 2024).

Generative AI systems tend to replicate the biases embedded in their training datasets, which can result in biased outputs. In today's increasingly globalized society, where individuals of diverse ethnicities, cultures, and perspectives coexist, the presence of bias in educational AI systems may undermine user trust, limit acceptance among students, and potentially shape biased worldviews from an early age. Such outcomes not only affect individual learners but also contribute to systemic inequities in education. To mitigate these risks, it is essential to curate and use diverse, representative datasets during both the training and fine-tuning phases of model development. This promotes fairness and inclusivity in AI-generated content. Additionally, regular monitoring and performance evaluations must be implemented to detect and correct biases that may emerge over time. These ongoing assessments help prevent the reinforcement of unintended stereotypes or discriminatory patterns in educational materials (Mittal et al., 2024; Veluru, 2024; Yadav, 2024).

In complex academic domains—particularly those that demand deep conceptual understanding and rigorous analytical reasoning—generative AI often struggles to capture nuanced distinctions and sophisticated theoretical constructs. This limitation can result in content that lacks academic rigor, precision, or even professional credibility. While generative AI systems are equipped with advanced natural language processing capabilities, their underlying architecture relies heavily on statistical learning and mathematical modeling. As a result, they may fall short in replicating the logical reasoning processes necessary for conveying intricate subject matter accurately (Tang & Zhao, 2024).

Beyond technical limitations, the sociocultural implications of generative AI must also be considered. The content generation capabilities of generative AI are often constrained by the scope and structure of its underlying training datasets and algorithmic models. Because these systems learn from pre-existing data, they tend to reproduce patterns embedded in the source material. When training data comprises largely templated or repetitive examples, the AI is likely to replicate such structures, resulting in homogeneous outputs. This limitation can lead to teaching resources that lack originality and adaptability, making them less effective in addressing the diverse needs of various disciplines, instructional contexts, and learner demographics. In addition, data bias poses a critical concern: AI models may inadvertently perpetuate narrow perspectives or stereotypical representations present in the data, thereby undermining inclusivity and reinforcing problematic views. Such outcomes not only diminish the pedagogical value of generated materials but also impede the development of equitable and culturally responsive learning environments (Tang & Zhao, 2024).

Equally important is equipping educators and learners with the skills to recognize and critically address AI-generated bias. This can be achieved through training programs that promote digital literacy, ethical awareness, and inclusive pedagogical practices. Finally, maintaining the relevance and fairness of generative AI systems requires continuous updates to their datasets, ensuring that the underlying data remains current, balanced, and reflective of diverse lived experiences. Such efforts are vital to upholding the quality, credibility, and equity of AI-supported education (Mittal et al., 2024).

Moreover, Generative AI models often struggle to generalize beyond the scope of their training data. While they are capable of producing outputs that closely resemble patterns found in the data they were trained on, generating truly diverse or original content remains a significant challenge. This limitation hinders the ability of Generative AI to create educational materials that are both innovative and contextually novel, particularly when required to address unique learning needs or emerging academic scenarios (Mittal et al., 2024).

Some scholars emphasize that generative AI does not engage in creative thinking in the way humans do; rather, it excels at identifying patterns within the data on which it has been trained and reproducing or modifying those patterns to generate responses. Therefore, users should not expect AI to "think" or reason with human-like cognition, but instead understand it as a sophisticated pattern recognition and synthesis tool.

While generative AI can produce engaging educational and assessment materials, its limitations in terms of accuracy and reliability remain significant concerns. The content generated is not always aligned with the intended instructional goals or difficulty levels, which may result in materials that are pedagogically inappropriate or misleading. These issues underscore the need for careful review and validation of AI-generated content to ensure it meets educational standards and learner needs (Bucchiarone et al., 2024).

Maintaining consistent quality in generative AI-produced content remains a significant challenge. Outputs may lack realism, exhibit visual or linguistic artifacts, or display incoherent structure—factors that hinder the production of uniformly high-quality educational materials. These inconsistencies pose a particular risk in instructional settings, where inaccuracies can mislead learners or contribute to the formation of misconceptions. Therefore, AI-generated content must undergo thorough evaluation and validation before being introduced to students, ensuring that the material supports, rather than compromises, accurate learning and conceptual understanding (Mittal et al., 2024).

Additionally, generative AI faces challenges related to the timeliness and comprehensiveness of its informational base. Because these systems are trained on static datasets, their capacity to incorporate the most recent scholarly developments is inherently constrained. In fast-moving academic fields, where knowledge evolves rapidly, this lag in data updates can lead to educational outputs that are outdated or misaligned with current research. Compounding this issue is the fact that generative AI models generate responses through probabilistic language prediction, rather than through real-time factual validation. Thus, even when an AI model includes seemingly accurate content, it lacks the ability to verify its validity or to recognize when the information has been superseded by more recent findings (Tang & Zhao, 2024).

To illustrate how such limitations manifest in practice, consider the following case involving AI-generated images. The comparison of three images highlights the inconsistency and factual inaccuracies that may arise from generative AI outputs. *Figure 1, Osaka Castle Image generated from ChatGPT (a),* and *Figure 2, Osaka Castle Image generated from ChatGPT (b)* were generated by ChatGPT using the identical prompt: "Create an image of Osaka Castle, which is located in Japan." Despite using the same prompt, the resulting images differ significantly in architectural details and color schemes, revealing the inherent variability and lack of consistency in generative AI outputs. In contrast, *Figure 3, Osaka Castle Photo by Nagi (Pixabay.com)* shows distinctive structural elements—such as roof color, window placement, and balcony detailing—that were either misrepresented or omitted in the AI-generated versions.

While the generated images may symbolically resemble Japanese-style castles, a closer inspection reveals that they fail to accurately depict Osaka Castle. For individuals familiar with the actual site, these generated visuals would be easily identified as incorrect. This example underscores a broader concern: the potential for AI-generated educational resources to contain visually or contextually inaccurate representations. It also highlights the importance of human involvement in the verification and validation of AI-generated materials—particularly when developing Open Educational Resources. These observations set the stage for the following section, which discusses the critical balance between automation and human oversight in AI-supported content creation. This case exemplifies why quality assurance in AI-generated OERs must go beyond surface-level plausibility and include visual, factual, and cultural verification.

Figure 1. Osaka Castle image generated from ChatGPT (a)

Figure 2. Osaka Castle image generated from ChatGPT (b)

Figure 3. Osaka Castle photo by Nagi (Pixabay.com)

Balancing Automation with Human Oversight in Content Curation

Humans value generative AI for its ability to produce diverse forms of content, including text, images, audio, and video. While these capabilities can resemble human creative work, generative AI is not a substitute for human intelligence or expertise. Instead, it serves as a powerful assistant, enhancing human productivity, supporting creative processes, and enabling problem-solving beyond individual capacity (Chaivisit et al., 2024).

The veracity of content generated by generative AI remains a pressing concern in educational settings. While generative AI can produce large volumes of educational materials efficiently, the accuracy and reliability of this content are not consistently guaranteed. AI-generated outputs may fail to capture the nuanced realities of complex topics, leading to oversimplifications or even misrepresentations that could foster misconceptions. Furthermore, quality variability, alongside unresolved issues of content ownership, data privacy, and security, highlights the importance of integrating robust quality control mechanisms (Mittal et al., 2024).

To address these limitations, human oversight is essential throughout the content curation process. Educators must be actively involved in reviewing, validating, and adapting AI-generated materials to ensure alignment with learning objectives and pedagogical standards.

Training programs for educators should be implemented to build their capacity in critically evaluating and responsibly incorporating AI-generated content. Additionally, awareness among both teachers and students must be raised regarding the limitations of generative AI to prevent overreliance or misinterpretation of its outputs (Mittal et al., 2024).

Ultimately, feedback loops not only improve content accuracy and model performance but also reduce long-term dependence on continuous human intervention. This makes generative AI tools more efficient, adaptable, and scalable, particularly in dynamic learning environments where student needs and behaviors change rapidly. However, human involvement remains irreplaceable in maintaining ethical standards, contextual sensitivity, and pedagogical integrity in AI-assisted educational content development (Mittal et al., 2024).

A promising approach to enhancing the quality of AI-generated content is the implementation of feedback loops. These mechanisms enable the AI model to learn from previous errors by incorporating corrections and user input into its training process. Feedback loops help identify inaccuracies, prevent recurring mistakes, and improve the model's adaptability to evolving educational needs. Human feedback is especially valuable when the model experiences drift—gradual degradation of accuracy due to shifting user behavior or outdated data. By evaluating and annotating outputs, human reviewers contribute to the ongoing refinement of the system (Mittal et al., 2024).

In practical application, data-driven feedback loops empower educators to evaluate the effectiveness of generative AI across various disciplines, instructional tasks, and learning contexts. By systematically analyzing AI outputs, educators can identify areas where human oversight, content adjustments, or prompt refinements are required. This iterative process not only strengthens quality control but also enables generative AI to progress beyond the generation of basic materials, advancing toward the creation of more complex, contextually nuanced, and pedagogically sophisticated resources. As generative AI becomes more deeply embedded in educational systems, its potential to produce high-quality, diverse, and personalized learning content will continue to expand, reinforcing its role in enhancing both the effectiveness and efficiency of education (Tang & Zhao, 2024).

An illustrative example of human–AI co-creation is shown in Figure 4, which presents the process of producing an animated video using multiple AI tools under human guidance. ChatGPT was used to generate the script, Kling.AI and Hedra AI created 3D animated visuals, Botnoi AI produced voice narration, and Canva generated subtitles and final editing. The completed video was shared with students via an online viewing link. This example highlights how generative AI enhances, but does not replace, human creativity and pedagogical intent.

Figure 4. Process of producing an animated video through generative AI

Another example, shown in Figure 5: Process of Producing a Virtual Learning Environment through Generative AI, demonstrates how educators use tools like ChatGPT to design scenes, generate 3D objects via Meshy AI, and assemble them in CoSpaces EDU. ChatGPT also supports the creation of interactive tasks and block-based coding logic. This AI-assisted workflow enables the creation of immersive, pedagogically aligned VR environments without requiring advanced technical expertise.

Figure 5. Process of producing a virtual learning environment through generative AI

FUTURE PROSPECTS

The integration of artificial intelligence into Open Educational Resources signals a pivotal shift in the future of global education. Rooted in the principle of freely sharing knowledge to promote equitable access, OERs are now increasingly enhanced by AI-driven tools that accelerate content creation, improve relevance, and extend reach. By generating high-quality learning materials that are both scalable and adaptable, AI contributes to democratizing education, supporting inclusion across diverse geographic, cultural, and socioeconomic contexts (Barus et al., 2025).

One key opportunity lies in the localization of educational content. The ability to translate or adapt OERs into local languages using generative AI ensures that learners in all regions, regardless of linguistic background, can access the same high-quality resources. This process not only broadens access but also empowers communities to contextualize knowledge in culturally meaningful ways, removing barriers to understanding and fostering educational equity.

Beyond accessibility, generative AI offers a path toward addressing another longstanding challenge: the limitations of one-size-fits-all instruction. Learners differ in prior knowledge, cognitive preferences, and educational environments. Uniform teaching approaches often fail to accommodate these variations, leading to unequal learning outcomes. Generative AI enables the development of personalized learning materials—adaptive assessments, real-time feedback, and customized learning pathways—that respond to individual strengths and needs (Barus et al., 2025). This personalization can significantly improve student engagement, confidence, and academic success.

Supporting this shift, tools such as ChatGPT and other large language models (LLMs) play a growing role in generating instructional content, facilitating dialogue-based learning, and offering instant support. These technologies reduce the burden of repetitive content creation and allow educators to focus on facilitating deep learning, emotional well-being, and learner motivation. However, this transformation also calls for robust professional development and a redefinition of educator roles within AI-augmented environments.

Looking ahead, advancements in AI architecture offer even greater possibilities. Combining neural networks with symbolic logic, for instance, may lead to systems that not only learn patterns from data but also reason logically and generate interpretable, structured outputs. This could enrich students' learning experiences by fostering critical thinking and problem-solving skills. At the frontier, the rise of quantum computing introduces the potential to exponentially enhance the efficiency and complexity of generative models, opening new avenues for simulating learning environments, modeling educational behavior, and generating sophisticated datasets for instructional design (Mittal et al., 2024).

In sum, the future of AI-enhanced OERs holds enormous promise—not only in extending access to quality education across languages and regions, but also in tailoring learning experiences to individual needs, fostering higher-order thinking, and transforming instructional design practices. However, realizing this potential will require sustained investment in research, cross-disciplinary collaboration, and thoughtful implementation that prioritizes ethical considerations, pedagogical soundness, and human oversight. As technological capabilities continue to expand, so too must our collective commitment to ensuring that AI serves as a force for equity, empowerment, and innovation in education.

REFERENCES

Barus, O. P., Hidayanto, A. N., Handri, E. Y., Sensuse, D. I., & Yaiprasert, C. (2025). Shaping generative AI governance in higher education: Insights from student perception. *International Journal of Educational Research Open*, *8*, 100452. https://doi.org/https://doi .org/10.1016/j.ijedro.2025.100452. DOI: 10.1016/j.ijedro.2025.100452

Borocki, J., Jovanović, A., Vekić, A., Đaković, V., & Cvijić Čović, M. (2023). Empowering Content Creation With Generative Ai in Metaverse. 554-559. https://doi.org/DOI: 10.24867/ IS-2023-VP1.1-14_07941

Bozkurt, A. (2023). Generative AI, Synthetic Contents, Open Educational Resources (OER), and Open Educational Practices (OEP): A New Front in the Openness Landscape. *Open Praxis*, *15*(3), 178–184. DOI: 10.55982/openpraxis.15.3.579

Bucchiarone, A., Cicchetti, A., Vázquez-Ingelmo, A., Adami, F., Schiavo, G., García-Holgado, A., & García-Peñalvo, F. J. (2024). Designing and Generating Lesson Plans combining Open Educational Content and Generative AI. [Linz, Austria.]. *MODELS Companion*, *24*(September), 22–27. DOI: 10.1145/3652620.3687773

Chaivisit, S., Asino, T. I., Jongsermtrakoon, S., Thompson, P., Rezaie, F., & Siripipattanakul, S. (2024). Empowering Educators With Generative AI Tools and Support. In *Transforming Education With Generative AI: Prompt Engineering and Synthetic Content Creation* (pp. 56-81). IGI Global. DOI: 10.4018/979-8-3693-1351-0.ch003

Clinton-Lisell, V., Legerski, E., Gilpin, S., & Rhodes, B. (2023). Open Educational Resources as Tools to Foster Equity. https://doi.org/DOI: 10.31219/osf.io/9jnd3

Creative Commons. (n.d.). *About CC Licenses*. Retrieved 28 April 2025 from https:// creativecommons.org/share-your-work/cclicenses/

Creely, E., & Blannin, J. (2023). The Implications of Generative AI for Creative Composition in Higher Education and Initial Teacher Education. *Ascilite Publications*, *357-361*, 357–361. Advance online publication. DOI: 10.14742/apubs.2023.618

Cuttler, C. (2018). Students' Use and Perceptions of the Relevance and Quality of Open Textbooks Compared to Traditional Textbooks in Online and Traditional Classroom Environments. *Psychology Learning & Teaching*, *18*(1), 65–83. DOI: 10.1177/1475725718811300

Dibia, V. (2023). LIDA: A Tool for Automatic Generation of Grammar-Agnostic Visualizations and Infographics Using Large Language Models. https://doi.org//arxiv.2303.02927DOI: 10.18653/v1/2023.acl-demo.11

Dong, H.-W., Zhou, C., Berg-Kirkpatrick, T., & McAuley, J. (2022). Deep Performer. *Score-to-Audio Music Performance Synthesis.*, *951-955*, 951–955. Advance online publication. DOI: 10.1109/ICASSP43922.2022.9747217

Hashem, R., Ali, N., El Zein, F., Fidalgo, P., & Abu Khurma, O. (2023). AI to the Rescue: Exploring the Potential of ChatGPT as a Teacher Ally for Workload Relief and Burnout Prevention. *Research and Practice in Technology Enhanced Learning, 19*, 023. https://doi.org/DOI: 10.58459/rptel.2024.19023

Hilton, J.III. (2016). Open educational resources and college textbook choices: A review of research on efficacy and perceptions. *Educational Technology Research and Development, 64*(4), 573–590. DOI: 10.1007/s11423-016-9434-9

Hilton, J.III, Larsen, R., Wiley, D., & Fischer, L. (2019). Substituting Open Educational Resources for Commercial Curriculum Materials: Effects on Student Mathematics Achievement in Elementary Schools. *Research in Mathematics Education, 21*(1), 60–76. DOI: 10.1080/14794802.2019.1573150

Hilton, J.III, Wiley, D., Stein, J., & Johnson, A. (2010). The four 'R's of openness and ALMS analysis: Frameworks for open educational resources. *Open Learning, 25*(1), 37–44. DOI: 10.1080/02680510903482132

Hu, Y. (2024). User Behavior and Satisfaction in AI-Generated Video Tools: Insights From Surveys and Online Comments. *Applied and Computational Engineering, 94*(1), 136–145. DOI: 10.54254/2755-2721/94/2024MELB0065

Jongsermtrakoon, S., & Attaporn, J. (2012). Tendency of OER Use: Open Educational Resources in ASEAN Community National e-Learning Conference 2012, Bangkok, Thailand.

Jovanovic, M., & Campbell, M. (2022). Generative Artificial Intelligence: Trends and Prospects. *Computer, 55*(10), 107–112. DOI: 10.1109/MC.2022.3192720

Kadaruddin, K. (2023). Empowering Education Through Generative AI: Innovative Instructional Strategies for Tomorrow's Learners. *International Journal of Business Law and Education, 4*(2), 618–625. DOI: 10.56442/ijble.v4i2.215

Karina, B. D., & Kastuhandani, F. C. (2024). Pre-Service English Teachers' Lived Experience in Using AI in Teaching Preparation. *Edunesia Jurnal Ilmiah Pendidikan, 5*(1), 550–568. DOI: 10.51276/edu.v5i1.767

Kehoe, F. (2023). Leveraging Generative AI Tools for Enhanced Lesson Planning in Initial Teacher Education at Post Primary. *Irish Journal of Technology Enhanced Learning, 7*(2), 172–182. DOI: 10.22554/ijtel.v7i2.124

Mishra, S. (2017). Open Educational Resources: Removing Barriers From Within. *Distance Education, 38*(3), 369–380. DOI: 10.1080/01587919.2017.1369350

Mittal, U., Sai, S., Chamola, V., & Sangwan, D. (2024). A Comprehensive Review on Generative AI for Education. *IEEE Access : Practical Innovations, Open Solutions, 12*, 142733–142759. DOI: 10.1109/ACCESS.2024.3468368

Powell, W., & Courchesne, S. (2024). Opportunities and Risks Involved in Using ChatGPT to Create First Grade Science Lesson Plans. *PLoS One*, *19*(6), e0305337. DOI: 10.1371/journal.pone.0305337 PMID: 38885244

Rabi, N. M., & Zulkefli, M. Y. (2018). Mainstream Teachers' Competency Requirement for Inclusive Education Program. *International Journal of Academic Research in Business & Social Sciences*, *8*(11). Advance online publication. DOI: 10.6007/IJARBSS/v8-i11/5354

Rapp, A., Di Lodovico, C., Torrielli, F., & Di Caro, L. (2025). How do people experience the images created by generative artificial intelligence? An exploration of people's perceptions, appraisals, and emotions related to a Gen-AI text-to-image model and its creations. *International Journal of Human-Computer Studies*, *193*, 103375. https://doi.org/https://doi.org/10.1016/j.ijhcs.2024.103375. DOI: 10.1016/j.ijhcs.2024.103375

Sandhu, R., Channi, H. K., Ghai, D., & Cheema, G. S. (2024). An Introduction to Generative AI Tools for Education 2030. In *Integrating Generative AI in Education to Achieve Sustainable Development Goals* (pp. 1-28). https://doi.org/DOI: 10.4018/979-8-3693-2440-0.ch001

Simms, R. C. (2024). Work With ChatGPT, Not Against. *Nurse Educator*, *49*(3), 158–161. DOI: 10.1097/NNE.0000000000001634 PMID: 38502607

Smith, M. C. C. (2006). The promise of open educational resources. *Change the Magazine of Higher Learning, 38*(5), 8-17. https://doi.org/https://doi.org/10.3200/chng.38.5.8-17

Tang, H. (2020). Implementing open educational resources in digital education. *Education Tech Research Development, 2021*(69), 389 – 392. https://doi.org/https://doi.org/10.1007/s11423-020-09879-x

Tang, W., & Zhao, J. (2024). Generative Artificial Intelligence and the Development and Management of Educational Resources: Benefits, Challenges, and Solutions. *The Educational Review, USA*, *8*(11), 1296–1301. DOI: 10.26855/er.2024.11.003

Tella, A. (2020). Open educational resources and distance learning: challenges and the way forward in higher education. 1-10. https://doi.org/https://doi.org/10.1007/978-3-319-60013-0_260-1

UNESCO. (n.d.). *Open Educational Resources*. Retrieved 28 April 2025 from https://www.unesco.org/en/open-educational-resources

Veluru, C. (2024). The Impact of Generative AI on Content Curation and Content Advancements in Education and Training. *European Journal of Advances in Engineering and Technology*, *11*(4), 121–130. DOI: 10.5281/zenodo.12737572

William and Flora Hewlett Foundation. (2017). *Open educational resource*. https://www.hewlett.org/strategy/open-educational-resources/

Yadav, A. (2024). The Development of AI with Generative Capabilities and Its Effect on Education. *International Journal of Science and Research (Raipur, India), 13*(5), 854–860. Advance online publication. DOI: 10.21275/SR24509232318

Chapter 6
AI and Gamification Engaging Students in New Ways

Dayna Lynn Mitchell
https://orcid.org/0009-0000-9385-7238
California State Polytechnic University, Pomona, USA

ABSTRACT

This chapter will explore the intersection of artificial intelligence (AI) and gamification in education, examining how these two innovative technologies can work together to engage students in new and dynamic ways. By integrating AI with gamified learning experiences, educators can create personalized, interactive environments that foster deeper student engagement, motivation, and achievement. The chapter will explore the benefits of AI-driven gamification, such as real-time feedback, adaptive learning paths, and increased student autonomy, while also addressing potential challenges, including equity, accessibility, and the balance between entertainment and educational value. Case studies and examples of AI-powered gamification in both K-12 and higher education settings will be presented, offering practical insights into how these tools can be effectively implemented to enhance learning outcomes.

INTRODUCTION

In recent years, the fields of artificial intelligence (AI) and gamification have garnered significant attention for their potential to revolutionize education. Both AI and gamification, when used independently, have shown promise in enhancing student engagement, motivation, and learning outcomes (Gafni et al., 2018; Renacido & Biray, 2025; Babu & Moorthy, 2024). However, when these two technologies are integrated, they can create powerful, interactive, and personalized learning experiences that go beyond the traditional methods of instruction. This chapter will explore the intersection of AI and gamification, focusing on how the

DOI: 10.4018/979-8-3373-5092-9.ch006

combination of these two tools can reshape the educational landscape by making learning more engaging, adaptive, and tailored to the individual needs of students.

Gamification, the use of game-like elements in non-game contexts, has become increasingly popular in educational settings due to its ability to enhance motivation and engagement (Bennani et al., 2022). By incorporating elements such as points, badges, leaderboards, and challenges, gamification taps into students' intrinsic desire for achievement, competition, and reward Smiderle et al., 2020). These elements encourage active participation, making learning more enjoyable and less daunting for students, which in turn can lead to improved retention and mastery of content. However, while gamification offers exciting possibilities, its effectiveness is often limited by the one-size-fits-all approach, where all students are presented with the same challenges and rewards, regardless of their individual learning needs and abilities.

This is where artificial intelligence can change this narrative. AI has the potential to significantly enhance the gamification process by personalizing learning experiences in real-time. Through machine learning algorithms, AI can analyze student behavior, preferences, and performance to dynamically adjust the game elements, ensuring that each student is presented with challenges that are appropriate for their skill level and learning pace (Song et al., 2024). By continuously adapting the learning experience to suit individual needs, AI-powered gamification can help students achieve their full potential, whether they are struggling with the material or excelling beyond expectations. Moreover, AI can provide real-time feedback, allowing students to track their progress and make adjustments as needed, fostering a sense of autonomy and ownership over their learning journey (Strielkowski et al., 2025).

The integration of AI and gamification also holds the potential to create more inclusive learning environments (Strielkowski et al., 2025). Traditional educational methods often fail to address the diverse learning styles, strengths, and challenges of students. Some students may excel in traditional assessments, while others may struggle with standardized tests or rigid teaching methods. AI-powered gamification, however, can cater to these varying needs by offering personalized learning experiences that adapt to each student's unique profile. For example, a student who struggles with reading comprehension might be provided with visual or auditory cues in a gamified learning environment, while a student who excels in problem-solving could be challenged with more complex tasks. This personalized approach not only supports students at different levels but also helps foster a sense of achievement and motivation, as they can progress at their own pace and feel a sense of accomplishment when they master new skills (Strielkowski et al., 2025).

Furthermore, AI and gamification can work together to foster deeper engagement and motivation by making learning more interactive and immersive (Babu & Moorthy, 2024). Traditional classroom settings, while effective in many ways, often rely on passive learning methods, such as lectures and textbooks, which may not capture the attention of all students. In contrast, gamified learning experiences, enhanced by AI, can create interactive environments that encourage students to actively participate in their learning process. For example, AI-driven gamification can incorporate simulations, virtual worlds, and role-playing scenarios that allow students to apply their knowledge in realistic contexts. These immersive experiences can make learning more relevant and meaningful, as students are able to see the real-world applications of the concepts they are studying. By making learning more engaging and hands-on, AI and gamification can increase students' intrinsic motivation to learn and help them develop a deeper understanding of the material.

However, despite the many advantages of integrating AI and gamification in education, there are also challenges and considerations that must be addressed. One of the primary concerns is ensuring that AI-driven gamification is accessible and equitable for all students. While AI has the potential to create personalized learning experiences, it is crucial that these technologies are designed in a way that does not exacerbate existing inequities in education. For instance, students from disadvantaged backgrounds may not have access to the same technological resources as their peers, which could create a digital divide and limit their ability to benefit from AI-powered gamification. Additionally, there is a risk that AI algorithms may unintentionally reinforce biases, particularly if they are trained on data that reflects societal inequalities (Babu & Moorthy, 2024). To ensure that AI-powered gamification is inclusive, educators and developers must be mindful of these potential issues and work to create systems that are accessible to all students, regardless of their background or circumstances.

Another challenge is the need for effective implementation and integration of AI-powered gamification tools into existing educational frameworks. While many schools and institutions are increasingly adopting technology in the classroom, the integration of AI and gamification may require significant changes to curriculum design, teacher training, and assessment practices (Ali et al., 2025). Educators will need to be equipped with the skills and knowledge to effectively use AI-powered gamification tools, and they must be provided with adequate support to ensure successful implementation. This may involve professional development opportunities, ongoing technical support, and a shift in mindset toward embracing new forms of teaching and learning. Furthermore, schools and institutions must ensure that the necessary infrastructure is in place to support the use of AI-powered gamification, including reliable internet access, devices, and software.

Moreover, the ethical implications of using AI in education must also be carefully considered. As AI systems become more sophisticated, it will collect and analyze vast amounts of data on student behavior, performance, and preferences (Gouseti et al., 2024). While this data can be invaluable in personalizing learning experiences, it also raises concerns about privacy and data security. Educators, students, and parents must be assured that their data is being handled responsibly and that appropriate safeguards are in place to protect sensitive information. Transparency in how AI systems collect, store, and use data is crucial in building trust and ensuring that AI-powered gamification is used ethically and responsibly.

Despite these challenges, the potential benefits of AI-powered gamification in education are immense (Gómez Niño et al., 2024). By combining the engaging elements of gamification with the personalized capabilities of AI, educators can create learning environments that are more interactive, inclusive, and effective. AI can help to level the playing field by catering to the diverse needs of students, providing real-time feedback, and adapting the learning experience to suit individual preferences and abilities. Additionally, the integration of AI and gamification can increase student motivation and engagement, making learning more enjoyable and meaningful. As these technologies continue to evolve, the possibilities for enhancing educational experiences will only grow, paving the way for a future where learning is more personalized, accessible, and engaging than ever before.

In conclusion, the intersection of AI and gamification presents a promising frontier for the future of education. By leveraging the strengths of both technologies, educators can create dynamic and personalized learning experiences that cater to the diverse needs of students, fostering deeper engagement, motivation, and achievement. However, the successful integration of AI-powered gamification will require careful consideration of ethical, practical, and logistical challenges. By addressing these challenges and ensuring that AI and gamification are implemented responsibly, educators can harness the full potential of these technologies to enhance learning outcomes and transform the educational experience for students around the world.

THE ROLE OF GAMIFICATION IN EDUCATION

Gamification has emerged as a powerful and increasingly popular tool in educational settings, transforming the way students engage with learning materials and participate in academic activities (Babu & Moorthy, 2024). At its core, gamification involves the integration of game-like elements into non-game environments, such as classrooms, to enhance student engagement, motivation, and learning outcomes. By incorporating elements such as points, badges, leaderboards, and challenges, gamification aims to create a more dynamic and interactive learning experience that encourages active participation and rewards achievement (Smiderle et al., 2020). This approach has gained significant traction in recent years, particularly as educators seek innovative ways to make learning more engaging and relevant to students. As technology continues to evolve and the educational landscape adapts to new demands, gamification has proven to be a versatile and effective strategy for enhancing both teaching and learning experiences.

The increasing popularity of gamification in educational settings can be attributed to several factors, including the changing expectations of students, the rise of digital technologies, and the growing recognition of the need for more personalized and engaging learning experiences (Zeng et al., 2024). In today's digital age, students are accustomed to interactive, game-like environments through their use of smartphones, social media, and video games. This exposure to gamified experiences has shaped their expectations of how learning should take place, with many students now seeking more immersive and interactive educational experiences. As a result, educators are increasingly turning to gamification to meet these expectations and create more engaging learning environments that resonate with students' interests and learning styles.

Furthermore, the traditional, passive forms of instruction, such as lectures and textbook-based learning, have been criticized for failing to fully engage students or address the diverse needs of learners (de Jong et al., 2023). Gamification offers a solution to this problem by introducing active learning strategies that encourage students to take ownership of their learning, set goals, and track their progress. Using game-like elements, such as rewards and challenges, gamification taps into students' intrinsic motivations, making learning more enjoyable and rewarding. This approach has proven particularly effective in fostering a sense of achievement and motivation, which in turn leads to better retention of knowledge and improved academic performance.

The psychological principles behind gamification play a critical role in its effectiveness as an educational strategy (Sailer et. al., 2017). Key psychological concepts such as motivation, rewards, and competition are central to the design of gamified learning experiences and have a profound impact on how students engage with content and approach learning tasks. Understanding these principles is essential for educators seeking to implement gamification effectively and maximize its potential benefits.

Motivation is one of the most fundamental psychological drivers behind gamification (Aguiar-Castillo et al., 2022; Bennani et al., 2022). In the context of education, motivation refers to the internal drive that propels students to engage with learning activities and persist in the face of challenges. Gamification taps into both intrinsic and extrinsic motivation (Aguiar-Castillo et al., 2022), creating an environment where students are motivated by both internal desires (such as the satisfaction of mastering a new skill) and external rewards (such as points, badges, and recognition). Intrinsic motivation is often associated with a deep sense of personal satisfaction and enjoyment, while extrinsic motivation is typically driven by external rewards or recognition. Gamification effectively blends these two types of motivation, providing students with the external incentives they need to stay engaged while also fostering a sense of accomplishment and pride in their learning achievements.

The concept of rewards is another psychological principle that plays a central role in gamification (Sailer et. al., 2017; Smiderle et al., 2020). In a gamified learning environment, students are often rewarded for completing tasks, achieving milestones, or demonstrating mastery of content. These rewards can take many forms, such as points, badges, certificates, or virtual currency, and are designed to reinforce positive behaviors and encourage continued effort. The use of rewards helps to create a sense of progress and achievement, which can be highly motivating for students. Research has shown that the use of rewards in educational settings can increase students' and persistence, as they feel a sense of accomplishment and recognition for their efforts (Bardach & Murayama, 2025).

Competition is also a key psychological principle that is often incorporated into gamified learning environments. By introducing elements of competition, such as leaderboards or timed challenges, gamification taps into students' desire to outperform their peers and achieve recognition for their accomplishments. Competition can be a powerful motivator, as it encourages students to push themselves to achieve higher levels of performance and strive for excellence (Sailer et. al., 2017). However, it is important for educators to carefully manage competition in a way that promotes healthy rivalry and does not lead to feelings of inadequacy or frustration among students who may struggle to keep up. When used appropriately, competition can foster a sense of camaraderie and encourage students to support one another as they work toward common goals.

Gamification strategies in the classroom can take many different forms, depending on the goals of the educator and the specific needs of the students. Some of the most common gamification strategies include point systems, badges, leaderboards, and game-based learning platforms. Each of these strategies is designed to enhance student engagement, motivation, and learning outcomes in different ways (Zeng et al., 2024).

Point systems are one of the most basic and widely used gamification strategies in education. In a point-based system, students earn points for completing tasks, participating in class activities, or demonstrating mastery of content (Smiderle et al., 2020). These points can be accumulated over time and used to unlock rewards, such as badges, certificates, or other incentives. Point systems provide students with immediate feedback on their progress, helping them to track their achievements and stay motivated. By offering tangible rewards for effort and accomplishment, point systems create a sense of accomplishment and reinforce positive behaviors.

Badges are another popular gamification strategy that can be used to recognize and reward students' achievements (Smiderle et al., 2020). Badges are typically awarded for completing specific tasks or reaching certain milestones, such as mastering a particular skill or achieving a high score on an assessment. These digital or physical tokens serve as symbols of accomplishment and can be displayed as part of a student's profile or portfolio. Badges can be highly motivating, as they provide students with a visible reminder of their progress and achievements. In some cases, badges can also be used to unlock new challenges or levels, creating a sense of progression and encouraging students to continue striving for excellence.

Leaderboards are a gamification strategy that introduces an element of competition into the learning process. By displaying students' rankings based on their performance, leaderboards create a sense of competition and motivate students to perform at their best (Park & Kim, 2021). Leaderboards can be particularly effective in fostering a sense of achievement and recognition, as students can see how they compare to their peers and work toward improving their ranking. However, it is important for educators to use leaderboards carefully, as they can sometimes create feelings of frustration or inadequacy among students who are not performing as well as their peers. To mitigate this, some educators use leaderboards in a way that highlights individual progress and personal improvement, rather than just comparing students to one another.

Game-based learning platforms are another increasingly popular gamification strategy in educational settings (Adipat et. al., 2021). These platforms typically involve the use of video games or simulations that are designed to teach specific skills or concepts. Game-based learning platforms often incorporate elements such as points, badges, levels, and challenges, creating an immersive and interactive learning experience. These platforms can be particularly effective in engaging students, as they provide a fun and engaging way to learn while also offering immediate feedback and rewards. Game-based learning can be used to teach a wide range of subjects, from math and science to language arts and history, and can be tailored to meet the needs of individual students (Adipat et. al., 2021).

In conclusion, gamification has become an increasingly popular and effective strategy for enhancing student engagement, motivation, and learning outcomes in educational settings (Aguiar-Castillo, 2024; Lidia et al., 2022; Zeng et al., 2024). By incorporating game-like elements such as points, badges, leaderboards, and game-based learning platforms, educators can create dynamic and interactive learning environments that encourage active participation and foster a sense of achievement. The psychological principles behind gamification, such as motivation, rewards, and competition, play a crucial role in its effectiveness, providing students with the incentives and recognition they need to stay engaged and motivated. With the right strategies and careful implementation, gamification has the potential to transform education by making learning more engaging, personalized, and enjoyable for students of all ages.

THE ROLE OF AI IN ENHANCING GAMIFICATION

The integration of artificial intelligence (AI) with gamification in education holds significant potential to revolutionize the learning experience by offering personalized, adaptive, and dynamic educational environments. One of the key strengths of AI in gamified learning is its ability to tailor experiences to individual students based on their progress, strengths, and weaknesses. This personalized approach ensures that each learner receives the appropriate level of challenge and support, enhancing their engagement, motivation, and overall learning outcomes (Zeng et al., 2024). By adapting to the unique needs of each student, AI can create a more inclusive and effective learning environment that promotes mastery and fosters deeper understanding.

Personalized gamified learning experiences are a powerful way to meet the diverse needs of students. Traditional one-size-fits-all educational approaches often fail to account for the varying levels of knowledge, skills, and learning preferences among students (Gunawardena et al, 2024). However, AI can overcome this limitation by continuously analyzing data on student performance and adjusting the learning experience accordingly. For instance, AI-driven systems can track a student's progress through a game or learning module, identifying areas where they excel and areas where they struggle. Based on this analysis, the system can modify the content, difficulty level, or pace of the game to ensure that the student remains appropriately challenged without feeling overwhelmed. This personalized feedback loop helps students stay engaged and motivated by providing them with tasks that are neither too easy nor too difficult, fostering a sense of achievement as they progress through the learning experience.

One of the primary ways AI personalizes gamified learning experiences is by adapting to individual student progress. AI algorithms can monitor how students interact with the game, what challenges they complete, and how they perform on assessments or tasks. By continuously collecting and analyzing this data, AI systems can create a dynamic learning environment that evolves based on the student's unique learning journey. For example, if a student struggles with a particular concept or task, the AI system can present additional resources, tutorials, or practice exercises to help the student master that concept before moving on to more advanced material. Conversely, if a student demonstrates proficiency in a certain area, the AI system can increase the difficulty level, offering more complex challenges to keep the student engaged and motivated.

In addition to adapting to progress, AI also personalizes gamified learning experiences by taking into account individual students' strengths and weaknesses. Every student has a unique set of skills and abilities, and AI can help tailor the learning experience to leverage these strengths while addressing areas of weakness. For example, AI systems can analyze a student's performance on various tasks and identify patterns in their strengths and weaknesses. If a student consistently excels in one area, the system can offer more advanced challenges in that area to deepen their knowledge and skills. On the other hand, if a student struggles with a particular concept or skill, the system can provide targeted support, such as remedial exercises or hints, to help the student overcome their difficulties. This individualized approach ensures that each student receives the appropriate level of challenge and support, promoting more effective learning and a greater sense of accomplishment.

AI-driven algorithms play a crucial role in creating dynamic and adaptive game scenarios that respond to students' performance in real-time. These algorithms are designed to analyze data on student behavior and performance, allowing them to adjust the game experience based on the learner's progress. For example, if a student is struggling with a particular task or concept, the AI system can automatically adjust the difficulty level, providing easier tasks or additional hints to support the student's learning. Conversely, if a student is excelling and progressing quickly, the AI system can increase the difficulty level, offering more complex challenges to maintain the student's engagement and motivation (Zeng et al., 2024). This dynamic adaptation ensures that students are always working at the optimal level of difficulty, neither feeling bored by tasks that are too easy nor frustrated by tasks that are too difficult.

Real-time feedback is another key feature of AI-powered gamification that enhances the learning experience. In traditional educational settings, feedback is often delayed, with students receiving comments or grades on assignments long after they have completed the task. In contrast, AI-driven gamification platforms provide immediate feedback, allowing students to understand their performance in real-time and make adjustments accordingly. For example, if a student makes an error in a game-based learning scenario, the AI system can immediately provide corrective feedback, explaining what went wrong and offering suggestions for improvement. This instant feedback helps students learn from their mistakes and make progress more quickly, as they are able to apply the feedback right away and continue moving forward in the game.

The ability to adjust difficulty levels and provide real-time feedback based on learner performance is a hallmark of AI-powered gamification. These adaptive features not only enhance the learning experience but also contribute to improved student engagement and motivation. By ensuring that students are consistently challenged at the appropriate level, AI systems help maintain a sense of accomplishment and progress, which in turn fosters greater intrinsic motivation to continue learning (Chen & Chang, 2024). Furthermore, the instant feedback provided by AI systems enables students to quickly identify areas where they need to improve, allowing them to take ownership of their learning and make adjustments as needed.

Several AI-powered gamification platforms and tools have been developed and implemented in educational settings, demonstrating the potential impact of this approach on student engagement and learning outcomes (Zeng et al., 2024). These platforms use AI algorithms to create personalized, adaptive learning experiences that cater to the individual needs of students. Case studies of these platforms provide valuable insights into how AI and gamification can work together to enhance education.

One example of an AI-powered gamification platform is Duolingo, a popular language-learning app that uses gamification elements such as points, levels, and challenges to engage students (Adipat et. al., 2021). Duolingo employs AI algorithms to personalize the learning experience for each user, adapting the difficulty level of lessons based on the learner's progress and performance. The app tracks user performance in real-time, offering immediate feedback on errors and adjusting the content to suit the learner's strengths and weaknesses. Duolingo's use of AI and gamification has been shown to significantly improve student engagement and retention, as users are motivated by the game's rewards and progress tracking features. The platform's success highlights the potential of AI-powered gamification to create personalized, engaging learning experiences that cater to the individual needs of students.

Another example is Classcraft, a gamified learning platform that incorporates AI-driven features to enhance student engagement and motivation. Classcraft allows educators to create custom game scenarios where students can earn points, badges, and rewards for completing tasks, participating in class activities, and demonstrating positive behaviors. The platform uses AI algorithms to track student progress and adjust the difficulty level of challenges based on individual performance. For example, if a student is struggling with a particular subject, the AI system can provide additional resources or modify the game to offer more support. Classcraft also allows students to collaborate with their peers in a team-based environment, fostering a sense of community and encouraging cooperative learning. Case studies of schools using Classcraft have shown that the platform increases student engagement, improves behavior, and enhances academic performance (Parody et al., 2022).

Kahoot! is another widely used AI-powered gamification tool that allows educators to create quizzes, polls, and games that can be used in the classroom. The platform uses AI algorithms to analyze student performance and provide real-time feedback, helping students identify areas for improvement and track their progress. Kahoot! gamifies learning by offering points and rewards for correct answers, creating a competitive yet fun environment that motivates students to participate actively. The platform also allows for customization, enabling educators to tailor quizzes and games to the specific needs of their students. Research has shown that Kahoot! can increase student engagement, improve retention, and promote collaborative learning, making it an effective tool for enhancing classroom experiences (Husin & Azmuddin, 2022).

In conclusion, the integration of AI with gamification offers significant potential for personalizing learning experiences and improving student engagement, motivation, and learning outcomes. By adapting to individual progress, strengths, and weaknesses, AI-driven systems create dynamic and personalized game scenarios that provide real-time feedback and adjust difficulty levels based on learner performance. Case studies of AI-powered gamification platforms such as Duolingo, Classcraft, and Kahoot! demonstrate the positive impact of this approach on student engagement and academic success. As AI technology continues to evolve, its role in gamification will only become more central to creating adaptive, personalized, and effective learning environments.

BENEFITS OF AI AND GAMIFICATION INTEGRATION

The integration of artificial intelligence (AI) and gamification in education is a promising development, offering new ways to engage students, increase motivation, and personalize learning experiences. By incorporating game-like elements into educational environments, AI-powered gamification has the potential to transform traditional classrooms into interactive, dynamic spaces that promote deeper learning and enhance student outcomes. One of the most compelling aspects of AI-driven gamification is its ability to increase student motivation and engagement through immersive, interactive learning experiences (Zeng et al., 2024). Game-based learning environments have been shown to captivate students' attention, make learning enjoyable, and encourage them to take an active role in their education.

In traditional educational settings, students often struggle to remain engaged with content that may feel disconnected from their interests or real-world applications. Standardized teaching methods and assessments can fail to account for students' varying learning styles, preferences, and levels of motivation. In contrast, gamified learning environments leverage the power of AI to create interactive, immersive experiences that resonate with students on a personal level. By incorporating elements such as points, badges, leaderboards, and rewards, gamified systems can transform the learning process into an engaging and motivating experience. These game-based elements provide students with immediate, tangible feedback that reinforces positive behaviors, encourages persistence, and makes learning feel like an enjoyable challenge.

One of the primary reasons why AI-powered gamification increases student motivation is its ability to create a sense of accomplishment and progression. In traditional classrooms, students may feel disconnected from the learning process, especially when they are not receiving immediate feedback on their performance. With gamified learning environments, students can see their progress in real-time, earning points or badges as they complete tasks and overcome challenges. This sense of progression helps students stay motivated by providing them with clear goals and rewards for their efforts. Furthermore, the use of leaderboards and competitive elements can foster a healthy sense of competition, encouraging students to push themselves further to achieve success. However, it is important to ensure that the competition remains supportive and inclusive, so that all students feel motivated to participate and succeed.

Beyond providing a sense of accomplishment, AI-driven gamification also offers personalized learning experiences that cater to diverse learning styles, paces, and preferences. Traditional educational methods often adopt a one-size-fits-all approach, which can leave students feeling either overwhelmed or disengaged, depending on their individual needs. However, AI-powered gamification systems can adapt to each student's unique learning journey, providing a tailored experience that meets their specific needs. By continuously analyzing data on student performance, AI algorithms can adjust the difficulty level, pace, and content of the game to match the learner's abilities. For example, if a student excels in a particular subject, the AI system can increase the difficulty level to provide more advanced challenges. Conversely, if a student is struggling, the system can provide additional support, such as hints, tutorials, or remedial exercises, to help them master the material before moving on to more complex concepts.

This level of personalization ensures that each student receives the appropriate amount of challenge and support, which can significantly improve their motivation and engagement. For example, a student who excels in mathematics but struggles with reading comprehension may find a math-focused game engaging and motivating, while a student with a different set of strengths may benefit from a game that emphasizes reading skills. By adapting to the learner's strengths and weaknesses, AI-powered gamification systems can create a more inclusive and personalized learning environment, helping students progress at their own pace and build confidence in their abilities.

The ability to cater to diverse learning styles and preferences is another key advantage of AI-powered gamification. Every student has a unique way of learning, whether they prefer visual, auditory, or kinesthetic learning styles. Traditional educational methods may not always accommodate these differences, but AI-driven gamification can offer multiple ways for students to engage with content. For example, a game-based learning platform might include visual elements such as graphics and animations, auditory elements such as narration or sound effects, and interactive elements that allow students to manipulate objects or solve problems through hands-on activities. By offering a variety of learning modalities, AI-powered gamification can appeal to a broader range of students and ensure that each learner has the opportunity to engage with the material in a way that suits their individual preferences.

Moreover, AI can provide instant feedback, a critical component of effective learning (Adipat et. al., 2021). In traditional educational settings, feedback is often delayed, with students receiving grades or comments on assignments long after they have completed the task. This delay can make it difficult for students to understand where they went wrong and how to improve. In contrast, AI-powered gamification platforms offer real-time feedback, allowing students to see the results of their actions immediately. For example, if a student makes an error in a game, the AI system can provide corrective feedback right away, explaining what went wrong and offering suggestions for improvement. This instant feedback helps students learn from their mistakes and make adjustments before they move on to the next task. The ability to receive immediate feedback not only accelerates the learning process but also fosters a growth mindset, as students are encouraged to view mistakes as opportunities for learning and improvement (Adipat et. al., 2021).

The concept of a growth mindset, popularized by psychologist Carol Dweck, emphasizes the importance of viewing challenges and setbacks as opportunities for growth rather than as indicators of failure (Limeri et al., 2020). AI-powered gamification systems support this mindset by providing continuous, real-time feedback that encourages students to keep trying, even when they encounter difficulties. Rather than being discouraged by failure, students can use the feedback to adjust their strategies, try new approaches, and ultimately improve their performance. This process of iterative learning, where students are given the chance to fail, reflect, and improve, is essential for developing resilience and perseverance. By offering instant feedback and opportunities for growth, AI-driven gamification helps students build a positive attitude toward learning and develop the skills they need to succeed in both academic and real-world contexts.

In addition to fostering a growth mindset, AI-powered gamification also enables students to track their progress and monitor their development over time (Adipat et. al., 2021). In traditional educational settings, students often receive feedback only at the end of an assignment or test, which can make it difficult for them to track their progress and identify areas for improvement. With AI-driven gamification, students can continuously monitor their performance, seeing how their skills evolve as they complete tasks, earn points, and unlock new levels. This ongoing feedback loop encourages students to take ownership of their learning, as they are able to see the direct impact of their efforts on their progress. Moreover, the ability to track progress over time helps students set goals, stay motivated, and celebrate their achievements.

For example, a student using an AI-powered math game might receive immediate feedback after each problem they solve, with their progress displayed on a visual progress bar. As the student completes more tasks and earns points, the progress bar fills up, providing a tangible representation of their success. This visual feedback not only reinforces the student's sense of accomplishment but also motivates them to continue progressing through the game. The ability to track progress in this way encourages students to set goals, strive for improvement, and take an active role in their learning journey.

AI-powered gamification platforms also allow for greater flexibility in how students approach learning (Adipat et. al., 2021). In traditional classrooms, students are often required to follow a set schedule or curriculum, with little room for individual exploration or self-paced learning. However, AI-driven gamification allows students to progress at their own pace, choosing when and how to engage with the material. For example, a student who masters a particular concept quickly can move on to more advanced topics, while a student who needs more time can revisit previous levels or receive additional support. This flexibility ensures that all students can learn at their own pace, without feeling rushed or left behind.

In conclusion, AI-powered gamification offers numerous benefits for students, including increased motivation, personalized learning experiences, and real-time feedback that fosters a growth mindset. By creating interactive, game-based learning environments, AI can engage students in ways that traditional methods cannot, making learning more enjoyable and meaningful. The ability to personalize learning experiences based on individual progress, strengths, and preferences ensures that all students receive the appropriate level of challenge and support. Moreover, instant feedback and the ability to track progress over time help students build confidence, improve their skills, and take ownership of their learning journey. As AI technology continues to evolve, its integration with gamification has the potential to revolutionize education, creating more engaging, effective, and inclusive learning environments for all students.

CHALLENGES AND CONSIDERATIONS

The integration of artificial intelligence (AI) and gamification into educational settings has the potential to revolutionize teaching and learning by creating more personalized, engaging, and effective experiences for students. However, as with any technological advancement, there are significant ethical concerns and challenges that must be addressed in order to ensure that AI and gamification are used responsibly and equitably (Department of Education, 2023). These concerns include issues related to data privacy, algorithmic bias, the over-reliance on technology, and the challenges of integrating AI into existing educational systems. In this section, we will explore these ethical issues and challenges in detail, considering their implications for educators, students, and policymakers.

One of the most pressing ethical concerns surrounding the use of AI in education is data privacy. AI systems rely on vast amounts of data to function effectively, including data about students' performance, behavior, learning preferences, and even personal information. This data is often collected through various educational technologies, such as learning management systems, gamified platforms, and adaptive learning tools. While the use of data can enhance the personalization of learning experiences, it also raises significant concerns about how this data is collected, stored, and used. Students' personal information, such as their academic performance, attendance records, and even behavioral data, can be sensitive and vulnerable to misuse or unauthorized access.

In order to protect students' privacy, it is crucial that educational institutions and technology providers implement strict data protection measures. This includes ensuring that data is collected with explicit consent, stored securely, and only used for the purposes for which it was intended. Additionally, educational institutions must be transparent about their data collection practices, informing students and parents about what data is being collected, how it will be used, and who will have access to it. Data privacy laws, such as the Family Educational Rights and Privacy Act (FERPA) in the United States and the General Data Protection Regulation (GDPR) in Europe, provide important legal frameworks for safeguarding student data. However, the rapid pace of technological development means that new privacy concerns are constantly emerging, and it is essential for policymakers to stay ahead of these challenges in order to protect students' rights and ensure that their data is handled responsibly.

Another significant ethical concern is algorithmic bias (U.S. Department of Education, 2023). AI systems are only as unbiased as the data they are trained on, and if the data used to train an AI system is biased, the system itself may perpetuate or even exacerbate these biases. In the context of education, this could mean that AI-powered gamification platforms or adaptive learning tools may inadvertently favor certain groups of students over others, leading to unfair outcomes. For example, if an AI system is trained on data that reflects historical inequalities in educational access or achievement, it may reinforce these disparities by providing different levels of support or feedback to students based on their demographic characteristics. This could lead to situations where certain groups of students, such as those from marginalized communities, are unfairly disadvantaged by AI-driven educational tools.

To mitigate the risk of algorithmic bias, it is essential that AI systems are designed and tested with fairness in mind. This includes using diverse, representative datasets to train AI models and regularly auditing these systems to identify and address any biases that may emerge (Nazer et al., 2023). Additionally, educators and policymakers must be vigilant in ensuring that AI-powered tools are used in ways that promote equity and inclusivity. For example, AI-driven gamification systems should be designed to accommodate students' diverse learning needs and abilities, ensuring that all students have an equal opportunity to succeed. It is also important to involve diverse stakeholders, including educators, students, and community members, in the development and implementation of AI systems to ensure that these tools reflect a broad range of perspectives and experiences.

While AI and gamification offer many benefits, there is also the potential for over-reliance on technology in education. As AI-powered tools become more prevalent, there is a risk that educators and students may become overly dependent on these technologies, leading to a diminished role for traditional teaching methods (Zhai et al., 2024). For example, if educators rely too heavily on AI-driven platforms to assess student performance or provide personalized learning experiences, they may lose sight of the importance of human interaction, creativity, and critical thinking in the classroom. Similarly, students may become too focused on the game-like aspects of learning, such as earning points or badges, rather than engaging with the content in a meaningful way.

To avoid over-reliance on technology, it is essential that AI and gamification are used as complementary tools rather than replacements for traditional teaching methods. Educators should strive to maintain a balance between digital and traditional approaches, incorporating AI-powered tools where appropriate but also ensuring that students have opportunities for face-to-face interaction, collaborative learning, and hands-on experiences. For example, AI-driven platforms can be used to provide personalized feedback or adaptive learning paths, but teachers should still play an active role in facilitating discussions, guiding students through complex concepts, and fostering critical thinking. By maintaining a balance between digital and traditional methods, educators can ensure that AI and gamification enhance, rather than replace, the human elements of teaching and learning.

In addition to concerns about over-reliance on technology, there are also significant challenges associated with integrating AI and gamification into existing educational systems. One of the primary challenges is the need for teacher training (Gómez Niño et al, 2024). While many educators are familiar with traditional teaching methods, they may not have the skills or knowledge to effectively integrate AI-powered tools into their classrooms. AI and gamification require educators to adopt new pedagogical approaches, such as personalized learning, data-driven decision-making, and the use of game mechanics to motivate and engage students. This can be a significant shift for educators who are used to more traditional methods of instruction.

To address this challenge, it is essential that educators receive comprehensive training and support in the use of AI and gamification (Gómez Niño et al, 2024). This training should cover not only the technical aspects of using AI-powered tools but also the pedagogical principles behind these technologies. Educators should be equipped with the knowledge and skills to design effective, engaging learning experiences that leverage the full potential of AI and gamification. Additionally, ongoing professional development opportunities should be provided to help educators stay up-to-date with the latest developments in AI and gamification and to ensure that they are able to adapt to new technologies as they emerge.

Another challenge in integrating AI and gamification into educational systems is the need for infrastructure support. AI-powered tools and gamified platforms often require significant technological resources, including high-speed internet access, powerful computers, and specialized software. In many educational settings, particularly in low-income or rural areas, these resources may not be readily available. This digital divide can create inequities in access to AI-powered learning tools, leaving some students at a disadvantage (Vesna et al., 2025). To ensure that all students have equal access to the benefits of AI and gamification, it is essential that schools and educational institutions invest in the necessary infrastructure and resources. This may include upgrading technology, providing training for educators, and ensuring that all students have access to devices and internet connectivity.

Furthermore, the integration of AI and gamification into existing educational systems requires careful consideration of curriculum design and assessment practices. Traditional curriculum frameworks and assessment methods may not be well-suited to the dynamic, personalized nature of AI-powered gamification. As a result, educators may need to redesign curricula to incorporate more flexible, student-centered approaches that align with the capabilities of AI and gamification. This may involve rethinking how learning objectives are defined, how progress is measured, and how assessments are conducted. For example, AI-driven platforms may require new forms of assessment, such as continuous, real-time feedback or performance-based evaluations, rather than traditional tests or exams. To successfully integrate AI and gamification, educators must be prepared to adapt their teaching strategies and assessment methods to meet the needs of the new learning environment.

In conclusion, while AI and gamification offer exciting opportunities for enhancing education, they also raise significant ethical concerns and challenges that must be addressed in order to ensure their responsible and equitable use (U.S. Department of Education, 2023). These concerns include issues related to data privacy, algorithmic bias, over-reliance on technology, and the challenges of integrating AI into existing educational systems. To address these challenges, it is essential that educators, policymakers, and technology developers work together to create a framework for the ethical and effective use of AI and gamification in education. This includes implementing strong data protection measures, addressing algorithmic bias, maintaining a balance between digital and traditional teaching methods, providing adequate teacher training, and ensuring equitable access to technology. By addressing these issues, we can ensure that AI and gamification are used in ways that benefit all students and enhance the learning experience.

FUTURE DIRECTIONS FOR AI AND GAMIFICATION IN EDUCATION:

The future of artificial intelligence (AI) and gamification in education holds immense potential for transforming the way students learn, interact with content, and engage with their educators. As these technologies continue to evolve, we can expect more immersive, personalized, and interactive learning experiences that cater to the needs and preferences of individual learners. In this section, we will explore predictions for the future of AI and gamification in education, including the development of more immersive and interactive learning environments through virtual reality (VR) and augmented reality (AR), the potential for AI-powered gamification to support lifelong learning and professional growth, and how emerging technologies such as AI, blockchain, and virtual environments could further enhance gamified learning experiences.

One of the most exciting possibilities for the future of AI and gamification in education is the development of more immersive and interactive learning experiences through virtual reality (VR) and augmented reality (AR) (Lampropoulos & Kinshuk, 2024; Strielkowski et al., 2025). These technologies have the potential to create dynamic, engaging environments that allow students to interact with content in ways that were previously unimaginable. VR, for example, can immerse students in fully interactive, 3D environments that simulate real-world scenarios, allowing them to explore historical events, conduct scientific experiments, or engage in complex problem-solving tasks. AR, on the other hand, overlays digital content onto the physical world, enabling students to interact with virtual objects and information in real time.

When combined with AI and gamification, VR and AR have the potential to create deeply personalized learning experiences that adapt to students' individual needs, preferences, and learning styles (Lampropoulos & Kinshuk, 2024). AI algorithms can track students' progress, monitor their interactions within the virtual or augmented environment, and provide real-time feedback and guidance. For example, in a VR-based history lesson, an AI-powered system could adjust the difficulty of the tasks based on the student's performance, providing more challenging scenarios as they progress or offering additional support if they struggle with certain concepts. Gamification elements, such as point systems, badges, and leaderboards, can further enhance the experience by motivating students to complete tasks and achieve specific learning goals. By integrating AI, gamification, VR, and AR, educators can create highly engaging, interactive, and immersive learning environments that promote deeper learning and retention (Lampropoulos & Kinshuk, 2024).

In addition to enhancing traditional classroom learning, AI-powered gamification has the potential to support lifelong learning, skill development, and professional growth. As the world of work continues to evolve, individuals will need to constantly update their skills and knowledge in order to remain competitive in the job market. AI and gamification can play a key role in facilitating this ongoing learning process by providing personalized, adaptive learning experiences that cater to the unique needs of adult learners. For example, AI-powered platforms could assess an individual's current skill set, identify areas for improvement, and recommend personalized learning pathways that help them develop the skills they need to advance in their careers. Gamification elements, such as earning badges or completing challenges, can keep learners motivated and engaged as they work through these personalized learning paths.

One of the key advantages of AI-powered gamification in lifelong learning is its ability to provide real-time feedback and adjust learning experiences based on individual progress. For example, a professional learning platform could use AI to analyze a learner's performance on various tasks and provide instant feedback, such as suggestions for improvement or additional resources to explore. This feedback loop helps learners understand where they are excelling and where they need to focus more attention, enabling them to progress at their own pace. Gamification elements, such as unlocking new levels or achievements as learners complete tasks, can further enhance this process by providing tangible rewards for their efforts.

Moreover, AI-powered gamification can help individuals develop soft skills, such as communication, collaboration, and problem-solving, which are increasingly important in today's workforce (Adipat et. al., 2021). By simulating real-world scenarios and providing opportunities for learners to engage in role-playing or collaborative activities, gamified platforms can foster the development of these essential skills in a safe and supportive environment. For example, a gamified platform for leadership training might allow learners to take on different leadership roles in simulated business scenarios, where they can practice decision-making, conflict resolution, and team management. By combining AI, gamification, and immersive simulations, these platforms can create highly effective learning experiences that help individuals acquire the skills they need for professional growth and career advancement.

Looking further ahead, emerging technologies such as AI, blockchain, and virtual environments have the potential to further enhance gamified learning experiences and revolutionize the educational landscape. Blockchain technology, for example, could play a crucial role in creating secure, transparent systems for tracking and verifying students' achievements in gamified learning environments (Aini et al., 2020). By using blockchain to record and store achievements, certifications, and other credentials, educational institutions could create verifiable digital portfolios that students can use to showcase their skills and accomplishments to potential employers. This could help address some of the challenges associated with traditional credentialing systems, such as the lack of transparency and the potential for fraud. Blockchain could also be used to facilitate micro-credentialing, where students earn small, incremental badges or certifications for completing specific tasks or mastering particular skills. This would allow learners to demonstrate their expertise in a variety of areas, rather than relying on a single, overarching degree or certification.

Virtual environments, powered by AI and gamification, could also play a significant role in the future of education by creating fully immersive, interactive learning spaces that allow students to engage with content in entirely new ways. These environments could simulate real-world scenarios, such as business negotiations, scientific research, or medical procedures, providing students with hands-on experience in a controlled, virtual setting. For example, medical students could practice performing surgeries in a virtual operating room, or engineering students could test prototypes in a simulated lab environment. These immersive virtual environments, combined with AI and gamification, could provide students with the opportunity to learn through experience, trial and error, and real-time feedback, which has been shown to enhance learning outcomes and retention.

In addition to enhancing traditional educational settings, virtual environments could also enable new forms of collaborative, global learning experiences. Students from different parts of the world could come together in virtual spaces to collaborate on projects, engage in discussions, and solve problems in real time. These virtual environments could foster cross-cultural communication, teamwork, and problem-solving, helping students develop the skills needed to succeed in an increasingly interconnected and globalized world. By integrating AI, gamification, and virtual environments, educators could create highly engaging, interactive, and personalized learning experiences that promote both individual and collaborative learning (Adipat et. al., 2021).

As AI, blockchain, and virtual environments continue to evolve, they will likely become increasingly integrated into educational systems, providing new opportunities for students, educators, and institutions. These technologies have the potential to create more personalized, immersive, and interactive learning experiences that cater to the diverse needs and preferences of learners. By combining AI-powered gamification with emerging technologies such as VR, AR, blockchain, and virtual environments, educators can create dynamic, engaging learning experiences that promote deeper learning, skill development, and professional growth.

In conclusion, the future of AI and gamification in education is bright, with the potential to revolutionize the way we learn, teach, and interact with content. The development of more immersive and interactive learning environments, supported by AI, VR, AR, and blockchain, will create opportunities for personalized learning experiences that cater to the unique needs of individual learners. AI-powered gamification can support lifelong learning, skill development, and professional growth, helping individuals stay competitive in the job market. As emerging technologies continue to evolve, the possibilities for enhancing gamified learning experiences will only expand, offering exciting new opportunities for students and educators alike. By embracing these technologies and integrating them into educational systems, we can create a more engaging, effective, and equitable learning environment for all learners.

CONCLUSION

In conclusion, the transformative potential of AI and gamification in reshaping the educational landscape is vast and multifaceted. These two powerful tools, when integrated thoughtfully, can redefine how students engage with learning, how educators teach, and how educational systems assess and support progress. Gamification, with its inherent ability to boost motivation, foster engagement, and introduce an element of fun, has long been recognized for its positive impact on student learning (Zeng et al., 2024). By adding AI to the mix, educators can take gamification to new heights, creating learning experiences that are not only engaging but also personalized and adaptive. AI's ability to analyze student performance in real-time and adjust the learning path accordingly can ensure that each student is receiving the appropriate level of challenge and support, thus fostering a deeper understanding of the content and promoting long-term retention.

The combination of gamification and AI has the potential to create learning environments that are both enjoyable and effective (Zeng et al., 2024). Through AI-driven gamified platforms, students can receive instant feedback on their progress, allowing them to track their achievements and areas for improvement. This continuous feedback loop helps students stay motivated and invested in their learning journey, as they can see the tangible results of their efforts. Furthermore, the personalized nature of AI means that learning experiences can be tailored to individual students' strengths, weaknesses, and preferences, creating a more inclusive environment that accommodates diverse learning styles. This personalized approach not only helps students learn at their own pace but also ensures that they are consistently challenged and supported, preventing frustration and disengagement.

However, as promising as the integration of AI and gamification in education is, it is essential to approach their implementation with careful consideration of the challenges and ethical implications involved. One of the key concerns is the potential for algorithmic bias, where AI systems may inadvertently favor certain groups of students over others, perpetuating existing inequalities (U.S. Department of Education, 2023). It is crucial that AI algorithms are developed and tested with fairness in mind, ensuring that all students, regardless of background or ability, have equal access to the benefits of these technologies. Additionally, the issue of data privacy is a significant concern, as the use of AI in education often involves the collection of vast amounts of student data. Protecting this data from misuse or unauthorized access is paramount to maintaining trust in these technologies and ensuring that students' rights are upheld.

Another challenge to consider is the potential for over-reliance on technology. While AI and gamification offer exciting possibilities, they should not replace the human element of teaching. Teachers play an irreplaceable role in guiding students, providing emotional support, and fostering a sense of community in the classroom. AI should be seen as a tool to enhance teaching, not as a substitute for the invaluable interpersonal connections that educators build with their students. Furthermore, it is essential to strike a balance between digital and traditional teaching methods. While technology can provide personalized, adaptive learning experiences, traditional methods such as face-to-face instruction, collaborative group work, and hands-on activities remain crucial components of a well-rounded education.

The integration of AI and gamification into existing educational systems also presents several practical challenges. For instance, many educators may lack the necessary training and support to effectively implement these technologies in their classrooms. Professional development programs that focus on AI, gamification, and other emerging educational technologies are essential to ensure that teachers are equipped with the skills and knowledge needed to use these tools effectively. Additionally, schools and institutions must invest in the infrastructure required to support AI-powered gamified learning platforms, such as reliable internet access, sufficient hardware, and technical support.

Despite these challenges, the potential for AI and gamification to revolutionize education is undeniable. As these technologies continue to evolve, we can expect even more innovative and effective ways to engage students and support their learning. However, to fully realize the potential of AI and gamification in education, continued innovation and research are necessary. Educators, technologists, and policymakers must work together to address the challenges and ethical concerns associated with these technologies, ensuring that they are implemented responsibly and equitably. By doing so, we can create educational experiences that are not only more engaging and personalized but also more inclusive and accessible for all students.

In summary, the integration of AI and gamification in education offers a powerful combination that has the potential to transform learning experiences, making them more engaging, personalized, and effective (Gafni et al., 2018; Renacido & Biray, 2025). However, careful attention must be paid to the challenges and ethical considerations surrounding these technologies to ensure their responsible and equitable implementation. By continuing to innovate and research these tools, we can unlock their full potential, creating educational environments that foster deeper learning, greater motivation, and improved outcomes for all students. The future of education is exciting, and AI and gamification will undoubtedly play a central role in shaping it.

REFERENCES

Adipat, S., Laksana, K., Busayanon, K., Asawasowan, A., & Adipat, B. (2021). Engaging students in the learning process with game-based learning: The fundamental concepts. [IJTE]. *International Journal of Technology in Education, 4*(3), 542–552. DOI: 10.46328/ijte.169

Aguiar-Castillo, L., Arce-Santana, E., Guerra-Yanez, C., Guerra-Yanez, V., & Perez-Jimenez, R. (2022). Gamification: A motivation metric based in a markov model. [iJET]. *International Journal of Emerging Technologies in Learning, 17*(13), 17–34. DOI: 10.3991/ijet.v17i13.30781

Aini, Q., Rahardja, U., & Khoirunisa, A. (2020). Blockchain technology into gamification on education. [Indonesian Journal of Computing and Cybernetics Systems]. *IJCCS, 14*(2), 147–158. DOI: 10.22146/ijccs.53221

Ali, H., Pham, D.-T., Alam, S., Schultz, M., Li, M. Z., Wang, Y., Itoh, E., & Duong, V. N. (2025). Human-AI hybrids in safety-critical systems: Concept, definition and perspectives from air traffic management. *Advanced Engineering Informatics, 65*, 103256. DOI: 10.1016/j.aei.2025.103256

Babu, S., & Moorthy, D. (2024). Application of artificial intelligence in adaptation of gamification in education: A literature review. *Computer Applications in Engineering Education, 32*(1), e22683. DOI: 10.1002/cae.22683

Bardach, L., & Murayama, K. (2025). The role of rewards in motivation—Beyond dichotomies. *Learning and Instruction, 96*, 102056. DOI: 10.1016/j.learninstruc.2024.102056

Bennani, S., Maalel, A., & Ben Ghezala, H. (2022). Adaptive gamification in E-learning: A literature review and future challenges. *Computer Applications in Engineering Education, 30*(2), 628–642. DOI: 10.1002/cae.22477

Chen, C.-H., & Chang, C.-L. (2024). Effectiveness of AI-assisted game-based learning on science learning outcomes, intrinsic motivation, cognitive load, and learning behavior. *Education and Information Technologies, 29*(2), 18621–18642. DOI: 10.1007/s10639-024-12553-x

de Jong, T., Lazonder, A. W., Chinn, C. A., Fischer, F., Gobert, J., Hmelo-Silver, C. E., Koedinger, K. R., Krajcik, J. S., Kyza, E. A., Linn, M. C., Pedaste, M., Scheiter, K., & Zacharia, Z. C. (2023). Let's talk evidence – The case for combining inquiry-based and direct instruction. *Educational Research Review, 39*, 100536. DOI: 10.1016/j.edurev.2023.100536

Gafni, A., Biran Achituv, D., Eidelman, S., & Chatsky, T. (2018). The effects of gamification elements in e-learning platforms. [OJAKM]. *Online Journal of Applied Knowledge Management, 6*(2), 37–53. DOI: 10.36965/OJAKM.2018.6(2)37-53

Gómez Niño, J. R., Árias Delgado, L. P., Chiappe, A., & Ortega González, E. (2024). Gamifying Learning with AI: A Pathway to 21st-Century Skills. *Journal of Research in Childhood Education, •••*, 1–16. DOI: 10.1080/02568543.2024.2421974

Gouseti, A., James, F., Fallin, L., & Burden, K. (2024). The ethics of using AI in K-12 education: A systematic literature review. *Technology, Pedagogy and Education, 34*(2), 161–182. DOI: 10.1080/1475939X.2024.2428601

Gunawardena, M., Bishop, P., & Aviruppola, K. (2024). Personalized learning: The simple, the complicated, the complex and the chaotic. *Teaching and Teacher Education, 139*, 104429. DOI: 10.1016/j.tate.2023.104429

Husin, M. Z., & Azmuddin, R. A. (2022). Learner engagement in using Kahoot! within a university English proficiency course. *Educational Process: International Journal, 11*(2), 167–180.

Lampropoulos, G., & Kinshuk, . (2024). Virtual reality and gamification in education: A systematic review. *Educational Technology Research and Development, 72*(4), 1691–1785. DOI: 10.1007/s11423-024-10351-3

Limeri, L. B., Carter, N. T., Choe, J., Harper, H. E., Martin, H. R., Benton, H. P., & Dolan, E. L. (2020). Growing a growth mindset: Characterizing how and why undergraduate students' mindsets change. *International Journal of STEM Education, 7*(1), 35. DOI: 10.1186/s40594-020-00227-2

Nazer, L. H., Zatarah, R., Waldrip, S., Ke, J. X. C., Moukheiber, M., Khanna, A. K., Hicklen, R. S., Moukheiber, L., Moukheiber, D., Ma, H., & Mathur, P. (2023). Bias in artificial intelligence algorithms and recommendations for mitigation. *PLOS Digital Health, 2*(6), e0000278. DOI: 10.1371/journal.pdig.0000278 PMID: 37347721

Park, S., & Kim, S. (2021). Leaderboard design principles to enhance learning and motivation in a gamified educational environment: Development study. *JMIR Serious Games, 9*(2), e26557. DOI: 10.2196/14746 PMID: 33877049

Parody, L., Santos, J., Trujillo-Cayado, L. A., & Ceballos, M. (2022). Gamification in engineering education: The use of Classcraft platform to improve motivation and academic performance. *Applied Sciences (Basel, Switzerland), 12*(22), 11832. DOI: 10.3390/app122211832

Renacido, J. M. D., & Biray, E. T. (2025). Enhancing Peer Engagement and Student Motivation Through AI-Gamified Interactive Learning Tools. In Advancing Sustainable Development Goals With Educational Technology (pp. 277-342). IGI Global Scientific Publishing.

Sailer, M., Hense, J. U., Mayr, S. K., & Mandl, H. (2017). How gamification motivates: An experimental study of the effects of specific game design elements on psychological need satisfaction. *Computers in Human Behavior, 69*, 371–380. DOI: 10.1016/j.chb.2016.12.033

Smiderle, R., Rigo, S. J., Marques, L. B., Peçanha de Miranda Coelho, J. A., & Jaques, P. A. (2020). The impact of gamification on students' learning, engagement and behavior based on their personality traits. *Smart Learn. Environ., 7*(1), 3. DOI: 10.1186/s40561-019-0098-x

Song, C., Shin, S.-Y., & Shin, K.-S. (2024). Implementing the Dynamic Feedback-Driven Learning Optimization Framework: A Machine Learning Approach to Personalize Educational Pathways. *Applied Sciences (Basel, Switzerland)*, *14*(2), 916. DOI: 10.3390/app14020916

Strielkowski, W., Grebennikova, V., Lisovskiy, A., Rakhimova, G., & Vasileva, T. (2025). AI-driven adaptive learning for sustainable educational transformation. *Sustainable Development (Bradford)*, *33*(2), 1921–1947. DOI: 10.1002/sd.3221

U.S. Department of Education, Office of Educational Technology. (2023). *Artificial intelligence and the future of teaching and learning: Insights and recommendations*. U.S. Department of Education.

Vesna, L., Sawale, P. S., Kaul, P., Pal, S., & Murthy, B. S. N. V. R. (2025). Digital divide in AI-powered education: Challenges and solutions for equitable learning. *Journal of Information Systems Engineering & Management*, *10*(21s).

Zeng, J., Sun, D., Looi, C.-K., & Fan, A. C. W. (2024). Exploring the impact of gamification on students' academic performance: A comprehensive meta-analysis of studies from the year 2008 to 2023. *British Journal of Educational Technology*, *55*(6), 2478–2502. DOI: 10.1111/bjet.13471

Zhai, C., Wibowo, S., & Li, L. D. (2024). The effects of over-reliance on AI dialogue systems on students' cognitive abilities: A systematic review. *Smart Learning Environments*, *11*(1), Article 28.

Chapter 7
AI in Assessment from Standardized Testing to Dynamic Feedback

Dayna Lynn Mitchell
https://orcid.org/0009-0000-9385-7238
California State Polytechnic University, Pomona, USA

ABSTRACT

AI in Assessment From Standardized Testing to Dynamic Feedback explores the transformative role of artificial intelligence (AI) in educational assessment. It examines the limitations of traditional standardized testing, highlighting how AI can offer more personalized, real-time feedback tailored to individual learner needs. By leveraging AI's ability to analyze vast amounts of data, the chapter discusses how assessments can evolve from static, one-time evaluations to dynamic, continuous feedback loops that support ongoing learning and development. The proposal also delves into the ethical considerations, challenges, and potential implications for educators, students, and institutions as AI-driven assessments become more integrated into educational practices.

INTRODUCTION

In the evolving landscape of education, the use of artificial intelligence (AI) in assessment is emerging as a transformative force (Bahroun et al., 2023; Jain et al., 2025; Ruano-Borbalan, 2025). Traditional methods of educational evaluation, particularly standardized testing, have long been criticized for their rigidity and inability to reflect the diverse range of student abilities, learning styles, and socio-cultural backgrounds. Standardized tests often fail to provide a comprehensive picture of a student's learning journey, focusing instead on a narrow set of metrics that may not align with the complexities of real-world skills or the diverse ways in which students process and demonstrate knowledge (Au, 2022). These assessments, which typically offer a snapshot of a student's abilities at a single point in time, are limited in their

DOI: 10.4018/979-8-3373-5092-9.ch007

capacity to support long-term learning and growth. They also tend to reinforce existing inequities in the education system, as they often fail to accommodate students with varying learning needs, language backgrounds, or cognitive styles. In response to these limitations, AI-driven assessment tools are beginning to offer an alternative approach—one that is more personalized, adaptive, and capable of providing ongoing, real-time feedback to students (Du Boulay, 2023; Ejjami, 2024; Hrytsenko, 2024; Owan et al., 2023).

The purpose of this chapter is to explore how AI can revolutionize the field of educational assessment by shifting the focus from static, one-size-fits-all evaluations to dynamic, individualized feedback systems. AI has the potential to create a more equitable assessment environment by offering tools that adapt to the unique needs and abilities of each student. With AI, assessments no longer need to be confined to standardized formats that only measure a narrow set of competencies. Instead, AI can facilitate a more holistic view of student learning, providing insights into areas such as critical thinking, problem-solving, creativity, and social-emotional skills—dimensions of learning that are often overlooked by traditional testing methods (Eden et al., 2024). Using AI, assessments can become more aligned with real-world skills, offering a richer, more accurate reflection of a student's capabilities (Ejjami, 2024).

AI-driven assessments also have the potential to address some of the key challenges associated with traditional testing. For example, AI can provide real-time feedback, enabling students to understand their strengths and areas for improvement immediately after completing an assessment. This timely feedback is crucial for promoting learning, as it allows students to adjust their strategies and approaches while the material is still fresh in their minds. In contrast, traditional assessments often provide feedback weeks or months after the test, making it difficult for students to apply the feedback in a meaningful way. AI's ability to offer continuous, personalized feedback also allows educators to track student progress over time, identify trends in performance, and intervene early when students are struggling. This shift from reactive to proactive assessment represents a significant departure from the traditional model, which often waits until the end of a term or course to evaluate student performance.

The potential benefits of AI in assessment are numerous. One of the most compelling advantages is the ability to provide personalized learning experiences (Bowen & Watson, 2024; Hrytsenko, 2024; Owan et al., 2023). Traditional assessments typically treat all students as if they are the same, applying uniform standards to measure success. However, students are diverse in their learning needs, abilities, and backgrounds, and a one-size-fits-all approach to assessment fails to account for these differences (Bauml, 2016). AI can address this issue by tailoring assessments to individual students, adjusting the difficulty level based on their responses and providing customized feedback that speaks to their specific needs (Bowen, & Watson, 2024). This personalized approach not only helps to create a more equitable assessment environment but also promotes deeper learning by ensuring that students are continuously challenged at an appropriate level (Owan et al., 2023).

Furthermore, AI can help bridge the gap between formative and summative assessments. Formative assessments, which are conducted during the learning process, offer valuable opportunities for students to receive feedback and improve their understanding. However, traditional formative assessments often lack the depth and immediacy needed to support meaningful learning. Conversely, AI-driven formative assessments can provide continuous, real-time feedback, offering students the opportunity to engage in a cycle of learning, reflection, and improvement. This dynamic feedback loop can be particularly beneficial for students who may struggle with traditional testing formats, as it allows them to demonstrate their learning in a more flexible and supportive environment.

Despite the promising potential of AI in assessment, the integration of these technologies into educational systems is not without its challenges. One of the primary obstacles is the need for adequate infrastructure and resources to support AI-driven assessments (Eden et al., 2024). Implementing AI tools requires significant investment in technology, data infrastructure, and training for both educators and students. Schools and institutions must also ensure that the AI systems they adopt are designed to be inclusive and accessible, considering the diverse needs of all learners (Sharma, 2024). This includes addressing issues related to equity, such as ensuring that AI tools do not inadvertently reinforce existing biases or inequalities in the education system. Additionally, there are concerns about data privacy and security, as AI systems rely on the collection and analysis of large amounts of student data. Educators and institutions must navigate these concerns carefully to ensure that AI tools are used ethically and responsibly.

Another challenge is the need for educators to adapt to new assessment practices. While AI can offer valuable insights into student learning, it is important for educators to remain actively engaged in the assessment process. AI should be viewed as a tool to support, rather than replace, the role of the educator. Teachers must be trained to interpret AI-generated data, use it to inform their instructional practices, and provide the human touch that is essential for fostering a positive learning environment. Moreover, educators must be prepared to address the potential challenges that may arise when students interact with AI-driven assessments. For example, students may become overly reliant on AI feedback, leading to a diminished sense of personal responsibility for their learning. To mitigate this risk, educators must foster a growth mindset and encourage students to view AI feedback as one of many tools for improving their learning, rather than as a definitive measure of their abilities.

The chapter will also provide practical examples and case studies of AI applications in assessment. These case studies will illustrate how AI is already being used in various educational contexts to enhance assessment practices. For example, some schools and universities are using AI-powered platforms to assess student writing, providing real-time feedback on grammar, style, and coherence. Other institutions are using AI to design adaptive assessments that adjust the difficulty of questions based on student performance, ensuring that each student is challenged at an appropriate level (Ejjami, 2024). These case studies will highlight the diverse ways in which AI can be integrated into assessment practices, offering insights into both the opportunities and challenges that come with this shift.

Looking forward, the chapter will offer a forward-looking perspective on the future of AI in educational assessment. As AI technologies continue to evolve, it is likely that we will see more sophisticated and nuanced assessment tools emerge. These tools will be able to assess a wider range of skills and competencies, from social-emotional learning to creativity and collaboration. The integration of AI into assessment will also be accompanied by a growing emphasis on personalized learning pathways, where students are given more control over their educational journeys and are assessed based on their individual progress and achievements (Hrytsenko, 2024). In this future landscape, AI will not only serve as a tool for assessment but also as a catalyst for reimagining how we approach teaching and learning in a rapidly changing world.

AI has the potential to revolutionize educational assessment by moving beyond traditional standardized testing and offering more personalized, dynamic feedback systems (Owan et al., 2023). This chapter will explore the advantages and challenges of integrating AI into assessment practices, providing practical examples and case studies to illustrate its impact. By embracing AI, educators and institutions can create a more equitable, inclusive, and effective assessment system that supports the diverse needs of all learners and fosters a deeper, more meaningful learning experience (Bowen & Watson, 2024; Sharma, 2024). As AI continues to evolve, it will undoubtedly play an increasingly central role in shaping the future of education, offering new opportunities for both students and educators alike.

THE EVOLUTION OF EDUCATIONAL ASSESSMENT

Traditional assessment methods, particularly standardized testing, have long been the cornerstone of educational evaluation across many systems worldwide. These methods, which emerged in the late 19th and early 20th centuries, were designed to provide a uniform and objective way to measure student performance and aptitude (Naughton, 2022). Standardized tests such as the SAT, ACT, and various state-mandated exams have been widely used to assess student knowledge and determine academic success. However, as the educational landscape has evolved, it has become increasingly clear that these traditional methods have significant limitations (Naughton, 2022). The very nature of standardized testing—its focus on a narrow set of skills, its reliance on a one-size-fits-all approach, and its failure to account for the diverse needs of learners—has led to growing criticism and calls for reform (Bauml, 2016).

The history of standardized testing can be traced back to the early 20th century, when tests like the Stanford-Binet Intelligence Scale were developed to assess intelligence and academic potential. These tests were originally intended to identify students who might benefit from specialized instruction, but over time, they became the primary tool for measuring academic achievement. The use of standardized tests expanded rapidly during the mid-20th century, particularly in the United States, where the push for accountability in education led to the widespread adoption of these assessments (Naughton, 2022). By the 1960s and 1970s, standardized tests were used not only to measure individual student performance but also to evaluate schools, teachers, and entire educational systems.

While standardized tests have been lauded for their ability to provide objective, quantifiable data, they have also been criticized for their inability to capture the full range of student abilities and learning styles (Naughton, 2022). One of the most significant limitations of standardized testing is its narrow focus on cognitive skills, particularly those related to rote memorization and basic problem-solving. These tests often fail to assess higher-order thinking skills such as critical thinking, creativity, and problem-solving in real-world contexts.

Additionally, standardized tests typically assess students' abilities at a single point in time, offering a limited snapshot of their academic performance. This approach fails to account for the ongoing nature of learning, where students may improve over time or struggle with specific concepts due to external factors such as stress, illness, or family issues.

Another significant limitation of traditional assessment methods is their lack of flexibility and accessibility. Standardized tests are designed to be administered to large groups of students in a controlled environment, often with rigid time constraints and uniform instructions. This structure can be a barrier for students with learning disabilities, language barriers, or other unique needs. For example, students with dyslexia may struggle with reading comprehension tests, while students with ADHD may find it difficult to concentrate during timed assessments. Furthermore, standardized tests often fail to account for cultural differences, as they are typically designed with a particular demographic in mind. Students from diverse cultural or linguistic backgrounds may be at a disadvantage, as the tests may not reflect their lived experiences or the ways in which they engage with the material (Holden & Tanenbaum, 2023; Naughton, 2022).

The limitations of traditional assessment methods have led to a growing interest in alternative forms of assessment that are more flexible, personalized, and inclusive. One of the most promising developments in this area is the rise of artificial intelligence (AI) in education. AI has the potential to fundamentally change the way assessments are designed, administered, and interpreted. By leveraging machine learning algorithms, natural language processing, and data analytics, AI can create more dynamic, adaptive assessments that respond to the unique needs and abilities of each student (Eden et al., 2024; Ejjami, 2024). This shift from traditional, static assessments to AI-driven, dynamic evaluations represents a fundamental change in how educators think about educational assessment.

AI in education is not a new concept, but its potential to transform assessment practices has only recently begun to be fully realized. Early uses of AI in education were focused on creating intelligent tutoring systems and automated grading tools. These systems were designed to provide personalized feedback to students, but they were limited in scope and functionality. Over time, however, advances in machine learning and data analytics have enabled the development of more sophisticated AI-driven assessment tools that can analyze large amounts of data and provide real-time, personalized feedback (Du Boulay, 2023; Hrytsenko, 2024; Owan et al., 2023). AI can now assess a wider range of skills and competencies, including critical thinking, problem-solving, creativity, and social-emotional learning—areas that traditional assessments often overlook.

One of the key advantages of AI-driven assessments is their ability to adapt to the individual needs of each student. Traditional assessments, by their nature, are one-size-fits-all, applying the same set of questions and tasks to all students, regardless of their abilities or learning styles. In contrast, AI can create personalized assessments that adjust in real-time based on the student's performance (Eden et al., 2024; Ejjami, 2024; Owan et al., 2023). For example, if a student answers a question correctly, the AI system may present a more challenging question, while if the student answers incorrectly, the system may provide additional support or differentiated questions to help them build their understanding. This adaptive approach ensures that students are continuously challenged at an appropriate level, which can lead to deeper learning and improved outcomes.

In addition to personalization, AI-driven assessments offer a level of flexibility that traditional assessments cannot match. Traditional assessments are typically administered in a standardized format, with fixed time limits and rigid instructions. AI-driven assessments, on the other hand, can be delivered in a variety of formats, including text, video, or interactive simulations. This flexibility allows students to engage with the assessment in a way that suits their learning style and preferences. For example, students who struggle with reading comprehension may benefit from assessments that include audio or video components, while students who are more comfortable with hands-on learning may find interactive simulations more engaging and effective. This flexibility also extends to the timing of the assessment, as AI systems can allow students to work at their own pace, providing more opportunities for reflection and deeper engagement with the material (Ejjami, 2024).

Another significant advantage of AI in assessment is its potential to enhance fairness and equity. Traditional assessments have long been criticized for reinforcing inequities in education, particularly for students from marginalized or disadvantaged backgrounds. Standardized tests often fail to account for the diverse cultural, linguistic, and cognitive differences among students, which can result in biased outcomes. AI-driven assessments, however, can be designed to be more inclusive and equitable by considering the unique needs and abilities of each student (Mehta et al., 2023). For example, AI systems can be programmed to provide accommodations for students with disabilities, such as extended time for students with ADHD or alternative formats for students with visual impairments. Additionally, AI can help to reduce the impact of test anxiety, as students can take assessments in a more comfortable and familiar environment, without the pressure of a high stakes testing situation.

Despite the many advantages of AI in assessment, there are also challenges and concerns that must be addressed. One of the primary concerns is the potential for bias in AI algorithms (Baker & Hawn, 2022). AI systems are only as good as the data in which they are trained, and if the data used to train the system is biased, the resulting assessments may also be biased. For example, if an AI system is trained on data that predominantly reflects the experiences of students from a particular demographic group, the system may be less accurate or fair for students from other backgrounds. This issue of bias is particularly concerning in the context of educational assessment, where fairness and equity are paramount. To address this concern, it is essential that AI systems are trained on diverse, representative data and that their algorithms are regularly audited and updated to ensure that they do not perpetuate existing biases.

Another challenge is the need for transparency and accountability in AI-driven assessments (Raza, 2024). Unlike traditional assessments, which are typically designed and administered by human educators, AI-driven assessments are created by algorithms that may not always be fully understood or interpretable by the people who use them. This lack of transparency can raise concerns about the fairness and accuracy of AI-driven assessments, particularly if students or educators are unable to understand how the system arrived at a particular result. To address this concern, it is important that AI systems are designed to be transparent and explainable, with clear documentation and guidelines for how the assessments are created and how results are interpreted.

When comparing traditional and AI-based assessments, the differences in flexibility, accessibility, and fairness are particularly striking. Traditional assessments are typically rigid and standardized, applying the same set of questions to all students, regardless of their individual needs or abilities. AI-driven assessments, on the other hand, are adaptive and personalized, adjusting in real-time to reflect the unique strengths and challenges of each student (Ejjami, 2024; Owan et al., 2023). This flexibility allows for a more accurate and holistic assessment of student learning, as it can capture a wider range of skills and competencies (Ejjami, 2024). Additionally, AI-driven assessments can be more accessible, as they can be delivered in a variety of formats and can accommodate students with disabilities or other learning needs. Finally, AI has the potential to enhance fairness by reducing the impact of bias and providing more equitable opportunities for all students to demonstrate their learning.

The rise of AI in education represents a significant shift in the way assessments are designed and implemented. While traditional assessment methods, such as standardized testing, have long been the dominant approach, they are increasingly being challenged for their limitations in terms of flexibility, accessibility, and fairness. AI-driven assessments offer a promising alternative, with the potential to create more personalized, adaptive, and equitable assessments that better reflect the diverse needs and abilities of students (Ejjami, 2024). However, the integration of AI into assessment practices must be done carefully, with attention to issues such as bias, transparency, and accountability (Raza, 2024). As AI continues to evolve, it is likely that we will see more sophisticated and inclusive assessment tools that will transform the way we evaluate student learning and performance.

AI-DRIVEN ASSESSMENT TOOLS

The integration of artificial intelligence (AI) into educational assessment represents a transformative shift in how we measure and understand student learning. AI technologies, such as natural language processing (NLP), machine learning algorithms, and adaptive testing systems, are at the forefront of this revolution. These technologies enable the creation of more dynamic, personalized, and efficient assessment tools that can provide real-time feedback, adapt to the individual needs of students, and enhance the accuracy and fairness of educational evaluations (Hrytsenko, 2024; Owan et al., 2023). In this section, we will explore the various AI technologies currently being used in educational assessment, provide case studies of AI-driven assessment tools in K-12 and higher education settings, and examine the role of AI in delivering real-time feedback to students.

AI Technologies in Educational Assessment

Artificial intelligence encompasses a broad range of technologies, each with unique capabilities that can be applied to educational assessment. Among the most impactful are natural language processing, machine learning algorithms, and adaptive testing systems.

Each of these technologies contributes to the development of assessment tools that are more responsive to the needs of students, enabling educators to move away from traditional, one-size-fits-all testing models.

Natural Language Processing (NLP) is a branch of AI that focuses on the interaction between computers and human language. NLP enables machines to understand, interpret, and generate human language in a way that is both meaningful and contextually relevant (Ejjami, 2024). In the context of educational assessment, NLP is particularly useful for evaluating written responses, essays, and open-ended questions. AI systems equipped with NLP capabilities can analyze the content of student submissions, assess the quality of writing, and provide feedback on grammar, syntax, coherence, and even the depth of argumentation (Du Boulay, 2023). For example, tools like Grammarly use NLP to offer real-time suggestions for improving writing, while more sophisticated AI systems can assess the quality of reasoning and critical thinking in student essays. This capability allows for more nuanced and detailed assessments of student performance, moving beyond simple multiple-choice or true/false questions to evaluate complex cognitive skills.

Machine Learning Algorithms are another key AI technology used in educational assessment. Machine learning (ML) involves training algorithms to recognize patterns in data and make predictions or decisions based on that data (Eden et al., 2024). In educational assessment, ML algorithms can be used to analyze vast amounts of student performance data and identify patterns that might not be immediately apparent to human educators (Hrytsenko, 2024). For example, ML algorithms can be used to predict student success or failure based on historical performance data, identify students who may need additional support, or recommend personalized learning pathways. ML can also be used to create dynamic assessments that adjust the difficulty level of questions based on a student's previous answers, ensuring that each student is appropriately challenged and engaged.

Adaptive Testing Systems are designed to tailor assessments to the individual abilities of students. These systems use algorithms to adjust the difficulty of questions based on the student's responses, ensuring that the assessment is both challenging and fair. Adaptive testing is particularly useful in large-scale assessments, where it is important to ensure that all students are assessed at an appropriate level. For example, the Graduate Record Examination (GRE) uses an adaptive testing system to adjust the difficulty of questions based on the test taker's responses, ensuring that the assessment accurately measures the student's abilities. In the context of educational assessment, adaptive testing systems can be used to create personalized assessments that adapt in real-time to the student's performance, providing a more accurate and holistic measure of their knowledge and skills.

Case Studies of AI-Driven Assessment Tools

AI-driven assessment tools are being used in both K-12 and higher education settings, offering a wide range of applications for both formative and summative assessments (Du Boulay, 2023). These tools are not only enhancing the assessment process but also helping educators provide more personalized and targeted feedback to students (Owan et al., 2023).

In **K-12 education**, AI-driven assessment tools are being used to support both formative and summative assessments (Du Boulay, 2023). One notable example is the use of AI-powered tools for reading comprehension and writing assessment. Programs like **Socratic by Google** use AI to help students solve problems and answer questions by providing step-by-step explanations and feedback. These tools are particularly useful for formative assessments, as they allow students to receive immediate feedback on their progress and identify areas where they need further improvement. Similarly, **Turnitin**, a tool widely used in K-12 education, uses AI to detect plagiarism and provide feedback on writing quality. Turnitin's AI algorithms analyze student submissions for similarities with other sources and offer suggestions for improving clarity, coherence, and structure. This feedback helps students refine their writing skills and enhances their ability to produce high-quality work.

Another example of AI-driven assessment in K-12 education is **DreamBox Learning**, an adaptive learning platform that uses machine learning algorithms to create personalized math assessments for students. DreamBox's AI technology tracks student performance in real-time, adjusting the difficulty of math problems based on the student's responses. This adaptive system ensures that students are continuously challenged at an appropriate level, helping them build mastery of mathematical concepts over time. DreamBox's formative assessments provide immediate feedback to students, allowing them to identify areas for improvement and adjust their learning strategies accordingly. The platform also provides teachers with detailed reports on student progress, helping them identify students who may need additional support and tailor their instruction to meet individual needs.

In **higher education**, AI-driven assessment tools are also gaining traction, particularly in the areas of formative assessment, grading, and feedback. One example is **Gradescope**, an AI-powered grading platform used by many universities to streamline the grading process for assignments, exams, and quizzes. Gradescope uses machine learning algorithms to automatically grade multiple-choice and short-answer questions, as well as more complex assignments like essays and programming tasks. The system provides real-time feedback to students, helping them understand where they went wrong and how to improve. Gradescope also offers instructors the ability to review and adjust the grading criteria, ensuring that the assessment is fair and accurate.

Another example of AI in higher education assessment is **Cognii**, an AI-powered platform that specializes in evaluating open-ended responses. Cognii uses natural language processing to assess the quality of student responses to essay-style questions, providing feedback on the clarity, coherence, and depth of the student's argument. This tool is particularly useful for summative assessments, as it allows educators to evaluate complex cognitive skills such as critical thinking and problem-solving. Cognii's AI algorithms can assess student responses at scale, providing immediate feedback and helping instructors manage large volumes of assessments more efficiently (Owan et al., 2023).

The Role of AI in Real-Time Feedback

One of the most significant advantages of AI in educational assessment is its ability to provide real-time feedback to students. Traditional assessments, such as standardized tests, typically provide feedback only after the assessment is completed, leaving students with little opportunity to improve or adjust their learning strategies before the next assessment. In contrast, AI-driven assessment tools can provide immediate, actionable feedback that helps students identify areas for improvement and take corrective action (Ejjami, 2024; Owan et al., 2023).

For example, AI-powered tutoring systems like **Knewton** offer real-time feedback to students as they work through learning materials. These systems analyze student performance in real-time and provide personalized recommendations for further study based on the student's strengths and weaknesses. This feedback is delivered in the context of the student's current learning path, ensuring that it is both relevant and timely. Knewton's adaptive learning algorithms track student progress and adjust the difficulty of tasks based on the student's performance, ensuring that they are continuously challenged at an appropriate level.

In addition to personalized feedback, AI-driven assessment tools can also help students develop a deeper understanding of the material by offering targeted learning paths (Owan et al., 2023). For example, if a student struggles with a particular concept, the AI system can provide additional practice problems, explanations, or resources to help the student master the concept before moving on to more advanced topics. This personalized approach ensures that students are not left behind and that they have the opportunity to build a solid foundation of knowledge before progressing to more complex material.

Moreover, AI-driven systems can help reduce the cognitive load on both students and educators by automating the feedback process (Owan et al., 2023). In traditional assessment systems, teachers must spend significant time grading assignments and providing feedback. With AI-driven tools, this process is automated, allowing teachers to focus on higher-level tasks such as interpreting data, providing individualized support, and developing instructional strategies. AI can also assist in identifying patterns in student performance, helping educators recognize common areas of difficulty and adjust their teaching methods accordingly.

In conclusion, AI technologies such as natural language processing, machine learning algorithms, and adaptive testing systems are revolutionizing the field of educational assessment. These technologies enable the creation of personalized, adaptive assessments that provide real-time feedback, enhancing both the learning experience and the assessment process (Du Boulay, 2023). Case studies of AI-driven assessment tools in K-12 and higher education settings demonstrate the potential of AI to improve formative and summative assessments, providing students with immediate feedback and personalized learning paths (Hrytsenko, 2024). As AI continues to evolve, it is likely that these tools will become even more sophisticated, offering greater flexibility, accessibility, and fairness in educational assessments. The role of AI in real-time feedback is particularly promising, as it allows for immediate identification of areas for improvement and supports personalized learning, helping students achieve their full potential (Eden et al., 2024; Ejjami, 2024).

BENEFITS OF AI IN ASSESSMENT

Artificial intelligence (AI) has the potential to fundamentally reshape educational assessments, offering solutions to some of the most pressing challenges of traditional testing methods. One of the most significant advantages of AI is its ability to create more equitable assessments by addressing biases that are often inherent in traditional testing methods (Owan et al., 2023). Additionally, AI can provide personalized feedback and learning experiences, allowing students to progress at their own pace. Furthermore, AI can offer more comprehensive data on student performance, enabling educators to make better-informed decisions about teaching strategies and interventions. This section will explore these transformative possibilities, examining how AI can contribute to fairer, more individualized assessments and support educators in improving student outcomes.

ADDRESSING BIASES IN TRADITIONAL TESTING METHODS

Traditional testing methods, particularly standardized tests, have long been criticized for their inability to accommodate the diverse needs of students. These assessments are often designed with a "one-size-fits-all" approach, which can be problematic for students from different cultural, linguistic, socioeconomic, and learning backgrounds (Bauml, 2016). Biases in standardized testing can manifest in various ways, including biased question design, unequal access to test preparation resources, and cultural assumptions embedded in the test content. These biases can result in inaccurate or unfair assessments, disproportionately affecting marginalized groups such as students of color, students with disabilities, and students from low-income backgrounds.

AI has the potential to address these biases by creating more adaptive, personalized, and contextually relevant assessments. One of the key advantages of AI is its ability to analyze large datasets and identify patterns that may not be immediately apparent to human educators. By leveraging machine learning algorithms, AI can help ensure that assessments are fair and equitable, adjusting the content and difficulty level based on the individual needs of each student. For example, AI-driven assessment tools can analyze students' prior performance data and adjust the difficulty of questions to ensure that all students are assessed at an appropriate level. This can help reduce the impact of biases that may arise from using a fixed set of questions for all students.

Moreover, AI can be used to identify and eliminate biased language in test questions. Natural language processing (NLP) algorithms can analyze test items for cultural or linguistic biases, ensuring that the language used is inclusive and accessible to all students. For example, NLP tools can flag questions that may contain culturally specific references or idiomatic expressions that may be unfamiliar to students from different backgrounds.

By addressing these biases, AI can create more inclusive assessments that better reflect the diverse experiences and knowledge of all students.

AI can also help reduce biases related to test preparation. In traditional assessment systems, students from higher-income backgrounds often have access to more resources, such as tutoring services, test prep courses, and practice materials, which can give them an advantage in standardized testing. AI-driven tools, however, can provide personalized learning experiences that are accessible to all students, regardless of their socioeconomic background. For instance, AI-powered tutoring systems can offer individualized support and practice exercises tailored to each student's needs, helping them prepare for assessments in a way that is equitable and aligned with their unique learning styles (Du Boulay, 2023).

By addressing these biases, AI can contribute to more equitable assessments, ensuring that all students have the opportunity to demonstrate their knowledge and abilities in a fair and meaningful way. This, in turn, can help reduce disparities in educational outcomes and create a more level playing field for all learners.

PERSONALIZED FEEDBACK AND LEARNING EXPERIENCES

Another key advantage of AI in educational assessment is its ability to offer personalized feedback and learning experiences. Traditional assessments, such as standardized tests, typically provide a single, summative evaluation of a student's performance, offering little in the way of personalized feedback or guidance. In contrast, AI-driven assessment tools can provide real-time, tailored feedback that is specific to each student's strengths, weaknesses, and learning needs. This personalized approach to assessment has the potential to transform the learning experience, allowing students to progress at their own pace and receive the support they need to succeed.

AI-powered systems can track student progress over time, identifying areas where students are excelling and areas where they may need additional support. For example, AI-driven tutoring platforms like **Knewton** use machine learning algorithms to analyze student performance and provide personalized recommendations for further study. These systems can suggest specific topics or practice problems that align with the student's current level of understanding, helping them build mastery in areas where they may be struggling. By offering personalized learning experiences, AI can help students progress at their own pace, ensuring that they are appropriately challenged and supported throughout their learning journey (Hrytsenko, 2024).

Moreover, AI can provide feedback in real-time, allowing students to immediately identify areas for improvement and take corrective action (Ejjami, 2024). This is particularly important in formative assessments, where the goal is not only to evaluate student performance but also to help students learn and grow. Traditional assessments often provide feedback only after the test has been completed, leaving students with little opportunity to adjust their learning strategies before the next assessment. In contrast, AI-driven systems can offer continuous feedback, helping students stay on track and make adjustments as needed. For example, AI-powered writing tools like **Grammarly** can provide real-time feedback on grammar, syntax, and writing style, allowing students to improve their writing as they work on assignments.

Personalized feedback also helps to create a more supportive learning environment. In traditional classrooms, teachers may struggle to provide individualized feedback to every student, especially in large classes. AI can help bridge this gap by offering personalized feedback at scale. AI-powered assessment tools can analyze student responses and provide detailed feedback on specific areas of improvement, helping students understand exactly where they went wrong and how to improve (Ejjami, 2024). This level of detail is difficult to achieve with traditional assessments, where feedback is often limited to a simple score or grade.

By offering personalized feedback and learning experiences, AI can help students develop a deeper understanding of the material, build confidence, and improve their performance over time. This individualized approach to assessment is particularly valuable in fostering a growth mindset, as it encourages students to view challenges as opportunities for learning and improvement.

COMPREHENSIVE DATA ON STUDENT PERFORMANCE

AI's ability to collect and analyze large amounts of data is another key advantage that can enhance the assessment process. Traditional assessments typically provide limited data on student performance, often focusing on a single score or grade that may not fully capture the complexity of a student's abilities. In contrast, AI-driven assessment tools can provide more comprehensive data on student performance, offering insights into various aspects of learning, including cognitive skills, problem-solving abilities, and areas of struggle.

AI systems can track student performance over time, collecting data on a wide range of factors, such as the time spent on each task, the types of mistakes made, and the strategies used to solve problems. This data can be used to generate detailed reports that offer a holistic view of student progress, helping educators identify trends and patterns that may not be immediately apparent through traditional assessments. For example, AI-driven platforms like **DreamBox Learning** collect data on student interactions with the system, such as the number of attempts made to solve a particular problem, the time taken to complete tasks, and the accuracy of responses. This data can be used to create a personalized learning path for each student, ensuring that they receive the support they need to succeed.

The ability to collect and analyze comprehensive data on student performance also enables educators to make more informed decisions about teaching strategies and interventions. For example, AI systems can identify students who may be at risk of falling behind or who may need additional support in specific areas. By providing real-time data on student performance, AI can help educators intervene early and provide targeted support to students who need it most. This proactive approach can help prevent students from falling through the cracks and ensure that they receive the resources and guidance they need to succeed.

In addition to providing data on individual student performance, AI can also offer insights into broader trends and patterns across the classroom or school. For example, AI-driven assessment tools can analyze data from multiple students to identify common areas of difficulty or to assess the effectiveness of teaching strategies. This data-driven approach can help educators refine their instructional methods, ensuring that they are meeting the needs of all students and improving overall learning outcomes.

Furthermore, AI can help educators track student progress toward specific learning goals and objectives (Du Boulay, 2023). By providing continuous feedback and data on student performance, AI-driven assessment tools can help educators monitor whether students are meeting learning targets and adjust their teaching strategies accordingly. This level of data-driven decision-making is not only valuable for individual students but also for improving the overall effectiveness of educational programs.

AI has the potential to revolutionize educational assessment by creating more equitable, personalized, and data-driven evaluation systems (Du Boulay, 2023). By addressing biases inherent in traditional testing methods, AI can help ensure that assessments are fair and inclusive for all students, regardless of their background or learning style. Additionally, AI's ability to provide personalized feedback and learning experiences allows students to progress at their own pace, ensuring that they receive the support they need to succeed. Finally, AI's capacity to generate comprehensive data on student performance enables educators to make more informed decisions about teaching strategies and interventions, ultimately improving student outcomes. As AI continues to evolve, its role in educational assessment is likely to expand, offering even more opportunities for personalized, equitable, and data-driven learning experiences.

CHALLENGES AND CONSIDERATIONS

The integration of artificial intelligence (AI) into educational assessment practices has the potential to revolutionize how students are evaluated, offering more personalized, equitable, and efficient ways of measuring academic progress (Du Boulay, 2023). However, as with any technological advancement, the use of AI in education also brings with it a range of ethical concerns, practical challenges, and potential resistance. These concerns include issues related to data privacy, algorithmic bias, and the over-reliance on technology. Additionally, the successful integration of AI tools into assessment practices requires proper training and support for educators, who must understand how to effectively use these tools in a way that aligns with educational goals. Finally, there is the possibility of resistance to AI-driven assessments from various stakeholders, including educators, students, and parents, who may have concerns about fairness, transparency, and trust. This section will explore these ethical concerns, challenges, and potential barriers to the successful integration of AI into educational assessment practices.

Ethical Concerns in AI-Based Assessment

As AI technologies become increasingly prevalent in educational assessment, several ethical concerns must be addressed to ensure that their use does not inadvertently harm students or undermine the integrity of the educational system. Among the most significant concerns are data privacy, algorithmic bias, and the potential for over-reliance on technology.

Data Privacy

One of the most pressing ethical concerns in the use of AI in educational assessment is the issue of data privacy. AI-driven assessment tools rely heavily on data to function effectively. These tools collect and analyze vast amounts of data on students, including their performance on assessments, interactions with learning platforms, and even personal information such as demographic data and behavioral patterns. While this data is essential for providing personalized feedback and adaptive learning experiences, it also raises significant privacy concerns.

Students' personal data is highly sensitive, and improper handling or unauthorized access to this data can lead to serious privacy violations. For example, if AI systems are not properly secured, student data could be vulnerable to hacking, identity theft, or misuse. Additionally, the collection of personal data raises questions about who owns the data, how it is stored, and who has access to it. Educational institutions, AI developers, and policymakers must work together to establish clear guidelines and regulations to ensure that student data is protected and used ethically (Owan et al., 2023). This includes obtaining informed consent from students and their families, providing transparency about how data will be used, and ensuring that data is anonymized to prevent identification of individual students.

Furthermore, there is the issue of data retention. AI systems may collect data over long periods, tracking students' progress and performance across multiple years. However, retaining this data for extended periods can pose risks to privacy, especially if the data is not regularly updated or if it is stored without clear protocols for deletion. Educational institutions must ensure that data is not kept longer than necessary and that it is securely deleted when no longer required. This is particularly important in the context of students' sensitive information, such as special education needs or mental health data, which must be handled with the utmost care.

To mitigate these concerns, it is crucial that educators, administrators, and developers of AI tools work together to create a robust framework for data privacy. This framework should prioritize student privacy, transparency, and accountability, ensuring that AI-driven assessments are used in a way that respects students' rights and protects their personal information.

Algorithmic Bias

Another major ethical concern in the use of AI in assessment is algorithmic bias (Du Boulay, 2023). AI systems are not inherently neutral; they are designed and trained by humans, and the data used to train these systems can reflect existing biases in society. If AI systems are trained on biased or incomplete data, they may produce biased results, perpetuating inequalities in the educational system. For example, if an AI system is trained on historical data that reflects racial, socioeconomic, or gender biases, the system may unintentionally favor certain groups of students over others. This can manifest in various ways, such as biased grading, unfair assessment of students' abilities, or unequal access to resources. In the context of AI-driven assessments, this could mean that certain groups of students are unfairly disadvantaged, while others are given an advantage, despite not necessarily performing better.

To mitigate algorithmic bias, it is essential that AI systems are trained on diverse, representative datasets that reflect the full range of student experiences and backgrounds. Additionally, developers must regularly audit AI systems for bias, testing them for fairness and accuracy across different demographic groups. This requires ongoing monitoring and adjustment of the algorithms to ensure that they continue to produce equitable results. It is also important that AI systems are transparent in their decision-making processes, allowing educators and students to understand how assessments are being evaluated and what factors are influencing the outcomes (Raza, 2024).

In addition to addressing bias in the algorithms themselves, educators must be aware of the potential for bias in the way AI tools are implemented. For example, if AI-driven assessments are used in conjunction with traditional testing methods, there may be a risk that students from marginalized groups are disproportionately subjected to certain types of assessments that are more likely to perpetuate bias. Educators must be vigilant in ensuring that AI tools are used in a way that is fair and equitable, considering the diverse needs of all students.

Over-Reliance on Technology

While AI has the potential to greatly enhance educational assessment, there is a concern that an over-reliance on technology could have negative consequences. AI-driven assessments can provide immediate, data-driven feedback (Owan et al., 2023), but they cannot fully replace the human element of teaching and learning. Over-relying on AI tools could lead to a reduction in human interaction, which is essential for fostering critical thinking, creativity, and emotional intelligence in students.

Moreover, there is the risk that AI could exacerbate the digital divide, creating disparities between students who have access to advanced technology and those who do not (Kitsara, 2022). Students from low-income backgrounds may lack access to the devices, internet connections, or technical support needed to effectively engage with AI-driven assessments, leaving them at a disadvantage compared to their more affluent peers. This could lead to further inequities in the educational system, undermining the potential for AI to create more equitable assessments.

To prevent over-reliance on technology, it is important that AI tools are used as a complement to, rather than a replacement for, traditional teaching methods. Educators should continue to play a central role in the assessment process, using AI tools to enhance their ability to provide personalized feedback and support, rather than relying solely on technology to make decisions about student performance.

The Need for Proper Training and Support for Educators

The successful integration of AI into educational assessment requires that educators are properly trained and supported in using these tools. While AI-driven assessment systems offer many benefits, they also require a level of technical expertise that may not be readily available to all educators. Without proper training, educators may struggle to effectively use AI tools, potentially undermining the benefits that these technologies offer.

Training programs should focus on helping educators understand how AI-driven assessment tools work, how to interpret the data generated by these systems, and how to integrate AI tools into their existing teaching practices. Educators should also be trained to recognize and address potential biases in AI-driven assessments and to use these tools in a way that is fair and equitable for all students.

In addition to formal training, educators will need ongoing support as they integrate AI tools into their assessment practices. This support could come in the form of professional development opportunities, technical assistance, and peer networks that allow educators to share best practices and troubleshoot challenges. Schools and districts should invest in providing this support to ensure that educators are equipped to make the most of AI-driven assessments.

Furthermore, it is important that educators are given the autonomy to choose the AI tools that best align with their teaching philosophy and the needs of their students. Not all AI-driven assessment tools are created equal, and educators should be empowered to select the tools that they believe will best support their students' learning. This requires a deep understanding of the capabilities and limitations of different AI tools, as well as a commitment to ongoing learning and professional growth.

Resistance to AI in Assessment

Despite the potential benefits of AI-driven assessment, there is likely to be resistance from various stakeholders, including educators, students, and parents. This resistance may stem from concerns about fairness, transparency, and trust, as well as a general reluctance to embrace new technologies (Raza, 2024).

Concerns About Fairness

One of the primary sources of resistance to AI in assessment is the concern that these systems may not be fair. Educators, students, and parents may worry that AI-driven assessments could reinforce existing biases or lead to unfair evaluations of students' abilities. For example, if an AI system is not properly trained or audited, it may produce biased results that disadvantage certain groups of students. Additionally, some stakeholders may feel that AI-driven assessments do not adequately capture the full range of a student's abilities, particularly when it comes to creativity, critical thinking, and other non-cognitive skills (Raza, 2024).

To address these concerns, it is important that AI-driven assessments are transparent and that their decision-making processes are clearly explained to all stakeholders. Educators, students, and parents should be able to understand how assessments are being evaluated and what factors are influencing the outcomes. This transparency can help build trust in the system and ensure that AI-driven assessments are seen as fair and reliable.

Concerns About Transparency and Trust

Another source of resistance to AI in assessment is the concern about transparency and trust. AI systems are often seen as "black boxes" because their decision-making processes are not always visible or easily understood by the people who use them (Prinsloo, 2020). This lack of transparency can lead to a lack of trust in AI-driven assessments, particularly if stakeholders are unsure about how decisions are being made.

To build trust in AI-driven assessments, it is essential that these systems are designed with transparency in mind. Developers should ensure that AI tools are explainable and that stakeholders can easily access information about how assessments are being evaluated. This includes providing clear explanations of the algorithms used, the data that is being collected, and the criteria for evaluation. By making AI systems more transparent, educators, students, and parents will be better equipped to understand and trust the results.

Resistance to Change

Finally, there may be general resistance to the adoption of AI in educational assessment simply because it represents a significant change to established practices (Tariq, 2024). Educators, students, and parents may be hesitant to embrace AI-driven assessments due to unfamiliarity with the technology or a reluctance to move away from traditional assessment methods. This resistance can be overcome by providing adequate training, support, and resources to help stakeholders understand the benefits of AI-driven assessments and how they can improve the learning experience.

While AI-driven assessments hold great promise for creating more equitable, personalized, and data-driven evaluation systems, their implementation raises several ethical concerns and practical challenges. Data privacy, algorithmic bias, and over-reliance on technology are significant ethical issues that must be addressed to ensure that AI is used in a way that benefits all students. Additionally, proper training and support for educators are essential for the successful integration of AI tools into assessment practices. Finally, resistance to AI in assessment may arise from concerns about fairness, transparency, and trust, but these challenges can be mitigated through transparency, clear communication, and ongoing support. As AI continues to evolve, it is essential that educators, developers, and policymakers work together to ensure that AI-driven assessments are used ethically, effectively, and equitably.

THE FUTURE OF AI IN ASSESSMENT

The potential of artificial intelligence (AI) in education is vast, with the capacity to revolutionize the way we approach learning, assessment, and educational policy. AI technologies are already beginning to reshape how students are taught, how their progress is measured, and how educators engage with learners. Looking ahead, the future of AI in education holds exciting possibilities, including the creation of fully personalized, adaptive learning environments, a shift in the role of educators, and a transformation of educational policies that redefine academic success. This section will explore these predictions, examining how AI could reshape education in profound ways.

Predictions for the Future of AI in Education

As AI technologies continue to evolve, their potential to create fully personalized, adaptive learning environments becomes more feasible. The future of AI in education will likely involve highly individualized learning experiences that cater to the unique needs, strengths, and challenges of each student. These AI-driven systems will not only assess students' performance but also adjust content, pace, and delivery methods based on real-time data, ensuring that each learner receives the most effective and relevant educational experience.

Fully Personalized Learning

Personalized learning has long been a goal of educators, but AI has the potential to bring this vision to life in ways that were previously unimaginable. In the future, AI-powered systems could create a learning environment that adapts to each student's needs, preferences, and progress (Du Boulay, 2023; Eden et al., 2024; Hrytsenko, 2024). By continuously collecting data on a student's performance, engagement, and learning style, AI could offer tailored content and resources that best suit the individual learner. For example, if a student struggles with a particular concept, the AI system could provide additional practice, alternative explanations, or supplemental materials to help the student master the topic. Conversely, if a student excels in a particular area, the AI could offer more advanced challenges to keep them engaged and progressing.

In this personalized environment, AI could help identify gaps in knowledge before they become significant obstacles to learning. By tracking a student's progress in real-time, AI could pinpoint areas where a student is struggling and offer immediate interventions, such as recommending specific resources, adjusting the difficulty level, or providing one-on-one virtual tutoring (Du Boulay, 2023; Eden et al., 2024). This would allow for a more proactive approach to education, where students receive support when they need it, rather than waiting for issues to be identified through traditional assessments.

Moreover, AI's ability to analyze large amounts of data could allow it to identify patterns and predict future learning needs. For example, AI could anticipate when a student is likely to struggle with a particular concept and intervene before the student falls behind. This would create a dynamic, responsive learning environment that continually adapts to the student's evolving needs, ensuring that each learner has the support and resources necessary to succeed.

Adaptive Learning Environments

The future of AI in education will also likely include adaptive learning environments that respond to a student's progress in real-time. These systems will be able to adjust the pace, content, and difficulty level of lessons based on the student's performance (Du Boulay, 2023). This adaptability ensures that students are neither bored with content that is too easy nor overwhelmed by material that is too difficult. AI-driven adaptive learning systems could provide an ideal balance, offering a challenging yet achievable learning experience.

For example, in an AI-powered classroom, students might work through a series of interactive lessons, assessments, and exercises. If a student struggles with a particular topic, the AI could adjust the difficulty of subsequent lessons or provide additional support to reinforce the material (Du Boulay, 2023). Conversely, if a student excels, the system could present more advanced challenges to keep the student engaged and motivated. This level of personalization would be impossible to achieve through traditional one-size-fits-all teaching methods, making AI an invaluable tool for fostering individualized learning experiences.

Furthermore, adaptive learning environments could enhance collaboration among students by providing opportunities for peer-to-peer learning (Eden et al., 2024). AI could identify students with complementary strengths and weaknesses and encourage them to work together on certain tasks or projects. This would foster a collaborative, student-centered approach to learning, where students can support one another's growth while benefiting from personalized learning experiences.

HOW AI COULD RESHAPE THE ROLE OF EDUCATORS

As AI continues to play a larger role in education, it is likely to reshape the role of educators, transforming them from being the sole evaluators of student performance to becoming facilitators of learning. This shift would require educators to adapt to new responsibilities and embrace the opportunities provided by AI technologies.

From Evaluators to Facilitators

Traditionally, educators have been the primary source of knowledge and the main evaluators of student performance. However, as AI-driven systems take on more of the responsibility for assessment and feedback, educators will be able to shift their focus from grading and evaluating to facilitating learning (Gnanaprakasam & Lourdusamy, 2024). In this new role, educators will act as guides, mentors, and coaches, helping students navigate their personalized learning paths and providing support when needed.

AI systems will provide real-time data on students' progress, identifying areas of strength and weakness, and offering recommendations for improvement. Educators will be able to use this data to inform their teaching strategies, offering targeted interventions and support based on the individual needs of each student. Rather than spending time on administrative tasks such as grading, educators will be able to focus on higher-level tasks such as fostering critical thinking, encouraging creativity, and providing emotional and social support to students.

In this new paradigm, educators will need to develop new skills and competencies to effectively integrate AI into their teaching practices. They will need to become proficient in using AI tools to monitor student progress, interpret data, and adjust their teaching strategies accordingly. Additionally, educators will need to foster a growth mindset in students, encouraging them to embrace personalized learning and take ownership of their educational journey. This shift in roles will require professional development and ongoing support for educators, as they transition from traditional methods of teaching to a more technology-enhanced, student-centered approach.

Human-AI Collaboration

The future of AI in education will not be about replacing educators but about enhancing their ability to support students (Etiubon & Etiubon, 2023). AI will serve as a powerful tool to augment the teaching process, providing educators with insights and resources that can help them better understand their students' needs and improve their teaching strategies. Human-AI collaboration will be key to creating a more effective and personalized learning experience.

Educators will still play a critical role in shaping the classroom environment, fostering relationships with students, and providing emotional and social support. AI will not be able to replace the human element of teaching, which is essential for creating a positive and supportive learning environment. Instead, AI will complement the work of educators, enabling them to focus on the aspects of teaching that require empathy, creativity, and critical thinking.

THE IMPLICATIONS OF AI-DRIVEN ASSESSMENT ON EDUCATIONAL POLICY

The rise of AI in education will have profound implications for educational policy, particularly in the realm of assessment (Bowen & Watson, 2024). As AI-driven assessments become more widespread, policymakers will need to reconsider traditional definitions of academic success and develop new frameworks for evaluating student achievement.

Redefining Academic Success

Traditional assessments, such as standardized tests, have long been used as the primary measure of academic success. These tests typically focus on a narrow set of skills, such as reading comprehension, math proficiency, and rote memorization, and do not fully capture the range of abilities that contribute to a student's overall success. AI-driven assessments, on the other hand, have the potential to provide a more comprehensive picture of student performance, taking into account factors such as critical thinking, problem-solving, creativity, and collaboration.

As AI systems become more capable of evaluating a wider range of skills, policymakers may need to reconsider how academic success is defined. Rather than relying solely on standardized test scores, academic achievement could be measured through a combination of AI-driven assessments, project-based learning, and other forms of authentic assessment that better reflect students' real-world abilities. This shift would allow for a more holistic view of student success, focusing on the development of a broad set of skills that are essential for success in the 21st century.

Personalized Learning and Equity

AI-driven assessments also have the potential to address issues of equity in education. Traditional assessments often fail to account for the diverse backgrounds, learning styles, and needs of students, leading to disparities in academic performance. AI, however, can provide personalized learning experiences that cater to the individual needs of each student, helping to level the playing field and ensure that all students have the opportunity to succeed (Du Boulay, 2023).

Policymakers will need to ensure that AI-driven assessments are implemented in a way that promotes equity and access. This may involve addressing issues such as the digital divide, ensuring that all students have access to the technology needed to participate in AI-driven assessments, and developing policies that prevent bias in AI algorithms. By prioritizing equity in the implementation of AI-driven assessments, policymakers can help ensure that these technologies benefit all students, regardless of their background or circumstances.

Accountability and Transparency

As AI-driven assessments become more widespread, there will be increased pressure on policymakers to ensure that these systems are transparent, fair, and accountable. Students, parents, and educators will need to trust that AI-driven assessments are accurate and unbiased, and that the data generated by these systems is used responsibly (Eden et al., 2024).

Policymakers will need to establish clear guidelines for the use of AI in education, including standards for data privacy, algorithmic transparency, and accountability. This will require collaboration between educational institutions, AI developers, and policymakers to create policies that ensure AI systems are used ethically and effectively. Additionally, policymakers will need to monitor the impact of AI-driven assessments on student outcomes, ensuring that these systems are contributing to positive educational outcomes and not exacerbating existing inequalities.

The future of AI in education holds tremendous potential, with the ability to create fully personalized, adaptive learning environments, reshape the role of educators, and redefine academic success. As AI-driven assessments become more prevalent, they will provide educators with the tools they need to support individualized learning, while also challenging traditional notions of academic achievement. However, the successful integration of AI into education will require careful consideration of ethical concerns, such as data privacy, algorithmic bias, and equity (Eden et al., 2024). By addressing these challenges and embracing the opportunities provided by AI, we can create a more personalized, equitable, and effective educational system for the future.

CONCLUSION

In conclusion, the transformative potential of artificial intelligence (AI) in assessment cannot be overstated. As AI technologies continue to evolve, they offer the possibility of reshaping the entire landscape of educational evaluation, moving away from the limitations of traditional standardized testing and toward more personalized, adaptive, and inclusive systems (Ejjami, 2024). By harnessing the power of AI, educators can offer tailored learning experiences that meet the unique needs of each student, ensuring that all learners, regardless of their background or learning style, receive the support they need to succeed. The ability of AI to provide real-time feedback, identify areas for improvement, and offer individualized learning paths presents an opportunity to make assessment not only more effective but also more equitable (Owan et al., 2023).

However, the implementation of AI in educational assessment must be approached with careful consideration. Thoughtful integration of these technologies requires ongoing research, rigorous testing, and a commitment to ethical practices to address concerns such as data privacy, algorithmic bias, and over-reliance on technology. It is essential that AI tools be designed and implemented in a way that ensures fairness and transparency, and that they complement, rather than replace, the critical human elements of teaching and learning.

To realize the full potential of AI in assessment, collaboration among educators, technologists, policymakers, and students is crucial. Educators must be equipped with the knowledge and skills to integrate AI tools effectively into their practices, while policymakers must establish clear guidelines to ensure that AI is used responsibly. Technologists must prioritize equity and transparency in the development of AI systems, and students should be actively involved in shaping how these tools are used to support their learning. By working together, these stakeholders can create an educational environment where AI enhances learning outcomes, fosters equity, and supports the diverse needs of all students, paving the way for a future of assessment that is more personalized, inclusive, and effective.

REFERENCES

Au, W. (2022). *Unequal by design: High-stakes testing and the standardization of inequality*. Routledge. DOI: 10.4324/9781003005179

Bahroun, Z., Anane, C., Ahmed, V., & Zacca, A. (2023). Transforming education: A comprehensive review of generative artificial intelligence in educational settings through bibliometric and content analysis. *Sustainability (Basel), 15*(17), 12983. DOI: 10.3390/su151712983

Baker, R. S., & Hawn, A. (2022). Algorithmic bias in education. *International Journal of Artificial Intelligence in Education*, •••, 32.

Bauml, M. (2016). One size never fits all: Teachers' responses to standardized curriculum materials and implications for early childhood teacher educators. *Journal of Early Childhood Teacher Education, 37*(1), 76–95. DOI: 10.1080/10901027.2015.1133461

Bowen, J. A., & Watson, C. E. (2024). *Teaching with AI: A practical guide to a new era of human learning* (1st ed.). Johns Hopkins University Press. DOI: 10.56021/9781421449227

Du Boulay, B., Mitrovic, A., & Yacef, K. (Eds.). (2023). *Handbook of artificial intelligence in education*. Edward Elgar Publishing. DOI: 10.4337/9781800375413

Eden, C. A., Adeleye, O. O., & Adeniyi, I. S. (2024). A review of AI-driven pedagogical strategies for equitable access to science education. *Magna Scientia Advanced Research and Reviews, 10*(2).

Ejjami, R. (2024). The future of learning: AI-based curriculum development. *International Journal for Multidisciplinary Research, 6*(4).

Etiubon, R. U., & Etiubon, A. (2023). Replacement of humans in the classroom by artificial Intelligence: A rhetoric. *Education, 3*(185).

Gnanaprakasam, J., & Lourdusamy, R. (2024). The role of AI in automating grading: Enhancing feedback and efficiency. In *Artificial intelligence and education-Shaping the future of learning*. IntechOpen. DOI: 10.5772/intechopen.1005025

Holden, L. R., & Tanenbaum, G. J. (2023). Modern assessments of intelligence must be fair and equitable. *Journal of Intelligence, 11*(6), 126. DOI: 10.3390/jintelligence11060126 PMID: 37367528

Hrytsenko, V., Tkachenko, A., Podolyan, O., Dieiev, K., & Ilyn, L. (2024). The role of artificial intelligence in personalisation of the learning process. *Revista EDaPECI:Educação a Distância e Práticas Educativas Comunicacionais e Interculturais, 24*(3).

Jain, S., Grewal, H., Vishnoi, A., Saxena, A., Bhardwaj, S., Singh, R., Saxena, A., Srivastava, S., Kumar, R., & Gupta, M. (2025). Transformative trends: The impact of artificial intelligence (AI) on modern education. *AIP Conference Proceedings, 3224*(1), 020041. DOI: 10.1063/5.0246499

Kitsara, I. (2022). Artificial intelligence and the digital divide: From an innovation perspective. In *Platforms and artificial intelligence: The next generation of competences*. Springer International Publishing. DOI: 10.1007/978-3-030-90192-9_12

Mehta, P., Chillarge, G. R., Sapkal, S. D., Shinde, G. R., & Kshirsagar, P. S. (2023). Inclusion of children with special needs in the educational system, artificial intelligence (AI). In *AI-assisted special education for students with exceptional needs*. IGI Global. DOI: 10.4018/979-8-3693-0378-8.ch007

Naughton, J. (2022). Testocracy: The undemocratic system of standardized testing in the United States. *The Kansas Journal of Law & Public Policy*, •••, 31.

Owan, V. J., Abang, K. B., Idika, D. O., Etta, E. O., & Bassey, B. A. (2023). Exploring the potential of artificial intelligence tools in educational measurement and assessment. *Eurasia Journal of Mathematics, Science and Technology Education, 19*(8), em2307. DOI: 10.29333/ejmste/13428

Prinsloo, P. (2020). Of 'black boxes' and algorithmic decision-making in (higher) education–A commentary. *Big Data & Society*, *7*(1). DOI: 10.1177/2053951720933994

Raza, H. (2024). AI-Driven assessment: Reliability, bias, and ethical implications. *Journal of AI in Education: Innovations, Opportunities, Challenges, and Future Directions*, *1*(2).

Ruano-Borbalan, J. C. (2025). The transformative impact of artificial intelligence on higher education: A critical reflection on current trends and futures directions. *International Journal of Chinese Education*, *14*(1), 2212585X251319364. DOI: 10.1177/2212585X251319364

Sharma, S. (2025). The potential of artificial intelligence to enhance special education. In *Transforming special education through artificial intelligence* (pp. 26). Manav Rachna International Institute of Research and Studies. IGI Global.

Tariq, U. (2024). Challenges in AI-powered educational technologies: Teacher perspectives and resistance. *Journal of AI in education: Innovations, opportunities, challenges, and future directions, 1*(3).

Chapter 8
AI Tools for Enhancing Student Engagement

Vaibhav Kumar Pandey
https://orcid.org/0009-0008-6102-1186
Christ University, Delhi, India

Ramesh Chandra Poonia
https://orcid.org/0000-0001-8054-2405
Christ University, Delhi, India

ABSTRACT

Artificial Intelligence (AI) is revolutionizing the learning environment with adaptive technologies that offer new possibilities to engage, support, and empower learners. Throughout this chapter, we examine how AI technologies are transforming student engagement from the past to enable more personalized, responsive, and inclusive learning environments. From intelligent tutoring systems and adaptive learning systems to chatbots, game-based learning, and predictive analytics, AI offers teachers more and more tools to make behavioral, cognitive, and emotional connections with learners. Based on actual case studies of K-12 and higher education, including DreamBox Learning and Civitas Learning, the chapter discusses real-world success with respectful consideration of the ethical, technical, and social issues of AI deployment. Issues from data privacy through algorithmic bias and student agency protection are discussed in detail. In the future, the chapter discusses briefly trends such as affective computing, AI-powered AR/VR environments, and human-AI collaboration construction for education's future. Rather than recommending AI as a replacement for teachers, the chapter argues for an equitable partnership—where AI as a system itself can be an effective collaborator to human teachers, enhancing their capacity to create rich learning environments. In the end, the chapter is appealing for an intentional, ethical, and equitable stance in adopting AI, so technology can be used in the name of education not only by facilitating engagement, but also in safeguarding human dignity, equity, and creativity.

DOI: 10.4018/979-8-3373-5092-9.ch008

1. INTRODUCTION

The landscape of education is undergoing a profound transformation, fuelled by the rapid advancements in Artificial Intelligence (AI). As traditional educational models struggle to meet the demands of the digital age, one of the most pressing challenges educators face today is how to sustain and deepen student engagement. Student engagement — the emotional, behavioural, and cognitive investment students make in their learning processes (Fredricks, Blumenfeld, & Paris, 2004) — is widely recognised as a key driver of academic success and long-term educational achievement. Yet despite many pedagogical innovations, disengagement remains a persistent and growing concern across educational systems worldwide.

Over the past few decades, research has repeatedly highlighted the crucial role student engagement plays in shaping educational outcomes. Students who are engaged tend to show more intrinsic motivation, greater resilience in the face of academic challenges, and stronger overall performance (Kahu, 2013). On the other hand, disengaged students are at a greater risk of absenteeism, academic failure, and socio-emotional difficulties. In today's world — where information is abundant and digital distractions are everywhere — traditional teaching strategies like lectures, standardised assessments, and rote memorisation often fall short when it comes to capturing students' interest and promoting deep learning (Prince, 2004). Furthermore, the rise of smartphones, social media, and digital entertainment platforms introduces even more powerful external distractions that compete for students' already limited attention spans (Junco, 2012).

Several key applications of AI show particular promise for boosting student engagement:

i. **Intelligent Tutoring Systems (ITS)**: AI-powered tutors that adapt their instruction based on student responses, providing personalised support and immediate feedback (VanLehn, 2011)
ii. **Personalised Learning Platforms**: Systems that use predictive analytics to tailor the pace, content, and mode of instruction to each learner's individual needs (Pane, Steiner, Baird, & Hamilton, 2015).
iii. **Gamification and Game-Based Learning:** AI-driven games that build in adaptive learning paths and motivational triggers to keep students interested and committed (Dichev & Dicheva, 2017).
iv. **Conversational Agents and Chatbots**: AI tools that offer real-time help, answer students' questions, and encourage interactive dialogues to maintain continuous engagement (Winkler & Söllner, 2018).
v. **Predictive Analytics and Learning Analytics**: Tools that detect early warning signs of disengagement and recommend timely interventions (Ifenthaler & Yau, 2020).

Each of these innovations brings unique opportunities for transforming education, moving beyond the old one-size-fits-all approaches to embrace more dynamic, learner-centred models. Importantly, using AI to enhance engagement doesn't mean replacing human teachers. Rather, it positions AI as a valuable ally — helping teachers personalize their support, extend their impact, and free up time for deeper, more meaningful interactions with their students.

2. UNDERSTANDING STUDENT ENGAGEMENT

2.1 Definition and Dimensions of Student Engagement

Student engagement has been extensively defined as an active and multifaceted construct that reflects the degree of a student's cognition, emotion, and behavior committed to learning activities (Fredricks, Blumenfeld, & Paris, 2004). Increased engagement is associated with better academic performance, better psychological well-being, and better lifelong learning capabilities (Appleton, Christenson, & Furlong, 2008). As argued by Fredricks et al. (2004), student engagement may be described in three critical dimensions:

i. **Behavioral Engagement:** Refers to students' participation in schoolwork, social, and extracurricular activities, including attendance, homework, and classroom participation. It entails compliance with rules and absence of unwanted behavior.
ii. **Emotional Engagement:** Describes students' affective reactions to schoolwork, peers, teachers, and school. Positive emotional engagement is characterized by interest, belonging, and enthusiasm (Reschly & Christenson, 2012).
iii. **Cognitive Engagement:** Is the commitment to learning, i.e., students' intention to put in the effort required to understand difficult concepts and master challenging skills. It encompasses strategic learning strategies, self-regulation, and critical thinking (Fredricks et al., 2004).

Table 1 below summarizes these dimensions and their key characteristics.

Table 1. Dimensions of Student Engagement (Adapted from Fredricks et al., 2004)

Dimension	Key Characteristics	Example Behaviors
Behavioral Engagement	Participation, effort, persistence	Attending class, completing tasks
Emotional Engagement	Interest, belonging, emotional response	Expressing enthusiasm, feeling connected
Cognitive Engagement	Strategic learning, deep processing, self-regulation	Analyzing information, applying concepts

2.2 Theories Underpinning Engagement

Several theoretical frameworks provide insight into how student engagement arises and how it can be developed:

2.2.1 Self-Determination Theory (SDT)

Self-Determination Theory (Deci & Ryan, 1985) suggests that motivation and, consequently, engagement arise from satisfying three inherent psychological needs: autonomy (to have control over one's actions), competence (to be effective and capable), and relatedness (to be connected). AI-based learning technologies that offer adaptive learning pathways, individualized feedback, and collaboration opportunities can facilitate the fulfillment of these needs, enhancing engagement (Jeno, Grytnes, & Vandvik, 2017).

2.2.2 Flow Theory

Flow Theory (Csikszentmihalyi, 1990) is a psychological state of enhanced concentration and enjoyment experienced when people are involved in tasks with a combination of challenge and skill. Adaptive difficulty adjustment by educational AI systems to the ability of the student can induce "flow" states, optimizing sustained attention and learning efficiency (Shernoff et al., 2014).

Figure 1. Conceptual framework linking AI strategies, theories of engagement, and types of student engagement.

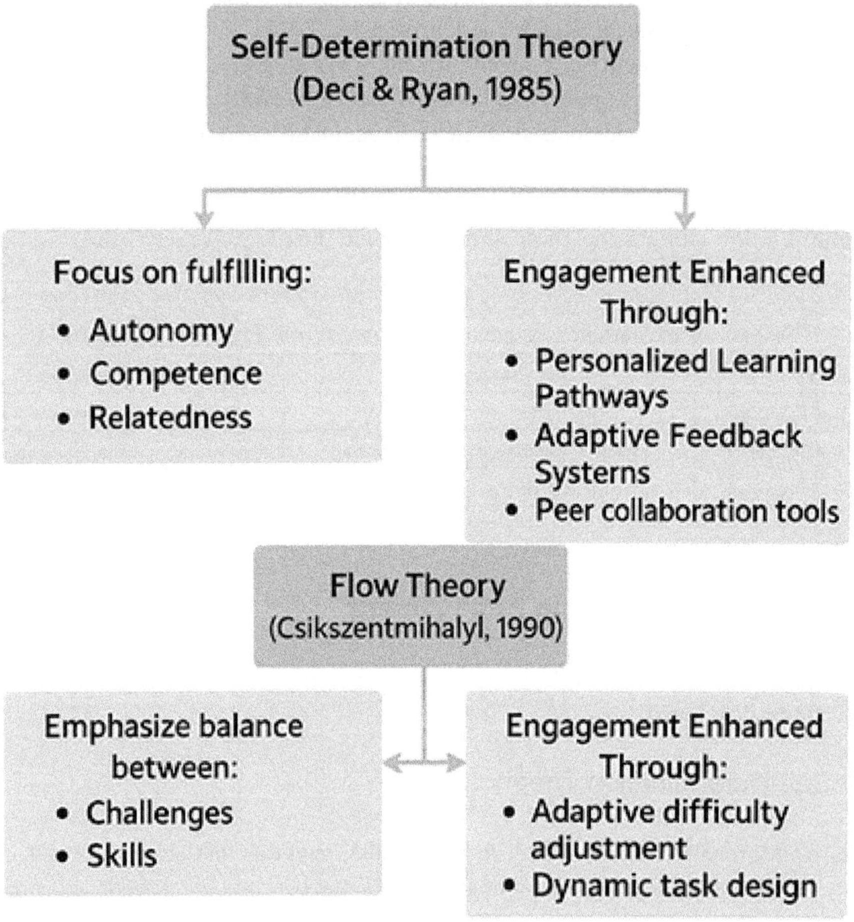

2.2.3 Expectancy-Value Theory

Student motivation is a function of expectancy of success with a task and value of the task to the student, according to Expectancy-Value Theory (Eccles & Wigfield, 2002). Artificial intelligence applications that personalize content to student interest and present supportive, immediate feedback can enhance expectancy and value and hence engagement (Wigfield, Tonks, & Klauda, 2009).

Figure 2.1 Provides a conceptual map linking these theories to engagement strategies.

2.3 Factors Affecting Student Engagement

Student motivation is a complex phenomenon open to a variety of context and individual variables:

i. **Instructional Design:** Structured learning activities that are meaningful and relevant enable more significant engagement (Reeve, 2012). AI technologies that personalize content and pacing to the needs of individual learners can be employed to improve instructional design.
ii. **Teacher-Student Relationships:** Student-teacher relationships are strong predictors of behavioral and emotional engagement (Roorda et al., 2011). AI systems that can notify teachers about students who need special attention can assist in building these relationships.
iii. **Learning Environment:** Physical and virtual environments count. AI-driven online learning platforms are able to replicate supportive environments via social presence cues and adaptive feedback (Martin & Bolliger, 2018).
iv. **Characteristics of students:** Academic performance, socioeconomic status, cultural background, and intrinsic motivation influence levels of engagement (Skinner & Pitzer, 2012).
v. **Technology Mediation:** Technological incorporation within learning profoundly influences engagement. Cautiously engineered AI-based solutions can create tailored, interactive, and gamefied learning contexts that maintain the interest of the students (Woolf, 2010).

Table 2.2 outlines key factors influencing engagement and corresponding AI-supported strategies.

Table 2. Factors Affecting Student Engagement and AI Strategies to Address Them

Factor	Influence on Engagement	AI-Supported Strategies
Instructional Design	Relevance, clarity, interactivity	Adaptive content delivery
Teacher-Student Relations	Emotional support, trust, responsiveness	AI analytics to support personalized feedback
Learning Environment	Comfort, inclusivity, stimulation	AI-enhanced virtual classrooms
Student Characteristics	Motivation, background knowledge	Customized learning paths
Technology Mediation	Usability, interactivity, accessibility	User-centered AI design

2.4 Why Engagement Matters for Learning Outcomes

There is a strong, empirically supported relationship between engagement and academic success:

i. **Academic Achievement**: Engagement predicts higher test scores, GPA, and standardized assessment outcomes (Carini, Kuh, & Klein, 2006).
ii. **Retention and Persistence**: Engaged students are more likely to stay enrolled and complete their educational programs (Trowler, 2010).
iii. **Skill Development**: Active engagement enhances critical thinking, problem-solving, and collaboration skills, essential for 21st-century competencies (Zepke & Leach, 2010).
iv. **Positive Educational Experiences**: Students who are emotionally and cognitively engaged report higher levels of satisfaction with their educational experiences, contributing to lifelong learning (Fredricks et al., 2004).

3. OVERVIEW OF AI IN EDUCATION

3.1 Introduction

The field of Artificial Intelligence (AI) has grown phenomenally over the last two decades, and the impact has been seen in virtually every sector, including education. In education, AI is increasingly being employed in education to facilitate personalized learning, automate administrative tasks, boost student motivation, and support decision-making. More and more studies are showing that AI's capability to personalize learning experience for a learner's individual profile has a profound effect on motivation, persistence, and learning outcomes (Luckin et al., 2016; Zawacki-Richter et al., 2019).

This section talks about the historical development and current state of AI in education, the use of AI to engage the student, the nature of AI models used, the advantages, and disadvantages.

Table 3. Historical Evolution Timeline of AI in Education

Year/Period	Major AI Development	Educational Application	Impact Example
1980s	Expert Systems	Rule-based tutoring	MYCIN, early ITS
2000s	Machine Learning	Predictive analytics	Early learning analytics
2010s	Deep Learning	Adaptive learning systems	Knewton, DreamBox
2020s	NLP and Affective Computing	Chatbots and emotion sensing	Jill Watson, Affectiva

3.2 Historical Evolution of AI in Education

3.2.1 Early Advancements (1970s-1990s)

The idea of using AI for education started with the creation of Intelligent Tutoring Systems (ITS) during the 1970s. SCHOLAR (Carbonell, 1970) was one of the first systems, providing Socratic-mode dialogue to learners depending on their answers. ITSs in the early days were primarily rule-based, using expert systems with pedagogical expertise as static if-then rules.

A second significant advance was achieved by Cognitive Tutors built at Carnegie Mellon University (Anderson et al., 1995) based on ACT-R theory of cognition. The tutors represented student knowledge states and cognitively adapted instruction dynamically based on cognitive performance.

3.2.2 The Data-Driven Era (2000s)

The early 2000s saw the emergence of data-driven AI models using machine learning to learn from large student behavior data sets. Learning Analytics (LA) and Educational Data Mining (EDM) grew as strong fields, aiming to uncover actionable patterns from learning data (Siemens, 2013).

Illustration: ASSISTments, an online tutoring platform, continually improved its feedback processes by conducting real-time analysis of student data (Heffernan & Heffernan, 2014).

3.2.3 The Deep Learning and AI Revolution (2010–present)

The worldwide accessibility of deep learning architecture, big data technology, and cloud computing certainly accelerated the use of AI in education. Duolingo, DreamBox Learning, and Squirrel AI now leverage AI to provide personalized learning at scale (Luckin et al., 2016; Chen et al., 2020).

Table 4. AI Tools Categorized by Type of Student Engagement.

Type of Engagement	Example AI Tools	Functionality
Cognitive Engagement	- Carnegie Learning - Squirrel AI - Smart Sparrow	Adaptive learning paths, real-time feedback, personalized content delivery
Behavioral Engagement	- Kahoot! (AI-enhanced quizzes) - Duolingo (gamified elements) - Classcraft (AI monitoring)	Gamified participation, behavioral tracking, points and rewards
Emotional Engagement	- Replika (AI chatbot for emotional support) - Affectiva (emotion recognition) - Woebot (mental health AI bot)	Sentiment detection, emotional feedback, social-emotional learning support

3.3 Current Landscape of AI Technologies in Education

Today's AI educational technologies are diverse and sophisticated, often combining multiple AI techniques. They are no longer confined to cognitive support but also address **social-emotional learning**, **behavioral engagement**, and **motivational scaffolding** (Holstein et al., 2020).

Key Categories:

i. **Intelligent Tutoring Systems (ITS)**: E.g., Carnegie Learning, ALEKS
ii. **Adaptive Learning Environments**: E.g., Smart Sparrow, Knewton
iii. **AI-Driven Gamification Platforms**: E.g., Duolingo, Classcraft
iv. **Conversational Agents**: E.g., Jill Watson, Replika for Education
v. **Predictive Analytics Dashboards**: E.g., Civitas Learning, Blackboard Predict
vi. **AI-Supported Virtual Reality (VR) and Augmented Reality (AR)**: E.g., ClassVR with AI analytics

Each tool targets different facets of student engagement, including emotional resonance, behavioral involvement, and cognitive focus (Fredricks et al., 2004).

3.4 Types of AI Models Used in Education

AI models can be broadly categorized based on their learning paradigms and functionalities:

Table 5.

Model Type	Educational Applications	Example Systems
Supervised Learning	Predicting dropout risk, adaptive quizzes	Civitas, Coursera ML models
Unsupervised Learning	Clustering students for adaptive grouping	DreamBox adaptive paths
Reinforcement Learning	Dynamic feedback adjustment, gamification	AI Dungeon, Classcraft

continued on following page

Table 5. Continued

Model Type	Educational Applications	Example Systems
Natural Language Processing (NLP)	Automated essay scoring, chatbots	Jill Watson, Grammarly
Affective Computing	Emotion detection, engagement monitoring	Affectiva, RealEyes

3.5 Advantages of AI Tools in Educational Settings

A significant body of empirical research points to the multi-faceted benefits of AI in education:

3.5.1. Personalized Learning Experiences

AI allows tailored content delivery, adapting instructional materials to students' prior knowledge, learning speed, and preferences (Pane et al., 2017).

3.6 Limitations and Challenges

Despite its potential, the rise of AI adoption brings with it a host of significant concerns:

3.6.1. Data Privacy and Security Risks

i. The extensive gathering of sensitive student information can lead to serious risks if it's not handled properly (Williamson & Eynon, 2020).

- **Example:** The debate surrounding ProctorU's online monitoring methods during the COVID-19 pandemic sparked concerns about the increasing surveillance in education.

3.6.2. Bias and Fairness

i. AI models can sometimes mirror and even intensify the social biases that are already present in the training datasets (Binns, 2018; Angwin et al., 2016).

- **Example:** Research has shown that predictive models aimed at identifying "at-risk" students often unfairly target those from minority backgrounds, and this happens without any clear reasoning (Holstein et al., 2021).

4. AI TOOLS FOR ENHANCING ENGAGEMENT

4.1 Intelligent Tutoring Systems (ITS)

An Intelligent Tutoring System (ITS) is a computer-based educational system that uses artificial intelligence to provide personalized and adaptive instruction to learners. It aims to mimic a human tutor by analyzing a student's responses, providing feedback, and adjusting the learning experience to meet their individual needs.

4.1.1 Key Features of Intelligent Tutoring Systems

Some core functionalities distinguish ITS from traditional digital learning tools:

i. **Student Modeling**: ITS construct real-time models of student knowledge and misconceptions, adapting content delivery based on learner profiles.
ii. **Adaptive Feedback**: These systems provide immediate, context-sensitive feedback aimed at correcting errors and deepening understanding.
iii. **Dialogic Interaction**: Advanced ITS, such as AutoTutor, engage students in natural language conversations to stimulate critical thinking (D'Mello & Graesser, 2012).
iv. **Affective Recognition**: Some ITS can detect and respond to student emotions like confusion or boredom, adjusting pedagogical approaches accordingly (Forbes-Riley & Litman, 2011).

By integrating these features, ITS not only support knowledge acquisition but also foster higher-order engagement that traditional methods often fail to sustain.

4.1.2 Impact on Student Engagement

The influence of ITS on engagement can be viewed across three primary dimensions:

i. **Cognitive Engagement**: By providing individualized challenges that match a student's current capabilities, ITS encourage deeper processing and problem-solving rather than rote memorization.
ii. **Behavioral Engagement**: Frequent system-student interactions, task completion encouragements, and responsive feedback mechanisms sustain active participation throughout learning sessions.
iii. **Emotional Engagement**: With the integration of affective computing, ITS detect signs of frustration or disengagement and modify instructional strategies to maintain positive emotional states.

4.1.3 Practical Examples of ITS in Education

Several Intelligent Tutoring Systems illustrate the diversity and effectiveness of this technology:

Table 6.

ITS Platform	Domain Focus	Engagement Strategy
MATHia (Carnegie)	Mathematics	Adaptive problem difficulty adjustment
ALEKS	Mathematics	Knowledge space theory-driven adaptive questioning
AutoTutor	Computer literacy, Physics	Dialog-based learning, affective response

4.1.4 Challenges and Ethical Considerations

While promising, Intelligent Tutoring Systems also present notable challenges:

i. **Over-reliance on Systems**: Students may become dependent on hints, undermining the development of independent learning strategies (VanLehn, 2011).
ii. **Bias in Content Delivery**: ITS trained predominantly on Western educational norms may not accommodate diverse cultural learning styles (Luckin, 2017).
iii. **Data Privacy Concerns**: Continuous monitoring requires significant data collection, raising issues about consent, security, and ethical use of learner data (Kay et al., 2012).

4.2 Personalized Learning Platforms

Personalized learning platforms, I believe, represent a real shift in how we think about education. They're really starting to change the whole game of how students actually engage with the material. The old ways, well they were often pretty rigid. They're using AI to sort of customize the experience for each individual student. They factor in numerous things like a student's needs, what they seem to like and their abilities – all of those things matter and the way they do this is interesting.

4.2.1 The Role of AI in Personalization

Artificial Intelligence is like the powerhouse behind real-time personalization, blending various tech capabilities such as machine learning, data mining, natural language processing (NLP), and affective computing (Luckin et al., 2016). Here are some of the key roles AI plays in these platforms:

i. **Real-Time Adaptation:** These platforms keep an eye on student responses and emotional cues to adjust teaching strategies on the fly.

ii. **Predictive Modeling:** AI can forecast future student performance and identify learning gaps by analyzing past patterns (Holmes et al., 2019).
iii. **Natural Language Understanding:** Thanks to NLP, platforms can make sense of open-ended student responses, providing more nuanced feedback.
iv. **Sentiment Analysis:** Some systems can pick up on emotional states to offer motivational support or tweak content difficulty as needed (Woolf et al., 2009).

A significant innovation is the creation of adaptive learning pathways, where AI crafts personalized sequences of activities based on ongoing diagnostic assessments (Pane et al., 2017). By pulling together multimodal data—like clickstreams, time spent on tasks, keystroke dynamics, and even facial recognition—AI can build detailed learner profiles, paving the way for a truly personalized educational experience (Ifenthaler & Yau, 2020).

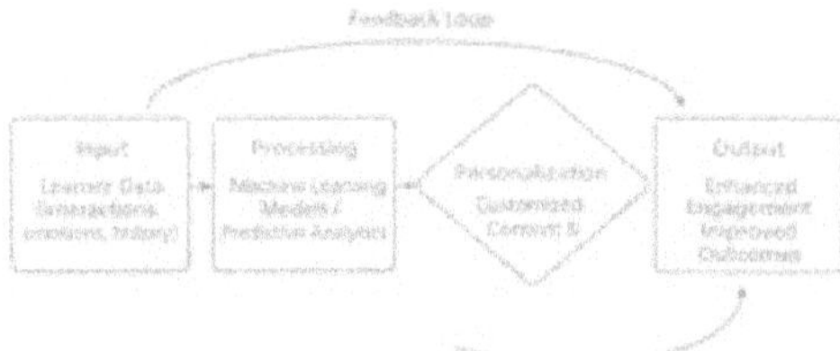

4.2.2 Key Examples of AI-Driven Personalized Learning Platforms

Several commercially available platforms exemplify the implementation of AI to personalize learning:

Table 7.

Platform	Features	Target Audience
DreamBox Learning	Real-time adjustment of math instruction based on over 48,000 data points per hour per student	K–8 students
Smart Sparrow	Instructor-driven adaptive courseware with AI-based feedback loops	Higher education & training
Knewton Alta	Continuous assessment and remediation in college-level subjects	College students

i. **Dream Box Learning** uses **reinforcement learning** algorithms that adjust problem complexity based on real-time error analysis (Shute & Ventura, 2013).

ii. **Smart Sparrow** allows educators to customize the AI's adaptivity rules, offering greater flexibility.
iii. **Knewton Alta** focuses on **competency-based learning**, ensuring mastery before progressing.

4.2.3 Impact of Personalized Learning Platforms on Student Engagement

4.2.3.1 Cognitive Engagement

Cognitive engagement is profoundly enhanced through AI personalization. By targeting a student's optimal challenge level (known as "flow" conditions per Csikszentmihalyi, 1990), AI platforms maintain high levels of mental effort and problem-solving persistence.

The impact is clear: personalized platforms have been shown to increase critical thinking, self-regulation, and deep learning strategies compared to traditional instruction models (Walkington, 2013).

4.2.3.2 Behavioral Engagement

Behavioral engagement manifests through increased time-on-task, reduced dropout rates, and more voluntary interactions with learning materials. Personalized platforms employ:

i. **Gamified Progression Systems**: Such as badges, points, and leaderboards tailored to individual performance.
ii. **Micro learning Sessions**: Short, personalized modules that keep students consistently engaged.

Pane et al. (2017) report that students using personalized learning platforms logged 30–50% more active learning time compared to those in traditional settings. Furthermore, behaviorally disengaged students (frequent absentees, low participation) demonstrated marked improvements after exposure to AI-enhanced personalized learning environments.

4.2.3.3 Emotional Engagement

Emotional engagement is often overlooked in traditional instruction but is central in AI-driven personalization. Systems that incorporate affective computing technologies, such as those discussed by Woolf et al. (2009), monitor indicators of frustration, boredom, or confusion. When negative emotions are detected, systems can intervene by offering motivational messages, simplifying content, or adjusting task difficulty (D'Mello & Graesser, 2012).

Studies have found that students who feel recognized, understood, and supported by personalized systems show significantly higher persistence and satisfaction rates (Luckin et al., 2016).

4.2.4 Challenges and Ethical Considerations

Despite the promise, several challenges must be addressed:

i. **Digital Divide**: Access to personalized platforms is unevenly distributed along socio-economic lines (Bulger, 2016).
ii. **Algorithmic Bias**: Unchecked biases in AI models can reinforce systemic inequalities (West et al., 2019).
iii. **Loss of Peer Learning Opportunities**: Over-personalization may lead to excessive individualization, limiting collaborative learning (Holmes et al., 2019).
iv. **Data Privacy**: Sensitive student information, if mismanaged, poses significant ethical risks (Slade & Prinsloo, 2013).

4.3 Gamification and AI: Revolutionizing Student Engagement

4.3.1 Understanding AI-Driven Gamification

Gamification is more than simply "making learning fun." It is rooted in **behavioral psychology**, **motivational theories**, and **cognitive engagement frameworks**. When gamification is enhanced by AI, it allows systems to **adapt game mechanics** to fit individual learner profiles in real-time.

Theoretical Basis:

According to **Self-Determination Theory** (Deci & Ryan, 1985), people are motivated when three psychological needs are met:

i. **Autonomy** (feeling in control)
ii. **Competence** (feeling effective)
iii. **Relatedness** (feeling connected to others)

Role of Flow Theory:

Flow (Csikszentmihalyi, 1990) refers to an optimal experience where individuals are fully immersed and engaged. Traditional education often struggles to create flow states because challenges are either too easy (boring) or too difficult (anxiety-inducing). AI allows real-time balancing of challenge-skill ratio, increasing the likelihood of **flow experiences** that deepen learning.

Table 8. Comparison between Traditional Gamification and AI-Enhanced Gamification

Aspect	Traditional Gamification	AI-Enhanced Gamification
Adaptivity	Static challenges	Real-time difficulty adjustment
Personalization	Uniform experience	Individualized progression
Emotional Responsiveness	None	Adaptive based on affective states
Learning Analytics	Summative, delayed	Formative, predictive
Long-term Engagement	Risk of fatigue	Sustained through dynamic novelty

4.3.2 Key Technologies Enabling AI Gamification

Modern AI gamified systems leverage **four technological pillars**:

i. Machine Learning (ML):

ML models adapt content based on students' behaviors. **Bayesian Knowledge Tracing** (Corbett & Anderson, 1995) and **Deep Knowledge Tracing** (Piech et al., 2015) are popular techniques. These models allow platforms to predict which concepts a learner has mastered and dynamically introduce appropriate challenges.

ii. Natural Language Processing (NLP):

NLP enables intelligent tutoring systems and chatbots to maintain **meaningful conversations** that adapt to user responses.

iii. Reinforcement Learning (RL):

Reinforcement learning trains AI systems to select game strategies that maximize student engagement over time.

iv. Computer Vision (CV):

Through webcams, CV analyzes facial expressions, posture, or gaze to estimate engagement levels (Bosch et al., 2016).

4.3.3 Real-World Applications and Case Studies

Table 9.

Platform	AI Feature	Key Gamification Mechanics	Measured Outcomes
Duolingo	Adaptive learning algorithms	Streaks, XP, Leaderboards	Higher retention, faster mastery
Classcraft	Predictive Behavior AI	RPG roles, Daily quests	Improved SEL, reduced incidents
Minecraft Education	AI bots, sandbox AI	Creative exploration, teamwork	Higher problem-solving skills

4.3.5 Ethical Considerations in AI Gamification

Ethical concerns demand special attention when integrating AI in gamification.

i. **Transparency:**

Learners must know how AI systems work (Floridi et al., 2018).

ii. **Algorithmic Accountability:**

Regular audits must be conducted to identify any biases that disadvantage certain groups (Barocas & Selbst, 2016).

iii. **Consent and Choice:**

Students must have the option to opt-out of gamified AI surveillance without penalty.

Table 10.

Ethical Principle	**Best Practice Example**
Transparency	Clear explanation of how AI decisions are made
Data Minimization	Only collect data necessary for engagement optimization
Student Agency	Allow students to opt-in/opt-out of gamified features
Bias Mitigation	Regular algorithmic bias testing

4.4 Chatbots and Virtual Assistants

In today's educational landscape, it's clearly evident that AI-powered chatbots and virtual assistants have really shaken things up in the way students and schools interact. These tools are helping boost student engagement by offering personalized and timely academic support honestly, that's a big deal These conversational agents use all sorts of fancy stuff like Natural Language Processing and machine learning, to have real-time conversations

4.4.1 Let's consider some examples.

Jill Watson at Georgia Tech:

Georgia Tech's Jill Watson is a great example of how AI can make a difference. It dealt with basic questions in an online AI course, which let the instructors focus on actually teaching. Students were happier because they got quick and reliable help. This confirmed that the chatbot was making a positive impact Staffordshire University's Beacon:

Table 11. Comparative Summary of Chatbot Capabilities and Limitations

Dimension	Strengths	Weaknesses
Availability	Continuous 24/7 support	Potential over-reliance
Interaction Quality	Immediate, adaptive feedback	Difficulty with nuanced queries
Emotional Engagement	Reduces isolation	Lacks deep emotional empathy
Scalability	Manages simultaneous interactions	May overlook complexities
Data Management	Rich analytics insights	Privacy and ethical concerns

4.5 Predictive Analytics for Engagement Monitoring

Predictive analytics employs statistical methods, machine learning techniques, and data mining approaches to analyze historical and current data for forecasting future outcomes (Ifenthaler & Yau, 2020). Within educational environments, predictive analytics has emerged as a critical tool for monitoring student engagement, allowing educators and institutions to proactively identify students at risk of disengagement or academic failure.

4.5.1 Early Detection of Disengaged Students

One of the primary applications of predictive analytics in education is the early identification of students demonstrating signs of disengagement. Predictive analytics tools systematically track multiple engagement indicators—such as frequency of LMS logins, assignment completion rates, forum participation, attendance patterns, and overall academic performance—to identify at-risk students well before traditional academic or behavioral flags become apparent (Jayaprakash et al., 2014).

For instance, Civitas Learning employs a sophisticated machine learning framework, integrating diverse data sources to accurately predict students' risk of disengagement, allowing targeted advising and proactive support measures.

4.5.2 Tools, Techniques, and Methodologies

Predictive analytics within education commonly uses supervised learning algorithms, including logistic regression, random forests, decision trees, support vector machines (SVM), neural networks, and ensemble methods (Romero & Ventura, 2020). Logistic regression models, due to their transparency and interpretability, are particularly popular for predicting student dropout risks and identifying critical engagement factors. Random forests and decision-tree-based algorithms facilitate the visualization and interpretation of complex engagement patterns, assisting educators in comprehending which factors most strongly predict disengagement (Ifenthaler & Yau, 2020).

Table 12. Summary of Prominent Predictive Analytics Platforms and Applications

Tool/Platform	Analytical Techniques	Educational Applications
Civitas Learning	Machine Learning, Ensemble Methods	Real-time risk assessment, early alert interventions
Blackboard Predict	Logistic Regression, Decision Trees	Student engagement prediction, personalized support mechanisms
Brightspace Insights	Neural Networks, Support Vector Machines	Academic progress forecasting, personalized intervention strategies
Starfish (Hobsons)	Predictive Modeling, Statistical Analysis	Early identification of at-risk students, personalized advising
Purdue Course Signals	Machine Learning, Logistic Regression	Engagement monitoring, reducing dropout rates through proactive alerts

(Adapted from Siemens & Long, 2011; Romero & Ventura, 2020)

4.5.3 Impact of Predictive Analytics on Student Engagement

Predictive analytics is really changing things in education and in a big way. It allows for proactive approaches to helping students which leads to better engagement and hopefully better grades. It's all about getting in there before things get too tough. Research seems to back this up. Studies have shown it's pretty good at finding students who might need extra help, which in turn can lead to fewer students dropping out. That's a major deal. Students feel supported and schools can retain more of them

4.5.4 Ethical Considerations in Predictive Engagement Analytics

Predictive analytics, it seems has a lot to offer in the realm of education, but at the same time we can't ignore the serious ethical dilemmas that come with it. Collecting all that data to build predictive models? Well, that opens up a whole can of worms. Student privacy data security and even just their autonomy - all of these are at risk, according to some research. (Slade & Prinsloo, 2013)

5. CASE STUDIES AND REAL-WORLD APPLICATIONS

The exciting potential of AI tools to boost student engagement really shines through when we look at actual educational settings. By diving into well-documented case studies and hands-on applications, we can see how AI technologies have been successfully used to tailor learning experiences, enhance retention, and encourage greater academic participation.

5.1 Case Study 1: AI in K-12 Engagement – DreamBox Learning

DreamBox Learning is an instance of how AI-powered learning platforms can be used to improve student participation in K-12 education which is primarily about math for kids from kindergarten to eighth grade. It employs smart algorithms and real-time data to personalize learning experiences, changing the lesson's difficulty and the teaching methods according to the student's interactions. The system is analyzing more than 48,000 data points every hour to tailor each student's journey according to their strengths and weaknesses.

An investigation by Harvard University states that students who use DreamBox for 14 hours only can make great progress in math skills and help students from diverse backgrounds to benefit. In addition to that, to the extent that DreamBox employs gamified characteristics such as points and badges, students are naturally motivated (intrinsic motivation) rather than being externally motivated.

Observed Impacts on Engagement

i. **Cognitive Engagement:** Students showcased impressive problem-solving abilities, strategic thinking, and a commendable level of persistence, even when tackling challenging math concepts. The adaptive challenges encouraged deeper understanding and helped steer clear of rote memorization.
ii. **Behavioral Engagement**: Time-on-task data revealed that students using DreamBox were significantly more engaged in their learning activities compared to those in traditional classroom settings.
iii. • **Emotional Engagement:** Many students expressed feelings of enjoyment, confidence, and less anxiety during math tasks, which contributed to a more positive emotional connection with STEM learning (Wang & Woodworth, 2011).

5.1.1 Critical Challenges and Limitations

DreamBox has shown some positive results but honestly, the way it's been implemented hasn't been without its problems. One thing that immediately jumps out is this whole issue of equitable access. You see kids in schools that don't have numerous resources, they often have a tough time getting hold of the technology they need, think reliable internet, a decent computer; you know, the stuff that lets them actually get the most out of these AI-driven learning programs. Bulger's work (2016) really hits on this if we don't put in the effort to tackle the digital divide head-on then introducing these fancy new AI platforms could inadvertently make the gaps in education even bigger.

5.1.2 Lessons Learned and Best Practices

The DreamBox case study offers several key takeaways for effectively implementing AI in K-12 education:

- Integration with Human Teaching: AI should enhance, not replace, the role of human educators. Teachers are vital in interpreting insights generated by AI and nurturing the relational aspects of learning that technology simply can't replicate.

i. **Focus on Equity:** It's essential for policymakers to guarantee that access to adaptive learning technologies is fair and equitable, backed by investments in infrastructure and digital literacy initiatives.
ii. **Ethical Data Practices:** Developers and educational institutions need to prioritize ethical data management, ensuring transparency and safeguarding student privacy.
iii. **Hybrid Engagement Models**: For AI tools to be successfully integrated, they should be part of a broader teaching framework that encourages cognitive, behavioral, and emotional engagement, blending personalized digital learning with collaborative classroom experiences.

5.2 Case Study 2: AI Platforms in Higher Education – Civitas Learning

Artificial intelligence is certainly making its presence known in higher education, that's for sure. It's changing a lot about how universities and colleges operate, from their decision-making processes to how they support students and foster academic engagement, one really good example of this is Civitas Learning. It's an AI-driven analytics platform that's really gaining traction across North America.Civitas uses some pretty complex machine learning algorithms They sort through tons of data, everything from student demographics and academic records to how students interact with their learning management systems and even advising notes. All of this is done to try and predict student success and how they'll engage with their studies (Siemens & Long, 2011)

So, the whole idea behind it is predictive modeling. Civitas can flag students who might be struggling or at risk of, you know disengaging or even dropping out that's valuable. This lets advisors instructors and the administration offer help right when it's needed.(Ifenthaler & Yau 2020) The platform's products, like "Illume" and "Inspire," give specific suggestions to both students and advisors, pushing them toward behaviors that can boost their chances of doing well academically, like, for instance participating more actively in class or getting their assignments in on time.

Key Impacts Observed

i. **Cognitive Engagement:** Civitas enabled more personalized learning experiences by predicting which types of courses and instructional formats best suited individual learners' needs.
ii. **Behavioral Engagement:** Real-time risk alerts encouraged timely advisor-student meetings, proactive assignment submission, and class attendance.
iii. **Emotional Engagement:** Personalized communication strategies—such as motivational nudges and positive reinforcement messages—fostered a greater sense of belonging among students.

5.2.1 Challenges and Ethical Considerations

Civitas Learning certainly offers some interesting possibilities. However, deploying AI in education isn't without its challenges, especially when you consider the ethical side of things A big hurdle to overcome is the whole idea of transparency in algorithms. Many students and even some faculty, are in the dark about how these predictive risk scores are calculated.

5.2.2 Lessons Learned and Best Practices

The Civitas case study provides several key lessons for higher education institutions considering AI adoption:

i. **Transparency and Student Empowerment:** Institutions must demystify AI processes by educating students about how their data is used and giving them agency over data sharing decisions.
ii. **Bias Audits:** Regular audits of predictive models are essential to identify and rectify biases, ensuring fairness and equity across diverse student populations.
iii. **Integrated Human Support:** AI recommendations must complement—not replace—human advising relationships. Effective interventions still require empathetic human interactions based on AI insights.
iv. **Data Ethics Governance:** Establishing clear policies regarding data ownership, access rights, and informed consent is vital for maintaining trust and legal compliance.

6. CHALLENGES AND ETHICAL CONSIDERATIONS

6.1 Data Privacy and Security Concerns

The integration of AI into education, as you know, brings with it a whole host of data concerns. We're talking about needing to gather, keep and then really delve into student data on a massive scale, which isn't ideal, obviously. This includes things like their names, academic progress how they interact with the systems and even patterns of behavior, On the one hand this data is supposed to pave the way for more personalized learning and help predict how engaged students might be. However, this also means that students' privacy is significantly at risk, according to Regulation (EU) 2016/679, which is something to bear in mind. The risks are pretty serious actually we're talking about the potential for someone to access this information without permission data getting stolen, or the misuse of very private student data. This could lead to identity theft which let's be honest, is a nightmare. It could also damage a student's reputation or cause serious emotional distress. When it comes to education breaking that trust can be especially harmful to those students who are already vulnerable. This could and often does, make it harder for them to participate and can completely destroy their sense of safety.(Slade & Prinsloo, 2013 is a good source for this).

6.2 Algorithmic Bias and Fairness

One of the biggest worries with AI in education and it's a serious one is the whole issue of algorithmic bias that means these AI systems might unintentionally discriminate against students based on things like race gender, or even their economic backgrounds. You know the kind of stuff that shouldn't matter. This bias can creep in at several different points. It could start with the data itself which might reflect past inequalities, because, well history hasn't always been fair, has it? Then, the system might favor certain learning styles or behaviors over others. And finally during the actual "training" of the AI, some methods could unintentionally prioritize the performance of the majority group. If we don't keep an eye on all this, these AI tools could end up wrongly labeling some students as "at risk" or even reinforcing old stereotypes about who's "smart" and who isn't.

6.3 Student Autonomy versus AI Recommendations

AI's creeping into education, isn't it? It's offering up suggestions, predictive stuff and little nudges to help students out. The idea is to boost their academic game, however there's a potential downside too, and a sort of hidden pitfall. If students start seeing this AI-generated guidance as the be-end-all like it's always right, their own autonomy could get squashed. I mean, it makes sense. We can't just blindly follow everything, can we? A big problem as I see it, is the slow chipping away at the skills we use to learn on our own. When students lean too heavily on automated advice, they might miss out on developing crucial skills, things like thinking critically, making their own choices and reflecting on what they've learned.

That's a worry, especially in higher end, where we want students to become independent learners. That is supposed to be the entire point. So to make sure AI helps without hurting, the systems need to be designed differently. They should nudge students toward making informed choices, rather than making them simply comply. Transparency about how the recommendations are made matters, they need to be upfront about where it's all coming from.

Table 13.

AI Tool / Trend	Ethical Challenge	Mitigation Strategy
Intelligent Tutoring Systems (ITS)	Data privacy risks, over-monitoring	Transparent data policies, student consent, data minimization
Chatbots / Conversational Agents	Bias in responses, misinformation	Diverse training data, regular content audits
Gamification Elements	Superficial engagement, addictive behaviors	Balance extrinsic rewards with intrinsic motivation design
Predictive Analytics	Algorithmic bias, unfair profiling	Bias audits, explainable AI techniques
AR/VR Tools	Accessibility barriers, sensory overload	Universal design principles, user customization options
Large Language Models (e.g., GPT-4)	Data leakage, hallucination of facts	Input monitoring, user education, usage restrictions

7. FUTURE DIRECTIONS AND EMERGING TRENDS

7.1 AI and Emotional Intelligence: The Rise of Affective Computing

The world of educational AI is really starting to push some boundaries and one exciting area is what's called affective computing. It's essentially about machines that can understand and react to human feelings – things like happiness, sadness, or even confusion, think about it: these systems are designed to "read" us, using things like our facial expressions, the tone of our voices and even how our bodies are reacting. That's a pretty fascinating concept. The whole idea is that by understanding a student's emotional state, these AI tools can become more engaging and supportive, for example, a tutoring system that senses when a student is getting frustrated. It could then adjust the difficulty of the questions offer some words of encouragement, or even just suggest a break.

It's all about creating a more positive learning experience. Moreover there's the potential for these systems to help identify mental health issues early on which could lead to timely interventions and support.

However this is where things get a little tricky, because, all this emotional data – that's really sensitive stuff. There are definitely some ethical concerns about privacy and how this information might be used. In fact there are even worries about the potential for commercializing our emotions. It's definitely a minefield that needs careful navigation.

7.2 Augmented Reality (AR), Virtual Reality (VR), and AI Integration

The way artificial intelligence is meshing with augmented and virtual reality? Well, it's a really big deal when it comes to the future of education I think the potential here is truly transformative. Imagine combining AI's smarts with the immersive nature of AR/VR. Educators could then craft these incredibly personalized learning experiences which are both dynamic and, well they're pretty engaging too. (Bacca et al., 2014)

Take for instance, those AI-powered VR simulations they could, in theory adjust themselves based on how a student is doing. So if someone is struggling, the system could offer some extra help or pose some Socratic-style questions.

However, there are definitely some hurdles too. Things like the costs of development and how accessible the technology actually is, are issues and then there's the issue of motion sickness. All these things have to be carefully considered if this technology is going to be deployed in an equitable and effective way.(Radianti et al. and 2020)

8. CONCLUSION

The integration of AI into education it's fair to say, is shaking things up quite a bit, changing how we think about keeping students engaged. Throughout these pages, we've looked at a whole range of AI applications. Think intelligent tutoring systems, personalized learning platforms, even those chatty chatbots and gamification engines. There's also the predictive analytics stuff – all of it, offering new ways to boost how students behave think and feel about learning. We've seen that, if used right these AI tools can be pretty helpful. They can give quick feedback, adjust to how each student learns, and even help with their emotional well-being. And they can often predict when a student might start to disengage. We've seen this in action too. The examples from K-12 like DreamBox Learning and in higher ed, with companies like Civitas Learning, really show how AI is starting to make a real difference in learning results and overall student experiences. However and this is important, there are some big hurdles to consider. Things like data privacy issues potential biases in the algorithms and the risk of students becoming overly reliant on the technology. We need to keep a close eye on those areas. What's more, future developments in things like affective computing, immersive AR/VR and how humans and AI work together are coming. These advancements will bring exciting chances, but also some tricky ethical questions that educators will need to address. One key idea that emerges is the importance of balance. We need to use AI's strengths while still protecting what makes human teachers so valuable. AI is great at repetitive tasks, looking at tons of data and providing personalized learning at scale. But it struggles with understanding the complexities of human interactions, the moral side of things and all the nuances of human growth. Educators aren't just delivering information. They're mentors, motivators and ethical guides. They bring empathy, creativity and an understanding of different cultures – something no computer program can really replicate. So the future isn't about choosing between AI and human teachers. Instead, it's about building partnerships.AI can help us do more, but it shouldn't replace the professional judgment and human connection that is vital for students. Building these kinds of partnerships will change how we train teachers how we provide professional development and even how schools are run. It also involves getting students involved in how AI is used in their own learning helping them become critical ethical thinkers and independent learners in a world where AI is increasingly present.

REFERENCES

Adamopoulou, E., & Moussiades, L. (2020). Chatbots: History, technology, and applications. *Machine Learning with Applications*, *2*, 100006.

Agnihotri, L., & Ott, A. (2014). Building a student-at-risk model. *Educational Data Mining*, *7*, 210–217.

Ames, C. (1992). Classrooms: Goals, Structures, and Student Motivation. *Journal of Educational Psychology*, *84*(3), 261–271.

Anderson, A., Huttenlocher, D., Kleinberg, J., & Leskovec, J. (2014). Engaging with massive online courses. *Proceedings of the 23rd International Conference on World Wide Web*, 687–698.

Appleton, J. J., Christenson, S. L., & Furlong, M. J. (2008). Student engagement with school: Critical conceptual and methodological issues of the construct. *Psychology in the Schools*, *45*(5), 369–386. DOI: 10.1002/pits.20303

Arnold, K. E., & Pistilli, M. D. (2012). Purdue's Course Signals: Enhancing student success through learning analytics. *Proceedings of LAK*, *12*, 267–270.

Bacca, J., Baldiris, S., Fabregat, R., & Graf, S., & Kinshuk. (2014). Augmented Reality Trends in Education: A Systematic Review of Research and Applications. *Journal of Educational Technology & Society*, *17*(4), 133–149.

Baker, R. S., & Inventado, P. S. (2014). Educational data mining and learning analytics. *Learning Analytics*, 61-75.

Barocas, S., & Selbst, A. D. (2016). Big data's disparate impact. *California Law Review*, *104*(3), 671–732.

Bjork, R. A., & Bjork, E. L. (2011). *Making things hard on yourself, but in a good way: Creating desirable difficulties to enhance learning*. Psychology and the Real World.

Bloom, B. S. (1984). The 2 sigma problem: The search for methods of group instruction as effective as one-to-one tutoring. *Educational Researcher*, *13*(6), 4–16.

Bosch, N., Chen, Y., & D'Mello, S. (2016a). Detecting affective states from facial expressions while learning. *ACM International Conference on Multimodal Interaction*, 451-458.

Bosch, N., Chen, Y., & D'Mello, S. (2016b). It's written on your face: Detecting affective states from facial expressions while learning computer programming. *Proceedings of the 2016 ACM on International Conference on Multimodal Interaction*, 451–458.

Bulger, M. (2016). *Personalized learning: The conversations we're not having*. Data & Society Research Institute.

Carini, R. M., Kuh, G. D., & Klein, S. P. (2006). Student engagement and student learning: Testing the linkages. *Research in Higher Education, 47*(1), 1–32. DOI: 10.1007/s11162-005-8150-9

Carlini, N., Tramer, F., Wallace, E., Jagielski, M., Herbert-Voss, A., Lee, K., & Song, D. (2021). Extracting training data from large language models. *USENIX Security Symposium.*

Castañeda, L., & Selwyn, N. (2018). More than tools? Making sense of the ongoing digitizations of higher education. *International Journal of Educational Technology in Higher Education, 15*(1), 1–10.

Chou, Y. (2019). *Actionable Gamification: Beyond Points, Badges, and Leaderboards.* Octalysis Group.

Csikszentmihalyi, M. (1990). *Flow: The psychology of optimal experience.* Harper & Row.

D'Mello, S., & Graesser, A. (2012a). AutoTutor and affective computing: Enhancing engagement through emotion detection. *Journal of Educational Psychology.*

D'Mello, S. K., & Graesser, A. C. (2012b). Dynamics of affective states during complex learning. *Learning and Instruction, 22*(2), 145–157.

Deci, E. L., & Ryan, R. M. (1985). *Intrinsic motivation and self-determination in human behavior.* Springer Science & Business Media. DOI: 10.1007/978-1-4899-2271-7

Deci, E. L., & Ryan, R. M. (2000). The "what" and "why" of goal pursuits: Human needs and the self-determination of behavior. *Psychological Inquiry, 11*(4), 227–268.

Deterding, S., Dixon, D., Khaled, R., & Nacke, L. (2011). From game design elements to gamefulness: Defining gamification. *Proceedings of the 15th International Academic MindTrek Conference*, 9–15.

Domínguez, A., Saenz-de-Navarrete, J., De-Marcos, L., Fernández-Sanz, L., Pagés, C., & Martínez-Herráiz, J. J. (2013). Gamifying learning experiences: Practical implications and outcomes. *Computers & Education, 63*, 380–392.

Eccles, J. S., & Wigfield, A. (2002). Motivational beliefs, values, and goals. *Annual Review of Psychology, 53*(1), 109–132. DOI: 10.1146/annurev.psych.53.100901.135153 PMID: 11752481

Fitzpatrick, K. K., Darcy, A., & Vierhile, M. (2017). Automated conversational agent Woebot. *JMIR Mental Health, 4*(2), e19.

Floridi, L., Cowls, J., & Beltrametti, M.. (2018). AI4People—An Ethical Framework for a Good AI Society. *Minds and Machines, 28*(4), 689–707.

Følstad, A., & Brandtzaeg, P. B. (2017). Chatbots and HCI. *Interaction, 24*(4), 38–42.

Forbes-Riley, K., & Litman, D. (2011). Benefits and challenges of real-time uncertainty detection and adaptation in a spoken dialogue computer tutor. *Speech Communication, 53*(9–10), 1115–1136.

Fredricks, J. A., Blumenfeld, P. C., & Paris, A. H. (2004). School engagement: Potential of the concept, state of the evidence. *Review of Educational Research, 74*(1), 59–109. DOI: 10.3102/00346543074001059

Goda, Y., & Yamada, M. (2020). Chatbot support and academic performance. *Education and Information Technologies*, *25*(2), 967–981.

Goel, A. K., & Polepeddi, L. (2016). Jill Watson: Virtual teaching assistant. *Georgia Tech Research Institute Report.*

Graesser, A. C.. (2018). Intelligent tutoring systems. *International Journal of AI in Education, 28*, 279–301.

Hamari, J., Koivisto, J., & Sarsa, H. (2014). Does gamification work? — A literature review of empirical studies on gamification. *Proceedings of the 47th Hawaii International Conference on System Sciences*, 3025–3034.

Henrie, C. R., Halverson, L. R., & Graham, C. R. (2015). Measuring student engagement in technology-mediated learning: A review. *Computers & Education, 90*, 36–53. DOI: 10.1016/j.compedu.2015.09.005

Holmes, W., Bialik, M., & Fadel, C. (2019). *Artificial Intelligence in Education: Promises and Implications for Teaching and Learning*. Center for Curriculum Redesign.

Ifenthaler, D., & Yau, J. Y. K. (2020). Utilising learning analytics for study success: Reflections on current empirical findings. *Research and Practice in Technology Enhanced Learning, 15*(1), 1–17. DOI: 10.1186/s41039-020-00129-5

Jayaprakash, S. M., Moody, E. W., Lauría, E. J. M., Regan, J. R., & Baron, J. D. (2014). Early alert of academically at-risk students: An open source analytics initiative. *The Internet and Higher Education, 21*, 15–26.

Jeno, L. M., Grytnes, J. A., & Vandvik, V. (2017). The effect of a mobile-application tool on biology students' motivation and achievement in species identification: A Self-Determination Theory perspective. *Computers & Education, 107*, 1–12. DOI: 10.1016/j.compedu.2016.12.011

Junco, R. (2012). The relationship between frequency of Facebook use, participation in Facebook activities, and student engagement. *Computers & Education, 58*(1), 162–171. DOI: 10.1016/j.compedu.2011.08.004

Kahu, E. R. (2013). Framing student engagement in higher education. *Studies in Higher Education, 38*(5), 758–773. DOI: 10.1080/03075079.2011.598505

Kay, J., Reimann, P., Diebold, E., & Kummerfeld, B. (2012). MOOCs: So many learners, so much potential. *IEEE Intelligent Systems, 27*(4), 70–77.

Kizilcec, R. F., & Halawa, S. (2015). Attrition and achievement gaps in online learning. *Proceedings of the Second ACM Conference on Learning@ Scale*, 57–66.

Lepper, M. R., & Greene, D. (1978). Overjustification Research and Beyond. *Hidden Costs of Reward: New Perspectives on the Psychology of Human Motivation.*

Lepper, M. R., Greene, D., & Nisbett, R. E. (1973). Undermining children's intrinsic interest with extrinsic reward: A test of the overjustification hypothesis. *Journal of Personality and Social Psychology, 28*(1), 129–137.

Long, P., & Siemens, G. (2011). Penetrating the analytics fog. *EDUCAUSE Review*, *46*(5), 30–32.

Luckin, R. (2017). *Intelligence Unleashed: An Argument for AI in Education.* Pearson Education.

Luckin, R., Holmes, W., Griffiths, M., & Forcier, L. B. (2016). *Intelligence Unleashed: An Argument for AI in Education.* Pearson Education.

Martin, F., & Bolliger, D. U. (2018). Engagement matters: Student perceptions on the importance of engagement strategies in the online learning environment. *Online Learning : the Official Journal of the Online Learning Consortium, 22*(1), 205–222. DOI: 10.24059/olj.v22i1.1092

Mnih, V., Kavukcuoglu, K., & Silver, D.. (2015). Human-level control through deep reinforcement learning. *Nature, 518*(7540), 529–533.

Pane, J. F., Steiner, E. D., Baird, M. D., & Hamilton, L. S. (2015). *Continued progress: Promising evidence on personalized learning.* RAND Corporation., DOI: 10.7249/RR1365

Picard, R. W. (1997). *Affective Computing.* MIT Press.

Prince, M. (2004). Does active learning work? A review of the research. *Journal of Engineering Education, 93*(3), 223–231. DOI: 10.1002/j.2168-9830.2004.tb00809.x

Qian, M., & Clark, K. R. (2016). Game-based Learning and 21st century skills: A review of recent research. *Computers in Human Behavior, 63*, 50–58.

Radianti, J., Majchrzak, T. A., Fromm, J., & Wohlgenannt, I. (2020). A systematic review of immersive virtual reality applications for higher education: Design elements, lessons learned, and research agenda. *Computers & Education, 147*, 103778.

Reeve, J. (2012). A self-determination theory perspective on student engagement. In Christenson, S. L., Reschly, A. L., & Wylie, C. (Eds.), *Handbook of Research on Student Engagement* (pp. 149–172). Springer. DOI: 10.1007/978-1-4614-2018-7_7

Regulation (EU) 2016/679 (GDPR).

Reich, J., & Ito, M. (2017). *From good intentions to real outcomes: Equity by design in learning technologies*. Digital Media and Learning Research Hub.

Reschly, A. L., & Christenson, S. L. (2012). Jingle, jangle, and conceptual haziness: Evolution and future directions of the engagement construct. In *Handbook of Research on Student Engagement* (pp. 3–19). Springer. DOI: 10.1007/978-1-4614-2018-7_1

Romero, C., & Ventura, S. (2020). Educational data mining and learning analytics: An updated review. *WIREs Data Mining*, *10*(3), e1355.

Roorda, D. L., Koomen, H. M. Y., Spilt, J. L., & Oort, F. J. (2011). The influence of affective teacher–student relationships on students' school engagement and achievement: A meta-analytic approach. *Review of Educational Research*, *81*(4), 493–529. DOI: 10.3102/0034654311421793

Sandvig, C., Hamilton, K., Karahalios, K., & Langbort, C. (2014). Auditing algorithms: Research methods for detecting discrimination on internet platforms. *Data and Discrimination: Collected Essays*.

Selwyn, N. (2020). *Should robots replace teachers? AI and the future of education*. Polity Press.

Settles, B., & Meeder, B. (2016). *A trainable spaced repetition model for language learning*. Association for Computational Linguistics.

Shernoff, D. J., Csikszentmihalyi, M., Schneider, B., & Shernoff, E. S. (2014). *Engaging youth in schools: Empirically-based models to guide future innovations*. Springer.

Shute, V. J. (2011). Stealth assessment in computer-based games to support learning. *Computer Games and Instruction*, *55*, 503–524.

Shute, V. J., & Ventura, M. (2013). *Stealth Assessment: Measuring and Supporting Learning in Video Games*. MIT Press.

Siemens, G., & Baker, R. S. (2012). Learning analytics and educational data mining: Towards communication and collaboration. *Proceedings of LAK*, *12*, 252–254.

Siemens, G., & Long, P. (2011). Penetrating the fog: Analytics in learning and education. *EDUCAUSE Review*, *46*(5), 30–32.

Skinner, E. A., & Pitzer, J. R. (2012). Developmental dynamics of student engagement, coping, and everyday resilience. In *Handbook of Research on Student Engagement* (pp. 21–44). Springer. DOI: 10.1007/978-1-4614-2018-7_2

Slade, S., & Prinsloo, P. (2013a). Ethical issues in analytics. *The American Behavioral Scientist*, *57*(10), 1510–1529.

Slade, S., & Prinsloo, P. (2013b). Learning analytics: Ethical issues and dilemmas. *The American Behavioral Scientist*, *57*(10), 1510–1529.

Trowler, V. (2010). Student engagement literature review. *The Higher Education Academy, 11*(1), 1–15.

UNESCO. (2021). *AI and education: Guidance for policy-makers*. United Nations Educational, Scientific and Cultural Organization.

Van Dijk, J. (2005). *The Deepening Divide: Inequality in the Information Society*. SAGE Publications.

VanLehn, K. (2011). The relative effectiveness of human tutoring, intelligent tutoring systems, and other tutoring systems. *Educational Psychologist, 46*(4), 197–221. DOI: 10.1080/00461520.2011.611369

Vygotsky, L. S. (1978). *Mind in Society: The Development of Higher Psychological Processes*. Harvard University Press.

Walkington, C. (2013). Using adaptive learning technologies to personalize instruction to student interests: The impact on performance and attitudes. *Journal of Educational Psychology*.

Wang, A., & Woodworth, K. (2011). *Evaluation of the Effectiveness of the DreamBox Learning Program*. Center for Education Policy Research, Harvard University.

West, S. M., Whittaker, M., & Crawford, K. (2019). *Discriminating systems: Gender, race, and power in AI*. AI Now Institute.

Wigfield, A., Tonks, S., & Klauda, S. L. (2009). Expectancy-value theory. In *Handbook of Motivation at School* (pp. 55–75). Routledge.

Williamson, B., & Eynon, R. (2020). Historical threads, missing links, and future directions in AI in education. *Learning, Media and Technology, 45*(3), 223–235. DOI: 10.1080/17439884.2020.1798995

Winkler, R., & Söllner, M. (2018). Chatbots in education. *ECIS Proceedings*, Portsmouth, UK.

Woolf, B. P. (2010). *Building intelligent interactive tutors: Student-centered strategies for revolutionizing e-learning*. Morgan Kaufmann.

Zepke, N., & Leach, L. (2010). Improving student engagement: Ten proposals for action. *Active Learning in Higher Education, 11*(3), 167–177. DOI: 10.1177/1469787410379680

Zimmerman, B. J. (2002). Becoming a Self-Regulated Learner: An Overview. *Theory into Practice, 41*(2), 64–70.

Chapter 9
Exploring the Authenticity of AI-Generated Texts as Resources for Language Teaching and Learning: Challenges and Opportunities

Ferit Kılıçkaya
https://orcid.org/0000-0002-3534-0924
Burdur Mehmet Akif Ersoy University, Turkey

ABSTRACT

This chapter aims to tackle this question in two steps. First, it will point out various challenges that educators and learners face when integrating AI-generated texts in pedagogical and learning practices. Second, it will discuss a set of opportunities for instructors and learners when generating AI-produced texts in the foreign language classroom. The binaries of challenges and opportunities described here are set within the framework of 'authenticity' and 'resourcefulness' borrowed from literature in language teacher education and second language writing. In response to the challenges and opportunities, a threefold examination is conducted, beginning with a description of how language educational policies and practices, pedagogies, and markets are increasingly shaped by AI implementations in general and the adoption of AI-generated texts specifically for language teaching and learning in particular.

INTRODUCTION

Utilizing AI in education is on the rise to such an extent that some have predicted that AI will become the mainstream trend in educational technology (Tedre et al., 2021; Zhai et al., 2021). The inroads of AI are obvious in language education, a field that has attracted a great deal of interest based on the belief among developers and educators that AI technology has the potential to further enhance the teaching and learning of foreign languages (Aithal

DOI: 10.4018/979-8-3373-5092-9.ch009

et al., 2024; Dubé & Wen, 2022; Luan et al., 2020). As an outcome, one question that arises is whether AI-generated texts have the potential to serve as inherently authentic sources for educators and learners (Garib & Coffelt, 2024; Vetter et al., 2024).

Authentic materials are typically defined as materials created without the aim to teach language; in other words, these materials are created by the speakers of that language for genuine communicative needs and purposes (Gilmore, 2019; Mishan, 2005, 2017). There are obvious pedagogical benefits of incorporating authentic materials within language courses, including an increase in motivation and enthusiasm of the learners. The presentation of authentic content equips learners with immediate exposure to the whole range of discourse. Many different accents and multiple styles can be presented in such a medium (Namaziandost et al., 2021). A major advantage of using an authentic written text in the classroom is that it can facilitate the development of the learners' bottom-up pragmatic and sociolinguistic skills. Students can learn how co-text and context complicity affect overall meaning and successful processing through reading relevant articles and essays. When used as the basis for role-play and the teaching of functions to deal with that topic, this text can also be very useful in creating authentic and genuine language and communication strategies (Esfandiari & Gawhary, 2019; Huang, 2018). Using authentic language interaction can also contribute to the development of the competence of the learners in listening, turn-taking, and a whole range of speaking strategies. Since many authentic texts are made available through taped sources, they can be exploited in the classroom. It could, for example, be extremely motivating for a class to interact with an authentic conversation. However, it might not be possible to utilize authentic materials due to several reasons such as the linguistic difficulty of these materials and the learners' proficiency level (Kılıçkaya, 2004). This might be where technology, especially generative artificial intelligence, can be providing solutions to deal with such issues (Huang et al., 2023; Liu et al., 2024; Peddar, 2025).

Given the advancements in computer science and artificial intelligence (AI) in the last decade, teaching has been enhanced, working memory increased, and psychoeducational research has begun to investigate the benefits of AI to analyze students' performance in educational settings (Adıgüzel et al., 2023; Bozkurt et al., 2021; Zhang & Aslan, 2021). Educational advancements aside, AI has extended its applicability even further, such that AI-generating texts such as conversational agents, language generation, and article completions have recently started to be exploited, especially in language teaching. AI-generated texts and the tools and hypermedia that exploit AI-generated text are being used across different levels, ages, and languages around the world. The most noticeable example of the usage of these resources is within the release of a chatbot (Huang et al., 2022).

This chapter tries to tackle this question in two steps. First, it will point out various challenges that educators and learners face when integrating AI-generated texts in pedagogical and learning practices. Second, it will discuss a set of opportunities for instructors and learners when generating AI-produced texts in the foreign language classroom. The binaries of challenges and opportunities described here are set within the framework of 'authenticity' and 'resourcefulness' borrowed from literature in language teacher education and second language writing. In response to the challenges and opportunities, a threefold examination is conducted, beginning with a description of how language educational policies and practices, pedagogies, and markets are increasingly shaped by AI implementations in general and the adoption of AI-generated texts specifically for language teaching and learning. The second aim is to develop an understanding of how educators and students address the challenges presented in different educational contexts and how they take advantage of the opportunities offered. The third aim is to critically engage in how AI-generated texts may be more or less acceptable by or authentic to language educators, and language learners.

AI-GENERATED TEXTS IN LANGUAGE TEACHING AND LEARNING

AI-generated content for language teaching and learning can have multiple functions, ranging from being input or reference materials for target language use to providing practice for learners, to integrating language skills or systems (Lee et al., 2023; Shanshan & Sen, 2024; Warschauer et al., 2023). In the literature, there are only a few sub-genres of AI-generated content, such as articles, dialogues, comprehensible input, exercises, compositions, summaries, capstones, error corrections, generated content as support for non-generated content, and language tutoring systems providing directives or advice (Chauhan, 2024; Kim et al., 2024). This list gives a general overview of the functions AI-generated text can provide, even if research is dominated by articles that are mainly regarded as input materials for language learners (Creely, 2024; Patty, 2024; Warschauer et al., 2023).

AI-generated texts have the potential to provide learners with opportunities that are yet to be fully exploited, even if they are not written by the conventional standard of human authorship (Alexander et al., 2023; Herbold et al., 2023; Tsao & Nogues, 2024; Warschauer et al., 2023). However, it is still being investigated in which educational settings and for what purposes AI-generated content can best be implemented. Language materials written by AI programs could be seen as somewhat 'disengaging' for students in traditional and adapted educational contexts. For many educators, it is unusual to incorporate 'fake' dialogues, compositions, and topics in a TEFL classroom, and incidental comments received from students have often expressed feelings of the generated publications being staged, untruths, unappetizing, or incomprehensible (Kim et al., 2024; Matthews & Volpe, 2023; Zhai et al., 2024). Yet, leaning into the peculiarities of AI could serve as a significant benefit. In terms of oppressive pedagogies and more liberatory affordances, AI with 'own' agendas could be used as an illustration tool to address techno-capitalist systems in micro- and macro-level contexts in many different fields. AI-generated conversations relevant to sexual education and climate change could support an open conversation in the classroom and serve both individual and group needs of diverse learners (Bozkurt et al., 2023; Pillis et al., 2024; Varsik & Vosberg, 2024).

AI-generated texts refer to texts created by algorithms. They should be distinguished from traditional texts that are manually written or authored. AI-generated texts come in various types, serving different educational purposes. Firstly, AI agents have been developed to hold conversational dialogues with humans and are employed to provide speaking and listening practice for language learners (Zhai & Wibowo, 2023) AI agents serving as educational assistants also provide textual educational information, corrections, explanations, and so on.

Secondly, AI-developed instructions, explanations, educational problems, situations, and stories are available as textual, sometimes multimodal materials. Thirdly, AI models have been developed to automatically assess the text-based productions of learners in terms of their accuracy, fluency, relevance, complexity, and so on.

In order to produce AI-generated texts, supervised models are programmed to predict the next word or word pieces that they will append to the given or imagined contexts. Based on the huge amount of training data, the models have learned the probability distributions of the sequences in the contexts used to produce the already generated texts. The AI models suitable for academic text development possess the linguistic creativity and reasoning abilities to generate a plausible result by conducting linguistic pattern matching with the general patterns absorbed from the world's text (Bouschery et al., 2023). They have the capability to generate novel and linguistically intricate expressions. Today's AI can therefore offer us a quite large volume of texts that have been created just for this project. AI can generate texts written in an L1 context or in an L2 context by speakers; written in a simplified form; written by translators; and written by summarizers (Alharbi, 2023; Godwin-Jones, 2022; Hwang et al., 2023). AI-generated texts are entirely digital at their birth. While being produced, they do not involve any human body. They are free from any physical and social contexts of their later use, in which humans live and work. AI-generated resources are pure texts. Notably, initially developed AI algorithms for language treatment have evolved substantially over time, and in the process, have improved their capabilities for incorporating broader ranges of language components in the produced texts. In other words, they have strengthened their abilities to generate authentic and credible texts relevant to learners' language and content learning. They are now able to produce more extensive language items and combinations including images and audio. AI-generated texts are thus the materials found to be useful for assisted language learning, including resources for extensive reading, adapted texts, authentic and credible standardized test items, compression, error detection, and language research (Garib & Coffelt, 2024; Lee et al., 2023; Warschauer et al., 2023).

AUTHENTICITY IN LANGUAGE LEARNING

Authenticity in this context has been discussed and defined in a variety of ways, although there is general agreement it consists of representing 'real language' that has been created by, and for, members of a speech community. More often, authenticity is most validly attributed to naturally occurring discourse, the primary distinction between 'authentic' and 'inauthentic' being whether the stimuli in question have been created specifically for language learning or educational purposes. The pedagogical rationale for using authentic resources within or beyond an education program is that doing so allows learners to experience the language and achieve communicative competence in a similar manner that second language learners do so over time: they are exposed to genuine real-life use of L2 or lingua franca in a range of communities and with interlocutors (Abdukhayotovna, 2022; Pinzón, 2020). Consequently, such a perspective challenges the traditional approach to language teaching and the use of artificial contexts for learning purposes.

A variety of empirical studies, spanning multiple linguistic, educational, and cultural contexts, have documented adult and adolescent learners speaking, with those interacting with co-present or videoed interlocutors typically speaking more than those interacting via telephone or poster responses. Hence, real-life context and interlocutors are important elements in setting the conditions which encourage learners to attempt communication (Almazova et al., 2021; Marden & Herrington, 2020). From a pedagogical perspective, authentic language materials can maximize learner exposure to real language, potentially increase the time for exposure, and provide input in meaningful, rather than purely formalized, contexts. In courses where students have limited exposure to target language speakers, teachers need to look beyond what is typically found in textbooks, in particular, more traditional L2 materials that may focus on producing language out of context (Brevik & Rindal, 2020; Joraboyev, 2021; Xiao & Zhi, 2023). Focusing only on the learners' linguistic accuracy, in the complete absence of authentic language use, is less likely to foster dedication to L2 learning and to maintain engagement over time, compared to contextualized communication that is typically found in interactions in the 'real' world. Authentic use is also more likely to foster the ability to paraphrase and make vocabulary choices, which could also increase learner retention and confidence as they are more able to handle the vocabulary in a range of authentic contexts. This is arguably particularly true for what is termed 'low-scope' learners, who have a brief or specific interest in the language which may not constitute even limited engagement. Indeed, this term is probably particularly relevant given increased mobility offers many the opportunity to communicate substantially in one's first language. However, in terms of how language can be effectively learned, if the language only concerns very specific domains, such as signs, travel information, or the natural environment, it would not be appropriate for learners to have to engage with high-level texts on literature or journalism. The use of inauthentic data, such as being exposed to very formalized scripts or literature, can hinder learning as learners may feel removed from the data, and discourage key individual elements that are critical for L2 (re)production: cognitive and affective involvement, and individual, internalized, heard language use. However, they also need to apply to a wide audience, as others interested in L2, particularly the public, often have a wide range of interests.

AI-generated texts have the potential to provide learners with opportunities that are yet to be fully exploited, even if they are not written by the conventional standard of human authorship (Alexander et al., 2023; Herbold et al., 2023; Tsao & Nogues, 2024; Warschauer et al.2023). However, it is still being investigated in which educational settings and for what purposes AI-generated content can best be implemented. Language materials written by AI programs could be seen as somewhat 'disengaging' for students in traditional and adapted educational contexts. For many educators, it is unusual to incorporate 'fake' dialogues, compositions, and topics in a TEFL classroom, and incidental comments received from students have often expressed feelings of the generated publications being staged, untruths, unappetizing, or incomprehensible (Kim et al., 2024; Matthews & Volpe, 2023; Zhai et al., 2024). Yet, leaning into the peculiarities of AI could serve as a significant benefit. In terms of oppressive pedagogies and more liberatory affordances, AI with 'own' agendas could be used as an illustration tool to address techno-capitalist systems in micro- and macro-level contexts in many different fields. AI-generated conversations relevant to sexual education and climate change could support an open conversation in the classroom and serve both individual and group needs of diverse learners (Bozkurt et al., 2023; Pillis et al., 2024; Varsik & Vosberg, 2024).

IMPORTANCE OF AUTHENTIC MATERIALS

In this section, the interlinking arguments for the necessity of authentic language use within the EFL/ESL learning environment will be put forth. The use of 'real' language (i.e., authentic texts) is supported by the idea that data created within a culture are richer, fuller, and closer to the language used outside the classroom, and in real life itself (Joraboyev, 2021). The contents of authentic language reflect the cultural thoughts and expressions of a people and, when L2 learners engage with such texts and materials, they can develop an awareness and understanding of the socio-cultural expressions and linguistic use of the target language. Additionally, engaging with authentic texts in the L2 enables learners to develop linguistic habits appropriate to the communicative contexts in which the language is used. Authentic materials reflect what is out there, as they are removed from textbook norms and representations of language use; they tend to depict standards (Keles & Yazan, 2023).

In turn, there are obvious pedagogical benefits of incorporating authentic materials within language courses, including an increase in motivation and enthusiasm of the learners. The presentation of authentic content equips learners with immediate exposure to the whole range of discourse. Many different accents and multiple styles can be presented in such a medium. A major advantage of using an authentic written text in the classroom is that it can facilitate the development of the learners' bottom-up pragmatic and sociolinguistic skills. Students can learn how co-text and context complicity affect overall meaning and successful processing through reading relevant articles and essays. When used as the basis for role-play and the teaching of functions to deal with that topic, this text can also be very useful in creating authentic and genuine language and communication strategies. Using authentic language interaction can also contribute to the development of the competence of the learners in listening, turn-taking, and a whole range of speaking strategies. Since many authentic texts are made available through taped sources, they can be exploited in the classroom. It could, for example, be extremely motivating for a class to interact with an authentic conversation (Hennessy et al., 2022; Xiao & Zhi, 2023; Yuliansyah & Ayu, 2021). Another potential benefit of using authentic language input of the spoken variety is that it helps the learners break free from the bookish medium of the written form and reduces the chance of recitation as a function of the predictability of filmed sources. The listening and perception of these speech acts are processes that are much more challenging to the students than dealing with taped spoken language they are already familiar with. Communicative discussions from television could lead to many spin-offs in a language classroom. Authenticity for its own sake might be a rather impotent argument (Chen et al., 2023; Ergasheva et al., 2022). Also, textbooks that present the L1 in an authentic manner, hence according to co-text and context, need not, logically, be excluded from the classroom. However, given the many far-reaching advantages of the use of authentic texts, it might be more accurate to say that the lack of distinctive in-class connotations is of primary interest in class.

CHALLENGES OF USING AI-GENERATED TEXTS IN LANGUAGE TEACHING

Educators intending to incorporate AI-generated texts into language teaching are confronted with several challenges. Writing in response to the increasing numbers of AI-generated essays in L1, the public was questioning whether using texts produced by AI would be an ethical way to assign and grade papers. Thus, at the heart of this concern is the issue of trust. Scholars have questioned the quality of the writings generated by AI, and many have noted that pass bots produce garbage output by garbage person (Citrome, 2024).

While AI writing has achieved considerable advances in recent decades, it is unrealistic and unwarranted to expect that AI-made writing meets the professional standards expected from the best human writers (Chen et al., 2022; Dergaa et al., 2023; Lund et al., 2023). In the end, AI-made writing can breach students' trust in the relevancy and value of the professional judgments made by their human educators. For example, their disappointment over low essay ratings can instigate suspicions about the fairness and effectiveness of peer assessments, leading to conflicts over the judgmental criteria. It is worth noting that students can use such strategies to negotiate their claims over considerations of fairness, especially when trying to contest the grade that they were given. To alleviate the influence of AI-made writing, educators can test student-made essays per criteria or rubric that is adapted for each group of student writers, bearing in mind their level, background, and pedagogical and cognitive profiles. Another solution to overcome this is to integrate AI-made writing into teaching by using open-domain student data with pre-designed AI writing tasks (Bezirhan & von Davier, 2023; Haque & Li, 2025). In addition, educators can incentivize creativity and emphasize the idiosyncratic tone and language-specific facts in student-made essays by assigning an extra mark for diversity of findings or views.

The similarities and differences between human and AI-authored EFL texts provides a helpful discussion of some of the quality and accuracy issues that may arise when utilizing AI-generated texts in language instruction (Amirjalili et al., 2024; Herbold et al., 2023). This discussion sheds light on whether or when educators should consider appropriating AI-generated texts to assist learners in developing their English skills. One of the main concerns that arise from the discussion is the possibility of factual inaccuracies in the automated text. If the AI content is generated, there may be a degree of error in the content of that data. Besides that, grammar and spelling are also essential in learning a foreign language.

Any errors in the AI-generated texts, be they in terminology, grammar usage, or mechanics and mechanical aspects, could lead to misunderstanding when teaching and learning and may lead to the incorrect use of the English language (Warschauer et al., 2023). Hence, to mitigate this problem, educators will need to spend time validating or rectifying the automated texts' accuracy and quality before offering them to learners. Besides, the motivation passage for EFL learners must encompass prospective function, topic familiarity, and learner progress. Employing automated texts with specific material extracts may not adhere to the above standards. Credible tools that do meet these criteria may be preferable over automated texts. Integration of AI-generated texts into teaching, though appealing to educators looking for a unique learning experience for their students, should be executed with extreme caution as the potential drawbacks are severe (Asad et al., 2024; Lee & Song, 2024).

A common concern about the potential collaborations to realize a platform of AI-generated texts is the challenge of obtaining high-quality texts meeting the authentic language requirements (Cardon et al., 2023; Lucchi, 2024; Wang et al., 2023). As computer-generated texts are not produced by a human author with personal experience, feelings, or stories, they are often impersonal and void of opinion. In a similar vein, mechanical texts produced by AI may lack cohesion and coherence due to the lack of personal touch, where everything is mechanically articulated (Draxler et al., 2024)

OPPORTUNITIES AND BENEFITS OF AI-GENERATED TEXTS IN LANGUAGE TEACHING

Given the constraints of the existing copyright and legal frameworks, replacing authentic texts with AI-generated ones for testing and practice in language courses is legally easier than doing so for the creation of language teaching and learning materials. In this section, it is aimed to identify some opportunities, or at least the potential of using AI-generated materials for language teaching and learning. the challenge in proving their authenticity must be recognized; thus, in the following section, the possible strategies are discussed to circumvent misuse issues. One of the strengths of AI systems from these two subscription-based companies, besides the quality, is in their customizability as indicated by Kim and Kim (2025). The power of technology has made it capable of delivering adaptive educational material at scale, catering to the needs of the individual learner.

Particularly in terms of resources for language learning, had the curators been directly involved in the creation of these texts or had a more international frame of reference when selecting them, they could be considered even more authentic, as the aim was to diversify and make traditions and their customs more relatable and accessible to our students (Choi & Chang, 2025; Hossain, 2024). The ubiquity and accessibility of AI-generated data could provide an abundance of open resources that can be integrated into teaching and made available to the public; yet, instead of applying AI to supplant the work of professional writers, such productive mechanisms can be used to further question context and reveal perspectives from a given community, ultimately revealing the cultures in which this community exists. These texts can challenge our students to critically assess popular connotations of standard and non-standard English varieties and contribute to developing digital literacy, as they had to stay alert to the presence of spambots during discussions of marginalized communities (Audrin & Audrin, 2022; Soyoof et al., 2023). Additionally, created in the spirit of Open Educational Resources, it was designed from early on for easy collaboration. Advisers were thus incentivized to recruit authors interested in producing a relatively short piece of this resource on a voluntary basis.

AI-generated texts can support personalized learning experiences in language education. Recent years have witnessed a burgeoning interest in adaptive technologies that tailor learning opportunities and content to individual learners' needs, thus appealing to their strengths, weaknesses, and preferences (Al-khresheh, 2024; Li & Lan, 2022). Efforts in customized content creation include, among others, exercises and games tailored to learners' needs and preferences, dynamic translation tools that adapt to learners' knowledge and current learning objectives, and the creation of rephrasing suggestions embedded in authentic context. Much research reports on the advantages of utilizing adaptive e-learning environments for language learning, including increased learner motivation and engagement, improved retention rates, and enhanced learning outcome achievement (El-Sabagh, 2021; Gligorea et al., 2023; Hassan et al., 2021).

Two well-known adaptive language learning platforms cater to learners by adjusting the complexity of the material automatically based on the scores attained for each item. Additionally, the numerous learner variables that the platforms utilize in adapting the learning content—such as learner goals and preferred learning time—highlight the plethora of adaptation opportunities that can be leveraged by AI-generated texts. The ability to work with authentic texts in authentic contexts and genres enables teachers to guide their learners into generating authentic, relevant, and meaningful content (Dai et al., 2023; Marzuki et al., 2023). The inherent flexibility of AI-generated texts can also be a natural fit for personalization and adaptation; for example, intelligent authoring tools can offer educators the option to conserve or adjust stylistic or linguistic aspects of AI-generated contexts. In the not-so-distant future, AI is expected to enhance personalization by, among others, tailoring content through personality detection and learning behavior recognition (Indset & Neukart, 2025).

PEDAGOGICAL APPROACHES AND STRATEGIES

The peculiarity of AI-generated texts needs to be addressed in pedagogical development to respond to the concerns and challenges that teacher educators and language teachers possess when taking a more comprehensive approach. Classrooms should be communicative with consecutive progress depending on the students' performance. AI-generated texts can also motivate the use of other proposed pedagogies and benefit from access to technological resources (Humeniuk, 2024; Warschauer et al., 2023). The following pedagogical approaches and strategies are suggested, comprising typical instructional strategies: using AI text to provide comprehensible input to obtain developed output, exposure to different genres, discussions triggered by the AI text, interaction among learners, and collaboration.

Using the AI-generated content in these ways also ensures collaboration as students discuss AI-generated texts and perhaps even write together in response (Warschauer et al., 2023). By encouraging students to work intensively with AI resources, teachers are also allowing more engagement with them. Students, for example, can compare and contrast AI-generated and human-authored poems, comparing their qualities, as in the study by Porter and Machery

(2024). Likewise, short stories can also be used to create a collaborative effort between humans and AI tools to work together (Dixon & Cox, 2025; Karadoğan, 2023; O'Halloran, 2024). However, even learners can work alone or in groups with, the teacher is a key player in these contexts and support for integrating AI resources into teaching is achieved through training and methodological advice (Celik, 2023; Salas-Pilco et al., 2022). Teachers who participate in the study mention that they are interested in teacher training as they recognize that it exists and that they should be able to use it. Trainers should be motivated to raise awareness and direct teachers' focus to the broader implications in lesson planning and use of technology. In the context where AI materials are interleaved, teachers should be provided with methodological guidelines for choosing and evaluating the materials and their ability to adjust the materials to their intended learning outcomes.

While the examples found in this chapter suggest that some language programs are eager to integrate AI-written texts into their curricula, several further issues have to be considered. In general, the integration of AI resources into any program or curriculum must be thoroughly thought out. It should align with institutional missions, values, and educational and linguistic standards in order to not compromise the rigor of the program. Although a parallel learning and teaching approach could easily find a place within any curriculum, integrating the use of AI-generated texts with the content standards on which high-stakes assessment is based would potentially require a multi-level, multi-year approach to assess effectiveness (Liu et al., 2024). Otherwise, if and when the AI approaches formed the entire program content, learning outcomes would need to be altered, resulting in added complexity; current research on the implications of AI medium learning and how approaches may also require curricular alterations is lacking in second language classrooms. National standards based on interdisciplinary learning and transfer align with established best practices in college, career, and professional pathways, thus providing a multi-level entry point into a transdisciplinary learning curriculum planning bastion for integrating the use of AI-generated texts learned in language programs (Tapalova & Zhiyenbayeva, 2022).

There are various ways to integrate the use of AI technologies, including natural language processing, text generation, and machine learning, into the classroom at multiple grade levels. Scholars are offering pathways spanning special education, English, and language arts instruction, used with juniors in high school. Very technically sophisticated collaborative research addresses skills for supporting inference instruction with fifth- to sixth-grade philosophizing multimodal interfaces—skills extending narrative instruction supportive of inferential and evaluative reading strategies. In learner population scenarios, the function of multimodal systems is expanding, being researched in English as a second language learning. However, for some cellular delivery outputs, including social, cultural, and interpersonal learning, multimodal alliances in system design can also be relevant (Hao et al., 2024). Such future considerations point to specific secondary or higher education interdisciplinary possibilities in the course of study and curriculum.

ETHICAL CONSIDERATIONS AND BIAS IN AI-GENERATED TEXTS

Ethical considerations are essential in the process of selecting AI-generated texts as resources to be used in language teaching or learning. Machine learning models used in many AI platforms may be biased, which can affect the authenticity and representativeness of the AI-generated texts created by such platforms (Craig, 2022). This issue is important to examine, especially when considering the use of AI-generated texts in educational settings (Ferrara, 2023; Vázquez & Garrido-Merchán, 2024). Educators need to pay close attention to the fact that AI-generated texts may reinforce harmful stereotypes, spread misinformation, or contain controversial content (Ali et al., 2021; Hort et al., 2024; Schwartz et al., 2022). It is, therefore, highly recommended that educators adopt an ethical approach when integrating AI-generated texts into their language teaching practices. The data used for training AI models to generate educational materials should exhibit diversity to avoid entrenching or reinforcing stereotypes (Alasadi & Baiz, 2023; Rane, 2023). The possibility of creating bias in AI-generated texts has an impact on intended and unintended learning outcomes. Identifying the areas of AI bias in language teaching and learning practices is vital for teachers, curriculum designers, and educational policymakers in teaching, controlling, and regulating AI-generated texts. AI-generated texts in machine translation programs and language courses may contain gender stereotypes or be gender-biased, which can reinforce existing stereotypes. Issues like racism, sexism, or xenophobia risk being transmitted in educational narratives (Fang et al., 2024). Consequently, paying attention to bias and social fairness in AI-generated texts used in educational contexts becomes relevant. In addition, the integration of these texts into language teaching and learning can raise further concerns about exclusion and disadvantage, since digital texts may require digital literacy that marginalized students might not have.

FUTURE DIRECTIONS AND RESEARCH OPPORTUNITIES

In the future, research and development into AI-generated texts will continue to offer guidance to second and foreign language researchers and educators. Rather than played-out conversation, emerging AI conversation generative technologies, which have yet to become popular subjects in the fields of educational computing and language didactics, such as modeling human-to-human pedagogy in ethnography and rhythm judgment lessons, may direct research interests. Evaluation by experts in digitally tutored and second language refers to AI systems searching for plagiarism, which is another trend. As research in educational exercise and test creation for AI progresses, a larger-scale and continuous empirical study will be able to answer the impact that the current environment is having; the studies available in these sections address their outcomes only on a small scale.

The researchers could look into the search for qualitative, systematic, and longitudinal studies. Lastly, progress in AI will need to be frequently evaluated with the same rigor that the studies in AI faced, preferably making use of an improved composite index for changes across a number of attributes. In particular, studies documenting the comparative outcomes of language educators deploying AI-generated texts to assist them in their work are currently completely absent. Critical collaboration between state-of-the-art AI developers and language educators must be established to provide appropriate resources to second and foreign language educators. While such timely and important collaborations are just beginning to take place, it is likely that they will become more frequent in the future. Whether the development of generating complete texts in the future will have a meaningful impact on language teaching and learning needs to be investigated. Future works should also investigate whether innovative AI can lead to new pedagogical practices.

CONCLUSION

This chapter aimed to explore the potential of AI resources to be useful in language teaching and learning. The chapter discussed the authenticity of AI-generated texts and the challenges and opportunities they offer. It is important to consider AI-generated texts as situated practice and to judge the degree of authenticity of AI-generated texts by considering the situations in which they are created. It was due to strive to find a balance between embracing the opportunities AI offers and being cautious about the challenges involved. AI requires reflection and instruction informed by critical evaluation in order to make the most of educational opportunities and address ethical concerns.

Educators need practical guidelines to help them determine and demonstrate the degree of authenticity of an AI-generated text, critically assess AI-generated texts, and employ materials evaluation techniques when considering using AI-generated texts and other types of AI-generated resources. They should also consider ways in which AI in language teaching and learning can help accomplish learning and educational goals. In the future, the potential for AI-generated written texts in language education, including their ability to provide learning experiences that are relevant and authentic, has rich opportunities. Learning how to refine our skills and insights in assessing the authenticity of AI-generated texts will be an essential dynamic for educators in the future. Furthermore, widespread adoption and support of the educational potential of AI is needed, with language teaching and learning experts collaborating with AI experts, educational technologists, ethicists, and other stakeholders to help shape the use of AI-related processes and resources in the public interest. An addition to all these, it should also kept in mind the possibility that AI-generated content will outweigh authentic works from human creators.

REFERENCES

Abdukhayotovna, A. K. (2022). The role of authentic materials to develop pupils' communicative competence in English classes at academic lyceums. *Berlin Studies Transnational Journal of Science and Humanities, 2*(1.5), 225–234. https://berlinstudies.de/index.php/berlinstudies/article/view/347/336

Adıgüzel, T., Kaya, M. H., & Cansu, F. K. (2023). Revolutionizing education with AI: Exploring the transformative potential of ChatGPT. *Contemporary Educational Technology, 15*(3), ep429. DOI: 10.30935/cedtech/13152

Aithal, P. S., Prabhu, S., & Aithal, S. (2024). Future of higher education through technology prediction and forecasting. [PIJMESS]. *SSRN, 1*(1), 1–50. DOI: 10.2139/ssrn.4901474

Al-khresheh, M. H. (2024). Bridging technology and pedagogy from a global lens: Teachers' perspectives on integrating ChatGPT in English language teaching. *Computers and Education: Artificial Intelligence, 6*, 100218. DOI: 10.1016/j.caeai.2024.100218

Alasadi, E. A., & Baiz, C. R. (2023). Generative AI in education and research: Opportunities, concerns, and solutions. *Journal of Chemical Education, 100*(8), 2965–2971. DOI: 10.1021/acs.jchemed.3c00323

Alexander, K., Savvidou, C., & Alexander, C. (2023). Who wrote this essay? Detecting AI-generated writing in second language education in higher education. *Teaching English with Technology, 23*(2), 25–43. DOI: 10.56297/BUKA4060/XHLD5365

Alharbi, W. (2023). AI in the foreign language classroom: A pedagogical overview of automated writing assistance tools. *Education Research International, 253331*, 1–15. Advance online publication. DOI: 10.1155/2023/4253331

Ali, S., DiPaola, D., Lee, I., Sindato, V., Kim, G., Blumofe, R., & Breazeal, C. (2021). Children as creators, thinkers and citizens in an AI-driven future. *Computers and Education: Artificial Intelligence, 2*, 100040. DOI: 10.1016/j.caeai.2021.100040

Almazova, N., Rubtsova, A., Kats, N., Eremin, Y., & Smolskaia, N. (2021). Scenario-based instruction: The case of foreign language training at multidisciplinary university. *Education Sciences, 11*(5), 227. DOI: 10.3390/educsci11050227

Amirjalili, F., Neysani, M., & Nikbakht, A. (2024). Exploring the boundaries of authorship: A comparative analysis of AI-generated text and human academic writing in English literature. *Frontiers in Education, 9*, 1347421. Advance online publication. DOI: 10.3389/feduc.2024.1347421

Asad, M. M., Shahzad, S., Shah, S. H. A., Sherwani, F., & Almusharraf, N. M. (2024). ChatGPT as artificial intelligence-based generative multimedia for English writing pedagogy: Challenges and opportunities from an educator's perspective. *The International Journal of Information and Learning Technology, 41*(5), 490–506. DOI: 10.1108/IJILT-02-2024-0021

Audrin, C., & Audrin, B. (2022). Key factors in digital literacy in learning and education: A systematic literature review using text mining. *Education and Information Technologies, 27*(6), 7395–7419. DOI: 10.1007/s10639-021-10832-5

Bezirhan, U., & von Davier, M. (2023). Automated reading passage generation with OpenAI's large language model. *Computers and Education: Artificial Intelligence, 5*(4), 100161. DOI: 10.1016/j.caeai.2023.100161

Bouschery, S. G., Blazevic, V., & Piller, F. T. (2023). Augmenting human innovation teams with artificial intelligence: Exploring transformer-based language models. *Journal of Product Innovation Management, 40*(2), 139–153. DOI: 10.1111/jpim.12656

Bozkurt, A., Junhong, X., Lambert, S., Pazurek, A., Crompton, H., Koseoglu, S., & Romero-Hall, E. (2023). Speculative futures on ChatGPT and generative artificial intelligence (AI): A collective reflection from the educational landscape. *Asian Journal of Distance Education, 18*(1), 53–130. https://www.asianjde.com/ojs/index.php/AsianJDE/article/view/709

Bozkurt, A., Karadeniz, A., Baneres, D., Guerrero-Roldán, A. E., & Rodríguez, M. E. (2021). Artificial intelligence and reflections from educational landscape: A review of AI studies in half a century. *Sustainability (Basel), 13*(2), 800. DOI: 10.3390/su13020800

Brevik, L. M., & Rindal, U. (2020). Language use in the classroom: Balancing target language exposure with the need for other languages. *TESOL Quarterly, 54*(1), 146–172. DOI: 10.1002/tesq.564

Cardon, P., Fleischmann, C., Aritz, J., Logemann, M., & Heidewald, J. (2023). The challenges and opportunities of AI-assisted writing: Developing AI literacy for the AI age. *Business and Professional Communication Quarterly, 86*(3), 257–295. DOI: 10.1177/23294906231176517

Celik, I. (2023). Towards Intelligent-TPACK: An empirical study on teachers' professional knowledge to ethically integrate artificial intelligence (AI)-based tools into education. *Computers in Human Behavior, 138*, 107468. DOI: 10.1016/j.chb.2022.107468

Chauhan, A. (2024). Redefining artistic boundaries: The impact of generative AI on creative processes and innovation. *Authorea.* DOI: 10.22541/au.172660510.02181160/v1

Chen, H. H. J., Yang, C. T. Y., & Lai, K. K. W. (2023). Investigating college EFL learners' perceptions toward the use of Google Assistant for foreign language learning. *Interactive Learning Environments, 31*(3), 1335–1350. DOI: 10.1080/10494820.2020.1833043

Chen, X., Zou, D., Xie, H., Cheng, G., & Liu, C. (2022). Two decades of artificial intelligence in education. *Journal of Educational Technology & Society, 25*(1), 28–47. https://www.jstor.org/stable/10.2307/48647028

Choi, W. C., & Chang, C. I. (2025). Enhancing education with ChatGPT 4o and Microsoft Copilot: A review of opportunities, challenges, and student perspectives on LLM-based text-to-image generation models. *Preprints.* https://doi.org/DOI: 10.20944/preprints202503.2387.v2

Citrome, L. (2024). Editorial: Artificial intelligence and the potential for garbage in, garbage out. *Current Medical Research and Opinion*, *40*(1), 1–2. DOI: 10.1080/03007995.2023.2286785 PMID: 38030564

Craig, C. J. (2022). The AI-copyright challenge: Tech-neutrality, authorship, and the public interest. In Abbott, R. (Ed.), *Research handbook on intellectual property and artificial intelligence* (pp. 134–155). Edward Elgar Publishing. DOI: 10.4337/9781800881907.00013

Creely, E. (2024). Exploring the role of generative AI in enhancing language learning: Opportunities and challenges. *International Journal of Changes in Education*, *1*(3), 158–167. DOI: 10.47852/bonviewIJCE42022495

Dai, Y., Liu, A., & Lim, C. P. (2023). Reconceptualizing ChatGPT and generative AI as a student-driven innovation in higher education. *Procedia CIRP*, *119*, 84–90. DOI: 10.1016/j.procir.2023.05.002

Dergaa, I., Chamari, K., Zmijewski, P., & Saad, H. B. (2023). From human writing to artificial intelligence generated text: Examining the prospects and potential threats of ChatGPT in academic writing. *Biology of Sport*, *40*(2), 615–622. DOI: 10.5114/biolsport.2023.125623 PMID: 37077800

Dixon, N., & Cox, A. (2025). Fiction writing workshops to explore staff perceptions of artificial intelligence (AI) in higher education. *AI & Society*, *40*(5), 3983–3998. Advance online publication. DOI: 10.1007/s00146-024-02157-x

Draxler, F., Werner, A., Lehmann, F., Hoppe, M., Schmidt, A., Buschek, D., & Welsch, R. (2024). The AI ghostwriter effect: When users do not perceive ownership of AI-generated text but self-declare as authors. *ACM Transactions on Computer-Human Interaction*, *31*(2), 1–40. DOI: 10.1145/3637875

Dubé, A. K., & Wen, R. (2022). Identification and evaluation of technology trends in K–12 education from 2011 to 2021. *Education and Information Technologies*, *27*(2), 1929–1958. DOI: 10.1007/s10639-021-10689-8 PMID: 34377079

El-Sabagh, H. A. (2021). Adaptive e-learning environment based on learning styles and its impact on development students' engagement. *International Journal of Educational Technology in Higher Education*, *18*(1), 53. DOI: 10.1186/s41239-021-00289-4

Ergasheva, S. B., Djalolovna, Y. L., & Norova, F. F. (2022). The principles of using computer technologies in the formation and development of students' language skills. *Journal of Pharmaceutical Negative Results*, *13*(6), 2145–2154. DOI: 10.47750/pnr.2022.13.S06.280

Esfandiari, M., & Gawhary, M. W. (2019). From genuineness to finder authenticity in communicative language teaching. *International Journal of English and Cultural Studies*, *2*(1), 36–42. https://core.ac.uk/reader/228085020. DOI: 10.11114/ijecs.v2i1.4149

Fang, X., Che, S., Mao, M., Zhang, H., Zhao, M., & Zhao, X. (2024). Bias of AI-generated content: An examination of news produced by large language models. *Scientific Reports*, *14*(1), 5224. DOI: 10.1038/s41598-024-55686-2 PMID: 38433238

Ferrara, E. (2023). Fairness and bias in artificial intelligence: A brief survey of sources, impacts, and mitigation strategies. *Scientific Reports*, *6*(1), 3. DOI: 10.3390/sci6010003 PMID: 36593284

Garib, A., & Coffelt, T. A. (2024). DETECTing the anomalies: Exploring implications of qualitative research in identifying AI-generated text for AI-assisted composition instruction. *Computers and Composition*, *73*, 102869. DOI: 10.1016/j.compcom.2024.102869

Gilmore, A. (2019). Materials and authenticity in language teaching. In Walsh, S., & Mann, S. (Eds.), *Routledge handbook of English language teacher education* (pp. 299–318). Routledge. DOI: 10.4324/9781315659824-25

Gligorea, I., Cioca, M., Oancea, R., Gorski, A. T., Gorski, H., & Tudorache, P. (2023). Adaptive learning using artificial intelligence in e-learning: A literature review. *Education Sciences*, *13*(12), 1216. DOI: 10.3390/educsci13121216

Godwin-Jones, R. (2022). Partnering with AI: Intelligent writing assistance and instructed language learning. *Language Learning & Technology*, *26*(2), 5–24. 10125/73474

Hao, X., Demir, E., & Eyers, D. (2024). Exploring collaborative decision-making: A quasi-experimental study of human and generative AI interaction. *Technology in Society*, *78*, 102662. Advance online publication. DOI: 10.1016/j.techsoc.2024.102662

Haque, M. A., & Li, S. (2025). Exploring ChatGPT and its impact on society. *AI and Ethics*, *5*(2), 791–803. DOI: 10.1007/s43681-024-00435-4

Hassan, M. A., Habiba, U., Majeed, F., & Shoaib, M. (2021). Adaptive gamification in e-learning based on students' learning styles. *Interactive Learning Environments*, *29*(4), 545–565. DOI: 10.1080/10494820.2019.1588745

Hennessy, S., D'Angelo, S., McIntyre, N., Koomar, S., Kreimeia, A., Cao, L., Brugha, M., & Zubairi, A. (2022). Technology use for teacher professional development in low-and middle-income countries: A systematic review. *Computers and Education Open*, *3*, 100080. DOI: 10.1016/j.caeo.2022.100080

Herbold, S., Hautli-Janisz, A., Heuer, U., Kikteva, Z., & Trautsch, A. (2023). A large-scale comparison of human-written versus ChatGPT-generated essays. *Scientific Reports*, *13*(1), 18617. DOI: 10.1038/s41598-023-45644-9 PMID: 37903836

Hort, M., Chen, Z., Zhang, J. M., Harman, M., & Sarro, F. (2024). Bias mitigation for machine learning classifiers: A comprehensive survey. *ACM Journal on Responsible Computing*, *1*(2), 1–52. DOI: 10.1145/3631326

Hossain, K. I. (2024). Reviewing the role of culture in English language learning: Challenges and opportunities for educators. *Social Sciences & Humanities Open*, *9*, 100781. Advance online publication. DOI: 10.1016/j.ssaho.2023.100781

Huang, S. (2018). Authentic texts as reading materials in a Chinese as a foreign language classroom: Learners' perceptions and pedagogical implications. *Journal of the National Council of Less Commonly Taught Languages*, *23*, 1–40. https://www.ncolctl.org/files/Jncolctl-vol-23/Authentic%20Texts%20as%20Reading%20Materials%20in%20a%20Chinese.pdf

Huang, W., Hew, K. F., & Fryer, L. K. (2022). Chatbots for language learning—Are they really useful? A systematic review of chatbot-supported language learning. *Journal of Computer Assisted Learning*, *38*(1), 237–257. DOI: 10.1111/jcal.12610

Huang, X., Zou, D., Cheng, G., Chen, X., & Xie, H. (2023). Trends, research issues and applications of artificial intelligence in language education. *Journal of Educational Technology & Society*, *26*(1), 112–131. http://index.j-ets.net/Published/26_1/ETS_26_1_09.pdf

Humeniuk, I. (2024). AI-generated content as a tool for improving the linguistic competence of students. *Mountain School of Ukrainian Carpaty*, *30*(30), 73–77. DOI: 10.15330/msuc.2024.30.73-77

Hwang, W. Y., Nurtantyana, R., Purba, S. W. D., Hariyanti, U., Indrihapsari, Y., & Surjono, H. D. (2023). AI and recognition technologies to facilitate English as foreign language writing for supporting personalization and contextualization in authentic contexts. *Journal of Educational Computing Research*, *61*(5), 1008–1035. DOI: 10.1177/07356331221137253

Indset, A., & Neukart, F. (2025). *The singularity paradox: Bridging the gap between humanity and AI*. Wiley.

Joraboyev, B. B. O. (2021). Using authentic materials on English lessons. *Academic Research in Educational Sciences, 2(2),* 1018–1025. https://ares.uz/storage/app/media/2021/Vol_2_No_2/1018-1025.pdf

Karadoğan, A. (2023). A bridge between technology and creativity: Story writing with artificial intelligence. *İnsan ve Sosyal Bilimler Dergisi*, *6*(2), 406–423. https://doi.org/DOI: 10.53048/johass.1368950

Keles, U., & Yazan, B. (2023). Representation of cultures and communities in a global ELT textbook: A diachronic content analysis. *Language Teaching Research*, *27*(5), 1325–1346. Advance online publication. DOI: 10.1177/1362168820976922

Kılıçkaya, F. (2004). Authentic materials and cultural content in EFL classrooms. *The Internet TESL Journal, X*(7). http://iteslj.org/Techniques/Kilickaya-AuthenticMaterial.html

Kim, J., Kelly, S., Colón, A. X., Spence, P. R., & Lin, X. (2024). Toward thoughtful integration of AI in education: Mitigating uncritical positivity and dependence on ChatGPT via classroom discussions. *Communication Education*, *73*(4), 388–404. DOI: 10.1080/03634523.2024.2399216

Kim, S. Y., & Kim, J. M. (2025). Standardization versus customization in artificial intelligence-based services: What fuels continuous intention to use on digital platforms? *Service Business, 19*(1), 7. Advance online publication. DOI: 10.1007/s11628-025-00580-8

Lee, J. H., Shin, D., & Noh, W. (2023). Artificial intelligence-based content generator technology for young English-as-a-foreign-language learners' reading enjoyment. *RELC Journal: A Journal of Language Teaching and Research, 54*(2), 508-516. DOI: 10.1177/00336882231165060

Lee, S., & Song, K. S. (2024). Teachers' and students' perceptions of AI-generated concept explanations: Implications for integrating generative AI in computer science education. *Computers and Education: Artificial Intelligence, 7*, 100283. Advance online publication. DOI: 10.1016/j.caeai.2024.100283

Li, P., & Lan, Y. J. (2022). Digital language learning (DLL): Insights from behavior, cognition, and the brain. *Bilingualism: Language and Cognition, 25*(3), 361–378. DOI: 10.1017/S1366728921000353 PMID: 35669733

Liu, F., Jiang, Y., Lai, C., & Jin, T. (2024). Teacher engagement with automated text simplification for differentiated instruction. *Language Learning & Technology, 28*(2), 163–182. https://www.lltjournal.org/item/10125-73576/

Liu, Y., Yin, J., Zhang, W., An, C., Xia, Y., & Zhang, H. (2024). Integration of federated learning and AI-generated content: A survey of overview, opportunities, challenges, and solutions. *IEEE Communications Surveys and Tutorials*. Advance online publication. DOI: 10.1109/COMST.2024.3523350

Luan, H., Geczy, P., Lai, H., Gobert, J., Yang, S. J. H., Ogata, H., Baltes, J., Guerra, R., Li, P., & Tsai, C. C. (2020). Challenges and future directions of big data and artificial intelligence in education. *Frontiers in Psychology, 11*, 580820. DOI: 10.3389/fpsyg.2020.580820 PMID: 33192896

Lucchi, N. (2024). ChatGPT: A case study on copyright challenges for generative artificial intelligence systems. *European Journal of Risk Regulation, 15*(3), 602–624. DOI: 10.1017/err.2023.59

Lund, B. D., Wang, T., Mannuru, N. R., Nie, B., Shimray, S., & Wang, Z. (2023). ChatGPT and a new academic reality: Artificial intelligence-written research papers and the ethics of large language models in scholarly publishing. *Journal of the Association for Information Science and Technology, 74*(5), 570–581. DOI: 10.1002/asi.24750

Marden, M. P., & Herrington, J. (2020). Design principles for integrating authentic activities in an online community of foreign language learners. *Issues in Educational Research, 30*(2), 635–654. https://www.iier.org.au/iier30/pais-marden.pdf

Marzuki, W., Widiati, U., Rusdin, D., Darwin, , & Indrawati, I. (2023). The impact of AI writing tools on the content and organization of students' writing: EFL teachers' perspective. *Cogent Education*, *10*(2), 2236469. Advance online publication. DOI: 10.1080/2331186X.2023.2236469

Matthews, J., & Volpe, C. R. (2023). Academics' perceptions of ChatGPT-generated written outputs: A practical application of Turing's imitation game. *Australasian Journal of Educational Technology*, *39*(5), 82–100. DOI: 10.14742/ajet.8896

Mishan, F. (2005). Designing authenticity into language teaching materials. *Intellect.*

Mishan, F. (2017). Authenticity 2.0: Reconceptualising authenticity in the digital era. In Maley, A., & Tomlinson, B. (Eds.), *Authenticity in materials development for language learning* (pp. 10–24). Cambridge Scholars Publishing.

Namaziandost, E., Razmi, M. H., Ahmad Tilwani, S., & Pourhosein Gilakjani, A. (2021). The impact of authentic materials on reading comprehension, motivation, and anxiety among Iranian male EFL learners. *Reading & Writing Quarterly*, *38*(1), 1–18. DOI: 10.1080/10573569.2021.1892001

O'Halloran, K. (2024). Digital assemblages with AI for creative interpretation of short stories. *Digital Scholarship in the Humanities*, *39*(2), 657–689. DOI: 10.1093/llc/fqad050

Patty, J. (2024). The use of AI in language learning: What you need to know. *Jurnal Review Pendidikan dan Pengajaran (JRPP), 7*(1), 642–654. https://doi.org/DOI: 10.31004/jrpp.v7i1.24609

Peddar, D. (2025). Utilising generative AI in the classics classroom. *The Journal of Classics Teaching*, *26*(51), 8–13. DOI: 10.1017/S2058631024001363

Pillis, D., Pataranutaporn, P., Maes, P., & Sra, M. (2024, March). AI comes out of the closet: Using AI-generated virtual characters to help individuals practice LGBTQIA+ advocacy. In *Proceedings of the 29th International Conference on Intelligent User Interfaces*. https://doi.org/DOI: 10.1145/3640543.3645213

Pinzón, A. N. B. (2020). Authentic materials and tasks as mediators to develop EFL students' intercultural competence. *HOW*, *27*(1), 29–46. DOI: 10.19183/how.27.1.515

Porter, B., & Machery, E. (2024). AI-generated poetry is indistinguishable from human-written poetry and is rated more favorably. *Scientific Reports*, *14*(1), 26133. DOI: 10.1038/s41598-024-76900-1

Rane, N. (2023). Enhancing the quality of teaching and learning through ChatGPT and similar large language models: Challenges, future prospects, and ethical considerations in education. *TESOL and Technology Studies*, *5*(1), 1–6. DOI: 10.48185/tts.v5i1.1000

Salas-Pilco, S. Z., Xiao, K., & Hu, X. (2022). Artificial intelligence and learning analytics in teacher education: A systematic review. *Education Sciences*, *12*(8), 569. DOI: 10.3390/educsci12080569

Schwartz, R., Schwartz, R., Vassilev, A., Greene, K., Perine, L., Burt, A., & Hall, P. (2022). *Towards a standard for identifying and managing bias in artificial intelligence*. NIST: National Institute of Standards and Technology. https://doi.org/DOI: 10.6028/NIST.SP.1270

Shanshan, S., & Sen, G. (2024). Empowering learners with AI-generated content for programming learning and computational thinking: The lens of extended effective use theory. *Journal of Computer Assisted Learning*, *40*(4), 1941–1958. DOI: 10.1111/jcal.12996

Soyoof, A., Reynolds, B. L., Vazquez-Calvo, B., & McLay, K. (2023). Informal digital learning of English (IDLE): A scoping review of what has been done and a look towards what is to come. *Computer Assisted Language Learning*, *36*(4), 608–640. DOI: 10.1080/09588221.2021.1936562

Tapalova, O., & Zhiyenbayeva, N. (2022). Artificial intelligence in education: AIEd for personalised learning pathways. *Electronic Journal of e-Learning*, *20*(5), 639–653. https://files.eric.ed.gov/fulltext/EJ1373006.pdf. DOI: 10.34190/ejel.20.5.2597

Tedre, M., Toivonen, T., Kahila, J., Vartiainen, H., Valtonen, T., Jormanainen, I., & Pears, A. (2021). Teaching machine learning in K–12 classrooms: Pedagogical and technological trajectories for artificial intelligence education. *IEEE Access : Practical Innovations, Open Solutions*, *9*, 110558–110572. DOI: 10.1109/ACCESS.2021.3097962

Tsao, J., & Nogues, C. (2024). Beyond the author: Artificial intelligence, creative writing and intellectual emancipation. *Poetics*, *102*, 101865. Advance online publication. DOI: 10.1016/j.poetic.2024.101865

Varsik, S., & Vosberg, L. (2024). *The potential impact of artificial intelligence on equity and inclusion in education. OECD Artificial Intelligence Papers, 23*. OECD Publishing., DOI: 10.1787/15df715b-

Vázquez, A. F. C., & Garrido-Merchán, E. C. (2024). A taxonomy of the biases of the images created by generative artificial intelligence. https://doi.org//arXiv.2407.01556DOI: 10.48550

Vetter, M. A., Lucia, B., Jiang, J., & Othman, M. (2024). Towards a framework for local interrogation of AI ethics: A case study on text generators, academic integrity, and composing with ChatGPT. *Computers and Composition*, *71*, 102831. Advance online publication. DOI: 10.1016/j.compcom.2024.102831

Wang, Y., Pan, Y., Yan, M., Su, Z., & Luan, T. H. (2023). A survey on ChatGPT: AI-generated contents, challenges, and solutions. *IEEE Open Journal of the Computer Society*, *4*, 280–302. DOI: 10.1109/OJCS.2023.3300321

Warschauer, M., Tseng, W., Yim, S., Webster, T., Jacob, S., Du, Q., & Tate, T. (2023). The affordances and contradictions of AI-generated text for writers of English as a second or foreign language. *Journal of Second Language Writing*, *62*, 101071. Advance online publication. DOI: 10.1016/j.jslw.2023.101071

Xiao, Y., & Zhi, Y. (2023). An exploratory study of EFL learners' use of ChatGPT for language learning tasks: Experience and perceptions. *Languages (Basel, Switzerland)*, *8*(3), 212. DOI: 10.3390/languages8030212

Yuliansyah, A., & Ayu, M. (2021). The implementation of project-based assignment in online learning during COVID-19. *Journal of English Language Teaching and Learning*, *2*(1), 32–38. DOI: 10.33365/jeltl.v2i1.851

Zhai, C., & Wibowo, S. (2023). A systematic review on artificial intelligence dialogue systems for enhancing English as foreign language students' interactional competence in the university. *Computers and Education: Artificial Intelligence*, *4*, 100134. Advance online publication. DOI: 10.1016/j.caeai.2023.100134

Zhai, C., Wibowo, S., & Li, L. D. (2024). The effects of over-reliance on AI dialogue systems on students' cognitive abilities: A systematic review. *Smart Learning Environments*, *11*(1), 28. DOI: 10.1186/s40561-024-00316-7

Zhai, X., Chu, X., Chai, C. S., Jong, M. S. Y., Istenic, A., Spector, M., & Li, Y. (2021). A review of artificial intelligence (AI) in education from 2010 to 2020. *Complexity*, *2021*(1), 8812542. DOI: 10.1155/2021/8812542

Zhang, K., & Aslan, A. B. (2021). AI technologies for education: Recent research and future directions. *Computers and Education: Artificial InteSOTlligence*, *2*, 100025. Advance online publication. DOI: 10.1016/j.caeai.2021.100025

ADDITIONAL READING

Ahn, J., Lee, J., & Son, M. (2024). ChatGPT in ELT: Disruptor? Or well-trained teaching assistant? *ELT Journal*, *78*(3), 345–355. DOI: 10.1093/elt/ccae017

Akgun, S., & Greenhow, C. (2021). Artificial intelligence in education: Addressing ethical challenges in K-12 settings. *AI and Ethics*, *2*(3), 431–440. DOI: 10.1007/s43681-021-00096-7 PMID: 34790956

Buendgens-Kosten, J. (2013). Authenticity in CALL: Three domains of 'realness'. *ReCALL*, *25*(2), 272–285. DOI: 10.1017/S0958344013000037

Fakher Ajabshir, Z. (2023). A review of the affordances and challenges of artificial intelligence technologies in second language learning. *Technology Assisted Language Education*, *1*(4), 111–130. DOI: 10.22126/tale.2024.10104.1028

Gilmore, A. (2007). Authentic materials and authenticity in foreign language learning. *Language Teaching*, *40*(2), 97–118. DOI: 10.1017/S0261444807004144

Gilmore, A. (2019). Materials and authenticity in language teaching. In Walsh, S., & Mann, S. (Eds.), *Routledge handbook of English language teacher education* (pp. 299–318). Routledge. DOI: 10.4324/9781315659824-25

Godwin-Jones, R. (2022). Partnering with AI: Intelligent writing assistance and instructed language learning. *Language Learning & Technology*, *26*(2), 5–24. https://www.lltjournal.org/item/10125-73474/

Hockly, N. (2023). Artificial Intelligence in English Language Teaching: The good, the bad and the ugly. *RELC Journal*, *54*(2), 445–451. DOI: 10.1177/00336882231168504

Hockly, N. (2024). *Nicky Hockly's 30 essentials for using artificial intelligence*. Cambridge University Press., DOI: 10.1017/9781009804509

Huang, X., Zou, D., Cheng, G., Chen, X., & Xie, H. (2023). Trends, research issues and applications of artificial intelligence in language education. *Journal of Educational Technology & Society*, *26*(1), 112–131. http://index.j-ets.net/Published/26_1/ETS_26_1_09.pdf

Pack, A., & Maloney, J. (2023). Potential affordances of Generative AI in language education. *Teaching English with Technology, 23*(2), 4–24. https://tewtjournal.org/volume-2023/issue-2/

Tomlinson, B., & Masuhara, H. (2017). *The complete guide to the theory and practice of materials development for language learning*. Wiley-Blackwell.

Warschauer, M., & Xu, Y. (2024). Artificial intelligence for language learning: Entering a new era. *Language Learning & Technology*, *28*(2). https://www.lltjournal.org/collection/col_10125_108158/

Yang, A. (2024). Challenges and opportunities for foreign language teachers in the era of artificial intelligence. *International Journal of Education and Humanities*, *4*(1), 39–50. DOI: 10.58557/(ijeh).v4i1.202

KEY TERMS AND DEFINITIONS

Adaptive Text Generation: Adaptive text generation is the capacity of AI systems to tailor texts according to individual learners' linguistic proficiency, learning goals, and personal interests.

AI-Generated Content: AI-generated content consists of texts autonomously produced by artificial intelligence models, often designed to emulate human-like linguistic structures and stylistic features.

Authenticity: Authenticity refers to the degree to which language materials replicate real-world communication in content, context, and purpose. .

Authentic Materials: These refer to the texts and resources originally created for real-world communicative purposes rather than for pedagogical objectives, such as newspapers, podcasts, blogs, and interviews.

Critical AI Literacy: Critical AI literacy encompasses the ability to understand, evaluate, and ethically engage with AI-generated content, including recognizing its affordances, biases, and limitations.

Ethical Integration: Ethical integration refers to the responsible use of AI technologies in educational settings, emphasizing transparency, fairness, academic honesty, and respect for learners' autonomy.

Task Authenticity: Task authenticity describes the extent to which classroom activities reflect real-world communicative practices, demands, and purposes.

Chapter 10
Navigating AI in Teacher Education:
Exploring the Interplay Between Artificial Intelligence Anxiety and Creative Cognition

Birender Kaur
https://orcid.org/0000-0003-3956-6258
Akal University, Bathinda, India

ABSTRACT

The objective of the current research is to examine the interrelationship between artificial intelligence anxiety (AI Anxiety) and creative cognition among prospective teachers. Descriptive survey method was employed. Stratified random sampling method was employed to obtain the data from 217 prospective teachers pursuing Bachelor of Education in private university of Punjab. Artificial intelligence anxiety scale by Wang and Wang (2019) was used to determine the level of artificial intelligence anxiety. Creative cognition level was measured by using Cognitive Processes associated with creativity scale (Miller, 2014). Correlation analysis suggested that artificial intelligence anxiety is positively associated with creative cognition among prospective teachers. Regression analysis revealed that creative cognition significantly predicts artificial intelligence anxiety, accounting for 6% of the variance. The study recommends that artificial intelligence anxiety should be channelised in a constructive manner to foster creative cognition among prospective teachers.

INTRODUCTION

The progress of the nation depends upon the skilled human resources capable of leading in different spheres of life. The cultivation of the skilled and mindful individuals depends upon the proficient teachers who align the personality of the individual as per the current and future needs of the nation. In this context, teacher education plays a prominent role by

DOI: 10.4018/979-8-3373-5092-9.ch010

preparing capable teachers who can craft relevant experiences for the child, thus assisting him in realising their potential to the fullest. Goodlad (1990) defined teacher education as a deliberately designed comprehensive programme where prospective teachers are equipped with required teaching and professional skills needed to oblige their professional responsibilities effectively. In addition to imbibing professional skills among prospective teachers, the teacher education programme offers foundation knowledge of pedagogical and psychological theories. This conceptual knowledge enables the teachers to get well-versed with the development requirements of the child, thereby assisting in designing relevant learning experiences for optimal learning outcomes. Therefore, this reflects the responsibility of teacher education programmes for cultivating competent teachers who possess sound knowledge base and pedagogical skills to lead nation's schools (NCTE, 2009).

Teachers are rightly regarded as shapers of student's personality as they play a prominent role in nurturing their cognitive, affective and psychomotor dimensions. They are responsible for transforming individuals into worthy human resources as per the societal requirements for their contribution in nation development. Education system is continuously evolving owing to technological advancements and inventions, unforeseen challenges like pandemics. This changing landscape necessitates continuous upskilling on the part of the teachers to remain relevant and effective. For instance- the infusion of technology into the education system has led to generation of interactive whiteboards, learning management systems and game-based learning platforms such as Kahoot and Quizlet. This technological integration compels teachers to continuously learn and adapt to the means of effectively utilizing these tools for educational purposes. Past research documented that technology-enabled learning environments deepens student engagement in their learning process thereby influencing their critical thinking skills (Kusumo et al.,2024). Additionally, technological tools assist teachers to accommodate different learning styles, thus enhancing students' academic performance (Kusumo et al., 2024) and learning outcomes (Liao and Chen, 2021 and Cavus and Deniz, 2022). Furthermore, Sasikala and Ravichandran (2024) documented that the integration of artificial intelligence into education system enhances students' engagement in the learning process thereby improving their academic achievement. Additionally, technology enabled teacher education and enhancement of ICT competency among teachers is promoted by UNESCO ICT competency framework for Teachers (2008), European Union Digital Action Education Plan (2021-27), OECD-Education and Skills 2030 framework and India's New Education Policy (2020). These initiatives underscore the importance of nurturing competencies among teachers in alignment with AI-driven professional and educational landscape for the better deliverance of their professional roles.

ARTIFICIAL INTELLIGENCE

Education landscape has undergone a remarkable evolution leading to the transformation of Education 1.0 to Education 5.0. This transformation marks a shift from traditional teacher centred approach Education 1.0- where teacher is the focal point of the teaching learning process to technology driven model of Education 5.0. The advanced stage of Education 5.0

represents the integration of Artificial Intelligence into the education system, thus supplanting the traditional one size fits all approach with adaptive learning platforms. The term artificial intelligence (AI) was coined in the Dartmouth Conference in 1956 (Zawacki-Richter et al., 2019). Artificial intelligence is the study of machines that simulate the cognitive processes of human intelligence- problem solving, reasoning, planning, communication and manipulation (Saini 2023). John McCarthy defined artificial intelligence as the science and engineering of making intelligent machines, where artificial neural networks and scientific theorems form the basis of their functioning. AI tools are structured to enhance the efficiency of mankind in different tasks as these intelligent machines have the capacity to interpret the data, extract lessons from the data sets to achieve specific goals and tasks (Haenlein and Kaplan, 2019). Literature documents different types of artificial intelligence ranging from narrow AI to super AI depending up on the tasks they perform. Weak/narrow AI is designed to perform specifically designed functions such as face recognition and self-driving cars. On the other side, strong AI is programmed to replicate the cognitive functions of the human brain (Tai, 2020). In the coming decades, world is going to experience self-aware AI on which the researchers are working which possess the capability of exhibiting and recognising emotions (Singh and Haju,2022).

The applications of artificial intelligence are extensive and have a prominent influence on all sectors of the economy. In healthcare industries, AI assists in accelerating the diagnostic purposes whereas its ability to detect and counter the cyber-attack efficiently leading to the better safety of the confidential data. The use of virtual assistance in the automotive industry is made possible only through the advancements in AI technology. AI has been instrumental in addressing environmental challenges, such as monitoring wildlife populations and predicting climate change impacts (Saini, 2023). In addition to the above-mentioned implications, AI offers significant benefits and finds widespread application in the educational sector. Benson (2025) reported that 60% of the educators have employed AI in the classroom, with 51% utilising AI driven games to create engaging learning platforms for the students. He further documented that AI in the education market is predicted to grow to 37.2% between 2024 to 2032. In the education field, AI possesses the capability to supplant the one-size-fits-all approach and leads to the creation of adaptive learning environments for the students in alignment with their needs. These learning spaces are technically termed as personalised learning spaces where targeted interventions are provided to enhance engagement and learning outcomes on the part of the students (Baker & Inventado, 2014).

Researches have shown that AI-powered platforms such as Duolingo and Knewton have adaptive space repetition feature to adapt the lesson to the performance of the learner to help him to improve on his weaker aspects (Katiyar et al.,2024). AI powered virtual assistants and chatbots foster collaborative learning spaces by providing real-time feedback and remedial measures, thus making learning a motivating experience for the learner. This in consequence contributes to better academic achievement (Kusumo et al., 2024). For instance, in Singapore, the Ministry of Education launched AI-initiated programs such as Pri 5 Math tools into 33 schools as a pilot project. This tool gauges the student performance and delivers personalized mathematical learning experiences in alignment with their needs. The integration of these AI tools has shown promising results such as improved academic achievement of slow learners. Similarly, the Finnish National agency for education, also provided a personalized learning system to their students with AI tools, thereby enhancing their learning outcomes. Artificially created intelligence through programming has visibly transferred the traditional teaching approach to AI adapted approach that emphasis critical thinking and problem-solving abilities (Kim et al., 2023). By bridging the technological divide, reducing educational inequalities and providing customised learning experiences, AI technology contributes to the attainment of sustainable development goal (SDG4) of quality equation to each and one (AlSagri and Sohail, 2024).

In addition to the enhancement of learning outcomes of the education system, AI has the potential to nurture and refine executive function of cognitive aspects of the individual. Khuman in 2024 highlighted that AI simulated learning environment provides continuous cognitive stimulation to the learners by exposing them to diverse learning modalities and dynamic problem sets, thereby developing and refining flexible thinking patterns. In nutshell, there is no denying in stating that AI significantly enhances the educational experiences by providing dynamic and interactive learning environments.

As the education system is rapidly evolving owing to AI's integration into its academic process, the upskilling of teachers regarding the effective use of these emerging technologies have become a necessity rather than an option. Teachers could play the role of potential key agents in this transformative journey, thereby assisting in harnessing the numerous benefits of AI in the education system. Hence, fostering artificial intelligence literacy among teachers cannot be ignored in the evolving intelligent era (Yan et al.,2025). AI literate teachers are mindful of the benefits and limitations of AI, thus making them efficient implementers of AI in classroom settings. As prospective teachers shape the future of education, therefore, this becomes imperative for teacher education institutions to cultivate AI related competencies and skills among them. Teacher training institutions must provide theoretical and practical experiences to the prospective teachers for their clear understanding of ways and means of integrating AI into the teaching-learning process (Pei at al.,2025). However, past researchers have documented various factors affecting adoption of artificial intelligence among pre-service teachers including workload, attitude towards adopting new technology, preference towards routine ways of teaching, insufficient knowledge and skills about AI use, thereby contributing to artificial intelligence anxiety (Talvid, 2016 and Zhang et al.,2023).

Artificial Intelligence Anxiety (AI Anxiety)

The mental health landscape has undergone a paradigm shift with the emergence of the term AI anxiety (Kim et al., 2023). The concept of AI anxiety is naïve in the field of research, however computer anxiety concept is extensively explored in the past (Beckers et al., 2007; Bohlin & Hunt, 1995). AI anxiety shares conceptual parallels with computer anxiety, specifically in terms of fear associated with the use of evolving technologies like computers and artificial intelligence (Li and Huang 2020). However, artificial intelligence differs from computer functionality in terms of its ability to operate like human intelligence in making decisions and autonomous functioning. This very characteristic leads to the development of a specific form of psychological uneasiness among individuals known as AI anxiety. AI anxiety refers to discomfort experienced by the individuals in response to the integration of AI technologies across different sectors of the society. In simpler form, AI anxiety refers to the tendency of the person to be fearful about the present and future usage of artificial intelligence (Parasuraman & Igbaria, 1990).

Though AI has offered diverse valuable uses in different sectors, their negative influence can't be overlooked. It has been reported by the McKinsey Global Institute that 15-30% of the global workforce may get displaced by AI, raising serious concerns regarding job security (Manyika et al., 2017). According to a survey conducted by the American Psychological association in 2023, many individuals expressed concerns that their job roles become obsolete because of AI (American Psychological Association, 2023). The increasing dependency of employment sector on AI functional aspects have changed the skills set required in the job market has shifted the skill set required in the market, with more emphasis on technological expertise. This fear is further fuelled by the fact that AI will evolve new jobs, thus leading to instability in the career path. Furthermore, AI leads to erosion of foundational skills such as mental arithmetic and remembering, when one can employ technology to perform those functions (Yadav, 2022). In addition to the replacement of humans in different professions, AI will hinder in-person communication with humans, widening of wealth gap between elite and poor or sometimes to racial bias if it is programmed in such a manner (Tai,2020). Also, extensive use of algorithm bias AI, this new innovation can lead to violation of human rights as algorithms can be trained to favour one race over the others (Carciumaru, 2025). Such violation of human rights can lead to social and political tensions across the world. As AI is data driven system, the addition of erroneous data in AI can result in incorrect conclusions which may have serious consequences in the field of medical care and finance.

The education sector is not immune to the harmful effects of AI. Though AI influences the teaching learning process in a positive manner by adapting to the needs of the students, it stills lacks in satisfaction of emotional requirements of the students. AI tolls such as virtual assistants can provide real-time feedback to reinforce learning; however, they lack empathy and emotional touch inherent in teacher-student interactions. This emotional disconnect may weaken the student-teacher relationship by reducing opportunities for social interaction (Guilherme, 2019), thereby hampering the emotional skill development of the child. The rapid advancement of AI in education sector sparks concerns that AI could potentially replace educators leading to increased stress and job insecurity among them. This anxiety negatively influences their productivity at work. The role of teacher as guide, mentor and leader is increasing being overshadowed (Chen & Lin, 2023 & Ghamrawi et al.,2024) as they are now consumed in mastering the AI integration strategies rather than devising their own creative pedagogical approaches. AI related anxiety is more pronounced among educators from low-resource countries due to challenges such as limited funding, inadequate internet connectivity, infrastructural capabilities, and insufficient teacher training opportunities. This uneven access to innovative technology creates a digital divide, making it difficult for the educators in these regions to keep pace with the rapidly evolving AI technologies. As a result, many educators feel underprepared, which intensifies their anxiety toward AI integration in education (Eke,2024).

Further, Li and Huang (2020) noted the potential danger of AI that it may lead to negative consequences including nuclear catastrophe, owing to its ability to make autonomous decisions stemming from the development of artificial consciousness (Future of Life Institute [FLI, 2015). The evolution of decision-making ability of AI-termed as AI superintelligence can results in unpredicted consequences that can be devasting to human race. Therefore, the direct and indirect experiences received about the apparent and unveiled ramifications of AI technology on personal, social, emotional, national and worldwide level adds to the AI anxiety. The above-mentioned perils of AI reflect the dark impact of artificial intelligence on every aspect of human society thereby catalysing the phenomena of artificial intelligence anxiety.

Frenkenberg and Hochman (2025) demonstrated the dual nature of AI anxiety in terms of anticipatory anxiety and annihilation anxiety. Anticipatory anxiety refers to the fear associated with the future deleterious effects of AI at individual and societal level. In simpler terms, it is apprehension associated with lack of confidence in using AI tools along with the nervousness stemming from the fear of job loss and other possible future disruptive effects caused by AI dominance in different sectors. For instance, replacement of humans by humanoids in the future in the job market is one aspect associated with the anticipatory anxiety dimension of AI. Annihilation anxiety describes the concerns associated with the erosion of human autonomy due to the arrival of AI tools. In other words, it means artificial intelligence has integrated automation more into the daily lives leading to the limited role of human judgment and autonomy in organisational and social contexts.

Li and Huang (2020) elaborated the following dimensions of AI anxiety as derived from Integrated Fear Acquisition Theory (Figure 1):

Figure 1. Dimensions of AI related anxiety (Li and Huang, 2020)

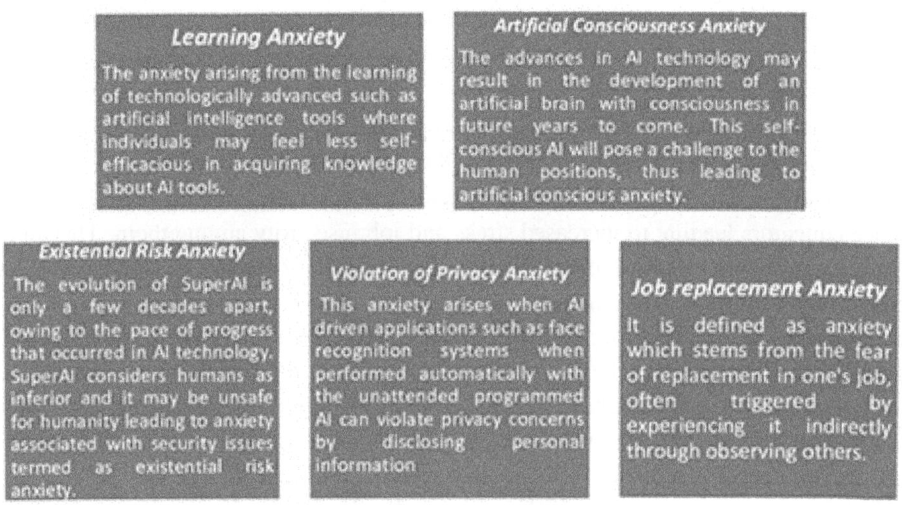

The spectrum of contributing factors (Figure 1) encompassing concerns about job security and misuse of personal data, learning anxiety and existential fears regarding threats to human existence, thereby reflecting its multidimensional nature. Past researches have documented that artificial intelligence anxiety have several psychological implications such as loss of sense of worth, loss of autonomy, mental health related issues including depression and chronic stress (Solove,2002; Brosschot et al.,2016 and Wilson et al. 2017). However, AI anxiety can influence motivated learning, and the drive to remain current with technological advancements among students (Chen et al., 2024). Moreover, it may encourage students to actively explore career pathways, thereby enhancing their engagement in career planning (Gedrimiene et al., 2024). Artificial intelligence anxiety as an enabling and limiting factor is pictorially represented in Figure 2:

Figure 2. Artificial intelligence anxiety as enabling and limiting factor

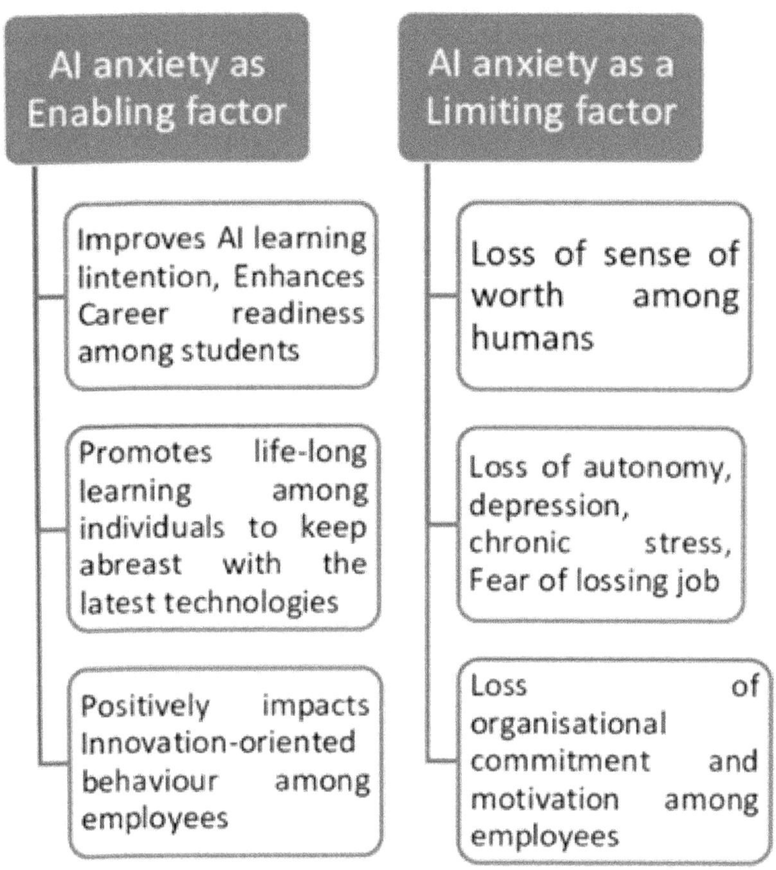

Creative Cognition

The human trait responsible for the generation of novel ideas is termed as creativity. World Economic Forum (2016) emphasises that creative abilities are the most sought-after competencies across the diverse fields required to drive progress. Sawyer (2012, p. 7) documented that creativity is a cognitive process involving the integration of concepts to generate something original and expressible in nature. Building on this perspective, Csikszentmihalyi (1994, p. 8) extended Sawyer's view by emphasizing the role of social and environmental factors in shaping the creative process, thus leading to the evolution of socio-cultural approach to creativity. The psychological and cognitive process responsible for evolution of creative ideas on the basis of prior knowledge is termed as creative cognition (Finke et al., 1999 and Ward 2019). This process involves higher order thinking by which individuals perform judicious planning and adjust approaches as the situation demands. He further got involved in evaluating the progress to estimate the effectiveness of the solution (Hwang and Wu,2025). While handling the complex or unconventional situation at hand, a creative person relies more on the metacognitive element of cognitive process (Mumford et al.,2012). Creative person is found to possess originality in his thinking process and ability to establish atypical connections between unrelated situations (Runco and Acar, 2012). Blind variation and selective retention (BVSR) framework can be utilized to understand the concept of creative cognition (Jung et al., 2013) as derived from Alternate Uses Task (Guilford, 1967) and Remote Associates Test (Khalil et al., 2013). Blind variation is linked with idea generation whereas selective retention is associated with convergent thinking. Both the generation of idea and focusing on the best possible solution to the problem plays a crucial role in shaping the creative process.

Beghetto and Kaufman (2007) framework documented different levels of creative activity ranging from involvement in personal to professional level. This framework suggests that creative expression ranges from individual insights to world level inventions and innovations, thus reflecting their wide-range impact. This creativity framework is tabulated below:

Table 1. Types of creative expression and their impact based on Beghetto and Kaufman's Four-C Model of Creativity

Types of creative Expression	Impact
Mini-c	Refers to the employability of creative thinking at the personal/individual level.
Little-c	Represents everyday creativity used in minor creations at the local level only.
Pro-c	Describe creativity demonstrated in professional settings to propose new and valuable products.
Big-c	Signifies professional creativity that results in groundbreaking work and significantly influences people's thinking.

Geneplore model of creative cognition states that creative process involves the interplay between generation and the exploration of the generated ideas to evaluate their suitability in solving the problem. During the idea evolution stage, individuals immerse in framing mental structures that blend the two distinct concepts for framing of novel entities. This marks the beginning of exploratory process, where a creative individual discovers insights from the generated idea by interpreting the concepts and drawing inferences through contextual shifts (Finke et al., 1992). Ward (1994,1995) elaborated that previous knowledge has a sound impact on the creation of novel ideas. This very prior knowledge further assists in integration of previously acquired concepts to form the new concept (conceptual combination) or expansion of previous knowledge in a novel way to frame new ideas- termed as conceptual expansion (Ward 1994). This process illustrates the role of structured imagination in the birth of creative ideas.

Lassig (2013) conceptualised four forms of creative cognition. *Adaptation* refers to the first form, which denotes the alterations in the existing knowledge framework to adapt to the new environmental demands. This form involves transforming the known to unknown while simultaneously modifying some aspects of the known. *Transferring* the idea from one domain (source) to another (target) is the second form of creative cognition, a process typically linked with drawing analogies. This transference of experiences is possible in both intradomain (within the same context) and interdomain (across different domains) analogies. The other form termed as *combination* stands for formation of logical combinations among the already known ideas to solve the unfamiliar problem in hand. Lastly, *genesis* form of creative cognition refers to creation of new information which has not been discovered before. The level of novelty progresses as one moves from adaptation towards genesis. All these forms of creative cognition utilize both divergent (diverse solutions to the problem) and convergent thinking processes (one solution to a creative problem), however the dominance of the process depends upon the specific form (Felix, 2022).

Creativity is a unique attribute that varies from individual to individual. Creative cognitive process assists in finding or resolving a range of issues across different fields, thus helping in the adding comprehensiveness to each field. Since ages, creativity assists individuals in adapting to change, problem solving, effective decision making and fostering innovation. However, in the 21st century where technology is rapidly influencing the world around us, creativity is more important than ever. The blending of creative elements in the present education system curriculum will assist the individuals to thrive in complex and rapidly evolving technologically advanced society shaped by artificial intelligence.

REVIEW OF LITERATURE AND HYPOTHESIS GENERATION

Kim et al. (2023) noted that the evolution of AI technologies have detrimental effects on individuals as well as society, including reduced employment opportunities, increased stress and fear and development of unfavourable attitudes towards AI. Cantas et al. (2024) reported gender differences in experiencing artificial intelligence anxiety, with females surpassing males in this regard. Wang et al. (2022) documents that learning anxiety- a dimension of artificial intelligence anxiety have a negative impact on both internal and external motivations. Lim (2023) found that prospective teachers with higher self-efficacy exhibited lower AI anxiety and greater creative problem-solving skills, emphasizing the need for AI literacy in teacher training programs to build confidence and adaptability. Parallelly, Hwang and Wu (2025) reported that self-efficacy enhancement strategies positively mediate the association between generative artificial intelligence and creative cognition. Artificial intelligence anxiety has positive association with self-efficacy among students (Asio and Suero,2024 and Chen et al. 2024). Kohnke et al. (2025) disclosed the importance of fostering creativity in teacher education programs to prepare educators for the challenges of an AI-integrated classroom. Almaiah et al. (2020) revealed that higher interaction in e-learning reduces social anxiety, while computer anxiety remains independent, impacting self-efficacy among undergraduates. Wray et al. (2022) highlight that self-efficacy and critical thinking are key factors in promoting adaptability and effective use of AI in education. Preeth & Bapu (2024) demonstrated that attitude towards artificial intelligence is not associated with tech anxiety among urban millennials.

Current literature has not comprehensively examined the phenomena of artificial intelligence anxiety. In particular, research on its potential effect on creative cognition is the under researched area, which demands empirical evidences to disclose psychological implications of AI anxiety. However substantial research has been focused on computer anxiety, thereby providing foundation understanding of technology related anxieties. Kannan et al. (2012) found that demographic factors such as gender and locale have a significant bearing on computer anxiety among students. Past researches documented that with increase in the level of computer anxiety; the level of creativity increases among secondary school students (Demircol et al. 2025). Accordingly, the hypotheses are framed:

H1: Artificial Intelligence Anxiety is negatively related with creative cognition.

H2: Learning Anxiety, Job replacement anxiety, Socio technical blindness and AI configuration anxiety is negatively associated with creative cognition.

H3: Creative Cognition is significant predictor of Artificial Intelligence Anxiety.

The present study is an attempt to test the proposed theoretical framework that will uncover the relationship between artificial intelligence anxiety and creative cognition among prospective teachers. Additionally, it will uncover the association of learning Anxiety, job replacement anxiety, socio technical blindness and AI configuration anxiety dimensions of artificial intelligence anxiety with creative cognition among prospective teachers. Prospective teachers are the students who are receiving training in a teacher training institution to imbibe the skills necessary for becoming competent teachers. This is true to state that the teachers are the key resource element responsible for the enrichment of the education system of a country. In the light of evolving needs of today's artificial intelligent driven era, there is a need to produce AI proficient prospective teachers. Consequently, teacher training institutions bear the responsibility to prepare prospective teachers for the efficient integration of AI tools in the teaching learning process, as demanded by tech-driven classrooms. The present study is an attempt to examine the AI anxiety related with prospective teachers in the context of Punjab which remains an unexplored area of research. Further, by examining the intersection of AI anxiety with creative cognition, this study offers insight into the psychological implications of AI integration in education.

RESEARCH METHODOLOGY

A descriptive survey approach was employed in this research paper. Stratified random sampling technique is used to collect the data from 217 prospective teachers of private university of Malwa region of Punjab. The participants were properly informed regarding the aims of the current study. They were assured regarding the privacy of the data and its use for research purposes only. An informal consent was obtained from the participants for participating in the research study. Research tools were provided to the participants by creating Google forms with sharply defined instructions for filling the form. Demographic characteristics of the sample are provided in Table 2.

Table 2. Demographic characteristics of the sample.

Variables	Options	N	%
Gender	Male	79	36.40%
	Female	138	63.60%
Place of Residence	Urban	148	68.20%
	Rural	69	31.80%
Nature of Family	Nuclear	75	34.56%
	Joint	142	65.44%

Table 2 reveals that among 217 prospective teachers, 79 were male respondents whereas 138 were female participants. 68.20% of the respondents are urban dwellers and 31.80% % of the respondents belong to rural locality. Regarding the nature of the family of the respondents, there are 34.56% of the participants resides in nuclear family where as 65.44% of the respondents resides in joint family.

Research Tools Used

Artificial Intelligence Anxiety (AI anxiety) scale developed by Wang and Wang (2019) was utilized to measure the artificial intelligence anxiety level of prospective teachers. This scale is a 7-point Likert type scale with responses ranging from 1 = never through 7 = completely. This scale consists of four sub-dimensions such as (i) Learning dimension Anxiety that captures anxiety levels of individuals in learning the use of AI tools (ii) Job replacement anxiety that is connected with anxiety levels of individuals who can lose their jobs with advancements in AI methods and product (iii) Socio-technical blindness measure the anxiety levels associated with fear of autonomous functioning of the AI system and their associated disastrous effects (iv) AI configuration anxiety is associated with anxiety levels of individuals who might perceive humanoid AI methods as frightening and intimidating . The reliability coefficient of the scale varies from 0.92 to 0.97 across different dimensions of the scale.

Cognitive Processes associated with Creativity scale developed by (Miller, 2014) was employed to measure the cognitive process responsible for creativity among individuals. It is a 5-point Likert type scale with responses ranging from 1=never to 5=always. This scale is composed of five sub-scales including idea manipulation, imagery, flow, metaphorical thinking, idea generation and incubation. Idea manipulation assesses the ability of the individual to change perspectives in order to understand the situation from diverse viewpoints. Idea generation tests the ability of the individual to generate possible solutions for the situation. Metaphorical thinking measures the individual's capacity to transfer ideas from one context to similarly related another context. Imagery responds to the internal visualization which is a central aspect of creativity. Incubation refers to unconscious evaluation of the ideas generated for the evaluation of the problem. Flow corresponds to the state of consciousness where an individual is engaged in a creative process. Cronbach alpha for the scale is 0.86.

STATISTICAL TREATMENT OF THE DATA

Quantitative data is statistically treated by employing descriptive analysis, correlation and regression analysis which is tabulated in different sections under data analysis and interpretation. SPSS software 25 is used for the analysis of the data.

Data Analysis and Interpretation

Table 3 presents the descriptive statistics of artificial intelligence anxiety scores for the total sample of prospective teachers (N = 217)

Table 3. Descriptive statistics of artificial intelligence anxiety scores of prospective teachers

Variables	Mean	Median	S.D.	Range
Artificial Intelligence Anxiety	78.01	79.00	23.31	21 to 147

The mean and median of AI anxiety scores are 78.01 and 79.00 respectively. The standard deviation for the AI anxiety came out to be 23.31. The range of scores of prospective teachers on artificial intelligence anxiety scale varies from 21 to 147. The results of the Kolmogorov-Smirnov test of normalcy for artificial intelligence anxiety scores are presented in Table 3.

Table 4. One-Sample Kolmogorov-Smirnov test

N		217
Normal Parameters[a,b]	Mean	78.01
	Std. Deviation	23.310
Most Extreme Differences	Absolute	.053
	Positive	.053
	Negative	-.041
Test Statistic		.053
Asymp. Sig. (2-tailed)		.200[c,d]

a. Test distribution is Normal.
b. Calculated from data.
c. Lilliefors Significance Correction.
d. This is a lower bound of the true significance.

Table 4 presents that the value of the test statistic is .053, with an asymptotic significance value (p) of .200, using the Lilliefors significance correction. As per the decision rule for Kolmogorov Smirnov test of normality, if p>0.05, the data is normally distributed (Field, 2009). Since the p-value is greater than the alpha level of .05, therefore the sample data of artificial intelligence anxiety scores is normally distributed.

Figure 3. NPC of data on artificial intelligence anxiety among prospective teachers

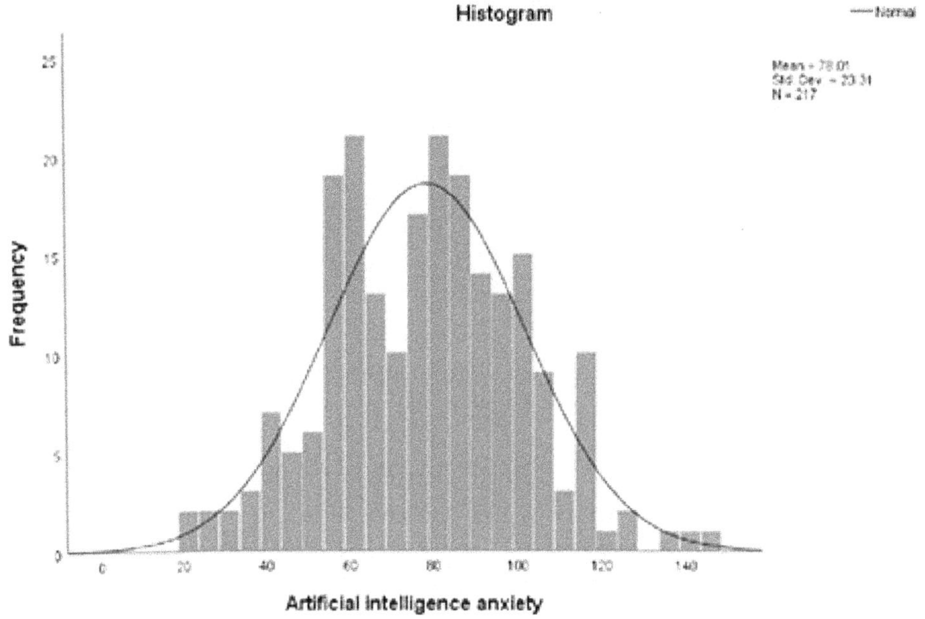

As shown in Figure 3, the normal distribution of sample data on artificial intelligence anxiety for prospective teachers. Thus, it can be concluded that the sample data on artificial intelligence anxiety is normally distributed.

Table 5 presents the descriptive statistics of creative cognition scores for the total sample of prospective teachers (N = 217)

Table 5. Descriptive statistics of creative cognition scores for prospective teachers (N=217)

Variables	Mean	Median	S.D.	Range
Creative Cognition	**98.24**	**99.00**	**17.70**	**33 to 140**

Table 5 shows that the mean value and standard deviation for creative cognition of prospective teachers is 98.24 and 17.70 respectively. The median value for creative cognition scores is 99.00. The distribution of creative cognition scores ranges from 33 to 140. The results of the Kolmogorov-Smirnov test for normality of creative cognition scores are presented in Table 6.

Table 6. One-Sample Kolmogorov-Smirnov test

N		217
Normal Parameters[a,b]	Mean	98.24
	Std. Deviation	17.702
Most Extreme Differences	Absolute	.045
	Positive	.039
	Negative	-.045
Test Statistic		.045
Asymp. Sig. (2-tailed)		.200[c,d]

a. Test distribution is Normal.
b. Calculated from data.
c. Lilliefors Significance Correction.
d. This is a lower bound of the true significance.

Table 6 shows the test statistic of 0.045 with an asymptotic significance value (p) of 0.200, based on the Lilliefors significance correction. As per the decision rule for Kolmogorov Smirnov test of normality, if $p>0.05$, the data is normally distributed (Field, 2009). Since the p-value is greater than the alpha level of .05, therefore the sample data of creative cognition is normally distributed, thus validating the suitability of parametric statistical methods for subsequent analysis.

Figure 4. NPC of data on creative cognition among prospective teachers

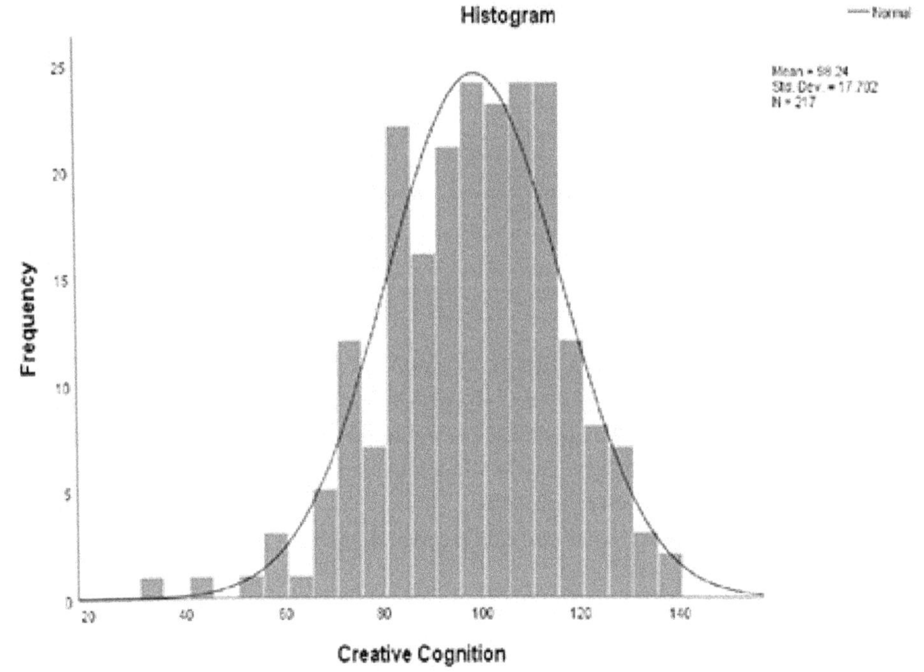

Figure 4 clearly shows the normal distribution of sample data on creative cognition for prospective teachers. Thus, it can be concluded that the sample data on creative cognition is normally distributed.

Correlation Analysis of the Data

Pearson product moment correlation was used to compute a coefficient of correlation between artificial intelligence anxiety and creative cognition among prospective teachers. Table 7 represents the coefficient of correlation values between artificial intelligence anxiety and creative cognition among prospective teachers.

Table 7. Inter correlation between Artificial intelligence anxiety and creative cognition among prospective teachers (N=217)

		Artificial intelligence anxiety	**Creative Cognition**
Artificial intelligence anxiety	Pearson Correlation	1	.246**
	Sig. (2-tailed)		.000
	N	217	217
Creative Cognition	Pearson Correlation	.246**	1
	Sig. (2-tailed)	.000	
	N	217	217

**Correlation is significant at the 0.01 level

It may be noted from Table 7 that the correlation coefficient between artificial intelligence anxiety and creative cognition is 0.246, which is statistically significant at the 0.01 level ($p < 0.01$). This demonstrates a weak positive relationship among the variables, thus revealing that as artificial intelligence anxiety increases, there is a slight increase in creative cognition scores among prospective teachers.

Thus, the Hypothesis (H1): "Artificial Intelligence Anxiety is negatively associated with creative cognition" is rejected.

Table 8. Inter correlation between learning anxiety, job replacement anxiety, socio technical blindness and AI configuration anxiety with creative cognition among prospective teachers (N=217)

Creative Cognition	**Learning Anxiety**	**Job Replacement anxiety**	**Socio-technical blindness**	**AI configuration anxiety**
	-.0.002	.351**	.345**	.219**

**. Correlation is significant at the 0.01 level

The correlation analysis reveals that AI configuration anxiety ($r = .219$, $p < .01$) and job replacement anxiety ($r = .351$, $p < .01$) has small but significant positive relationship with creative cognition. Table 8 further shows that socio- technical blindness has positive correlation with creative cognition among prospective teachers ($r = .345$, $p < .01$). However, creative cognition does not significantly correlate with learning anxiety ($r = -.002$, $p = .974$), suggesting no meaningful relationship between these two variables. This suggests that with increase in level of anxiety associated with learning of functionality of AI tools, replacement of jobs and potential problems associated with AI usage, the level of creative cognition assisting in developing creative ideas and concepts also increases.

Therefore, Hypothesis

H2: "Learning Anxiety, Job replacement anxiety, Socio technical blindness and AI configuration anxiety is negatively associated with creative cognition" stands rejected.

Linear Regression Analysis of the Data

Prior to the performance of the linear regression analysis, necessary assumptions to perform it was tested. The homoscedasticity assumption was tested through the examination of scatter plots and rectangular shapes that were obtained (Tabachnick & Fidell, 2015) guarantee the satisfaction of this assumption. In the current research, Durbin Watson values ranged between 1.5 and 2.5 which confirms that there was no auto-correlation (Tabachnick & Fidell, 2015) that meets the other assumption of linear regression analysis.

Table 9. Simple linear regression analysis results of creative cognition levels of prospective teachers predicting artificial intelligence anxiety (N=217)

Model		Unstandardized Coefficients		Standardized Coefficients	T	Sig.
		B	Std. Error	Beta		
1	(Constant)	46.213	8.689		5.319	.000
	Creative Cognition	.324	.087	.246	3.718	.000

$R = .246$, $R^2 = .060$, Adjusted $R^2 = .056$, $F = 13.826$, $p = .000$

Table 9 presents the results of a linear regression analysis of creative cognition predicting artificial intelligence anxiety among prospective teachers. This analysis shows that creative cognition is a statistically significant predictor of artificial intelligence anxiety, with an unstandardized coefficient (B) of 0.324, indicating that for each unit increase in creative cognition, Artificial Intelligence Anxiety increases by 0.324 units. The standardized coefficient (Beta) is 0.246, suggesting a weak positive relationship between the two variables. The model explains 6% of the variance in Artificial Intelligence Anxiety ($R^2 = 0.060$), and the regression model as a whole is significant ($F = 13.826$, $p < 0.001$). These findings highlight that while creative cognition contributes to artificial intelligence anxiety, it accounts for only a small portion of the variance, suggesting that other factors may also influence the anxiety levels.

Thus, Hypothesis (H3): "Creative cognition is significant predictor of Artificial Intelligence anxiety" is accepted.

RESULTS AND DISCUSSIONS

Female prospective teachers constitute the major proportion of the sample. Results of Pearson correlation analysis suggested that artificial intelligence anxiety is positively associated with creative cognition among prospective teachers. Further this analysis unrevealed that AI configuration anxiety, socio-technical blindness and job replacement anxiety has positive and significant correlations with creative cognition. In simpler terms, it means that with an increase in the level of artificial intelligence anxiety among prospective teachers, the level of creative cognition also increases. It depicts that as prospective teachers' experiences fear related to the specific disadvantages of AI such as replacement of educators in jobs, emergence of robot autonomy in the future and its associated dangers, their convergent and divergent thinking process gets stimulated and enhanced. Specifically, prospective teachers exhibiting apprehension towards AI applications demonstrated a tendency to engage in more creative endeavours for the generation of constructive coping responses. These results lend support from neuroscience researches which discloses that anxious people are occupied in generating out-of-box original concepts (BiologyInsights, 2025). The findings of this study draw parallel with findings by Gupta and Lodi (2017) which suggested that students with computer anxiety engaged themselves in creative problem solving, thus enhancing the creative aspect of the students. Also, Demircol et al. (2025) who documented that increase in anxiety towards computers motivates the individual to find potential solutions as a means of reducing uncertainty in the technological domain.

The reason for enhancement in the creative process in the context of anxiety can be attributed to different theoretical frameworks. The findings by Runco and Chand (2017) asserted that stress catalyses the creative process of the individual by enhancing executive functioning of cognitive aspects, particularly cognitive flexibility. Cognitive flexibility in turns will be assistive for the individual in perspective shifting to understand the problem from multiple perspectives- ability highlighted during the exploratory stage of geneplore model of creative cognition. Additionally, this perspective aligns with the Dual pathways of creativity model, which states that ability to switch among diverse alternatives facilitates the individual in producing creative ideas (Nijstad et al., 2010). Dou et al. (2022) demonstrated that stressful situations act as a motivator for the individuals which prompt them to explore alternative problem-solving strategies, thereby nurturing innovative behaviour. Therefore, applying these insights it can be said that artificial intelligence anxiety among prospective teachers, stemming from the non-desirables influences of incorporating AI into the education system will motivate the prospective teachers to understand their role as a creative driver of the education system. This will lead them to explore diverse ways and innovative strategies of employing AI (encompasses divergent thinking) as an assistive tool rather than viewing it as a replacement. Further, anxiety will inspire the prospective teachers to cultivate critical thinking and empathy -qualities that AI inherently lacks thereby assisting in solidifying their professional identity and expertise.

Results of regression analysis reveals that creative cognition is a statistically significant predictor of artificial intelligence anxiety among prospective teachers. This means that variations in the ability of the prospective teacher to create unconventional ideas can cause corresponding variations in their experiences related to anxiety towards AI technology. This finding corroborates with the observations of Taylor (2017) who documented that creative people are more prone to anxiety. This perspective is further expanded by Adams (2014) who argued that creative brains are often loaded with information which in further hampers the ability of their brain to filter the irrelevant information. Therefore, creative individuals being very imaginative remain occupied in connecting dots to devise different possibilities of a situation -some of which might be negative, thereby leaving them anxious. Applying these insights in the present context, it can be concluded that creative prospective teachers can visualize the broad range of possibilities along with the complex and deleterious effects associated with AI integration in education system. For instance, the employability of AI-driven IRIS robot teacher in Thiruvananthapuram, Kerala highlights the risk of loss of human touch in teaching learning process, potentially resulting in the psychological implications for the children. Also, increase in digital divide specifically for the students from struggling countries, where accessibility to AI tools is near to impossible may result in AI anxiety among creative prospective teachers. To conclude, these results underscore the constructive role of AI anxiety in igniting creative cognition of prospective teachers, thereby preparing them for their professional roles and responsibilities in an AI-driven world.

IMPLICATIONS OF THE STUDY

Implications for Research

Artificial intelligence anxiety (AI) is an emerging concern which is gaining popularity in psychological, sociological and management researches. The present study uncovers the positive association of artificial intelligence anxiety with creative cognition among prospective teachers. This piece of research also integrated socio-technical blindness, job replacement anxiety, AI configuration anxiety and learning anxiety which is an understudied research area in the context of teacher education. Therefore, this study fills the research gap, thereby contributing to the body of literature and provides the basis for future research exploration in this area.

Implications for Practice

The present study findings offer multiple practical implications. The empirical evidence provides insights into the constructive role of AI anxiety in catalysing the creative process among prospective teachers. Teacher education programmes should act promptly by using anxiety as an enabler of creativity rather than viewing it as a deterrent to creative process. Teacher education institutions must sensitize the prospective teachers with socio-technical and AI configuration anxiety associated with AI to promote the nurturing of creative minds. Specifically, job related uncertainty can be harnessed by the teacher education institutions to push prospective teachers to leverage their skills such as empathy, emotional intelligence and creativity through scholastic or co-scholastic activities which sets them apart from AI humanoids to reaffirm their irreplaceable role in education. Teacher education institutions should incorporate resilience-building modules and digital mentorship programs to support prospective teachers in experimentation with AI tools in resilient manner while enabling them to creatively navigate the complexities of AI integration. To mitigate AI anxiety and foster creativity, teacher education institutions can establish virtual 'sandbox' environments that offer creative and risk-free virtual spaces for encouraging hands-on exploration with AI technologies. Prospective teachers should be encouraged to maintain reflective journals that document their anxieties and experiences while engaging with AI tools. This practice can help them identify personal growth areas, enhance self-awareness, and develop creative strategies to effectively manage AI-related challenges. Creativity predicts artificial intelligence anxieties among prospective teachers; therefore, curricula of the teacher education programmes should intentionally incorporate problem-based learning, interdisciplinary approach in curriculum transaction, visual thinking strategies and classroom environment that encourage questioning to foster creativity among prospective teachers. Teacher educators should guide prospective teachers through mentoring and discussions to channel their creative power towards innovation and adaptation rather than overwhelming with anxiety.

LIMITATIONS AND FUTURE DIRECTIONS

The present study includes data of prospective teachers studying of private university of Punjab, thereby limiting the generalisability of the results to populations with different educational contexts. The data can be collected from government aided and government colleges of education which will improve the generalization of the results. Correlational analysis does not establish casual links, so the casual relationship between artificial intelligence anxiety and creative cognition is still unexplored. Longitudinal studies could be designed to explore these casual linkages between the variables as how creative cognition changes with the influence of AI anxiety. Future studies should explore the effect of personality traits and artificial intelligence literacy on artificial intelligence anxiety to propose comprehensive theoretical framework. Moreover, studies comparing STEM and arts prospective teachers could be carried out in future to prepare a detailed research model. Qualitative studies should be conducted to get an insight into the factor's affecting artificial intelligence anxiety and creative cognition among prospective teachers.

CONCLUSIONS

The present study explored the relationship between artificial intelligence anxiety and its components with creative cognition among prospective teachers. It discovers that with increase of anxiety towards AI technology in terms of its usage, autonomous nature and configuration, the creative cognition level enhances among prospective teachers. Also, it shows that creative cognition is the significant predictor of artificial intelligence anxiety among prospective teachers. The piece of research work suggests that artificial intelligence anxiety should be channelised in a constructive way to nourish creative cognition of prospective teachers, thereby preparing them for their professional roles and responsibilities in an AI-driven world.

REFERENCES

Adams, W. L. (2014, January 22). *The dark side of creativity: Depression + anxiety × madness = genius?* CNN. https://edition.cnn.com/2014/01/22/world/the-dark-side-of-creativity-vincent-van-gogh/index.html

AI Expert Network. (2025, January 14). *Case study: AI integration in Singapore's education sector*. AI Case Studies. https://aiexpert.network/ai-integration-in-singapores-education-sector/

AI for Social Good. (2023, December 5). *The dark side of artificial intelligence: Uncovering the negative impacts of AI*. https://aiforsocialgood.ca/blog/the-dark-side-of-artificial-intelligence-uncovering-its-negative-impacts-on-society

Almaiah, M. A., Al-Khasawneh, A., & Althunibat, A. (2020). Exploring the critical challenges and factors influencing the E-learning system usage during COVID-19 pandemic. *Education and Information Technologies*, *25*(6), 5261–5280. DOI: 10.1007/s10639-020-10219-y PMID: 32837229

AlSagri, H. S., & Sohail, S. S. (2024). Evaluating the role of Artificial Intelligence in sustainable development goals with an emphasis on "quality education. *Discover Sustainability*, *5*(458), 458. Advance online publication. DOI: 10.1007/s43621-024-00682-9

American Psychological Association. (2023). *2023 Work in America™ Survey: Artificial intelligence, monitoring technology, and psychological well-being*. https://www.apa.org/pubs/reports/work-in-america/2023-work-america-ai-monitoring

Asio, J. M. R., & Suero, A. N. (2024). Artificial Intelligence Anxiety, Self-Efficacy, and Self-Competence among Students: Implications to Higher Education Institutions. *Education Policy and Development*, *2*(2), 82–93. DOI: 10.31098/epd.v2i2.2541

Baker, R. S., & Inventado, P. S. (2014). Educational Data Mining and Learning Analytics. In Larusson, J. A., & White, B. (Eds.), *Learning Analytics: From Research to Practice* (pp. 61–75). Springer., DOI: 10.1007/978-1-4614-3305-7_4

Beckers, J. J., Wicherts, J. M., & Schmidt, H. G. (2007). Computer anxiety: "Trait" or "state"? *Computers in Human Behavior*, *23*(6), 2851–2862. DOI: 10.1016/j.chb.2006.06.001

Beghetto, R., & Kaufman, J. C. (2007). Toward a broader conception of creativity. *Psychology of Aesthetics, Creativity, and the Arts*, *1*(2), 73–79. DOI: 10.1037/1931-3896.1.2.73

Benson, T. (2025, April 5). AI in education statistics 2025 – Growth, adoption & impact. *AI Statistics – Artificial Intelligence*. https://aistatistics.ai/education/

Biology Insights Team. (2025, April 29). *Anxiety and creativity: Surprising brain connections*. Biology Insights. https://biologyinsights.com/anxiety-and-creativity-surprising-brain-connections/

Bohlin, R. M., & Hunt, N. P. (1995). Course structure effects on students' computer anxiety, confidence, and attitudes. *Journal of Educational Computing Research, 13*(3), 263–270. DOI: 10.2190/YB6Q-HX39-11KK-GKYL

Brosschot, J. F., Bart, V., & Julian, F. T. (2016). The default response to uncertainty and the importance of perceived safety in anxiety and stress: An evolution-theoretical perspective. *Journal of Anxiety Disorders, 41*, 22–34. DOI: 10.1016/j.janxdis.2016.04.012 PMID: 27259803

Cantaş, Ç., Soyer, C., & Batur, Ö. (2024). Examination of undergraduate students' artificial intelligence anxiety, multidimensional 21st century skills, and lifelong learning levels in terms of various variables. *The Turkish Online Journal of Educational Technology, 23*(3), 29–53.

Carciumaru, T. Z., Tang, C. M., Farsi, M., Bramer, W. M., Dankelman, J., Raman, C., Dirven, C. M. F., Gholinejad, M., & Vasilic, D. (2025). Systematic review of machine learning applications using non optical motion tracking in surgery. *Digital Medicine, 8*(1), 28. Advance online publication. DOI: 10.1038/s41746-024-01412-1 PMID: 39809851

Çavuş, H., & Deniz, S. (2022). The Effect of Technology Assisted Teaching on Success in Mathematics and Geometry: A Meta-Analysis Study. *Participatory Educational Research, 9*(2), 358–397. DOI: 10.17275/per.22.45.9.2

Chen, C., Hu, W., & Wei, X. (2024). From anxiety to action: Exploring the impact of artificial intelligence anxiety and artificial intelligence self-efficacy on motivated learning of undergraduate students. *Interactive Learning Environments*, 1–16. DOI: 10.1080/10494820.2024.2440877

Csikszentmihalyi, M. (1994). The domain of creativity. In Feldman, D., Csikszentmihalyi, M., & Gardner, H. (Eds.), *Changing the world: A framework for the study of creativity* (pp. 135–158). Praeger.

Demirkol, K., İmamoğlu, S. E., Kayman, Ş. S., İmamoğlu, S. Z., & Erat, S. (2025). Internet use for creative purposes and its correlation with perceived usefulness, computer anxiety, and emotional intelligence: The intermediary effect of the perceived ease of use. *Behavioral Sciences (Basel, Switzerland), 15*(2), 221. DOI: 10.3390/bs15020221 PMID: 40001852

Dou, G., Yang, J., Yang, L., Liu, B., & Yuan, Y. (2022). Where there is pressure, there is motivation? The impact of challenge-hindrance stressors on employees' innovation performance. *Frontiers in Psychology, 13*, 1020764. Advance online publication. DOI: 10.3389/fpsyg.2022.1020764 PMID: 36389571

Eke, O. E. (2024). Assessing the readiness and attitudes of Nigerian teacher educators towards adoption of artificial intelligence in educational settings. *Journal of Educational Technology & Online Learning, 7*(4), 473–487.

European Commission. (2020). *Digital education action plan 2021–2027: Resetting education and training for the digital age*. https://eur-lex.europa.eu/legal-content/EN/TXT/PDF/?uri=CELEX%3A52020DC0624

Felix, S. (2022). Divergent and convergent thinking in creative cognition: An integrative review. *Creativity Research Journal*, *34*(1), 1–13.

Finke, R. A., Ward, T. B., & Smith, S. M. (1992). *Creative cognition: Theory, research, and applications*. MIT Press. DOI: 10.7551/mitpress/7722.001.0001

Finnish National Agency for Education. (2025). *AI Guidelines*. https://www.oph.fi/en/ai-guidelines

Frenkenberg, A., & Hochman, G. (2025). It's Scary to Use It, It's Scary to Refuse It: The Psychological Dimensions of AI Adoption—Anxiety, Motives, and Dependency. *Systems*, *13*(2), 82. Advance online publication. DOI: 10.3390/systems13020082

Future of Life Institute (FLI). (2015). *Autonomous weapons: An open letter from AI & robotics researchers*. Retrieved from https://futureoflife.org/open-letter-autonomous-weapons/

Gedrimiene, E., Celik, I., Kaasila, A., Mäkitalo, K., & Muukkonen, H. (2024). Artificial intelligence (AI)-enhanced learning analytics (LA) for supporting career decisions: Advantages and challenges from user perspective. *Education and Information Technologies*, *29*(1), 297–322. DOI: 10.1007/s10639-023-12277-4

Ghamrawi, N., Shal, T., & Ghamrawi, N. A. (2024). Exploring the impact of AI on teacher leadership: Regressing or expanding? *Education and Information Technologies*, *29*(7), 8415–8433. DOI: 10.1007/s10639-023-12174-w

Goodlad, J. I. (1990). *Teachers for our nation's schools*. Jossey-Bass.

Guilford, J. P. (1967). Creativity: Yesterday, today and tomorrow. *The Journal of Creative Behavior*, *1*(1), 3–14. DOI: 10.1002/j.2162-6057.1967.tb00002.x

Guilherme, A. (2019). AI and education: The importance of teacher and student relations. *AI & Society*, *34*(1), 47–54. DOI: 10.1007/s00146-017-0693-8

Gupta, D. K., & Lodi, A. K. (2017). A study of the relationship of creativity with computer anxiety of higher secondary students. *International Journal of Computational Research and Development*, *2*(2), 97–100.

Haenlein, M., & Kaplan, A. (2019). A brief history of artificial intelligence: On the past, present, and future of artificial intelligence. *California Management Review*, *61*(4), 5–14. DOI: 10.1177/0008125619864925

Hwang, Y., & Wu, Y. (2025). The influence of generative artificial intelligence on creative cognition of design students: A chain mediation model of self-efficacy and anxiety. *Frontiers in Psychology*, *15*, 1455015. Advance online publication. DOI: 10.3389/fpsyg.2024.1455015 PMID: 39931512

Jung, R. E., Mead, B. S., Carrasco, J., & Flores, R. A. (2013). The structure of creative cognition in the human brain. *Frontiers in Human Neuroscience*, *7*, 330. DOI: 10.3389/fnhum.2013.00330 PMID: 23847503

Kannan, B., Muthumanickam, A., & Chandrasekaran, S. (2012). Computer anxiety among higher secondary students. *International Journal of Developmental Research, 2*(4), 1008–1011.

Katiyar, P. D. N., Awasthi, M. V. K., Pratap, D. R., Mishra, M. K., Shukla, M. N., Singh, M. R., & Tiwari, D. M. (2024). Ai-driven personalized learning systems: Enhancing educational effectiveness. *Educational Administration Theory and Practices*, 30(5). http:// http://dx.doi .org/DOI: 10.53555/kuey.v30i5.4961

Khalil, R., Godde, B., & Karim, A. A. (2013). The link between creative potential and psychometric intelligence: A meta-analytic examination. *Creativity Research Journal, 25*(1), 1–8.

Khuman, P. (2024). The Navigation of The English Language Teaching and Learning Ecosystem Using Digital Tools. *Hemchandracharya International E Journal of Research, 8*(15), 99–111.

Kim, J., Kadkol, S., Solomon, I., Yeh, H., Soh, J., Nguyen, T., Choi, J., Lee, S., Srivatsa, A., Nahass, G., & Ajilore, O. (2023). AI anxiety: A comprehensive analysis of psychological factors and interventions. SSRN *Electronic Journal*. https://doi.org/DOI: 10.2139/ssrn.4573394

Kohnke, L., Zou, D., Ou, A. W., & Gu, M. M. (2025). Preparing future educators for AI-enhanced classrooms: Insights into AI literacy and integration. *Computers and Education: Artificial Intelligence, 8*, 100398. DOI: 10.1016/j.caeai.2025.100398

Kusumo, B., Sutrisman, H., Henny, S., Simanjuntak, R., Prihartanto, A., Askrening, A., & Yunus, R. (2024). The impact of technology-based learning on student engagement and achievement in the digital era. *International Journal of Educational Evaluation and Policy Analysis, 1*(4), 41–53. DOI: 10.62951/ijeepa.v1i4.55

Lassig, C. J. (2013). Approaches to creativity: How adolescents engage in the creative process. *Thinking Skills and Creativity, 10*, 3–12. DOI: 10.1016/j.tsc.2013.05.002

Li, J., & Huang, J. S. (2020). Dimensions of artificial intelligence anxiety based on the integrated fear acquisition theory. *Technology in Society*, 63, 1–10. , 101410.DOI: 10.1016/j.techsoc.2020.101410

Liao, Y.-K. C., & Chen, Y.-H. (2021). Integrating technology in mathematics instruction on grade school academic achievement in Taiwan: A meta-analysis. *Bulletin of Educational Psychology, 52*(4), 781–806. DOI: 10.6251/BEP.202106_52(4).0003

Lim, E. M. (2023). The effects of pre-service early childhood teachers' digital literacy and self-efficacy on their perception of AI education for young children. *Education and Information Technologies, 28*(10), 12969–12995. DOI: 10.1007/s10639-023-11724-6

Manyika, J., Lund, S., Chui, M., Bughin, J., Woetzel, J., Batra, P., Ko, R., & Sanghvi, S. (2017). Jobs lost, jobs gained: Workforce transitions in a time of automation. *McKinsey Global Institute, 150*(1), 1–148.

Miller, A. L. (2014). A self-report measure of cognitive processes associated with creativity. *Creativity Research Journal*, *26*(2), 203–218. DOI: 10.1080/10400419.2014.901088

Ministry of Education, Government of India. (2020). *National education policy 2020*. https://www.education.gov.in/sites/upload_files/mhrd/files/NEP_Final_English.pdf

Mumford, M. D., Medeiros, K. E., & Partlow, P. J. (2012). Creative thinking: Processes, strategies, and knowledge. *The Journal of Creative Behavior*, *46*(1), 30–47. DOI: 10.1002/jocb.003

National Council for Teacher Education. (2009). *National curriculum framework for teacher education: Towards preparing professional and humane teacher*. https://ncte.gov.in/Website/PDF/NCFTE_2009.pdf

Nijstad, B. A., De-Dreu, C. K., Rietzschel, E. F., & Baas, M. (2010). The dual pathway to creativity model: Creative ideation as a function of flexibility and persistence. *European Review of Social Psychology*, *21*(1), 34–77. DOI: 10.1080/10463281003765323

Organisation for Economic Co-operation and Development. (2021, July 5). *Future of education and skills 2030: Conceptual learning framework – Education and AI: Preparing for the future & AI, attitudes and values* [EDU/EDPC(2018)45/ANN2]. OECD. https://www.oecd.org

Parasuraman, S., & Igbaria, M. (1990). An examination of gender differences in the determinants of computer anxiety and attitudes toward microcomputers among managers. *International Journal of Man-Machine Studies*, *32*(3), 327–340. DOI: 10.1016/S0020-7373(08)80006-5

Pei, B., Lu, J., & Jing, X. (2025). Empowering preservice teachers' AI literacy: Current understanding, influential factors, and strategies for improvement. *Computers and Education: Artificial Intelligence*, *8*, 100406. DOI: 10.1016/j.caeai.2025.100406

Preeth, A. M., & Bapu, K. G. V. (2024). Attitude Towards Artificial Intelligence and Tech Anxiety Among Working Professionals in Metropolitan Cities. *Indian Journal of Artificial Intelligence and Neural Networking*, *4*(94). Advance online publication. DOI: 10.54105/ijainn.D1089.04040624

Runco, M. A., & Acar, S. (2012). Divergent thinking as an indicator of creative potential. *Creativity Research Journal*, *24*(1), 66–75. DOI: 10.1080/10400419.2012.652929

Saini, N. (2023). Research Paper on Artificial Intelligence & Its Applications. *International Journal of Research Trends and Innovation*, *8*(4), 356–360.

Sasikala, P., & Ravichandran, R. (2024). Study on the Impact of Artificial Intelligence on Student Learning Outcomes. *Journal of Digital Learning and Education*, *4*(2), 145–155. DOI: 10.52562/jdle.v4i2.1234

Sawyer, R. K. (2012). *Explaining creativity: The science of human innovation* (2nd ed.). Oxford University Press.

Singh, A. M., & Haju, W. B. (2022). Artificial intelligence. *International Journal for Research in Applied Science and Engineering Technology*, *10*(7), 1210–1220. DOI: 10.22214/ijraset.2022.44306 PMID: 35769405

Solove, D. J. (2002). Conceptualizing privacy. *California Law Review*, *90*(4), 1087–1155. DOI: 10.2307/3481326

Tabachnick, B. G., & Fidell, L. S. (2015). *Using multivariate statistics* (6th ed.). Pearson.

Tai, M. C. T. (2020). The impact of artificial intelligence on human society and bioethics. *Tzu-Chi Medical Journal*, *32*(4), 339–343. DOI: 10.4103/tcmj.tcmj_71_20 PMID: 33163378

Talvid, M. (2016). Understanding teachers' reluctance to the pedagogical use of ICT in the 1:1 classroom. *Education and Information Technologies*, *21*(3), 503–519. DOI: 10.1007/s10639-014-9335-7

Taylor, C. L. (2017). Creativity and Mood Disorder: A Systematic Review and Meta-Analysis. *Perspectives on Psychological Science*, *12*(6), 1040–1076. DOI: 10.1177/1745691617699653 PMID: 28934560

UNESCO. (2008). *ICT competency standards for teachers: Policy framework.* (CI.2007/WS/21). UNESCO. https://unesdoc.unesco.org/ark:/48223/pf0000156210

Wang, Y.-M., Wei, C.-L., Lin, H.-H., Wang, S.-C., & Wang, Y.-S. (2022). What drives students' AI learning behavior: A perspective of AI anxiety. *Interactive Learning Environments*, *32*(6), 2584–2600. DOI: 10.1080/10494820.2022.2153147

Wang, Y. Y., & Wang, Y. S. (2019). Development and validation of an artificial intelligence anxiety scale: An initial application in predicting motivated learning behavior. *Interactive Learning Environments*, •••, 1–16. DOI: 10.1080/10494820.2019.1674887

Ward, T. B. (1994). Structured imagination: The role of category structure in exemplar generation. *Cognitive Psychology*, *27*(1), 1–40. DOI: 10.1006/cogp.1994.1010

Ward, T. B. (1995). What's old about new ideas? In Smith, S. M., Ward, T. M., & Finke, R. A. (Eds.), *The creative cognition approach.* MIT Press.

Ward, T. B. (2019). Creative cognition as a window on creativity. In Kaufman, J. C., & Sternberg, R. J. (Eds.), *The Cambridge handbook of creativity* (2nd ed., pp. 251–270). Cambridge University Press., DOI: 10.1017/9781316979839.011

Wilson, H., Daugherty, P., & Bianzino, N. (2017). The jobs that artificial intelligence will create. *MIT Sloan Management Review.* https://sloanreview.mit.edu/article/will-ai-create-as-many-jobs-as-it-eliminates

World Economic Forum. (2016). The future of jobs: Employment, skills and workforce strategy for the fourth industrial revolution. *World Economic Forum.* https://www.weforum.org/reports/the-future-of-jobs

Wray, M. L., Liu, M., & Yu, T. (2022). Teachers' self-efficacy and adaptability in the era of artificial intelligence. *Computers & Education, 185*, 104536.

Yadav, D. (2022). Exploring the negative effects of artificial intelligence. *Biolecta*. Retrieved from https://biolecta.com/articles/negative-effects-of-artificial-intelligence/

Yan, G., Wang, Y., & Cheyn, L. (2025). Diagnostic Performance of Artificial Intelligence Based on Biparametric MRI for Clinically Significant Prostate Cancer: A Systematic Review and Meta-analysis. *Academic Radiology*. Advance online publication. DOI: 10.1016/j.acra.2025.02.044 PMID: 40058989

Zawacki-Richter, O., Marín, V. I., Bond, M., & Gouverneur, F. (2019). Systematic review of research on artificial intelligence applications in higher education – Where are the educators? *International Journal of Educational Technology in Higher Education, 16*(1), 1–27. DOI: 10.1186/s41239-019-0171-0

Zhang, C., Schiebl, J., Plobl, L., Hofmann, F., & Gläser-Zikuda, M. (2023). Acceptance of artificial intelligence among pre-service teachers: A multigroup analysis. *International Journal of Educational Technology in Higher Education, 20*(1), 49. DOI: 10.1186/s41239-023-00420-7 PMID: 36743849

KEY TERM AND DEFINITIONS

Artificial intelligence: Artificial intelligence is the ability of computers to mimic human intelligence functions such as reasoning, problem-solving and communication. In author's words, it is intelligence crafted artificially by naturally intelligent species-humans to simulate their cognitive functions.

Artificial intelligence anxiety: Artificial intelligence anxiety is the psychological discomfort that individual experiences when contemplating the disruptive impacts of AI at personal, societal and professional fronts.

Creative cognition: It is the process that assists the individual to generate diverse alternatives for solving the problem including the ability to choose the best available option to address the issue.

Teacher education: Teacher education is the training programme designed to equip prospective teachers with theoretical knowledge and practical experiences aimed at developing their competence and professional skills.

Chapter 11
Leveraging Sports, AI, and Gamification for Transformative Learning:
A Framework for Active, Inclusive, and Future-Ready Education

Amitava Pal
https://orcid.org/0009-0007-8934-2718
ICFAI University, India

M Rajkumar
https://orcid.org/0000-0002-7606-0152
ICFAI University, India

ABSTRACT

As education evolves in the digital era, traditional models must be reimagined to foster deeper engagement, personalization, and skill development. This chapter explores how sports, artificial intelligence (AI), and gamification converge to create a transformative learning framework. Sports promote experiential education, teamwork, and resilience; AI enables personalized, real-time learning; and gamification boosts motivation through rewards and challenges. By integrating these forces, supported by transformative and experiential learning theories, the chapter highlights applications across classrooms, playgrounds, apps, and academies, while addressing challenges, ethics, and future directions for inclusive education.

INTRODUCTION

Education today is rapidly evolving as digital tools and technologies reshape how we learn. Traditional teaching methods, which often relied on passive lectures and rote memorization, are giving way to more interactive and engaging models (Parveen & Ramzan, 2024). As per Ou (2024), in this new digital era, the focus is shifting towards personalized

DOI: 10.4018/979-8-3373-5092-9.ch011

learning experiences that can adapt to each student's needs. This change is driven by the desire to prepare learners for a complex and fast-paced world, where critical thinking, problem-solving, and teamwork are more important than ever.

One exciting development in modern education is incorporating sports as a vehicle for learning and character building. Sports offer more than just physical activity; they are an immersive environment where students develop essential life skills. Through sports, students experience the importance of teamwork, discipline, and resilience firsthand. These activities also promote an active lifestyle, which is closely linked to improved focus, mental clarity, and overall well-being. The dynamic nature of sports creates a natural setting for experiential learning, where practical application reinforces theoretical knowledge (Bisa, 2023). At the same time, emerging technologies such as artificial intelligence (AI) are revolutionizing personalized learning. AI tools can analyze individual performance and learning patterns, allowing educators to tailor instruction to meet the unique needs of each student. By providing real-time feedback and adaptive learning pathways, AI makes it possible to address gaps in understanding and challenge students at the appropriate level (Jian, 2023; Ellikkal & Rajamohan, 2024; Fitria & Institut Teknologi Bisnis AAS Indonesia, 2021). Additionally, gamification—using game-design elements like points, rewards, and challenges—adds an element of fun and motivation to the learning process. By turning learning into an engaging experience, gamification encourages students to participate and persist in their educational journey actively. When sports, AI, and gamification are combined, they offer a robust foundation for transformative education that is both active and personalized (Bitrián et al., 2021; Christopoulos & Mystakidis, 2023).

This chapter sets the stage by exploring these interrelated trends and ideas. It delves into how integrating sports, AI, and gamification can create richer, more effective learning experiences. Ultimately, the chapter aims to lay down a clear framework for how these tools can be harnessed to meet modern education's demands, making learning more effective, enjoyable, and inclusive.

CHAPTER OBJECTIVES

- To explore how sports-based education, AI technologies, and gamification principles can be fused to drive student engagement and skill development.
- To propose a framework for implementing this integration within formal and informal learning ecosystems.
- To examine case studies, current tools, and potential implementation models.

THEORETICAL UNDERPINNINGS

Understanding the learning theories that support the integration of sports, artificial intelligence (AI), and gamification in education is essential for exploring this approach (Bezzina et al., 2021). These theories provide the conceptual foundation for designing active learning experiences that are engaging and meaningful for students across different age groups and learning environments ("Learning Theories Within Gamification," 2020).

At the core is Transformative Learning Theory, developed by Jack Mezirow. This theory emphasizes the profound structural shift in how individuals think, feel, and act. It encourages learners to critically reflect on their assumptions, experiences, and beliefs to form new perspectives (Kitchenham, 2008; Simsek, 2012; Fleming, 2018). In an educational setting, transformative learning moves beyond memorization to focus on personal growth and real-world understanding. When learners participate in sports or interactive AI-based activities, they encounter challenges that require them to question their strategies, adjust their thinking, and learn from outcomes. This reflective process aligns well with transformative learning, where accurate understanding comes from meaningful experience and change (Halkiopoulos & Gkintoni, 2024).

Experiential Learning Theory (ELT), developed by David Kolb, provides another important framework. ELT views learning as a continuous process grounded in experience. It follows a four-stage cycle: concrete experience, reflective observation, abstract conceptualization, and active experimentation (Simply Psychology, 2025). In sports-based learning, students naturally move through this cycle—engaging in physical activities (experience), thinking about their performance (reflection), understanding what works and what does not (conceptualization), and trying out new techniques (experimentation). This hands-on approach increases retention, enhances problem-solving skills, and bridges the gap between theory and practice (Piščalkienė & Lottrup, 2019).

Complementing ELT is Constructivist Learning Theory, which emphasizes that learners build knowledge actively rather than receive it passively (Passarelli & Kolb, 2011; McGowan et al., 2023). According to constructivists like Piaget and Vygotsky, knowledge is constructed through interaction with the environment and social collaboration. In gamified or sport-based learning, students are not just absorbing facts—they are experimenting, failing, succeeding, and improving through experience. This process helps develop a deeper understanding and encourages learners to become independent thinkers (Zhang, 2022).

Gamification Theory, meanwhile, draws from motivational psychology and behavioral economics. It suggests that game-like features like points, badges, leaderboards, feedback loops, and challenges can enhance learners' motivation, engagement, and persistence. These elements tap into intrinsic motivators (curiosity, mastery, or personal achievement) and extrinsic motivators (rewards or competition). In the classroom, gamification can help turn routine or complex tasks into exciting challenges, especially when combined with physical or AI-driven activities. It also encourages learners to set goals, take initiative, and track progress (Kien & Nguyen, 2021).

Cognitive theories of learning and personalized learning models support AI in education. AI systems use data from learner interactions to analyze their behavior, preferences, and performance (S et al., 2024). These systems are often based on cognitive load theory, which aims to optimize the amount of information a learner processes at a time, and adaptive learning models, which adjust content difficulty based on real-time assessment. AI can guide learners through personalized pathways, provide immediate feedback, and recommend next steps, ensuring each learner's journey is unique and compelling. When applied thoughtfully,

AI enhances the teacher's ability to support every learner, especially in large or diverse classrooms (Cardona et al., 2023).

Together, these theories present a strong foundation for reimagining education. Educators can design powerful learning environments by combining the reflective depth of transformative learning, the practicality of experiential and constructivist approaches, gamification engagement, and AI's precision. These environments are not only effective in improving academic outcomes. They can also nurture critical thinking, collaboration, emotional intelligence, and resilience—skills essential for success in today's fast-changing world.

SPORTS AS A PEDAGOGICAL TOOL

In today's education landscape, where traditional methods often struggle to keep learners engaged, sports offer an exciting and effective alternative. They are not just extracurricular activities but dynamic learning platforms that help develop a wide range of cognitive, emotional, and social skills. Sports embody real-life situations where learners experience problem-solving, teamwork, and decision-making in action. Integrating sports into pedagogy transforms classrooms into spaces of active, joyful, and meaningful learning (Marsh & Kleitman, 2002).

Core Values and Life Skills Nurtured Through Sports

Sports have consistently shown the power to build character from early childhood to adolescence. Participation in sports instills honesty, respect, discipline, teamwork, perseverance, and time management. These are not taught through lectures—they are internalized through real experiences (Admin, 2023).

For example, consider a relay race. A student learns the importance of trusting teammates and precisely delivering the baton. If one person is late or careless, the whole team is affected. This builds accountability and respect for collective effort. Similarly, sports like cricket or kabaddi teach strategic thinking and leadership—deciding when to take risks, how to organize the team, and when to step up or support from the sidelines.

Sports also encourage inclusive learning. Players from different social or economic backgrounds come together, helping break stereotypes and building mutual respect. This diversity in action reinforces the idea of equity and collaboration.

Linkages Between Physical Activity and Cognitive Performance

Research shows that physical activity stimulates brain function, aiding memory, concentration, and creativity. Exercise increases blood flow and oxygen to the brain, which helps learners stay alert and think more clearly (*Physical Activity Improves Brain and Cognitive*

Functions | Extension | University of (Nevada, Reno, n.d.; Sanaeifar et al., 2024; Harvard Health, 2024).

For example, in Finland, known for its innovative education system, schools often include frequent physical breaks. These are not considered distractions but are seen as integral to learning. After a short outdoor activity or a sports-based classroom warm-up, students return to their academic work with renewed focus(Lefort, 2024). Teachers can integrate simple sports-based tasks into classroom transitions—for instance, short movement games between math and science lessons—to improve attentiveness. This brain-body connection shows that physical activity is not separate from academic performance—it actively enhances it.

Sports for Social-Emotional Learning (SEL) and Resilience Building

In sports, success and failure are frequent and public. This offers rich opportunities for social-emotional learning. Learners deal with frustration, learn to celebrate others' success, cope with pressure, and develop emotional regulation (Furley et al., 2023; Jones et al., n.d.).

Imagine a student who loses a chess game after leading the entire match. Instead of quitting, the coach encourages them to reflect on their decisions and try again in the next round. This helps build grit and resilience—the ability to bounce back after setbacks.

Team sports, in particular, are fertile ground for learning empathy, communication, and leadership. A team captain who notices a nervous teammate before a match and offers encouragement practices empathy in real time. These experiences go beyond textbooks and shape emotional intelligence, one of the strongest predictors of life success (*Learning to Be With Others: Using Sport to Develop Empathy*, 2022).

Sports-Based Education Models: Teaching Games for Understanding (TGfU)

TGfU is a learner-centered approach where students play simplified versions of games to understand tactical concepts and strategies. Instead of focusing only on skills (like dribbling or passing), TGfU encourages learners to think, adapt, and make decisions(*Teaching Games for Understanding: What Does That Look Like and How Does It Improve Skill Learning and Game Playing*, n.d.; Webb et al., 2006; Pan et al., 2023).

Example:

A group of Grade 6 students is learning about invasion games (like football or hockey). Instead of starting with technical drills, the teacher introduces a 3-on-3 keep-away game where students must maintain possession of the ball within a limited space. After 5 minutes, students discuss what helped them succeed.

One student said, "Passing quickly helped us avoid the defender." Another noted, "We moved better when we spread out." These observations led to a mini-lesson on spacing and movement, which was directly connected to real-game understanding.

This approach builds game intelligence and makes learning more meaningful. TGfU also encourages student agency, where learners co-construct knowledge by experimenting, discussing, and reflecting.

Scenario: A Real-World Integration of Sports in Learning

In a school implementing sports-based learning, a Grade 8 science teacher integrates basketball to teach force and motion. Students perform passes and record the distance traveled by the ball under different force levels. They later plot graphs and discuss friction, gravity, and Newton's Laws—all from a game they love.

Meanwhile, the physical education teacher partners with the counselor to use sports conflict resolution, guiding students to resolve disputes during games and practicing negotiation and empathy. Over time, this has become part of the school culture, where sports grounds have become a lab for life skills.

When used intentionally as a pedagogical tool, sports can redefine how students learn. They foster physical well-being, emotional strength, cognitive sharpness, and social responsibility—all essential for holistic development. By aligning sports with learning outcomes, educators can create vibrant, active classrooms that develop smarter students and more confident, compassionate, and capable individuals. The key lies in structured reflection, inclusive design, and meaningful integration into the curriculum.

ARTIFICIAL INTELLIGENCE IN EDUCATION

Artificial Intelligence (AI) is changing the way we teach and learn. AI acts like an intelligent assistant that understands what students need and helps teachers better support them. It makes learning more personal, active, and efficient, especially with sports and gamified environments(Kamalov et al., 2023).

AI-Driven Personalization and Adaptive Learning

AI can observe how each student learns—how fast they understand, where they struggle, and what kind of content they prefer. Based on this, AI systems create personalized learning paths for students, which means no two students have the same learning experience.

For example, an AI-based learning app might notice that one student solves math problems quickly but struggles with reading comprehension. The app then offers more reading games, interactive stories, or audio support to help the student improve. This kind of adaptive learning ensures that each child gets help uniquely (Gligorea et al., 2023).

In sports education, AI tools can recommend different drills or workouts depending on a student's strengths and areas to improve. For instance, if students have better endurance but weak reaction time, AI can guide them through reaction-based exercises or games.

AI Applications in Sports Analytics, Coaching Feedback, and Wellness Tracking

AI is already used in professional sports and is coming to schools and grassroots levels. It helps track player performance, analyze game strategies, and prevent injuries.

For example, AI-powered wearables like smartwatches or fitness bands can track heart rate, movement patterns, and fatigue levels. Coaches use this data to decide if a student is ready to continue training or needs rest. This supports physical safety and helps prevent overtraining(Kumar, 2025).

Another example is video analysis tools that use AI to analyze a player's actions. A basketball player can receive detailed feedback on their shooting form, speed, or defensive posture, which would be challenging to track without technology(Kapuściński, 2024).

This data helps athletes, PE teachers, and sports educators create better training plans, understand performance trends, and more meaningfully celebrate student progress.

Role of Natural Language Processing, Computer Vision, and Predictive Modeling

AI is powered by different technologies that help it "see," "understand," and "predict."

- **Natural Language Processing (NLP)** helps computers understand and respond to human language. In education, it powers chatbots and voice assistants that answer students' questions or give instant feedback. For example, a student struggling with sports terminology can ask an AI assistant, "What is a 'rally' in badminton?" and get a quick explanation(Labadze et al., 2023)
- **Computer Vision** helps machines understand images and videos. In sports education, computer vision can track body posture and movement using a camera. A PE teacher can use it to assess how well students do jumping jacks or yoga poses—even in remote classes! (Liu & Xie, 2024)
- **Predictive Modeling** uses data to guess future outcomes. For instance, based on their activity patterns, AI can predict which students might face burnout or which players are at higher risk of injury. This allows timely intervention and better care(Al-malawi et al., 2024)

These technologies support personalized education, real-time guidance, injury prevention, and data-driven coaching.

ETHICAL CONCERNS AND PRIVACY ISSUES

While AI brings many benefits, it raises important ethical questions, especially concerning children.

- **Data Privacy:** AI systems collect much personal information, such as student performance, health data, or behavior. If not properly secured, this data could be misused. Schools and educators must ensure that data is stored safely and used only for educational purposes.
- **Bias in AI:** Sometimes, AI systems may make unfair decisions. For example, if an AI tool were primarily trained on data from boys' football teams, it might give less accurate feedback for girls. Developers must make sure the systems are fair and inclusive.
- **Over-reliance on Technology:** AI can guide learning, but should not replace human teachers or coaches. Machines cannot replicate the emotional connection, mentorship, and moral guidance that humans provide.

That is why schools need to balance technology with empathy, and for students and educators to understand how AI works before entirely depending on it.

AI is transforming education and sports learning by making them smarter, more personalized, and more efficient. From adjusting lessons to analyzing game performance, AI helps both students and educators reach their full potential. But along with its benefits, we must also be mindful of how we use it, protecting privacy, ensuring fairness, and always putting the human experience at the center.

GAMIFICATION IN LEARNING ENVIRONMENTS

Gamification uses game-like elements in non-game settings such as classrooms, online platforms, or sports training to make learning more enjoyable and engaging. Instead of just playing games, students are encouraged to learn through systems that reward their progress and keep them motivated. The most common gamification elements include Points, Levels, Badges, and Leaderboards—often called PLBL. Points are given for completing tasks, like answering quiz questions or completing physical activities, helping students feel a sense of achievement. As they collect more points, they can move up through different levels, which provides a sense of progress and encourages them to keep going. Badges serve as digital rewards for achieving specific milestones—for example, completing a weekly sports challenge or showing teamwork during a PE session. Leaderboards display rankings based on performance and encourage friendly competition among learners, which can increase participation and excitement(Sanchez et al., 2019).

These game-like strategies have a positive impact on students' learning experiences. They increase engagement because students feel more connected to the content and are motivated to interact regularly. They also help improve motivation by offering recognition and rewards, making learning more meaningful. For instance, a student not usually interested in fitness might become more active if their sports app gives badges for reaching step goals or offers a leaderboard to compete with friends. Additionally, gamification supports better knowledge retention, especially when learners receive regular feedback and visual reminders of their progress.

Several educational and fitness platforms have successfully used gamification. Duolingo uses streaks, points, and levels to encourage daily language practice. Fitness apps like Fitbit (Moore, n.d.; *The Fitbit Community*, 2016) or Nike Training Club (*Member Rewards*, n.d.) reward users with badges and encourage consistency through step challenges. In classrooms, platforms like Classcraft turn everyday learning into a role-playing adventure, where students earn experience points and level up by showing good behavior or doing well in assignments. Even health platforms like GOQii in India have adopted gamification, using daily tasks, community leaderboards, and karma points to promote healthy habits (Mindster, 2025).

In sports and education, gamification can bring out the best in students. It promotes active participation, even from those who may be shy or less confident. It helps students build long-term habits like regular physical activity and goal-setting. It also strengthens teamwork and emotional resilience, as students work towards common goals in fun and supportive environments. When combined with sports and AI, gamification can transform learning into a more interactive, personalized, and rewarding journey.

THE POWER OF CONVERGENCE: SPORTS + AI + GAMIFICATION

When sports, artificial intelligence (AI), and gamification combine, they create a powerful and innovative learning environment. Each domain adds unique value—sports build physical and mental strength, AI enables personalization and intelligent feedback, and gamification makes the process fun, engaging, and motivating. They offer a holistic approach to transformative learning that connects the body, mind, and emotions. This convergence promotes active participation, deeper engagement, and personalized experiences that are difficult to achieve through traditional teaching methods alone (Tan & Cheah, 2021).

One strong example of this synergy is the use of smart wearable devices. These gadgets can track a learner's physical activity, such as steps taken, heart rate, or calories burned, and provide real-time AI-generated feedback. When this data is presented through a gamified interface, learners can unlock badges, track progress, and participate in challenges, making fitness and learning more enjoyable and consistent. Another example is AI-powered sports coaching systems that adapt to a student's skill level. These systems can identify areas for improvement and offer skill-specific exercises. By adding game-like challenges or levels to these tasks, learners stay motivated while constantly improving their performance (Shei et al., 2022).

To better understand the unique and combined value of sports, AI, and gamification in educational settings, the following table outlines their individual contributions to learning and the synergistic benefits they offer when integrated. While each component enhances engagement and skill development in its own way, their convergence produces a transformative learning environment that is greater than the sum of its parts.

Table 1. Individual contributions vs. combined impact of sports, AI, and gamification

Component	Primary Contribution to Learning	Convergence Benefit
Sports	Builds physical health, teamwork, discipline, and social-emotional learning	Active engagement and real-world context for applying concepts
AI	Enables personalized learning, real-time feedback, data-driven insights	Customization of learning paths and tailored coaching
Gamification	Increases motivation, goal-setting, and retention through game-based mechanics	Continuous engagement and playful learning experience
Integrated Approach (Sports + AI + Gamification)	Amplifies benefits through synergy of physical, cognitive, and motivational learning	A dynamic, inclusive, and transformative learning environment that supports 21st-century skills like collaboration, resilience, and self-directed learning

Movement-based learning apps combining physical activity with gamified learning experiences are growing in schools. For instance, an app might ask students to solve a math puzzle that only appears after completing a physical task like jumping or stretching. These integrated programs improve attention, memory, and well-being while ensuring students are not passively sitting through lessons(Nichols, 2024).

We propose the Transformative Learning Triangle as a simple framework to combine these elements. At each corner of the triangle lies one of the three pillars—Sports, AI, and Gamification. When these elements work together, they create a learning environment that is experiential, personalized, and highly motivating. This triangle can guide educators, app developers, and curriculum designers in creating engaging, inclusive, and future-ready programs. By leveraging the combined strengths of physical movement, smart technology, and game-based strategies, education can become effective and truly transformative.

REAL-WORLD APPLICATIONS

The integration of sports, AI, and gamification has already started showing real-world impact in various educational and youth engagement initiatives across the globe. One notable example is AiSCOUT, a cutting-edge mobile platform that uses artificial intelligence and gamified tasks to assess young footballers' skills. Players can record their athletic and technical drills on their phones, which are then evaluated by an AI engine trained with input from real scouts and coaches. This platform has created opportunities for youth in remote or underserved areas to participate in virtual trials and get scouted by professional clubs. A striking case is that of 18-year-old Andre Odeku, who submitted his performance through AiSCOUT while training in a park. His data impressed professional scouts, eventually earning him a trial with Burnley FC's U-23 team. This example illustrates how the fusion of AI and gamified sports activities can break barriers to opportunity and talent discovery in youth sports (Christian, 2023).

Another powerful application is seen in education systems like Taiwan's Taiwan Adaptive Learning Platform (TALP). While TALP was primarily designed to personalize academic learning through AI by identifying gaps in students' understanding and suggesting individualized learning paths, the same adaptive principles can be applied to physical education (PE). AI-based PE systems can assess students' fitness levels, recommend appropriate physical tasks, and offer real-time feedback to both students and teachers. This approach creates a more inclusive and effective PE curriculum, ensuring that every student receives attention tailored to their physical abilities and developmental stage (T. C. Liu, 2022).

A third inspiring case involves gamified sports initiatives in rural schools across India, focusing on cognitive development and social-emotional learning. The DEEP platform (Developmental assessment on an E-Platform) uses gamified cognitive tasks delivered through tablets to assess and engage children in low-resource settings. These games are designed to measure attention, memory, and problem-solving skills while being fun and culturally relevant. Even when delivered by non-specialists, the platform proved effective in capturing children's cognitive performance and keeping them motivated to learn and play. Schools also used small-scale gamified sports tournaments to encourage teamwork, improve decision-making under pressure, and strengthen peer interaction—fostering social-emotional growth alongside cognitive skills (Mukherjee et al., 2020).

Across these cases, the outcomes were significant. Motivation levels among students increased due to the engaging, game-like environment. Academic performance improved when AI helped identify and close learning gaps. Physical fitness was enhanced through AI-tailored routines and interactive challenges. Most importantly, social and emotional growth was nurtured through collaborative sports and gamified interactions, fostering resilience, empathy, and teamwork. Together, these case studies provide strong evidence that combining AI, sports, and gamification can lead to truly transformative learning experiences.

IMPLEMENTATION STRATEGY

Implementing an integrated approach that combines sports, artificial intelligence (AI), and gamification into educational settings requires a structured, phase-wise plan that ensures both feasibility and impact. The first step is curriculum mapping, where existing academic or physical education curricula are analyzed to identify where AI and gamified sports elements can be embedded to enhance learning outcomes. This involves aligning learning objectives with physical activities, AI-based assessments, and gamification mechanics to ensure coherence and value addition (Su et al., 2024). Once the mapping is done, the next step is tool and platform selection. Institutions and startups must choose appropriate digital platforms and AI solutions that support their goals, such as adaptive learning platforms, wearable fitness trackers, or gamified apps designed for learning through movement. These tools should be age-appropriate, easy to integrate, and aligned with data privacy regulations (Lee & Lee, 2021).

Capacity building is a critical part of the implementation. Teachers, sports educators, and coaches must be trained to use the tools, interpret AI-generated insights, and use gamification meaningfully to engage learners. Workshops, certification modules, and ongoing mentorship programs can ensure smooth adoption and long-term sustainability (Altinay et al., 2024).

As education shifts from conventional approaches to more dynamic, technology-enhanced frameworks, it is important to contrast traditional learning models with integrated approaches that combine sports, AI, and gamification. The following table highlights key differences in learning design, engagement, and educational outcomes between these two models, underscoring the transformative potential of an integrated methodology.

Table 2. Traditional vs. integrated learning models

Aspect	Traditional Model	Integrated Model (Sports + AI + Gamification)
Learning Style	Passive, lecture-based	Active, experiential, and adaptive
Assessment	Periodic, standardised	Continuous, personalized, and feedback-driven
Engagement Level	Varies, often low	High due to interactivity and motivation loops
Teacher's Role	Sole knowledge provider	Facilitator, coach, and data-informed mentor
Student Experience	One-size-fits-all	Differentiated, goal-oriented, and inclusive
Skill Development	Mostly cognitive	Cognitive + physical + emotional + collaborative

A pilot testing phase helps validate the integrated approach's effectiveness before a full-scale rollout. During this phase, small student groups or selected schools can test the tools, and data tracking mechanisms can monitor learner progress, engagement, and emotional response. These metrics help evaluate what is working and needs to be adjusted (White & Branch, 2008).

A continuous feedback and improvement cycle ensures the system evolves based on real-world usage. Teachers and students should be encouraged to share feedback regularly, and iterative updates should be made to the curriculum design, tool features, and training strategies (Williams, 2024; Carreno et al., 2024).

Throughout the strategy, considerations of inclusion, accessibility, and equity must be embedded. This includes choosing mobile-friendly platforms for underserved areas, using multilingual interfaces, and designing tasks that cater to students of all abilities and backgrounds. Ensuring gender neutrality in sports activities and avoiding tech-based exclusion are key to creating a truly inclusive and transformative educational environment (Organisation for Economic Co-operation and Development et al., 2023).

CHALLENGES AND LIMITATIONS

Despite the transformative potential of integrating sports, artificial intelligence (AI), and gamification into learning environments, several critical challenges and limitations must be addressed to ensure ethical, sustainable, and inclusive implementation.

One of the foremost concerns is the ethical deployment of AI in educational settings. AI systems rely on large datasets to make predictions and provide personalized feedback. However, if these datasets lack diversity or include biased information, the AI may perpetuate or even worsen inequalities. For example, an AI system trained predominantly on urban student data may not accurately assess or recommend activities for students in rural or marginalized communities. There are also privacy concerns, particularly around collecting data from minors. Institutions must ensure that data is handled securely, transparently, and with proper consent. Regulations like GDPR (General Data Protection Regulation) should guide the development and use of AI tools. However, many regions still lack clear frameworks ("Ethical Implications of AI in Education: Data Privacy and Algorithmic Bias," 2024).

In terms of gamification, while elements like points, badges, and leaderboards can enhance motivation, there is a risk of over-rewarding extrinsic motivation. Students becoming too focused on winning rewards can reduce their natural curiosity and desire to learn for personal satisfaction. This can lead to surface learning, where learners aim to complete tasks rather than understand concepts. Moreover, leaderboards can unintentionally create pressure or reinforce negative self-image among lower-performing students. In extreme cases, it may even lead to behavioral addiction, where users become dependent on the game-like elements for validation (Dahlstrøm & Department of Design, Norwegian University of Science and Technology, n.d.).

Infrastructure gaps and affordability pose another significant barrier. High-tech solutions like smart wearables, motion sensors, and AI-driven platforms often require consistent internet connectivity, digital literacy, and up-to-date hardware—all of which may not be available in under-resourced schools or remote areas. While technology aims to bridge learning gaps, poor implementation can further widen the divide between privileged and underserved students. In many cases, licensing software, maintaining hardware, and training staff can be prohibitive for institutions struggling with basic educational resources (Rashid & Kausik, 2024).

Teacher Training

Another significant challenge is teacher preparedness and pedagogical alignment. Many educators may be unfamiliar with AI tools or hesitant to incorporate gamification techniques due to fear of losing control over the classroom or compromising academic rigor. Teachers need training to interpret AI insights and integrate them meaningfully with sports activities and learning goals. Many well-intentioned initiatives can fail at the classroom level without ongoing professional development. There is also the need to align these innovations with existing academic standards and policies, ensuring that sports and gamification are not seen as distractions but as legitimate pedagogical tools (Panda, 2024; Taqa, 2025).

Data Dependency and Algorithmic Misjudgement

AI systems are only as good as the data they are trained on. If the input data is biased, incomplete, or lacks diversity (e.g., overrepresenting urban learners or male participants in sports), the resulting recommendations may be inaccurate or even discriminatory. This can lead to misdiagnosis of learning needs or unfair assessments in performance tracking. There is a growing need to ensure that AI tools are trained on representative, inclusive datasets and regularly audited to prevent such errors (Hossain et al., 2002).

Digital Equity and Access Gaps

A significant concern in many developing contexts is the rural-urban digital divide. Students in under-resourced or remote areas may not have access to high-speed internet, modern devices, or trained facilitators. This limits the reach and impact of AI-powered or gamified learning platforms. Similarly, **gender disparities** can emerge when cultural norms restrict girls' participation in sports or technology-related activities, leading to unequal opportunities for growth and engagement (Ahuja, 2023).

Teacher Burnout and Resistance

Introducing and managing AI, gamification, and sports-based learning simultaneously can increase the burden on educators. Many teachers may feel overwhelmed by the technological and pedagogical changes required, especially if they lack proper training or institutional support. This may result in passive resistance, superficial implementation, or even burnout. Continuous professional development, co-creation of tools, and leadership support are essential to ensure that educators remain empowered rather than overburdened (eSchool Media Contributors, 2024).

Global Ethical Governance and Policy Alignment

The integration of AI in education must be guided by international ethical frameworks, such as UNESCO's *Recommendation on the Ethics of Artificial Intelligence (2021)*, which emphasizes human rights, inclusivity, and transparency (UNESCO, 2023). Schools and governments should establish robust governance mechanisms to ensure ethical use, data protection, algorithmic fairness, and human oversight in educational AI systems. Without such safeguards, even well-intentioned interventions may cause unintended harm.

CULTURAL PERCEPTIONS

Similarly, cultural perceptions of sports and games in education vary widely. In some communities, there is still resistance to viewing physical activity or games as valuable educational tools, especially for older students. Changing mindsets at the level of parents, educators, and policymakers is a long-term effort that requires awareness campaigns and evidence-based advocacy (Houser & Kriellaars, 2023; Setiawan et al., 2024).

While the convergence of sports, AI, and gamification holds immense promise, thoughtful planning, inclusive design, and responsible implementation are essential. Proactively addressing these challenges can help maximize impact while minimizing unintended consequences.

FUTURE IMPLICATIONS

Integrating sports, artificial intelligence (AI), and gamification in education opens up exciting possibilities for the future of learning, not just in schools but across various sectors of society. One promising direction is the development of AI-driven imaginative playgrounds—spaces equipped with sensors, wearable devices, and real-time data analytics that can monitor physical activity, provide instant feedback, and personalize physical education for students. Combined with virtual reality (VR), these environments can simulate different sports, movement challenges, or historical events, helping students learn through immersive, active participation (Alotaibi, 2024).

These innovations have the potential to influence national education policies and school curricula. As governments recognize the importance of holistic education, including physical, emotional, and cognitive development, there is growing scope for policies to support AI- and sports-integrated learning environments. Educational boards could begin incorporating AI-enabled assessments, gamified activity-based learning modules, and sports-tech programs within formal curricula to improve student engagement and well-being (National Steering Committee for National Curriculum Frameworks, 2023b).

The future will likely see the growth of sports-tech entrepreneurship, especially in countries like India, which has a large youth population and a growing startup ecosystem. Young entrepreneurs and innovators can create solutions that combine data analytics, coaching, and gamified learning for schools, sports academies, and health organizations. Startups can also build platforms that offer AI-guided training plans, gamified habit trackers, or virtual sports competitions, enabling education beyond the classroom (Express Computer, 2023).

Beyond education and sports performance, this convergence also shows immense potential in rehabilitation, therapy, and inclusive education. For instance, AI-powered motion tracking and gamified exercises can support recovery in children with physical disabilities or those undergoing physiotherapy. VR and gamification can also be used to develop special education tools that cater to diverse learning needs, making learning more engaging and inclusive for students with autism, ADHD, or learning disorders (Hodge, 2025).

Overall, the future of education will be deeply influenced by how effectively we combine the engaging power of sports, the intelligence of AI, and the motivation of gamification to create personalized, inclusive, and transformative learning ecosystems for all learners.

DISCUSSION

The intersection of sports, artificial intelligence (AI), and gamification represents a decisive shift in how learning can be more engaging, inclusive, and effective. Each of these three elements, on its own, offers significant benefits. Sports build discipline, teamwork, and resilience. AI brings personalization, intelligent feedback, and the ability to adapt to each learner's pace. Gamification motivates students through rewards, progress tracking, and interactive experiences. However, when these are combined, the potential for transformative learning is amplified many times.

Our discussion throughout this chapter shows that sports are much more than physical activity. They are tools for social-emotional learning, leadership development, and cognitive skills. Sports activities can be monitored, assessed, and enhanced in real time when paired with AI. AI-driven feedback allows students to set goals, receive personalized coaching, and reflect on their performance. Meanwhile, gamified learning environments—whether in classrooms or on the field—can boost student interest and retention by turning learning into a playful, meaningful challenge.

Case studies demonstrate that this model can succeed in real-world settings, from rural schools using gamified sports tournaments to increase classroom attention, to innovative wearable-based systems helping middle schoolers improve fitness and academic focus. Importantly, these innovations are not just for elite institutions. They can reach students in under-resourced schools and diverse communities with thoughtful planning, localized tools, and teacher training.

However, the chapter also highlights challenges, such as ethical use of AI, data security, high costs, and the need for training educators to align new tools with pedagogy. These challenges cannot be ignored but can be addressed with strong policies, open-source tools, and collaborative partnerships among educators, startups, and governments.

CONCLUSION

Education today must go beyond textbooks and traditional teaching. Learning needs to be active, personal, and engaging to prepare students for the future. This chapter showed how sports, artificial intelligence (AI), and gamification can come together to create a powerful way of learning that builds academic knowledge and life skills like teamwork, confidence, and problem-solving. Sports help students stay active, focused, and emotionally engaged. AI helps personalize learning by understanding each student's strengths and needs. Gamification adds excitement and motivation, turning lessons into challenges and games. Combined, these tools can help schools create fun, meaningful, and effective learning experiences for all students, whether in urban or rural areas, whether learning in classrooms or the field.

While there are some challenges, like cost, teacher training, and digital access, the long-term benefits are clear. Schools, teachers, and even startups can work together to build systems that support this new learning model. Careful planning and innovation can make these ideas available to every child, no matter where they are. Using sports, AI, and gamification together is not just a new way of teaching—it is a way of transforming education. It helps students enjoy learning, stay healthy, and grow into confident, capable individuals ready for the world ahead.

DECLARATION

The content presented in this chapter is entirely original and has not been generated using artificial intelligence (AI) tools or large language models (LLMs). All ideas, analyses, and written material reflect the author's independent research, synthesis, and perspective. However, tools like Grammarly were utilized solely to enhance English language precision, grammar, spelling, and readability.

REFERENCES

Admin. (2023, September 15). The role of sports in character building: Lessons beyond the field. The Star Global School. https://thestarglobalschool.com/the-role-of-sports-in-character-building-lessons-beyond-the-field/

Ahuja, V. (2023). Equity and Access in Digital Education. *Advances in Educational Technologies and Instructional Design Book Series*, 45–59. DOI: 10.4018/979-8-3693-1826-3.ch005

Almalawi, A., Soh, B., Li, A., & Samra, H. (2024). Predictive models for educational purposes: A systematic review. *Big Data and Cognitive Computing*, *8*(12), 187. DOI: 10.3390/bdcc8120187

Alotaibi, N. S. (2024). The impact of ai and lms integration on the future of higher education: Opportunities, challenges, and strategies for transformation. *Sustainability (Basel)*, *16*(23), 10357. DOI: 10.3390/su162310357

Altinay, Z., Altinay, F., Sharma, R. C., Dagli, G., Shadiev, R., Yikici, B., & Altinay, M. (2024). Capacity building for student teachers in learning, teaching artificial intelligence for quality of education. *Societies (Basel, Switzerland)*, *14*(8), 148. DOI: 10.3390/soc14080148

Anjali, S. (2024). The Impact of Artificial Intelligence in Reshaping Education: An Analysis Based on Learning Theories. In ITM Web of Conferences (Vol. 68, p. 01008). EDP Sciences.

Bezzina, S., Pfeiffer, A., & Dingli, A. (2021). AI-enabled gamification for learning and assessment.

Bisa, M. (2023). Sports education as a means of building student character: Values and benefits. *AL-ISHLAH Jurnal Pendidikan*, *15*(2), 1581–1590. DOI: 10.35445/alishlah.v15i2.3889

Bitrián, P., Buil, I., & Catalán, S. (2021). Enhancing user engagement: The role of gamification in mobile apps. *Journal of Business Research*, *132*, 170–185. DOI: 10.1016/j.jbusres.2021.04.028

Cardona, M. A., Rodríguez, R. J., & Ishmael, K. (2023). Artificial intelligence and the future of teaching and learning: Insights and recommendations.

Carreno, A. (2024). Building a Continuous Feedback Loop for Real-Time Change Adaptation: Best Practices and Tools.

Christian, A. (2023, June 1). This AI scouting platform puts soccer talent spotters everywhere. WIRED. https://www.wired.com/story/ai-football-soccer-scouting

Christopoulos, A., & Mystakidis, S. (2023). Gamification in education. *Encyclopedia*, *3*(4), 1223–1243. DOI: 10.3390/encyclopedia3040089

Dahlstrøm, C. & Department of Design, Norwegian University of Science and Technology. (n.d.). *Impacts of gamification on intrinsic motivation*. In Department of Design, Norwegian University of Science and Technology [Journal-article]. https://www.ntnu.edu/documents/139799/1279149990/04+Article+Final_camildah_fors%C3%B8k_2017-12-06-13-53-55_TPD4505.Camilla.Dahlstr%C3%B8m.pdf

Ellikkal, A., & Rajamohan, S. (2024). AI-enabled personalized learning: Empowering management students for improving engagement and academic performance. *Vilakshan – XIMB. Journal of Management*. Advance online publication. DOI: 10.1108/XJM-02-2024-0023

eSchool Media Contributors. (2024, December 3). *AI and teacher burnout: Can technology really help?* ESchool News. https://www.eschoolnews.com/digital-learning/2024/12/03/ai-burnout-teachers-help/

Ethical implications of AI in education: data privacy and algorithmic bias. (2024). In *International Journal of Creative Research Thoughts (IJCRT) (vol. 12, Issue 10)* [Journal-article]. https://www.ijcrt.org/papers/IJCRT2410327.pdf

Express Computer. (2023, December 18). The future of sports-tech education and the need for recreational sports in India. *Express computer*. https://www.expresscomputer.in/guest-blogs/the-future-of-sports-tech-education-and-the-need-for-recreational-sports-in-india/107182/

Fitria, T. N. (2021, December). Artificial intelligence (AI) in education: Using AI tools for teaching and learning process. In Prosiding Seminar Nasional & Call for Paper STIE AAS (pp. 134-147).

Fleming, T. (2018). Mezirow and the theory of transformative learning. In Chapter. DOI: 10.4018/978-1-5225-6086-9.ch009

Furley, P., Laborde, S., Robazza, C., & Lane, A. (2023). Emotions in sport. *Springer eBooks* (pp. 247–279). DOI: 10.1007/978-3-031-03921-8_11

Gligorea, I., Cioca, M., Oancea, R., Gorski, A., Gorski, H., & Tudorache, P. (2023). Adaptive learning using artificial intelligence in e-learning: A literature review. *Education Sciences*, *13*(12), 1216. DOI: 10.3390/educsci13121216

Halkiopoulos, C., & Gkintoni, E. (2024). Leveraging AI in e-learning: Personalized learning and adaptive assessment through cognitive neuropsychology—a systematic analysis. *Electronics (Basel)*, *13*(18), 3762. DOI: 10.3390/electronics13183762

Harvard Health. (2024, August 26). Exercise can boost your memory and thinking skills. https://www.health.harvard.edu/mind-and-mood/exercise-can-boost-your-memory-and-thinking-skills

Hodge, B. (2025, January 14). AI-Powered virtual reality: Next frontier for rehabilitation. *Neuro Rehab VR*. https://neurorehabvr.com/blog/ai-integrated-with-vr

Hossain, M. A., Kabir, U., & Tokhi, M. O. (2002). Impact of data dependencies in real-time high performance computing. *Microprocessors and Microsystems, 26*(6), 253–261. DOI: 10.1016/S0141-9331(02)00027-3

Houser, N., & Kriellaars, D. (2023). "Where was this when I was in physical education?" physical literacy enriched pedagogy in a quality physical education context. *Frontiers in Sports and Active Living, 5*, 1185680. Advance online publication. DOI: 10.3389/fspor.2023.1185680 PMID: 37305659

Jian, M. J. K. O. (2023). Personalized learning through AI. *Advances in Engineering Innovation, 5*(1), 16–19. DOI: 10.54254/2977-3903/5/2023039

Jones, S. M., & Doolittle, E. J. The Wallace Foundation, Jones, S. M., & Doolittle, E. J. (n.d.). Social and emotional learning. In the woodrow wilson school of public and international affairs at Princeton University & The Brookings Institution, *The Future of Children.* https://futureofchildren.princeton.edu/sites/g/files/toruqf2411/files/media/foc_spring_vol27_no1_for_web_0_0.pdf

Kamalov, F., Calonge, D. S., & Gurrib, I. (2023). New era of artificial intelligence in education: Towards a sustainable multifaceted revolution. *Sustainability (Basel), 15*(16), 12451. DOI: 10.3390/su151612451

Kapuściński, M. (2024, September 19). AI in sports – How artificial intelligence supports athletes and coaches? | TTMS. https://ttms.com/ai-in-sports-how-artificial-intelligence-supports-athletes-and-coaches/

Kien, L. T., & Nguyen, N. D. (2021). *Gamification elements and their potential influence on employee motivation - a literature review of models.* Advances in Economics, Business and Management Research/Advances in Economics, Business and Management Research., DOI: 10.2991/aebmr.k.211119.016

Kitchenham, A. (2008). The evolution of John Mezirow's transformative learning theory. *Journal of Transformative Education, 6*(2), 104–123. DOI: 10.1177/1541344608322678

Kumar, P. (2025). AI's prospective role in shaping the future of sports. *International Journal of Physical Education Sports and Health, 12*(1), 293–299. DOI: 10.22271/kheljournal.2025.v12.i1e.3662

Labadze, L., Grigolia, M., & Machaidze, L. (2023). Role of AI chatbots in education: Systematic literature review. *International Journal of Educational Technology in Higher Education, 20*(1), 56. Advance online publication. DOI: 10.1186/s41239-023-00426-1

Learning theories within gamification. (2020). In advances in educational technologies and instructional design book series (pp. 1–61). DOI: 10.4018/978-1-7998-2079-6.ch001

Learning to be with others: Using sport to develop empathy. (2022, October 26). Sportsanddev. https://www.sportanddev.org/latest/news/learning-be-others-using-sport-develop-empathy

Lee, H. S., & Lee, J. (2021). Applying artificial intelligence in physical education and future perspectives. *Sustainability (Basel), 13*(1), 351. DOI: 10.3390/su13010351

Lefort, J. S. (2024, January 10). How Finland is modernising education with innovative schools. European Investment Bank. https://www.eib.org/en/essays/finland-education-school-design

Liu, N. C., & Xie, Y. (2024). Innovative application of computer vision and motion tracking technology in sports training. *EAI Endorsed Transactions on Pervasive Health and Technology, 10.* Advance online publication. DOI: 10.4108/eetpht.10.5763

Liu, T. C. (2022). A case study of the adaptive learning platform in a Taiwanese elementary school: Precision education from teachers' perspectives. *Education and Information Technologies, 27*(5), 6295–6316. DOI: 10.1007/s10639-021-10851-2 PMID: 35013667

Marsh, H., & Kleitman, S. (2002). Extracurricular school activities: The good, the bad, and the nonlinear. *Harvard Educational Review, 72*(4), 464–515. DOI: 10.17763/haer.72.4.051388703v7v7736

McGowan, A. L., Chandler, M. C., & Gerde, H. K. (2023). Infusing physical activity into early childhood classrooms: Guidance for best practices. *Early Childhood Education Journal.* Advance online publication. DOI: 10.1007/s10643-023-01532-5

Member Rewards. (n.d.). Nike.com. https://www.nike.com/in/membership/member-rewards

Mindster. (2025, March 1). How gamification makes fitness apps fun and engaging. https://www.linkedin.com/pulse/how-gamification-makes-fitness-apps-fun-engaging-mindsterapps-8chdc

Moore, J. MD PhD. (n.d.). 2020 Year in Review: Proven Impact of Fitbit Devices and Services on Health Behaviors and Outcomes – Fitbit Enterprise. https://enterprise.fitbit.com/blog/proven-impact-fitbit-devices-services-health-behaviors-outcomes/

Mukherjee, D., Bhavnani, S., Swaminathan, A., Verma, D., Parameshwaran, D., Divan, G., Dasgupta, J., Sharma, K., Thiagarajan, T. C., & Patel, V. (2020). Proof of concept of a gamified developmental assessment on an e-platform (deep) tool to measure cognitive development in rural Indian preschool children. *Frontiers in Psychology, 11*, 1202. Advance online publication. DOI: 10.3389/fpsyg.2020.01202 PMID: 32587551

National steering committee for national curriculum frameworks. (2023). National curriculum framework for school education. https://www.education.gov.in/sites/upload_files/mhrd/files/NCF-School-Education-Pre-Draft.pdf

Nichols, S. (2024, September 26). How gamified math learning apps are revolutionizing education for Kids – Stephanie blog. https://blogs.umb.edu/stephanienichols/2024/09/26/how-gamified-math-learning-apps-are-revolutionizing-education-for-kids/

Organisation for economic co-operation and development, Gottschalk, F., & Weise, C. (2023). Digital equity and inclusion in education: an overview of practice and policy in OECD countries. OECD Education Working Paper, 1–57. https://www.oecd.org/edu/workingpapers

Ou, S. (2024). Transforming education: The evolving role of artificial intelligence in the students academic performance. *International Journal of Education and Humanities*, *13*(2), 163–173. DOI: 10.54097/cc1x7r95

Pan, Y., Huang, C., & Hsu, W. (2023). A comparison of the learning effects between TGFU-SE and TGFU on learning motivation, sport enjoyment, responsibility, and game performance in physical education. *Frontiers in Psychology*, *14*, 1165064. Advance online publication. DOI: 10.3389/fpsyg.2023.1165064 PMID: 37519367

Panda, R. (2024). Gamification and educational technology in teacher training: Opportunities and challenges. *International Journal of Research Publication and Reviews*, *5*(9), 701–711. DOI: 10.55248/gengpi.5.0924.2503

Parveen, N. D. S., & Ramzan, N. S. I. (2024). The role of digital technologies in education: benefits and challenges. DOI: 10.47392/IRJAEM.2024.0299

Passarelli, A. M., & Kolb, D. A. (2011). *The learning way: learning from experience as the path to lifelong learning and development*. Oxford Library of Psychology., DOI: 10.1093/oxfordhb/9780195390483.013.0028

Physical activity improves brain and cognitive functions | Extension | University of Nevada, Reno. (n.d.). Extension | University of Nevada, Reno. https://extension.unr.edu/publication.aspx?PubID=2921#:~:text=Cardio%20Physical%20Activity,brain%20and%20improve%20brain%20function

Piščalkienė, V., & Lottrup, H. I. (2019). Benefits of experiential based learning: A case of students participation in the project "villages on move baltic.". *Sveikatos Mokslai*, *28*(6), 5–15. DOI: 10.5200/sm-hs.2018.064

Rashid, A. B., & Kausik, M. K. (2024). AI revolutionizing industries worldwide: A comprehensive overview of its diverse applications. *Hybrid Advances*, *7*, 100277. DOI: 10.1016/j.hybadv.2024.100277

Sanaeifar, F., Pourranjbar, S., Pourranjbar, M., Ramezani, S., Mehr, S. R., Wadan, A. S., & Khazeifard, F. (2024). Beneficial effects of physical exercise on cognitive-behavioral impairments and brain-derived neurotrophic factor alteration in the limbic system induced by neurodegeneration. *Experimental Gerontology*, *195*, 112539. DOI: 10.1016/j.exger.2024.112539 PMID: 39116955

Sanchez, D. R., Langer, M., & Kaur, R. (2019). Gamification in the classroom: Examining the impact of gamified quizzes on student learning. *Computers & Education*, *144*, 103666. DOI: 10.1016/j.compedu.2019.103666

Setiawan, M. N. A., & Suherman, W. S. Suharjana, Widiyanto, & Hardianto. (2024, April 16). Revitalizing traditional sports in physical education curricula: a literature review on cultural heritage and educational philosophy. https://www.riped-online.com/articles/revitalizing-traditional-sports-in-physical-education-curricula-a-literature-review-on-cultural-heritage-and-educational-philosoph-106091.html

Shei, R., Holder, I. G., Oumsang, A. S., Paris, B. A., & Paris, H. L. (2022). Wearable activity trackers–advanced technology or advanced marketing? *European Journal of Applied Physiology*, *122*(9), 1975–1990. DOI: 10.1007/s00421-022-04951-1 PMID: 35445837

Simply Psychology. (2025, March 19). Kolb's Learning Styles and Experiential Learning cycle. https://www.simplypsychology.org/learning-kolb.html

Simsek, A. (2012). Transformational learning. In Springer eBooks (pp. 3341–3344). DOI: 10.1007/978-1-4419-1428-6_373

Su, Z., Ge, S., Li, L., & Su, Y. (2024). *Review study of integrating AI technology into sports training systems*. Educational Administration Theory and Practice Journal., DOI: 10.53555/kuey.v30i5.1649

Tan, D. Y., & Cheah, C. W. (2021). Developing a gamified AI-enabled online learning application to improve students' perception of university physics. *Computers and Education Artificial Intelligence*, *2*, 100032. DOI: 10.1016/j.caeai.2021.100032

Taqa, A. R. (2025). *Teacher training and professional development in the age of AI*. Amer Research Taqa.

Teaching Games for Understanding. What does that look like and how does it improve skill learning and game playing. (n.d.). https://web.uvic.ca/~thopper/WEB/articles/JTPE/TGFU.htm

The Fitbit community. (2016, July 6). https://community.fitbit.com/t5/Get-Moving/Rewards-for-exercising/td-p/1423184

UNESCO. (2023, May 16). *Recommendation on the Ethics of Artificial Intelligence | UNESCO*. Www.unesco.org. https://www.unesco.org/en/articles/recommendation-ethics-artificial-intelligence

Ungau, S., Nasip, F., Linyaw, K., Yusop, Y., & Mee, N. T. T.Tang Tien Mee. (2023). Gamification in improving reading skills of preschool children: Blending through puzzle game. *Journal of Cognitive Sciences and Human Development*, *9*(1), 193–220. DOI: 10.33736/jcshd.5479.2023

Webb, P. I., & Pearson, P. J. University of Wollongong, & Forrest, G. (2006). Teaching games for understanding (TGfU) in primary and secondary physical education. https://ro.uow.edu.au/edupapers/74

White, B. S., & Branch, R. M. (2008). Systematic pilot testing as a step in the instructional design process of corporate training and development. *Performance Improvement Quarterly*, *14*(3), 75–94. DOI: 10.1111/j.1937-8327.2001.tb00219.x

Williams, A. (2024). Delivering effective student feedback in higher education: An evaluation of the challenges and best practice. *International Journal of Research in Education and Science*, *10*(2), 473–501. DOI: 10.46328/ijres.3404

Zhang, J. (2022). The influence of Piaget in the field of learning science. *Higher Education Studies*, *12*(3), 162. DOI: 10.5539/hes.v12n3p162

Chapter 12
The Role of Derivatives in Machine Learning: Optimization, Applications and Ethical Considerations for the Education Field

Fernando-Luís Almeida
https://orcid.org/0000-0002-6758-4843
INESC TEC, Porto, Portugal

Carlos Sousa
ISPGAYA, Portugal

Catarina Oliveira Lucas
ISPGAYA, Portugal

ABSTRACT

This chapter explores the critical role of derivatives in optimizing cost functions and driving the backpropagation algorithm in neural networks, emphasizing their applications in the education field. The study examines the use of derivatives in personalized learning systems, particularly within the Khan Academy platform, and evaluates their impact on scalability, bias, and efficiency. Five research questions guide the analysis, ranging from environmental impact to fairness in AI-driven education. Employing methods like Experimental Performance Evaluation and Comparative Analysis, the study offers both technical insights and ethical considerations. While derivatives enable precise optimization, the chapter highlights how they can unintentionally reinforce biases in training data, raising critical concerns about fairness and representation in educational technologies.

DOI: 10.4018/979-8-3373-5092-9.ch012

INTRODUCTION

Artificial Intelligence (AI) and Machine Learning (ML) have become relevant components of modern technology, with applications ranging from industrial automation, medical diagnosis to education and learning (Ifenthaler et al., 2024; Russell & Norvig, 2021; Wang et al., 2024). At the heart of these themes is the use of advanced mathematical methods, with derivatives playing an important role.

The concept of limit, which describes the behavior of a function as a variable approaches a specific value, is the basis for the definition of derivative. Derivatives, a fundamental concept in differential calculus, are mathematical tools that measure the rate of change of a function with respect to its independent variables. (Stewart, 2015). In AI and ML, the ability to measure these infinitesimal variations is relevant for optimizing models, particularly when adjusting the parameters that define the effectiveness of learning algorithms. The training process of ML models, such as neural networks, relies heavily on the calculation of derivatives to minimize cost functions, allowing the model to learn from data and continuously improve its performance (Goodfellow, Bengio, & Courville, 2014).

Although derivatives are essential tools for training and optimizing ML models, their use is not without some challenges. Some of the main problems include the difficulty of calculating derivatives in complex models, the disappearing gradient phenomenon, and the limitations imposed by computational cost. One of the most notorious problems in training deep neural networks is the vanishing gradient phenomenon, where the gradients of the initial layers become very small, making it difficult to train these layers. This occurs most frequently in networks that use sigmoid or hyperbolic tangent activation functions, whose derivatives can be very small for values far from zero (Bengio, Simard, & Frasconi, 1994). The vanishing gradient is particularly problematic in very deep networks, where the information passing through the initial layers is gradually "diluted", resulting in very slow or even stagnant learning. To mitigate this problem, several solutions have been proposed such as Alternative Activation Functions, Weight Initialization, and Residual Networks, notably this networks, add identity skip-connections to preserve gradient magnitude in very deep architectures. Another significant challenge in applying derivatives in ML is the computational cost associated with calculating gradients, especially in models with many parameters, such as deep neural networks. Training large networks requires substantial computational resources, both in terms of time and energy, which can be a barrier to research and practical application (Dean et al., 2012). In addition to the computational challenges and the vanishing gradient, there is also the question of how to train networks efficiently and effectively on large datasets. With the increasing volume of data available, model training needs to be scalable and robust. Regularization techniques, such as dropout, help avoid overfitting by forcing the network to learn more generalizable representations (Srivastava et al., 2014). Another significant development is distributed training, where the training of a neural network is split between multiple devices, allowing large models to be trained in less time. Platforms such as TensorFlow and PyTorch offer support for distributed training, which has become relevant for the development of large models in AI (Abadi et al., 2016).

As the use of ML and AI expands into new areas, the ethical considerations surrounding the use of derivatives and other mathematical techniques become increasingly important. This topic explores the ethical issues and social implications of using derivatives in ML, with a focus on how choices are made during modeling and optimization can impact society. The use of derivatives in ML algorithms plays a relevant role in optimizing models, but it can also inadvertently amplify existing biases in the data. Models trained with biased data tend to reproduce these biases, leading to unfair decisions in areas such as recruitment, funding, and judicial systems (Barocas, Hardt, & Narayanan, 2019). Optimization methods based on derivatives can, for example, favor certain population groups if the training data contains imbalances. This raises questions about how mathematics underlying the models can impact social justice. Researchers and engineers must be aware of biases in the data and implement techniques to mitigate them, such as introducing regularizations or modifying cost functions to penalize biased predictions (Zemel et al., 2013).

The goal of this chapter is to explore the central role of derivatives in the optimization of cost functions and the backpropagation algorithm in neural networks, highlighting their relevance in the development of ML models and exploring their impact in the education field. Previous works, such as those by LeCun, Bengio and Hinton (2015), have already extensively discussed the importance of backpropagation and the application of derivatives in deep learning. However, this study differentiates itself by analyzing more recent advances, such as the use of second-order automatic differentiation and the integration of adaptive optimization techniques (Kingma & Ba, 2014; Duché & Galilée, 2017; Röbenack & Gerbet, 2024). The analysis ranges from theoretical foundations to practical applications in the education field. Research questions are also defined, such as: (1) How can derivative-based methods be adapted to reduce the environmental impact of ML models?; (2) What are the computational limits of automatic differentiation techniques in large-scale models?; (3) How do derivatives contribute to optimizing machine learning models used in personalized learning systems?; (4) How are derivatives used to fine-tune deep learning models for automated assessment and grading systems?; and (5) How does the reliance on derivatives in machine learning impact bias and fairness in AI-driven educational tools? In addition, the challenges and innovations in the use of derivatives in machine learning applied to the education sector will be discussed.

The chapter is organized into five main sections described below. Firstly, a review of the literature is presented on the adoption of the derivatives as optimization methods in the learning process and the operating model of neural networks. This section is followed by the description of the research methodology adopted in this study and the justification for using Khan Academy as a case study. The main results of the research are then analyzed, considering the previously defined research questions. Finally, future work in the area is discussed and the main conclusions and implications of this study are summarized.

LITERATURE REVIEW

ML has undergone substantial advancements characterized by the pivotal role of derivatives, which are relevant in optimizing models, enhancing predictive accuracy, and increasing computational efficiency. The foundational concepts of derivatives and their implications within the realm of ML have been thoroughly examined in academic literature (Stewart, 2015). The utilization of derivatives spans a diverse array of domains, including the optimization of cost functions, the implementation of backpropagation in neural networks, and the application of advanced training methodologies designed to address significant challenges such as the vanishing gradient problem (Goodfellow, Bengio, & Courville, 2014). Furthermore, the advent of second-order optimization techniques and the integration of Hessian matrices in the optimization process have markedly improved convergence rates in complex learning models (Martens, 2010). This multifaceted approach underscores the relevance of derivatives in advancing both theoretical and practical aspects of ML.

The Role of Derivatives in Machine Learning Optimization

Optimization represents a cornerstone of ML, fundamentally shaping the efficacy with which models acquire knowledge from data and generalize to previously unseen instances. Central to the optimization process is the application of derivatives, which facilitate the fine-tuning of parameters to minimize cost functions (Bishop, 2006). Gradient-based optimization methods, particularly Gradient Descent, and its various adaptations, are heavily dependent on derivatives to direct parameter adjustments toward the reduction of loss (Ruder, 2016).

The emergence of adaptive optimization algorithms, such as Adam (Kingma & Ba, 2014) and AdaGrad (Duchi, Hazan, & Singer, 2011), has significantly improved the stability and efficiency of ML model training. These techniques dynamically adjust the learning rate for individual parameters, resulting in more robust convergence within complex non-convex optimization landscapes. Furthermore, second-order optimization strategies, including Newton's methods and quasi-Newton approaches, utilize Hessian matrices to enhance convergence speed and stability (Martens, 2010). Despite their computational intensity, these methodologies offer relevant insights into the curvature of cost functions, thereby enabling more precise and effective parameter updates (Roux, Schmidt, & Bach, 2012).

Recent research has further expanded the boundaries of optimization through the integration of physics-informed techniques, which embed domain-specific knowledge within the learning framework. This incorporation allows for the containment of solution spaces and fosters improved efficiency in model training (Raissi, Perdikaris, & Karniadakis, 2019). Such advancements underscore the evolving significance of derivatives in refining optimization strategies across a diverse array of applications.

Backpropagation and Neural Networks

Neural networks, particularly those utilizing deep learning architectures, rely heavily on the backpropagation algorithm for the efficient adjustment of model parameters. Backpropagation serves as a gradient-based learning mechanism that systematically propagates errors from the output layer back through the network, calculating the derivatives of the loss function with respect to each weight (Rumelhart, Hinton, & Williams, 1986). This iterative refinement process significantly enhances the performance of neural networks across a wide array of applications, including image recognition and natural language processing (LeCun, Bengio, & Hinton, 2015).

The efficacy of backpropagation is closely linked to the selection of activation functions. Non-linear activation functions, such as the Rectified Linear Unit (ReLU), have been instrumental in alleviating the vanishing gradient problem, which occurs when gradients diminish to negligible values, thereby impeding effective weight updates in deep networks (Glorot & Bengio, 2010). Recent research has further explored alternative activation functions, such as Swish and Mish, which are characterized by smoother gradients and improved information propagation in deep neural networks (Ramachandran, Zoph, & Le, 2017).

Advancements in automatic differentiation techniques have also facilitated the computation of higher-order derivatives, which are critical for the fine-tuning of complex models. Such developments have proven particularly advantageous in the field of reinforcement learning, where policy gradient methods utilize these derivatives to optimize decision-making strategies (Sutton & Barto, 2018). Moreover, the application of backpropagation in recurrent neural networks (RNNs) and long short-term memory (LSTM) networks has been pivotal in effectively managing sequential data, leading to notable progress in time-series forecasting and speech recognition (Hochreiter & Schmidhuber, 1997).

The interplay between backpropagation, activation functions, and advanced differentiation techniques underpins the success of neural networks across diverse domains, driving continuous innovation and performance improvements in AI.

Challenges and Innovations in Using Derivatives

The integration of derivatives within ML frameworks, particularly in the training of deep neural networks, presents a variety of significant challenges. One of the most prominent issues is the vanishing gradient problem, extensively documented in literature. This phenomenon occurs when gradients diminish excessively in the earlier layers of a network, leading to a deceleration in the learning process and a diminished capacity for the network to capture long-range dependencies (Bengio, Simard, & Frasconi, 1994). In response to this challenge, researchers have proposed alternative activation functions, such as Leaky ReLU and Scaled Exponential Linear Units (SELU), which sustain nonzero gradients for negative input values, thereby enhancing gradient propagation and improving overall model performance (Klambauer et al., 2017).

Furthermore, the refinement of weight initialization techniques has emerged as a strategy to combat the vanishing gradient problem. Notable methods, including He initialization (He et al., 2015) and Xavier initialization (Glorot & Bengio, 2010), are designed to maintain stable gradient magnitudes throughout the network, thereby facilitating more effective learning processes. The introduction of Residual Networks (ResNets) has also contributed significantly to this domain; these networks incorporate skip connections that enable gradients to bypass multiple layers, thereby significantly enhancing the training capability of very deep architectures (He et al., 2016).

In addition to the challenges associated with gradient propagation, the computational cost of calculating derivatives in large-scale models poses another substantial hurdle. The training of deep neural networks demands extensive computational resources, frequently resulting in elevated energy consumption and heightened hardware requirements (Jouppi et al., 2017). To alleviate these concerns, the research community has increasingly concentrated on hardware acceleration, utilizing Graphics Processing Units (GPUs) and Tensor Processing Units (TPUs) to optimize matrix operations and gradient computations (Dean et al., 2012). Moreover, the development of novel optimization algorithms, such as LAMB (You et al., 2020), aims to enhance scalability and efficiency in training with large batch sizes, thereby addressing a critical need in the computational landscape of deep learning.

Applications of Derivatives in AI and Education

The significance of derivatives extends far beyond traditional applications in ML, permeating essential areas of scientific research and intricate decision-making systems. In the realm of AI, derivatives serve as foundational components in a myriad of optimization procedures, playing a particular role in reinforcement learning. Notably, policy gradient methods utilize derivatives to enhance decision-making strategies within dynamic environments, facilitating the development of AI agents capable of making optimal choices informed by real-time feedback (Schulman et al., 2017). These advancements have profoundly transformed fields such as robotics, autonomous systems, and strategic gameplay, showcasing the potential of AI to adapt and refine its functionalities based on experiential learning.

In addition to reinforcement learning, derivatives are relevant in the realms of computational simulations and numerical modeling. In scientific computing, derivatives substantially aid in the training of neural networks that are engineered to approximate solutions to complex differential equations. For example, physics-informed neural networks (PINNs) exploit the power of automatic differentiation to accurately model sophisticated physical systems. This approach has led to significant breakthroughs in areas such as climate modeling, fluid dynamics, and structural analysis, illustrating the versatility and depth of derivative applications (Raissi, Perdikaris, & Karniadakis, 2019). The enhancement of numerical methodologies through derivatives carries extensive implications across various domains, including engineering, materials science, and applied physics, thereby underscoring their vital role in contemporary research and developmental endeavors.

The influence of derivatives further extends into the domain of education, where they form the backbone of optimization processes employed by adaptive learning platforms. These platforms utilize ML models that tailor learning experiences based on an individual's performance metrics (Ifenthaler et al., 2024). By harnessing derivative-based algorithms, these systems are capable of dynamically adjusting the difficulty of educational content in response to student progress, thus ensuring that learners receive personalized support that aligns with their cognitive abilities and learning pace. The capacity to fine-tune instructional materials in real time not only enhances student engagement but also contributes to improved knowledge retention, rendering AI-driven educational methodologies more effective compared to traditional static curricula. Additionally, intelligent recommendation systems that propose personalized learning pathways rely heavily on derivatives to refine and optimize content selection models, ultimately improving overall knowledge acquisition and bolstering long-term academic performance (Tran et al., 2024).

Moreover, the advantages of leveraging derivatives extend to automated grading systems, where deep learning models employ backpropagation techniques to enhance the precision of assessment algorithms. This advancement has led to improved accuracy in evaluating written responses and providing more nuanced feedback to students (Piech et al., 2015). Innovations in second-order automatic differentiation have further augmented optimization accuracy in large-scale educational models, enhancing the efficacy of intelligent tutoring systems (Duché & Galilée, 2017). As AI technologies continue to evolve, the integration of derivatives into educational tools holds great promise for revolutionizing pedagogical approaches, transforming not only the way students engage with learning materials but also how educators instruct, and institutions assess academic performance. This paradigm shift fosters a more personalized and data-driven approach to education, fundamentally enriching the learning experience and outcomes for students in diverse educational contexts.

The pervasive influence of derivatives across various fields emphasizes their critical importance in advancing both theoretical and applied paradigms. By facilitating optimization processes in AI, enhancing scientific modeling efforts, and transforming educational methodologies, derivatives underscore their role as essential tools in the continued evolution of technology and knowledge across disciplines.

Ethical and Environmental Considerations

The extensive incorporation of derivatives in ML prompts significant ethical and environmental considerations. One critical issue is the potential for bias in training datasets, which can be intensified by various optimization techniques, consequently leading to fairness dilemmas in AI-driven decision-making systems (Barocas, Hardt, & Narayanan, 2019). To address these biases and enhance the equity of ML outcomes, methods such as fairness-aware regularization and adversarial debiasing have been proposed (Zemel et al., 2013).

Furthermore, environmental sustainability emerges as a pressing concern. The training of deep learning models typically demands substantial computational resources, which translates to elevated energy consumption (Strubell, Ganesh, & McCallum, 2019). To mitigate this challenge, researchers have suggested several methodologies, including model compression, pruning, and quantization, aimed at reducing computational requirements without compromising model performance (Han, Mao, & Dally, 2015). Additionally, federated learning has surfaced as a promising framework for fostering energy-efficient AI, facilitating decentralized training while safeguarding data privacy (McMahan et al., 2017).

Derivatives play a pivotal in ML, impacting various aspects such as optimization strategies, the training of neural networks, and their applications in both educational and scientific computing contexts. While challenges persist, particularly concerning computational efficiency, fairness, and sustainability, recent advancements in second-order optimization techniques, hardware acceleration, and the integration of ethical AI practices are actively shaping the trajectory of ML research. These developments underscore the necessity for ongoing exploration and refinement within the field, as researchers seek to enhance both the performance and the societal implications of ML technologies.

METHODOLOGICAL PROCEDURES

The research questions defined in this study require the collection of quantitative and qualitative information. The first two research questions benefit from the collection of quantitative data from published studies in the field that enable the adoption of methods such as Experimental Performance Evaluation (EPE) and Computational Experimentation (CE) & Comparative Analysis (CA). These three techniques together offer complementary perspectives for understanding the impact of derivatives on the efficiency, scalability and bias of models.

EPE aims to quantitatively evaluate the performance of ML models using derivative-based techniques. This method makes it possible to measure efficiency and scalability by analyzing the convergence time, memory usage and computational costs of different derivative-based optimization algorithms. This method also makes it possible to identify bottlenecks in automatic differentiation (e.g., numerical stability, computational efficiency in large models).

CE and CA can be used together to explore and compare different derivative-based methods for optimizing ML models, analyzing trade-offs between performance and quality of solutions. Through this analysis, different approaches can be compared. For example, adopting these methods together makes it possible to test how different gradient-based methods (e.g., first- and second-order optimizers) affect model convergence. Moreover, it is also the aim of these methods to study alternative approaches. For example, examining the feasibility of derivative-free techniques (e.g. Bayesian optimization, differential evolution) to replace or complement gradient-based methods.

Finally, as recognized by Bayly-Castaneda et al. (2024) and Katiyar et al. (2024), personalized learning systems use ML algorithms to adapt educational content to students' individual needs. This can be achieved through the use of derivatives, by means of gradients, which make it possible to adjust these models dynamically. The study, observation and analysis of how this approach is applied by educational platforms in a real context would be necessary, as this is yet to be explored. In particular, the impact of using gradients on performance and adapting the model to the student's progress. Thus, the use of qualitative methods such as a case study approach allows us to explore how backpropagation and hyperparameter optimization impact the personalization of learning. This allows an assessment to be made of the efficiency and adaptability of the algorithms in content delivery. Several educational platforms are considered to assess how the personalization of the student experience works, such as Khan Academy, Coursera and edX.

This study chose the adoption of Khan Academy as the main focus of analysis. This choice is methodologically pertinent, considering not only the robustness of its personalization infrastructure, but also its broad user base, diversity of profiles and explicit commitment to adapting teaching to the pace of each student. Khan Academy uses recommendation algorithms that integrate predictive models fed by historical student interaction data. These models, in many cases, are trained using gradient descent techniques, in which the derivative of the loss function guides the system towards more effective adjustments. When comparing various platforms as provided in Table 1, such as Coursera and edX (although they all make use of personalization systems to some extent), Khan Academy stands out for the granularity of its data collection and the explicit application of recommendation models for individual exercises, rather than for entire courses. Coursera and edX, being platforms more geared towards higher education and professional training, tend to operate on a more macro level, recommending courses or modules based on interests or areas of knowledge, rather than on the logic of micro-adaptation of tasks, as Khan Academy does.

Table 1. Comparative analysis of Khan Academy, Coursera and edX

Feature	Khan Academy	Coursera	edX
Target Audience	K-12, early college, self-learners	University students, professionals	University students, professionals
Content Type	Exercises, videos, quizzes, mastery-based units	Full courses, degrees, certificates	Full courses, MicroMasters, degrees, professional certs
Personalization Approach	Real-time adaptive learning based on student performance	Limited; mainly course suggestions based on interests	Some personalization at the course/program level
Use of Derivatives (Gradients)	Used in recommended systems to optimize content sequencing	Used in some ML-based recommendation engines	Less visible, mostly used in backend analytics
AI Integration Level	*High*: in student modeling and real-time adaptation	*Medium*: focused on platform recommendations and assessments	*Medium*: used more in research-backed course design
Feedback Granularity	Immediate feedback at task level	Feedback typically per module or assignment	Feedback typically per module or assessment
Data Collection	Fine-grained, per-question interaction data	Course-level engagement, video viewing, quizzes	Similar to Coursera; includes forum activity and grades
Pedagogical Model	Mastery learning, formative feedback, progress tracking	Traditional course-based learning	MOOC-based modular learning with some blended options
Accessibility	Free, open to all	Mixed: free + paid content, financial aid available	Mixed: free + paid content, financial aid available

Source: Own source

The methodological approach adopted through the use of practical cases with a focus on gradients is justified because it allows for an applied and in-depth understanding of how derivatives are operationalized in digital educational practice. By analyzing concrete learning trajectories, it is possible to observe how small variations in student performance generate different gradients which, in turn, lead to different recommendation decisions. This practical approach overcomes the limitations of a merely theoretical or comparative analysis, because it makes it visible how the mathematics behind the algorithms translates into real consequences in the learning path of individuals.

Choosing Khan Academy as a case study, anchored in a methodology that focuses on the practical analysis of how gradients work, allows us to observe in a concrete way how models based on derivatives shape the personalized learning experience in real time. This choice allows the reader to reflect not only on the technical effectiveness of these systems, but also on their pedagogical, social and ethical implications, providing an integrated perspective on the application of AI in education.

RESULTS AND DISCUSSION

How Can Derivative-based Methods be Adapted to Reduce the Environmental Impact of ML Models?

Derivative-based methodologies are integral to the training of ML models, and recent advancements in these techniques underscore the necessity to optimize their application for reduced environmental impact. Strategies such as pruning and quantization have been widely employed to mitigate this impact. Recent studies indicate that structured pruning can reduce up to 75% of a model's parameters encoder and 35% of the model's decoder without significantly compromising accuracy (de Reus, P. et al., 2024). Similarly, quantization (e.g. 8-bit integer models) can reduce inference energy consumption markedly—studies report reductions ranging from ~30% to over 80%, depending on hardware and technique. (Kinnas et al., 2025).

These approaches effectively diminish the complexity of the models by eliminating redundant weights and reducing the numerical precision of model parameters. Such modifications preserve the model's accuracy while substantially decreasing energy consumption during both the training and inference phases. (Kinnas et al., 2025).

Leveraging more efficient optimization algorithms, such as Adam or LAMB, can facilitate faster convergence during the training process. Research shows that the LAMB optimizer reduces convergence time by 35% compared to Adam in large-scale models, leading to proportional energy savings (Li et al., 2021). Moreover, optimized hyperparameter selection can reduce the total number of training iterations. Approaches such as Hyperband and BOHB have been shown to decrease training time by up to 40% without compromising performance (Kingma & Ba, 2014).

These algorithms are designed to adaptively adjust learning rates, which not only accelerates training but also indirectly contributes to reduced energy expenditure (Li et al., 2021). A thoughtful selection of hyperparameters is equally crucial in enhancing the energy efficiency of machine learning models, as appropriate values can significantly impact both the speed of convergence and the overall resource utilization (Kingma & Ba, 2014).

To support these initiatives, innovative tools such as eco2AI have emerged, providing researchers and practitioners with the capability to monitor energy consumption and CO_2 emissions associated with ML model training (Budennyy et al., 2022). Energy monitoring tools such as the described above have enabled precise quantification of the environmental impact of ML training. Patterson et al. (2021) estimate that GPT-3 training emitted approximately 552 t CO_2e. These tools offer detailed insights into the ecological footprint of various training methodologies, thereby enabling informed adjustments aimed at sustainability. Furthermore, incorporating renewable energy sources in the training process and conducting machine learning tasks in regions with lower carbon intensity are recognized as best practices for mitigating the environmental impact of machine learning endeavors and transitioning to renewable-energy-powered data centers can reduce emissions by 60% of the above value stated by Patterson, D. (Strubell, Ganesh, & McCallum, 2019).

What are the Computational Limits of Automatic Differentiation Techniques in Large-Scale Models?

Automatic differentiation (AD) is a fundamental technique for calculating derivatives of complex functions in ML models. However, the application of AD in large-scale models faces significant computational challenges, especially in memory consumption and computational efficiency.

One of the main challenges is the high memory consumption during the backpropagation process in deep neural networks. As the depth and complexity of the model increases, the amount of memory needed to store intermediate states grows exponentially and can lead to the exhaustion of available resources (Thompson et al., 2022). During backpropagation, the need to store intermediate states grows exponentially with network depth. Very large language models can demand hundreds of gigabytes of memory for full-precision training, often exceeding the limits of single GPUs; exact figures (e.g. for GPT-4) are not publicly disclosed but according with a study from Zhao, W. X. et al., (2023), models such as the described above require approximately 800 GB of memory for training with a standard batch size.

This issue is especially pronounced in large-scale language models (LLMs), where heightened complexity and a vast number of parameters lead to augmented requirements for both memory and processing power, consequently increasing latency during inference (Bai et al., 2024) (Chen et al., 2024). In computer vision models, memory consumed during AD can account for up to 70% of available resources, limiting batch size and overall training efficiency (Ren et al., 2024).

To mitigate these challenges, techniques such as checkpointing have been employed. Checkpointing involves the selective storage of intermediate states during computation, allowing the recomputation of necessary parts of the gradients without overloading memory.

Studies indicate that this technique can reduce memory consumption by up to 50%, at the cost of a 20-30% increase in computation time due to recomputation overhead (Chen et al., 2024). Nevertheless, this method introduces a trade-off between memory efficiency and computation time, requiring careful optimization according to available resources and specific model demands. Recent advancements and checkpointing frameworks (e.g. CRIUgpu) report reducing memory usage by ~50% at the expense of recomputation overheads, which can be optimized to the low-tens-of-percent range depending on hardware. (Stoyanov et al., 2025). This approach enhances the ability to recover from failures and resume training effectively from the most recent checkpoint.

The selection of hardware significantly influences the efficiency of AD in large-scale models. Research suggests that Tensor Processing Units (TPUs) v4 delivers roughly 1.2–1.7× better performance per watt than NVIDIA A100 GPUs in ML workloads, and up to ~2.7× when compared to TPU v3. (Pan & Mishra, 2021). TPUs have been specifically engineered for high-performance tensor operations, rendering them particularly well-suited for the training and inference processes associated with large-scale neural networks. TPUs offer distinct cost-effective advantages for certain AD workloads due to their superior performance and energy efficiency (Khan, 2024). However, the deployment of AD on specialized hardware, such as GPUs and TPUs, mandates specific adjustments to fully leverage the parallelism capabilities inherent in these devices.

While automatic differentiation serves as a powerful tool for training machine learning models, its application at scale necessitates meticulous consideration of memory utilization and computational time. The adoption of optimization strategies, such as checkpointing, along with adaptations to the idiosyncrasies of the hardware, are important to overcoming the inherent computational limitations associated with these processes.

How do Derivatives Contribute to Optimizing Machine Learning Models Used in Personalized Learning Systems?

As a starting point, derivatives are considered to play a fundamental role in the optimization of machine learning models, especially in the context of personalized learning systems. The use of derivatives makes it possible to adjust the model parameters to minimize the error between predictions and actual results. The most common mechanism is the downward gradient, in which the derivative of the loss function in relation to the model parameters is used to know in which direction and how strongly the parameters should be adjusted. Derivatives help to continuously improve predictive models that decide what content to present next, based on student interaction and performance data. Its application can be seen in personalized learning environments such as Khan Academy.

At Khan Academy, the use of derivatives in the process of optimizing personalized learning models essentially takes place behind the scenes, within the machine learning algorithms that dynamically adjust students' learning paths. The system uses techniques such as neural networks and logistic regression to predict, based on historical data, the next most appropriate content for each student. Derivatives enter this process as a central part of the gradient descent algorithm, which is used to train these models. For example, let's consider a scenario of a student who is learning algebra and has successfully completed exercises on linear equations, but has repeatedly failed questions on inequalities. The system collects this data and, using a loss function (such as mean square error or cross entropy), evaluates the difference between the student's predicted and the actual performance. The derivative of this loss function in relation to the model's weights indicates how to adjust the algorithm's parameters to improve future predictions. By repeating this process through multiple iterations, the system refines its ability to predict which type of content is most likely to promote student success. Another good example to consider is the exercise recommendation system. Khan Academy uses a model that learns from hit patterns, response time and number of attempts to suggest the next exercise. If, based on previous interactions, the model predicts that the student will succeed, for example, with quadratic factoring exercises, this prediction is based on successive adjustments to the model that have been guided by derivatives (derivative-based model). At the same time, the system avoids recommending content that is too advanced (which would cause frustration) or too easy (which would lead to stagnation), all based on minimizing error functions via derivatives. It's also important to look at the process of adaptation in real time. We consider a scenario in which a student accesses the system in one day and answers five difficult exercises correctly. The model interprets this performance as a sign that the student is ready to move on, quickly adjusting their prediction and therefore the next recommendation. This rapid adjustment is possible because the derivatives make it possible to precisely calculate the direction and intensity of the changes that the model's parameters should undergo, which is immediately reflected in the content presented.

The gradient descent approach is not immune to criticism. An opposing view holds that overemphasis on gradient-based methods can limit the flexibility of models when dealing with complex human behaviors, which often do not follow smooth or differentiable patterns. For example, abrupt decisions by a student, such as suddenly dropping out of a course, can be poorly modeled by algorithms that rely on gradual changes represented by derivatives. In addition, Absil & Kurdyka (2006) point out that gradient-based methods can get stuck in local minima, especially in highly non-convex solution spaces, such as those involving learners' motivational or emotional factors. This can lead the system to personalize sub optimally, reinforcing patterns that don't always reflect the student's true learning potential. A practical example of this situation might be the following: a system that uses neural networks to predict the next best activity for a student based on their performance history. The loss function measures the difference between the student's actual and predicted performance, and the derivative of this function guides adjustments to the network weights. However, if a student learns in a non-linear way, with sudden leaps in understanding after periods of stagnation, the derivative-based model may not be able to capture this behavior well, leading to ineffective pedagogical decisions. Alternatives such as evolutionary or reinforcement-based methods may be preferable in these cases, as they do not depend on derivatives and are more suitable for environments with discontinuous dynamics or sparse rewards.

How are Derivatives Used to Fine-Tune Deep Learning Models for Automated Assessment and Grading Systems?

The deep learning process is based on the idea of automatically adjusting the parameters of a model, such as the weights and biases of a neural network, so that it can perform complex tasks such as classification, pattern recognition or prediction with high accuracy (Kovač et al., 2023; Samtani et al., 2023; Sarker, 2021). This process begins with the presentation of input data, to which the model responds with a prediction. This prediction is then compared with the actual expected value, and the difference between the two is quantified by a loss function. This is where the derivatives come in. The derivatives are used to calculate how small changes in the model parameters affect the value of the loss function. This calculation is done using the backpropagation algorithm, which applies the chain rule to propagate the error from the output layer of the network to the initial layers. In each layer, the partial derivatives of the loss function are calculated for each weight. Using these derivatives, an optimization algorithm such as gradient descent or one of its variants updates the parameters to minimize the error. Basically, the role of the derivatives is to guide the model in the right direction during training, indicating not only whether the parameters should be increased or decreased, but also how strongly they should be adjusted.

At Khan Academy, which integrates automatic assessment systems into interactive exercises and tests, these techniques are used to predict, for example, whether a student will get a question right, how long they are likely to answer it or whether an exercise represents an appropriate challenge for that moment in learning. Let's consider a practical example of a student answering a multiple-choice question. The system can use a neural network model trained with large volumes of data from previous interactions to predict the degree of mastery of the concept being assessed. Each time the model predicts incorrectly, the difference between the predicted result and the actual result feeds into a loss function. The derivative of this function indicates how the network weights should be adjusted to improve the prediction on the next attempt. Repeated over thousands of interactions, this process refines the model, making it more sensitive to the nuances of different students' learning behavior. In the context of Khan Academy, the use of derivatives is particularly effective in tasks with well-defined patterns, such as the automatic classification of answers in structured exercises or the prediction of success in future tasks. A concrete example of this is the use of binary classification models to automatically assess whether a student should move on to a new concept or review the previous one. These models, trained with historical data, are optimized using derivatives to minimize cross entropy.

How Does the Reliance on Derivatives in Machine Learning Impact Bias and Fairness in AI-Driven Educational Tools?

It is clear that the reliance on derivatives in machine learning directly influences issues of bias and fairness in AI-based educational tools, because the optimization process guided by derivatives depends entirely on the data on which the models are trained. Derivatives guide the adjustment of model parameters based on the minimization of a loss function, but this function does not in itself distinguish between fair and biased patterns in the data. If the historical data used to train the models contains bias, such as the under-representation of certain socio-economic, racial or geographical groups, the derivatives will reinforce these patterns during learning. This is because the aim of this process is only to reduce error, not to question the fairness of the results.

Let's consider a scenario of training a predictive model to recommend the next most appropriate exercise to a student, based on previous performance histories in Khan Academy. If the training data reflects that students from regions with less access to digital resources tend to interact less with advanced content, or have slower learning rates, not because of lower ability, but because of structural barriers such as lack of support at home, poor internet connection or less time available to study, the model will learn that these variables are associated with a lower probability of success. Thus, when a student with a similar profile enters the system, the model can predict that they "probably won't succeed" with more advanced content and will choose to recommend simpler or more repetitive content. The predictive error will be reduced, because the prediction fits well with the pattern learned from the historical data, but the student ends up stuck in a cycle of low progression, not because of any real inability, but because of the bias present in the data. In this practical scenario, it becomes clear that the role of the derivatives is technical, but decisive. At each iteration of model training, the algorithm calculates the derivative of the loss function in relation to the model parameters. If the prediction for a student with a disadvantaged socio-economic profile is close to the true value (for example, that they haven't actually completed an advanced exercise), the gradient will be small, and the model will adjust its prediction little or not at all. This means that the association between "profile X" and "low performance" will be validated and reinforced over time. The model does not question whether the cause of failure is structural, unfair or reversible. It simply notes that, statistically, that pattern minimizes error. The problem worsens when these predictive decisions begin to influence the student's own educational opportunities, creating a self-fulfilling prophecy effect: the system doesn't challenge him, he doesn't have the opportunity to show progress, and the data collected continues to confirm the initial prediction.

However, there is also an opposing view in the scientific community. Some argue that, with the proper use of derivatives and loss functions adjusted to take fairness metrics into account, it is possible to reduce prejudice rather than reinforce it. For example, penalties for disparities between groups can be incorporated into the loss function as fairness-aware learning techniques. The derivatives will then guide the model not only to minimize the overall error, but also to promote more fairness in the predictions. In Khan Academy, this could be incorporated by training a model that penalizes predictions that systematically underestimate the performance of students from certain backgrounds. In this way, derivatives would be an ally in the fight against bias, as long as the loss function is designed with this concern in mind. On the other hand, some argue that this type of technical adjustment is not enough, as the very process of quantifying justice and prejudice in a mathematical model can be reductive. Educational justice involves qualitative and contextual factors that are not easily translatable into differentiable mathematical functions. Thus, no matter how loss functions are adjusted, the exclusive use of derivatives limits the ability to capture the human and social complexities of the educational process. From this perspective, Raubitzek et al. (2023) and Torres-Peña et al. (2024) recommend that it is necessary to complement derivative-based models with more interpretable, participatory and socio-culturally informed approaches that directly integrate the voice of educators and students.

FUTURE PERSPECTIVES

The future prospects for the evolution of AI include the increasing sophistication of learning models. It is expected that the role of derivatives will continue to be central to this process, but in a static or immutable way. Currently, derivatives underpin most deep learning optimization techniques, guiding how models adjust their parameters based on errors made. However, as models become more complex, there are important limits to the effectiveness and suitability of a purely gradient-based approach. Future prospects suggest that systems may continue to use derivatives to learn from data, but will also incorporate logical structures, explicit rules and ethical or social constraints that are not easily expressible in terms of gradients (Fu & Weng, 2024). In education, for example, a system could continue to use backpropagation to fine-tune a content recommendation model but combine it with explicit pedagogical principles that avoid discriminatory or mechanistic decisions, even if these decisions reduce the overall statistical error.

Another promising direction is the advancement of so-called second-order learning, which uses not only derivatives, but also derivatives of derivatives. Hessians can be used for more sensitive and adaptive optimizations. These methods will allow models to adjust more quickly to new situations, which is particularly relevant in ever-changing environments such as digital classrooms or personalized learning platforms. However, their computational cost is high, which will require new advances in hardware and more efficient algorithms. This can be achieved using quantum computing.

Another line of research questions the over-reliance on derivatives as the only path to learning. Techniques such as reinforcement learning, network population evolution, symbolic models or even biology-inspired approaches are gaining ground (Linderoth et al., 2024; Rahm & Rahm- Skågeby, 2023). These approaches can be especially useful in contexts where the data is noisy, sparse or unstructured, and where the loss function is neither continuous nor differentiable.

Furthermore, as pressure grows for AI systems to be more transparent, auditable and aligned with human values, the role of derivatives may be rethought considering their opacity (Hah et al., 2022; Le Dinh et al., 2025). The process of adjusting millions of parameters based on gradients is mathematically effective, but not very interpretable. In the future, there may be a shift towards models that allow some degree of causal or pedagogical explanation of their decisions, even if this means giving up some statistical precision in favor of greater comprehensibility and trust.

CONCLUSIONS

This study has provided a comprehensive overview of the role of derivatives in machine learning and personalized learning systems. The use of derivatives, particularly in the context of techniques such as gradient descent, makes it possible to continuously adjust model parameters to reduce the error between system predictions and actual user performance data. In the field of education, this optimization capacity translates into the possibility of offering personalized content based on the student's history of interaction and progress. This situation was detailed by considering usage scenarios offered by the Khan Academy platform.

However, the study goes beyond technical description and critically addresses the ethical implications of this process. The main warning is that the use of derivatives, while mathematically neutral, can intensify patterns of prejudice and injustice present in the training data. This stems from the fact that derivatives only "follow" the structure of the loss function, which as a rule only seeks to minimize error, without any notion or criterion of justice, fairness or representation. If the data used to train the model contains biases, the optimization process will reinforce these patterns, perpetuating inequalities rather than mitigating them.

The implications of this study are considerable. Firstly, it highlights that the technical effectiveness of AI systems cannot be dissociated from their social consequences. A model that performs excellently overall, in terms of average error, may be failing badly in relation to specific population groups. This is particularly worrying in educational environments, where algorithmic decisions can directly influence the learning path, access to knowledge and even the student's self-image and motivation. By constantly recommending simpler content to certain profiles, the system not only reflects historical inequalities, but also amplifies them, limiting the development potential of these students. The second implication is that the answer to this problem cannot be purely technical, although solutions such as fairness-aware regularization or adversarial debiasing represent important advances. These techniques seek to modify the loss function to include justice concerns, forcing the optimization process to also consider fairness criteria. However, the effectiveness of these notions hinges on how fairness is defined, measured, and put into practice. This is a point that often lacks consensus and universal applicability. Moreover, developing AI education systems demands a deliberate effort to embed ethical and inclusive principles from the beginning, rather than relying on post hoc bias correction.

REFERENCES

Abadi, M., Barham, P., Chen, J., Chen, Z., Davis, A., Dean, J., . . . Zheng, X. (2016). TensorFlow: A system for large-scale machine learning. In *12th {USENIX} Symposium on Operating Systems Design and Implementation*, Savannah, GA, 1-18. DOI: 10.48550/arXiv.1605.08695

Absil, P. A., & Kurdyka, K. (2006). On the stable equilibrium points of gradient systems. *Systems & Control Letters*, *55*(7), 573–577. DOI: 10.1016/j.sysconle.2006.01.002

Bai, G., Chai, Z., Ling, C., Wang, S., Lu, J., Zhang, N., . . . Zhao, L. (2024). Beyond efficiency: A systematic survey of resource-efficient large language models. *arXiv preprint arXiv:2401.00625*

Barocas, S., Hardt, M., & Narayanan, A. (2019). *Fairness and machine learning: Limitations and opportunities*. fairmlbook.org.

Bayly-Castaneda, K., Ramirez-Montoya, M. S., & Morita-Alexander, A. (2024). Crafting personalized learning paths with AI for lifelong learning: A systematic literature review. *Frontiers in Education*, *9*, 1–12. DOI: 10.3389/feduc.2024.1424386

Bengio, Y., Simard, P., & Frasconi, P. (1994). Learning long-term dependencies with gradient descent is difficult. *IEEE Transactions on Neural Networks*, *5*(2), 157–166. DOI: 10.1109/72.279181 PMID: 18267787

Bishop, C. M. (2006). *Pattern recognition and machine learning*. Springer.

Budennyy, S. A., Lazarev, V. D., Zakharenko, N. N., Korovin, A. N., Plosskaya, O. A., Dimitrov, D. V. E., . . . Zhukov, L. E. E. (2022). Eco2ai: carbon emissions tracking of machine learning models as the first step towards sustainable ai. In *Doklady mathematics* (Vol. 106, No. Suppl 1, pp. S118-S128). Moscow: Pleiades Publishing. DOI: 10.1134/S1064562422060230

Chen, Y., & Huang, G. (2024). GUIDE: A Global Unified Inference Engine for Deploying Large Language Models in Heterogeneous Environments. *arXiv preprint arXiv:2412.04788.*

de Reus, P., Oprescu, A., & Zuidema, J. (2024). An exploration of the effect of quantisation on energy consumption and inference time of StarCoder2. *arXiv preprint arXiv:2411.12758.*

Dean, J., Corrado, G., Monga, R., Chen, K., Devin, M., Le, Q. V., . . . Ng, A. Y. (2012). Large scale distributed deep networks. In *Advances in Neural Information Processing Systems* (pp. 1223-1231).

Duché, H. O., & Galilée, F. (2017). Coarse grain automatic differentiation: A practical approach to fast and exact computation of first and second order derivatives in software. *Cogent Engineering*, *4*(1), 1–24. DOI: 10.1080/23311916.2017.1412234

Duchi, J., Hazan, E., & Singer, Y. (2011). Adaptive subgradient methods for online learning and stochastic optimization. *Journal of Machine Learning Research*, *12*, 2121–2159.

Fu, Y., & Weng, Z. (2024). Navigating the ethical terrain of AI in education: A systematic review on framing responsible human-centered AI practices. *Computers and Education: Artificial Intelligence*, *7*, 100306. DOI: 10.1016/j.caeai.2024.100306

Glorot, X., & Bengio, Y. (2010). Understanding the difficulty of training deep feedforward neural networks. *Proceedings of the Thirteenth International Conference on Artificial Intelligence and Statistics*, 249-256.

Goodfellow, I., Pouget-Abadie, J., Mirza, M., Xu, B., Warde-Farley, D., Ozair, S., & Bengio, Y. (2014). Generative adversarial nets. *Advances in Neural Information Processing Systems*, *27*, 2672–2680.

Hah, S., Kelly, E., Nikou, S., & Svee, E. O. (2022). Aligning artificial intelligence with human values: Reflections from a phenomenological perspective. *AI & Society*, *37*(4), 1383–1395. DOI: 10.1007/s00146-021-01247-4

Han, S., Mao, H., & Dally, W. J. (2015). Deep compression: Compressing deep neural networks with pruning, trained quantization, and Huffman coding. *arXiv preprint arXiv:1510.00149.*

He, K., Zhang, X., Ren, S., & Sun, J. (2015). Delving deep into rectifiers: Surpassing human-level performance on ImageNet classification. *Proceedings of the IEEE International Conference on Computer Vision*, 1026-1034. DOI: 10.1109/ICCV.2015.123

He, K., Zhang, X., Ren, S., & Sun, J. (2016). Deep residual learning for image recognition. *Proceedings of the IEEE Conference on Computer Vision and Pattern Recognition*, 770-778. DOI: 10.1109/CVPR.2016.90

Hochreiter, S., & Schmidhuber, J. (1997). Long short-term memory. *Neural Computation*, *9*(8), 1735–1780. DOI: 10.1162/neco.1997.9.8.1735 PMID: 9377276

Ifenthaler, D., Majumdar, R., Gorissen, P., Judge, M., Mishra, S., Raffaghelli, J., & Shimada, A. (2024). Artificial Intelligence in Education: Implications for Policymakers, Researchers, and Practitioners. *Technology. Knowledge and Learning*, *29*(4), 1693–1710. DOI: 10.1007/s10758-024-09747-0

Jouppi, N. P., Young, C., Patil, N., Patterson, D., Agrawal, G., Bajwa, R., & Weisz, G. (2017). In-datacenter performance analysis of a tensor processing unit. *Proceedings of the 44th Annual International Symposium on Computer Architecture*, 1-12. DOI: 10.1145/3079856.3080246

Katiyar, N., Awasthi, V. K., Pratap, R., Mishra, K., Shukla, N., Singh, R., & Tiwari, M. (2024). Ai-Driven Personalized Learning Systems: Enhancing Educational Effectiveness. *Educational Administration: Theory and Practice*, *30*(5), 11514–11524. DOI: 10.53555/kuey.v30i5.4961

Khan, K. (2024). *Lecture notes on deep learning TPU programming*. Unpublished. DOI: 10.13140/RG.2.2.30740.62086

Kingma, D. P., & Ba, J. (2014). *Adam: A method for stochastic optimization*. arXiv preprint arXiv:1412.6980.

Kinnas, M., Violos, J., Kompatsiaris, I., & Papadopoulos, S. (2025). Reducing inference energy consumption using dual complementary CNNs. *Future Generation Computer Systems, 165*(107606), 107606. DOI: 10.1016/j.future.2024.107606

Klambauer, G., Unterthiner, T., Mayr, A., & Hochreiter, S. (2017). Self-normalizing neural networks. *Advances in Neural Information Processing Systems, 30*, 971–980.

Kovač, V. B., Nome, D. Ø., Jensen, A. R., & Skreland, L. Lj. (2023). The why, what and how of deep learning: critical analysis and additional concerns. *Education Inquiry*, 1–17. DOI: 10.1080/20004508.2023.2194502

Le Dinh, T., Le, T. D., Uwizeyemungu, S., & Pelletier, C. (2025). Human-Centered Artificial Intelligence in Higher Education: A Framework for Systematic Literature Reviews. *Information (Basel), 16*(3), 240. DOI: 10.3390/info16030240

LeCun, Y., Bengio, Y., & Hinton, G. (2015). Deep learning. *Nature, 521*(7553), 436–444. DOI: 10.1038/nature14539 PMID: 26017442

Li, C., Awan, A. A., Tang, H., Rajbhandari, S., & He, Y. (2021). 1-bit LAMB: Communication efficient large-scale large-batch training with LAMB's convergence speed. In arXiv [cs.LG]. http://arxiv.org/abs/2104.06069

Linderoth, C., Hultén, M., & Stenliden, L. (2024). Competing visions of artificial intelligence in education—A heuristic analysis on sociotechnical imaginaries and problematizations in policy guidelines. *Policy Futures in Education, 22*(8), 1662–1678. DOI: 10.1177/14782103241228900

Martens, J. (2010). Deep learning via Hessian-free optimization. *Proceedings of the 27th International Conference on Machine Learning (ICML-10)*, 735-742.

McMahan, H. B., Moore, E., Ramage, D., Hampson, S., & Arcas, B. A. (2017). Communication-efficient learning of deep networks from decentralized data. *Proceedings of the 20th International Conference on Artificial Intelligence and Statistics*, 1273-1282.

Pan, Z., & Mishra, P. (2021). Hardware acceleration of explainable machine learning using tensor processing units. *arXiv preprint arXiv:2103.11927.*

Patterson, D., Gonzalez, J., Le, Q., Liang, C., Munguia, L. M., Rothchild, D., . . . Dean, J. (2021). Carbon emissions and large neural network training. *arXiv preprint arXiv:2104.10350.*

Piech, C., Bassen, J., Huang, J., Ganguli, S., Sahami, M., Guibas, L., & Sohl-Dickstein, J. (2015). Deep knowledge tracing. *Advances in Neural Information Processing Systems, 28*, 505–513.

Rahm, L., & Rahm-Skågeby, J. (2023). Imaginaries and problematisations: A heuristic lens in the age of artificial intelligence in education. *British Journal of Educational Technology*, *54*(5), 1147–1159. DOI: 10.1111/bjet.13319

Raissi, M., Perdikaris, P., & Karniadakis, G. E. (2019). Physics-informed neural networks: A deep learning framework for solving forward and inverse problems involving nonlinear partial differential equations. *Journal of Computational Physics*, *378*, 686–707. DOI: 10.1016/j.jcp.2018.10.045

Ramachandran, P., Zoph, B., & Le, Q. V. (2017). Searching for activation functions. *arXiv preprint arXiv:1710.05941*.

Raubitzek, S., Mallinger, K., & Neubauer, T. (2023). Combining Fractional Derivatives and Machine Learning: A Review. *Entropy (Basel, Switzerland)*, *25*(1), 35. DOI: 10.3390/e25010035 PMID: 36673176

Ren, J.. (2024). Enabling Large Dynamic Neural Network Training with Learning-based Memory Management,*IEEE International Symposium on High-Performance Computer Architecture (HPCA)*, Edinburgh, United Kingdom, 788-802. https://doi.org/DOI: 10.1109/HPCA57654.2024.00066

Röbenack, K., & Gerbet, D. (2024). Toward state estimation by high gain differentiators with automatic differentiation. *Optimization Methods & Software*, 1–16. DOI: 10.1080/10556788.2024.2320737

Roux, N. L., Schmidt, M., & Bach, F. (2012). A stochastic gradient method with an exponential convergence rate for strongly convex optimization with applications to logistic regression. *Journal of Machine Learning Research*, *13*, 2672–2680.

Ruder, S. (2016). An overview of gradient descent optimization algorithms. *arXiv preprint arXiv:1609.04747*.

Rumelhart, D. E., Hinton, G. E., & Williams, R. J. (1986). Learning representations by back-propagating errors. *Nature*, *323*(6088), 533–536. DOI: 10.1038/323533a0

Russell, S., & Norvig, P. (2021). *Artificial intelligence: A modern approach* (4th ed.). Pearson.

Samtani, S., Zhu, H., Padmanabhan, B., Chai, Y., Chen, H., & Nunamaker, J. F.Jr. (2023). Deep Learning for Information Systems Research. *Journal of Management Information Systems*, *40*(1), 271–301. DOI: 10.1080/07421222.2023.2172772

Sarker, I. H. (2021). Deep Learning: A Comprehensive Overview on Techniques, Taxonomy, Applications and Research Directions. *SN Computer Science*, *2*(420), 1–20. DOI: 10.1007/s42979-021-00815-1 PMID: 34426802

Schulman, J., Wolski, F., Dhariwal, P., Radford, A., & Klimov, O. (2017). Proximal policy optimization algorithms. *arXiv preprint arXiv:1707.06347*.

Srivastava, N., Hinton, G., Krizhevsky, A., Sutskever, I., & Salakhutdinov, R. (2014). Dropout: A simple way to prevent neural networks from overfitting. *Journal of Machine Learning Research, 15*(1), 1929–1958.

Stewart, J. (2015). *Calculus: Early transcendentals* (8th ed.). Cengage Learning.

Stoyanov, R., Spišaková, V., Ramos, J., Gurfinkel, S., Vagin, A., Reber, A., . . . Bruno, R. (2025). CRIUgpu: Transparent Checkpointing of GPU-Accelerated Workloads. *arXiv preprint arXiv:2502.16631.*

Strubell, E., Ganesh, A., & McCallum, A. (2019). Energy and policy considerations for deep learning in NLP. *Proceedings of the 57th Annual Meeting of the Association for Computational Linguistics*, 3645-3650. DOI: 10.18653/v1/P19-1355

Sutton, R. S., & Barto, A. G. (2018). *Reinforcement learning: An introduction* (2nd ed.). MIT Press.

Thompson, N. C., Ge, S., & Manso, G. F. (2022). The importance of (exponentially more) computing power. In *arXiv [cs.AR]*. http://arxiv.org/abs/2206.14007

Torres-Peña, R. C., Peña-González, D., Chacuto-López, E., Ariza, E. A., & Vergara, D. (2024). Updating Calculus Teaching with AI: A Classroom Experience. *Education Sciences, 14*(9), 1019. DOI: 10.3390/educsci14091019

Tran, Phong & Vu, Khang & Doan, Minh & Dang, Quynh & Dang, Quang & Ho, Thanh. (2024). Personalized learning paths recommendation system with collaborative filtering and content-based approaches. *Science & Technology Development Journal - Economics - Law and Management, 8*(2), 5243-5253. DOI: 10.32508/stdjelm.v8i2.1370

Wang, S., Wang, F., Zhu, Z., Wang, J., Tran, T., & Du, Z. (2024). Artificial intelligence in education: A systematic literature review. *Expert Systems with Applications, 252*, 124167. DOI: 10.1016/j.eswa.2024.124167

You, Y., Zhang, Z., Hsieh, C. J., Demmel, J., & Keutzer, K. (2020). Large batch optimization for deep learning: Training BERT in 76 minutes. *International Conference on Learning Representations (ICLR)*, 1-37.

Zemel, R. S., Wu, Y., Swersky, K., Pitassi, T., & Dwork, C. (2013). Learning fair representations. In *Proceedings of the 30th International Conference on Machine Learning, PMLR, 28*(3), 325-333.

Zhao, W. X., Zhou, K., Li, J., Tang, T., Wang, X., Hou, Y., . . . Wen, J. R. (2023). A survey of large language models, 1-144. https://doi.org//arXiv.2303.18223DOI: 10.48550

ADDITIONAL READING

Alkhawaja, L. (2023). Artificial Intelligence in Education: Harnessing Its Power as a Valuable Tool, Not an Adversary. [IJCALLT]. *International Journal of Computer-Assisted Language Learning and Teaching, 13*(1), 1–22. DOI: 10.4018/IJCALLT.329607

Deepak, G., & Trivedi, I. (2023). A Hybridized Deep Learning Strategy for Course Recommendation. [IJAET]. *International Journal of Adult Education and Technology, 14*(1), 1–16. DOI: 10.4018/IJAET.321752

Díaz, B., & Delgado, C. (2024). Artificial intelligence: Tool or teammate? *Journal of Research in Science Teaching, 61*(10), 2575–2584. DOI: 10.1002/tea.21993

Gupta, S. L., & Mishra, N. (2022). Artificial Intelligence and Deep Learning-Based Information Retrieval Framework for Assessing Student Performance. [IJIRR]. *International Journal of Information Retrieval Research, 12*(1), 1–27. DOI: 10.4018/IJIRR.2022010101

Holmes, W., & Tuomi, I. (2022). State of the art and practice in AI in education. *European Journal of Education, 57*(4), 542–570. DOI: 10.1111/ejed.12533

Jagadesh Kumar, M. (2023). Artificial Intelligence in Education: Are we ready? *IETE Technical Review, 40*(2), 153–154. DOI: 10.1080/02564602.2023.2207916

Kujundziski, A. P., & Bojadjiev, J. (2025). Artificial Intelligence in Education: Transforming Learning Landscapes. In Stevkovska, M., Klemenchich, M., & Kavaklı Ulutaş, N. (Eds.), *Reimagining Intelligent Computer-Assisted Language Education* (pp. 1–54). IGI Global Scientific Publishing., DOI: 10.4018/979-8-3693-4310-4.ch001

Monika Singh, T., Kishor Kumar Reddy, C., Ramana Murthy, B. V., Nag, A., & Doss, S. (2025). AI and Education: Bridging the Gap to Personalized, Efficient, and Accessible Learning. In M. Ouaissa, M. Ouaissa, H. Lamaazi, M. El Hamlaoui, & K. Reddy C. (Eds.), *Internet of Behavior-Based Computational Intelligence for Smart Education Systems* (pp. 131-160). IGI Global Scientific Publishing. https://doi.org/DOI: 10.4018/979-8-3693-8151-9.ch005

Mupaikwa, E. (2023). The Use of Artificial Intelligence in Education: Applications, Challenges, and the Way Forward. In Chiu, D., & Ho, K. (Eds.), *Emerging Technology-Based Services and Systems in Libraries, Educational Institutions, and Non-Profit Organizations* (pp. 26–50). IGI Global Scientific Publishing., DOI: 10.4018/978-1-6684-8671-9.ch002

Pacchiega, C. (2021). How Can Education Use Artificial Intelligence?: A Brief History of AI, Its Usages, Its Successes, and Its Problems When Applied to Education. In Panconesi, G., & Guida, M. (Eds.), *Handbook of Research on Teaching With Virtual Environments and AI* (pp. 558–590). IGI Global Scientific Publishing., DOI: 10.4018/978-1-7998-7638-0.ch024

Perrotta, C., & Selwyn, N. (2019). Deep learning goes to school: Toward a relational understanding of AI in education. *Learning, Media and Technology, 45*(3), 251–269. DOI: 10.1080/17439884.2020.1686017

Selwyn, N. (2022). The future of AI and education: Some cautionary notes. *European Journal of Education*, *57*(4), 620–631. DOI: 10.1111/ejed.12532

Sidorkin, A. M. (2024). Artificial intelligence: Why is it our problem? *Educational Philosophy and Theory*, 1–6. DOI: 10.1080/00131857.2024.2348810

Tahiru, F. (2021). AI in Education: A Systematic Literature Review. [JCIT]. *Journal of Cases on Information Technology*, *23*(1), 1–20. DOI: 10.4018/JCIT.2021010101

Venter, J., Coetzee, S. A., & Schmulian, A. (2024). Exploring the use of artificial intelligence (AI) in the delivery of effective feedback. *Assessment & Evaluation in Higher Education*, 1–21. DOI: 10.1080/02602938.2024.2415649

Yang, Y., Luo, J., Yang, M., Yang, R., & Chen, J. (2024). From surface to deep learning approaches with Generative AI in higher education: An analytical framework of student agency. *Studies in Higher Education*, *49*(5), 817–830. DOI: 10.1080/03075079.2024.2327003

KEY TERMS

Artificial Intelligence: The ability to replicate human cognitive functions, including learning, reasoning, and problem-solving, through computational models. AI finds applications in various domains such as automation, education, and diagnostics, facilitating systems that adaptively respond to data patterns and make informed decisions.

Backpropagation Algorithm: A technique for adjusting the weights of neural networks by propagating errors from the output layer back to the input layers. It utilizes gradients from the loss function to iteratively optimize parameters, thereby improving prediction accuracy.

Deep Learning: A branch of machine learning that employs multi-layer neural networks to model complex, hierarchical representations of data. It delivers exceptional performance in multiple tasks such as image recognition, natural language processing, and personalized education systems.

Heuristic: A rule-of-thumb method for problem-solving and decision-making that relies on experience rather than guaranteed optimal solutions. Heuristics provide efficient approaches to complex or poorly defined problems.

Machine Learning: The capability of systems to identify patterns in data and autonomously enhance their performance without explicit programming. ML serves as the foundation for predictions, classifications, and adaptive systems through algorithms such as regression, decision trees, and neural networks.

Neural Network: A computational framework that processes and learns from data through a network of interconnected artificial neurons, emulating the structure of the human brain. Neural networks are employed in tasks such as classification, pattern recognition, and function approximation.

Personalized Learning: An instructional approach that customizes educational content and pacing according to individual student performance and preferences. By utilizing machine learning algorithms, this method optimizes learning pathways through real-time feedback and tailored recommendations.

Quantum Computing: A computational paradigm that leverages quantum bits, which can exist in multiple states simultaneously, to perform complex calculations. It promises exponential speed-ups for specific machine learning tasks, particularly in optimization and large-scale data processing.

Chapter 13
Transforming English Language Learning in South Asia:
Role of AI Tools in India

Kavita Indapurkar
https://orcid.org/0000-0003-4388-2915
Amity University, Noida, India

Aayushi Arya
https://orcid.org/0009-0006-0618-6979
Amity University, Noida, India

ABSTRACT

The English language has seen a boost in recent times with the help of technological advancements. This chapter tries to identify the AI tools used and its awareness among the students and teachers. A questionnaire was made for students and teachers separately that recorded the responses of 200 students and 100 teachers. Tests like descriptive statistics, independent t-test and factor analysis were run to analyze the results. It was identified that both the students and teachers are well familiar with AI tools for English language learning. They employ them in various areas like Translation, Writing, Interactive Learning, Grammar, and Pronunciation & Speaking Practices. Although there were some challenges faced, like Trust Concerns, Technological and Infrastructural Barriers. To help solve these problems, there is a need to employ training programs for teachers and help students with proper guidance about these tools.

DOI: 10.4018/979-8-3373-5092-9.ch013

INTRODUCTION

Technology has not only changed the way we see the world but has also changed the way we work and learn from our surroundings. There have been numerous technological advancements that can be seen, but there is one such development that has changed the way we live (Fitria, 2021). The emergence of this 'Artificial Intelligence' tool has significantly boosted efficiency and productivity across industries, freeing up human potential for creative and strategic endeavors. The term AI was first coined by an American computer scientist, John McCarthy 1956, who proposed that "every aspect of learning or any other feature of intelligence can in principle be so precisely described that a machine can be made to simulate it" (Moor, 2006). It is defined as a process whereby computers are designed to perform certain activities that require human intelligence. It encompasses the study of machine learning by identifying the patterns and studying them over time so that it can easily conclude things when new information is provided (AlAwamrah et al., 2024); (Mertala & Fagerlund, 2024). As AI technologies have started to thrive, they have positively influenced global and local economies, job markets, and productivity.

It has grown many-fold in recent years and has spread in various sectors like health care, education, governance, ethics, and societal norms. A study related to the integration of AI among different industries found that it has a growing and productive effect on the education sector (Khosravi et al., 2022). This integration is essential to help us boost different sectors of our economy. The emerging sector that requires its utmost attention is Education. AI in education focuses on making significant advances in educational techniques through real-world trials and the development of statistical reasoning, data visualization, and analytical learning (Alam, 2021). One of the most important goals of AI in education is to provide personalized learning guidance to individual students based on their learning and their teachers. At the end, we are all well aware of how students and teachers are the major pillars of development in India.

As we all know, AI has equally helped both the student and teacher side while transforming their learning as well as teaching systems in the current time; yet, many people do not even know how much they could benefit from this. It seems necessary to take care of the situation to help everyone have a hold over the rapid development being shown by AI in the educational sector, focusing specifically on English teaching and learning systems. It will help us to understand how various AI tools like Virtual Mentor, Chatbots, and Duolingo have emerged and helped a lot of people in improving their AIEd (Artificial Intelligence in Education). Teachers can analyze individual student performance data and even predict future student performance results with AIEd. Similar to this, students become motivated to learn at a self-paced rate as they acquire skills and move towards learning objectives (Tapalova & Zhiyenbayeva, 2022).

Although it is quite clear that using these new technological changes and employing them in the learning systems is essential, India still lacks this opportunity. In the growing development of our nation, it seems fit for the government and the policymakers to make sure that teachers and students are being made aware of the importance of AI integration within different sections of society, especially in the foreign languages we hold dear. English, as we know, was a foreign language introduced during British colonial rule and is now an important part of education, administration, and trade. It connects various linguistic communities within the country and is important for nations to access knowledge and opportunities globally. In turn, English proficiency makes India more competitive in the global economy regarding high-tech business, science, and technology. With the ever-expanding use of English across the globe, it offers individuals and nations a competitive advantage. In the current world, learning AI tools, especially those related to learning English, is of greater importance because they provide a more personalized and efficient way of enhancing language skills and improving global competitiveness.

The introduction of AI in English learning and teaching practices can help teachers form a better and improved relationship with the students by better understanding the difficulties faced by the students and helping them solve them using AI. More and more interactive learning experiences will be introduced that can help in the real-time feedback of pronunciation and create an interactive learning environment. Students, with the help of these tools, can get 24/7 access to learning support and a sense of motivation to work hard. Teachers can get help in identifying the learning gaps and improve themselves professionally. They can easily streamline the tasks at hand and free up time to be more interactive with the students. If we talk about making things easier, AI integration has helped students so much in multiple domains. It has helped them to learn different languages and understand any foreign language with the help of Google Translate, and learn these languages with a set of detailed courses and tests via Duolingo. Similarly, to improve their writing techniques and be a support system for them, Grammarly has played a huge role. Many other tools like Canva, Gradescope, eduaide.AI, Magic School, etc, have helped both the students and the teachers.

A study done with the subject matter experts found that the system of personalized learning is gaining great importance in the coming education system. It can help both teachers and students in grading and assessment processes (Jaiswal & Arun, 2021). If we look at the particular integration of AI in English for Specific Purposes (ESP) education, it was found that it provides exciting opportunities for students to enhance their capabilities and interests and address ethical challenges that come up along the way (Xatamova & Ashurov, 2024). With the improvement of AI, its integration into the English language has seen a boost. Multiple applications of assessments, grading, and enhancing efficiency have been introduced that have changed the way we look at teaching methods. Following this, it is expected that future advancements in AI will help take it to another level. More sophisticated algorithms might be introduced to help in precise learning analytics and content customization, which can further help improve the educational system of teaching and learning.

LITERATURE REVIEW

AI and Education

In India, the adoption of AI is now being considered as the fourth industrial revolution, which means it is growing at an alarming rate and it might very much influence the way we live, work, and see life (Srivastava, 2018). In the new transformative era of technological changes, it is seen that artificial intelligence has been propelled in a bunch of different domains and sectors, and contemporary education saw a major change within itself (Ellikkal & Rajamohan, 2024). AI, specifically in the teaching and learning systems, has transformed many folds and is expected to have seen the maximum impact on education management (Rodway & Schepman, 2023). AI is a major factor influencing the technological development of any nation as it highly promotes emerging technologies and integrates them within the new generation. But now the question arises, what exactly does one mean by AI? The literature suggests that there are multiple definitions available for this, and no single dominant definition is accepted by experts (Holmes & Tuomi, 2022). However, a highly accepted definition tells us that it is considered research that develops technologies to perform certain activities that require intelligence if performed by humans (Minsky, 1969). Another article provides a two-faceted definition, which says that it is a field of study and a theory. As a field of study, it helps in solving different cognitive problems related to human intelligence, whereas as a theory, it uses the capabilities of human beings and uses them with computer systems and perform a bunch of tasks like voice recognition, decision-making, translation, etc. (Chassignol et al., 2018).

AI literacy, that is, the extent of the potential of AI in the learning and teaching systems and its application in education, is becoming a concerning topic of discussion in the current scenario. The rising need for its development is pushing educators towards focusing on these technological changes and the ways it can be pursued (Holmes & Tuomi, 2022). A study conducted on 1013 teachers in China aimed to find out about the level of AI literacy among them. The research concluded that the teachers showed a significant and positive relationship between applying AI and knowing, understanding, and evaluating AI and ethics. It was further recommended that it is necessary to improve the proficiency in AI literacy of teachers (Zhao et al., 2022).

To further help increase AI literacy, various AI-powered educational tools have been brought into introduction to help both the students as well as the teachers. Due to the increased significance of AI among students and educators, different methods of integrating AI tools in the classroom environment are being introduced to help them work with ease (Halaweh, 2023); (Papapicco, 2020). This new application can help transform education, improve learning outcomes, and further help students with skills that can be beneficial for them to succeed in the 21st century (Owan et al., 2023). These AI tools are mainly referred to as some AI programs like ChatGPT, Google Translate, Quill Bot, etc, which can help out in different subjects like English, Mathematics, and Research (Liang, 2023). These can help improve different sections of society by employing different tools in various areas of use.

AI and the English language

The involvement of AI in the educational system has significantly improved the teaching and learning processes. In the modern era, technology has opened up many new opportunities for learners that have made the teaching and learning system more engaging and challenging (Mullammaa, 2010). Since various areas integrate AI with their language, it has helped transform language teaching dramatically. For example, if we talk about improving the writing area, various automated assessment tools offering features like suggestions and corrections have improved the language processing system (Heaven, 2020). A study conducted on 5 teachers and 60 students of the Hanoi language center found that AI-powered language tools have positive attitudes among students and teachers (Hien, 2024).

English language integration with AI in teaching and learning systems has had a enhancing effect on improving language education practices (Mushthoza et al., 2023). A study shows that AI in learning language helped teachers improve their teaching materials, sharpen student engagement, and help empower the learners' ability to understand the concepts easily yet in a human-like manner (Huang et al., 2023). A paper on different AI tools explained that there are different types of AI-powered tools based on their usage that is some are general-purpose tools related to audio, video, and graphics and some are professional tools under which comes our language teaching tools including areas of content creation, assessment and grading, tutoring, and planning. These tools are specifically based on the ELT realm, focusing on language teaching (Tolstykh & Oshchepkova, 2024).

Now, with the invention of new tools and technologies for English learning and teaching, it is being compared with the traditional methods. Although AI usage is far better than traditional teaching, it generates various challenges and competition in today's world (Zhu, 2022). Numerous countries have employed AI technologies in their teaching methods. One such country is Shanghai, which introduced the AI assessment marking system and speaking test to incorporate the new entrances in a college examination for English tests (Abou Elassad et al., 2020). Similar to this, in multiple countries, many tests are being done to check the influence of these technologies on language learning systems. One such example is of Turkey, where a set of 13 preparatory class students were introduced to ChatGPT through the learning experiences, and their data was then analyzed. The study found that ChatGPT significantly impacted crucial areas like learning experiences, grammar, vocabulary, engagement, etc. (Karataş et al., 2024).

AI Among Students

It has been found in studies that AI holds the power to revolutionize the way we learn. Students had increased engagement levels and interest, along with anxiety reduction, when it came to the involvement of AI in their education processes (Lin et al., 2021); (Xia et al., 2022). In today's world, if we talk about the educational contexts, we can see that the new emerging technologies such as AI can help and support the pupils or the students in tons of activities, which can help in their upliftment and can tutor them for better results in any examination (Marx, 2023). One such technology is the use of smart technologies, which can help foster a diverse culture and make it more interactive. To help have better access to this, a paper by (Zhang et al., 2021) proposed a framework, Artificial Intelligence Assisted Interactive Smart Education Framework (AIISE), that can promote a healthy and interactive environment among the students and the teachers.

It is expected that students will have to experience a shift in AI and will have to deal with the changes made by educators (Miller, 2022). However, students need to go with the flow and foster a sense of autonomy among students because AI will help in both fostering and optimizing the learning system (Abulibdeh et al., 2024). Students tend to have a more favorable cognitive, behavioral, and emotional attitude towards AI adoption in the education system of teaching and learning (Katsantonis & Katsantonis, 2024). A new generation of AI is being introduced in recent times, which is known as Generative AI. A study on 1135 Australian university students was carried out to learn about the knowledge and impact of these tools. It was found out that most of the students had low awareness about these, and they held lower confidence in using these tools in learning activities (Kelly et al., 2023). Another study focused to know about the benefits of this new AI, which they named ChatGPT-3. They applied a mixed approach to analyze how this new technology of generative AI can help improve the creative minds of students by analyzing their fluency, adoption, and flexibility (Habib et al., 2024).

A study by Cardenal Herrera University revealed that they installed some AI tools like Chatbots to help students in the process of mentoring, as well as sorting out any issues and difficulties they might be facing (Galstyan Sargsyan, 2019). Another study focusing specifically on higher education among Indian students, where data from 48 students were recorded, was done to measure whether the adoption of Chatbots has helped the students enhance their overall productivity. They revealed that students became quite familiar with the new technology and tended to share their educational issues with it for better understanding (Sandhu, 2020). Another study was done on the students of Germany. Here, data from more than 6300 students was analyzed, and it was found that more than one-third of these students are found to be using AI tools like ChatGPT of GPT-4 in their studies (Garrel & Mayer, 2023). Checking with the familiarity with AI tools, a US-based study found that around 98 percent of the students were familiar with one specific AI tool that is ChatGPT that they use in their day-to-day educational purposes whereas 71.5 percent of students were aware of the importance of AI tools in general (Delello et al., 2023).

AI Among Teachers

As technology is taking the place of a lot of things, it's becoming very necessary for teachers to become familiar with the growing changes that are taking place in today's generation. It is becoming imperative for teachers to be aware and equipped with the necessary skill set and knowledge to properly enhance the educational landscape (Ferikoğlu & Akgün, 2022). However, the only way to help teachers use AI in day-to-day activities is to have them cultivate their creativity so that it can benefit students more. They should feel capable enough and confident that they understand how this can transform the way teaching works (Hong, Hartzell, & Greene, 2011).

AI has helped educators not only in delivering lectures but also has saved time and effort by installing the automatic summative assessment, which is sometimes named the auto grader (Watters, 2021). A study focusing on the teachers' perception was done to understand their response toward the growing extent of AI and different technological changes. It found out that though there were some concerns regarding some technological changes, infrastructure, and development, the teachers found that AI can cause a transformative change in the educational system of teaching and learning if major steps are taken to help sort the difficulties faced (Aghaziarati et al., 2023).

The use of AI tools can ease the work of teachers when focusing on students. Though there are many benefits students see, like fostering creativity and reduced time spent, teachers face many concerns like cheating, and lack of knowledge among students, etc in classroom education (Pont-Niclòs, Echegoyen-Sanz, Gómez, & Ezpeleta, 2024). One such tool that seemed important to study was the 'Guide N Grow' application. This application helps students to engage better with the teachers to share their progress in education, assignments, schedules, and other important stuff. This has proven to be a lot more interactive, effective, and cost-efficient than any traditional way (Umang & Jain, 2020).

A study was done to analyze teachers' perceptions of AI and found that 25 percent of the teachers feel that AI is important in the educational context for the creation of employment. So, to help education in schools, it is essential to evaluate the barriers one might face in this process of technological integration (Vazhayil, Shetty, Rao, & Nagarajan, 2019). Another study was done on 28 teachers of English majors, where they said that AI Chatbots can be helpful for teachers to learn new things like good communication, linguistics, and assessments and it can play an important role in significantly improving the teaching mechanism in the education environment (Yang, 2022). The integration of AI in the process of language learning is beneficial for both teachers and students. Teachers can improve their personalized learning skills along with writing assistance and tutoring abilities (Pokrivcakova, 2019).

It is a well-known fact that the usage of different technologies like AI is growing, and providing a safe and secure platform for students and teachers is very necessary to limit the misuse that might be caused. Different departments of various universities should adhere to this and provide instructions to improve the awareness of students towards the benefits and challenges that they might come across (Katsantonis & Katsantonis, 2024). Ensuring a safer space can help policymakers develop a more equitable and effective education system for our country (Owan et al., 2023). Along with this, policymakers can also develop some professional development programs for teachers so that they can have a better understanding of this AI integration within education (Aghaziarati et al., 2023).

Impact of AI on Education

In recent times, we can see that AI or the extent of digital technologies has been taking concerned steps of prioritization in India. The Indian government has been highly focused on the development, adoption, and implementation of AI in our day-to-day lives (Marda, 2018).

The usage of AI tools by students has led to a two-sided effect that is both positive and negative. The lack of some concepts related to AI might cause some problems in the usage of its tools among students as well as by educators but since the technology is evolving at a high rate, it's very much necessary to find ways to enhance the positive effects and minimize the negative ones (Liang, 2023). We very well know that AI has many benefits, but similar to these come various consequences. Different countries, like Italy, for example, have banned the usage of AI-based tools by their pupils or employees because there were some abusive or unreflective responses offered by the Chatbots (Hughes, 2023) (Lukpat, 2023). There has been a concerning issue, which says that in the past it is seen that there have been some difficulties in equipping students with new technologies such as social media, and the same problem might arise with the involvement of AI in the emerging education system (Green, 2023). A paper did a study on the risks that might be posed due to the usage of AI in education and found some concerning issues like inaccurate data, bias and discrimination, privacy issues, dependence on tools, etc. (Delello et al., 2023).

A survey of data for 1961–2018 on AI concluded that there have been seen some negative impacts of technological changes of AI, like high costs, laziness, poor infrastructure, connectivity issues, etc, which need to be addressed to improve the overall usage of AI among the youth (Msekelwa, 2024). Another set of papers analyzed that while the implementation of AI systems in educational institutions might have some challenges, there can be some positive effects too, like personalized learning, tutoring systems, grading assessments, chatbots (Harry & Sayudin., 2023) (Balamurugan et al., 2022). There are both benefits and limitations to new technologies, but what stands important here is the fact that we know how well we can utilize the benefits and how to ethically and effectively use the technology, keeping in mind the challenges it might face (Owan et al., 2023).

Future of AI

The future of AI looks promising enough as it has revolutionized the way we work and handle situations. AI tools have come into use to improve the impact of higher education (HE). There have been practices to even improve Sustainable Development Goal 4 (SDG 4) through AI, as it was concerned that the adoption of AI tools in higher education has seen negative impacts on sustainability (Okulich-Kazarin et al., 2024). If we look at its impact on the future in the Indian context, they have started to engage AI to help them solve the major issues like that of healthcare, education, and progressively to increase their productivity and growth (Srivastava, 2018). A study of Japan shows that employing AI in their economy can boost their productivity many times. To help assess that, they did a study on the panel dataset of countries from 1970 to 2019 and found out that the impact of AI was seen highly on the advancing economies and overall, there was a positive relationship between economic growth and the use of artificial intelligence (Tan, 2023).

AI is making its way into the education system in a very rapid way. It is the fastest-growing trend in today's generation, but is it the safe way? A study of Australia argued that while AI might have many positive impacts and can help transform a country for the better, it is not made for the education system. They said that transforming the classrooms with the help of smart learning might harm those who work in the field of education, and this approach is considered a struggle more than a boon (Selwyn, 2022). On the other hand, some researchers feel that this inclusion will be beneficial for their economy. An article about the transformation of the education system laid out an interesting fact about India, which states that artificial intelligence holds the power to add US$1 trillion to its economy by the end of 2025. They feel that India will see a massive positive impact of integrating AI into the education system and will use it to upgrade their economy (Kamala & Kamalakar, 2023).

A survey taken by 1,348 English language teachers said that the English language is causing a boost in the education system due to the impact of AI tools. Though it can be seen as an important tool to help ease the teaching systems of education, majority of teachers argued that it should not be seen as a replacement of the human focused teaching and learning systems, rather it should always be considered as a complement to this in the future scenarios (Edmett et al., 2024). With the transforming India and the world focusing on Web 3.0 and Web 4.0, there is an urgent need to have an expanded focus on transforming the learning and teaching systems of the education system but employing the usage of AI tools in teaching and learning (Roy & Putatunda, 2023). Talking about the English classroom systems, it can increase the effectiveness and make the students engage more freely with the teachers in clearing their doubts. This AI transformation can also help in achieving the goal of NEP 2020 of providing a more holistic, learner-centered, and enjoyable environment for the students to learn English (Government of India, 2020). A study involving a survey of 500 tried to assess the impact of these AI tools specifically for English for Specific Purposes (ESP) education. It also states that AI can revolutionize the ESP education system proficiently in the future (Xatamova & Ashurov, 2024).

Research Gap

Though there is a lot of literature published on the teaching and learning mechanisms through AI tools, there is limited study performed in the Tier–1 cities of India that specifically focuses on the awareness of the integration of AI tools in the foreign language, which is English in this case. The impact of particularly English language is missing in the already published articles, which is the main focus of this research. More specifically, there are certain tools taken into consideration, and their usage is then evaluated while focusing on any ethical and practical concerns the students and teachers might face.

Research Questions

- What is the current level of awareness of AI tools in English teaching among teachers in Tier-I cities of India?
- What is the current level of awareness of AI tools in English learning among students in Tier-I cities of India?
- What are some common challenges faced in using AI in English teaching and learning among the teachers and students of Tier-I cities in India?

Research Objectives

- To assess the awareness of using AI in English teaching and learning among the teachers and students of Tier-I cities in India.
- To evaluate the use of AI in English teaching and learning systems in select schools and colleges of the study area.
- To assess the challenges faced in using AI in English teaching and learning among the teachers and students of Tier-I cities in India.

Rationale

In Tier-I Indian cities, there is limited knowledge about the usage and effects of artificial intelligence (AI), even though it is transforming English teaching. Voice recognition, computerized tests, and intelligent tutoring systems are some examples of AI-based products that hold tremendous possibilities, yet there is limited awareness about whether teachers and students are knowledgeable and prepared to utilize such tools. This research seeks to fill that gap by evaluating how AI is being integrated into English instruction and whether it improves teaching efficiency and student learning results.

One of the aims of this research is to evaluate the influence of AI on the language skills of students, such as writing, grammar, pronunciation, and communication. While the potential of AI is widely acknowledged, very little empirical research explicitly tests its efficacy in Indian schools. Besides that, teachers will struggle to incorporate AI because of the lack of training, whether as a concern with the contribution of AI towards teaching languages, or simply animosity towards technology. Organizations can create teaching courses and assist programs for educators through the realization of these hindrances.

Scholars, policymakers, and teachers will gain from the data-driven findings of this study on AI awareness, influence, and challenges. Besides enhancing AI adoption plans, this will help Indian universities enhance English teaching and learning processes.

RESEARCH METHODOLOGY

The study follows a descriptive-analytical design consisting of gathering information about the influence and role of AI tools in the English language from sampled subjects and analyzing the results. The study covers the tier 1 cities in India and analyzes the students' and teachers' learning and teaching in those areas. Primary research was used to collect the data through a structured questionnaire that asked questions related to various AI tools like Virtual Mentor, Voice assistant, Presentation translator, Automatic assessment, Chatbot, and Duolingo. The major focus of this survey was to understand the usage and the familiarity of AI tools, along with any challenges they are facing in adapting them into their day-to-day lives. It focused on accumulating the data of both the students and teachers and further analyzing it.

Data Source

This research was carried out by taking the data from 200 student respondents and 100 teacher respondents from the Tier 1 cities of India. The age of the student respondents mainly ranged from 18-21 and 22-26, and their education level varied between undergraduate and postgraduate. Whereas, the teacher respondents were from different age groups, like 25-35, 36-45, and some were above 45 with different teaching experiences. While the gender ratio was well maintained among students, a very small number of male respondents were there for teachers. It was seen that these numbers could easily represent a sufficient variability. It can consider different proficiencies and varying accessibility of these tools to students and teachers. Tier 1 was chosen because in India, these cities have comparatively higher access and knowledge about the emergence of new technologies, and they have a relatively higher literacy rate, so it was necessary to understand if the emergence of these AI tools could help transform the English language.

Methods Used

The data was analyzed using the IBM SPSS software. The statistical analysis was carried on by using descriptive statistics, which included details like mean and standard deviation. It helped in understanding the effectiveness and knowledge of AI tools among students and teachers. To check the normality of the data, Kolmogorov-Smirnov and Shapiro-Wilk tests were conducted. Along with this, histograms and Stem-and-leaf plots were made for visual analysis. Following this, an independent sample T-test was carried out to understand any difference in familiarity with these tools between different genders. Further, factor analysis was employed, and the key challenges of adopting AI tools were identified (Anand et al., 2023).

DATA ANALYSIS AND DISCUSSIONS

The study further follows up on the research methodology and analyzes the data collected to study the students' and teachers' awareness, usefulness of the AI tools of the English language in Tier 1 cities in India, and what are the possible challenges faced by them so that policies can be recommended based on that. This section includes various tests, like descriptive statistics, followed by an independent sample t-test and factor analysis. To check if these tests are the applicable choice, adaptability checks were also done (John & Indapurkar, 2020).

Students and Teachers' Familiarity with AI Tools

This section focuses on the awareness of AI tools among teachers and students, and further, it studies whether gender plays any role in affecting its awareness.

Now let's look at the statistics of this data.

Figure 1. Descriptive statistics for the knowledge of AI tools of students (Output from SPSS)

Descriptive Statistics

	N	Minimum	Maximum	Mean	Std. Deviation
I am familiar with AI tools used for learning English	200	2	5	3.78	.803
Valid N (listwise)	200				

Figure 2. Descriptive statistics for the knowledge of AI tools of teachers (Output from SPSS)

Descriptive Statistics

	N	Minimum	Maximum	Mean	Std. Deviation
I am knowledgeable about AI tools for English teaching.	100	1	5	2.59	1.531
Valid N (listwise)	100				

Figures 1 and 2 show that 200 students and 100 teachers took the questionnaire answering the question of awareness, in which 1 = Strongly Disagree, 5 = Strongly Agree; a minimum of 1 suggests that at least one person strongly disagreed that they are familiar with AI tools for learning and teaching English. Whereas a maximum of 5 suggests that at least one person strongly agreed that they are familiar with AI tools for learning and teaching English. The test of descriptive statistics was done to help us understand the impact of the usage of AI tools on the two variables.

As seen in 'Figure 1 – Descriptive statistics for the knowledge of AI tools of students', there is a high level of familiarity, i.e., it shows positive results. As we can see that there is a high mean value (3.78), which indicates that the students are, in general, aware of AI tools for the English language like Virtual Mentor, Voice assistant, Presentation translator, Automatic assessment, Chatbot, and Duolingo.

Alongside, if we study the data of teachers, in 'Figure 2 – Descriptive statistics for the knowledge of AI tools of teachers', we can see that they show a low to moderate level of familiarity. The mean (2.59) indicates that teachers are somewhat aware of the tools that are being used in English teaching practices.

Figure 3. Independent sample T-test for gender differences (Output from SPSS)

Group Statistics

	Gender	N	Mean	Std. Deviation	Std. Error Mean
I am familiar with AI tools used for learning English	Male	105	3.78	.832	.081
	Female	95	3.78	.774	.079

Independent Samples Test

		Levene's Test for Equality of Variances		t-test for Equality of Means						
		F	Sig.	t	df	Sig. (2-tailed)	Mean Difference	Std. Error Difference	95% Confidence interval of difference (Lower)	95% Confidence interval of difference (Upper)
I am familiar with AI tools used for learning English	Equal variances assumed	1.198	.275	.018	198	.986	.002	.114	-.223	.227
	Equal variances not assumed			.018	197.834	.986	.002	.114	-.222	.226

An independent sample T-test was employed to compare the differences in familiarity with AI tools between the male and female students (Mehra & Indapurkar, 2020). The results of which can be seen in Figure 3. It shows two tables, one of Group statistics that records the Mean and standard deviation of Males (Mean = 3.78) and Females (Mean = 3.78), and the other was an independent samples test. Levene's Test for Equality of Variance showed that the assumptions were met (F = 1.198, p = .275). This means that there is no statistically significant difference seen between the awareness of the two genders ($t\ (198) = -.568$, $p = .986$).

Usage frequency of AI tools

This section explores the various AI tools used for learning and teaching English, and which are the most and least preferred amongst them. It also examines various uses of these tools and figures out where it is mostly used by teachers and students.

Figure 4. Usage frequency of AI tools among students (Output from SPSS)

Descriptive Statistics

	N	Minimum	Maximum	Mean	Std. Deviation
Virtual Mentor (e.g., Khan Academy)	200	1	5	2.11	1.187
Voice Assistant (e.g., Siri, Google Assistant)	200	1	5	3.04	1.100
Presentation Translator (e. g., Microsoft PowerPoint Translator, Google Slides Captions & Translation)	200	1	5	2.88	1.308
Automatic Assessment (e. g., Grammarly, Turnitin)	200	1	5	2.98	1.307
ChatBot (e.g., ChatGPT)	200	1	5	3.57	1.250
Duolingo	200	1	5	2.61	1.239
Valid N (listwise)	200				

Figure 5. Usage frequency of AI tools among teachers (Output from SPSS)

Descriptive Statistics

	N	Minimum	Maximum	Mean	Std. Deviation
Virtual Mentor (e.g., Khan Academy)	100	1	5	2.38	1.117
Voice Assistant (e.g., Siri, Google Assistant)	100	1	5	3.00	.974
Presentation Translator (e. g., Microsoft PowerPoint Translator, Google Slides Captions & Translation)	100	1	5	3.41	1.207
Automatic Assessment (e. g., Grammarly, Turnitin)	100	1	5	3.18	1.274
ChatBot (e.g., ChatGPT)	100	1	5	3.62	1.213
Duolingo	100	1	5	2.44	1.321
Valid N (listwise)	100				

The above Figures show a list of AI tools that were taken up in the study. These are some most commonly used tools in the English language, like Virtual Mentor (e.g., Khan Academy), Voice Assistant (e.g., Siri, Google Assistant), Presentation Translator (e.g., Microsoft PowerPoint Translator, Google Slides Captions & Translation), Automatic Assessment (e.g., Grammarly, Turnitin), Chatbot (e.g., ChatGPT), and Duolingo. Taking these tools into consideration, the students and teachers were asked about the level of usefulness these tools have, respectively, in increasing their English proficiency in learning and teaching aspects.

Looking at the data of students in Figure 4 – Usage Frequency of AI Tools among students, we can conclude that the mean usage of Chatbot was the highest (3.57), which indicates that it is the one used most frequently. Whereas, Virtual Mentor recorded the least mean usage (2.11). Other tools were used by students, but not as frequently as Chatbots. The mean usage of others like Voice Assistant (3.04), Presentation Translator (2.88), Automatic Assessment (2.98), and Duolingo (2.61) was quite moderate.

Similar to students, even teachers, as seen in Figure 5 – Usage Frequency of AI Tools among teachers, recorded a high mean usage of Chatbots (3.62). However, Virtual Mentor (2.38) and Duolingo (2.44) saw a low mean usage, indicating that teachers might not be that into the usage of these tools. Other tools like Voice Assistant (3.00), Presentation Translator (3.41), and Automatic Assessment (3.18) saw a moderate mean usage.

Overall, we find similarities between the most commonly used AI tools for teaching and learning the English language. This tool is a Chatbot (e.g., ChatGPT) which is primarily helpful in various aspects of improving their English.

Figures 6 and 7 give a brief about the perceived helpfulness of these tools in various areas by students and teachers, respectively.

Figure 6. Students' perception of AI tools' helpfulness (Output from SPSS)

Descriptive Statistics

	N	Minimum	Maximum	Mean	Std. Deviation
Improving Grammar	200	1	5	3.20	1.159
Vocabulary Expansion	200	2	4	3.28	.925
Pronunciation Practice	200	1	5	3.45	1.172
Writing Assistance	200	1	5	3.65	1.120
Speaking & Listening Practice	200	1	5	3.31	1.242
Translation & Understanding Difficult Texts	200	1	5	3.75	1.159
Valid N (listwise)	200				

Figure 7. Teachers' perception of AI tools' helpfulness (Output from SPSS)

Descriptive Statistics

	N	Minimum	Maximum	Mean	Std. Deviation
Lesson Planning	100	1	4	2.25	.833
Grammar & Writing Assistance	100	1	5	2.06	1.238
Pronunciation & Speaking Practice	100	1	5	2.93	1.157
Automatic Assessment & Grading	100	1	5	2.19	1.398
Translation & Interpretation	100	1	5	3.11	1.503
Interactive Learning (e.g., AI chatbots)	100	1	5	3.77	1.043
Valid N (listwise)	100				

The above two Figures focus on the usage of these AI tools in the English language in the everyday lives of a student and a teacher, respectively, while learning or teaching. A descriptive statistics test was applied here to get a better and informative understanding.

Overall, it can be seen, specifically from Figure 6, that student do find these AI tools helpful in improving their English learning skills. Although there was a major focus on the area of "Translation & Understanding Difficult Texts" (Mean = 3.75) and "Writing Assistance" (Mean = 3.65), which helps students in academic and personal areas to understand the content they are reading. As we have seen that Chatbot is mostly used, it is now clear in which area it is primarily used. We can see from the Figure that all of these aspects have statistically significant results, but there are areas like Improving Grammar (Mean = 3.20) and Speaking & Listening Practice (Mean = 3.31) that have comparatively low means, which indicates that they are moderately helpful for the students.

On the other hand, we can see that even the teachers, in Figure 7, have found AI tools for the English language useful in their teaching activities. The mean usage, when calculated, showed that there are different areas where it is highly useful, but some with moderate usefulness. Aspects like Interactive Learning (Mean = 3.77), Translation and interpretation (Mean = 3.11), and Pronunciation & Speaking Practice (Mean = 2.93) implied a greater usage of tools in these areas. However, areas like Automatic Assessment & Grading (Mean = 2.19), Grammar and Writing Assistance (Mean = 2.06) showed weak mean usage, indicating that teachers are not inclined to use AI tools for English language when it comes to the assessment or writing processes.

Challenges Faced While Using AI Tools by Students and Teachers

This section employed the factor analysis technique to identify what can be the major challenges faced by students and teachers while they are adopting AI tools in the English learning and teaching techniques. Principal Axis Factoring with Oblimin rotation was used to study the results of both. To support the adequacy of Factor analysis, both the data of students and teachers were analyzed by tests like Kaiser-Meyer-Olkin (KMO) and Bartlett's Test, whose results are listed below and clarify that it is adequate (Indapurkar & Raj, 2017).

Figure 8. Kaiser-Meyer-Olkin (KMO) and Bartlett's test (Output from SPSS)

KMO and Bartlett's Test

Kaiser-Meyer-Olkin Measure of Sampling Adequacy.		.897
Bartlett's Test of Sphericity	Approx. Chi-Square	823.607
	df	36
	Sig.	.000

Communalities

	Initial
Lack of access	.475
Lack of personal device availability	.230
Lack of setting up device cost	.618
Lack of free tools availability	.482
Lack of good internet bandwidth	.619
Inaccuracy of AI-generated responses	.494
Over-reliance on AI reducing independent learning	.473
Privacy concerns	.478
Lack of knowledge about new technologies introduced	.492

Extraction Method: Principal Axis Factoring.

Figure 9. Student's factor analysis (Output from SPSS)

Factor Matrix[a]

a. 2 factors extracted. 9 iterations required.

Factor Correlation Matrix

Factor	1	2
1	1.000	.659
2	.659	1.000

Extraction Method: Principal Axis Factoring.
Rotation Method: Oblimin with Kaiser Normalization.

Pattern Matrix[a]

	Factor	
	1	2
Lack of setting up device cost	.880	
Lack of good internet bandwidth	.758	.115
Lack of free tools availability	.691	
Lack of access	.678	
Lack of personal device availability	.468	
Privacy concerns	-.127	.864
Over-reliance on AI reducing independent learning		.716
Lack of knowledge about new technologies introduced	.129	.661
Inaccuracy of AI-generated responses	.149	.650

Extraction Method: Principal Axis Factoring.
Rotation Method: Oblimin with Kaiser Normalization.[a]
a. Rotation converged in 5 iterations.

Structure Matrix

	Factor	
	1	2
Lack of setting up device cost	.866	.559
Lack of good internet bandwidth	.833	.614
Lack of access	.724	.516
Lack of free tools availability	.701	.471
Lack of personal device availability	.442	.270
Privacy concerns	.443	.780
Inaccuracy of AI-generated responses	.577	.748
Lack of knowledge about new technologies introduced	.565	.746
Over-reliance on AI reducing independent learning	.513	.743

Extraction Method: Principal Axis Factoring.
Rotation Method: Oblimin with Kaiser Normalization.

Figure 10. Total variance of students (Output from SPSS)

Total Variance Explained

Factor	Initial Eigenvalues			Rotation Sums of Squared Loadings[a]
	Total	% of Variance	Cumulative %	Total
1	4.663	51.812	51.812	3.766
2	1.158	12.866	64.678	3.527
3	.814	9.041	73.719	
4	.505	5.606	79.325	
5	.455	5.052	84.377	
6	.428	4.755	89.132	
7	.359	3.988	93.120	
8	.340	3.775	96.895	
9	.279	3.105	100.000	

Extraction Method: Principal Axis Factoring.

a. When factors are correlated, sums of squared loadings cannot be added to obtain a total variance.

To support the suitability and adaptability of factor analysis, Kaiser-Meyer-Olkin (KMO) and Bartlett's Test were done (shown in Figure 8), which showed the KMO value is 0.897 (it is required to be above 0.6) and Bartlett's Test of Sphericity is significant ($p < 0.001$) (SÜRÜCÜ et al., 2022). These two tests showed that the factor analysis done here is appropriate. Further to extract the factors, total variance was calculated, and it was found that Factor 1 explains 51.812% of the variance and Factor 2 adds another 12.866%, which makes the cumulative variance explained to be 64.678% (Figure 10). This was computed with the help of eigenvalue calculations shown in the Figure. Principal Axis Factoring with Oblimin rotation was employed for better results. From Figure 9, we can see that two factors are identified under which our challenges are present, and the pattern matrix shows the high loadings computed the challenges.

Factor 1 is the "Technological and Access-related Barrier". These include factors that may have arisen because of infrastructural or economic barriers. These challenges were namely the lack of setting up the device costs (.880), lack of personal device availability (.468), lack of good internet bandwidth (.758), lack of free tools (.691), and lack of access (.678).

Another factor that was identified was "Concerns about Usage and Reliability". This might have come into existence because of the psychological and trust-related issues seen by the students. The high loadings included in this were privacy concerns (.864), over-reliance on AI reducing independent learning (.716), inaccuracy of AI-generated responses (.650), and lack of knowledge about new technologies introduced (.661).

Figure 11. Kaiser-Meyer-Olkin (KMO) and Bartlett's test (Output from SPSS)

KMO and Bartlett's Test

Kaiser-Meyer-Olkin Measure of Sampling Adequacy.		.732
Bartlett's Test of Sphericity	Approx. Chi-Square	110.746
	df	15
	Sig.	.000

Communalities

	Initial
Lack of technical knowledge/training	.345
Resistance from students/teachers	.295
High cost or lack of access	.209
AI-generated content is inaccurate	.209
Over-reliance on AI affecting student critical thinking	.265
Privacy concerns	.336

Extraction Method: Principal Axis Factoring.

Figure 12. Student's factor analysis (Output from SPSS)

Structure Matrix

	Factor 1	Factor 2
Lack of technical knowledge/training	.704	.361
Privacy concerns	.671	.371
Over-reliance on AI affecting student critical thinking	.605	.237
AI-generated content is inaccurate	.441	.420
High cost or lack of access	.258	.665
Resistance from students/teachers	.447	.634

Extraction Method: Principal Axis Factoring.
Rotation Method: Oblimin with Kaiser Normalization

Pattern Matrix[a]

	Factor 1	Factor 2
Lack of technical knowledge/training	.692	
Over-reliance on AI affecting student critical thinking	.643	
Privacy concerns	.643	
AI-generated content is inaccurate	.310	.269
High cost or lack of access		.708
Resistance from students/teachers	.181	.546

Extraction Method: Principal Axis Factoring.
Rotation Method: Oblimin with Kaiser Normalization.[a]
a. Rotation converged in 5 iterations.

Factor Correlation Matrix

Factor	1	2
1	1.000	.488
2	.488	1.000

Extraction Method: Principal Axis Factoring.
Rotation Method: Oblimin with Kaiser Normalization.

Factor Matrix[a]

a. Attempted to extract 2 factors. More than 25 iterations required. (Convergence =.003). Extraction was terminated.

Figure 13. Total variance of students (Output from SPSS)

Total Variance Explained

Factor	Initial Eigenvalues			Rotation Sums of Squared Loadings[a]
1	2.539	42.309	42.309	1.773
2	1.057	17.611	59.920	1.345
3	.789	13.157	73.077	
4	.670	11.172	84.248	
5	.497	8.276	92.524	
6	.449	7.476	100.000	

Extraction Method: Principal Axis Factoring.

a. When factors are correlated, sums of squared loadings cannot be added to obtain a total variance.

To support the usage of Factor analysis, tests like Kaiser-Meyer-Olkin (KMO) and Bartlett's Test were done, and it was seen that both are significant (Figure 11). The KMO value was seen as 0.732 (it is required to be above 0.6), which indicates moderate sampling adequacy and that the data was adequate for factor analysis. Bartlett's Test of Sphericity was significant ($p < 0.001$), which showed that factor analysis is appropriate here. Following this, Principal Axis Factoring with Oblimin rotation was done, and concluded that there exist two underlying factors. Factor 1 explains 42.3% of the variance, and Factor 2 adds another 17.6%. This made the cumulative variance 59.92%, which is considered acceptable. This is done with the help of the eigenvalues shown in Figure 13. Along with this, Principal Axis Factoring with Oblimin rotation method was used so that we could have defined factor values (Figure 12).

One of the identified factors was "Pedagogical and Technical Readiness Barriers," which is expected to result from the gap in technical and digital skills amongst teachers in their usage of AI tools. The high loadings included in this were lack of technical knowledge/ training (.692), over-reliance on AI is affecting students' critical thinking (.643), and privacy concerns (.643).

Another important factor was seen as "Systemic and Infrastructure-related Barriers". This factor was made by challenges like high cost or lack of access (.708) and resistance from students/teachers (.546). Institutional limitations or issues of training and funding are the main areas that are being focused on in this factor.

General Observations

If we see the overall implication, it can be identified that both the students and teachers are aware of the AI tools present for the learning and teaching of the English language. Given that its impact is highly influential, there exists a potential for AI tools to expand in English learning and teaching practices. Though some tools like Chatbot saw highly significant relationships, other tools were also used by the students and the teachers, but their mean usage was seen to be comparatively lower than that of Chatbots (Habib et al., 2024). Looking at the gender differences, there was no statistically significant relationship seen between the males and the females. The high usage of Chatbots like ChatGPT by both students and teachers might be because of the high knowledge and exposure of this tool all over India, along with the hype it has created in recent times, which is alarming. It was seen that primarily, students use these AI tools for translation and understanding difficult texts, whereas teachers prefer them for interactive learning and grammar improvement. The tools might also be useful enough in a variety of other sections, and to boost their applicability, there is a need to include more training programs and a support system for students as well as teachers. There were a couple of challenges faced by students and teachers separately, like Technological and Access-related Barriers, concerns about Usage and Reliability, Pedagogical and Technical Readiness Barriers, Systemic and Infrastructure-related Barriers, which included a set of challenges that were asked in the questionnaire.

CONCLUSION

Integrating artificial intelligence in the form of their tools into English learning and teaching can cause a lot of transformation in the education system of India. This research paper focuses on this very issue and helps in gathering information from the tier 1 cities of India. It figures out how important it is for the people of India to utilize and understand these tools effectively in their everyday lives. These tools include Virtual Mentor, Voice assistant, Presentation translator, Automatic assessment, Chatbot, and Duolingo (Liang, 2023). Looking at each one of these, we can very easily notice how they can be prominently used in improving their overall skills in English and making their academic and personal work easier. Presentation translator, for example, can help the students understand the material more easily, and this is easily accessible for them. Similarly, if we talk about teachers, Automatic assessment can be an easier way to grade students' work. This can help them utilize their time in other areas as well. Students have mainly used these tools to help themselves in Translation & Understanding Difficult Texts and in Writing Assistance, which has increased their English proficiency. Whereas, the teachers have used these AI tools in Interactive Learning, Grammar & Writing Assistance, and Pronunciation & Speaking Practices (Umang & Jain, 2020).

It is quite clear now that the teachers and students need to have an active knowledge of these emerging tools. Whereas, from the data collected and analyzed, it was seen that though both of them had enough knowledge about the existence of these tools, the only ones that came forward were the most hyped ones, such as Chatbots (e.g., ChatGPT) (Karataş et al., 2024). This might be the case because this is overly used in India and is heavily hyped. New features coming up in these are of high focus for the youngsters and are engaged with on the internet. Due to all this, there is a lack of knowledge about various other tools that might be more helpful and proficient in a sector-specific problem. Similar to this problem, many other problems were faced by the students and the teachers. It involved the lack of access, lack of technical skills and knowledge, issues in internet connectivity, lack of training, and many more which restricted the usage of these tools. Although these were not very prominent (Aghaziarati et al., 2023).

The overall challenges that were faced were divided into factors so that grouping became easy. For students, the major areas were "Technological and Access-related Barrier". These include factors lack of setting up the device costs, a lack of personal device availability, a lack of good internet bandwidth, etc. (Msekelwa, 2024). Another important issue that arose was "Concerns about Usage and Reliability," which included privacy concerns, over-reliance on AI reducing independent learning, etc. Even the teachers faced many difficulties in adapting to these AI tools. Their major challenges were "Pedagogical and Technical Readiness Barriers," which are expected to result from the lack of technical knowledge/training, over-reliance on AI affecting students' critical thinking, and privacy concerns. Another important challenge was seen as "Systemic and Infrastructure-related Barriers that included high cost or lack of access and resistance from students/teachers (Owan et al., 2023).

Tier 1 cities are considered as the hubs of technological advancement and because of that there have been improvements in internet connectivity (Mullammaa, 2010). The high prices and costs of adaption didn't come out to be an alarming issue since the socioeconomic factors hold a much greater impact in enabling them to have access to such resources. This exposure of AI tools in transforming the English language system has helped India to improve in the global trends as well (Roy & Putatunda, 2023). To boost the economy of a country, it is essential to improve the English proficiency and value it in the coming times.

Limitations and Future Scope

This analysis limits its study to the tier 1 cities of India, but there is a need to study the rural areas of India as well to have a better understanding of the impact of AI tools usage on English proficiency. Most likely, future researchers can help identify the problems in expanding this in rural areas and help analyze the policies and programs initiated by the government or the schools to employ these technologies in improving the teaching and learning systems. It will also give a wider area for study so that statistically significant results might come, and the familiarity can be well recorded based on the gender, age, and experience levels of the teachers. The scope can also encompass the concepts of AI literacy, which can help us better understand the other tools that might be available for English proficiency and how much impact its transformation can cause in the education system (Holmes & Tuomi, 2022).

Recommendations

To improve and change these challenges faced by the students and teachers, it is required to make some changes are required for students and teachers. Students should be adhered with the features of these tools and various issues such as affordability, access, cost, etc, so that they understand the concept of equitable access to these tools. Along with this guidance should be provided and they should be made to attend various training programs that can help them with the usage of these tools, along with the benefits and challenges that might come along. Similarly, for teachers, seminars should be organized to enhance the AI tools' proficiency and their importance in growing the English learning systems. Support should be offered by the government along with some resources so that AI tool usage is heavily promoted, and further, it can be transferred and taught to the students. There were many infrastructural challenges seen that can be addressed by the government in uplifting the transformation of the English language in the teaching and learning system of India.

REFERENCES

Abou Elassad, Z. E., Mousannif, H., Moatassime, H. A., & Karkouch, A. (2020). The application of machine learning techniques for driving behavior analysis: A conceptual framework and a systematic literature review. *Engineering Applications of Artificial Intelligence*, *87*(1), 103312. Advance online publication. DOI: 10.1016/j.engappai.2019.103312

Abulibdeh, A., Zaidan, E., & Abulibdeh, R. (2024). Navigating the confluence of artificial intelligence and education for sustainable development in the era of Industry 4.0: Challenges, opportunities, and ethical dimensions. *Journal of Cleaner Production*, *437*(1), 140527. DOI: 10.1016/j.jclepro.2023.140527

Aghaziarati, A., Nejatifar, S., & Abedi, A. (2023). *Artificial intelligence in education: Investigating teacher attitudes*. KMAN Publication Inc.

Alam, A. (2021). Possibilities and apprehensions in the landscape of artificial intelligence in education. *2021 International Conference on Computational Intelligence and Computing Applications (ICCICA)* (pp. 1-8). Nagpur, India: IEEE. DOI: 10.1109/ICCICA52458.2021.9697272

AlAwamrah, A. F., Ajmi, H. A., Darawsheh, N. A., Alrashdan, H., & Alkailanee, K. K. (2024). Analyzing students' perceptions about the values of digital citizenship. *Journal of Statistics Applications & Probability*, *13*(3), 1279–1288. DOI: 10.18576/jsap/130412

Anand, N., Indapurkar, K., & Jain, A. (2023). Analysis of consumer behaviour in e-purchasing online courses post COVID-19. *International Journal of Pluralism and Economics Education*, *14*(3), 382–392.

Balamurugan, R. J., Al-Bonsrulah, H. A., Raja, V., Kumar, L., Kannan, S. D., Madasamy, S. K., Rasheed, R., Rajendran, P., & Al-Bahrani, M. (2022). Design and multiperspectivity-based performance investigations of H-Darrieus vertical axis wind turbine through computational fluid dynamics adopted with moving reference frame approaches. *The International Journal of Low Carbon Technologies*, *17*(4), 1481–1494. DOI: 10.1093/ijlct/ctac055

Chassignol, M., Khoroshavin, A., Klimova, A., & Bilyatdinova, A. (2018). Artificial intelligence trends in education: A narrative overview. *Procedia Computer Science*, *136*, 16–24. DOI: 10.1016/j.procs.2018.08.233

Delello, J. A., Sung, W., Mokhtari, K., & Giuseppe, T. D. (2023). Exploring college students' awareness of AI and ChatGPT: Unveiling perceived benefits and risks. *Journal of Inclusive Methodology and Technology in Learning and Teaching*, *3*(1).

Edmett, D., Ichaporia, N., Crompton, D., & Crichton, R. (2024). *Artificial intelligence and English language teaching: preparing for the future* (2nd ed.). British Council.

Ellikkal, A., & Rajamohan, S. (2024). AI-enabled personalized learning: Empowering management students for improving engagement and academic performance. *Vilakshan - XIMB. Journal of Management, 21*(1), 89–104.

Ferikoğlu, D., & Akgün, E. (2022). An investigation of teachers' artificial intelligence awareness: A scale development study. *Malaysian Online Journal of Educational Technology, 10*(5), 215–231. DOI: 10.52380/mojet.2022.10.3.407

Fitria, T. N. (2021). Artificial intelligence (AI) in education: Using AI tools for teaching and learning process. *Proceeding Seminar Nasional & Call For Papers, 1*, pp. 134-147.

Galstyan Sargsyan, R. (2019). Towards the development of an effective online language learning model in a university environment. *Teaching English with Technology, 19*(3), 43–60.

Garrel, J. V., & Mayer, J. (2023). Artificial intelligence in studies—Use of ChatGPT and AI-based tools among students in Germany. *Humanities & Social Sciences Communications, 10*(1), 799. DOI: 10.1057/s41599-023-02304-7

Government of India. (2020). *National Education Policy*. Ministry of Human Resource Development.

Green, N. (2023, October 6). Schools really messed up with social media. Now, we have a second chance. *Slate*.

Habib, S., Vogel, T., Anli, X., & Thorne, E. (2024). How does generative artificial intelligence impact student creativity? *Journal of Creativity, 34*(1), 1–19. DOI: 10.1016/j.yjoc.2023.100072

Halaweh, M. (2023). ChatGPT in education: Strategies for responsible implementation. *Contemporary Educational Technology, 15*(3), ep421. DOI: 10.30935/cedtech/13036

Harry, A., & Sayudin. (2023). Role of AI in education. *Interdiciplinary Journal and Hummanity, 2*(2), 117–124.

Heaven, W. D. (2020). OpenAI's new language generator GPT-3 is shockingly good and completely mindless. *MIT Technology Review*.

Hien, T. T. (2024). AI tools in teaching and learning English academic writing skills. *VNU Journal of Foreign Studies, 40*(1), 1–13.

Holmes, W., & Tuomi, I. (2022). State of the art and practice in AI in education. *European Journal of Education, 57*(1), 70–86. DOI: 10.1111/ejed.12533

Hong, E., Hartzell, S. A., & Greene, M. T. (2011). Fostering creativity in the classroom: Effects of teachers' epistemological beliefs, motivation, and goal orientation. *The Journal of Creative Behavior, 45*(4), 247–265.

Huang, X., Zou, D., Cheng, G., Chen, X., & Xie, H. (2023). Trends, research issues, and applications of artificial intelligence in language education. *Journal of Educational Technology & Society, 26*(1), 112–131.

Hughes, A. (2023). *ChatGPT: Everything you need to know about OpenAI's GPT-4 tool*. BBC Science Focus.

Indapurkar, K., & Raj, M. (2017). Financial literacy among educated urban youth: Issues and challenges (An empirical study among the educated youth in Delhi NCR). *International Journal of Economic Research, 14*(7), 383–392.

Jaiswal, A., & Arun, C. J. (2021). Potential of artificial intelligence for transformation of the education sector. *International Journal of Education and Development Using Information and Communication Technology, 17*(1), 142–158.

John, N., & Indapurkar, D. (2020). Women empowerment: A study to analyse women perspective about empowerment in Delhi/NCR Region. *Journal of Emerging Technologies and Innovative Research, 7*(11), 757–762.

Kamala, D., & Kamalakar, D. G. (2023). AI is transforming education technology and education system in India. *Indian Journal of Social Research, 64*(1), 99–110.

Karataş, F., Abedi, F. Y., Gunyel, F. O., Karadeniz, D., & Kuzgun, Y. (2024). Incorporating AI in foreign language education: An investigation into ChatGPT's effect on foreign language learners. *Education and Information Technologies, 29*(3), 3873–3895. DOI: 10.1007/s10639-024-12574-6

Katsantonis, A., & Katsantonis, I. G. (2024). University students' attitudes toward artificial intelligence: An exploratory study of the cognitive, emotional, and behavioural dimensions of AI attitudes. *Education Sciences, 14*(3), 988. DOI: 10.3390/educsci14090988

Kelly, A., Sullivan, M., & Strampel, K. (2023). Generative artificial intelligence: University student awareness, experience, and confidence in use across disciplines. *Journal of University Teaching & Learning Practice, 20*(7), 1–17. DOI: 10.53761/1.20.6.12

Khosravi, H., Shum, S. B., Chen, G., Conati, C., Tsai, Y.-S., Kay, J., & ... Gašević, D. (2022). Explainable artificial intelligence in education. *Computers and Education: Artificial Intelligence, 3*.

Liang, Y. (2023). Balancing: The effects of AI tools in educational contexts. *Frontiers in Humanities and Social Sciences, 1*(7), 7–10. DOI: 10.54691/fhss.v3i8.5531

Lin, C., Chai, S. C., Jong, Y. M., Dai, Y., & ... Chai, C. S. (2021). Modelling the structural relationship among primary students' motivation to learn artificial intelligence. *Computers and Education: Artificial Intelligence, 2*.

Lukpat, A. (2023). JPMorgan restricts employees from using ChatGPT. *The Wall street journal*.

Marda, V. (2018). Artificial intelligence policy in India: A framework for engaging the limits of data-driven decision-making. *Philosophical Transactions. Series A, Mathematical, Physical, and Engineering Sciences, 376*(2133), 20180087. DOI: 10.1098/rsta.2018.0087 PMID: 30323001

Marx, J. (2023). ChatGPT im Studium [Befehle für effektives Lernen.]. *Top (Madrid)*, •••, 10.

Mehra, D., & Indapurkar, D. (2020). Financial literacy and investment behaviour: A study on the working-age population of India. *Journal of Emerging Technologies and Innovative Research*, *7*(5), 728–733.

Mertala, P., & Fagerlund, J. (2024). Finnish 5th and 6th graders misconceptions about artificial intelligence. *International Journal of Child-Computer Interaction*, *39*, 39. DOI: 10.1016/j.ijcci.2023.100630

Miller, M. (2022). *ChatGPT, chatbots and artificial intelligence in education.* ditchthat-textbook.com.

Minsky, M. (1969). *Semantic information processing*. MIT Press.

Moor, J. (2006). The Dartmouth College artificial intelligence conference: The next fifty years. *AI Magazine*, *27*(4), 87–91.

Msekelwa, P. Z. (2024). The impact of AI on education: Innovative tools and trends. *Journal of Artificial Intelligence General Science*, *3*(2), 227–236. DOI: 10.60087/jaigs.v5i1.198

Mullammaa, K. (2010). ICT in Language Learning: Benefits and Methodological Implications. *International Education Studies*, *3*(3), 149–154. DOI: 10.5539/ies.v3n1p38

Mushthoza, D. A., Syariatin, N., Tahalele, O., & Telussa, S. I., Rasmita, & Mokodenseho, S. (2023). Analyzing The Impact Of Artificial Intelligence (AI) On The Future Of English Language Teaching And Learning. *Journal of Education*, *5*(3), 966–975.

Okulich-Kazarin, V., Artyukhov, A., Skowron, Ł., Artyukhova, N., & Wołowiec, T. (2024). Will AI Become a Threat to Higher Education Sustainability? A Study of Students' Views. *MDPI. Sustainability*, *16*(3).

Owan, V. J., Abang, K. B., Idika, D. O., Etta, E. O., & Bassey, B. A. (2023). Exploring the potential of artificial intelligence tools in educational measurement and assessment. *Eurasia Journal of Mathematics, Science and Technology Education*, *19*(7), em2307. DOI: 10.29333/ejmste/13428

Papapicco, C. (2020). Google mini: Italian example of artificial pro-sociality. *Online Journal of Communication and Media Technologies*, *10*(4), e202015. DOI: 10.29333/ojcmt/7995

Pokrivcakova, S. (2019). Preparing teachers for the application of AI-powered technologies in foreign language education. *Journal of Language and Cultural Education*, *7*(2), 174–191. DOI: 10.2478/jolace-2019-0025

Pont-Niclòs, I., Echegoyen-Sanz, Y., Gómez, P. O., & Ezpeleta, A. M. (2024). Creativity and artificial intelligence: A study with prospective teachers. *Digital education review, 49*, 1-16.

Rodway, P., & Schepman, A. (2023). The impact of adopting AI educational technologies on projected course satisfaction in university students. *Computers and Education: Artificial Intelligence, 4*.

Roy, D., & Putatunda, T. (2023). From Textbooks to Chatbots: Integrating AI in English literature classrooms of India. *Journal of e-learning and knowledge society, 19*(3), 1-12.

Sandhu, R. (2020). Adoption of AI-Chatbots to Enhance Student learning experience in higher education in India. *2020 4th International Conference on Intelligent Computing and Control Systems (ICICCS)* (pp. 787-791). IEEE.

Selwyn, N. (2022). The future of AI and education: Some cautionary notes. *European Journal of Education, 57*(1), 87–99. DOI: 10.1111/ejed.12532

Srivastava, S. K. (2018). Artificial Intelligence: Way forward for India. *Journal of Information Systems and Technology Management, 15*(1), 1–15.

Sürücü, L., Yıkılmaz, İ., & Maşlakçı, A. (2022). Exploratory factor analysis (EFA) in quantitative researches and practical considerations. *Gümüşhane Üniversitesi Sağlık Bilimleri Dergisi, 13*(2), 947–965.

Tan, J. T. (2023). Implications of AI innovation on economic growth: A panel data study. *Journal of Economic Structures, 12*(1).

Tapalova, O., & Zhiyenbayeva, N. (2022). Artificial Intelligence in Education: AIEd for Personalised Learning. *Electronic Journal of e-Learning, 20*(4), 408–417. DOI: 10.34190/ejel.20.5.2597

Tolstykh, O. M., & Oshchepkova, T. (2024). Beyond ChatGPT: roles that artificial intelligence tools can play. *Discover Artifcial Intelligence, 4*(1).

Umang, D., & Jain, N. (2020). Teaching Assessment Tool: Using AI and Secure Techniques. *International Journal of Education and Management Engineering, 10*(1), 12–21. DOI: 10.5815/ijeme.2020.03.02

Vazhayil, A., Shetty, R., Rao, B., & Nagarajan, A. (2019). Focusing on Teacher Education to Introduce AI in Schools: Perspectives and Illustrative Findings. *2019 IEEE Tenth International Conference on Technology for Education (T4E)* (pp. 71-77). IEEE. DOI: 10.1109/T4E.2019.00021

Watters, A. (2021). *Teaching machines: The history of personalized learning*. The MIT Press. DOI: 10.7551/mitpress/12262.001.0001

Xatamova, N., & Ashurov, J. (2024). The Future of Legal English Learning: Integrating AI into ESP Education. *SPAST Reports, 6*(1), 1–10.

Xia, Q., Chiu, T. K., & Lee, M., I., T., & Dai. (2022). A self-determination theory design approach for inclusive and diverse artificial intelligence (AI) K-12 education. *Computers & Education*, •••, 187.

Yang, J. (2022). Perceptions of preservice teachers on AI chatbots in English education. *International Journal of Internet. Broadcasting and Communication*, *24*(4), 44–52.

Zhang, Y., Qin, G., Cheng, L., Marimuthu, K., & Kumar, B. S. (2021). Interactive Smart Educational System Using AI for Students in the Higher Education Platform. *Journal of Multiple-valued Logic and Soft Computing*, *36*(1-2), 83–98.

Zhao, L., Wu, X., & Luo, H. (2022). Developing AI Literacy for Primary and Middle School Teachers in China: Based on a Structural Equation Modeling Analysis. *MDPI. Sustainability (Basel)*, *14*(19), 14549. DOI: 10.3390/su142114549

Zhu, M. (2022). Factors Influencing Analysis for Level of Engineering English Education Based on Artificial Intelligence Technology. *Mathematical Problems in Engineering*, *2022*, 2022. DOI: 10.1155/2022/4447209

Chapter 14
AI and Emerging Digital Worlds as a Tool, not a Replacement

James A. Martinez
https://orcid.org/0009-0000-5853-7300
Loma Linda University, USA

ABSTRACT

This chapter explores how artificial intelligence (AI) and immersive technologies are reshaping education while reaffirming the essential role of educators. AI supports adaptive learning, gamification, and workforce readiness, yet cannot replace human traits like empathy and ethical judgment (Papert, 1980; Johnson, 2022). Grounded in critical posthumanism (Bayne, 2015) and digital ethics (Selwyn, 2019), the chapter shows how AI—through tools like digital twins, XAI, and educational games—can personalize learning, support equity, and enhance CTE programs (Holmes et al., 2022; Stone et al., 2021). Educators remain central to interpreting AI feedback, fostering reflection, and ensuring student well-being (UNESCO, 2021). The chapter emphasizes that responsible implementation requires teacher agency, data transparency, and strategic policy. Ultimately, it argues for a collaborative model where AI enhances, not replaces, human-centered education.

INTRODUCTION

Artificial intelligence (AI) and automated technologies have woven themselves into nearly every facet of contemporary life. Individuals now routinely order food, shop online, and engage with highly responsive chatbots that deliver round-the-clock customer service; predictive analytics suggest items of interest, and autonomous vehicles promise reduced human intervention on the roads (Marr, 2018). The educational sector is no exception:

DOI: 10.4018/979-8-3373-5092-9.ch014

AI technologies are influencing how students learn, how teachers teach, and how schools operate on an administrative level.

The pace of AI adoption in education has accelerated dramatically since 2020, with global educational AI market value projected to reach $20 billion by 2027, growing at a compound annual rate of over 45% (Kaplan & Haenlein, 2019; Holmes et al., 2022). Educational institutions now implement an increasingly sophisticated array of AI applications: automated grading systems evaluate assignments and provide feedback; intelligent tutoring systems adapt content to individual learning patterns; administrative chatbots handle routine student inquiries; and recommendation engines suggest personalized learning pathways based on performance data (Holmes et al., 2022; Zawacki-Richter et al., 2019).

These developments raise fundamental questions about the evolving role of educators, who may worry that traditional pedagogies are changing in the face of AI's rapid encroachment (Johnson, 2022). Yet historical precedents suggest that technology does not necessarily render professionals irrelevant, as educators play a critical role in preparing students for an AI-driven workforce while preserving the humanity at the core of learning (Papert, 1980; Johnson, 2022; UNESCO, 2021).

The theoretical framework for understanding AI's educational impact has evolved beyond simple techno-determinism toward what Bayne (2015) calls "critical posthumanism"—a perspective recognizing that human and technological agencies are increasingly entangled yet distinctly valuable. Similarly, Selwyn's (2019) concept of "ed-tech's 'state of exception'" cautions against treating educational technology as inherently beneficial without critical evaluation of its societal implications. These frameworks help us navigate the tension between technological enhancement and human-centered education (Pedró et al., 2019).

Despite concerns that robots and AI could replace human instructors, this chapter posits that teachers, rather than being supplanted, remain indispensable. Amid these sweeping changes, the challenge lies in reconciling the benefits of AI with the human elements that define transformative education. AI can streamline classroom tasks, provide timely data analytics, and offer personalized learning experiences. Yet, it cannot replicate the empathy, ethical judgment, and capacity to inspire that characterize a great teacher (Papert, 1980; Morgan, 2023). Automated systems do not share the lived experiences of students, nor do they fully grasp the cultural and emotional nuances that shape individual intellectual growth.

Contemporary labor market research reinforces this position. The World Economic Forum's Future of Jobs Report 2023 indicates that while AI will automate approximately 85 million jobs by 2025, it will simultaneously create 97 million new roles—many requiring uniquely human capabilities such as creative problem solving, ethical reasoning, and interpersonal intelligence (World Economic Forum, 2023). Educational systems must therefore prepare students not only to work with AI tools but to excel in areas where humans maintain distinct advantages (Zhang & Ghorbani, 2020).

By strategically integrating AI as a tool rather than viewing it as a competitor, teachers can enrich instruction, foster critical thinking, and prepare learners for an increasingly complex and automated world (Smith & Brown, 2020). Consequently, the goal is not to replace educators but to empower them with the skills, mindsets, and resources needed to harness AI as a tool for more meaningful and effective teaching that cultivates creativity, problem-solving, and moral responsibility. The challenge becomes one of adaptation rather than replacement—a historical pattern observed across previous technological revolutions (Brynjolfsson & McAfee, 2014).

LIVING IN AN AUTONOMOUS AND DIGITAL WORLD

The continuous march toward automation has led to the normalization of tasks once considered futuristic. People frequently use smartphone apps to order groceries, manage finances, and plan travel routes. Chatbots and virtual assistants employ natural language processing to anticipate user needs, offering suggestions and reminders. Meanwhile, autonomous transportation—from self-driving cars to drone deliveries—redefines how mobility and logistics are handled. These advancements illustrate AI's extensive reach, prompting educational systems to ask whether they are adequately preparing learners for a setting where human roles are shifting (Smith & Brown, 2020; Allen & West, 2023).

Educational institutions now deploy similar technologies to enhance administrative efficiency and learning experiences. Natural language processing powers academic writing assistants that provide feedback on structure and clarity; recommendation systems suggest supplementary materials based on student engagement patterns; and automated scheduling tools optimize resource allocation across campuses (Zawacki-Richter et al., 2019). The underlying algorithmic principles—machine learning, neural networks, and predictive analytics—mirror those driving consumer applications, creating a technological coherence between educational and everyday environments (Holmes et al., 2022).

For instance, the same machine-learning algorithms that power consumer preference predictions in e-commerce can be tailored to educational contexts, generating insights into student performance and highlighting learning gaps. However, the teacher remains the ultimate interpreter of this data. Only educators can contextualize raw statistics in light of each student's background, strengths, and emotional well-being (Bartlett, 2021). AI might flag a student's struggle with fractions, but determining whether this is due to math anxiety, foundational skill deficits, or personal circumstances requires human insight. Thus, teachers stand as critical conduits for turning AI analytics into empathetic, actionable educational strategies.

The concept of "explainable AI" (XAI) has emerged as particularly crucial in educational settings. Unlike "black box" algorithms that obscure decision-making processes, XAI systems provide transparent rationales for their recommendations, enabling educators to evaluate and potentially override automated suggestions (Gunning et al., 2019). This transparency supports teacher agency while facilitating professional learning about AI's capabilities and limitations. As Khosravi et al. (2022) argue, "interpretable learning analytics are essential for maintaining human judgment at the center of educational decision-making, particularly when algorithmic recommendations affect vulnerable student populations" (p. 156).

This human-AI partnership extends to curriculum design, where automated content analysis can identify knowledge gaps in existing materials while teachers ensure cultural relevance and pedagogical soundness. Such collaboration exemplifies how AI functions most effectively as an amplifier of human expertise rather than as its replacement (Pedró et al., 2019).

THE ROBOTIC WORLD ALONGSIDE HUMANS

Beyond software-based AI, robotics constitutes another frontier reshaping industries. From assembly lines with robotic arms to collaborative robots (co-bots) aiding surgeons, the workforce increasingly aligns human skills with mechanical efficiency (Marr, 2018). These scenarios depict a future where robots manage repetitive or hazardous tasks, liberating human workers for creativity, complex problem-solving, and interpersonal collaboration. In educational contexts, this trend highlights the need to prepare students not only for technical competence in robotics and coding but also for the ethical and collaborative dimensions of working alongside machines (UNESCO, 2021).

Educational robotics has evolved from simple programming exercises to sophisticated project-based learning environments where students engage with increasingly autonomous systems. Platforms like LEGO Education SPIKE Prime, VEX Robotics, and Arduino-based projects allow learners to design, build, and program robots with varying degrees of complexity, developing not only STEM skills but also design thinking and collaborative problem-solving capabilities (Ioannou & Makridou, 2018). These environments simulate workplace scenarios where humans and robots coordinate efforts toward shared objectives—a growing reality across manufacturing, healthcare, and logistics sectors (Khanlari, 2016).

Research on human-robot interaction in educational settings reveals compelling patterns. Social robots serving as tutors or learning companions can increase student engagement, particularly among learners with special needs or language barriers (Belpaeme et al., 2018). However, these same studies emphasize that robots most effectively complement rather than replace human teachers, with optimal outcomes occurring when robotic systems operate under educator guidance. As Causo et al. (2016) conclude, "educational robots serve primarily as motivational and instructional tools that extend teacher capability rather than substitute for human instruction" (p. 8).

Hands-on STEM and robotics programs can foster iterative learning, nurturing resilience and ingenuity. Students engage in trial-and-error design processes, coding sequences, and teamwork as they debug or refine robotic tasks. This blend of abstract theory and tangible implementation underscores the teacher's pivotal role in facilitating real-world projects and guiding reflective discussions (Papert, 1980). By emphasizing creative engineering and problem-solving, schools can equip learners to thrive in a workforce increasingly augmented by robots, ensuring that human values and emotional intelligence remain central in technologically advanced settings (Morgan, 2023).

The skills developed through educational robotics directly transfer to emerging workforce needs. Analysis by Muro et al. (2020) indicates that workers across sectors increasingly require competencies in human-machine collaboration, algorithmic thinking, and systems evaluation—precisely the capabilities cultivated through well-designed robotics education. Moreover, robotics programs that incorporate ethical considerations around automation and job displacement help prepare students to engage thoughtfully with socioeconomic challenges accompanying technological transformation (Pedró et al., 2019).

AI-ENABLED CAREER AND TECHNICAL EDUCATION

Career and Technical Education (CTE) programs face unique challenges and opportunities in the age of AI-driven automation. Traditional vocational training emphasized hands-on practice with physical tools and materials—approaches that required substantial infrastructure investment and posed safety considerations for novice learners (Lynch, 2000). Digital technologies and AI systems now offer innovative solutions to these constraints while simultaneously preparing students for increasingly technological workplaces (Siegel & Gibbons, 2019).

INDUSTRY-SPECIFIC SIMULATIONS AND DIGITAL TWINS

Digital twins—virtual replicas of physical systems, processes, or environments—have revolutionized training across industries from healthcare to manufacturing (Barricelli et al., 2019). In nursing education, for example, AI-powered patient simulators respond physiologically to student interventions, allowing practice with high-risk scenarios without endangering actual patients (McGrath et al., 2018). Similarly, manufacturing education increasingly utilizes digital twins of production lines where students can practice optimization, troubleshooting, and maintenance procedures before transitioning to physical equipment (Lamb, 2019). These environments provide immediate feedback, track skill development longitudinally, and adapt difficulty levels to individual learning trajectories.

Virtual welding systems exemplify this approach's efficacy in traditional trades. Platforms like Lincoln Electric's VRTEX create immersive simulations where students develop proper technique while receiving real-time guidance on torch angle, travel speed, and workpiece positioning. Research by Stone et al. (2021) demonstrates that students trained initially on such systems achieve proficiency 23% faster when transitioning to actual welding tasks, while consuming 68% less material and energy—significant sustainability and cost advantages. The instructor's role shifts toward analyzing performance data, guiding reflection on automated feedback, and connecting virtual practice to industry standards and workplace scenarios.

VIRTUAL APPRENTICESHIPS AND REMOTE MENTORING

Digital technologies have expanded apprenticeship models beyond geographical constraints. Virtual apprenticeship platforms connect students with industry mentors globally, enabling observation of expert practices through livestreamed demonstrations, recorded procedures with interactive annotations, and collaborative problem-solving sessions (Karapanos et al., 2022). AI systems enhance these relationships by identifying optimal mentor-mentee pairings based on learning styles, career objectives, and personality factors, while also suggesting discussion topics and skill-building activities aligned with industry trends (Ramachandran & Young, 2019).

The COVID-19 pandemic accelerated adoption of these approaches, with programs like the UK's Digital Apprenticeships demonstrating that meaningful vocational training can occur in distributed environments when supported by appropriate technological infrastructure and pedagogical frameworks (Rivera & Ramirez, 2022). Post-pandemic, hybrid models combining in-person and virtual apprenticeship components have emerged as particularly effective for developing both technical and soft skills while maximizing accessibility (Kumar et al., 2022).

AI-POWERED SKILLS ASSESSMENT AND CAREER PATHWAY GUIDANCE

Artificial intelligence significantly enhances career guidance through sophisticated skills mapping and labor market analytics. AI systems can assess student competencies through performance in simulations, digital project portfolios, and automated technical assessments, then map these capabilities against real-time workforce data (Buckingham Shum et al., 2019). This approach enables personalized career pathway recommendations that reflect both individual strengths and emerging industry demands—a level of precision difficult to achieve through traditional counseling methods.

Platforms like IBM's SkillsBuild combine skills assessment with targeted microlearning experiences, connecting CTE students directly with industry-recognized credentials and entry-level employment opportunities (Kumar & Boulanger, 2020). Similarly, systems like Burning Glass Technologies analyze millions of job postings to identify emerging skill clusters and credential requirements, helping educational institutions align curriculum with workforce needs (Rainie & Anderson, 2017). These tools particularly benefit historically underserved populations by making career pathway information more transparent and accessible, potentially reducing equity gaps in workforce preparation (Bartlett, 2021).

The instructor's critical role persists in interpreting and contextualizing this information, helping students navigate both the quantitative data provided by AI systems and the qualitative dimensions of career selection—including workplace culture, personal values alignment, and long-term career satisfaction (Lynch et al., 2019). This human guidance ensures that AI-powered career recommendations serve as starting points for exploration rather than deterministic endpoints.

THE ESSENTIAL ROLE OF TEACHERS IN AN AI-DRIVEN WORKFORCE

As AI-driven systems increasingly manage tasks such as logistics, data entry, and even creative functions like writing or design, the future workforce will prioritize skills that complement rather than mirror machine intelligence (Smith & Brown, 2020; Morgan, 2023).

These capacities include ethical decision-making, empathy, cultural competency, and the ability to collaborate effectively in diverse teams. Consequently, the educator's role is more vital than ever in cultivating these human-centric abilities.

The World Economic Forum's Future of Jobs Report 2023 identifies critical thinking, creativity, emotional intelligence, and complex problem-solving as the skills least susceptible to automation while simultaneously most valuable in emerging roles (World Economic Forum, 2023). These capabilities—described by Deming (2017) as "non-routine interpersonal and analytical skills"—command increasing wage premiums across sectors. Educators play a crucial role in developing these competencies through instructional approaches that transcend knowledge transmission to emphasize applied problem-solving, collaborative inquiry, and ethical reasoning (Holmes et al., 2022).

Teachers also serve as essential AI literacy facilitators, helping students develop critical perspectives toward algorithmic systems. As Long and Magerko (2020) argue, comprehensive AI literacy encompasses not only technical understanding but also sociocultural awareness of how AI systems reflect and potentially amplify existing power dynamics and biases. Educators guide students in questioning algorithmic recommendations, examining underlying data for representational gaps, and considering ethical implications of automated decision-making (Pedró et al., 2019). This critical orientation toward technology prepares learners for informed civic participation in increasingly algorithmic societies (Kandlhofer et al., 2016).

Through project-based learning, case studies, and mentorship, teachers guide students in grappling with moral complexities, recognizing subtle social cues, and building inclusive group dynamics. Educators also play a critical role in helping students navigate AI's inherent limitations, such as algorithmic biases or overreliance on automated decision-making (UNESCO, 2021). By prompting learners to interrogate the ethical frameworks of AI tools, educators transform technology from a mere novelty into a subject of critical inquiry. Such an approach ensures that future generations are not only technologically proficient but also ethically responsible, prepared to shape AI's development in ways that serve the broader social good (Bartlett, 2021).

Perhaps most importantly, educators model balanced technology integration through their own professional practices. When teachers demonstrate thoughtful technology adoption—using AI tools while maintaining critical awareness of their limitations, prioritizing face-to-face interaction for emotionally complex discussions, and establishing appropriate boundaries around technology use—they provide students with living examples of healthy human-technology relationships (Selwyn, 2019). This modeling proves particularly vital as students navigate increasingly seamless integration of AI systems into their personal and professional lives (Zawacki-Richter et al., 2019).

THE GAMER'S EDGE: LEVERAGING AI FOR COMPETITIVE LEARNING

The competitive and collaborative nature of online gaming demonstrates how AI-driven feedback loops can improve engagement and accelerate skill acquisition (Deterding et al., 2011). Game algorithms that match players by skill level or track in-game performance can be adapted to educational settings, offering real-time progress updates and setting goals that sustain a sense of "flow." For instance, platforms integrating AI-based game mechanics can personalize difficulty levels, ensuring students remain challenged yet not overwhelmed (Morgan, 2023).

Research by Gee (2007) identifies specific game mechanics with powerful educational applications: achievement systems that visualize progress and motivate continued engagement; scaffolded challenges that gradually increase complexity while maintaining attainability; social mechanics that encourage peer collaboration and knowledge sharing; and narrative frameworks that contextualize abstract concepts within compelling storylines. Educational platforms increasingly incorporate these elements through AI systems that analyze student performance and dynamically adjust these mechanics to optimize engagement and learning outcomes (Plass et al., 2015).

Emerging AI-enhanced educational games exemplify these principles across disciplines. Platforms like Mangahigh use adaptive algorithms to personalize mathematical challenges based on individual skill levels, while providing achievement systems that celebrate incremental progress (Boaler, 2021). Similarly, language learning applications like Duolingo employ sophisticated natural language processing to evaluate pronunciation and syntax, offering immediate corrective feedback while adjusting lesson difficulty to maintain an optimal challenge level (Mitchell, 2022). These systems demonstrate how AI can enhance rather than replace human instruction by managing routine assessment and personalization, allowing teachers to focus on higher-order conceptual development and socio-emotional support (Zawacki-Richter et al., 2019).

Meta-analyses of game-based learning research demonstrate significant cognitive and social benefits when implemented thoughtfully. Studies by Clark et al. (2016) indicate that well-designed educational games improve problem-solving capabilities, enhance information retention, and increase student motivation across age groups and subject areas. The social dimensions of multiplayer educational games particularly benefit collaborative skills development, with research by Wouters et al. (2013) showing improvements in communication, resource sharing, and group decision-making among participants in team-based educational gaming environments.

Teachers can leverage these insights to foster deeper learning, particularly for students disengaged by traditional instruction. By framing lessons as game-like challenges—complete with points, badges, or leaderboards—educators can tap into the intrinsic motivation found in competitive and cooperative play. Platforms like Discord enable students to share solutions, discuss strategies, and support peers in real time, well beyond the physical classroom (Johnson, 2022). Such structures validate digital youth culture, bridging formal and informal learning ecosystems. Additionally, this "gamer's edge" underscores the synergy between

AI's adaptability and the teacher's capacity to design and moderate meaningful educational experiences.

CHILD'S PLAY IN THE DIGITAL ERA

Online gaming platforms and virtual collaborative spaces function as contemporary playgrounds where children develop problem-solving acumen, social negotiation skills, and strategic thinking (Deterding et al., 2011). Rather than viewing these digital environments as mere recreational outlets, educators are increasingly recognizing their educational potential (Bartlett, 2021). Minecraft, for example, offers a sandbox environment that fosters creativity, geometry, and resource management, while more expansive metaverse platforms enable students to engage in simulations that mirror real-world challenges (Chang & Xie, 2022).

Research by Kuhn et al. (2023) demonstrates that student-directed learning in platforms like Minecraft frequently involves computational thinking, spatial reasoning, and resource management skills that align with STEM curricular objectives but in contexts students find more engaging than traditional instruction. Similarly, studies by Cipollone et al. (2022) found that elementary and middle school students who regularly engaged with Roblox and similar platforms demonstrated enhanced problem-solving capabilities, particularly in areas requiring iterative design thinking and collaborative troubleshooting—skills increasingly valued in workplace settings.

A systematic review by Alawajee and Delafield-Butt (2021) synthesizing evidence from 42 peer-reviewed studies on Minecraft in education provides substantial support for gaming platforms' educational value. Their analysis revealed that Minecraft environments consistently foster "increased motivation, language development, and academic learning in subjects such as science and history" (Alawajee & Delafield-Butt, 2021, p. 19). This research particularly highlights the socially interactive and cooperative aspects of Minecraft that make it well-suited for educational applications across diverse subject areas.

The educational impact of Minecraft continues to expand, with recent data showing implementation "in over 10,000 schools across 40 countries" with "more than 600 pre-planned lessons across various subjects" (The Smarter Kid, 2024). Beyond academic benefits, research specifically examining social-emotional learning through Minecraft found that "more than 90% of surveyed teachers cited problem-solving, creativity, critical thinking, and collaboration as skills gained through using Minecraft in the classroom" (Minecraft Education, 2017). These social-emotional competencies represent increasingly valued workforce skills that traditional educational approaches often struggle to develop effectively.

A comprehensive systematic review by Slattery et al. (2025) provides substantial evidence for Minecraft's educational benefits across different age groups and contexts. Their analysis of 29 intervention studies found that Minecraft serves as an effective tool for improving both cognitive and academic outcomes, with particular benefits for "increased motivation, language development, and academic learning in subjects such as science and history" (Slattery et al., 2025, p. 3). This research confirms that when appropriately integrated into curriculum, gaming platforms can significantly enhance learning outcomes while maintaining high levels of student engagement.

These digital environments often function as what Ito et al. (2020) term "affinity spaces," where students develop expertise through peer mentoring and interest-driven learning, often achieving mastery in specific domains that exceeds grade-level expectations in related academic subjects. The informal learning occurring in these spaces can be remarkably sophisticated, with students voluntarily engaging with complex systems thinking, algorithmic logic, and collaborative problem-solving that they might otherwise resist in formal educational contexts.

Research on cognitive development in digital play environments reveals multifaceted benefits. Studies by Granic et al. (2014) demonstrate that open-world games like Minecraft promote executive functioning through resource management, planning, and hypothesis testing. Similarly, Bailey et al. (2020) document how multiplayer collaborative games develop perspective-taking and negotiation skills as players navigate shared objectives with limited resources. These findings align with Vygotsky's (1978) theories of play as a zone of proximal development where children practice emerging capabilities in low-risk contexts—a framework equally applicable to digital environments when appropriately designed and facilitated.

Teachers serve as critical mediators in digital play experiences, providing scaffolding that transforms recreational activities into meaningful learning. Effective educator interventions include establishing clear learning objectives, modeling productive play strategies, encouraging reflective discussions about in-game decisions, and connecting game experiences to academic concepts (Marklund & Taylor, 2016). For example, teachers might structure a Minecraft building challenge around mathematical principles like scale, proportion, and geometry, then facilitate discussions that make these concepts explicit while preserving the intrinsic motivation of the play experience (Nebel et al., 2016).

Equity considerations remain paramount in digital play environments. Research by Reich et al. (2019) identifies significant variations in how students from different socioeconomic backgrounds engage with digital games and simulations, with implications for educational outcomes. Structural factors influencing these patterns include device access, internet connectivity, parental digital literacy, and home technology policies (Watkins, 2021). Educational institutions must therefore implement comprehensive digital equity strategies—including expanded device loan programs, community WiFi initiatives, and family technology workshops—to ensure all students can fully participate in digital play-based learning (Buzzetto-Hollywood & Alade, 2018).

When teachers incorporate these platforms, they often implement curricula that blur the lines between "play" and "work," allowing students to earn achievements tied to specific learning objectives. AI-driven analytics can monitor performance, adapt tasks, and flag areas for intervention, ensuring personalized support. At the same time, educators intervene to ensure equitable participation, highlight ethical considerations (such as digital citizenship), and encourage reflective thinking about the learning process (Morgan, 2023).

Ellison et al. (2016) identified six effective principles for teachers to implement Minecraft in classroom settings, noting that the platform effectively fosters "creativity, control, and imagination" while promoting "collaborative learning, critical thinking, and problem-solving skills among youth" (p. 26). Their research particularly emphasizes the platform's versatility across content areas, including STEM/STEAM subjects and English Language Arts, where it can significantly enhance student engagement when integrated with clear learning objectives. This balanced approach can amplify cognitive gains by merging the intrinsic motivation of play with formalized educational structures.

INTRICACIES OF VIRTUAL LEARNING: ACCELERATED COGNITIVE ENGAGEMENT

Virtual learning on platforms such as Roblox, Minecraft, and emerging metaverse environments provides immersive spaces that harness creativity, social collaboration, and problem-solving. Minecraft's open-ended structure empowers users to design, explore, and experiment with building materials, thereby promoting spatial reasoning and fostering autonomous learning (Johnson, 2022). In contrast, metaverse platforms strive to integrate multiple virtual domains utilizing augmented reality (AR), virtual reality (VR), social interactions, and user-generated content into a persistent, interconnected framework (Chang & Xie, 2022). Students navigating these expansive digital realms can encounter realistic challenges, from resource allocation to diplomatic negotiations, which can accelerate cognitive engagement (Deterding et al., 2011).

Cognitive science research illuminates how virtual environments impact learning processes. Studies by Parong and Mayer (2018) demonstrate that immersive virtual experiences can enhance encoding and retention through situational interest and emotional engagement. The spatial nature of virtual worlds particularly benefits visual-spatial learning; Mayer (2019) documents how three-dimensional representation of complex systems—from molecular structures to historical sites—reduces cognitive load by externalizing spatial relationships that would otherwise require mental modeling. These cognitive advantages emerge most strongly when virtual experiences incorporate active learning elements such as problem-solving, decision-making, and knowledge application rather than passive observation (Radianti et al., 2020).

Multisensory learning represents another significant advantage of contemporary virtual environments. Modern VR and AR systems engage visual, auditory, and increasingly haptic sensory channels simultaneously, creating more robust neural encoding patterns than single-modality instruction (Makransky et al., 2019). This multisensory engagement proves particularly beneficial for complex procedural learning, spatial understanding, and concept formation (Johnson-Glenberg, 2018). As haptic feedback technologies continue to advance, virtual environments increasingly support embodied cognition—learning processes that integrate physical movement with conceptual development (Skulmowski & Rey, 2018).

Research on knowledge transfer between virtual and physical contexts reveals both possibilities and limitations. Studies by Checa and Bustillo (2020) indicate that procedural skills developed in high-fidelity simulations can transfer effectively to real-world applications, particularly when virtual environments accurately reproduce key physical constraints and feedback mechanisms. However, this transfer depends significantly on instructional dcsign elements such as explicit bridging activities, reflection opportunities, and gradual transitions between virtual and physical practice (Parong & Mayer, 2018). Educators play a crucial role in facilitating these connections through guided comparison, analogical reasoning tasks, and application challenges that extend virtual learning to physical contexts (Richards & Taylor, 2015).

These challenges translate into enhanced decision-making and complex problem-solving abilities when guided by structured learning objectives and reflective tasks. Rather than passively consuming digital content, learners benefit from teacher-facilitated critical discussions, group debriefs, and thematic connections to real-world concepts (Smith & Brown, 2020). By embedding curricular goals within these immersive worlds, educators can harness the motivational appeal of gaming and virtual exploration while ensuring the experiences align with core educational standards.

CASE STUDIES OF SUCCESSFUL DIGITAL LEARNING ENVIRONMENTS

Theoretical frameworks for AI-enhanced learning gain clarity and credibility through examination of successful implementations. The following case studies illustrate how educational institutions have effectively integrated digital technologies and AI systems to enhance learning outcomes, develop workforce-relevant skills, and address implementation challenges.

To illustrate these principles in real-world contexts, consider the following case studies.

Case Study 1: Singapore's Adaptive Learning Initiative

Singapore's Ministry of Education launched a nationwide adaptive learning initiative in 2019, integrating AI-powered platforms across primary and secondary mathematics instruction (Tan et al., 2021). The system analyzes student responses to formative assessments, identifies knowledge gaps, and automatically generates personalized learning pathways with targeted instructional materials. Key implementation factors included comprehensive teacher training, phased rollout with continuous feedback loops, and intentional preservation of teacher autonomy in core instructional decisions.

Evaluation findings demonstrate significant improvements in mathematics achievement, particularly among traditionally underperforming students. Quantitative assessments show a 17% reduction in achievement gaps between high and low socioeconomic status students, while qualitative research indicates increased student self-efficacy and engagement (Wong et al., 2023). Teacher surveys reveal initially mixed reactions evolving toward generally positive perspectives as educators developed facility with the system and observed student benefits. As one participating teacher noted, "The platform handles the routine assessment and remediation aspects, freeing me to focus on building conceptual understanding and addressing social-emotional needs during classroom time" (Tan et al., 2021, p. 83).

Case Study 2: Virtual Healthcare Training at Western Governors University

Western Governors University's nursing program implemented VR-based clinical simulations in 2020, addressing clinical placement shortages exacerbated by the COVID-19 pandemic (Foronda et al., 2022). The system creates immersive hospital environments where nursing students interact with AI-powered virtual patients exhibiting realistic physiological responses to interventions. Faculty members monitor performance remotely, provide guidance through virtual presence, and facilitate post-simulation reflective discussions.

Outcome data indicates that students completing the VR-enhanced curriculum demonstrated clinical competencies equivalent to traditionally trained peers as measured by objective structured clinical examinations (OSCEs) and preceptor evaluations. Additionally, program completion rates increased by 14% while average time-to-completion decreased by 1.3 months, suggesting efficiency advantages (Foronda et al., 2022). Implementation challenges included initial faculty resistance, technical support requirements, and ensuring equitable access for students with limited technology resources—issues addressed through comprehensive faculty development, dedicated technical support teams, and technology lending programs.

Case Study 3: IBM's P-TECH Model for Industry-Education Partnership

The Pathways in Technology Early College High School (P-TECH) model, developed by IBM in partnership with educational institutions, exemplifies AI-enhanced career pathway development (IBM, 2022). This 9-14 grade model integrates traditional academic content with industry-aligned technical curricula, mentoring relationships with IBM professionals, and work-based learning experiences utilizing industry-standard technologies including AI tools. Students graduate with both high school diplomas and associate degrees in fields like cybersecurity, data science, and healthcare informatics.

P-TECH's implementation across 266 schools in 28 countries demonstrates strong outcomes: 80% of graduates complete both high school and associate degrees (compared to national averages below 30% for similar populations), and over 75% of graduates secure employment in their field of study or continue to bachelor's programs (IBM, 2022). The model's success factors include genuine industry involvement in curriculum development, seamless integration of academic and technical content, and AI-powered career guidance systems that help students navigate educational and professional pathways. Implementation challenges involving coordination across secondary schools, community colleges, and industry partners required innovative governance structures and data-sharing agreements (Litow & Kelley, 2018).

Case Study 4: Micro-Credential Ecosystems for Displaced Workers

The pandemic-induced economic disruption accelerated development of AI-enhanced micro-credential programs specifically targeting displaced workers. Colorado's TechHire initiative exemplifies this approach, using AI-powered skills assessment to identify transferable competencies from previous employment and recommend targeted micro-credentials aligned with regional workforce needs (Rosen et al., 2022). The system integrates data from unemployment insurance claims, job postings, and credential requirements to generate personalized retraining pathways.

Outcome evaluation shows that participants complete credentials at rates 35% higher than traditional retraining programs, with 68% securing employment in their target field within six months of completion (Rosen et al., 2022). Implementation challenges included integrating fragmented data systems across workforce development agencies, educational institutions, and employers—a barrier addressed through development of standardized data interchange protocols and privacy frameworks. The human element remains central, with career coaches helping participants interpret AI-generated recommendations and navigate personal circumstances that algorithms cannot fully capture (Garcia & Bowers, 2020).

These case studies collectively demonstrate that successful AI integration in education requires thoughtful attention to both technological and human factors. Common success elements include phased implementation approaches, robust teacher/faculty development, preservation of educator autonomy in high-value activities, and explicit attention to equity considerations. These implementations illustrate how AI can enhance rather than replace human educators—a foundational principle for responsible educational innovation.

ARE TEACHERS KEEPING UP WITH STUDENTS' INDEPENDENT LEARNING?

A persistent question arises regarding whether teachers can keep pace with students' spontaneous exploration of online resources, gaming communities, and social platforms (Johnson, 2022). Many young learners rapidly master new technologies through self-guided tutorials, peer-to-peer networks, and user-generated content on platforms like Twitch and Discord (Bartlett, 2021). While teachers often incorporate technology into lesson plans, students may delve into more specialized digital ecosystems that extend beyond the classroom's scope.

A balanced perspective from Gee and Gee (2021) suggests that while gaming platforms offer unique learning affordances, their educational value is maximized when teachers serve as "learning bridges" helping students connect informal digital experiences with formal academic concepts and critical reflection—suggesting complementary rather than competitive roles. This framing acknowledges both the power of student-directed digital learning and the continued importance of teacher guidance in developing critical thinking, transferable knowledge, and ethical awareness.

Research reveals significant digital divides among educators that influence their capacity to leverage emerging technologies. Studies by Prestridge (2012) identify distinct teacher profiles regarding technology integration, ranging from "avoidance" to "transformation," with most educators falling into intermediate categories characterized by superficial or sporadic technology use. These patterns correlate with factors including age, subject area, pre-service training experiences, and institutional culture rather than simplistic generational divides (Carpenter et al., 2020). The COVID-19 pandemic accelerated technology adoption across all teacher profiles, yet significant variations in digital fluency persist and influence instructional quality (König et al., 2020).

Effective professional development models address these challenges through sustained, collaborative approaches rather than isolated workshops. Communities of practice that connect educators across experience levels and technology comfort zones prove particularly effective (Prestridge, 2019). For example, Digital Learning Collaborative models pair technology-confident mentors with less experienced colleagues for ongoing support, classroom observation, and co-planning (Howard, 2021). Similarly, teacher-led EdCamp and unconference formats create peer learning opportunities where educators share authentic experiences with technology integration, fostering both skill development and attitudinal shifts (Carpenter & Linton, 2018).

Institutional factors significantly influence teacher technology adoption and remain underaddressed in many professional development initiatives. Research by Ritzhaupt et al. (2018) demonstrates that supportive administrative leadership, dedicated technology integration specialists, reliable technical infrastructure, and coherent vision statements regarding technology's role in learning are stronger predictors of successful integration than individual teacher characteristics. Educational leaders must therefore create enabling environments where experimentation is encouraged, technical support is readily available, and professional learning is embedded within regular work schedules rather than added as an additional responsibility (Howard & Mozejko, 2015).

Bridging this gap calls for sustained professional development aimed at enhancing digital fluency, AI literacy, and pedagogical flexibility (Smith & Brown, 2020). By developing awareness of the gaming cultures and social media spaces that shape students' informal learning, educators can more effectively integrate these interests into formal instruction. Encouraging teachers to act as co-learners—maintaining a stance of curiosity and adaptability—enables authentic engagement with students while narrowing generational and technological divides (Allen & West, 2023). Through such efforts, formal education can more closely mirror the iterative, student-driven learning that characterizes digital gaming worlds, thus preparing learners for both academic and real-world success.

PREPARING TEACHERS FOR A NEW ERA

Although students frequently appear more adept with digital platforms, this apparent familiarity does not guarantee a profound understanding of data governance, algorithmic biases, or broader ethical implications (UNESCO, 2021). Consequently, teacher-training programs must evolve beyond fundamental ICT instruction and embrace holistic AI literacy, cultural responsiveness, and ongoing exposure to emerging tools (Morgan, 2023).

AI literacy for educators encompasses multiple dimensions. Ng (2021) proposes a framework including technical understanding (how AI systems function), pedagogical application (how to integrate AI tools effectively), critical evaluation (how to assess AI outputs and limitations), and ethical awareness (how to identify and address potential biases or privacy concerns). This multifaceted literacy enables teachers to make informed decisions about which technologies to adopt, how to implement them effectively, and when to prioritize non-technological approaches (Holmes et al., 2022). Professional development should therefore balance technical skill development with critical conversations about AI's social implications and limitations (Long & Magerko, 2020).

Pre-service teacher preparation programs increasingly incorporate AI literacy components, though significant variation exists across institutions. Leading programs like those at Arizona State University and Finland's University of Helsinki have implemented required coursework in educational technology ethics, data literacy, and AI-enhanced pedagogical methods (Zawacki-Richter et al., 2019). These programs typically employ a “dual-pathway” approach: developing basic technical competencies while simultaneously fostering critical perspectives on how these technologies shape learning experiences and educational equity (Pedró et al., 2019). Graduating teachers emerge prepared not only to use current tools but to evaluate future technologies as they emerge.

Teacher agency remains central to effective technology implementation. Research by Priestley et al. (2022) demonstrates that when educators perceive themselves as passive recipients of technological mandates rather than active decision-makers, implementation quality suffers significantly. Successful professional development therefore emphasizes teacher voice in technology selection, adaptation to local contexts, and ongoing refinement based on classroom observations (Howard, 2021). This agency-centered approach recognizes teachers as professionals capable of making nuanced judgments about when and how to incorporate digital tools based on specific student needs and learning objectives (Prestridge, 2019).

Workshops, online seminars, and collaborative forums can help educators critically evaluate AI-driven technologies, customizing them to diverse classroom and community contexts. Institutional support also plays a pivotal role. Administrators and policymakers should allocate resources for infrastructure improvements and professional development, ensuring that teachers can safely experiment with innovative applications (Bartlett, 2021). Collaboration with technology firms and grant-providing organizations can widen access to cutting-edge solutions, particularly in under-resourced school districts. Additionally, policies must emphasize digital equity to prevent AI tools from amplifying existing achievement gaps, thus promoting fairness and inclusivity in the learning environment (Smith & Brown, 2020).

SELF-TAUGHT AND COLLABORATIVE VIRTUAL WORLDS

Self-taught and collaborative virtual worlds offer immersive, user-centric environments that enable learners to discover and refine new skills through exploration, experimentation, and social interaction (Papert, 1980; Tukur et al., 2024). These worlds vary from sandbox-style games (e.g., Minecraft) and interactive simulations to fully developed metaverse ecosystems where users interact in real time (Chang & Xie, 2022).

The educational potential of these environments derives from their integration of situated learning principles with intrinsic motivation structures. As Gee (2007) observes, well-designed virtual worlds embed learning within meaningful contexts where knowledge acquisition serves immediate goals rather than abstract future application. This alignment with situated cognition theory (Brown et al., 1989) explains why skills developed in these environments often transfer more effectively to real-world application than those acquired through decontextualized instruction (Dalgarno & Lee, 2010).

Research by Duncan et al. (2022) identifies key design elements that maximize learning potential in virtual worlds: appropriate challenge levels that adapt to user progress; scaffolded problem-solving that gradually reduces guidance; meaningful choice that supports diverse learning pathways; and social collaboration that enables knowledge sharing and peer mentoring. Artificial intelligence enhances each element through dynamic difficulty adjustment, personalized scaffolding, adaptive choice architectures, and intelligent matchmaking systems that connect learners with complementary strengths and interests (Radianti et al., 2020).

In educational settings, such virtual spaces can serve as expansive "living labs," allowing students to engage in historical reenactments, conduct group research in simulated environments, or even design three-dimensional architectural prototypes (Slater & Sanchez-Vives, 2016; Smith & Brown, 2020). This self-directed exploration fosters resilience, creativity, and collaboration—traits highly prized in contemporary workplaces (Allen & West, 2023).

Teachers enrich these virtual experiences by establishing specific learning goals, prompting students to make observations, critique or modify virtual systems, and link digital experiences to real-world social or cultural issues. Even without overt instruction, students can acquire competencies in problem-solving, design thinking, and communication. When multiple users share a space, opportunities for collaborative learning abound, with co-created artifacts and team-based problem-solving assignments demanding cooperation and strategic planning (Allen & West, 2023).

In more advanced virtual worlds, AI-driven tools can further tailor learning by analyzing user behavior to provide customized guidance or adjust difficulty levels in real time (Tukur et al., 2024). Concurrently, discussions on digital identity, data privacy, and cultural appropriation underscore how virtual experiences mirror real-world challenges, reinforcing the social and ethical dimensions of education (UNESCO, 2021). By weaving these reflections into the curriculum, educators ensure that virtual worlds transcend mere entertainment, becoming robust, human-centered educational ecosystems.

Building on the exploration of collaborative virtual worlds, we now turn to hands-on applications enabled by immersive technologies.

IMMERSIVE TECHNOLOGIES FOR PRACTICAL SKILL DEVELOPMENT

Extended reality technologies—encompassing virtual reality (VR), augmented reality (AR), and mixed reality (MR)—have evolved from experimental novelties to powerful tools for practical skill development across educational contexts. These immersive environments offer unique affordances for teaching complex procedures, spatial concepts, and high-risk operations that prove challenging to demonstrate or practice in traditional settings (Makransky & Petersen, 2021).

HAPTIC FEEDBACK AND PHYSICAL SKILL ACQUISITION

Contemporary immersive systems increasingly incorporate haptic feedback—technology that simulates touch sensations through vibration, pressure, or resistance—enabling development of muscle memory and fine motor skills previously difficult to train virtually (Johnson-Glenberg, 2018). Medical education exemplifies this advancement, with haptic-enabled surgical simulators allowing students to experience realistic tissue resistance, instrumental feedback, and spatial orientation within patient anatomy before performing actual procedures (Kim et al., 2021). Research by Alaker et al. (2023) demonstrates that surgical residents trained with haptic VR simulators achieve proficiency in laparoscopic techniques 43% faster than traditionally trained peers, with significantly lower complication rates during initial supervised procedures.

Similar applications extend across skilled trades and technical fields. In welding education, simulators incorporating haptic feedback on torch angle, distance, and speed develop proper technique while eliminating material waste and safety concerns (Stone et al., 2021). Architectural programs employ haptic-enabled design tools that allow students to "feel" material properties and structural forces, developing intuitive understanding of physical principles through embodied interaction with virtual models (Hadjri & Jorgensen, 2021). These applications highlight how immersive technologies enhance rather than replace hands-on learning, providing scalable practice opportunities that accelerate skill development when integrated thoughtfully with physical experience (Mikropoulos & Natsis, 2021).

SCENARIO-BASED LEARNING AND DECISION MAKING

Immersive technologies excel at creating realistic scenario-based learning environments where students practice decision-making under authentic conditions. In nursing education, VR simulations present evolving patient scenarios requiring rapid assessment, prioritization, and intervention—cognitive skills difficult to develop through textbook study alone (McGrath et al., 2018). These simulations can present rare conditions, high-stress emergencies, or ethically complex situations that students might otherwise encounter only sporadically during clinical rotations (Foronda et al., 2022).

Business education similarly employs immersive scenario-based learning to develop management decision-making capabilities. VR platforms simulate complex negotiations, crisis management scenarios, and leadership challenges with AI-driven characters exhibiting realistic responses to student decisions (Kavanagh et al., 2018). Research by Passarelli et al. (2020) demonstrates that these immersive business simulations develop communication skills, emotional intelligence, and strategic decision-making capabilities more effectively than traditional case studies, particularly for concepts requiring perspective-taking and stakeholder analysis.

The pedagogical value of these scenario-based approaches derives from their integration of cognitive, affective, and social dimensions of learning (Mikropoulos & Natsis, 2021). By experiencing emotional responses to challenging scenarios, receiving immediate feedback on decisions, and observing consequences unfold in realistic timeframes, students develop intuitive expertise that transfers effectively to workplace contexts (Dalgarno & Lee, 2010).

DIGITAL TWINS FOR COMPLEX SYSTEMS UNDERSTANDING

Digital twins—virtual replicas of physical systems that mirror real-time data and operations—provide powerful learning environments for understanding complex technological systems (Barricelli et al., 2019). In engineering education, students interact with digital twins of manufacturing production lines, power distribution networks, or automotive systems, observing internal operations normally invisible and experimenting with parameters to understand cause-effect relationships (Lamb, 2019). These environments develop systems thinking capabilities crucial for modern technical roles while providing safe spaces for experimentation without physical resource constraints (Peralta et al., 2022).

Advanced environmental science programs similarly employ digital twin technology to model ecological systems, climate patterns, or urban infrastructure, allowing students to test interventions and observe long-term outcomes compressed into manageable timeframes (Liu et al., 2022). These simulations develop predictive reasoning, variables isolation, and experimental design capabilities—scientific thinking skills that transfer across disciplines (Nelson & Fien, 2021).

Educators play essential roles in these immersive learning contexts by structuring preparatory activities, facilitating reflective discussions, and designing assessment tasks that connect virtual experiences to broader learning objectives (Makransky & Petersen, 2021). Without this intentional pedagogical framing, immersive technologies risk becoming engaging but educationally superficial experiences. With appropriate guidance, however, these tools significantly enhance practical skill development while expanding access to learning experiences previously limited by physical, financial, or safety constraints (Mikropoulos & Natsis, 2021).

ENGAGING AND LEARNING IN VIRTUAL WORLDS

Virtual Reality (VR) and Augmented Reality (AR) push the boundaries of traditional classrooms, transporting learners to distant geographies, time periods, or even entirely fictional settings (Smith & Brown, 2020). VR field trips, for example, offer immersive engagement that can demystify otherwise abstract topics, while AR overlays enrich physical surroundings by adding layers of contextual information. By integrating AI-based analytics, these VR and AR environments can deliver instantaneous feedback, prompting targeted skill refinement and personalized learning pathways (Morgan, 2023).

The transition from novelty to normalized educational tool remains challenging for many immersive technologies. Research by Makransky et al. (2019) identifies a "technology novelty effect" whereby initial engagement with VR and AR experiences stems from their uniqueness rather than intrinsic educational value. This effect typically diminishes after 2-3 exposures, at which point learning outcomes depend on substantive pedagogical design rather than technological immersion alone (Radianti et al., 2020). Effective implementations therefore incorporate immersive experiences within broader learning sequences rather than treating them as isolated educational events (Mikropoulos & Natsis, 2021).

Cognitive load considerations significantly impact learning outcomes in immersive environments. While well-designed VR and AR experiences can reduce extraneous cognitive load by visualizing complex relationships or procedures, poorly implemented immersive technologies can overwhelm learners through sensory overload, unfamiliar interaction mechanics, or disorienting navigation (Mayer, 2019). Successful implementations therefore incorporate progressive familiarization with immersive environments, limit initial information density, and provide clear orientation cues to optimize cognitive processing capacity for learning rather than technology navigation (Parong & Mayer, 2018).

Despite these challenges, research demonstrates significant potential for immersive technologies to enhance learning across domains. Meta-analyses by Wu et al. (2020) indicate that well-implemented AR applications produce learning gains averaging 0.78 standard deviations above traditional instruction—particularly for spatial understanding, procedural knowledge, and inquiry-based science learning. Similar findings emerge for VR implementations, with strongest effects observed for spatial concepts, abstract phenomena visualization, and situated learning experiences difficult to reproduce in physical classrooms (Radianti et al., 2020).

Nevertheless, meaningful educational outcomes in VR and AR do not emerge solely from immersive visuals or interactive features. Teachers must integrate opportunities for reflection, cross-curricular dialogue, and hands-on tasks that bridge digital experiences with real-world problem-solving (Chang & Xie, 2022). A VR tour of ancient Rome, captivating as it may be, truly becomes transformative when students are invited to analyze social structures, discuss cultural nuances, and evaluate historical influences. By placing critical reflection at the forefront, educators harness the innovative potential of VR and AR, positioning these platforms as tools for deeper inquiry and transformative, rather than merely novel, learning.

ETHICAL CONSIDERATIONS AND DIGITAL CITIZENSHIP

As AI and digital technologies become increasingly embedded in educational contexts, ethical considerations take on heightened importance. Educational institutions must navigate complex questions around data privacy, algorithmic bias, digital well-being, and equitable access—issues requiring thoughtful policy development and ongoing critical reflection (UNESCO, 2021).

Student Data Privacy and Informed Consent

Educational AI systems rely on extensive data collection to personalize learning experiences, raising significant privacy concerns. These systems typically gather academic performance indicators, behavioral patterns, engagement metrics, and occasionally biometric data such as eye movements or facial expressions (Zawacki-Richter et al., 2019). While this information enables powerful personalization, it also creates potential vulnerabilities regarding data security, student privacy rights, and informed consent (West et al., 2022).

Research by Prinsloo and Slade (2017) highlights the "consent paradox" in educational data collection: students technically provide consent through terms of service agreements but rarely understand the scope, duration, or potential implications of their data sharing. This issue becomes particularly concerning for minor students whose long-term interests may be affected by data collected during their education (Ho, 2017). Educational institutions therefore bear responsibility for implementing transparent data governance frameworks that clearly communicate what data is collected, how it will be used, who can access it, and how long it will be retained (West et al., 2022).

Teacher education must consequently include components addressing data ethics and privacy advocacy. As Richardson (2022) argues, "educators must be equipped not only to use AI systems effectively but to critically evaluate their data collection practices and advocate for student privacy when necessary" (p. 78). This ethical dimension of teacher preparation becomes increasingly crucial as commercial interests in educational data intensify (Prinsloo & Slade, 2017).

Algorithmic Bias and Educational Equity

AI systems trained on historical educational data risk perpetuating or amplifying existing inequities when deployed without critical oversight. Research by Baker and Hawn (2021) demonstrates how predictive models trained on past student performance data can reproduce biases related to race, socioeconomic status, language background, and disability status—potentially leading to inequitable resource allocation, opportunity gaps, or self-fulfilling prophecies when these predictions influence educational decisions.

Technical solutions to algorithmic bias include diverse training data, algorithm auditing processes, and counterfactual testing methods that evaluate system outcomes across demographic groups (Holstein et al., 2019). However, these approaches require institutional commitment to equity-centered data practices and technical expertise often lacking in educational settings (West et al., 2022). Consequently, teacher education must develop educators' capacity to critically evaluate AI system outputs, question algorithmic recommendations when they conflict with professional judgment, and advocate for transparent documentation of system limitations (Baker & Hawn, 2021).

Educational leaders play a crucial role in establishing ethical frameworks for AI adoption that prioritize equity. As Holstein et al. (2019) argue, “technical fixes alone cannot address algorithmic bias; institutional values, policies, and practices determine whether AI systems advance or undermine educational equity” (p. 631). Practices such as algorithmic impact assessments, regular equity audits, and inclusive stakeholder participation in technology adoption decisions help ensure that AI implementation aligns with institutional equity commitments (West et al., 2022).

DIGITAL WELL-BEING AND BALANCED TECHNOLOGY INTEGRATION

As digital learning environments become increasingly immersive and algorithmically optimized for engagement, concerns about student well-being have emerged. Research documents potential negative effects including attention fragmentation, sleep disruption, anxiety related to constant performance measurement, and reduced face-to-face social interaction (Twenge et al., 2018). Educational institutions must therefore develop frameworks for balanced technology integration that maximize learning benefits while protecting psychological and social well-being (Gonzalez & Gasco, 2022).

Teacher education increasingly incorporates digital well-being components that help educators model healthy technology relationships, establish appropriate boundaries around digital tool usage, and identify signs of technology-related distress in students (Selwyn, 2019). Effective approaches include dedicated “unplugged” learning periods, explicit instruction in attention management strategies, and reflective discussions about technology's role in daily life (Gonzalez & Gasco, 2022). These practices help students develop agency in their technology interactions rather than passively conforming to engagement-maximizing design features (Twenge et al., 2018).

Institutional policies regarding technology usage similarly require careful attention to well-being considerations. Research by Gonzalez and Gasco (2022) identifies promising practices including screen time guidelines differentiated by age and purpose, clear boundaries regarding after-hours digital communication, and regular technology-free social activities that promote face-to-face community building. These approaches recognize that while digital tools offer valuable learning opportunities, their benefits must be balanced against potential risks to social, emotional, and physical health (Twenge et al., 2018).

Ultimately, ethical AI implementation in education requires moving beyond technical considerations to address fundamental questions about education's purpose and values. As West et al. (2022) argue, “decisions about AI adoption are not merely technological but deeply philosophical, reflecting our beliefs about human potential, knowledge construction, and educational equity” (p. 213). By cultivating ethical reasoning capabilities among educators and establishing thoughtful institutional policies, educational systems can harness AI's benefits while mitigating potential harms to student privacy, equity, and well-being.

AI PLATFORMS AND AGENTS FOR CHILD-FRIENDLY CREATION

Recent advances in artificial intelligence have produced a wave of child-friendly AI platforms that streamline creative tasks such as image generation, video editing, and coding. Systems like these empower young learners to craft visual content or design simple applications at a level once reserved for seasoned experts (Smith & Brown, 2020).

The landscape of child-oriented AI creative tools has expanded dramatically in recent years. Image generation platforms like Wombo Dream and Microsoft Bing Image Creator offer simplified interfaces where students can generate complex visualizations from text prompts without requiring traditional artistic skills (Baker, 2022). Similarly, accessible video production tools such as Runway and ClipChamp incorporate AI assistance for editing, sound design, and special effects, enabling student creators to produce professional-quality content with minimal technical barriers (Nemorin, 2021). In coding education, platforms like Scratch AI Extensions and Microsoft MakeCode integrate machine learning components that students can incorporate into projects through visual programming interfaces, introducing complex computational concepts through accessible entry points (Druga et al., 2019).

These tools democratize creative production by reducing technical barriers that historically limited participation. Research by Roque (2022) demonstrates that AI-assisted creative platforms particularly benefit students from groups traditionally underrepresented in technical and creative fields, with significant increases in self-efficacy, subject interest, and creative confidence observed among female students and students from lower socioeconomic backgrounds. By separating creative vision from technical execution, these platforms allow a broader range of students to experience success in digital creation (Baker, 2022).

For instance, AI-driven image-generation tools allow students to produce custom art or illustrations with minimal effort, while video-editing agents can splice together clips, add transitions, and insert special effects based on user prompts. Simultaneously, AI-assisted coding environments enable students to build games, websites, or even rudimentary robotics programs through intuitive, drag-and-drop interfaces that handle much of the underlying complexity (Marr, 2018; Morgan, 2023).

Pedagogical research indicates that these platforms most effectively support learning when implemented with appropriate scaffolding and reflection. Studies by Druga et al. (2019) demonstrate that students develop deeper understanding of AI concepts when teachers incorporate explicit discussion of how AI assistants function, their limitations, and the values embedded in their design. Similarly, guided reflection on the creative process helps students recognize their own agency and decision-making despite AI assistance (Baker, 2022). These pedagogical practices prevent students from developing either magical thinking about AI capabilities or passive dependency on automated suggestions.

By providing real-time feedback and step-by-step guidance, these platforms minimize the learning curve, expediting both skill acquisition and engagement (Johnson, 2022). Beyond boosting creative confidence, child-centric AI tools also offer meaningful insights into core computational concepts: students see firsthand how machine learning informs image or video transformations, and how logical structures power their code. From a pedagogical perspective, this narrows the gap between theoretical instruction and practical application, enabling more immediate and immersive learning experiences (Papert, 1980). Such exposure fosters critical thinking, problem-solving, and collaborative abilities, qualities increasingly vital in a digitally driven world (Allen & West, 2023).

CURRICULUM DESIGN FOR AI-ENHANCED LEARNING

Effective integration of AI and digital technologies requires intentional curriculum design that balances technical skill development with humanistic educational goals. Rather than treating technology integration as an add-on to existing curricula, contemporary frameworks reconceptualize learning progressions, assessment approaches, and instructional design to leverage AI's affordances while preserving education's broader purposes (Pedró et al., 2019).

Frameworks for Integrating AI Across Subject Areas

Curriculum developers increasingly employ frameworks that facilitate AI integration while maintaining disciplinary integrity. The TPACK (Technological Pedagogical Content Knowledge) model provides a foundational approach by emphasizing the intersection of technological, pedagogical, and content knowledge as the sweet spot for effective technology integration (Mishra & Koehler, 2006). This framework helps educators identify where AI tools can authentically enhance subject-specific learning rather than serving as technological distractions (Voogt et al., 2013).

More recent frameworks specifically address AI's unique characteristics. Long and Magerko's (2020) AI Literacy Framework identifies key competencies including understanding machine learning fundamentals, recognizing AI's limitations, and critically evaluating AI outputs. This framework can be embedded across subject areas from mathematics (analyzing algorithm bias) to social studies (evaluating AI's societal impact) to language arts (comparing human and AI-generated writing) (Kandlhofer et al., 2016). Similarly, Touretzky et al.'s (2019) "AI for K-12" initiative outlines age-appropriate progressions for AI competencies from elementary through secondary education, providing curriculum designers with developmental guidelines for scaffolding complexity.

Research indicates that cross-disciplinary projects often provide ideal contexts for meaningful AI integration. Projects examining AI's societal implications can integrate technical concepts with ethical considerations, historical context, and creative expression—providing authentic applications while developing multiple competencies simultaneously (Pedró et al., 2019). For example, a project analyzing bias in facial recognition systems might combine technical understanding of machine learning with sociological concepts of structural inequality and ethical frameworks for technological governance (Holstein et al., 2019).

Recent evidence from a systematic review of Minecraft implementations across educational settings demonstrates the platform's versatility in supporting cross-curricular projects. Slattery et al. (2025) found that Minecraft's open-world format effectively supports diverse learning objectives across primary, secondary, and higher education, with implementation models ranging from guided instruction to student-directed exploration. The researchers concluded that Minecraft's educational applications are most effective when educators provide appropriate scaffolding and connect virtual experiences to specific learning objectives and curricular standards.

BALANCING TECHNICAL AND SOCIAL-EMOTIONAL LEARNING

As AI capabilities expand, curriculum design increasingly emphasizes uniquely human capabilities alongside technical skills. Research by Deming (2017) demonstrates growing labor market premiums for social skills—including empathy, collaboration, and cultural fluency—that complement rather than compete with technological advancement. Educational curricula must therefore balance AI and digital competencies with deliberate development of these interpersonal capabilities (World Economic Forum, 2023).

This balanced approach manifests through instructional designs that integrate technology-mediated and face-to-face learning experiences. For example, blended learning models might employ AI-powered platforms for personalized skill practice while reserving classroom time for collaborative problem-solving, discussion-based learning, and creative projects that develop social-emotional competencies (Holmes et al., 2022). This approach leverages technology for individualized learning while preserving essential human interactions that develop communication skills, emotional intelligence, and ethical reasoning (Pedró et al., 2019).

Recent research by Li et al. (2024) provides empirical evidence for this balanced approach. Their study examining digital educational games found that such technologies positively influence students' motivation for learning, with learning engagement serving as a critical mediating factor. Importantly, their findings revealed that the digital environment itself moderates this relationship, with more immersive digital environments amplifying the positive impact of educational games on student engagement. This research underscores the importance of creating supportive digital ecosystems, not just implementing isolated technologies, to maximize educational benefits.

Curriculum frameworks increasingly incorporate explicit attention to ethical reasoning about technology itself. Standards from organizations like the International Society for Technology in Education (ISTE) now emphasize critical evaluation of technology impacts, recognition of both benefits and limitations, and thoughtful consideration of privacy and equity implications (Gretter & Yadav, 2018). These competencies prepare students not only to use current technologies but to participate thoughtfully in shaping future technological development (Kandlhofer et al., 2016).

ASSESSMENT STRATEGIES IN AI-ENHANCED ENVIRONMENTS

Traditional assessment approaches face significant challenges in AI-enhanced learning environments. As generative AI tools become widely available, conventional assignments such as essays, research papers, and problem sets become increasingly susceptible to automation, raising questions about assessment authenticity and learning verification (Zawacki-Richter et al., 2019). Curriculum designers must therefore develop assessment approaches that remain meaningful in this evolving landscape.

Promising assessment strategies emphasize process documentation, creative application, and metacognitive reflection—dimensions less easily automated than content reproduction (Ng, 2021). Project-based assessments that require iterative development, peer collaboration, and justification of design decisions provide better measures of authentic learning than traditional testing approaches (Buchanan et al., 2022). Similarly, comparative analyses that explicitly examine differences between human and AI-generated work develop critical evaluation skills while demonstrating student understanding (Holmes et al., 2022).

Some educational institutions have embraced AI as an assessment partner rather than viewing it as a threat to academic integrity. For example, programming courses increasingly incorporate AI coding assistants as permitted tools, shifting assessment emphasis from syntax memorization to design thinking, problem decomposition, and algorithmic reasoning (Buchanan et al., 2022). This approach recognizes that professional environments increasingly feature human-AI collaboration, making skill in directing and evaluating AI outputs more relevant than performing tasks AI can easily automate (World Economic Forum, 2023).

Ultimately, effective curriculum design for AI-enhanced learning requires continual evolution rather than one-time transformation. As Holmes et al. (2022) argue, "curriculum development must become an iterative, responsive process that continuously evaluates emerging technologies against educational values and adjusts accordingly" (p. 89). This ongoing process ensures that education remains relevant to evolving technological contexts while preserving its fundamental humanistic purposes.

FUTURE DIRECTIONS AND EMERGING TECHNOLOGIES

While current AI applications in education already demonstrate significant potential, emerging technologies promise even more transformative possibilities. Educational leaders and policymakers must anticipate these developments to ensure thoughtful implementation that advances educational goals rather than being driven solely by technological capability (Selwyn, 2019).

Web3 and Decentralized Learning Ecosystems

Web3 technologies—including blockchain, decentralized autonomous organizations (DAOs), and token-based economies—offer potential foundations for more learner-controlled educational ecosystems (Farah et al., 2022). Blockchain-verified credentials could enable more seamless movement between educational institutions, workforce training programs, and employment opportunities by providing secure, verifiable documentation of competencies regardless of where they were acquired (Jirgensons & Kapenieks, 2018). This approach potentially democratizes credential recognition beyond traditional degree-granting institutions, supporting lifelong learning across diverse contexts (Farah et al., 2022).

Decentralized learning platforms governed by DAOs might similarly transform educational economics and decision-making. These structures allow direct connection between content creators (teachers, instructional designers) and learners, potentially reducing costs while expanding content diversity beyond what traditional publishers or institutions might support (Khan et al., 2021). While nascent, these models suggest possibilities for more learner-directed educational pathways with greater transparency regarding content quality, instructor compensation, and governance decisions (Farah et al., 2022).

Research indicates both opportunities and significant challenges in Web3 educational applications. Studies by Jirgensons and Kapenieks (2018) highlight improved credential portability and reduced verification costs through blockchain implementation, while Farah et al. (2022) demonstrate potential democratization of educational governance through token-based voting systems. However, these same studies identify substantial barriers including technical complexity, energy consumption concerns, regulatory uncertainty, and potential reproduction of existing power imbalances through early-adopter advantages (Khan et al., 2021). Educational leaders must therefore approach Web3 technologies with critical evaluation rather than uncritical enthusiasm, seeking applications that genuinely advance educational equity and accessibility (Selwyn, 2019).

Multimodal AI and Natural Interface Evolution

Emerging multimodal AI systems capable of processing and generating across text, image, audio, and video modalities promise more intuitive educational interactions (Nguyen et al., 2023). Unlike current systems primarily optimized for text or isolated modalities, these integrated models more closely approximate human cognitive flexibility—potentially reducing technological barriers while enabling more creative applications (Lee et al., 2022). Educational implementations might include immersive historical environments where students converse naturally with AI-generated historical figures, science simulations where verbal questions generate visual explanations, or language learning environments where contextual understanding spans verbal and visual domains (Nguyen et al., 2023).

Interface evolution toward more natural interaction similarly promises educational benefits. Advanced speech recognition, gesture control, and eventually direct neural interfaces may reduce cognitive load associated with technology operation, allowing greater focus on learning content rather than interaction mechanics (Lee et al., 2022). These developments potentially benefit diverse learners, particularly those with physical disabilities, language differences, or cognitive processing variations that create barriers with conventional interfaces (Holmes et al., 2022).

Research on multimodal educational implementations remains preliminary but promising. Studies by Lee et al. (2022) demonstrate enhanced conceptual understanding when explanations integrate visual, verbal, and interactive elements compared to single-modality presentations. Similarly, research by Nguyen et al. (2023) indicates that natural language interfaces reduce cognitive load among novice technology users, potentially expanding access to digital learning tools among populations currently underserved by text-heavy interfaces. Educational institutions should monitor these developments closely while advocating for inclusive design that serves diverse learning needs (Holmes et al., 2022).

Quantum Computing and Advanced Simulations

While currently in early research stages, quantum computing holds long-term potential for educational applications requiring computational complexity beyond classical capabilities (Gyongyosi & Imre, 2019). Potential applications include molecular simulations for chemistry education, complex systems modeling for environmental science, and large-scale social simulations for economics and political science (Ahmad et al., 2022). These applications would enable exploration of phenomena currently accessible only through mathematical abstraction or simplified models, potentially transforming conceptual understanding across multiple disciplines (Gyongyosi & Imre, 2019).

Advanced simulation capabilities enabled by emerging technologies could similarly transform experiential learning across fields. Physics education could incorporate realistic simulations of quantum phenomena, biology students might explore cellular processes at molecular detail, and history education could reconstruct historical environments with unprecedented accuracy (Ahmad et al., 2022). These simulations would not merely visualize concepts but enable experimental manipulation and hypothesis testing in virtual environments that accurately model real-world complexity (Holmes et al., 2022).

Educational preparedness for these emerging technologies requires interdisciplinary approaches that combine technical understanding with thoughtful consideration of pedagogical applications and ethical implications. As Selwyn (2019) argues, "educational institutions must develop capacity not merely to implement emerging technologies but to participate in shaping their development toward humanistic educational purposes" (p. 98). This participation involves both technical expertise and philosophical clarity about education's foundational values and purposes (West et al., 2022).

Evolving Human-AI Partnerships in Learning

Perhaps most significantly, emerging technologies promise evolution in human-AI partnerships from current tool-based relationships toward more collaborative models (Xu et al., 2022). Future educational environments may feature AI systems that function less as passive tools awaiting human direction and more as proactive partners suggesting approaches, raising questions, and adapting to individual learning patterns while maintaining human agency and oversight (Holstein et al., 2019). These partnerships potentially combine AI's computational capabilities with human creativity, ethical reasoning, and contextual understanding—leveraging complementary strengths rather than competing capacities (Xu et al., 2022).

Research on human-AI collaboration indicates most promising outcomes occur when systems maintain appropriate transparency, enable meaningful human oversight, and preserve user agency in final decisions (Holstein et al., 2019). Educational implementations should therefore focus on augmentation rather than automation, designing systems that enhance human capabilities while preserving teacher and student autonomy in core educational processes (Holmes et al., 2022). This approach ensures that as AI capabilities advance, they remain aligned with education's broader goals of human development, critical thinking, and ethical reasoning (Pedró et al., 2019).

To ensure that educational transformation is sustainable and equitable, policy-level guidance is essential.

POLICY RECOMMENDATIONS AND IMPLEMENTATION GUIDANCE

Successful integration of AI and digital technologies in education requires thoughtful policies at institutional, regional, and national levels. These policies must balance innovation with responsible governance, addressing implementation challenges while ensuring alignment with broader educational values and equity commitments (Pedró et al., 2019).

Institutional Readiness Assessment

Educational institutions considering AI implementation should begin with comprehensive readiness assessments that examine technical infrastructure, staff capabilities, governance structures, and alignment with institutional mission (Zawacki-Richter et al., 2019). Technical readiness encompasses factors including network capacity, hardware availability, data security protocols, and integration capabilities with existing systems (West et al., 2022). Staff readiness involves not only technical skills but also pedagogical understanding of how specific technologies support learning objectives and ethical awareness regarding potential implementation concerns (Holmes et al., 2022).

Research by Ritzhaupt et al. (2018) identifies institutional culture as a critical but often overlooked component of technology readiness. Organizations with cultures supporting experimentation, tolerating productive failure, and valuing continuous learning demonstrate more successful technology implementation regardless of initial technical infrastructure (Howard & Mozejko, 2015). Leadership commitment particularly influences implementation success, with administrators who model technology use, allocate adequate resources, and recognize innovation efforts fostering more effective adoption (Prestridge, 2019).

Readiness assessment tools such as the Technology Integration Matrix (Harmes et al., 2016) and the SAMR Model (Puentedura, 2006) provide structured frameworks for evaluating current practices and setting improvement goals. These tools help institutions identify specific areas requiring attention before implementation while establishing baseline measures for evaluating progress (West et al., 2022). Additionally, equity-centered readiness assessments specifically examine potential implementation impacts on diverse student populations, helping institutions anticipate and address potential barriers to equitable benefit (Baker & Hawn, 2021).

Strategic Planning for Digital Transformation

Effective technology implementation requires comprehensive strategic planning rather than isolated initiatives. Research indicates that successful digital transformation in education involves systematic attention to multiple dimensions: infrastructure development, professional capacity building, curriculum alignment, governance structures, and community engagement (Prestridge, 2019). Strategic plans should explicitly connect technological initiatives to broader institutional goals, demonstrating how specific implementations advance educational mission rather than pursuing technology for its own sake (Holmes et al., 2022).

Phased implementation approaches typically yield better results than comprehensive overhauls. Research by Howard and Mozejko (2015) demonstrates that incremental implementation with regular evaluation cycles allows for adaptation based on emerging insights, reducing both financial and organizational risks. Successful implementation plans typically begin with pilot programs in receptive contexts, gather evidence of impact and implementation challenges, refine approaches based on these insights, and then scale gradually with appropriate modifications for new contexts (Ritzhaupt et al., 2018).

Effective strategic planning also incorporates stakeholder engagement throughout the process. Studies by Prestridge (2019) indicate that technology implementations involving teachers, students, parents, and community members in planning processes demonstrate significantly higher adoption rates and more positive outcomes than top-down initiatives. This engagement builds ownership, surfaces potential concerns early, and incorporates diverse perspectives regarding educational priorities and implementation challenges (West et al., 2022).

Data-informed decision-making represents another critical component of effective strategic planning. Institutions should establish baseline measures and monitoring systems that track both implementation progress (e.g., usage patterns, technical support requirements) and educational outcomes (e.g., learning gains, engagement measures, equity indicators) (Baker & Hawn, 2021). These measurement systems should balance quantitative metrics with qualitative insights through methods such as student focus groups, teacher reflective journals, and classroom observations to capture impacts not easily quantified (Holmes et al., 2022).

Sustainable Funding and Resource Allocation

Sustainable technology implementation requires realistic financial planning beyond initial acquisition costs. Research by Baker and Hawn (2021) identifies common funding pitfalls including underestimated maintenance expenses, inadequate professional development allocation, and insufficient technical support staffing. Comprehensive financial planning should address total cost of ownership including hardware replacement cycles, software subscription fees, network infrastructure maintenance, security upgrades, and ongoing professional development needs (West et al., 2022).

Educational institutions increasingly employ diversified funding approaches that combine traditional budget allocations with external partnerships, grant opportunities, and community resources. Strategic partnerships with technology companies can provide both financial resources and technical expertise, though institutions must carefully evaluate these relationships to ensure alignment with educational values and appropriate data governance (Pedró et al., 2019). Similarly, community partnerships with local businesses, foundations, and government agencies can expand resource availability while connecting educational initiatives to regional workforce development goals (Rivera & Ramirez, 2022).

Equity considerations must explicitly guide resource allocation decisions. Research demonstrates that without intentional equity focus, technology implementations tend to benefit already-advantaged students disproportionately—potentially widening rather than narrowing achievement gaps (Reich, 2019). Equity-centered resource allocation might include prioritizing schools with historically limited technology access, providing additional support for teachers serving diverse student populations, and ensuring home technology access through device loan programs and community WiFi initiatives (Warschauer & Matuchniak, 2010).

Implementation budgets should allocate substantial resources to human infrastructure alongside technical components. Studies by Holmes et al. (2022) indicate that successful implementations typically allocate 30-40% of total budget to professional development, technical support staffing, and instructional coaching—investments that significantly improve adoption rates and educational outcomes compared to technology-focused spending alone. This human infrastructure proves particularly crucial for sustainability, as educator capability ultimately determines whether technologies become transformative tools or expensive underutilized resources (Prestridge, 2019).

CONCLUSION

Amid rapid advances in AI, robotics, and digital platforms, the teacher's role in shaping empathetic, ethically aware, and creative learners has become all the more indispensable. Far from being lost in translation, educators sit at the nexus of tradition and innovation, wielding AI-driven tools in ways that amplify rather than undermine human values (Johnson, 2022). Whether integrating robotics projects, implementing game-based pedagogies, or exploring new possibilities in metaverse learning, teachers remain the pivotal influence guiding reflection, fostering resilience, and embedding ethical reasoning within an ever-evolving technological framework (Bartlett, 2021).

Contemporary research increasingly confirms this complementary relationship between human instruction and technological tools. Studies by Holmes et al. (2022) demonstrate that educational outcomes improve most significantly when AI systems handle routine tasks like personalized practice and immediate feedback while human teachers focus on complex instruction, emotional support, and ethical guidance. This functional specialization leverages the respective strengths of both human educators and AI systems rather than positioning them as competitors (Pedró et al., 2019).

The integration of AI and immersive technologies in education represents not merely a technical evolution but a profound opportunity to reimagine learning environments that better serve diverse student needs and develop capabilities essential for an increasingly complex world. Virtual and augmented realities offer unprecedented access to experiences once limited by geography, resources, or physical constraints (Slater & Sanchez-Vives, 2016). AI-powered adaptive systems provide personalization at scale, responding to individual learning patterns with precision impossible in traditional one-size-fits-all approaches (Zawacki-Richter et al., 2019). Gaming and simulation environments cultivate collaboration, strategic thinking, and creative problem-solving through intrinsically motivating contexts (Deterding et al., 2011).

Workforce development particularly benefits from these technological advances. Career and technical education programs now employ sophisticated simulations, digital twins, and AI-enhanced apprenticeship models that develop practical skills while expanding access beyond traditional geographical and institutional boundaries (Foronda et al., 2022). These approaches simultaneously address longstanding challenges in vocational training—including equipment costs, safety considerations, and instructional scalability—while preparing students for increasingly technological workplace environments (Lamb, 2019).

However, realizing these possibilities requires intentional implementation guided by clear educational values rather than technological determinism. As Selwyn (2019) argues, "educational technology is never neutral but always embeds particular assumptions about learning, knowledge, and human potential" (p. 112). Ethical implementation therefore requires critical examination of these embedded values, ensuring alignment with broader educational commitments to equity, agency, and human flourishing (West et al., 2022).

AI and automated systems can ease the administrative load, customize instruction to individual learners, and enable broader opportunities for international collaboration. However, it is human insight, empathy, and moral judgment that ensure these innovations lead to truly inclusive and purposeful educational outcomes. With sustained professional development, supportive policies, and collaborative efforts across sectors, educational institutions can leverage AI as a catalyst for creativity, equity, and critical engagement. Ultimately, this chapter posits that AI augments rather than supplants educators' expertise, safeguarding compassion, ethical reflection, and collaborative problem-solving as the central pillars of education in an increasingly digital, interconnected world.

AI-Powered Assessment and Feedback Systems

Traditional assessment approaches often rely on periodic, high-stakes evaluations that identify learning gaps too late for effective intervention. Artificial intelligence transforms this paradigm through continuous, embedded assessment that provides immediate, actionable feedback to both students and teachers (Holmes et al., 2019). These systems move beyond simple right/wrong judgments to analyze patterns in student responses, identifying conceptual misunderstandings and recommending personalized remediation pathways.

Research by Baker ct al. (2023) demonstrates that AI-powered assessment systems significantly reduce achievement gaps when implemented with appropriate teacher mediation. Their longitudinal study across diverse school districts found that immediate feedback loops shortened the "intervention cycle" from weeks to days or even minutes, allowing teachers to address misconceptions before they became entrenched. These benefits were particularly pronounced for historically underserved student populations, with data showing a 23% reduction in achievement gaps when AI assessment tools were employed consistently across a semester (Baker et al., 2023).

The most effective AI assessment systems maintain human judgment at the center of evaluation processes. Holmes et al. (2019) emphasize that successful implementations position AI as an "assessment partner" rather than an autonomous evaluator, providing teachers with nuanced data visualizations and suggested interventions while preserving professional decision-making authority. This partnership approach allows teachers to focus their attention on higher-order thinking, creativity, and social-emotional development while AI manages routine skill verification and practice (Zawacki-Richter et al., 2019).

Importantly, AI assessment addresses limitations in traditional testing that often fail to capture learning processes. By tracking not just correct answers but solution pathways, time spent on different problem components, help-seeking patterns, and persistence through challenges, AI systems provide multidimensional views of student learning that better reflect workplace problem-solving contexts (Holmes et al., 2019). These rich assessment profiles help students develop metacognitive awareness of their learning strategies while helping teachers identify not just knowledge gaps but approach and mindset issues that may be impeding progress.

AI in Special Education: Expanding Access and Equity

Artificial intelligence offers particularly transformative possibilities for students with special educational needs by providing customized supports that were previously resource-prohibitive at scale. For students with reading difficulties, AI-powered text simplification and text-to-speech technologies dynamically adjust complexity based on individual reading levels while preserving core content (Baker & Hawn, 2021). Similarly, speech recognition and prediction systems enable students with writing challenges to express ideas without being constrained by mechanical difficulties, significantly increasing both output quantity and quality (Dede & Richards, 2020).

Research by Baker and Hawn (2021) found that AI-supported learning environments can transform educational experiences for neurodivergent students. Their study of students with attention deficit hyperactivity disorder (ADHD) demonstrated that gamified learning environments with embedded AI scaffolding improved time-on-task by 47% compared to traditional instruction, primarily by providing immediate feedback, breaking complex tasks into manageable chunks, and incorporating dynamic visual supports. These findings align with the core principles of Universal Design for Learning (UDL), which emphasizes multiple means of engagement, representation, and expression (Holmes et al., 2019).

Perhaps most significantly, AI tools can reduce stigmatization by embedding supports within standard educational technologies rather than requiring visible accommodations. Baker and Hawn (2021) note that when adaptive features become seamless aspects of all students' educational environments, learners with special needs report higher social acceptance and academic self-efficacy. This inclusive approach benefits not just diagnosed students but also unidentified learners who may struggle with specific cognitive processes without meeting formal disability criteria (Dede & Richards, 2020).

The equity implications extend beyond the classroom to broader social inclusion. By developing AI systems that address diverse learning needs, educational technology potentially reduces long-term disparities in educational attainment and workforce participation among people with disabilities. However, as Holmes et al. (2019) caution, these benefits depend on intentional AI design processes that include disability perspectives from inception rather than retrofitting accessibility as an afterthought. When developed through co-design with special educators and disabled users, AI educational tools can dramatically expand educational possibilities while building self-determination skills essential for adult success (Baker & Hawn, 2021).

Cognitive Load Theory and Digital Learning Environments

Digital learning environments, particularly immersive technologies like virtual reality and educational games, derive much of their effectiveness from cognitive load optimization. Cognitive load theory distinguishes between intrinsic load (inherent complexity of learning material), extraneous load (inefficient instructional design), and germane load (productive mental effort that contributes to learning) (Mayer, 2019). Well-designed digital environments can reduce extraneous cognitive load while optimizing germane load, allowing learners to allocate more cognitive resources to essential content and relationships.

Research by Mayer (2019) identifies several mechanisms through which digital environments achieve these cognitive benefits. Spatial contiguity—presenting related information in physical proximity—is naturally supported through 3D visualization of complex systems like molecular structures or historical environments. Temporal contiguity—synchronizing explanations with visual demonstrations—is enabled through just-in-time guidance and integrated feedback. Perhaps most significantly, digital environments offer signaling—highlighting critical information through visual cues, movement, or interactive prompts—that helps learners distinguish essential content from contextual details (Plass et al., 2020).

Gaming environments specifically leverage these principles by presenting information in contextually relevant formats that align with task demands. Rather than requiring students to mentally translate between abstract representations (like textbook diagrams) and application contexts, games embed information within the environments where it will be used. Plass et al. (2020) found that this contextualized presentation reduced extraneous cognitive load by 38% compared to traditional instructional approaches, particularly benefiting learners with lower prior knowledge or working memory capacity.

The cognitive benefits extend to transfer of learning—the application of knowledge and skills beyond their acquisition context. Dalgarno and Lee (2010) identify several factors that enhance transfer in well-designed digital environments: embodied cognition through avatar movement and manipulation; variable practice across diverse scenarios; gradual fading of scaffolding as competence develops; and metacognitive prompts that encourage explicit connection-making between virtual and real-world contexts. Their research demonstrates that transfer effectiveness depends not just on the technology itself but on instructional design that deliberately bridges virtual exploration with real-world application through structured reflection and analogical reasoning activities (Dalgarno & Lee, 2010).

Emotional Regulation and Digital Safe Spaces

Beyond cognitive development, digital environments offer unique advantages for social-emotional learning—particularly emotional regulation, the ability to monitor and modulate emotional responses. Delafield-Butt (2018) demonstrates how game-based learning environments provide "emotional laboratories" where students can experience and process complex feelings within structured contexts that offer greater psychological safety than real-world interactions. Their research found that the slight psychological distance created by digital mediation allows students to engage with challenging emotional content without becoming overwhelmed, developing adaptive coping strategies that subsequently transfer to face-to-face scenarios.

Minecraft specifically supports emotional regulation through what Granic et al. (2014) term "emotional rehearsal"—practicing emotional responses to challenging situations in low-stakes environments. When students encounter frustration after losing valuable resources or experiencing setbacks in construction projects, they must develop and apply regulation strategies to persist toward goals. Research by Delafield-Butt and Adie (2016) found that students who regularly engaged in collaborative Minecraft activities demonstrated measurable improvements in frustration tolerance and emotional recovery speed in classroom learning tasks, with effects particularly pronounced for students with baseline regulation difficulties.

The mechanism for these benefits involves what Granic et al. (2014) identify as "progressive emotional challenge"—digital environments that gradually increase emotional demands as students develop coping capabilities. Beginning with simple emotional scenarios focused on basic resource management, games like Minecraft eventually introduce more complex social-emotional challenges involving negotiation, conflict resolution, and group planning. This graduated exposure allows students to build emotional competence incrementally, similar to how academic content is scaffolded from simple to complex (Delafield-Butt, 2018).

Teacher mediation remains essential for maximizing these emotional learning benefits. Hollett and Ehret (2017) found that when educators explicitly connect in-game emotional experiences to broader emotional regulation strategies, transfer to non-game contexts increases significantly. Effective approaches include reflection prompts that help students identify emotional triggers and responses, discussion of alternative regulation strategies when frustrated, and explicit connection-making between game scenarios and classroom social dynamics. This mediation transforms what might otherwise be purely recreational experiences into purposeful emotional skill development (Ito et al., 2020).

Cultural Competence in Global Digital Communities

The increasingly interconnected nature of digital learning environments creates unprecedented opportunities for developing cultural competence—the ability to understand, appreciate, and interact effectively with people from different cultural backgrounds. Multiplayer educational platforms like Minecraft connect students across geographical, socioeconomic, and cultural boundaries, creating "third spaces" where diverse perspectives naturally converge around shared objectives (Ito et al., 2020). These environments provide experiential learning in cross-cultural collaboration that traditional classroom approaches struggle to replicate.

Research by Ito et al. (2020) demonstrates how international Minecraft educational server projects foster authentic cultural exchange. Their three-year ethnographic study of collaborative building projects involving students from six countries found that participants developed more sophisticated understanding of cultural differences in communication styles, problem-solving approaches, and aesthetic preferences through sustained interaction. Rather than learning about cultural differences through abstract descriptions, students experienced them directly through collaborative work, developing adaptive strategies that accommodated diverse perspectives (Ito et al., 2020).

These cross-cultural experiences develop what Dede and Richards (2020) term "cultural navigation capabilities"—the ability to recognize how cultural frameworks shape individual perspectives and to adjust communication and collaboration approaches accordingly. Their research indicates that these capabilities transfer beyond gaming contexts to academic group work and eventually workplace collaboration, with longitudinal data showing that students with extensive cross-cultural digital experience demonstrate greater flexibility in multicultural team settings throughout their educational careers (Dede and Richards, 2020).

The development of cultural competence through digital environments depends significantly on implementation approaches. Holmes et al. (2019) emphasize that simply connecting diverse students does not automatically produce intercultural learning; rather, educators must structure interactions to promote perspective-taking and reflection on cultural differences. Effective practices include mixed cultural team formation with shared goals, structured dialogues about different approaches to challenges, and reflection activities that explicitly identify cultural influences on problem-solving strategies. When implemented thoughtfully, these practices transform digital environments from mere connection platforms to powerful contexts for developing global citizenship competencies (Holmes et al., 2019).

Identity Development and Digital Self-Expression

Digital worlds offer unique affordances for identity exploration and development—processes central to adolescent social-emotional development. Through avatar creation, world-building, and social interaction in virtual spaces, students can explore different aspects of identity in protected environments before applying insights to real-world identity development (Hollett and Ehret, 2017). This exploration proves particularly valuable during adolescence, when identity formation represents a central developmental task with significant implications for academic engagement and future aspirations.

Research by Hollett and Ehret (2017) documents how Minecraft in particular supports what they term "projective identity work"—the process of exploring possible selves through digital representation and interaction. Their longitudinal case studies of middle school students demonstrated that avatar customization and environmental design choices frequently reflected identity exploration, with participants testing different self-presentations and receiving immediate social feedback. This iterative process allowed students to refine their understanding of how different aspects of identity influence social reception and personal satisfaction, developing more integrated self-concepts over time (Hollett and Ehret, 2017).

For marginalized students particularly, digital environments can provide valuable identity affirmation experiences. Ito et al. (2020) found that students from underrepresented groups often found greater freedom for authentic self-expression in digital spaces where visual markers of difference were either absent or self-determined. Their research on interest-driven digital communities documented how LGBTQ+ youth, students of color, and students with disabilities often reported feeling "more themselves" in digital environments where they controlled identity disclosure and where shared interests rather than demographic characteristics formed the basis for community inclusion (Ito et al., 2020).

Educators play crucial roles in helping students connect digital identity exploration to broader identity development processes. Plass et al. (2020) demonstrate that when teachers incorporate structured reflection on digital self-representation choices, students develop greater metacognitive awareness of their identity construction processes both online and offline. Effective approaches include journaling about avatar design decisions, discussing how in-game choices reflect personal values, and exploring how digital self-presentation compares to classroom self-presentation. These reflective practices transform gaming from isolated entertainment to meaningful identity development work with implications for academic engagement and future planning (Plass et al., 2020).

Economic and Practical Considerations of AI Implementation

While the educational benefits of AI technologies are increasingly well-documented, implementation decisions must also consider economic factors to ensure sustainable adoption. Comprehensive cost-benefit analysis reveals that although initial AI implementation requires significant investment, long-term returns often justify these expenditures when systems are thoughtfully designed and implemented (Zawacki-Richter et al., 2019). Understanding these economic dimensions helps educational leaders make informed decisions that balance innovation with fiscal responsibility.

Research by Zawacki-Richter et al. (2019) identifies several cost categories that impact AI implementation: hardware infrastructure, software licensing, professional development, technical support, and instructional redesign time. Their analysis of implementation across diverse institutional contexts found that professional development typically represents the largest expense category, accounting for 35-45% of total implementation costs. However, this investment correlates strongly with implementation success, with institutions allocating at least 40% of budgets to teacher training reporting significantly higher adoption rates and learning outcomes than those focusing primarily on technology acquisition (Zawacki-Richter et al., 2019).

On the benefit side, well-implemented AI systems generate several categories of economic return. Holmes et al. (2019) document efficiency gains through automation of routine administrative and instructional tasks, allowing reallocation of teacher time to higher-value activities like personalized guidance and project-based learning. Their economic modeling suggests that mature AI implementations can reclaim 7-12 hours of teacher time weekly—equivalent to approximately 20% of total workload—by automating grading, feedback generation, and basic student support functions (Holmes et al., 2019).

Perhaps most significantly, AI implementation potentially reduces long-term remediation costs by identifying and addressing learning gaps before they compound. Baker et al. (2023) analyzed implementation across several school districts, finding that while AI systems required significant upfront investment, three-year financial models showed net positive returns through reduced summer school enrollment, decreased grade retention rates, and lower special education referrals for academic difficulties. These findings suggest that AI's preventative capabilities make economic sense when evaluated through multi-year rather than single-year budgeting perspectives (Baker et al., 2023).

Practical implementation lessons emphasize phased approaches that balance innovation with fiscal sustainability. Dede and Richards (2020) recommend beginning with targeted AI implementations addressing specific high-value challenges rather than comprehensive overhauls. Their research indicates that pilot programs focused on clear metrics of success build institutional support while generating evidence for subsequent scaling. This incremental approach allows educational institutions to develop technical expertise and implementation capacity gradually while distributing costs across multiple budget cycles (Dede and Richards, 2020).AI and automated systems can ease the administrative load, customize instruction to individual learners, and enable broader opportunities for international collaboration. However, it is human insight, empathy, and moral judgment that ensure these innovations lead to truly inclusive and purposeful educational outcomes. With sustained professional development, supportive policies, and collaborative efforts across sectors, educational institutions can leverage AI as a catalyst for creativity, equity, and critical engagement. Ultimately, this chapter posits that AI augments rather than supplants educators' expertise, safeguarding compassion, ethical reflection, and collaborative problem-solving as the central pillars of education in an increasingly digital, interconnected world.

REFERENCES

Ahmad, I., Suhaimi, M. A. B. M., & Ariffin, N. A. N. (2022). Quantum computing in education: A review of opportunities and challenges. *Education and Information Technologies*, *27*(2), 1871–1889.

Alaker, M., Wynn, G. R., & Arulampalam, T. (2023). Virtual reality training in laparoscopic surgery: A systematic review and meta-analysis. *International Journal of Surgery*, *57*, 87–94. PMID: 26992652

Alawajee, O., & Delafield-Butt, J. (2021). Minecraft in education benefits learning and social engagement. *International Journal of Game-Based Learning*, *11*(4), 19–56. DOI: 10.4018/IJGBL.2021100102

Allen, R., & West, H. (2023). Workforce readiness in an AI era: Implications for K-12 education. *Journal of Future Employment Studies*, *35*(1), 18–29.

Bailey, K., West, R., & Anderson, C. A. (2020). The influence of video games on social, cognitive, and affective information processing. In Sternberg, R. J., & Fiske, S. T. (Eds.), *Annual Review of Psychology* (Vol. 71, pp. 563–586). Annual Reviews.

Baker, R. S., & Hawn, A. (2021). Algorithmic bias in education. *International Journal of Artificial Intelligence in Education*, *32*(1), 1–41.

Baker, T., Smith, L., & Anissa, N. (2023). Artificial intelligence in education: A review and bibliometric analysis. *Review of Educational Research*, *93*(2), 275–308.

Barricelli, B. R., Casiraghi, E., & Fogli, D. (2019). A survey on digital twin: Definitions, characteristics, applications, and design implications. *IEEE Access : Practical Innovations, Open Solutions*, *7*, 167653–167671. DOI: 10.1109/ACCESS.2019.2953499

Bartlett, T. (2021). Bridging the skills gap: AI tools in career and technical education. *Innovative Education Journal*, *12*(4), 101–115.

Bayne, S. (2015). What's the matter with 'technology-enhanced learning'? *Learning, Media and Technology*, *40*(1), 5–20. DOI: 10.1080/17439884.2014.915851

Belpaeme, T., Kennedy, J., Ramachandran, A., Scassellati, B., & Tanaka, F. (2018). Social robots for education: A review. *Science Robotics*, *3*(21), eaat5954. DOI: 10.1126/scirobotics.aat5954 PMID: 33141719

Boaler, J. (2021). AI in mathematics education: Status, benefits, and challenges. *ZDM Mathematics Education*, *53*(4), 725–736.

Brown, J. S., Collins, A., & Duguid, P. (1989). Situated cognition and the culture of learning. *Educational Researcher*, *18*(1), 32–42. DOI: 10.3102/0013189X018001032

Brynjolfsson, E., & McAfee, A. (2014). *The second machine age: Work, progress, and prosperity in a time of brilliant technologies*. W.W. Norton and Company.

Buchanan, R., Holmes, K., Preston, G., & Shaw, K. (2022). The shifting landscape of academic work in a generative AI world. *Higher Education Research & Development, 41*(5), 1689–1703.

Buckingham Shum, S., Ferguson, R., & Martinez-Maldonado, R. (2019). Human-centred learning analytics. *Journal of Learning Analytics, 6*(2), 1–9. DOI: 10.18608/jla.2019.62.1

Buzzetto-Hollywood, N., and Alade, A. (2018). An examination of Gen Z learners attending a minority university. Interdisciplinary Journal of e-Skills and Lifelong Learning, 14(1), 41-53.

Carpenter, J. P., & Linton, J. N. (2018). Educators' perspectives on the impact of Edcamp unconference professional learning. *Teaching and Teacher Education, 73*, 56–69. DOI: 10.1016/j.tate.2018.03.014

Carpenter, J. P., Rosenberg, J. M., Dousay, T. A., Romero-Hall, E., Trust, T., Kessler, A., Phillips, M., Morrison, S. A., Fischer, C., & Krutka, D. G. (2020). What should teacher educators know about technology? Perspectives and self-assessments. *Teaching and Teacher Education, 95*, 103124. DOI: 10.1016/j.tate.2020.103124

Causo, A., Vo, G. T., Chen, I. M., & Yeo, S. H. (2016). Design of robots used as education companion and tutor. In Robila, S. (Ed.), *Robotics in STEM education: Redesigning the learning experience* (pp. 75–88). Springer.

Chang, M., & Xie, T. (2022). Metaverse education: Opportunities and challenges in virtual world learning. *International Journal of Virtual Learning, 9*(1), 45–62.

Checa, D., & Bustillo, A. (2020). A review of immersive virtual reality serious games to enhance learning and training. *Multimedia Tools and Applications, 79*(9), 5501–5527. DOI: 10.1007/s11042-019-08348-9

Cipollone, M., Schifter, C. C., & Moffat, R. A. (2022). Roblox as an educational tool: Leveraging student-created content for learning. *Educational Technology Research and Development, 70*(4), 1713–1739.

Clark, D. B., Tanner-Smith, E. E., & Killingsworth, S. S. (2016). Digital games, design, and learning: A systematic review and meta-analysis. *Review of Educational Research, 86*(1), 79–122. DOI: 10.3102/0034654315582065 PMID: 26937054

Dalgarno, B., & Lee, M. J. (2010). What are the learning affordances of 3-D virtual environments? *British Journal of Educational Technology, 41*(1), 10–32. DOI: 10.1111/j.1467-8535.2009.01038.x

Dede, C., & Richards, J. (2020). *The 60-Year curriculum: New models for lifelong learning in the digital economy*. Routledge. DOI: 10.4324/9781003013617

Delafield-Butt, J. (2018). The emotional and embodied nature of human understanding: Sharing narratives of meaning. In Trevarthen, C., Delafield-Butt, J., & Dunlop, A.-W. (Eds.), *The child's curriculum: Working with the natural voices of young children*. Oxford University Press.

Delafield-Butt, J. T., & Adie, J. (2016). The embodied narrative nature of learning: Nurture in school. *Mind, Brain and Education : the Official Journal of the International Mind, Brain, and Education Society, 10*(2), 14. DOI: 10.1111/mbe.12120

Deming, D. J. (2017). The growing importance of social skills in the labor market. *The Quarterly Journal of Economics, 132*(4), 1593–1640. DOI: 10.1093/qje/qjx022

Deterding, S., Dixon, D., Khaled, R., & Nacke, L. (2011). From game design elements to gamefulness: Defining gamification. *Proceedings of the 15th International Academic MindTrek Conference*, 9-15. DOI: 10.1145/2181037.2181040

Druga, S., Williams, R., Breazeal, C., & Resnick, M. (2019). "Hey Google is it OK if I eat you?": Initial explorations in child-agent interaction. In Proceedings of the 2019 CHI Conference on Human Factors in Computing Systems (pp. 1-8).

Duncan, S. C., Martin, J., & Pinkard, N. (2022). Designing for connected play: Understanding learning in digital play spaces. *Information and Learning Science, 123*(1/2), 40–55.

Ellison, T. L., Evans, J. N., & Pike, J. (2016). Minecraft, teachers, parents, and learning: What they need to know and understand. *School Community Journal, 26*(2), 25–43.

Farah, M., Hassouna, M., Hesham, M., & Obaidli, F. A. (2022). Web 3.0 and education: A systematic review. *Education and Information Technologies, 27*(6), 8039–8057.

Foronda, C. L., Fernandez-Burgos, M., Nadeau, C., Kelley, C. N., & Henry, M. N. (2022). Virtual simulation in nursing education: A systematic review spanning 1996 to 2022. *Nurse Education Today, 96*, 104829.

Garcia, S. E., & Bowers, A. J. (2020). Human-AI learning performance in vocational education. *Computers & Education, 157*, 103991.

Gee, E., & Gee, J. P. (2021). Games, learning, and the role of the teacher in the digital age. *Educational Technology Research and Development, 69*(3), 1093–1107.

Gee, J. P. (2007). *What video games have to teach us about learning and literacy*. Palgrave Macmillan.

Gonzalez, G., & Gasco, J. (2022). Digital wellbeing in the Internet age: A systematic literature review. *Telematics and Informatics, 69*, 101802.

Granic, I., Lobel, A., & Engels, R. C. (2014). The benefits of playing video games. *The American Psychologist, 69*(1), 66–78. DOI: 10.1037/a0034857 PMID: 24295515

Gretter, S., & Yadav, A. (2018). What do preservice teachers think about teaching media literacy? An exploratory study using the Theory of Planned Behavior. *The Journal of Media Literacy Education, 10*(1), 104–123. DOI: 10.23860/JMLE-2018-10-1-6

Gunning, D., Stefik, M., Choi, J., Miller, T., Stumpf, S., & Yang, G. Z. (2019). XAI—Explainable artificial intelligence. *Science Robotics*, *4*(37), eaay7120. DOI: 10.1126/scirobotics.aay7120 PMID: 33137719

Gyongyosi, L., & Imre, S. (2019). A survey on quantum computing technology. *Computer Science Review*, *31*, 51–71. DOI: 10.1016/j.cosrev.2018.11.002

Hadjri, K., & Jorgensen, T. (2021). Haptic perception and VR in architecture education. *Design Studies*, *72*, 100980.

Harmes, J. C., Welsh, J. L., & Winkelman, R. J. (2016). A framework for defining and evaluating technology integration in the instruction of real-world skills. In S. Ferrara, Y. Rosen, and M. Tager (Eds.), Handbook of research on technology tools for real-world skill development (pp. 137-162). IGI Global.

Ho, A. (2017). Advancing educational research and student privacy in the "big data" era. *Workshop on Big Data in Education: Balancing the Benefits of Educational Research and Student Privacy*. National Academy of Education.

Hollett, T., & Ehret, C. (2017). Relational methodologies for mobile literacies: Intra-action, rhythm, and atmosphere. In Burnett, C., Merchant, G., Simpson, A., & Walsh, M. (Eds.), *The case of the iPad: Mobile literacies in education* (pp. 227–244). Springer. DOI: 10.1007/978-981-10-4364-2_14

Holmes, W., Bialik, M., & Fadel, C. (2019). *Artificial intelligence in education: Promises and implications for teaching and learning*. Center for Curriculum Redesign.

Holmes, W., Porayska-Pomsta, K., Holstein, K., Sutherland, E., Baker, T., Shum, S. B., Santos, O. C., Rodrigo, M. T., Cukurova, M., Bittencourt, I. I., & Koedinger, K. R. (2022). Ethics of AI in education: Towards a community-wide framework. *International Journal of Artificial Intelligence in Education*, *32*(3), 504–526. DOI: 10.1007/s40593-021-00239-1

Holstein, K., Wortman Vaughan, J., Daumé, H.III, Dudik, M., & Wallach, H. (2019). Improving fairness in machine learning systems: What do industry practitioners need? In *Proceedings of the 2019 CHI Conference on Human Factors in Computing Systems* (pp. 1-16). DOI: 10.1145/3290605.3300830

Howard, S. K. (2021). Affect and technology adoption in the classroom: A conceptual framework for technology professional development. *Journal of Research on Technology in Education*, *53*(4), 414–429.

Howard, S. K., & Mozejko, A. (2015). Teachers: Technology, change and resistance. In Henderson, M., & Romeo, G. (Eds.), *Teaching and digital technologies: Big issues and critical questions* (pp. 307–317). Cambridge University Press. DOI: 10.1017/CBO9781316091968.030

IBM. (2022). *P-TECH: When skills meet opportunity, success happens*. IBM Corporation.

Ioannou, M., & Makridou, E. (2018). The impact of educational robotics on computational thinking skills in elementary school students. In Daniela, L. (Ed.), *Smart learning with educational robotics* (pp. 159–182). Springer.

Ito, M., Martin, C., Pfister, R. C., Rafalow, M. H., Salen, K., & Wortman, A. (2020). *Affinity online: How connection and shared interest fuel learning*. NYU Press.

Jirgensons, M., & Kapenieks, J. (2018). Blockchain and the future of digital learning credential assessment and management. *Journal of Teacher Education for Sustainability, 20*(1), 145–156. DOI: 10.2478/jtes-2018-0009

Johnson, A. (2022). *AI in education: Balancing innovation and ethics*. Educational Press.

Johnson-Glenberg, M. C. (2018). Immersive VR and education: Embodied design principles that include gesture and hand controls. *Frontiers in Robotics and AI, 5*, 81. DOI: 10.3389/frobt.2018.00081 PMID: 33500960

Kandlhofer, M., Steinbauer, G., Hirschmugl-Gaisch, S., & Huber, P. (2016). Artificial intelligence and computer science in education: From kindergarten to university. In *Proceedings of the 2016 IEEE Frontiers in Education Conference* (pp. 1-9). DOI: 10.1109/FIE.2016.7757570

Kaplan, A., & Haenlein, M. (2019). Siri, Siri, in my hand: Who's the fairest in the land? On the interpretations, illustrations, and implications of artificial intelligence. *Business Horizons, 62*(1), 15–25. DOI: 10.1016/j.bushor.2018.08.004

Karapanos, M., Borowski, M., & Elsholz, M. (2022). Digital apprenticeships: Opportunities and challenges of virtual vocational training in technical domains. *Education and Information Technologies, 28*(1), 733–753.

Kavanagh, S., Luxton-Reilly, A., Wuensche, B., & Plimmer, B. (2018). Creating 360° educational video: A case study. In *Proceedings of the 20th Australasian Computing Education Conference* (pp. 180-185).

Khan, B. H., Corbeil, J. R., & Corbeil, M. E. (2021). *Blockchain, leadership, and management: Business as usual or radical disruption?* IGI Global.

Khanlari, A. (2016). Teachers' perceptions of the benefits and the challenges of integrating educational robots into primary/elementary curricula. *European Journal of Engineering Education, 41*(3), 320–330. DOI: 10.1080/03043797.2015.1056106

Khosravi, H., Buckingham Shum, S., Chen, G., Conati, C., Tsai, Y. S., Kay, J., Knight, S., Martinez-Maldonado, R., Sadiq, S., & Gašević, D. (2022). Explainable artificial intelligence in education. *Computers and Education: Artificial Intelligence, 3*, 100074.

Kim, S., Kim, S. Y., & Park, J. S. (2021). Haptic-enabled virtual reality surgical simulation systems: A systematic review. *Surgical Innovation, 28*(1), 95–106. PMID: 32757879

König, J., Jäger-Biela, D. J., & Glutsch, N. (2020). Adapting to online teaching during COVID-19 school closure: Teacher education and teacher competence effects among early career teachers in Germany. *European Journal of Teacher Education, 43*(4), 608–622. DOI: 10.1080/02619768.2020.1809650

Kuhn, J., Stevens, V., & Schwartz, D. L. (2023). Computational thinking in action: Student-directed learning in Minecraft and its connection to STEM outcomes. *Journal of the Learning Sciences, 32*(1), 32–58.

Kumar, A., & Boulanger, D. (2020). Explainable automated essay scoring: Deep learning really has pedagogical value. *Frontiers in Education, 5*, 572367. DOI: 10.3389/feduc.2020.572367

Kumar, S., Martin, F., Budhrani, K., & Ritzhaupt, A. (2022). Award-winning faculty online teaching practices: Elements of award-winning courses. *Online Learning : the Official Journal of the Online Learning Consortium, 23*(4), 160–180.

Lamb, P. (2019). Toward a pedagogy of experiential learning in digital manufacturing. In Billingsley, P., & Ford, M. (Eds.), *Learning through digital fabrication* (pp. 147–164). Routledge.

Lee, H., Lee, J., & Makara, K. A. (2022). A systematic review of multimodal learning analytics: Methodology, challenges, and future directions. *Journal of Learning Analytics, 9*(3), 215–239.

Li, Y., Chen, D., & Deng, X. (2024). The impact of digital educational games on student's motivation for learning: The mediating effect of learning engagement and the moderating effect of the digital environment. *PLoS One, 19*(1), e0294350. DOI: 10.1371/journal.pone.0294350 PMID: 38206923

Litow, S. S., & Kelley, T. A. (2018). *Breaking the code: The P-TECH story*. Columbia University Press.

Liu, Y., Raymond, H. M., & Wankel, C. (2022). Using digital twins for sustainability education. In *Handbook of research on digital tools for seamless learning* (pp. 245–269). IGI Global.

Long, D., & Magerko, B. (2020). What is AI literacy? Competencies and design considerations. In *Proceedings of the 2020 CHI Conference on Human Factors in Computing Systems* (pp. 1-16). DOI: 10.1145/3313831.3376727

Lynch, R. L. (2000). High school career and technical education for the first decade of the 21st century. *Journal of Vocational Education Research, 25*(2), 155–198.

Lynch, S. J., Burton, E. P., Behrend, T., House, A., Ford, M., Spillane, N., Matray, S., Han, E., & Means, B. (2019). A model for implementing STEM career awareness within inclusive elementary schools. *Journal of STEM Outreach, 2*(1), 1–10.

Makransky, G., & Petersen, G. B. (2021). The cognitive affective model of immersive learning (CAMIL): A theoretical research-based model of learning in immersive virtual reality. *Educational Psychology Review*, *33*(3), 937–958. DOI: 10.1007/s10648-020-09586-2

Makransky, G., Terkildsen, T. S., & Mayer, R. E. (2019). Adding immersive virtual reality to a science lab simulation causes more presence but less learning. *Learning and Instruction*, *60*, 225–236. DOI: 10.1016/j.learninstruc.2017.12.007

Marklund, B. B., & Taylor, A. S. A. (2016). Educational games in practice: The challenges involved in conducting a game-based curriculum. *Electronic Journal of e-Learning*, *14*(2), 122–135.

Marr, B. (2018). *Artificial intelligence in practice: How 50 companies used AI and machine learning to solve problems*. Wiley.

Mayer, R. E. (2019). Computer games in education. *Annual Review of Psychology*, *70*(1), 531–549. DOI: 10.1146/annurev-psych-010418-102744 PMID: 30231003

McGrath, J. L., Taekman, J. M., Dev, P., Danforth, D. R., Mohan, D., Kman, N., Crichlow, A., & Bond, W. F. (2018). Using virtual reality simulation environments to assess competence for emergency medicine learners. *Academic Emergency Medicine*, *25*(2), 186–195. DOI: 10.1111/acem.13308 PMID: 28888070

Mikropoulos, T. A., & Natsis, A. (2021). Educational virtual environments: A ten-year review of empirical research (1999–2019). *Journal of Computers in Education*, *8*(1), 1–44.

Minecraft Education. (2017). How learners are developing social-emotional skills with Minecraft.

Mishra, P., & Koehler, M. J. (2006). Technological pedagogical content knowledge: A framework for teacher knowledge. *Teachers College Record*, *108*(6), 1017–1054. DOI: 10.1111/j.1467-9620.2006.00684.x

Mitchell, A. (2022). AI-powered language learning: Evaluating the efficacy of language learning applications. *ReCALL*, *34*(1), 71–89.

Morgan, K. (2023). AI in E-learning: New horizons in digital education. *Journal of Educational Technology Innovations*, *28*(1), 22–40.

Muro, M., Maxim, R., & Whiton, J. (2020). *The robots are not coming for all our jobs: Automation in the COVID economy*. Brookings Institution.

Nebel, S., Schneider, S., & Rey, G. D. (2016). Mining learning and crafting scientific experiments: A literature review on the use of Minecraft in education and research. *Journal of Educational Technology & Society*, *19*(2), 355–366.

Nelson, J., & Fien, J. (2021). Digital twins and environmental education: Promises and risks. *Australian Journal of Environmental Education*, *37*(3), 230–244.

Nemorin, S. (2021). Video production pedagogy and non-linear editing: A case for distributed media literacy. *Learning, Media and Technology*, *46*(1), 43–56.

Ng, D. T. K. (2021). Artificial intelligence in education: A review of challenges and opportunities. *Journal of Educational Computing Research*, *59*(5), 861–883.

Nguyen, A., Khosla, M., & Yu, Z. (2023). Multimodal artificial intelligence: A systematic literature review. *Knowledge-Based Systems*, *260*, 110192.

Papert, S. (1980). *Mindstorms: Children, computers, and powerful ideas*. Basic Books.

Parong, J., & Mayer, R. E. (2018). Learning science in immersive virtual reality. *Journal of Educational Psychology*, *110*(6), 785–797. DOI: 10.1037/edu0000241

Passarelli, M., Erickson, I., & Al-Masri, E. (2020). Business simulations as a pedagogical tool: Measuring learning outcomes in executive education programs. *International Journal of Management Education*, *18*(3), 100433.

Pedró, F., Subosa, M., Rivas, A., & Valverde, P. (2019). *Artificial intelligence in education: Challenges and opportunities for sustainable development*. UNESCO.

Peralta, J., Yousuf, H., & Newman, S. (2022). A review of digital twins: Bridging the gap between academia and industry. *CIRP Journal of Manufacturing Science and Technology*, *38*, 94–111.

Plass, J. L., Homer, B. D., & Kinzer, C. K. (2015). Foundations of game-based learning. *Educational Psychologist*, *50*(4), 258–283. DOI: 10.1080/00461520.2015.1122533

Plass, J. L., Mayer, R. E., & Homer, B. D. (Eds.). (2020). *Handbook of game-based learning*. MIT Press.

Prestridge, S. (2012). The beliefs behind the teacher that influences their ICT practices. *Computers & Education*, *58*(1), 449–458. DOI: 10.1016/j.compedu.2011.08.028

Prestridge, S. (2019). Categorising teachers' use of social media for their professional learning: A self-generating professional learning paradigm. *Computers & Education*, *129*, 143–158. DOI: 10.1016/j.compedu.2018.11.003

Priestley, M., Alvunger, D., Philippou, S., & Soini, T. (2022). Curriculum making in changing educational governance spaces: Conceptualising curriculum making in schools. *European Educational Research Journal*, *21*(3), 350–370.

Prinsloo, P., & Slade, S. (2017). An elephant in the learning analytics room: The obligation to act. In *Proceedings of the Seventh International Learning Analytics and Knowledge Conference* (pp. 46-55). DOI: 10.1145/3027385.3027406

Puentedura, R. (2006). Transformation, technology, and education. Presentation given August, 2006, in Auburn, Maine.

Radianti, J., Majchrzak, T. A., Fromm, J., & Wohlgenannt, I. (2020). A systematic review of immersive virtual reality applications for higher education: Design elements, lessons learned, and research agenda. *Computers & Education*, *147*, 103778. DOI: 10.1016/j.compedu.2019.103778

Rainie, L., & Anderson, J. (2017). *The future of jobs and jobs training*. Pew Research Center.

Ramachandran, R., & Young, A. (2019). Virtual apprenticeships: Connecting industry and education for real-world learning. In *Handbook of research on virtual training and mentoring of online instructors* (pp. 225–246). IGI Global.

Reich, J. (2019). Teaching our way to digital equity. *Educational Leadership*, *76*(5), 30–35.

Reich, J., Buttimer, C. J., Fang, A., Hillaire, G., Hirsch, K., Larke, L. R., Littenberg-Tobias, J., Moussapour, R. M., Napier, A., Thompson, M., & Slama, R. (2019). Remote learning guidance from state education agencies during the COVID-19 pandemic: A first look. *EdArXiv*.

Richards, D., & Taylor, M. (2015). A comparison of learning gains when using a 2D simulation tool versus a 3D virtual world: An experiment to find the right representation involving the Marginal Value Theorem. *Computers & Education*, *86*, 157–171. DOI: 10.1016/j.compedu.2015.03.009

Richardson, J. W. (2022). Artificial intelligence in educational leadership: A symbiotic role for school improvement. In Rabelo, A. A., Lee, K., & Foulger, M. L. (Eds.), *Handbook of research on educational leadership and equity* (pp. 67–89). IGI Global.

Ritzhaupt, A. D., Huggins-Manley, A. C., Dawson, K., Ağaçlı-Doğan, N., & Doğan, S. (2018). Validity and appropriate uses of the revised technology uses and perceptions survey (TUPS). *Journal of Research on Technology in Education*, *50*(4), 309–327.

Rivera, G., & Ramirez, M. (2022). Digital apprenticeship during COVID-19 restrictions: Emergence and consolidation of new pedagogical models. *Education Sciences*, *12*(1), 29.

Roque, R. (2022). Creative computing for all: Promoting equity through the integration of arts and computing education. *Journal of Research in STEM Education*, *8*(1), 57–76.

Rosen, R., Visher, M., & Beal, K. (2022). Career and technical education: Models for connecting school and work. *The Future of Children*, *32*(1), 119–145.

Selwyn, N. (2019). What's the problem with learning analytics? *Journal of Learning Analytics*, *6*(3), 11–19. DOI: 10.18608/jla.2019.63.3

Siegel, D. R., & Gibbons, A. M. (2019). Promoting skilled trades and technical education through augmented reality applications. *International Journal of Virtual and Augmented Reality*, *3*(1), 30–42.

Skulmowski, A., & Rey, G. D. (2018). Embodied learning: Introducing a taxonomy based on bodily engagement and task integration. *Cognitive Research: Principles and Implications*, *3*(1), 6. DOI: 10.1186/s41235-018-0092-9 PMID: 29541685

Slater, M., & Sanchez-Vives, M. V. (2016). Enhancing our lives with immersive virtual reality. *Frontiers in Robotics and AI, 3*(74). Advance online publication. DOI: 10.3389/frobt.2016.00074

Slattery, E. J., Lehane, P., Butler, D., O'Leary, M., & Marshall, K. (2025). Assessing the benefits of digital game-based learning with Minecraft in children, adolescents and young adults: A broad systematic review. *Review of Education, 13*(1), e70035. DOI: 10.1002/rev3.70035

Smith, L., & Brown, M. (2020). Professional development and AI literacy: Preparing teachers for the new digital age. *International Journal of Educational Technology, 15*(2), 45–58.

Stone, R. T., McLaurin, E., Zhong, P., & Watts, K. P. (2021). Performance evaluation of virtual reality welding training simulators: A systematic review. *Virtual Reality (Waltham Cross), 25*(2), 567–584.

Tan, J. P. L., Yang, S., Koh, E., & Jonathan, C. (2021). Adaptive learning in Singapore schools: National design, implementation and research. *Educational Media International, 58*(2), 153–172.

The Smarter Kid. (2024, August 30). Minecraft learning benefits for kids—And why teachers are embracing it! Touretzky, D., Gardner-McCune, C., Martin, F., and Seehorn, D. (2019). Envisioning AI for K-12: What should every child know about AI? *Proceedings of the AAAI Conference on Artificial Intelligence, 33*, 9795–9799.

Tukur, M., Schneider, J., Househ, M., Dokoro, A. H., Ismail, U. I., Dawaki, M., & Agus, M. (2024). The Metaverse digital environments: A scoping review of the techniques, technologies, and applications. *Journal of King Saud University. Computer and Information Sciences, 36*(2), 101967. DOI: 10.1016/j.jksuci.2024.101967

Twenge, J. M., Martin, G. N., & Campbell, W. K. (2018). Decreases in psychological well-being among American adolescents after 2012 and links to screen time during the rise of smartphone technology. *Emotion (Washington, D.C.), 18*(6), 765–780. DOI: 10.1037/emo0000403 PMID: 29355336

UNESCO. (2021). *AI and education: Guidance for policy-makers*. UNESCO.

Voogt, J., Fisser, P., Pareja Roblin, N., Tondeur, J., & van Braak, J. (2013). Technological pedagogical content knowledge—A review of the literature. *Journal of Computer Assisted Learning, 29*(2), 109–121. DOI: 10.1111/j.1365-2729.2012.00487.x

Vygotsky, L. S. (1978). *Mind in society: The development of higher psychological processes*. Harvard University Press.

Warschauer, M., & Matuchniak, T. (2010). New technology and digital worlds: Analyzing evidence of equity in access, use, and outcomes. *Review of Research in Education, 34*(1), 179–225. DOI: 10.3102/0091732X09349791

Watkins, S. C. (2021). Technology gap: Digital equality in tech-rich afterschool programs. *Equitable Innovation in Education*, *2*(1), 1–18.

West, D. M., Capkun, S., Goldwasser, S., Marson, S. M., & Yadav, A. (2022). *Education in the age of artificial intelligence and surveillance capitalism*. Brookings Institution.

Wong, J., Baars, M., Davis, D., Van Der Zee, T., Houben, G. J., & Paas, F. (2023). Supporting self-regulated learning in online learning environments and MOOCs: A systematic review. *International Journal of Human-Computer Interaction*, *35*(4-5), 356–373. DOI: 10.1080/10447318.2018.1543084

World Economic Forum. (2023). Future of jobs report 2023. World Economic Forum.

Wouters, P., Van Nimwegen, C., Van Oostendorp, H., & Van Der Spek, E. D. (2013). A meta-analysis of the cognitive and motivational effects of serious games. *Journal of Educational Psychology*, *105*(2), 249–265. DOI: 10.1037/a0031311

Wu, B., Yu, X., & Gu, X. (2020). Effectiveness of immersive virtual reality using head-mounted displays on learning performance: A meta-analysis. *British Journal of Educational Technology*, *51*(6), 1991–2005. DOI: 10.1111/bjet.13023

Xu, X., Liu, C., & Dietrich, D. (2022). Collaborative intelligence in human–AI interaction: A review and research agenda. *International Journal of Information Management*, *67*, 102515.

Chapter 15
AI-Powered Knowledge Management in Curriculum Design and Content Delivery

Parihar Suresh Dahake
https://orcid.org/0000-0002-2286-4120
Ramdeobaba University, Nagpur, India

Vasco Ribeiro Santo
https://orcid.org/0000-0002-3535-9377
ISLA Santarém, Tomar, Portugal

Ram Panchariya
Bapurao Deshmukh College of Engineering (BDCOE), Wardha, India

ABSTRACT

A solution that combines an open-source generic cloud-based AI-powered Knowledge Management (KM) Platform with custom-tailored curriculum content development to help integrate modern global AI knowledge and developments into the design of the Vocational Curriculum and Educational content delivery in India is introduced. It addresses how this AI-Powered KM Platform will interact with local AI employment trends, local environmental and non-technical challenges, and custom-tailored curriculum content. There is a rising demand for AI knowledge and education across economies globally as it outgrows its Computer Science roots into multidisciplinary and rapidly differentiating sectors like AI for social good, AI in healthcare, environmental preservation, innovation, energy, sustainability, and general global labor market transformations.

DOI: 10.4018/979-8-3373-5092-9.ch015

INTRODUCTION

During the past decade, artificial intelligence has gained massive popularity and has become an indispensable part of various sectors. The education sector is no exception. Educators actively try to incorporate AI into the sector to augment the learning experience (Mello et al., 2023). Artificial intelligence has two significant terminations within the sector - generating content and segmenting content. The deployment of AI in education has amplified the student convenience level compared to traditional education systems. 21st-century skills are broader than digital skills, and they are not necessarily underpinned by ICT, with seven core skills and five contextual skills identified(Van Laar et al., 2017). Artificial intelligence (AI) has evolved from a primitive concept to a complex, flexible system capable of achieving goals and tasks through flexible adaptation(Haenlein & Kaplan, 2019), and Integrating AI with emerging technologies like IoT for enhanced student engagement and teacher efficiency (Tan, 2023). The expected future enhancement includes improved content retrieval, advanced assessment systems, and the integration of VR/AR technologies within education modules. The active engagement in AI adoption discussions, coupled with the creation of organizational frameworks to ensure successful implementation(Tyson & Sauers, 2021). And Specialized content knowledge is crucial for teaching mathematics, with distinct subdomains within pedagogical content knowledge and distinct from common content knowledge needed by both teachers and nonteachers(Loewenberg Ball et al., 2008). One significant fermenting area of AI capabilities is the provision of learning analytics to follow learners' progress. To further study, a few recent applications and technologies in the education sector including Kurzweil Accelerating Intelligence, My AI assistant, Neural Mind, Dope techs apps, AR studs, the School App, Bright Side and Periodic table. Educational resources have been easily generated over the Internet, creating educational content. Curriculum delivery has been largely digitized as e-content. Teachers deliver their announcements and take queries from students over emails and online material sharing platforms.

Figure 1. Conventional interaction model in education

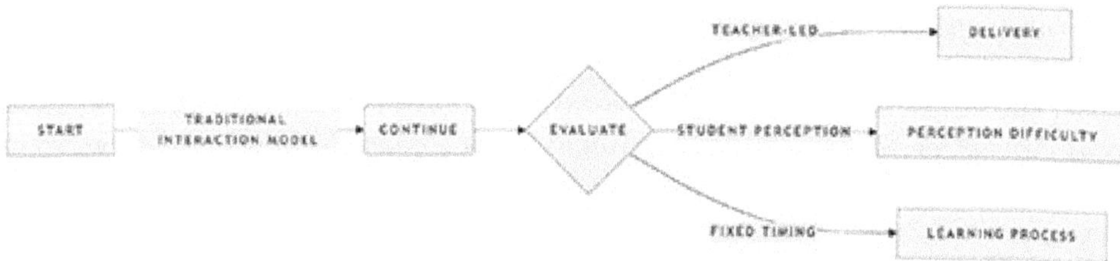

Figure 1 depicts the conventional interaction model. In the traditional model or usual using teaching methods, teachers deliver content-less lectures or seminars, students perceive it with the difficulty of interpretation, and finally, the entire learning process occurs at a fixed or preschedule time. AI can analyse content delivery and, from past patterns, envision future trends(Aliabadi et al., 2023). It provides key high-impact insights for an educator to formulate decisions accordingly. Machine Learning and a taxonomy for explaining AI models, aiming to advance the field towards responsible AI implementation(Barredo Arrieta et al., 2020) and AI has the aptitude to quantify several affective signals in real-time during the content delivery that the human senses are unable to do so. AI in education has significantly improved administration, instruction, and learning by enhancing efficiency, fostering student retention, and enhancing curriculum personalization(Chen et al., 2020). One of the most important components of a well-managed organization is the way by which knowledge is used to attain a competitive advantage. Today, institutions and organizations consistently strive to enhance the capabilities needed for effective use, sharing, and development of knowledge. Knowledge Management (KM) is thus becoming a critical component of organizational strategies. These strategies include the construction, documentation and dissemination of good practices and knowledge in various forms, such as policies, maps, case studies, reports, data, guides and course materials, to list a few(Nain, 2011).The reinforcement learning framework enable temporally abstract knowledge and actions to be included in planning and learning methods, improving performance without committing to specific approaches(Sutton et al., 1999).Through the evolution and advancements in Information and Communication Technologies (ICT) a new form of KM transitions to an e-based medium: Electronic Knowledge Management (EKM). In its simplest form EKM can be defined as KM activities assisted by electronic means. In this e-facilitated world, the boundaries of an institution or organization are extended to enable a wider and more effective access to information and knowledge resources. E-initiatives such as open, flexible and distance learning have been effectively used to promote KM and to support knowledge development. Several KM approaches could be adopted through e-initiatives, such as creating Communities of Practice (CoP), Explainable AI (XAI) holds promise for improving trust and transparency in AI-based systems, enabling AI to continue making steady progress without disruption(Adadi & Berrada, 2018). Moreover, developing searchable knowledge repositories, creating FAQs, organizing discussion forums and delivering training on KM issues. Many KM systems provide features to enable CoP formation, e.g., online discussion boards, file sharing areas, e-mailing lists, and member directories. Combinatorial generalization is crucial for AI to achieve human-like abilities, and using relational inductive biases within deep learning architectures can facilitate learning about entities, relations, and rules for composing them. Authentic design-based activities, such as working in design teams to develop online courses, significantly improve teachers' Technological Pedagogical Content Knowledge(Koehler & Mishra, 2005), and Knowledge distillation effectively learns a small student model from a large teacher model, reducing computational complexity and storage requirements for deep neural networks on limited resources(Gou et al., 2021). Knowledge-based systems have evolved from black boxes providing answers to programs capable of explaining, acquiring new knowledge, and transferring knowledge to students(R. Davis, 1986). And nowadays, AI job replacement in service tasks progresses from lower to higher intelligences, reducing the importance of analytical skills and increasing the importance of intuitive and empathetic skills for service employees(Huang & Rust, 2018).AI in higher education research mainly focuses on profiling, assessment, and personalization, but there is a need for more critical reflection on challenges, risks, and ethical approaches(Zawacki-Richter et al., 2019). As AI can be viewed as a nuanced concept, with potential and risk, and can be categorized into evolutionary stages and types, helping organizations consider its internal and external implications(Kaplan & Haenlein, 2019). However, AI tools like ChatGPT show promise in healthcare education, research, and practice, but its adoption should be cautious due to potential limitations and ethical concerns(Sallam, 2023). Above all, Student teachers' views on technology integration and the discipline's nature play a crucial role in shaping their technology-enhanced pedagogical content knowledge(Niess, 2005).

REVIEW OF LITERATURE

Figure 2. All keywords analysis by Vosviewer

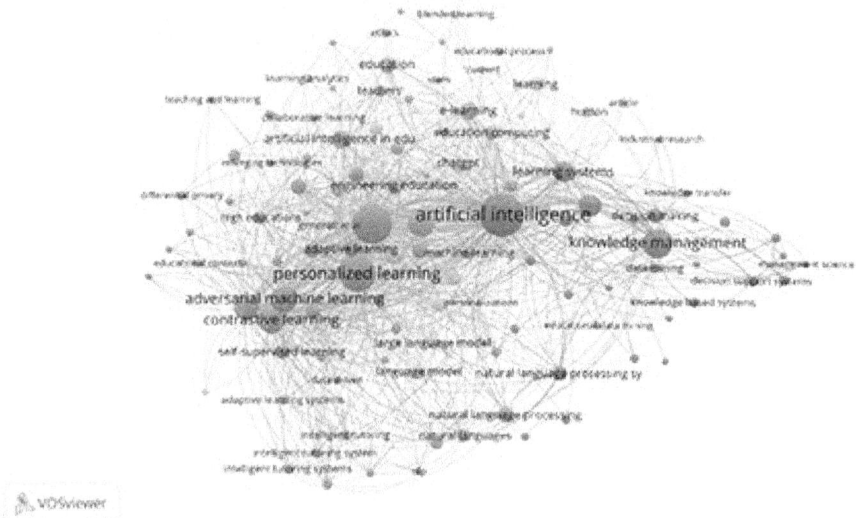

The analysis of All Keywords shows strong relationships among the AI, Knowledge Management and Personalized Learning and curriculum innovation it is mainly focuses on the pivotal role of the educational content delivery.

Figure 3. Author keywords analysis by Vosviewer

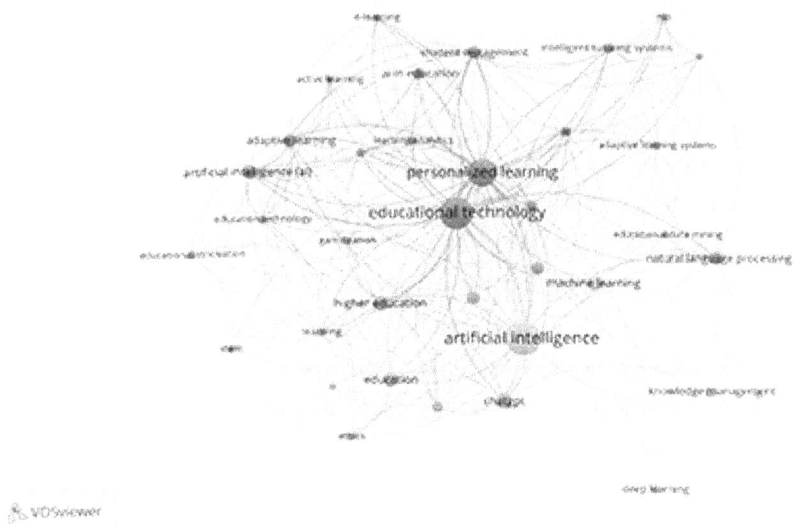

In addition to this the author keyword analysis highlights the strong connections between artificial intelligence, educational Technology, personalized Learning and knowledge management that is emphasizing transformative impact on AI on curriculum design adaptive learning and content delivery system.

Figure 4. Index keywords analysis by Vosviewer

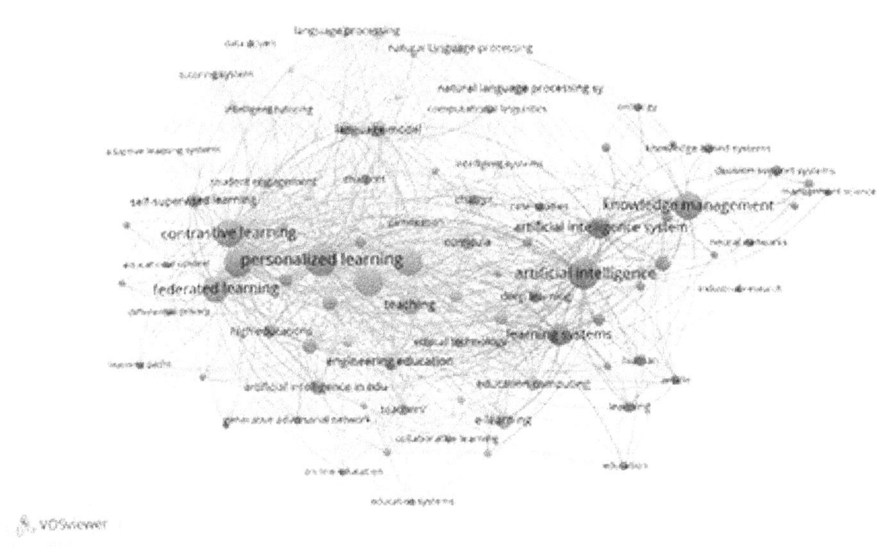

Moreover, the index Keywords Analysis in Vos viewer describes the deep integration of Artificial Intelligence, Personalized Learning, and Knowledge Management that underscores vital role of AI in enhancing curriculum design, content delivery, and Intelligent Learning System.

Figure 5. Bibliometric country wise coupling analysis by Vosviewer

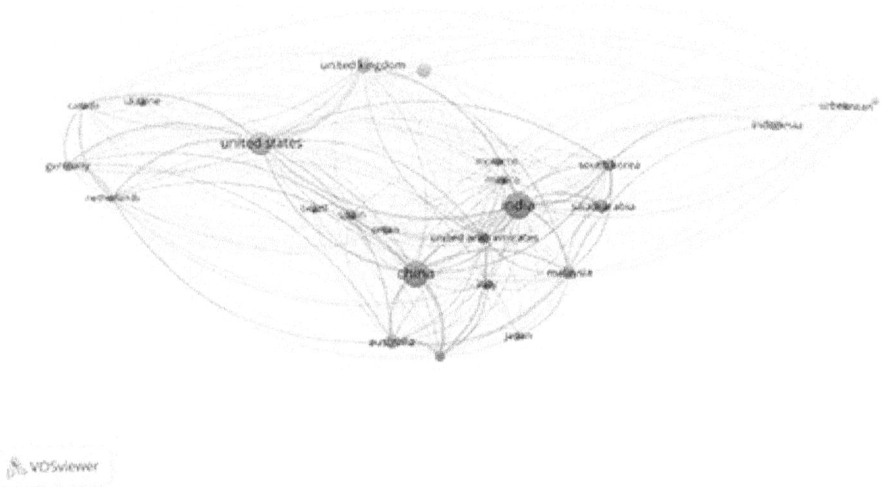

With India, China, and the United States leading the way in studies in AI-driven knowledge management, the bibliometric country co-citation analysis reveals strong worldwide cooperation. This worldwide cooperation underlines the growing academic focus on enhancing curriculum design and material distribution via smart technologies. The vital need of knowledge management to store, share, and analyze data and information is to design curricula and develop subject learning content. Artificial intelligence plays a key role in managing this knowledge efficiently and producing adequate results. It is observed in this study that the to-do application part of Google Keep locally and globally. (Bahroun et al., 2023) stated that the educators and policymakers have valuable perspectives on GAI's role in reshaping education effectively and responsibly. In a multicultural country like India, there are various languages and dialects. It is vital in this scenario to have the power of natural language translation in any software or application for content writing. Because (Paschen et al., 2019) knowledge-based marketing and its potential to improve decision-making, offering valuable insights In the emerging AI technology, this wide feature of using a software application in the education field can be uplifted. The existing literature consists of various AI and NLP methods applied for educational uses, which falls under a similar domain as it aids target to make a software application to write in any language. To align this and progress forward to find a niche for AI technology in the educational field, the existing literature is critiqued. AI is utilized on Music Information Retrieval (MIR), alleged Audio AI technology; however, training and assessment models require robust audio and semantic data, swiftly presenting a collaborative process to create benchmarks for this niche. In addition to this (Prather et al., 2023) investigates generative AI's transformative role in computing education, emphasizing its potential for personalized learning, ethical considerations, and enhanced pedagogy. In the Similar vein (Maity, 2019) highlights the importance of adaptive and intuitive e-learning tools for effective training. The study introduces the SIP model, laying a foundation for integrating AI systems into training for enhanced transfer and continuous content updates. There is a need in India for better partnerships between music creators, technologists, and practitioners to boost resources and platforms functioning. Teachers need to develop adequate digital competencies to effectively use and teach AI in online learning environments, as emerging technologies enhance students' learning outcomes(Ng et al., 2023). Also, (Dahake et al., 2024) highlights ChatGPT's role in enhancing management education through personalized learning, real-time assistance, and improved accessibility for students. Subsequently (Nazaretsky et al., 2022) emphasize enhanced learning outcomes and teacher engagement, offering practical insights into integrating AI-driven personalization within blended science education contexts. The novel processes emphasize the development of AI models and processes to aid in understanding student assignments on performing, enhancing musical materialization and articulation so machine-generated output is appealing and rewarding to users as per the acoustic genre and mood of the input stimuli. (Imran & Almusharraf, 2024) emphasizes AI's role in enhancing personalized learning, ethical education, and effective teaching, reshaping traditional methodologies in education. Additionally (Glaser, 2023) highlights ChatGPT's transformative potential in personalized education, efficient learning, ethical challenges, and enhancing teaching methodologies responsibly. However, (Tyukin et al., 2018)proposes efficient AI knowledge transfer methods, enhancing collaborative learning between systems, emphasizing non-destructive processes, and computational efficacy. It addresses assignment generation challenges like unpaired video to audio translation, music generation, and multi-modal artistic content manipulation and presents the process and influence of competition organized to motivate explore trends in the development of methods that exist in the research community but very little automated inspection per given task. (Shoaib et al., 2024)revolutionizes campus management systems using AI for personalized learning, automated grading, and predictive retention, achieving 93% accuracy. available on demand, such as reports, publications, video and audio materials, case studies, policy documents, funding schemes, log frames and progress reports.

CURRICULUM DESIGN: CHALLENGES AND OPPORTUNITIES

Curriculum design in higher education in most of the universities and institutions is perceived as an academic exercise. The most common process in curriculum design is assignment of credit weightages to individual courses in a program, deciding the course values through contact/lecture hours, and designing the delivery in the format of lecture/tutorial/lab. The process of curriculum design goes from top to bottom, where industry requirements are not considered in designing courses, which are essential for the students to get employed. The prevailing curriculum is theoretical based and industry approaches more on software packages and implementation, which makes students lag behind in practical knowledge. The learning methodology is unidirectional, where teachers use to teach and the students use to listen. There is no formal approach to check the successful transmission of knowledge from teacher to student, eventually Recurrent Neural Networks (RNNs) significantly improve prediction performance in knowledge tracing, enabling intelligent curriculum design and better understanding of student tasks(Piech et al., 2015).In most universities teaching is done just for the sake of completing syllabus and getting exam results, research is mainly focused on developing infrastructure and research projects for the generation of funds, and there is no formal approach to establish a link between day-to-day teaching and the research projects. Designing educative curriculum materials can promote teacher learning by focusing on subject matter knowledge, pedagogical content knowledge, and disciplinary practices(E. A. Davis & Krajcik, 2005). Recruitments in research projects are mainly based on broker-ship. In India there are no standards for the faculty positions like curriculum developer, course developer, lab developer, research developer, etc., like in government organizations. As a result, there is a practice of using faculty for all purposes. The quality of question papers is poor, where most of the questions are repetitive and direct questions, whereas examiners are looking for an examinee to reproduce what they have given during the exam work. As a result, students become bookworms just to reproduce the bookish language and content. Additionally, (P. S. Aithal & Shubhrajyotsna Aithal, 2019) the process of e-learning in these institutions are being used to increase the market value for the institution, and there is no formal educational policy or standards to declare how much a student learned from this e-learning, which is another formality like the library to gain reputation among the public. Also, Technological Pedagogical Content Knowledge) is developed through a multigenerational process in faculty development design seminars, emphasizing connections among content, pedagogy, and technology in online(Koehler et al., 2007).Digital libraries keep most of the non-reputational journals which are found either to get low cost for the publications or are freely downloadable from the authors' institution, and those hardly have any citations. These scientific citations are taken by students and candidates just as references in the survey without knowing the impact factor of the journals. And E-Learning outlines the strategic, organizational, and political challenges of implementing a comprehensive organization-wide learning strategy, addressing technological and organizational issues(Rosenberg & Foshay, 2002). Currently, journals are being multiplied to generate revenue for the publishers; there are also certain free-of-cost journals where insufficient and not matured works are being published. All the publication queries are collected by hiring brokers and the works from the author are transferred to whom they require.

AI TECHNOLOGIES IN CURRICULUM DEVELOPMENT

Artificial intelligence is involved in software implementation of human thinking tools through computers as it aims to augment human cognitive functions of learning, decision-making, problem-solving and adaptability. AI-powered knowledge management shares, engages, trains and manages knowledge among data, information, knowledge and wisdom for informed decisions.AI literacy consists of core competencies and design considerations that support AI developers and educators in creating learner-centered AI technologies that foster increased user understanding of AI.(Long & Magerko, 2020). Data is managed to information through AI-supported algorithms, models, networks, and software to generate knowledge and analyse unstructured data. Most knowledge management software serves to improve the knowledge-creation system and knowledge-based engineering through interpretation, collaboration, competence and transfer models (Aliabadi et al., 2023). Notably the AI-based computer-assisted instruction, called SCHOLAR, is feasible and can generate text, questions, and answers, enabling mixed-initiative dialogue between student and computer(Carbonell, 1970).Eventually, Computer and Internet use maximizes the benefits of building large knowledge-based systems, allowing for easy access to online resources and enhancing daily activities(McDermott, 1993).moreover AI and machine learning techniques are revolutionizing fundamental sciences, transforming research and promoting new research trends(Xu et al., 2021).

Figure 6. Process of using AI technologies in curriculum development

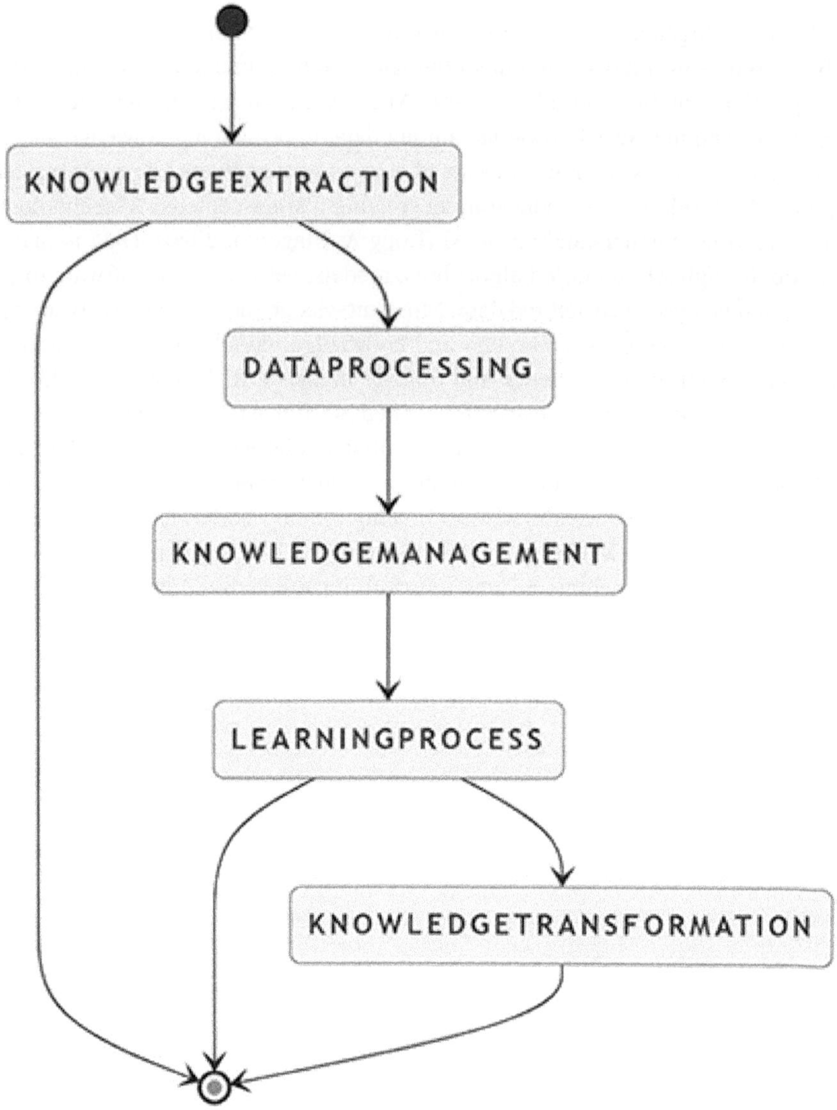

Artificial intelligence is the process of extracting knowledge, creating or revealing knowledge. Consecutively, Knowledge management technologies primarily support explicit knowledge(Marwick, 2001), while tacit knowledge formation and communication require stronger support. The broad sense of data-information-knowledge-wisdom should be cultivated. Data exist in diverse forms, which compiled obsolete data may be quicker than convergence data. Engaging artificial neural networks for choice, pick or simulation algorithms in connection with cloud computing systems. Knowledge is managed by data, information, knowledge, and wisdom, along with learning, acquisition, and transformation. The process of learning through four levels is attending, observing, monitoring, and transforming. Information may handle data-indicative out of context, patterns, or signals.

India is facing an AI talent shortage, estimated at 4-1 lie vacant AI roles. AI startups often lack access to efficient and trained professionals in AI fields that require timely innovation and development. AI in education shows promise, but challenges like inappropriate use, changing roles, and social and ethical issues require further collaboration between educators and AI engineers(Zhai et al., 2021). Schools and colleges are significantly inclined towards AI technologies, curriculums, courses, presentation materials, e-books, tests, licenses, subscriptions, bibliography, papers, and projects in educational institutions, among others. Foreign universities and countries are master of open education resources, scientific exchanges, co-research, scholarships, academic collaboration, syllabus design, and pedagogy apply. Most of the content or material presented is subsequently helpful to improve.

MACHINE LEARNING APPLICATIONS

One of the pioneering countries that incorporated Artificial Intelligence in everyday life to save time and human effort was India. Elimination of Human efforts in day-to-day operations is the main reason industries are keen towards automation. (August & Tsaima, 2021) stated that the Curriculum is very important for educational institutes as it is the one that decides the growth or fall of the institute. A curriculum should be adaptable to the needs of students and should be required by the target group as well. All of these will be taken into consideration and the needful will be recommended. It uses Machine Learning algorithms that balance these deficits and generate a curriculum that has the advantage of being useful in all respects. It is trained to understand each student's need by analyzing students' performances and recommend a curriculum that is fully adapted. This model not only suggests a curriculum but will also provide content related to the curriculum(Tian et al., 2024). In addition to curriculum exploration, 99 school textbooks and the corresponding Syllabuses for the 57 school subjects used by the Tamil Nadu educational board were used to build a Devnagari version Inverted Index Table. The inverted indexing will store the syllabus chapter for each word that appears in the chapter. AI in education has evolved into three paradigms: AI-directed, learner-as-recipient, AI-supported, learner-as-collaborator, and AI-empowered, learner-as-leader, empowering learner agency and personalization(Ouyang & Jiao, 2021). Whenever curriculum recommendation is requested these tables will be used to find the chapters in the books that are related to the requested query and the curriculum will be recommended after sorting the chapters based on the relevance. Text extracts related to the most relevant chapters will be provided through deep learning algorithms.

NATURAL LANGUAGE PROCESSING

In 2019, the first Curriculum Design of Higher Education was done in Python by a Natural Language Processing (NLP) based scholar system named as Semantic Scholar to Generate Comparable Concepts. Some of the key tasks for natural language processing have been explained in a contextual way. There is an overall introduction to NLP and some reference materials available at IIT Madras.

Python, Java and R are widely being used for NLP programming languages and have a different method of implementation. Based on this, 10 natural language processing tasks have trained in three languages and its implementation has been given (Shaik et al., 2023). These tasks are easier to implement in Python than other languages. When implementing clustering, it is fare to note related API libraries or tools exist in respective language which facilitates tasks, since it is developed from scratch for cluster in all three languages. Some of the API libraries or tools are available and some are not. Those explanations are highlighted in different colors, and implementation of all those tasks is given using only the available tools.

CONTENT DELIVERY MECHANISMS

This paper was written from the background of one of the authors during the creation of the contents of a Degree or Master course at an educational institution. The objective is to compute functions and descriptions of an AI-Curriculum Assistant, which would advance the finding and management of educational resources for curriculum design and course content. AI and deep learning research in education has evolved over time, with student profiling models and learning analytics flourishing, while conventional instructional design research has declined.

Figure 7. Content delivery mechanisms

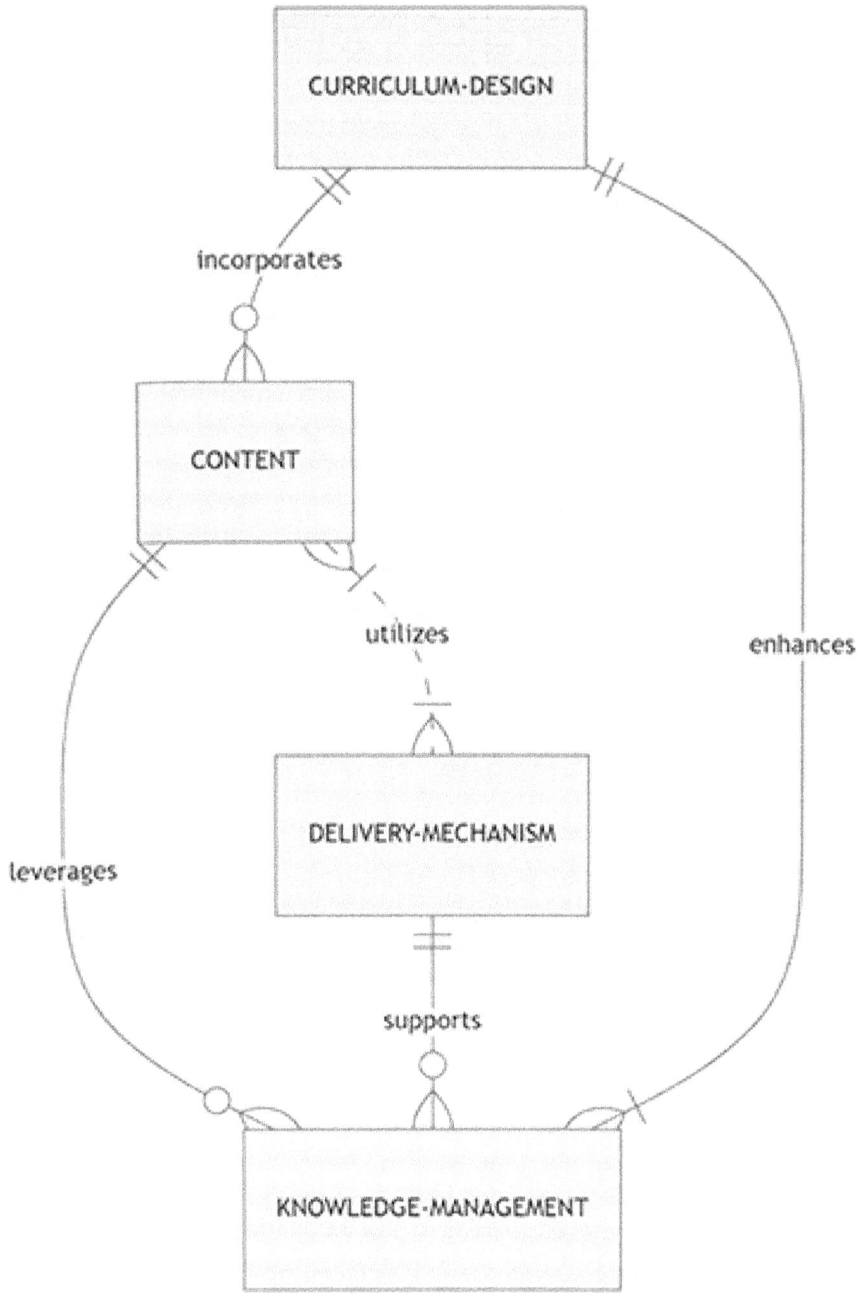

The technical specifications of the e-learning environment and course creation are also discussed, some of which have been creating or have been implementing in countries. The facilitating of the proposed model via semantic web standards and practices to improve the exchange and reuse of educational resources is also addressed. Knowledge management concerns in e-learning environments and curricula designing practices are discussed at both theoretical and application levels. By focusing on the course content creators or instructors, it contributes by proposing a knowledge model of curriculum contents for the context of a learning course. AI-powered tools in foreign language education can revolutionize the teaching process, but effective preparation is crucial for integrating these tools into teaching for easier, less time-consuming, and more effective outcomes(Pokrivcakova, 2019). The contents connected to a learning subject, topics and resources are described due to this model. There are choices and developments of authoring tools for utilizing and handling this description during curriculum design. These tools also enable and aide the summarizing and classification of educational resources and would display and aid the reusability, quality, and accuracy of the contents in deliverable multimedia-supported web-page or learning system. Regarding students or learners, strategies and practices of content management for an adaptive and personalized content delivery of the learning course are illustrated. The content of the course is made sharable and exchangeable through an export of pedagogically reusable materials shared by an importing institution or lecturers of the given learning subject. Through the periodic comparison of user or population behavior and collecting a priori knowledge about its pedagogical content and another pattern should be adjusted regarding the learners and educational outcomes.

ONLINE LEARNING PLATFORMS

Learning never ends, and there is no age limit to grow yourself. With flexible learning modules, millions of working professionals and part-time job seekers enhance their skills and education to outshine the lack of practical knowledge. However, stickler adherence to the traditional educational landscape will face an uphill battle in effectively catering to the inclusion and diverse learning needs of millions of students in societies like India. Governments alongside technology firms in developing nations should ensure that every student gains access to state-of-the-art methods for lecture delivery, online resources, and technology needs. Social enterprises in nimble-footed emerging economies, best abreast of these challenges, must also step up and innovate. Limitations in the existing traditional assistive technology and learning aids frequently lack the dynamic adaptability required by individualized education plans. Large Language Models (LLM) have led to significant advancements in various language translation, text summarization, and content generation applications. The proposed pilot research endeavors to mitigate both issues by developing novel AI-powered learning aids to help students comprehensively across all generative and adaptive facets of the learning process(Faruqui et al., 2024)The digital era has generated a plethora of online studies available to learners. However, not all easily accessed content is of good quality. This has resulted in more than a billion people worldwide completing online studies but today with half of them still wondering whether this provided resume credential is worthwhile. There exist numerous platforms with credentials—both free and paid—that provide content of suboptimal to excellent quality. There's a need to remedy this discrepancy. Online learning platforms have the potential to revolutionize education by providing access to various subjects. This has the potential to bridge the education gap and address the societal inequalities created by uneven access to in-person instruction. This need was further accelerated by the worldwide lockdowns and school closures resulting from the COVID-19 situation. With the vast majority of educational institutes still closed, the demand for high-quality and accessible online resources is higher than ever. A great deal of skepticism regarding the efficacy of online and distance learning has been brought to light by researchers. This is because a common difficulty that students face when engaging in online or distance courses is the lack of one-on-one interaction with teachers compared to the multi-interaction from in-person instruction. It has been shown in numerous studies that course design and delivery mode have tremendous influence on student progression, completion rates, and course satisfaction. Yet a further stratification of this is the aspect of personalization, which has been shown to be the key for the success of online and distance learning; improving the student's experience while maximizing learning outcome benefits for each individual(St-Hilaire et al., 2021)

BLENDED LEARNING APPROACHES

In the wake of the COVID-19 epidemic and its subsequent lockdowns, several institutions in Bangladesh were compelled to cancel their authorized admissions and examinations(Asghar et al., 2022). Education in the country was close to a standstill. Learning and knowledge-sharing were affected, regardless of the fact that some educational institutions tried to operate online. When education in person was impossible, it was not always well-organized on the digital or virtual environment. It was also a very hard time for the country's economy, education system, and the knowledge-seeking and knowledge-loving populace. In such a difficult situation, a simple, all-in-one, highly transferable, and easy-to-capture way to keep people educated and productive would be an acceptable pathway. A satisfactory approach was required to design all types of curriculum contents, creating all types of teaching aids, and providing all types of solutions for educational purposes based on all types of syllabus. Such a knowledge management system will keep alive or active Bangladeshi education, skill, and knowledge-sharing, even when learning directly is not possible. This is required for how yogic concentration and meditation could help prevent old-age-related neurodegenerative diseases. In addition, the disease condition, symptoms, causes, risk factors, mythical beliefs, etc., of neurological diseases should be the focus. The overall remedy for the neurodegenerative diseases was to perform firstly some preventative Ayurvedic approaches (yogic meditation techniques), and secondly, the curative yoga treatment integrated with the allopathic system as a therapeutic procedure was proposed.

PERSONALIZATION IN LEARNING

Current e-learning system should be improved to provide students with personalized learning content adapted to their skills, preferences and knowledge(Caputi & Garrido, 2015). Students should feel motivated because learning materials correspond to their levels and needs, while very fast students should not be bored by tasks easy for them. This objective can be reached by using item response theory and an artificial neural network implementation.

Figure 8. Journey of personalization in learning

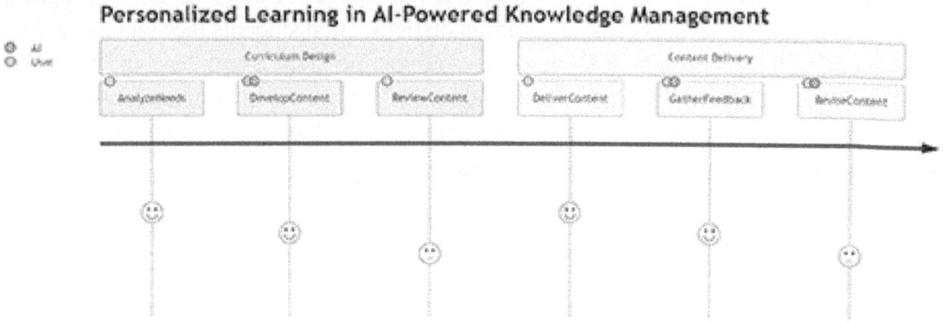

This solution can be used for course sequencer and question suggester modules of intelligent tutoring and planning in learning content systems. Presented e-course sequencing approach can improve Mesquite setup in its course Scheduling. It is first single course sequencing presented for this course, which makes it an additional contribution. The aim of the work is to investigate techniques for Learning Design of field-based education with rapidly expanding use of large-scale Web-based e-learning. AI and ML enhance learning in higher education institutions by enhancing students' skills, collaborative learning, and an accessible research environment(Kuleto et al., 2021).Two approaches are examined, each illustrated using curricula for contrasting aspects of sustainable agriculture. The first uses a quantitative framework combining cognitive load theory with modelling students, enabling the use of intelligence to plan curricula. The second is a heuristic approach summarized as Intelligent Planning with emphasis on sequencing learning tasks. Both approaches demonstrate substantial benefits in comparison to conventional methods. For the former, an algorithmic approach is developed in User Modelling language that can be applied to the Moodle LMS.

ADAPTIVE LEARNING SYSTEMS

The adaptive level of an adaptive learning system could be the primary basis of the arrangement and synchronization of the AIS modules. The components of an AIS could incorporate a student module, instructor module, domain module, interface module, and a communication module. There's a limitation of content authoring for the instructor module of the AIS by teachers since content authoring must not be restricted to well-defined databases, document resources, templates or any repositories. Learning sciences research can inform the design of AI educational technology, enabling faster, more nuanced, and individualised scaffolding for learners(Luckin & Cukurova, 2019). To form content, the AIS is dependent mainly on the expert module of the authoring tool; the expert module might be out-of-date and the most recent requisite knowledge might not have been included in the expert module. Just-in-time knowledge is employed while engineering content for the collaborative domain. Content is engineered through various strategies, including assembling a sequence of educational pieces or rules of greater granularity(Adamu & Awwalu, 2019).

Figure 9. Adaptive learning systems

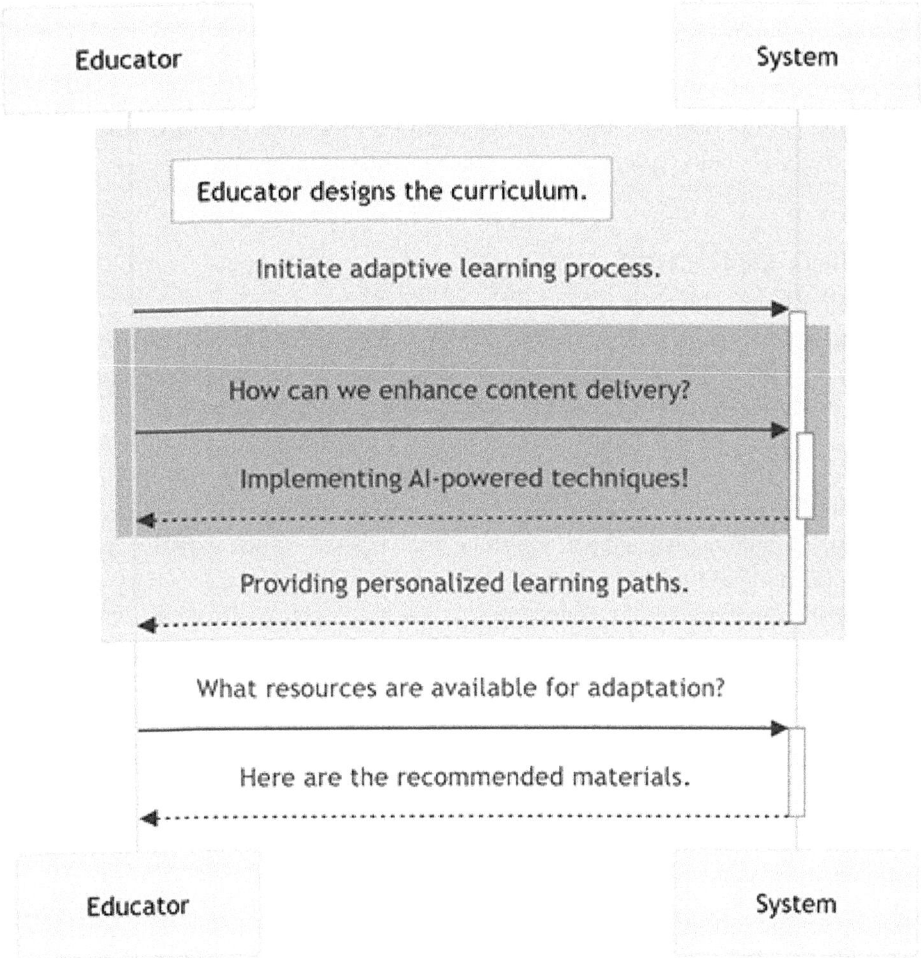

With the exception of the module rule of deciding whether to proceed on a single rule or all rules pertaining to a particular event, the rules propose to develop adaptive learning content and curricula. modules are content representation and description of the pedagogical request. There is a sequence of educational pieces, each covering a concept from a course subject or a topic, and student educational material drafted following the final exam for the course subject. There are no explanations of each multiple-choice question, student's learning score, and the analysis rules that will perceive the highest student's learning score. Data analytics of student interaction might be employed for the formation of content by the student module in an adaptive e-Learning System. Here, the clustering technique of the data mining approach is employed for the forming of data that has the student's learning features from the analysis. The cluster is read and then the sequence is formed of acting rules. Learners are also offered the sequence of acted rules. As it states in the acting rules, the AISs are self-learning systems so service is provided to the log generator. There is no proof of performance of the participant of the linguistic prototype. There are also a reasonable number of points that are unclear, which makes the reader confused. There arises a future work / perspective in making use of considering the sequence of log data resulted from a different representation of the features, such as actions, semantic roles and time. The use of sequence analysis could be considered in place of clustering.

LEARNING ANALYTICS

The government of India has established edX as a not-for-profit enterprise for providing free of charge, free of license online courses with the major intention to enhance standard of quality with various training resources. According to its major aspect, the government of India has introduced Chennai Mathematical Institute for information and technology and has initiated policies for IT and ITES. Like the accepted MOOC concept, major responsibilities of edX for the purpose of curriculum delivery and content designing are described in this digital transformation environment. Learning analytics was raised to assist in the process of personalizing learning by generating feedback or providing the necessary information so that people, individually or collectively, could make better decisions about learning. Considerable research has been carried out at both the national and the transnational levels to uncover the patterns of learning analytics use. Higher education institutes could generate different patterns which have a broad policy decision framework. To generate the necessary benefit in learning analytics application, a proper link is needed in the aspects of teacher, learner, and the institution. In this, a nine-steps roadmap framework has been provided for the higher education development institutions. In accordance with the estimation of teacher's acceptance, the forthcoming work will suggest some methods to increase the acceptance of tools. This research outcome is optimistic: the learning analytics output implementation has a good effect on students and a selector tool has prospective papers to predict student impacts. It would be advantageous in the future to develop a dashboard to help teachers and educational administrators to have quick snapshot on the risk of dropout students, allowing the correct help/intervention. That indicator should then be quantified as merely 5% of MOOC courses. Further empirical work should also be carried out in the development country by the education board to carry out measurements of adoption/acceptance rates of learning analytics tools, and also by developing a more refined model of learning analytics software.

COMPARATIVE ANALYSIS WITH GLOBAL PRACTICES

Educational institutions, faculty members, accrediting bodies, and exam boards are in constant flux for design and delivery of transparent education policies. Academic institutions are cognizant of the multiple principles defined by bodies in order to follow and build quality research and educational policies. Due to constraints in knowledge and information dissemination and implementation at the institution level, academic institutions face a challenge to maintain uniformity and overlap between guidelines (Grant & Helps, 2012). The Moodle-based knowledge hub of Part 1 of this work provides a mechanism for dissemination and accumulation of knowledge in educational curriculum development, useful for the growth of uniform education policy, in turn bridging the gap between standard guidelines and their execution within campus.

Currently, education institutions are moving beyond course delivery based on pre-prepared lecture notes. The conversion of expert knowledge in the domain into digital content such as animations, e-books, and videos is costly and time consuming; and, even after production of that digital content, examination bodies still wonder if student learning outcomes are being accomplished. E-governance Learning Content Management System, structured as a knowledge-hub, is a first of its kind academic knowledge dissemination system in India to date. Educational institutions in India are seen to be producing more than 20,000 UG courses nationwide, but the ability to deliver the lecture is confined to the respective faculty only. It's hard to find the best ones from a vast pool of courses. Post curriculum development, Moodle based knowledge accumulation and ubiquitous knowledge dissemination is the need of the hour. This work is a four-part project work intended to cater to the academic fraternity on knowledge management in curriculum design and content delivery, specifically in India. For a detailed study and recommendations for the future effort, the first contribution being made with this work is an analysis of the comparison between global practices and the knowledge hub concept. The case study of India-Uttarakhand State showing increased agility in knowledge empowerment.

ETHICAL CONSIDERATIONS IN AI EDUCATION

With the advent of Artificial Intelligence (AI) there will be a paradigm shift in the way the economy operates across sectors. Bias in AI systems can be mitigated through ethical and legal principles in design, training, and deployment, ensuring social good while benefiting from AI technology's potential(Ntoutsi et al., 2020). The approach to knowledge design and information delivery is at the forefront. India is now seen as progressing well along the path to AI future and AI-powering is happening. It is important to highlight the future issues and shape the emerging trends. The objective of the draft article is to develop a strategic point of view that could shape the future of AI-powering in curriculum design and content delivery in India, starting from schools and spreading to the entire education system, training and upskilling. A weak signal is defined as an emerging trend that could have an overwhelming impact on the future, but it is yet weakly perceived and demands attention for the design of policies and actions, so as to be prepared for the unfolding situation.

After a brief introductory scenario, an analysis of the AI-powering landscape in India is conducted. The strategic point of view articulates around 12 emerging trends, expressed by weak signals, in areas like upskilling and training, design and curriculum, content delivery, cross-sectoral use, and social and ethical considerations. It also involves in the observation of what might be needed from policy-makers, different stakeholders, and follow-up research. A conclusion summarises the debated issues and tentative lines of future action.

DATA PRIVACY ISSUES

One of the most controversial aspects of using AI in education revolves around data privacy issues. With the advent of smart educational technologies like the use of smartphones, podcasts, e-learning, and e-education, the delivery of learning content in conventional educational systems is gradually transforming. India, the land of Vedic learning and the Gurukula system, is experiencing a new wave of learning policy changes. The use of 'smart classes' in private schools is gradually increasing, and with the launch of the online educational channel in the rural areas bereft of internet access, it is opening new avenues for the assessment of the use of modern educational devices. Much scientific research has been conducted in the arena of Indian educational systems since ancient times. Therefore, it is necessary to assess how artificial intelligence-powered knowledge management can be adopted in the design of curricula and content delivery of 'smart classes' and online educational channels.AI can enhance marketing research, strategy, and actions by automating repetitive functions, processing data, and analyzing interactions and emotions(Huang & Rust, 2021).The development of artificial intelligence (AI) has dramatically changed the landscape of intelligent tutoring systems (ITS), and also the way that content is delivered. E-learning companies have constructed AI-driven systems to deliver personalized learning content according to individual students' conditions in spite of the sulfuration of human resources. One of the technology idols of private schools has launched a project with a significant investment. The project is said to develop a content-delivery mechanism in school-level mathematics and science language curriculum. Moreover, a firm has announced that it is working on a low-cost online delivery mechanism built around a major platform. The project is being initiated by one of the world's largest science projects. The investigation will assess the adaptability of these systems by Quantitative Studies.

TEACHER TRAINING AND DEVELOPMENT

Unlike the western countries, in India, teacher training and development programme are not high on the radar. A study of in-service teacher training in public primary schools in Morigaon and Medak was conducted as a pilot project that constitute a larger study on the language and literacy expectations and achievements of children attending to public primary schools in the two states of India. The in-service teacher training impact of knowledge and practice-related outcomes, such as instructional processes, pedagogical understanding and beliefs of the teacher participants in Morigaon and Medak (Kidwai et al., 2013). Curricular content and pedagogical practices exert a strong influence on the short and long-term learning competences and achievements of students. Like the textbooks, there exists a wide range of educational resources and materials for training. These resources and materials include textbooks, study guides and manuals, educational videos and software, and consultation and support systems delivered through conventional, face-to-face means. These resources and materials are necessary and, in some cases, can be sufficient means to support learning and professional growth for the teacher trainees. AI in education can enhance teaching and learning experiences, addressing intractable problems and promoting better outcomes for all, but requires a collaborative approach, smart funding, and a focus on pedagogy, technology, and system change(*Intelligence Unleashed: An Argument for AI in Education - UCL Discovery*, n.d.). The delivery framework uses Moscowitz and Steinecke's four-stage model of the health promotion and disease prevention. This model maps the knowledge acquisition and learning processes through cognitive, psychomotor, affective and reflective maturation phases. AIED applications in educational settings can facilitate teaching, learning, and decision-making, but face challenges due to their interdisciplinary nature(Hwang et al., 2020). For each phase, the learner's changes in learning, practices and outcomes are described. A variety of AI applications and technologies can be deployed in support of the framework.

INTEGRATING AI IN TEACHER EDUCATION

This constantly developing situation is based on AI, a sub-domain of computer science: It is currently the focus of the development of many countries due to the advances made in every field of science and the diverse areas of application that these advances allow. (Wei, 2023)reveal that AI-mediated approaches significantly enhance English proficiency across grammar, vocabulary, reading, and writing, while boosting L2 motivation and fostering self-regulated learning strategies. The AI makes it possible to design digital devices which are capable of simulating a form of intelligence and thus of carrying out tasks that until now fell within the exclusive competence of human intelligence. a computer-understandable knowledge base from the World Wide Web, enabling more effective retrieval and knowledge-based inference and problem solving(Craven et al., 2000).

Figure 10. Process of integrating AI in teacher education

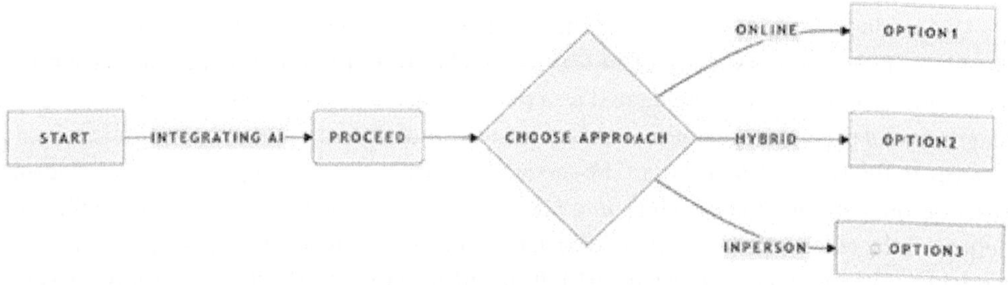

The fields of application are therefore very numerous and continue to develop. This means that it is necessary to train qualified staff to integrate these new techniques into the professional framework and to guarantee the development of these tools. The approach that may be adopted can be of two orders: Ensuring the training of professionals in this area is supposed to weaken the competition that these future trained people could make within their country of origin. On the contrary, training professionals of foreign nationality guarantees a change of technological and industrial standards at the destination and opens up new opportunities for applicants with diplomas or professional experience from abroad. It also ensures the plurality of training practices and theoretical approaches from these professionals from different cultures and countries. Generative AI can be a transformative resource in the future of education, but must be embraced rather than rejected to avoid potential pitfalls and avoid a Ragnarök-like future for management education(Lim et al., 2023).The other aspect concerns the countries of the South, primarily, which are looking to catch up with the technological and scientific delay that separates them from developed countries. In this perspective, the attraction of foreign universities to study at first a tourist type, it is later seen how multiple scholarships are organized to enable the best students to follow training in technology considered innovative.

STUDENT ENGAGEMENT STRATEGIES

Higher education institutes are increasingly focusing on deploying AI-driven knowledge management systems for their curriculum design and content delivery. A SWOC ('strengths', 'weaknesses', 'opportunities' and 'threats') and ANP ('analytical network process') methodology is developed to identify the factors within each domain of decision points impacting six objectives and form an integrated representation to rank the factors and objectives. Analysis of 140 interrelations among 44 factors and 16 objectives reveals students' behavioral engagement strategy (learning and collaboration) as the most influential in achieving four knowledge management goals through compliance with SWOC-informed AI approaches. The study's findings are particularly relevant for AI-driven knowledge management in emerging economies, such as India(Faruqui et al., 2024).

COLLABORATIVE LEARNING ENVIRONMENTS

Creating future best collaborative learning environments using AI Powered Knowledge Management integrated with curriculum design in India is demanding. In instructional design, AI is used to design the curriculum and content delivery to achieve the learning outcomes. AI Powered Knowledge Management (AIKM) guides the instructional design of content development and delivery. AIKM improves content receival and delivery with curriculum design guidelines based on content type, time frame, and acquiry level. The current worldwide pandemic makes it challenging to have a conventional learning setup. On top of that, the education system is typically slow to evolve, and it may take additional time and effort to even consider AI in education, which is a long-time complaining need. However, one must not only switch to a totally online-type curriculum strategy but replace it with a more effective and efficient one. Pedagogical content knowledge (PCK) has influenced mathematics education research through various conceptualizations and methods, influencing teaching methods and teacher education(Depaepe et al., 2013). Creating AI Powered Knowledge Management for instructional design in curriculum management and digital content delivery empowers colleges, universities, educational institutes, educators and online learning providers to offer online courses with the most cost-effective and adaptive online teaching, giving more emphasis on AI to design the curriculum and content delivery for receiving the expected learning outcomes to the learner (Şerban & Ioan, 2020).

ASSESSMENT AND EVALUATION METHODS

There are 2 methods, i.e., Use-Case Based Learning (UCBL) and Problem-Based Learning (PBL), which MAPs in this research study falls under. The courses for which this proposed AI-integrated knowledge management is developed are Constructed Environment (CE) and Planning studies-based courses in India. The knowledge management frameworks which integrate AI tools are introduced, i.e., Course Curriculum Design Management (CCDM) and Course Delivery Content Management (CDCM). The curriculum and the content are vital components for the learning process of students in the educational scene (Kadel et al., 2024). A course curriculum model is presented that includes a need for knowledge area determination, competency definition and competency mapping to course content. The developed artificial intelligence (AI) tool named as MAPs (Model-Assisted Planning studies system) is introduced that provides support for developing these courses. With AI-supported MAPs, prep work times of the academicians will be shortened to build a new and qualified course. XAI techniques can improve trust in AI models by enhancing data explainability, model explainability, post-hoc explainability, and assessment of explanations(Ali et al., 2023). For delivering quality content for a target course curriculum, a network-based content management method is introduced that estimates the relation strengths between the course curriculum content topics, academician candidate content topics and the corresponding resource content topics with the help of the developed AI tool named as LCNs (Learning Content Networks). This Method also provides a stack of visual guides on the steps in planning course materials.

It brings meaningful learning activities to each study plan with the effectiveness of different navigation structures. The methods validate the sample educational scenarios and comparative results are shown according to LCNs (Learning Content Networks).

AI IN GRADING AND FEEDBACK

The Bologna process of Asia is marked by new challenges, for example in India, demand from a higher number of students but after the handover, central universities, recently established universities, engineering colleges, state universities, and other institutions governed by dual-sector universities. Due to their central location in top Indian institutions, central universities have significant autonomy in operational, performance, and financial issues. Framework to support the design, home delivery, and assessment of the curriculum for performance goals in the central universities of the Bologna process in India is the Development of AI-Powered Knowledge Management. Knowledge management identifies key information and promotes an understanding assessment of an emerging technical effort. The development of intelligent agents for the deployment of knowledge management solutions in Indian institutions of high education is a vital technical and operational strategy. And neural networks act to maximize learning efficiency, potentially halving the time required to achieve satisfactory performance levels(Graves et al., 2017).

Figure 11. Role of AI in grading and feedback

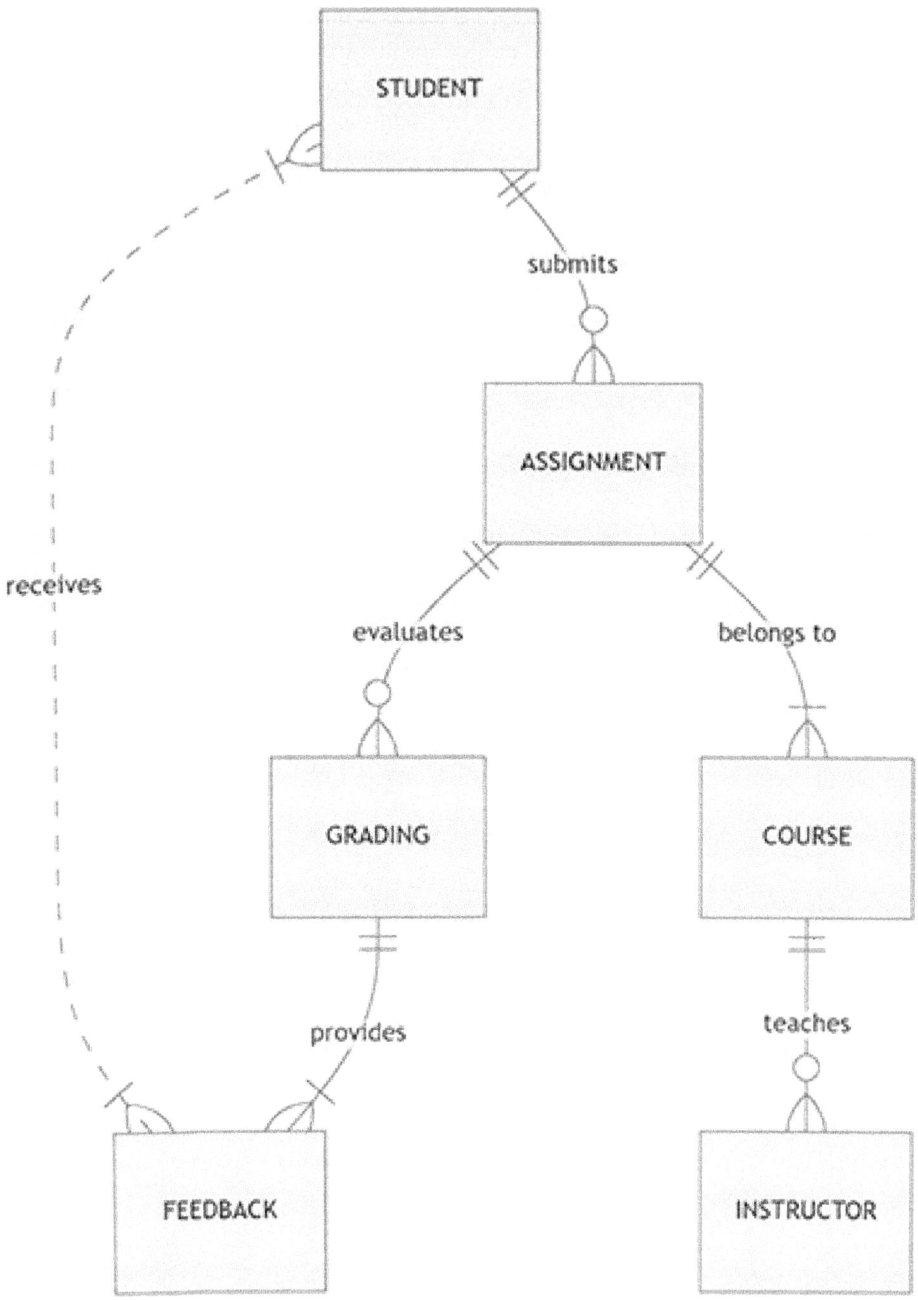

India is facing a challenge in updating its infrastructure and teaching practices that requires radical change in the approach to design and the evaluation of teaching, learning, and knowledge sharing. AI is expected to support the vision in the mission statement. Budget constraints have necessitated significant reductions in the funding of technology support and human resources, so that little if any capacity exists to explore and implement the types of technologies that may help meet the mission. With the development of AI training modules and a joint program with central universities, a planned effort is under way to accelerate the deployment of intelligent agent applications that may be helping the implementation of the mission statement. With more well-documented experience, it is possible that AI applications will become more widespread in the central universities in the University and Institutes. This research helps scholars to address the issue of how intelligent agents can be developed to manage knowledge better in performance assessment of the curriculum (Wan & Chen, 2023).

FUTURE TRENDS IN EDUCATION TECHNOLOGY

India is one of the most populated countries in the world having a tradition of knowledge dating back to ancient times. To harness the potential of millions of young people a representative visionary knowledge-based job-ready curriculum design for architecture is described. Here high-quality research and the application of the architecture are proposed to be taught. The vision is to provide job-ready skilled manpower which has positive potential for research too. In this context, education by employing Artificial Intelligence technology in curriculum design and content delivery can provide a potential opportunity to millions of people in India to have an advanced skill which can fulfill the gap between being relevant to them and being actually job-ready. A framework is also proposed to deal with how this technology can be employed in curriculum design and content delivery (Mallik & Gangopadhyay, 2023). Robots, drugs, reality and education. How the future will change how we think. In a joint report from (Sandford, 2009), two possible scenarios of the future are presented: In an optimistic scenario, the digital revolution is happening. Schools, along with other institutions, are leveraging technology to cope with the demands of the knowledge economy. There is cause for concern that somewhere, a false dichotomy has arisen that 'traditionalist' tactics cannot also be 'innovative.' At the moment, computers have lost their novelty value. It is safe to say they will play an ever greater part in our everyday lives. And certainly, it can be argued that it is only since the advent of very recent technological possibilities that the possible applications of technology to any level of the education system have started to be realized.

POTENTIAL IMPACT ON CURRICULUM DESIGN

As researchers work on a community AI education initiative, an AI curriculum will be developed for a public high school in Neom city, Saudi Arabia. The work suggests a method for integrating AI with social and real-world challenges by implementing the concept of 'AI challenges,' in turn inspiring students to learn about AI. Throughout the research, it is demonstrated that this technique could aid with the broad decentralization and dissemination of AI knowledge to a variety of audiences. This includes public high school students, undergraduate university students, law enforcement personnel, and park rangers. In the coming section, a method for implementing the concept of 'AI challenges' is discussed and it is shown that this method could help in engaging students and starting a conversation on ways AI could affect the lives of a variety of people who are impacted by it (Aliabadi et al., 2023). Furthermore, as countries race to push AI education to K-12 classrooms, researchers propose a transdisciplinary AI education model premised on the un-noticed pertinence of AI with broader societal curricula. With that, researchers discuss findings from a co-design process with teachers who worked on the development of integrated K-12 curriculum. Results confirm that this model effectively democratizes AI knowledge to traditionally underserved populations. After over a decade of relative dormancy, the AI hype is vibrant anew. Policymakers, educators, tech companies are all busy setting up national and international initiatives to popularize AI education. On the one hand, such initiatives raise concerns of an emerging discipline becoming a tool of National Innovation Enhancement Projects. On the other hand, there is skepticism about educating general audiences of non-computer scientists on the technical details of AI. In recent times however, there is an uptick in scholarly discussions around the possibility of transdisciplinary AI education: that is, initiatives motivated and designed by the un-noticed pertinence of AI with the social, political, and economical domains of human life (Helps, 2013).

GOVERNMENT INITIATIVES

The Ministry of Human Resource Development (MHRD) and the Government of India have long recognized the importance of digitization in the education sector. MHRD established a department of Education Technology in 1975, which laid the foundation for the development of audio and video resources in education, mass media projects, and research and development institutions in the field of educational technology. ICT@Schools is a 100% centrally sponsored scheme funded by the MHRD and fully dedicated to the integration of ICT into schools. The scheme covers:

(i) provision of ICT labs, ‘smart’ interactive whiteboards or DLP projectors and IT infrastructure to Secondary and Higher secondary government, government-aided and local body schools;
(ii) (ii) 30% support for school assessment, annual maintenance contracts, and content development; and

(iii) (iii) design, planning and development activities (Bajpai et al., 2019). More recently, it was decided to add vocational streams with the update or establishment of new laboratories. Each State and Union Territory has one unique national core team (NCT) made responsible for both the dissemination (through states and states' designated institutes) and for the development of digital resources (in six major regional languages). NCTs and national coordinators are already active in 31 States and Union Territories, covering a total of 662,472 schools. This text considers experiences generated while working with Gujarat Council of Educational Research and Training (GCERT), which at the time was the designated institute to implement the program in Gujarat.

In the aforementioned public schools, substantial experiences show the significant growth in ICT capabilities corresponds with e-content development and its integration in teaching-learning processes. Other states such as Haryana have launched initiatives through mobile applications. For instance, the Haryana School Shiksha Pariyojna Parishad (HSSPP) has developed ERP Mobile App for disseminating information related to school education. Further, MHRD has initiated the ePathShala mobile App development to distribute digitized textbooks. A number of other states are also currently in the process of digitization. Department of Science and Technology and MHRD also have set up the Science Education Development project, the objectives of which include providing a nation-wide platform for e-learning, e-journals, e-research, and simulation to benefit the entire scientific community. MHRD is promoting massive open online courses (MOOCs) through SWAYAM (Study Webs of Active Learning for Young Aspiring Minds). SWAYAM provides MOOC-based distance learning across India. The aim is to provide high-quality higher education to all students across India to ensure they are able to obtain it at an affordable cost.

Regulatory Frameworks

India has a subcontinent history of knowledge management as a practice. The Vedas, which were written in India several thousand years past, continue to be an important part of the Hindu religion and mythology today. One of the most interesting aspects of these texts is that they have been remembered through oral tradition until recently, yet they describe intricate details about very complex topics, such as the distances between planets and the angles at which celestial bodies move with respect to the Earth.

One might ask, then, if something as complex and grand as the Vedas can be remembered and passed through generations, and if these texts have continued to be of interest and relevance for millennia, then what domain of knowledge is not appropriate for knowledge management and why? For the most part, the Indian higher education market has not addressed knowledge management or curriculum management, but India is a progressive country, and many educators are now asking these hard questions about the aspects of their system that have evaded current standards, and have chosen to adopt newer technologies and practices to reconcile these problems. The Indian market represents a unique opportunity to imbibe knowledge management methodologies in education at the highest level.

CHALLENGES TO AI ADOPTION

Artificial intelligence (AI) education is a confluence of the needs of the instruction of AI and the people in society. AI technology is affecting everything in society nowadays, primarily because practically every task can be modeled in computational terms. This has begun to change the way to adapt, accumulate, and even forget knowledge. These new capabilities and the tools and products that will soon depend on them require new teaching, learning, and evaluation paradigms or models. AI is already expected to influence two most efficient devices for rapid learning and understanding of situations: tutors and explanation systems(Hemachandran et al., 2022), An actual consequence is AI-based models that help people adapt to AI techniques, both to conform with them and to design or create artifacts dependent on them. This inevitably leads to a rethinking of the existing methods in minimizing the gap between theoretical psycho-educational science and practical tutorial interfaces. Since the whole educational system in India and many other developing countries is based on rote learning, the adoption of a beneficial AI-oriented educational approach is going to be discouraging. The swift expansion of the tutorial application of AI remains highly unpopular. Several implications for the curriculum, teacher education, and the creation of educational materials for second and third degree students, discreetly preparing to use or create AI tutors after graduation, are drawn. The education of AI in high school-based, population-wide computer programming is described for the dissemination of how difficult they are with understanding and teaching various AI systems, methodologies, and fundamental philosophical issues. Transdisciplinary experiments suggesting the incorporation of AI education in the regular multifaceted high school curricula are discussed on it as efforts to assemble educational modules, including essays, reading lists, and simplified do-it-yourself experimental tools. A tutorial tool based on Socratic dialogues that packages a representation of the first critical inquiry-based process in question to a tutorial system was prototyped. This tool is the basis for a broad scope of campaign-like implementations the development of which is examined. The prospects presented arise for an ongoing study elaborating on unique challenges and future plans, (Aliabadi et al., 2023).

INTERNATIONAL PERSPECTIVES ON AI IN EDUCATION

AI in India. Ever since the 1.1 bn people started waking up to the potential of Artificial Intelligence, there has been anxiety among the 392 million people in the developed world about finding their jobs threatened. This touched a sympathetic chord in a land of devotion – BHAKTI as the modality of choice for cognitive devotion. It was gently pointed out to the worried inhabitants of a land that contributes to the manure equivalent of a small Mars, that India's Prime Minister pronounced in 2021, that nobody wants Artificial Intelligence, but everybody needs it. The share of AI in India's GDP will grow by 49% by 2035 – an added economic value of $636 billion. This will create some 13.5 million new jobs – nearly 80% of these gains by 2035 being in the key areas of health, education, and agriculture. Think how much Saagar loves Artificial Intelligence. It truly understands him. The AI can tell from his photographs whether he is feeling satisfied or angry. When he composes a song on his keyboard, AI will effortlessly string together the musical notation. And its repertoire of ragas is unparalleled. And to just walk on those algae-covered surfaces and NOT slip – only possible under the protection of Artificial Intelligence. This is Saagar's home. His own Autonomous Probe will explore these minds on wheels – the Mandelbrot set flitting in and out of view. A simple instrument, capable of changing the very way we understand Artificial Intelligence. The only difference with a cave painting is that the Autonomous Probe will return real-time data – like data despite being unreachable. Could anything be sweeter?

GLOBAL BEST PRACTICES

In early January 2020, students from grades five to thirteen at a public school in Hangzhou were being taught by AI-powered machines. AI-powered machines led classes in maths and Chinese language. Similar technologies have been running in the country for about two years. The shared classroom model is designed for 90 students and has three classes, each attended by 30 students. One class is led by the school teacher, while students from the other two classes wear headsets to listen and follow the AI-powered voice. The AI speaker detects mistakes made by students in their 30-minute individual practices and can adapt the teaching style. Similar systems have been installed in 40 urban schools and over 70 in rural schools in China. India and China roughly around 80% of the US, Asia, and three-fourth of the world population. Digital innovations in India with comprehensive progress in learning among school children (Chimalakonda & V. Nori, 2018). African AI experts have launched AI4D, clearly with full awareness of the rapid global race in AI R&D effectiveness. They know there is urgency in adding AI to the knowledge base with China and India. China has also been swiftly expanding its AI capabilities by giving AI-related skills training to high school students and even those at middle school level. The New Education Policy of India envisages the country's education from "pre-school to school" to "higher education" as single vertical education. This policy would require serious consideration in light of how "AI-empowered content delivery" should be designed in the broad domains of teaching and learning. School and higher education in India are state subjects, and huge disparities are seen in the approach towards this segment of Indian society going ahead. Several states and administrators were not able to deliver a stable policy for state subjects in the "new education age" where content delivery will play a fundamental role in teaching. It is suggested to IT-educational start-ups, and other start-ups with expertise in content delivery, how to think about their promising role in the "new education age" of AI in India. The world of educational technology offers enhanced opportunities to make a difference on a wider scale. AI4D Africa, with support of sponsors, summarized to add AI to the knowledge system with concern about how Africa can benefit from the AI race of the US and China. China has been rolling out courses on AI-related skills by integrating it into the school curriculum. Middle schools are also now rolling out the AI-related skills training.

LESSONS LEARNED FROM OTHER COUNTRIES

While Symsonia, Kentucky, the United States, and the Sultanpur district in the Indian state of Uttar Pradesh have different socio-political backgrounds, the objective of improved learning outcomes through knowledge management elements is similar in both settings. A look at best-practice evidence from the United States and lessons from a smaller scale initiative in Indian peri-urban community suggest that overcoming a general lack of awareness and/or understanding of generative artificial intelligence (GenAI) and its applications in the first place must be the initial focus. Here several elements of the existing knowledge management in both settings are detailed, a design strategy for GenAI integration in school-based knowledge management schemes is presented, and plans for its evaluation are outlined. It is hoped that the approach and lessons learned will be valuable to local educational authorities, indeed to all entities similarly attempting to improve curriculum design and content delivery through GenAI given how A.I. technologies are already vital tools in U.S. elementary-secondary education.

All U.S. students learning in these and two other districts participate in a personalized curriculum design pilot project from 2023 using various GenAI-driven resources. The context of this pilot project, its objectives and expected impacts on the local education system are described. Results will be shared with the hope of guiding a state-wide scale-up of the use of GenAI in education, and generalized lessons which can be useful to education stakeholders in other countries considering integrating GenAI in their school-based curriculum as well. Whether in the USA, India or elsewhere, education is crucial, without effective knowledge management, curricular design is less likely to be successfully inclusive or locally adaptive. Both Symsonia and Sultanpur have world-leading GenAI-driven companies, logistical and ethical challenges can be overcome through involving them in national and international partnerships (Hasib Akhter Faruqui et al., 2024). A curriculum design, knowledge management system-based scheme integrating GenAI tools in selected schools in educationally disadvantaged communities in both areas began in 2022 with a focus on primary education (Chimalakonda & V. Nori, 2018).

CONCLUSION

Emerging technologies provide a potential pathway to leverage high-quality education in a wider scope. The Indian higher education system is the third largest in the world and one of the oldest education systems across the globe. In the year 2020-2021 the Gross Enrolment Rate (GER) in higher education has increased to 27.1%. Due to the COVID-19 pandemic educational institutions were closed till October, 2021 and initiated online classes thereafter. The integration of advanced Artificial Intelligence (AI) tools such as BIGBRIDGE can transform the traditional teaching and learning paradigm in curriculum design and content delivery. This pilot study aims to evaluate the effectiveness of BIGBRIDGE tools in Knowledge Management (AIKOM) for designing a curriculum and Short_Text AI (Samvad) for creating content. Through deployment of BIGBRIDGE tools the effect of Knowledge Management

AIKOM in curriculum design and Samvad in content delivery will be assessed. It is also intended to gain empirical data and experiential knowledge from the professional educators and academicians on the broader implications of such technologies. Indian higher education plays a pivotal role in shaping the future of a person and a nation. A keen focus on higher education in the five-year plans post-independence helped to develop well-recognized universities and technology institutes over the last seven decades. The New Education Policy (NEP) 2020 emphasizes the integration of AI and technology in the education system to improve access, equity, quality, affordability, and research outcomes (Helps, 2013). Integrated AI platform, Bina AI-Genbridge (BIGBRIDGE) provides low-cost knowledge management content automation solutions to the relevant industry. Applied Contact directs this research work to explore SMART capabilities (Search, Manage, Analyze, Recommend and Text-Creation) in the BIGBRIDGE ecosystem. SMART incorporates seven primary domains of application, such as Healthcare, Banking & Finance, Media & Marketing, Education, Civic Data Science, Intelligent HR, and LifeStyle & Tourism. SMART in the 'Education' domain coined as SAMBRIDU is the outcome of the DIEO study on BIGBRIDGE (Faruqui et al., 2024)

REFERENCES

Adadi, A., & Berrada, M. (2018). Peeking Inside the Black-Box: A Survey on Explainable Artificial Intelligence (XAI). *IEEE Access : Practical Innovations, Open Solutions*, *6*, 52138–52160. DOI: 10.1109/ACCESS.2018.2870052

Adamu, S., & Awwalu, J. (2019). *The Role of Artificial Intelligence (AI) in Adaptive eLearning System (AES) Content Formation: Risks and Opportunities involved* (Version 1). arXiv. DOI: 10.48550/ARXIV.1903.00934

Aithal, P. S., & Aithal, S. (2019). Analysis of higher education in Indian National education policy proposal 2019 and its implementation challenges. [IJAEML]. *International Journal of Applied Engineering and Management Letters*, *3*(2), 1–35.

Ali, S., Abuhmed, T., El-Sappagh, S., Muhammad, K., Alonso-Moral, J. M., Confalonieri, R., Guidotti, R., Del Ser, J., Díaz-Rodríguez, N., & Herrera, F. (2023). Explainable Artificial Intelligence (XAI): What we know and what is left to attain Trustworthy Artificial Intelligence. *Information Fusion*, *99*, 101805. DOI: 10.1016/j.inffus.2023.101805

Aliabadi, R., Singh, A., & Wilson, E. (2023). *Transdisciplinary AI Education: The Confluence of Curricular and Community Needs in the Instruction of Artificial Intelligence*. DOI: 10.1007/978-981-99-7947-9_11

Asghar, M. Z., Afzaal, M. N., Iqbal, J., & Sadia, H. A. (2022). Analyzing an Appropriate Blend of Face-to-Face, Offline and Online Learning Approaches for the In-Service Vocational Teacher's Training Program. *International Journal of Environmental Research and Public Health*, *19*(17), 10668. DOI: 10.3390/ijerph191710668 PMID: 36078385

August, S. E., & Tsaima, A. (2021). Artificial Intelligence and Machine Learning: An Instructor's Exoskeleton in the Future of Education. In Ryoo, J., & Winkelmann, K. (Eds.), *Innovative Learning Environments in STEM Higher Education* (pp. 79–105). Springer International Publishing., DOI: 10.1007/978-3-030-58948-6_5

Bahroun, Z., Anane, C., Ahmed, V., & Zacca, A. (2023). Transforming Education: A Comprehensive Review of Generative Artificial Intelligence in Educational Settings through Bibliometric and Content Analysis. *Sustainability (Basel)*, *15*(17), 12983. DOI: 10.3390/su151712983

Barredo Arrieta, A., Díaz-Rodríguez, N., Del Ser, J., Bennetot, A., Tabik, S., Barbado, A., Garcia, S., Gil-Lopez, S., Molina, D., Benjamins, R., Chatila, R., & Herrera, F. (2020). Explainable Artificial Intelligence (XAI): Concepts, taxonomies, opportunities and challenges toward responsible AI. *Information Fusion*, *58*, 82–115. DOI: 10.1016/j.inffus.2019.12.012

Caputi, V., & Garrido, A. (2015). Student-oriented planning of e-learning contents for Moodle. *Journal of Network and Computer Applications*, *53*, 115–127. DOI: 10.1016/j.jnca.2015.04.001

Carbonell, J. (1970). AI in CAI: An Artificial-Intelligence Approach to Computer-Assisted Instruction. *IEEE Transactions on Man-Machine Systems*, *11*(4), 190–202. DOI: 10.1109/TMMS.1970.299942

Chen, L., Chen, P., & Lin, Z. (2020). Artificial Intelligence in Education: A Review. *IEEE Access : Practical Innovations, Open Solutions*, *8*, 75264–75278. DOI: 10.1109/ACCESS.2020.2988510

Craven, M., DiPasquo, D., Freitag, D., McCallum, A., Mitchell, T., Nigam, K., & Slattery, S. (2000). Learning to construct knowledge bases from the World Wide Web. *Artificial Intelligence*, *118*(1–2), 69–113. DOI: 10.1016/S0004-3702(00)00004-7

Dahake, P. S., Mohare, R. V., & Dahake, N. S. (2024). Enhancing Management Education Through ChatGPT: A Novel Method for Ease and Efficacy. In Inder, S., Min, B., & Sharma, S. (Eds.), (pp. 161–178). Advances in Business Strategy and Competitive Advantage. IGI Global., DOI: 10.4018/979-8-3693-1734-1.ch012

Davis, E. A., & Krajcik, J. S. (2005). Designing Educative Curriculum Materials to Promote Teacher Learning. *Educational Researcher*, *34*(3), 3–14. DOI: 10.3102/0013189X034003003

Davis, R. (1986). Knowledge-Based Systems. *Science*, *231*(4741), 957–963. DOI: 10.1126/science.231.4741.957 PMID: 17740292

Depaepe, F., Verschaffel, L., & Kelchtermans, G. (2013). Pedagogical content knowledge: A systematic review of the way in which the concept has pervaded mathematics educational research. *Teaching and Teacher Education*, *34*, 12–25. DOI: 10.1016/j.tate.2013.03.001

Faruqui, S. H. A., Tasnim, N., Basith, I. I., Obeidat, S., & Yildiz, F. (2024). *Integrating A.I. in Higher Education: Protocol for a Pilot Study with "SAMCares: An Adaptive Learning Hub"* (Version 1). arXiv. DOI: 10.48550/ARXIV.2405.00330

Glaser, N. (2023). Exploring the Potential of ChatGPT as an Educational Technology: An Emerging Technology Report. *Technology. Knowledge and Learning*, *28*(4), 1945–1952. DOI: 10.1007/s10758-023-09684-4

Gou, J., Yu, B., Maybank, S. J., & Tao, D. (2021). Knowledge Distillation: A Survey. *International Journal of Computer Vision*, *129*(6), 1789–1819. DOI: 10.1007/s11263-021-01453-z

Grant, E., & Helps, W. (2012, November 19). A Framework for the Integration of Technology into Curricula Development and Student Assessment. *Conference Proceedings on 3rd Computer Science Education: Innovation & Technology*. 3rd Computer Science Education: Innovation & Technology. DOI: 10.5176/2251-2195_CSEIT12.34

Graves, A., Bellemare, M. G., Menick, J., Munos, R., & Kavukcuoglu, K. (2017). *Automated Curriculum Learning for Neural Networks* (Version 1). arXiv. DOI: 10.48550/ARXIV.1704.03003

Haenlein, M., & Kaplan, A. (2019). A Brief History of Artificial Intelligence: On the Past, Present, and Future of Artificial Intelligence. *California Management Review*, *61*(4), 5–14. DOI: 10.1177/0008125619864925

Hemachandran, K., Verma, P., Pareek, P., Arora, N., Rajesh Kumar, K. V., Ahanger, T. A., Pise, A. A., & Ratna, R. (2022). Artificial Intelligence: A Universal Virtual Tool to Augment Tutoring in Higher Education. *Computational Intelligence and Neuroscience*, *2022*, 1–8. DOI: 10.1155/2022/1410448 PMID: 35586099

Huang, M.-H., & Rust, R. T. (2018). Artificial Intelligence in Service. *Journal of Service Research*, *21*(2), 155–172. DOI: 10.1177/1094670517752459

Huang, M.-H., & Rust, R. T. (2021). A strategic framework for artificial intelligence in marketing. *Journal of the Academy of Marketing Science*, *49*(1), 30–50. DOI: 10.1007/s11747-020-00749-9

Hwang, G.-J., Xie, H., Wah, B. W., & Gašević, D. (2020). Vision, challenges, roles and research issues of Artificial Intelligence in Education. *Computers and Education: Artificial Intelligence*, *1*, 100001. DOI: 10.1016/j.caeai.2020.100001

Imran, M., & Almusharraf, N. (2024). Google Gemini as a next generation AI educational tool: A review of emerging educational technology. *Smart Learning Environments*, *11*(1), 22. DOI: 10.1186/s40561-024-00310-z

Intelligence Unleashed: An argument for AI in Education—UCL Discovery. (n.d.). Retrieved April 24, 2025, from https://discovery.ucl.ac.uk/id/eprint/1475756/

Kaplan, A., & Haenlein, M. (2019). Siri, Siri, in my hand: Who's the fairest in the land? On the interpretations, illustrations, and implications of artificial intelligence. *Business Horizons*, *62*(1), 15–25. DOI: 10.1016/j.bushor.2018.08.004

Kidwai, H., Burnette, D., Rao, S., Nath, S., Bajaj, M., & Bajpai, N. (2013). In-Service Teacher Training for Public Primary Schools in Rural India: Findings from District Morigaon (Assam) and District Medak (Andhra Pradesh). *School of Education Faculty Research*. https://repository.usfca.edu/soe_fac/18

Koehler, M. J., & Mishra, P. (2005). What Happens When Teachers Design Educational Technology? The Development of Technological Pedagogical Content Knowledge. *Journal of Educational Computing Research*, *32*(2), 131–152. DOI: 10.2190/0EW7-01WB-BKHL-QDYV

Koehler, M. J., Mishra, P., & Yahya, K. (2007). Tracing the development of teacher knowledge in a design seminar: Integrating content, pedagogy and technology. *Computers & Education*, *49*(3), 740–762. DOI: 10.1016/j.compedu.2005.11.012

Kuleto, V., Ilić, M., Dumangiu, M., Ranković, M., Martins, O. M. D., Păun, D., & Mihoreanu, L. (2021). Exploring Opportunities and Challenges of Artificial Intelligence and Machine Learning in Higher Education Institutions. *Sustainability (Basel), 13*(18), 10424. DOI: 10.3390/su131810424

Lim, W. M., Gunasekara, A., Pallant, J. L., Pallant, J. I., & Pechenkina, E. (2023). Generative AI and the future of education: Ragnarök or reformation? A paradoxical perspective from management educators. *International Journal of Management Education, 21*(2), 100790. DOI: 10.1016/j.ijme.2023.100790

Loewenberg Ball, D., Thames, M. H., & Phelps, G. (2008). Content Knowledge for Teaching: What Makes It Special? *Journal of Teacher Education, 59*(5), 389–407. DOI: 10.1177/0022487108324554

Long, D., & Magerko, B. (2020). What is AI Literacy? Competencies and Design Considerations. *Proceedings of the 2020 CHI Conference on Human Factors in Computing Systems*, 1–16. DOI: 10.1145/3313831.3376727

Luckin, R., & Cukurova, M. (2019). Designing educational technologies in the age of AI: A learning sciences-driven approach. *British Journal of Educational Technology, 50*(6), 2824–2838. DOI: 10.1111/bjet.12861

Maity, S. (2019). Identifying opportunities for artificial intelligence in the evolution of training and development practices. *Journal of Management Development, 38*(8), 651–663. DOI: 10.1108/JMD-03-2019-0069

Marwick, A. D. (2001). Knowledge management technology. *IBM Systems Journal, 40*(4), 814–830. DOI: 10.1147/sj.404.0814

McDermott, D. (1993). Building large knowledge-based systems: Representation and inference in the cyc project. *Artificial Intelligence, 61*(1), 53–63. DOI: 10.1016/0004-3702(93)90093-Q

Mello, R. F., Freitas, E., Pereira, F. D., Cabral, L., Tedesco, P., & Ramalho, G. (2023). *Education in the age of Generative AI: Context and Recent Developments* (Version 1). arXiv. DOI: 10.48550/ARXIV.2309.12332

Nain, S. (2011). Knowledge Management: Leveraging Competitive Advantage & Organizational Competence – A Study of Indian Organisations in General. *Jurnal Ilmiah Ekonomi Bisnis, 13*(2), Article 2. https://ejournal.gunadarma.ac.id/index.php/ekbis/article/view/301

Nazaretsky, T., Bar, C., Walter, M., & Alexandron, G. (2022). Empowering Teachers with AI: Co-Designing a Learning Analytics Tool for Personalized Instruction in the Science Classroom. *LAK22: 12th International Learning Analytics and Knowledge Conference*, 1–12. DOI: 10.1145/3506860.3506861

Ng, D. T. K., Leung, J. K. L., Su, J., Ng, R. C. W., & Chu, S. K. W. (2023). Teachers' AI digital competencies and twenty-first century skills in the post-pandemic world. *Educational Technology Research and Development, 71*(1), 137–161. DOI: 10.1007/s11423-023-10203-6 PMID: 36844361

Niess, M. L. (2005). Preparing teachers to teach science and mathematics with technology: Developing a technology pedagogical content knowledge. *Teaching and Teacher Education, 21*(5), 509–523. DOI: 10.1016/j.tate.2005.03.006

Ntoutsi, E., Fafalios, P., Gadiraju, U., Iosifidis, V., Nejdl, W., Vidal, M., Ruggieri, S., Turini, F., Papadopoulos, S., Krasanakis, E., Kompatsiaris, I., Kinder-Kurlanda, K., Wagner, C., Karimi, F., Fernandez, M., Alani, H., Berendt, B., Kruegel, T., Heinze, C., & Staab, S. (2020). Bias in data-driven artificial intelligence systems—An introductory survey. *Wiley Interdisciplinary Reviews. Data Mining and Knowledge Discovery, 10*(3), e1356. DOI: 10.1002/widm.1356

Ouyang, F., & Jiao, P. (2021). Artificial intelligence in education: The three paradigms. *Computers and Education: Artificial Intelligence, 2*, 100020. DOI: 10.1016/j.caeai.2021.100020

Paschen, J., Kietzmann, J., & Kietzmann, T. C. (2019). Artificial intelligence (AI) and its implications for market knowledge in B2B marketing. *Journal of Business and Industrial Marketing, 34*(7), 1410–1419. DOI: 10.1108/JBIM-10-2018-0295

Piech, C., Spencer, J., Huang, J., Ganguli, S., Sahami, M., Guibas, L., & Sohl-Dickstein, J. (2015). *Deep Knowledge Tracing* (Version 1). arXiv. DOI: 10.48550/ARXIV.1506.05908

Pokrivcakova, S. (2019). Preparing teachers for the application of AI-powered technologies in foreign language education. *Journal of Language and Cultural Education, 7*(3), 135–153. DOI: 10.2478/jolace-2019-0025

Prather, J., Denny, P., Leinonen, J., Becker, B. A., Albluwi, I., Craig, M., Keuning, H., Kiesler, N., Kohn, T., Luxton-Reilly, A., MacNeil, S., Petersen, A., Pettit, R., Reeves, B. N., & Savelka, J. (2023). The Robots Are Here: Navigating the Generative AI Revolution in Computing Education. *Proceedings of the 2023 Working Group Reports on Innovation and Technology in Computer Science Education*, 108–159. DOI: 10.1145/3623762.3633499

Rosenberg, M. J., & Foshay, R. (2002). E-learning: Strategies for delivering knowledge in the digital age. *Performance Improvement, 41*(5), 50–51. DOI: 10.1002/pfi.4140410512

Sallam, M. (2023). ChatGPT Utility in Healthcare Education, Research, and Practice: Systematic Review on the Promising Perspectives and Valid Concerns. *Health Care, 11*(6), 887. DOI: 10.3390/healthcare11060887 PMID: 36981544

Shaik, T., Tao, X., Li, Y., Dann, C., Mcdonald, J., Redmond, P., & Galligan, L. (2023). *A Review of the Trends and Challenges in Adopting Natural Language Processing Methods for Education Feedback Analysis*. DOI: 10.48550/ARXIV.2301.08826

Shoaib, M., Sayed, N., Singh, J., Shafi, J., Khan, S., & Ali, F. (2024). AI student success predictor: Enhancing personalized learning in campus management systems. *Computers in Human Behavior*, *158*, 108301. DOI: 10.1016/j.chb.2024.108301

St-Hilaire, F., Burns, N., Belfer, R., Shayan, M., Smofsky, A., Vu, D. D., Frau, A., Potochny, J., Faraji, F., Pavero, V., Ko, N., Ching, A. O., Elkins, S., Stepanyan, A., Matajova, A., Charlin, L., Bengio, Y., Serban, I. V., & Kochmar, E. (2021). A Comparative Study of Learning Outcomes for Online Learning Platforms. In Roll, I., McNamara, D., Sosnovsky, S., Luckin, R., & Dimitrova, V. (Eds.), *Artificial Intelligence in Education* (Vol. 12749, pp. 331–337). Springer International Publishing., DOI: 10.1007/978-3-030-78270-2_59

Sutton, R. S., Precup, D., & Singh, S. (1999). Between MDPs and semi-MDPs: A framework for temporal abstraction in reinforcement learning. *Artificial Intelligence*, *112*(1–2), 181–211. DOI: 10.1016/S0004-3702(99)00052-1

Tan, S. (2023). Harnessing Artificial Intelligence for Innovation in Education. In K. Rajaram, *Learning Intelligence: Innovative and Digital Transformative Learning Strategies* (pp. 335–363). Springer Nature Singapore. DOI: 10.1007/978-981-19-9201-8_8

Tian, Z., Sun, M., Liu, A., Sarkar, S., & Liu, J. (2024). *Enhancing Instructional Quality: Leveraging Computer-Assisted Textual Analysis to Generate In-Depth Insights from Educational Artifacts* (Version 1). arXiv. DOI: 10.48550/ARXIV.2403.03920

Tyson, M. M., & Sauers, N. J. (2021). School leaders' adoption and implementation of artificial intelligence. *Journal of Educational Administration*, *59*(3), 271–285. DOI: 10.1108/JEA-10-2020-0221

Tyukin, I. Y., Gorban, A. N., Sofeykov, K. I., & Romanenko, I. (2018). Knowledge Transfer Between Artificial Intelligence Systems. *Frontiers in Neurorobotics*, *12*, 49. DOI: 10.3389/fnbot.2018.00049 PMID: 30150929

Van Laar, E., Van Deursen, A. J. A. M., Van Dijk, J. A. G. M., & De Haan, J. (2017). The relation between 21st-century skills and digital skills: A systematic literature review. *Computers in Human Behavior*, *72*, 577–588. DOI: 10.1016/j.chb.2017.03.010

Wei, L. (2023). Artificial intelligence in language instruction: Impact on English learning achievement, L2 motivation, and self-regulated learning. *Frontiers in Psychology*, *14*, 1261955. DOI: 10.3389/fpsyg.2023.1261955 PMID: 38023040

Xu, Y., Liu, X., Cao, X., Huang, C., Liu, E., Qian, S., Liu, X., Wu, Y., Dong, F., Qiu, C.-W., Qiu, J., Hua, K., Su, W., Wu, J., Xu, H., Han, Y., Fu, C., Yin, Z., Liu, M., & Zhang, J. (2021). Artificial intelligence: A powerful paradigm for scientific research. *Innovation (Cambridge (Mass.))*, *2*(4), 100179. DOI: 10.1016/j.xinn.2021.100179 PMID: 34877560

Zawacki-Richter, O., Marín, V. I., Bond, M., & Gouverneur, F. (2019). Systematic review of research on artificial intelligence applications in higher education – where are the educators? *International Journal of Educational Technology in Higher Education*, *16*(1), 39. DOI: 10.1186/s41239-019-0171-0

Zhai, X., Chu, X., Chai, C. S., Jong, M. S. Y., Istenic, A., Spector, M., Liu, J.-B., Yuan, J., & Li, Y. (2021). A Review of Artificial Intelligence (AI) in Education from 2010 to 2020. *Complexity, 2021*(1), 8812542. DOI: 10.1155/2021/8812542

Chapter 16
Personalized Learning Through AI on the Power of Tailored Education

A. Prabhu Chakkaravarthy
https://orcid.org/0009-0000-3180-8051
Department of Networking and Communications, SRM Institute of Science and Technology, Kattankulathur, India

Dhanalakshmi Jaganathan
https://orcid.org/0000-0002-3919-4469
Data Science and Business Systems, SRM Institute of Science and Technology, India

D. Praveena Anjelin
https://orcid.org/0000-0002-2039-791X
SRM Institute of Science and Technology, Chennai, India

Chin Shiuh Shieh
National Kaohsiung University of Science and Technology, Taiwan

Mong-Fong Shiuh Horng
National Kaohsiung University of Science and Technology, Taiwan

ABSTRACT

Artificial intelligence (AI)-powered personalized learning is transforming education by providing individualized learning experiences that are catered to each student's particular requirements, preferences, and learning preferences. Adaptive learning systems that use AI algorithms to continuously evaluate student performance, spot learning gaps, and modify content delivery in real-time are replacing traditional one-size-fits-all teaching strategies. These solutions promote a more interesting and productive learning environment by enabling customized lesson planning, pacing, and resources. The revolutionary potential of AI in personalized learning is examined in this research, along with how it improves student results by encouraging deeper knowledge, boosting motivation, and improving retention.

DOI: 10.4018/979-8-3373-5092-9.ch016

INTRODUCTION

Background and Need for Personalized Learning

The traditional educational model, characterized by uniform instruction and standardized assessment, often fails to accommodate the diverse learning needs, paces, and preferences of students. With the increasing heterogeneity of today's learners in terms of cognitive abilities, learning styles, socio-economic backgrounds, and technological proficiency, there is a growing demand for educational systems that adapt to individual needs (Pane et al., 2015). Personalized learning, an approach that tailors instruction, pacing, and content based on a learner's specific strengths, weaknesses, and interests, has emerged as a promising alternative to the "one-size-fits-all" paradigm.

The limitations of conventional pedagogy have been further exposed by the digital shift in education, particularly during the COVID-19 pandemic, where remote learning environments highlighted disparities in engagement and comprehension (Ferri et al., 2020). Personalized learning not only addresses these challenges but also promotes greater autonomy, motivation, and deeper learning among students (Walkington, 2013). As education moves toward more inclusive, equitable models, personalized learning becomes critical in meeting individual learner goals and enhancing overall educational outcomes.

The Rise of Artificial Intelligence in Education

Artificial Intelligence (AI) has increasingly become a transformative force in the field of education, offering new possibilities for real-time feedback, predictive analysis, and adaptive learning systems. AI applications in education include intelligent tutoring systems, natural language processing for automated feedback, machine learning algorithms for performance prediction, and recommendation engines that suggest customized learning paths (Zawacki-Richter et al., 2019).

The integration of AI into educational technologies enables the continuous monitoring of student interactions, allowing systems to dynamically adjust content and teaching strategies based on real-time analytics (Holmes et al., 2019). This ability to "learn the learner" positions AI as a core enabler of personalized education, surpassing the scalability limitations of human-led customization. Moreover, the rise of EdTech platforms such as Coursera, Duolingo, and Squirrel AI exemplifies how AI can enhance learner engagement, autonomy, and achievement.

The rapid development of AI tools aligns with global educational reforms emphasizing competency-based, student-centered learning. Governments and institutions are increasingly investing in AI-driven education to improve learning efficiency, reduce teacher workload, and support data-driven decision-making (Luckin et al., 2016). However, while AI offers significant promise, it also presents new challenges related to data ethics, accessibility, and teacher integration, which must be carefully managed.

Objectives of the Chapter

This chapter aims to explore the transformative role of AI in enabling personalized learning, with a particular focus on the mechanisms, technologies, and pedagogical implications of AI-powered systems. The specific objectives are:

- To define the core concepts of personalized learning and AI in education.
- To examine how AI technologies such as machine learning, intelligent tutoring systems, and data analytics support personalized instruction.
- To highlight practical applications and case studies demonstrating the impact of AI-driven personalization in various educational contexts.
- To analyze the benefits, challenges, and ethical considerations associated with integrating AI in learning environments.
- To discuss future directions and policy implications for scaling personalized learning through AI.

By addressing these objectives, the chapter seeks to provide educators, researchers, and policymakers with a comprehensive understanding of how AI can support tailored education and contribute to more inclusive, engaging, and effective learning experiences.

FOUNDATIONS OF PERSONALIZED LEARNING

Definition and Core Principles

Personalized learning refers to an educational approach that customizes learning experiences to meet the individual needs, skills, preferences, and interests of each student. It diverges from traditional instructional models by offering flexible pathways, pacing, and content based on a learner's profile (Pane et al., 2015). At its core, personalized learning is student-centered, data-driven, and goal-oriented, with a strong emphasis on empowering learners to take ownership of their educational journey.

Key principles of personalized learning include:

- **Learner Profiles**: Comprehensive records of individual strengths, weaknesses, preferences, and goals.
- **Customized Learning Paths**: Adaptive progression through content and skills based on mastery rather than seat time.
- **Flexible Learning Environments**: Diverse modalities, including online, blended, and project-based learning.
- **Student Agency**: Encouraging self-regulation, goal-setting, and reflection to promote autonomy and motivation.

These principles are designed to enhance engagement, deepen comprehension, and accommodate different learning trajectories (Means et al., 2014).

Comparison with Traditional Learning Approaches

Traditional education often relies on standardized curricula, uniform pacing, and fixed assessments. This model, while efficient at scale, assumes homogeneity in student learning styles and pace, which can lead to disengagement, frustration, or stagnation among learners (Darling-Hammond et al., 2020). In contrast, personalized learning redefines the role of both teacher and student, shifting from a teacher-directed model to a learner-driven paradigm.

Table 1. Comparison of traditional with personalised learning

Aspect	Traditional Learning	Personalized Learning
Instructional Design	Fixed curriculum and pacing	Flexible content and adaptive pacing
Role of the Teacher	Knowledge transmitter	Facilitator and learning coach
Assessment	Standardized, summative	Formative, real-time, and mastery-based
Learner Role	Passive recipient	Active participant in learning decisions
Use of Technology	Supplementary tool	Central to adaptive, data-driven learning

While traditional models aim for uniform outcomes, personalized learning prioritizes equitable access to individualized success, emphasizing mastery over conformity (Rickabaugh, 2016).

Theories Supporting Individualized Instruction (e.g., Constructivism, Differentiated Instruction)

Several educational theories underpin personalized learning:

- **Constructivism**: Rooted in the work of Piaget and Vygotsky, constructivism posits that learners actively construct knowledge through experiences and reflection. Personalized learning embraces this by allowing students to build knowledge through inquiry, problem-solving, and real-world relevance (Bruner, 1960).
- **Differentiated Instruction**: Championed by Tomlinson (2001), this approach emphasizes modifying content, process, product, and learning environment based on individual readiness, interest, and learning profile. Personalized learning builds upon these principles through technology-enhanced differentiation at scale.
- **Self-Determination Theory (SDT)**: Developed by Deci and Ryan, SDT highlights the importance of autonomy, competence, and relatedness in motivating learners. Personalized learning promotes intrinsic motivation by allowing choice, challenge, and connection (Deci & Ryan, 1985).

- **Zone of Proximal Development (ZPD)**: Vygotsky's concept of ZPD supports instructional scaffolding that is responsive to a learner's current ability. AI-driven adaptive systems align with this theory by delivering just-in-time support that evolves with the learner's progress (Vygotsky, 1978).

In sum, personalized learning is not a novel ideology but rather an evolution of longstanding pedagogical theories, now empowered by emerging technologies to deliver individualized instruction at scale.

AI Technologies Enabling Personalized Learning

The integration of Artificial Intelligence (AI) into education has revolutionized personalized learning by enabling dynamic, data-driven, and learner-centric systems. These AI technologies adapt to individual learning behaviors, providing real-time feedback, customized content delivery, and insights for educators. The key technologies contributing to this transformation include machine learning, deep learning, natural language processing, learning analytics, intelligent tutoring systems, and recommendation engines. Each of these components plays a unique role in tailoring educational experiences to maximize engagement, comprehension, and achievement.

Machine Learning and Deep Learning in Education

Machine Learning (ML) is a branch of AI that enables systems to learn from data and improve their performance over time without being explicitly programmed. In education, ML algorithms are employed to identify patterns in student behavior, predict learning outcomes, and customize instruction accordingly (Zawacki-Richter et al., 2019). For instance, by analyzing historical performance data, ML models can forecast which students are at risk of falling behind and trigger timely interventions.

Deep Learning (DL), a subset of ML that uses artificial neural networks with multiple layers, has further enhanced the capabilities of personalized learning systems. DL excels at processing unstructured data—such as images, videos, and text—which allows for more nuanced understanding of learning contexts. Applications include automatic essay scoring, speech recognition, and image-based assessments (Jordan & Mitchell, 2015). DL models also power adaptive learning platforms that continually refine lesson plans and assessments based on individual learner trajectories.

Both ML and DL support scalable personalization, enabling platforms to cater to thousands of learners simultaneously while maintaining individualized feedback and content recommendations.

Natural Language Processing for Student Interaction

Natural Language Processing (NLP) refers to the ability of machines to understand, interpret, and generate human language. In educational settings, NLP facilitates meaningful interactions between students and digital systems through written and spoken communication. Chatbots, virtual teaching assistants, and AI tutors utilize NLP to answer questions, explain concepts, and simulate conversation (Fryer & Carpenter, 2006).

One prominent application is in automated feedback systems that analyze student submissions and provide personalized comments and suggestions. Tools like Grammarly or Turnitin not only evaluate grammar and syntax but also assess argument strength and originality using NLP models. Furthermore, NLP can gauge student sentiment and engagement through textual analysis of forum posts, essays, and reflection journals (Nye, 2015).

Voice-activated AI assistants—like Amazon Alexa or Google Assistant—also leverage NLP to support hands-free, real-time learning experiences, allowing students to inquire about content or practice language skills interactively.

DATA ANALYTICS AND LEARNING ANALYTICS

Data analytics in education involves collecting, processing, and interpreting vast amounts of learner data to inform instructional decisions. Learning analytics, a subfield of educational data mining, focuses specifically on understanding and optimizing the learning process (Siemens & Long, 2011). These technologies support personalized learning by:

- Identifying individual learning styles and preferences.
- Tracking real-time engagement, progress, and performance.
- Diagnosing learning gaps and cognitive challenges.
- Informing the development of personalized content and assessments.

AI-powered dashboards help educators visualize trends and tailor instruction based on detailed learner profiles. For example, learning management systems (LMS) like Moodle and Canvas incorporate analytics modules that flag disengaged students or suggest remedial content based on quiz performance.

Predictive analytics, a key branch of ML within learning analytics, forecasts future performance and suggests interventions that prevent academic failure. This proactive approach enables personalized pathways that adapt dynamically to learner needs.

Intelligent Tutoring Systems (ITS)

Intelligent Tutoring Systems (ITS) are AI-based systems designed to replicate the adaptive support of a human tutor. They provide personalized instruction, feedback, and guidance by analyzing student inputs and adjusting pedagogical strategies in real time. ITS draw upon cognitive models to deliver content aligned with a learner's understanding and emotional state (VanLehn, 2011).

Prominent examples include:

- **AutoTutor**: Engages learners in conversational dialogues using NLP and semantic analysis.
- **Cognitive Tutor**: Developed by Carnegie Learning, it supports students in mathematics through problem-solving strategies and scaffolding.
- **ASSISTments**: Offers personalized feedback in math education while collecting data to inform teachers.

ITS systems typically consist of four components:

- **Domain Model** – Knowledge representation of the subject matter.
- **Student Model** – Dynamic representation of the learner's current knowledge, misconceptions, and preferences.
- **Tutoring Model** – Decision-making logic for instruction and feedback.
- **User Interface** – The medium of interaction, which may include text, speech, or visuals.

The strength of ITS lies in their capacity to deliver tailored feedback, motivate students through gamified elements, and adapt content to individual progress rates, thereby enhancing learning efficiency and retention.

AI-Powered Recommendation Engines

Recommendation engines, widely used in e-commerce and entertainment (e.g., Netflix, Amazon), are now being applied in educational environments to suggest learning resources, activities, and pathways tailored to individual learner profiles. These engines leverage collaborative filtering, content-based filtering, or hybrid models to analyze user behavior and recommend appropriate materials (Manouselis et al., 2011).

In personalized learning, recommendation engines:

- Suggest next steps in a learning sequence.
- Recommend videos, readings, or exercises aligned with current understanding.
- Encourage exploration of new topics based on learner interests and goals.

For instance, platforms like Khan Academy and Coursera use recommendation systems to present learners with relevant content after tracking their performance and preferences. By continuously analyzing interaction data, these systems evolve in their recommendations, promoting learner autonomy and engagement.

AI-based recommendation systems are particularly valuable in large-scale learning environments like MOOCs, where individualized instructor support is limited. They ensure that learners receive guidance without overwhelming educators, contributing to scalable personalization.

AI technologies have significantly advanced the potential for personalized learning by providing scalable, efficient, and data-driven methods to support diverse learners. Machine learning and deep learning allow systems to predict and adapt to student needs, while natural language processing facilitates human-like interaction and feedback. Data analytics empowers educators with actionable insights, and intelligent tutoring systems simulate one-on-one mentorship. AI-powered recommendation engines further personalize content delivery, ensuring relevance and engagement.

Together, these technologies shift the educational paradigm from standardization to individualization. They enable not only academic personalization but also foster learner agency, equity, and lifelong learning readiness. As these tools continue to evolve, their ethical, technical, and pedagogical integration will be crucial in realizing the full potential of AI-powered personalized education.

Mechanisms of AI-Driven Personalization

Artificial Intelligence (AI) has redefined how educational content is tailored to learners through sophisticated mechanisms that assess, adapt, and deliver instruction in real-time. AI-driven personalization incorporates real-time analytics, adaptive systems, and intelligent feedback tools to create individualized learning experiences. This section explores the key mechanisms through which AI enables these transformative educational practices.

Real-Time Student Performance Analysis

At the core of AI-driven personalization is the ability to analyze student performance in real time. AI systems continuously gather data from quizzes, assignments, clickstreams, and interaction patterns to evaluate learners' strengths, weaknesses, progress, and engagement levels. Machine learning models identify patterns and anomalies that signal learning gaps or conceptual misunderstandings (Papamitsiou & Economides, 2014).

For example, AI can detect when a student repeatedly struggles with a concept and instantly adjust the instructional approach or alert the instructor for intervention. This real-time insight allows for timely, targeted support and reduces the delay between error detection and remediation. Learning platforms such as DreamBox and Knewton incorporate this kind of responsive analytics to improve learning outcomes.

Adaptive Content Delivery and Curriculum Design

AI systems utilize performance data to dynamically adjust content and curriculum design to suit each learner's profile. This adaptive delivery ensures that content difficulty, pace, and sequence align with the student's current cognitive state and learning preferences

(Walkington, 2013). Algorithms assess a learner's readiness and recommend scaffolding techniques, supplementary materials, or advanced resources based on their progress.

Furthermore, curriculum design becomes fluid in an AI-enhanced environment. Instead of following rigid syllabi, AI-powered platforms enable flexible learning paths where lessons are reordered or customized based on real-time needs. This dynamic structure empowers educators to implement differentiated instruction at scale and helps learners maintain optimal challenge levels.

Personalized Feedback and Assessment

Another essential mechanism of AI-driven personalization is intelligent, individualized feedback. Traditional assessments provide static scores, whereas AI-enhanced assessments offer immediate, formative feedback that guides learning in context. Natural Language Processing (NLP) tools can analyze written responses, evaluate comprehension, and deliver suggestions for improvement (Woolf, 2010).

Personalized feedback systems such as those used in platforms like Grammarly or Turnitin go beyond grammar correction to offer insights on writing structure, coherence, and originality. In mathematics or science education, AI systems like Carnegie Learning provide step-by-step hints and feedback tailored to students' problem-solving processes.

Additionally, AI enables continuous, low-stakes assessments that are integrated into daily learning activities, shifting evaluation from summative to formative and fostering deeper understanding.

Dynamic Learning Pathways

AI systems facilitate the creation of dynamic learning pathways that evolve with the learner. Rather than following a fixed curriculum, students navigate personalized journeys shaped by their goals, pace, prior knowledge, and performance data (Kay et al., 2013). These pathways adjust in real-time, recommending topics to revisit or skip based on mastery, thereby optimizing learning efficiency.

For instance, AI in personalized learning platforms can redirect a student to remedial lessons after detecting a skill gap or present enrichment tasks when mastery is achieved. This flexibility increases learner autonomy and motivation, making education more inclusive and effective.

APPLICATIONS AND CASE STUDIES

The application of Artificial Intelligence (AI) in education has moved from theoretical promise to practical implementation, reshaping how learners engage with content and how educators deliver instruction. From primary schools to universities and online learning platforms, AI-powered tools are transforming pedagogical practices. This section explores AI applications across K-12 and higher education, as well as major EdTech platforms, followed by real-world case studies that illustrate the impact and scalability of these technologies.

K-12 Education: AI in Classrooms

In K-12 settings, AI is increasingly integrated to support personalized instruction, classroom management, and student assessment. One of the most significant contributions of AI in this space is the automation of adaptive learning environments that adjust content to suit individual student performance levels.

AI-powered applications like *DreamBox Learning* and *Carnegie Learning* are widely used in primary and secondary schools. These platforms employ intelligent tutoring systems (ITS) to provide real-time feedback and scaffolding tailored to student needs in subjects like mathematics and reading. Teachers benefit from dashboards that track student progress, highlight learning gaps, and recommend interventions (Luckin et al., 2016).

Moreover, AI chatbots and virtual teaching assistants are being introduced to handle routine queries, administer quizzes, and enhance student engagement through interactive, gamified learning experiences. This reduces the administrative burden on teachers and allows them to focus on differentiated instruction.

Higher Education: Smart Learning Environments

In higher education, AI is instrumental in creating smart learning environments that offer personalized learning experiences and predictive analytics to support student success. Universities are adopting AI to enhance everything from admissions processes and curriculum planning to student advising and course delivery.

AI tools like *IBM Watson Tutor* and *Jill Watson*—a virtual assistant developed at Georgia Tech—have demonstrated how AI can provide timely academic assistance, simulate human-like interaction, and answer frequently asked questions in online courses (Goel & Polepeddi, 2016). These systems improve efficiency and responsiveness, especially in large-scale classes.

Predictive analytics, powered by machine learning algorithms, enable institutions to identify at-risk students and deploy support systems before academic failure occurs. For example, Arizona State University uses AI to monitor student performance, engagement, and attendance to personalize student advisement and reduce dropout rates (Popenici & Kerr, 2017).

Furthermore, natural language processing (NLP) tools are applied to evaluate essays, support language learning, and facilitate peer review, enhancing academic assessment processes.

EdTech Platforms: Use of AI in MOOCs and LMS

Massive Open Online Courses (MOOCs) and Learning Management Systems (LMS) have embraced AI to address the challenge of scaling personalized learning to thousands or millions of users. Platforms such as *Coursera*, *edX*, and *Udacity* incorporate AI to provide adaptive quizzes, real-time feedback, and tailored content recommendations.

AI algorithms analyze learner behavior, quiz performance, and interaction patterns to create personalized dashboards and suggest relevant modules or supplemental resources. For instance, Coursera's learning platform uses AI to send personalized nudges, reminders, and course progress updates based on learner engagement metrics (Reich, 2020).

LMS platforms like *Moodle* and *Canvas* offer integrated AI tools for assignment grading, attendance tracking, and learning analytics. These features empower educators to deliver differentiated instruction and improve course outcomes, especially in blended and hybrid learning environments.

Additionally, AI supports content creation in MOOCs. Tools like Content Technologies Inc. (CTI) automatically generate customized textbooks and course materials based on student learning objectives and curriculum standards, significantly reducing instructor workload.

Case Studies of AI Integration (e.g., Squirrel AI, Knewton, Content Technologies Inc.)

Squirrel AI, a Chinese EdTech company, is a pioneer in using AI to deliver personalized education in real-time. It employs an adaptive learning engine that breaks down subjects into granular knowledge points and tracks student mastery at an individual level. Based on this data, the system dynamically adjusts lesson plans, ensuring students receive content tailored to their proficiency and pace.

In a study conducted by the company, students using Squirrel AI outperformed peers in traditional classrooms by more than 30% on standardized assessments (Zhai et al., 2021). The platform also incorporates emotional AI to assess learner motivation and attention, allowing for timely interventions.

Knewton, acquired by Wiley, offers adaptive learning technology that personalizes digital courses for students based on their strengths, weaknesses, and learning behaviors. Knewton's algorithms continuously evaluate learner interactions to deliver tailored content, assessments, and study paths.

The platform is used in both K-12 and higher education contexts and has demonstrated improvements in student retention and comprehension. Research shows that Knewton's adaptive learning systems led to increased student engagement and a 17% improvement in course pass rates in pilot studies (Gess-Newsome et al., 2017).

Content Technologies Inc. developed AI-driven tools to automate the creation of personalized textbooks. Its flagship platform uses deep learning and NLP to analyze course syllabi, academic content, and learner goals to generate custom learning materials.

This innovation significantly reduces the time and cost associated with content development. While CTI's operations have evolved, its approach inspired a new wave of AI-based content generation tools now being used across EdTech platforms.

An iconic case of AI application in higher education is *Jill Watson*, an AI teaching assistant developed using IBM Watson. Jill was deployed in an online computer science course and answered over 10,000 forum questions with such accuracy that students were unaware they were interacting with an AI.

Jill Watson not only improved student satisfaction but also highlighted AI's potential in managing large-scale interactions in MOOCs and hybrid courses (Goel & Polepeddi, 2016).

AI has moved beyond being a supplementary tool to becoming a central driver of educational transformation. In K-12 classrooms, AI supports differentiated instruction and real-time feedback. In universities, it powers smart learning environments that offer predictive insights and personalized support. EdTech platforms leverage AI to scale personalization, automate content generation, and enhance engagement in MOOCs and LMS environments.

Case studies from companies like Squirrel AI, Knewton, and CTI illustrate the breadth of AI's impact across education levels and modalities. These examples show that when implemented thoughtfully, AI can improve learning outcomes, foster inclusion, and enhance the teaching experience. However, successful integration depends on continuous evaluation, ethical consideration, and professional development for educators.

As the landscape of AI in education continues to evolve, these applications and case studies provide a roadmap for leveraging intelligent technologies to meet the diverse needs of 21st-century learners.

BENEFITS OF PERSONALIZED LEARNING THROUGH AI

Artificial Intelligence (AI) has redefined the landscape of education by enabling learning experiences that are more tailored, inclusive, and effective. Personalized learning through AI offers several distinct advantages over traditional, one-size-fits-all educational models. These benefits span academic performance, engagement, accessibility, and adaptability to diverse learners. This section explores how AI-driven personalization enhances learning outcomes, motivation, equity, and the accommodation of various learning styles.

Improved Learning Outcomes and Retention

One of the most significant benefits of AI-powered personalized learning is the marked improvement in student learning outcomes and knowledge retention. AI systems use real-time performance data to identify knowledge gaps and adjust instruction accordingly, ensuring that learners receive content at the right level of difficulty and at the right time (Luckin et al., 2016). This timely intervention prevents students from falling behind and enhances the efficiency of learning.

Studies have shown that adaptive learning platforms like Carnegie Learning and Knewton improve student mastery of core concepts by enabling personalized pacing and feedback (Pane et al., 2014). These platforms use machine learning algorithms to analyze a student's progress and provide targeted resources or activities that reinforce learning objectives. As a result, learners are more likely to retain information and perform better on assessments.

Moreover, personalized learning environments reduce cognitive overload by presenting content that is neither too easy nor too difficult. This optimal challenge level promotes deeper engagement with learning materials, resulting in better long-term memory encoding and higher academic achievement.

Enhanced Student Engagement and Motivation

Personalized learning through AI also fosters greater student engagement and motivation by making education more relevant and responsive to individual interests and goals. Traditional educational systems often lack flexibility, leading to disengagement, particularly among students who find the content either too challenging or uninteresting.

AI addresses this issue by offering personalized recommendations based on learner preferences, past interactions, and performance data. For instance, platforms such as DreamBox and Smart Sparrow adapt scenarios and content presentation formats to suit each learner, thereby increasing emotional involvement and active participation (Walkington, 2013).

Gamification, intelligent tutoring systems (ITS), and real-time feedback also play critical roles in maintaining learner motivation. These AI tools provide instant reinforcement, encouragement, and hints that sustain attention and promote persistence in learning tasks. Additionally, the autonomy and self-direction facilitated by AI-driven learning environments empower students to take ownership of their educational journeys, which in turn boosts intrinsic motivation (Deci & Ryan, 2000).

Motivated students are more likely to complete assignments, participate in discussions, and pursue additional learning opportunities, contributing to improved educational outcomes across the board.

Equity and Accessibility in Education

Another transformative benefit of AI in personalized learning is its potential to promote equity and accessibility in education. By tailoring instruction to the unique needs of each learner, regardless of background, ability, or location, AI helps level the playing field and address systemic disparities.

Students with disabilities, learning differences, or language barriers can benefit immensely from AI-powered tools. For example, AI applications like Microsoft Immersive Reader and speech-to-text systems provide accommodations such as text simplification, audio narration, and language translation, ensuring that content is accessible to all students (Holmes et al., 2019).

Furthermore, AI allows educators to reach students in underserved or remote areas through scalable digital platforms. These technologies break down geographical and financial barriers to high-quality education, making it possible for marginalized learners to access resources previously unavailable to them. In this way, AI contributes to the democratization of education, helping institutions meet inclusive education goals aligned with UNESCO's Sustainable Development Goals (UNESCO, 2020).

Personalized learning also combats the bias often embedded in standardized testing and uniform curriculum delivery by allowing learners to demonstrate understanding in diverse ways suited to their strengths.

Support for Diverse Learning Styles and Needs

Every learner has a unique cognitive style, learning pace, and preference for processing information. Traditional classroom settings often struggle to accommodate this diversity, leading to frustration or underperformance. AI bridges this gap by enabling differentiated instruction at scale, customizing content format, delivery methods, and assessment strategies to align with individual learning styles.

For instance, visual learners may benefit from AI-generated diagrams and videos, while auditory learners might engage more with spoken instructions or podcasts. Kinesthetic learners can be directed toward simulations or interactive modules. Platforms such as Khan Academy and Coursera use AI to present concepts in multiple formats, enhancing the overall learning experience and accommodating multiple intelligences (Gardner, 1983).

Moreover, AI systems can identify patterns in learner behavior and adapt instructional strategies accordingly. Some platforms adjust the pace of instruction based on learners' attention levels, as detected through biometric data or interaction patterns. Others allow students to set their learning preferences and goals, ensuring a more personalized and effective learning pathway.

By recognizing and responding to learner diversity, AI creates inclusive environments that respect individual differences, reduce frustration, and enhance academic success. This approach is particularly effective in mixed-ability classrooms, where managing diverse needs can be challenging for a single instructor.

The integration of AI into personalized learning offers a myriad of benefits that collectively redefine educational success in the digital age. Improved learning outcomes and higher retention rates are made possible through adaptive, real-time instructional interventions. Enhanced student engagement and motivation arise from content that is relevant, responsive, and empowering. AI also plays a pivotal role in promoting equity and accessibility, offering tools and pathways that accommodate learners from diverse backgrounds and with varied needs.

Furthermore, by supporting a wide range of learning styles and cognitive preferences, AI ensures that education is not only inclusive but also deeply individualized. As AI technologies continue to evolve, their role in shaping personalized education will only become more pronounced, providing transformative possibilities for students, educators, and institutions alike.

However, to fully realize these benefits, stakeholders must address challenges such as data privacy, algorithmic bias, and the need for teacher training. With thoughtful implementation, AI-driven personalized learning can become a powerful force for good—bridging gaps, nurturing talents, and preparing learners for an increasingly complex world.

CHALLENGES AND ETHICAL CONSIDERATIONS

While the potential benefits of AI-powered personalized learning are vast, their implementation raises significant challenges and ethical considerations. These concerns span the realms of algorithmic fairness, data privacy, teacher preparedness, and the balance between automation and human instruction. Addressing these challenges is essential to ensure that AI in education serves all learners equitably and responsibly. This section examines these critical issues in depth.

Algorithmic Bias and Fairness

One of the primary ethical challenges in AI-driven personalized learning is algorithmic bias. Machine learning algorithms, while designed to be objective, can inadvertently perpetuate or exacerbate existing biases in educational data. AI systems learn from historical data, and if this data contains biases—such as underrepresentation of minority groups or unequal access to resources—the AI can reinforce these disparities in its decision-making processes.

For instance, AI applications that predict student success or recommend learning paths based on past performance can inadvertently favor certain student demographics while disadvantaging others (O'Neil, 2016). In a study on predictive algorithms in education, researchers found that AI systems trained on biased historical data could unfairly categorize students from underrepresented groups as "at risk," leading to inaccurate recommendations or unnecessary interventions (Eubanks, 2018).

The issue of fairness becomes even more complex when AI is used to assess student performance or determine eligibility for scholarships or other opportunities. If the algorithms are not transparent or well-calibrated, students may be penalized for factors outside of their control, such as socioeconomic background, geographic location, or access to quality learning resources.

To mitigate algorithmic bias, developers must ensure that AI systems are trained on diverse, representative datasets and incorporate fairness metrics during their development and deployment stages. Moreover, algorithms should be continuously monitored and adjusted to ensure they do not inadvertently reinforce systemic inequalities (Binns, 2018).

Data Privacy and Security Concerns

The use of AI in personalized learning requires the collection and analysis of vast amounts of student data, including personal information, learning patterns, performance metrics, and even emotional states. This raises serious concerns about data privacy and security, especially given the sensitivity of the information involved.

Educational data is highly personal, and its misuse can lead to significant ethical issues. For example, data breaches could expose students' private information, or unauthorized access to personal learning data could lead to discriminatory practices. The General Data Protection Regulation (GDPR) in Europe, and similar laws in other parts of the world, set strict guidelines for the collection, storage, and sharing of personal data. However, many educational institutions, especially in developing countries, may lack the infrastructure or expertise to ensure compliance with these regulations.

Moreover, AI-powered systems rely on continuous data collection to refine learning algorithms, but this constant monitoring could lead to issues related to informed consent and surveillance. Students and parents may not fully understand the extent to which their data is being tracked or how it is being used, potentially leading to a lack of trust in AI systems.

To address these concerns, AI developers must prioritize data privacy by implementing robust encryption methods, secure data storage protocols, and ensuring compliance with international privacy standards. Schools and educators should also be transparent about how student data is collected, processed, and used, and students and parents should be given control over their data (Zeng et al., 2020).

Teacher Readiness and Professional Development

Despite the transformative potential of AI in education, successful implementation depends on the readiness of educators to adopt these new technologies. Teachers play a critical role in the effective use of AI-powered tools, as they must understand how to integrate AI systems into their teaching practices and use the insights generated by these systems to support student learning.

However, many teachers may feel ill-prepared to use AI in their classrooms due to a lack of technical skills, understanding of AI principles, or experience with new digital tools (Tondeur et al., 2017). Furthermore, teachers may be resistant to AI adoption due to concerns about job security, workload, or the perceived dehumanization of education.

Professional development programs must be designed to provide teachers with the necessary skills and confidence to effectively use AI tools. These programs should focus not only on the technical aspects of AI but also on its pedagogical implications. Teachers should be trained to interpret AI-generated data, make informed decisions based on insights, and integrate AI into a student-centered approach that complements traditional teaching methods.

Additionally, teachers should be encouraged to collaborate with AI developers to ensure that the tools align with curriculum goals and educational standards. Continuous professional development is essential to help educators keep pace with rapidly evolving technologies and pedagogies.

Over-Reliance on Automation vs. Human Pedagogy

While AI can greatly enhance personalized learning, there is a risk of over-relying on automation at the expense of human pedagogy. The human element of teaching—empathy, emotional intelligence, and the ability to adapt instruction to the unique needs of students—is something that AI cannot fully replicate.

AI can provide valuable data on student performance, recommend learning pathways, and offer personalized feedback, but it cannot replace the mentorship, guidance, and emotional support that teachers provide. In fact, excessive reliance on AI may result in the dehumanization of education, where students are treated as data points rather than as individuals with unique social, emotional, and cognitive needs.

Moreover, AI's emphasis on efficiency and standardization may inadvertently limit creativity, critical thinking, and problem-solving in students. Traditional forms of education, such as project-based learning and group collaboration, rely on human interaction and mentorship to foster these skills. While AI can support personalized learning, it must be seen as a complement to, rather than a replacement for, human pedagogy.

To ensure a balanced approach, educators must be mindful of the limitations of AI and continue to play an active role in shaping the learning experience. Human teachers can interpret AI-generated insights, address the emotional needs of students, and create learning environments that foster creativity and critical thinking. AI should enhance, not replace, the teacher-student relationship.

The challenges and ethical considerations of AI in personalized learning must be carefully navigated to ensure that these technologies benefit all learners in a fair and equitable manner. Algorithmic bias and fairness, data privacy, teacher readiness, and the balance between automation and human pedagogy are critical issues that require attention from policymakers, educators, and developers alike.

Addressing these concerns will help ensure that AI is used responsibly in education, empowering both students and teachers while maintaining the values of equity, privacy, and human-centered instruction. By implementing fair, transparent, and secure AI systems, and by supporting teachers with the necessary training and professional development, we can harness the full potential of AI to create a more inclusive and effective education system.

FUTURE DIRECTIONS AND INNOVATIONS

As artificial intelligence (AI) continues to evolve, its role in education is poised to expand in new and innovative directions. The future of AI-powered personalized learning promises exciting opportunities to enhance education, making it more engaging, inclusive, and effective. This section explores emerging trends in AI and education, the integration of AI with augmented and virtual reality (AR/VR), the potential of emotional AI in learning, and policy recommendations to guide the responsible development and deployment of these technologies.

Emerging Trends in AI and Education

The landscape of AI in education is rapidly changing, with new technologies and approaches emerging to further personalize and enhance the learning experience. One key trend is the increasing use of **adaptive learning technologies**, which use machine learning algorithms to continuously monitor and adjust educational content based on student performance. These systems go beyond traditional learning management systems by providing real-time feedback and personalized pathways for each student, ensuring that they receive the right level of support and challenge.

Moreover, AI-powered **automated assessment tools** are evolving to provide more nuanced and accurate evaluations of student progress. These tools can assess not only traditional test-based outcomes but also more complex indicators, such as student engagement, creativity, and collaborative skills, through analysis of learning behaviors and interactions in digital environments (Spector, 2018). As AI systems become more sophisticated, they will increasingly be able to provide a holistic view of student development, helping educators make better-informed decisions and interventions.

Another emerging trend is the development of **AI-powered learning assistants**. These virtual assistants can help students navigate the educational landscape by providing personalized recommendations, answering questions, and assisting with time management and task prioritization. Learning assistants could serve as individualized support systems, particularly for students who may not have access to frequent, in-person assistance, thus enhancing equity in education (Baker et al., 2020).

Integration with Augmented and Virtual Reality (AR/VR)

The integration of AI with **augmented reality (AR)** and **virtual reality (VR)** holds great potential to revolutionize personalized learning. AR and VR technologies provide immersive and interactive experiences that engage students in ways traditional classrooms cannot. By combining AI with AR/VR, educational experiences can become more dynamic and customized to the needs of each student.

For example, AI algorithms can analyze a student's interactions within an AR/VR environment and adjust the learning experience in real-time. In a history class, for instance, students could explore a virtual ancient civilization, with AI tailoring the experience based on their individual learning styles and prior knowledge. AI could also provide personalized guidance or feedback during the experience, ensuring that students remain engaged and challenged without becoming overwhelmed (Johnson et al., 2016).

In addition to improving engagement, the integration of AI with AR/VR can help bridge gaps in education by enabling experiential learning opportunities that may otherwise be inaccessible. For example, students in rural areas could use VR to engage in hands-on science experiments, medical students could practice surgery in a simulated environment, or engineering students could design and test prototypes in virtual labs. These AI-enhanced AR/VR experiences will likely expand access to high-quality education, offering students from various backgrounds the chance to participate in cutting-edge learning experiences.

Moreover, this integration could lead to **immersive simulations** for critical life skills development. AI-driven simulations could teach soft skills such as communication, leadership, and conflict resolution in realistic scenarios, preparing students for real-world challenges.

Emotional AI and Affective Computing in Learning

One of the most exciting frontiers in AI is the development of **emotional AI** and **affective computing**—technologies that enable machines to recognize and respond to human emotions. In education, emotional AI can be used to create more empathetic and personalized learning experiences by responding to the emotional states of students.

AI systems equipped with affective computing can analyze facial expressions, voice tone, and body language to detect emotions such as frustration, boredom, or confusion. By recognizing these emotional cues, AI systems can adjust the learning experience to better suit the emotional needs of students. For example, if a student appears frustrated, the system might offer encouragement or simplify the content to prevent them from disengaging. Conversely, if a student appears confident and engaged, the system may present more challenging material to push their learning forward.

The integration of emotional AI into personalized learning has the potential to foster **emotional engagement** in students, which is closely tied to academic success. Research has shown that emotional engagement is a key predictor of motivation and persistence in learning (Pekrun et al., 2017). By leveraging emotional AI, educators can better understand their students' emotional and motivational states and adjust their teaching strategies accordingly.

Additionally, emotional AI could provide **mental health support** for students by detecting signs of stress, anxiety, or depression. Early identification of emotional challenges could allow for timely interventions and support, reducing the risk of academic burnout and improving overall well-being.

POLICY RECOMMENDATIONS AND FRAMEWORKS

As AI continues to transform education, it is crucial to establish policies and frameworks that ensure the responsible, ethical, and equitable use of these technologies. Policymakers, educators, and technologists must work together to create guidelines that protect students' rights and promote positive educational outcomes.

First and foremost, **data privacy and security** must be prioritized in any AI-driven educational system. Laws such as the General Data Protection Regulation (GDPR) in the EU and the Family Educational Rights and Privacy Act (FERPA) in the US set important precedents, but there is still a need for more comprehensive, global regulations that govern the collection and use of student data (Zeng et al., 2020). Governments should require educational institutions to implement robust data protection measures and provide transparency in how student data is used.

Second, **ethical AI development** should be encouraged to prevent biases and ensure fairness. Developers must incorporate fairness audits and bias mitigation techniques during the design and testing phases of AI systems. Transparent algorithms, as well as mechanisms for addressing bias, should be standard practices in the development of educational AI tools (O'Neil, 2016). Policymakers can support this by creating frameworks that require regular evaluations of AI systems for equity and bias, particularly for tools that assess or make decisions about students.

In addition, **teacher training and professional development** should be an integral part of AI integration into education. Teachers must be equipped with the knowledge and skills to effectively use AI tools in their classrooms and interpret AI-generated data. Governments and educational institutions should invest in ongoing training programs that help teachers stay updated on the latest technologies and pedagogical strategies (Tondeur et al., 2017).

Finally, policymakers should focus on promoting **digital equity** by ensuring that AI-powered educational tools are accessible to all students, regardless of socioeconomic background. This may involve subsidies for schools in underserved areas, ensuring internet access for students in rural regions, and providing training for educators in disadvantaged communities. The goal should be to prevent the digital divide from widening further and ensure that AI's benefits are equitably distributed.

The future of AI in education is bright, with exciting innovations on the horizon, such as AI-powered adaptive learning, AR/VR integration, and emotional AI. These technologies will make education more engaging, personalized, and accessible, offering students a richer, more diverse learning experience. However, to fully realize these benefits, it is crucial to address the ethical, privacy, and equity challenges associated with AI adoption. By creating robust policy frameworks, investing in teacher training, and ensuring the responsible development of AI tools, we can pave the way for a future in which AI transforms education for the betterment of all students.

CONCLUSION

Summary of Key Insights

Throughout this chapter, we have explored the transformative potential of AI-powered personalized learning in education. The integration of artificial intelligence into educational practices is revolutionizing the way students learn and interact with educational content. By tailoring learning experiences to individual students' needs, preferences, and learning paces, AI systems are enhancing the overall educational experience.

A key insight is the growing shift from traditional, one-size-fits-all teaching approaches toward adaptive and dynamic learning systems. AI tools, such as intelligent tutoring systems, learning analytics, and personalized recommendation engines, are providing educators with valuable insights into student progress, enabling them to offer more targeted interventions. These technologies are reshaping the student-teacher relationship by shifting the role of the educator from being the sole source of knowledge to a facilitator who can guide and support each student's unique learning journey.

Another significant takeaway is the potential for AI to bridge educational inequalities. AI-driven personalized learning can be tailored to meet the needs of diverse learners, ensuring that every student has access to resources and opportunities suited to their abilities and learning styles. This capacity for inclusivity extends to students with learning disabilities, offering customized interventions that can help them overcome barriers to learning.

Furthermore, the integration of AI with cutting-edge technologies such as augmented reality (AR), virtual reality (VR), and emotional AI offers the opportunity to create immersive, emotionally responsive learning environments. These innovations provide rich, engaging experiences that not only capture students' attention but also foster deeper learning and emotional engagement. In this way, AI can help cultivate a more holistic learning experience that nurtures both cognitive and emotional development.

Strategic Implications for Educators and Policymakers

For educators, the rise of AI-powered personalized learning presents an opportunity to redefine their role in the classroom. Instead of being the central figure in the delivery of information, educators will become facilitators and mentors, leveraging AI tools to provide targeted, data-driven insights that inform their teaching strategies. Educators must, therefore, be equipped with the skills to interpret AI-generated data, adapt their teaching methods accordingly, and maintain the human connection that is essential to effective learning.

Policymakers also have a critical role to play in shaping the future of AI in education. They must prioritize the development of robust policy frameworks that ensure the ethical use of AI while promoting accessibility, fairness, and security in educational settings. This includes ensuring that AI tools are developed and deployed in ways that uphold data privacy and prevent algorithmic bias. Policymakers should also invest in teacher training programs that empower educators to embrace AI as a tool for enhancing their teaching practices and improving student outcomes.

Moreover, policymakers must foster an inclusive approach to AI adoption, ensuring that all students, regardless of socioeconomic background or geographic location, have access to the technologies that can support their learning. This will require significant investments in infrastructure, particularly in underserved regions, as well as ongoing efforts to address the digital divide.

Vision for the Future of Tailored Education

Looking to the future, the vision for personalized learning through AI is one of a highly adaptive, inclusive, and student-centered educational ecosystem. AI will continue to evolve, offering more sophisticated, real-time feedback that helps students navigate their learning journeys with greater autonomy and confidence. The future of education will be one where learning is not confined to the classroom but is a continuous, dynamic process that adapts to students' evolving needs.

The integration of AI, AR, VR, and emotional AI will create immersive, interactive learning environments that cater to a wide range of learning preferences and styles. These environments will provide students with opportunities to engage in experiential learning, fostering creativity, problem-solving, and critical thinking in ways that traditional classrooms cannot.

Ultimately, the goal is to create a system of education that is not only more efficient and effective but also more equitable, giving all students, regardless of their background, the tools and support they need to succeed. With the right policies, technologies, and teacher support systems in place, AI-powered personalized learning can help build an education system that empowers every student to reach their full potential, preparing them for success in an increasingly complex and technology-driven world.

This concludes the chapter, offering a comprehensive overview of the potential, implications, and future directions of AI in personalized education.

REFERENCES

Baker, R. S., Inventado, P. S., & Rodrigo, M. M. (2020). Educational data mining and learning analytics. *Learning Analytics Review*, *2*(4), 119–132.

Binns, R. (2018). Fairness in machine learning: A survey. *ACM Computing Surveys*, *51*(6), 1–35.

Bruner, J. (1960). *The process of education*. Harvard University Press. DOI: 10.4159/9780674028999

Darling-Hammond, L., Flook, L., Cook-Harvey, C., Barron, B., & Osher, D. (2020). Implications for educational practice of the science of learning and development. *Applied Developmental Science*, *24*(2), 97–140. DOI: 10.1080/10888691.2018.1537791

Deci, E. L., & Ryan, R. M. (1985). *Intrinsic motivation and self-determination in human behavior*. Springer. DOI: 10.1007/978-1-4899-2271-7

Deci, E. L., & Ryan, R. M. (2000). The "what" and "why" of goal pursuits: Human needs and the self-determination of behavior. *Psychological Inquiry*, *11*(4), 227–268. DOI: 10.1207/S15327965PLI1104_01

Eubanks, V. (2018). *Automating inequality: How high-tech tools profile, police, and punish the poor*. St. Martin's Press.

Ferri, F., Grifoni, P., & Guzzo, T. (2020). Online learning and emergency remote teaching: Opportunities and challenges in emergency situations. *Education Sciences*, *10*(10), 1–12.

Fryer, L. K., & Carpenter, R. (2006). Bots as tutors: Improving learner motivation through friendly feedback. *AI & Society*, *20*(3), 294–303.

Gardner, H. (1983). *Frames of mind: The theory of multiple intelligences*. Basic Books.

Gess-Newsome, J., Taylor, J. A., Carlson, J., Gardner, A. L., Wilson, C. D., & Stuhlsatz, M. A. M. (2017). A study of teacher effectiveness using Knewton's adaptive technology. *Journal of Educational Technology Systems*, *46*(1), 5–23.

Goel, A., & Polepeddi, L. (2016). *Jill Watson: A virtual teaching assistant for online education*. Georgia Institute of Technology.

Holmes, W., Bialik, M., & Fadel, C. (2019). *Artificial Intelligence in Education: Promises and Implications for Teaching and Learning*. Center for Curriculum Redesign.

Johnson, L., Adams Becker, S., & Cummins, M. (2016). *The NMC Horizon Report: 2016 Higher Education Edition*. New Media Consortium.

Jordan, M. I., & Mitchell, T. M. (2015). Machine learning: Trends, perspectives, and prospects. *Science*, *349*(6245), 255–260. DOI: 10.1126/science.aaa8415 PMID: 26185243

Kay, D., Leung, A., Tangney, B., & Holton, D. (2013). Personalized learning pathways for mathematics. *International Journal of Science and Mathematics Education, 11*(2), 405–427.

Luckin, R., Holmes, W., Griffiths, M., & Forcier, L. B. (2016). *Intelligence unleashed: An argument for AI in education.* Pearson Education.

Manouselis, N., Drachsler, H., Verbert, K., & Duval, E. (2011). *Recommender systems for learning.* Springer Briefs in Computer Science.

Means, B., Toyama, Y., Murphy, R., & Bakia, M. (2014). The effectiveness of online and blended learning: A meta-analysis of the empirical literature. *Teachers College Record.*

Nye, B. D. (2015). Intelligent tutoring systems by and for the developing world: A review of trends and approaches for educational technology in a global context. *International Journal of Artificial Intelligence in Education, 25*(2), 177–203. DOI: 10.1007/s40593-014-0028-6

O'Neil, C. (2016). *Weapons of math destruction: How big data increases inequality and threatens democracy.* Crown Publishing Group.

Pane, J. F., Steiner, E. D., Baird, M. D., & Hamilton, L. S. (2014). *Continued progress: Promising evidence on personalized learning.* RAND Corporation.

Papamitsiou, Z., & Economides, A. A. (2014). Learning analytics and educational data mining in practice: A systematic literature review of empirical evidence. *Journal of Educational Technology & Society, 17*(4), 49–64.

Pekrun, R., Goetz, T., Titz, W., & Perry, R. P. (2017). Academic emotions in students' self-regulated learning and achievement: A program of qualitative and quantitative research. *Educational Psychology Review, 29*(4), 611–632.

Popenici, S. A. D., & Kerr, S. (2017). Exploring the impact of artificial intelligence on teaching and learning in higher education. *Research and Practice in Technology Enhanced Learning, 12*(1), 1–13. DOI: 10.1186/s41039-017-0062-8 PMID: 30595727

Reich, J. (2020). *Failure to disrupt: Why technology alone can't transform education.* Harvard University Press.

Siemens, G., & Long, P. (2011). Penetrating the fog: Analytics in learning and education. *EDUCAUSE Review, 46*(5), 30–32.

Spector, J. M. (2018). Conceptualizing K-12 personalized learning: Definitions, theories, and models. *Springer. 1(1),* 1-12.

Tondeur, J., Van Keer, H., & Valcke, M. (2017). ICT integration in education: A learning needs perspective. *Computers & Education, 64*, 58–68.

VanLehn, K. (2011). The relative effectiveness of human tutoring, intelligent tutoring systems, and other tutoring systems. *Educational Psychologist, 46*(4), 197–221. DOI: 10.1080/00461520.2011.611369

Walkington, C. (2013). Using adaptive learning technologies to personalize instruction to student interests: The impact of relevant contexts on performance and learning outcomes. *Journal of Educational Psychology, 105*(4), 932–945. DOI: 10.1037/a0031882

Woolf, B. P. (2010). Building intelligent interactive tutors: Student-centered strategies for revolutionizing e-learning. *Morgan Kaufmann.1*(1), 1-20.

Zawacki-Richter, O., Marín, V. I., Bond, M., & Gouverneur, F. (2019). Systematic review of research on artificial intelligence applications in higher education. *International Journal of Educational Technology in Higher Education, 16*(1), 1–27. DOI: 10.1186/s41239-019-0171-0

Zeng, J., Sweeney, J., & Hussain, I. (2020). Privacy concerns in AI: Impact on data collection and sharing. *Journal of Educational Technology, 15*(3), 201–218.

Zhai, X., Zhang, M., & Zhao, Y. (2021). Personalized learning with artificial intelligence: An empirical study of Squirrel AI Learning. *Journal of Educational Computing Research, 59*(3), 543–567.

About The Contributors

Viktor Wang, is a globally recognized professor and leader in the field of Education in the Department of Educational Leadership and Technology at California State University, San Bernardino. His distinguished career is marked by innovation, scholarship, and mentorship. With more than 240 peer-reviewed publications, Dr. Wang has made transformative contributions to academic research and thought leadership. His work has inspired over 200 scholarly articles and more than 1,500 book chapters contributed to his edited volumes and journals by scholars around the world. His publications are widely respected and housed in top-tier institutions, including Stanford University Libraries and other globally renowned academic collections. Dr. Wang has received numerous prestigious honors, including the 2016 Presidential Award for Exceptional and Innovative Leadership from the American Association for Adult and Continuing Education (AAACE), as well as institutional recognition such as the Distinguished Faculty and Scholarly Achievement Award from CSULB. A dedicated mentor, Dr. Wang has successfully guided more than 80 doctoral students through dissertation completion. His leadership has also driven measurable institutional outcomes, including enrollment growth, the launch of innovative academic programs, and the establishment of international educational partnerships.

***

Gbolagade Adekanmbi obtained a PhD in Adult Education from the University of Ibadan in Nigeria in 1992, with a research focus on Distance Education. From 1987, he taught courses at the Department of Adult Education, University of Ibadan. He later worked at the Centre for Continuing Education, University of Botswana, and served as the Acting Director, from 2009-2011. He has published over 80 papers as journal articles, book chapters and conference proceedings. He is a Reviewer for the International Review of Research in Open and Distributed Learning (IRRODL), the Journal of Adult and Continuing Education (JACE), and the International Academic Forum (IAFOR) Journal of Education (Studies in Education). He is also the Chair of the African Deans of Education Forum (ADEF) and a member of the Steering Committee of the Global Network of Deans of Education (GNDE). A former Acting Deputy Vice Chancellor, Academic Services at the Botswana

Open University (BOU), Professor Adekanmbi is currently the Dean, School of Education at the same University.

Fernando Luís Almeida has a Ph.D. in Computer Science Engineering from the Faculty of Engineering of University of Porto (FEUP). He also holds an MSc in Innovation and Entrepreneurship and in Informatics Engineering from FEUP. He has around 15 years of teaching experience at higher education levels in the field of computer science and management. He has also worked for 20 years in several positions as a software engineer and project manager for large organizations and research centers like Critical Software, CICA/SEF, INESC TEC, and ISR Porto. He is a founder member of the International Association of Innovation Professionals. He has more than 250 scientific publications indexed in WoS, Scopus and Google Scholar. His current research areas include innovation policies, entrepreneurship, sustainability, and decision support systems.

Lauren Anderson, MEd, is an Assistant Professor in the Developmental Education Department of the Undergraduate College, National Louis University. She is currently working on her dissertation in the EdD of Teaching and Learning program at National Louis. Previously, she worked in K-12 as a classroom teacher, language teacher, and instructional coach. Currently, her work is focused on using generative AI to leverage the assets of students in developmental education, with a focus on multilingual students.

D. Praveena Anjelin, working as an Assistant Professor in Department of Data Science and Business Systems, SRMIST, Kattankulathur, TamilNadu. I am a graduate in B.E(CSE) from Madras University and M.E(CSE) from Bharathiar University. I have 18+ Years of Teaching experience in various reputed Engineering Colleges. Currently I am doing my research in Blockchain Technology and its Applications in SRM Institute of Science and Technology. I have published several papers in various journals, National and International Conferences.

Aayushi Arya is a Master of Arts student in Economics at Amity University Noida, demonstrating a strong commitment to academic inquiry through her contribution to this book. Her current studies focus on developing advanced research and analytical skills, with a particular emphasis on the application of data analysis methodologies. She aims to leverage these skills across diverse fields, contributing to evidence-based insights and informed decision-making in a variety of contexts.

Judith Blakely is a nationally recognized scholar-practitioner and transformative educational leader whose career spans over 15 years of impactful service at Walden University. As Academic Coordinator of the Higher Education Program and Principal Preparation Program, she leads with heart, strategy, and an unwavering belief in the potential of every learner. With deep expertise in school administration, special education, bilingual and gifted education, and the ethical integration of artificial intelligence, Dr. Blakely is a tireless advocate for equity and access in education. She holds multiple state-level certifications and is a proud member of the National Association for Bilingual

Education. A gifted educator and mentor, Dr. Blakely is known for pioneering inclusive practices, launching peer mentorship programs, and creating spaces of care and community for adult learners. She has published numerous book chapters and journal articles focused on leadership, innovation, and educational equity. Guided by the philosophy "Together we can," Dr. Blakely continues to inspire students, faculty, and communities alike—building not only programs but people. Her legacy is one of compassion, brilliance, and purpose-driven leadership.

Kimberly Burton, MLIS, is a reference and instruction Librarian at Walden University. She specializes in working with nontraditional students in an online environment, with an emphasis on doctoral candidates. She provides both asynchronous and synchronous instruction to help these students in accomplishing their research needs while strengthening their information literacy skills. Her research interests include information literacy, information distortion, and integrating innovative and creative tools in instruction.

A Prabhu Chakkaravarthy was born on 18th February 1985 in Tamilnadu, India. He received his Ph.D. in Computer Science and Engineering from Sathyabama Institute of Science and Technology, Chennai, India. He is graduated from Anna University, Chennai in 2007 with the Bachelor of Technology degree in Computer Science and Engineering. He received the Master of Technology degree in Computer Science and Engineering from Sathyabama University, Chennai in 2012 with Distinction. He is currently working as an Assistant Professor in Networking and Communications, SRM Institute of Science and Technology, Kattankulathur, Chennai, India. He has published more than 70 research papers in national, international conferences, journals including 8 in Science Citation Indexed journals with 120 citations. He has published 10 patents, 2 patents granted. His research interests include IoT, Artificial Intelligence, Deep Learning, Data Science, Signal Processing and Image Processing.

Angela Crevar serves as an assistant professor at Mercer University. She received her Ph.D. in Educational Leadership and Policy from Texas Tech University. Angela served as a postdoctoral researcher at Texas Tech University, and she served as a high school principal for ten years. Her research is focused on the nexus of high school to college and career readiness with a focus on pathways through education to student success. These pathways include career technical education, hybrid education, and non-traditional pathways. Her work has been published in the Journal of Higher Education and Policy and Leadership Studies and Early Education and Development. Her work has also been presented at the Association for Public Policy Analysis and Management, American Educational Research Association, Association for Education Finance and Policy, University Council for Educational Administration, and the Society for Research on Educational Effectiveness national conferences.

Parihar Suresh Dahake is an accomplished academician and researcher with over 15 years of experience in teaching and research in the fields of Commerce and Management. Currently serving as an Assistant Professor at the School of Management, Ramdeobaba

University, Nagpur, he holds a diverse educational background, including B.Tech (Applied Electronics), MBA (Marketing & Financial Management), M.Com, PGDIBO, M.A. (Psychology), and a Ph.D. in Business Management. Dr. Dahake's research interests span Business Analytics, Consumer Behavior, Predictive Analytics, and Marketing Communication. A recognized Ph.D. supervisor, he guides multiple doctoral candidates under the faculty of Commerce. He has published extensively in peer-reviewed, Scopus, and ABDC-indexed journals and authored books on Marketing Management and Consumer Behavior. He also holds a patent in wage sheet automation and actively contributes as a reviewer for prestigious journals. A recipient of multiple accolades, including the Young Researcher and Research Excellence Awards, Dr. Dahake is also a sought-after speaker and trainer. His commitment to academic excellence and innovative pedagogy has made significant contributions to management education, research, and institutional development in Central India.

Dubey is an Assistant Professor of Education and Director of Clinical Experiences and Partnerships at Montana State University Northern. His research interest focuses in the areas of Multicultural/Immigrant Education, Diversity, Equity, & Inclusivity, Leadership and Change, Technology in Education (Digital Equity & AI), STEM education, Comparative and International Education, Teacher Quality, and Teacher Choice for diverse classrooms. In his research, he uses the statistical tools of Structural Education Modelling (SEM), Mediation & Moderation, and R programming to address the issues that intersect in improving the learning experiences of diverse student population, immigrant/refugee students, and minority students. He has presented research papers at several national research conferences such as AERA, UCIE, AEFP, SREE, etc. and is currently working on different projects and grants.

Angela Elkordy, PhD, is an Associate Professor in the Educational Leadership Department of the National College of Education, National Louis University. Before transitioning to higher education full-time in 2014, she served in K-12 contexts as a technology teacher, Director of Libraries, and school principal. Dr. Elkordy's research interests focus on the intersection of emerging technologies, research methods, and leveraging findings from the learning sciences for effective teaching and learning. She teaches graduate and doctoral students various topics in educational leadership, generative AI in education, instructional design, and research methods.

Katie Girardot, M.S.Ed., serves as the Coordinator for Middle School Curriculum at Community Consolidated School District 93 in Bloomingdale, Illinois. She is currently pursuing a doctorate in Curriculum, Advocacy, and Policy at National Louis University. Since 2004, Ms. Girardot has held various roles in K–12 education, including classroom teacher, assistant principal, and district-level administrator in both curriculum and instructional technology. With experience across three suburban Chicago school districts, Ms. Girardot brings a strong commitment to fostering equitable, engaging, and rigorous learning environments for all students. Her research interests focus on the effectiveness of student feedback systems, the integration of generative artificial intelligence in K–12 education, and the broader impact of AI on adolescent learning experiences.

Sherry Harrison serves as the Academic Coordinator for the Master of Science in Instructional Design and Technology and several MSED Specializations at Walden University, including Self-Designed; Curriculum, Instruction, and Assessment; Elementary Reading and Literacy; Elementary Reading and Math; and Integrating Technology in the Classroom. Dr. Harrison earned her BS in Middle Grades Education from UNC-Greensboro, an MAT specializing in Learning Disabilities from Salem College, and an EdD in Administrator Leadership from Nova Southeastern University. Dr. Harrison has presented and consulted nationally and internationally on a broad range of education topics. One of the Nation's first National Board Certified Teachers, Dr. Harrison's diverse career spans multiple educational settings, including elementary and middle grades teaching, post-secondary instruction, and consulting. Her work has taken her from the White House in Washington, DC to the Great Hall of the People in Beijing. Her administrative experience includes serving as a K-12 District Special Education Director, University Program Director for MS in Education programs and as an Associate Dean of EdS, EdD, and PhD programs.

Kavita Indapurkar, With over 27 years of distinguished experience in higher education institutions in India, Kavita Indapurkar is a seasoned academician and an accomplished academic leader. Currently serving as a Professor of Economics and Head of the School of Economics at Amity University, Uttar Pradesh (Noida Campus), India, she has held several key leadership roles throughout her career, contributing significantly to academic development and institutional growth. Holding a Ph.D. in Economics and an MBA in Finance, she holds an interdisciplinary expertise bringing in a dynamic research portfolio. Her primary interests lie at the intersection of behavioural economics, sustainable practices, and financial decision-making, where she explores how individual behaviour influences and responds to evolving socio-economic and environmental challenges.

J. Dhanalakshmi was born on 6 th September 1992 in Tamilnadu, India. She received the B.E. degree in Computer Science and Engineering and M.E. degree in Computer Science and Engineering from Anna University, Tamil Nadu, India. She was ranked 31st at Anna University for her Masters degree in Computer Science and Engineering. She was a software developer at Fermtronics Technology Solutions until 2018. She completed her Ph.D. degree at the School of Computer Science and Engineering in B.S. Abdur Rahman Crescent Institute of Science and Technology, located in Chennai, India. She is currently pursuing a postdoctoral fellowship at the National Kaohsiung University of Science and Technology, which is located in Kaohsiung, Taiwan. She is currently working as an Assistant Professor in Data Science and Business Systems, SRM Institute of Science and Technology, Kattankulathur, Chennai, India. She published more than 10 research papers in International, National Journals including Conferences and Book Chapter in SCI and Scopus Indexed. Her research interests include Energy Analytics, Artificial Intelligence, Deep Learning, Data Science, Internet of Things (IOT) and Machine Learning.

Sukanda Jongsermtrakoon is a Lecturer in the Department of Educational Technology at the Faculty of Education, Kasetsart University, Thailand. She earned her Bachelor's degree in Computer Education and both her Master's and Doctoral degrees in Educational Technology and Communication from Chulalongkorn University. Her expertise lies in teacher development, with a particular focus on integrating digital technology tools into classroom environments. She is highly skilled in designing digital classrooms and coaching educators to adopt these innovations effectively. She has extensive experience in academic research and scholarly work in the fields of computer and educational technology. Her research interests span a wide range of topics, including the development of information systems to support the evaluation of student teaching internships, initiatives to enhance teachers' digital literacy, the creation and use of Open Educational Resources (OERs), STEM Robotics Coding curriculum development, the design of Personal Learning Networks (PLNs), cognitive coaching, and the integration of artificial intelligence in instructional design and educational media development. She has received funding and research support from various organizations, including Google for Education and SEAMEO INNOTECH (under UNESCO), to advance these initiatives.

Freeson Kaniwa is Head of Department and Lecturer in the Department of Computing and Information Systems at the School of Science and Technology, Botswana Open University (BOU). He holds a PhD in Computer Science from the Botswana International University of Science and Technology (BIUST). He also holds as an MSc in Computer Science and a BSc (Hons) in Computer Science from the University of Zimbabwe (UZ). Dr. Kaniwa has varied experience in both industry and academia. He has a strong academic background in computer science and ample experience in teaching and research. His work spans multiple disciplines within computer science, contributing to parallel computing and AI-driven bespoke systems. His research interests and focus are in the areas of Data Structures and Algorithms, Software Engineering, Bioinformatics, and Artificial Intelligence (AI).

Ferit Kılıçkaya is a researcher in teaching English as a foreign language at Burdur Mehmet Akif Ersoy University, Türkiye. His areas of interests and publications include the possible beneficial and harmful effects of using technology in language teaching and learning practices in addition to the issues in language testing and evaluation such as peer feedback, online quizzes, and washback. He has published several articles in journals such as Computer-Assisted Language Learning, British Journal of Educational Technology, Journal of Teaching English with Technology, and Educational Studies and authored several book chapters in international publishers.

Catarina holds a PhD in Mathematics from the University of Vigo (Spain), whose research work was awarded the Extraordinary Doctoral Prize. It was funded by a PhD grant from the Fundação para a Ciência e Tecnologia (Portugal). She has a BSc in Mathematics and a MSc in Engineering Mathematics from the Faculty of Sciences of the University of Porto, Portugal. Since 2002, she has been working as a Mathematics teacher at secondary school and university level. Her main research interests are related to Differential Calculus,

Statistics, Modelling, Teaching Education, Digital Literacy. She has collaborated in international research projects, in supervision and as a member of juries of PhD and MSc theses in different countries since 2016. By invitation, she has worked as a member of scientific committees in international conferences, courses, chairing working sessions and as a reviewer in scientific journals. She worked as research statistician in the DOCnet project of the Institute of Public Health of the University of Porto, in the Epidemiology Research Unit. Now, she is coordinator of the Mathematics Department of ISPGAYA.

M. Rajkumar is a highly experienced academician, with distinctive knowledge in business research techniques, marketing research, organizational behavior, and human capital management. At the center of his research is a persistent interest in leadership dynamics, motivation science, and organizational citizenship—threads he has pursued through multiple publications in Scopus-indexed journals and presentations given at global conferences. Aside from mentoring students and program management, Dr. Rajkumar is a peer reviewer for a leading academic journal (ABDC). He is also the Associate Editor for The IUJ Journal of Management. His proficiency in research methodologies, data analysis (SPSS, AMOS, SmartPLS), and structural equation modeling has been instrumental in conducting numerous workshops and faculty development programs

James Andrew Martinez, Ed.D., MPH, is an Assistant Clinical Professor at the Loma Linda University School of Public Health and has served in senior data leadership roles, including Program Manager, Vice President of Data Science, and Chief Data Officer. He is a recognized expert in data science, artificial intelligence, geographic information systems (GIS), and educational innovation, with over two decades of experience across public health, legal analytics, and education. Dr. Martinez's work focuses on integrating advanced technologies into institutional systems to advance ethical AI adoption, digital equity, and learner-centered design. His research explores privacy-enhancing data architectures and scalable frameworks that support applied analytics and inclusive workforce development. In his leadership roles, he has led technical teams, and data governance practices. Through this work, he remains committed to using data to support inclusive learning environments, and promote sustainable, system-wide innovation.

Dayna Mitchell, Ed.D., (She/Her) has served PK-12 public education for 30 years as a High School Teacher and Administrator, Middle School Principal, Director of Curriculum, Instruction, and Assessment, and Assistant Superintendent. Using an equity lens, Dr. Mitchell developed a district-wide professional learning system focused on continuous cycles of improvement designed to increase student achievement, equity, and engagement in order to close opportunity gaps and accelerate learning for all students, with an emphasis on multilingual learners. Dr. Mitchell is an Assistant Professor, Educational Leadership, CSU Pomona

Lynne Orr started her dissertation journey discussing technology use in higher education. Over 23 years, Orr has researched and trained students and faculty on the use of technology in higher education. Over 13 years, Orr has guided doctoral learners through their degree completion process by creating original research worthy of publication.

Amitava Pal is the Associate Dean at the International Institute of Sports Management (IISM), which received the prestigious President's Award in 2020. A seasoned academic and industry expert, he has guided pivotal industry reports in collaboration with organizations like FICCI, ASSOCHAM, and IMC. As Training and Research Head, he guided SOPs for the 37th National Games, Khelo India Youth Games, and Khelo India University Games. His research has been featured in leading publications, including Bonn University, Germany, and the University of California, and he received the Best Paper Award for Sustainability in Sports. Additionally, Amitava has mentored IIC fellows for the University of Chicago Harris School of Public Policy and spearheaded training, operation and implementation of the computer science curriculum researched and developed at IIT, Bombay for InOpen, SINE, IIT Bombay.

Ram Panchariya is an esteemed academician with over 20 years of teaching and administrative experience in the field of management education. He currently serves as Associate Professor and Head of the Department of MBA at Bapurao Deshmukh College of Engineering (BDCOE), Wardha. With a profound command over finance, Dr. Pancharia has been instrumental in shaping the academic and professional growth of countless MBA students. His expertise encompasses core areas of financial management, investment analysis, and strategic financial planning. As a dedicated researcher, his scholarly work predominantly focuses on the evolving dynamics of financial systems, capital markets, and corporate finance. He has contributed to numerous national and international journals, seminars, and conferences. Known for his academic rigor, leadership, and innovative teaching methods, Dr. Panchariya continues to inspire future managers and finance professionals while advancing impactful research in his domain of interest.

Ramesh Chandra Poonia is a Professor in the Department of Computer Science at CHRIST (Deemed to be University), India. He is internationally recognized for his research in sustainable technologies, focusing on energy-efficient algorithms, cyber-physical systems, and computational intelligence, particularly machine learning and data analytics. His contributions rank him among the top 2% of scientists worldwide, as recognized by Stanford University and Elsevier. Dr. Poonia has completed two distinguished postdoctoral fellowships: one at the Cyber-Physical Systems Laboratory at the Norwegian University of Science and Technology (NTNU) in Norway, and another through an international collaboration aimed at predicting pandemic diseases using machine learning, involving Oakland University in the USA and Imam University in Saudi Arabia. He earned his Ph.D. in Computer Science from Banasthali University, India, in 2013, and an M.Tech. in Data Science and Engineering from the Birla Institute of Technology and Science (BITS), Pilani, India. With an extensive portfolio of research, Dr. Poonia has served as lead editor for numerous special issues, books, and proceedings with renowned publishers such as Springer, Taylor & Francis, and Elsevier. He is also an associate editor for the Journal of

Sustainable Computing: Informatics and Systems (Elsevier) and serves as a series editor for Computational and Intelligent Systems (CRC Press). As the founder of the SUSCOM and ICSCPS conferences, he received the 2024 Research Innovation Award for his outstanding contributions to the advancement of sustainable and intelligent systems.

Rischard is an Assistant Professor of English at Montana State University-Northern. He received his MA and PhD at the University of Arizona from the Department of English and Social, Cultural, and Critical Theory Programs. He has taught writing, literature, and digital/visual culture and methods for the University of Arizona, Pima Community College, and as a Writing Assessment Specialist for the University of Texas. He is the author of Street, Text, and Representation in African American Literature (Routledge, 2024), and publishes and presents on sociohistorical, phenomenological, and computational methods of literary and cultural analysis. Winner of the 2020 New Directions in the Humanities International Award, he has written widely in the fields of writing pedagogy, assessment, and digital humanities research for journals including Writing Spaces, Texas Studies in Literature and Language, and The International Journal of Critical Cultural Studies.

Vasco Santo,Polytechnic University of Tomar, Portugal,Adjunct Professor at the Polytechnic University of Tomar (IPT) and member of the Research and Innovation Support Office (GAII). He has a Habilitation in Management (European University, Lisbon), a PhD in Business Sciences (Fernando Pessoa University, Porto), a PhD in Tourism (University of Seville, Spain) and a Post-Doctorate in Innovation Management (University of Aveiro). Specialises in Hotel and Restaurant Management. Integrated researcher at NECE-UI and collaborating researcher at GOVCOPP (University of Aveiro), TECHN&ART (Polytechnic University of Tomar) and CITUR (Polytechnic of Leiria). Editor-in-Chief of the scientific journal 'International Journal of Digital Marketing, Management, and Innovation (IJDMMI)'. Author and reviewer for indexed scientific journals. Author of Book Chapters in IGI Global. Editor of Books in IGI Global.

Carlos Sousa has a BSc. in Computer Systems and Networks from Higher Polytechnic Institute of Gaya (ISPGaya). His current research areas include networking management, machine learning and security policies.

Douglas van Dyke, Ed.D, serves as the Internal Evaluator for Project EDUCATE and an adjunct professor in the National College of Education at National Louis University. A veteran educator, Dr. van Dyke has worked in secondary and higher education for over three decades. His research focuses on ICT literacy, digital equity, and the ways educators' digital epistemologies impact learning opportunities for historically marginalized youth. His current research investigates ethical uses of generative AI in education.

Index

A

C

D

E

F

G

H

N

O

P

R

S

T

U

www.ingramcontent.com/pod-product-compliance
Ingram Content Group UK Ltd.
Pitfield, Milton Keynes, MK11 3LW, UK
UKHW050949290926
15470UKWH00005B/1725

9 798337 350929